걸프 사태

# 외국인 수송 및 난민 지원

걸프 사태

# 외국인 수송 및 난민 지원

한국학술정보

## | 머리말

걸프 전쟁은 미국의 주도하에 34개국 연합군 병력이 수행한 전쟁으로, 1990년 8월 이라크의 쿠웨이트 침공 및 합병에 반대하며 발발했다. 미국은 초기부터 파병 외교에 나섰고, 1990년 9월 서울 등에 고위 관리를 파견하며 한국의 동참을 요청했다. 88올림픽 이후 동구권 국교 수립과 유엔 가입 추진 등 적극적인 외교 활동을 펼치는 당시 한국에 있어 이는 미국과 국제사회의 지지를 얻기 위해서라도 피할 수 없는 일이었다. 결국 정부는 91년 1월부터 약 3개월에 걸쳐 국군의료지원단과 공군수송단을 사우디아라비아 및 아랍 에미리트 연합 등에 파병하였고, 군 · 민간 의료 활동, 병력 수송 임무를 수행했다. 동시에 당시 걸프 지역 8개국에 살던 5천여 명의 교민에게 방독면 등 물자를 제공하고, 특별기 파견 등으로 비상시 대피할 수 있도록 지원했다. 비록 전쟁 부담금과 유가 상승 등 어려움도 있었지만, 걸프전 파병과 군사 외교를 통해 한국은 유엔 가입에 박차를 가할 수 있었고 미국 등 선진 우방국, 아랍권 국가 등과 밀접한 외교 관계를 유지하며 여러 국익을 창출할 수 있었다.

본 총서는 외교부에서 작성하여 30여 년간 유지한 걸프 사태 관련 자료를 담고 있다. 미국을 비롯한 여러 국가와의 군사 외교 과정, 일일 보고 자료와 기타 정부의 대응 및 조치, 재외동포 철수와 보호, 의료지원단과 수송단 파견 및 지원 과정, 유엔을 포함해 세계 각국에서 수집한 관련 동향 자료, 주변국 지원과 전후복구사업 참여 등 총 48권으로 구성되었다. 전체 분량은 약 2만 4천여 쪽에 이른다.

2024년 3월

한국학술정보(주)

## | 일러두기

· 본 총서에 실린 자료는 2022년 4월과 2023년 4월에 각각 공개한 외교문서 4,827권, 76만 여 쪽 가운데 일부를 발췌한 것이다.

· 각 권의 제목과 순서는 공개된 원본을 최대한 반영하였으나, 주제에 따라 일부는 적절히 변경하였다.

· 원본 자료는 A4 판형에 맞게 축소하거나 원본 비율을 유지한 채 A4 페이지 안에 삽입하였다. 또한 현재 시점에선 공개되지 않아 '공란'이란 표기만 있는 페이지 역시 그대로 실었다.

· 외교부가 공개한 문서 각 권의 첫 페이지에는 '정리 보존 문서 목록'이란 이름으로 기록물 종류, 일자, 명칭, 간단한 내용 등의 정보가 수록되어 있으며, 이를 기준으로 0001번부터 번호가 매겨져 있다. 이는 삭제하지 않고 총서에 그대로 수록하였다.

· 보고서 내용에 관한 더 자세한 정보가 필요하다면, 외교부가 온라인상에 제공하는 『대한민국 외교사료요약집』 1991년과 1992년 자료를 참조할 수 있다.

# | 차례

| 정 리 보 존 문 서 목 록 | | | | | |
|---|---|---|---|---|---|
| 기록물종류 | 일반공문서철 | 등록번호 | 2017030042 | 등록일자 | 2017-03-21 |
| 분류번호 | 721.1 | 국가코드 | XF | 보존기간 | 영구 |
| 명 칭 | 걸프사태 : 외국인 수송 및 난민 지원, 1990-91. 전3권 | | | | |
| 생 산 과 | 중근동과/해외이주과/국제기구과 | 생산년도 | 1990~1991 | 담당그룹 | |
| 권 차 명 | V.1 IOM(국제이민기구) 지원 | | | | |
| 내용목차 | * 1990.9.27 50만불 특별기여금 출연 결정 사실 통보 | | | | |

0001

원 본

암호수신

# 외 무 부

종 별 :

번 호 : GVW-1629 일 시 : 90 0827 1500

수 신 : 장관(중근동,국기,영해)

발 신 : 주 제네바 대사

제 목 : 이라크 및 쿠웨이트 아국교민 안전 철수

연:GVW-1559

당지 소재 IOM(국제이민기구) PURCELL 사무총장은 별첨 본직앞 공한 및 AIDE MEMOIRE 를 본직앞 통해 IOM 을 걸프지역 국가에 갇혀있는 외국인 안전 철수를 지원키 위한 계획(PROGRAMME)를 착수할 준비가 되어 있으며 이를 위한 사전 조치로 외국인 철수를 위한 필요성 및 요건을 평가하기 위해 조사단을 걸프지역에 파견할 예정임을 통보하면서 회원국들에게 자발적 기여금등 지원을 요청하여 왔는바, 이라크 및 쿠웨이트에서 아국교민 안전철수와 관련 참고 바라며, 본부 검토의견 회시바람.

첨부: IOM 공한 및 AIDE MEMOIRE.(GVW(F)-0301). 끝.

(대사 이상옥-국장)

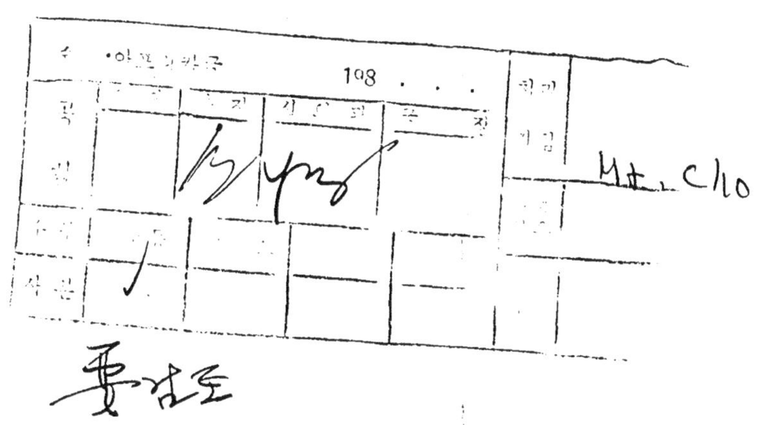

중아국 대책반 장관 차관 1차보 2차보 국기국 영교국 청와대 안기부

PAGE 1

90.08.28 01:29

외신 2과 통제관 CF

0002

GUW(F)-0371 00827 1500

INTERNATIONAL ORGANIZATION FOR MIGRATION

THE DIRECTOR GENERAL

GENEVA, SWITZERLAND

24 August 1990

Sir,

I have the honour to refer to the situation existing in the Middle East as a result of recent dramatic events, a situation which affects the fate of a great number of persons. Within the framework of its constitutional mandate, the International Organization for Migration (IOM) is prepared to undertake a programme to assist in the return of foreign nationals stranded in certain countries of the Gulf region.

These actions, prompted by enquiries from various governments, will be undertaken in close co-operation with the United Nations and other international organizations. They aim at assisting affected persons in the orderly return to their countries of origin or habitual residence in cases where such relocation is deemed necessary.

As a preliminary step, I will dispatch an assessment team to the region to evaluate needs and requirements for such an orderly return. The enclosed Aide Mémoire summarizes the actions IOM is prepared to take as well as the constitutional framework in which they will be implemented.

IOM requests the support of its Member States to ensure the successful completion of this humanitarian task. In view of the tens of thousands of persons for whom transportation is required, the voluntary contribution of funds needed to allow for the movement of such persons who are without adequate resources to finance their travel is especially important, and I am confident of being able to count on the assistance of your Government.

Please accept, Sir, the assurance of my highest consideration.

James N. Purcell, Jr.

His Excellency
Mr. Sang Ock Lee
Ambassador
Permanent Observer of the Republic of Korea
to the United Nations Office and
Permanent Delegate to the other
international organizations in Geneva
20, route de Pré-Bois
1215 GENEVA 15

34

0003

INTERNATIONAL ORGANIZATION FOR MIGRATION (IOM)
ORGANISATION INTERNATIONALE POUR LES MIGRATIONS (OIM)
ORGANIZACIÓN INTERNACIONAL PARA LAS MIGRACIONES (OIM)

Telephone: 717 91 11
Cable Address: Promigrant Geneva
Telex: 415 722
Telefax: 798 61 50

17, route des Morillons
P.O. Box 71
CH-1211 GENEVA 19
SWITZERLAND

AIDE MEMOIRE

The International Organization for Migration (IOM) hereby announces its readiness to undertake a programme of assistance in the return of foreign nationals stranded in certain countries of the Middle East as a result of the situation in the region. The aim of this special effort will be to assist such persons, in close co-operation with the United Nations and other international organizations, in the immediate and orderly return to their countries of origin or habitual residence in cases where such relocation is deemed necessary.

IOM would provide its services to such persons in accordance with Article 1, paragraph (a) and (b) of its Constitution which empowers the Organization to make arrangements for the organized transfer of migrants, for whom existing facilities are inadequate or who would not otherwise be able to move without special assistance, to countries offering opportunities for orderly migration, and to concern itself with the organized transfer of refugees, displaced persons and other individuals in need of international migration services for whom arrangements may be made between the Organization and the States concerned. The IOM Constitution further specifies that services can only be provided at the request, or with the agreement of the States concerned.

In light of the serious tension in this region and the urgent need to secure immediate relocation of affected foreign nationals outside of danger zones, the persons so stranded are in need of urgent international migration services and would not otherwise be able to move without special assistance.

In order to assess needs and requirements for such orderly return, IOM proposes to dispatch an assessment team to the region immediately. Such a team will be composed of professional transportation and logistics experts, skilled in the evaluation of needs.

0004

3-2

Based on past experience, services to be considered could be comprised of certain or all of the following, which would be undertaken in co-operation with local authorities and international organizations:

- enumeration of persons in need and determination of countries of destination;
- matching of transport requirements with "regularly scheduled" services or routes, including all modes of transport;
- determination of additional transport services which may be required;
- arranging for such additional services, as may be requested; and
- such other migration services as may be required for timely and orderly return.

In announcing its readiness to undertake this programme, IOM respectfully requests the support and assistance of governments and other entities necessary to the successful completion of this humanitarian task. Especially important would be the voluntary contribution of funds needed to allow the transportation of persons who are without adequate resources to finance their travel.

Information describing IOM and its worldwide migration services is enclosed.

Geneva, 24 August 1990

GVW(W)-301 — 3-3

0005

# 국제이민기구(IOM)를 통한 중동 아국교민 철수

90.8.28 국기과
중동국장 및 권병현
대책반장에 수교

1. 문제의 제기

o IOM 사무총장, 주제네바 아국 대사에게 다음 내용의 8.24자 Aide Memoire를 전달

- 걸프지역 국가에 억류되어 있는 외국인 안전 철수 계획 준비 일환으로 사전 조사단 중동에 파견

- 인도적인 상기 사업 시행 관련 각 회원국의 자발적 기금 요청

2. IOM 기구 성격

- 1951년 창설, 난민과 자국 이탈자등 개인의 질서있는 계획 이주 추진. 특히 개도국의 사회 경제 교육증진을 위한 전문인력 송출 및 기술협력 도모

- 본부 : 스위스 제네바

- 90년 현재 아국 포함 36개국 정부 회원, 14개국 정부 옵서버.

3. 상기 1항 IOM 사무총장의 제의 검토

가. IOM 제의내용

o 아국민 또는 서방국민 호송만을 위한것이 아니고 현 중동 사태로 인하여 이라크와 쿠웨이트를 떠나고자 하는 모든 타국인을 대상

o IOM 의 헌장상 동 기구의 원조를 청하는 국가의 국민에 관련한 업무만 관여(상기 Aide-Memoire 명기)

0006

나. 검토사항

- ㅇ 현 이라크 사태와 관련하여 이미 외국인 철수 업무로 관여하고 있는 ICRC(143개국 회원단체 가입) 업무와 중복

- ㅇ 단, ICRC가 관련 당사국(이라크)과의 정치적 교섭을 담당하고 호송차량등의 실무적 준비는 IOM에서 준비하는 공동업무 추진을 생각할 수도 있음.

- ㅇ 그러나 다음 이유에서 아국인 피난을 위하여 IOM 에 의존할 필요는 없다고 판단됨.

  - ICRC와 IOM의 공조 체제가 수립되어 있지 않음. 설령 현 단계에서 동 수립을 도모한다 하더라도 ICRC 의 호의적 반응이 나온다는 보장이 없음.

  - 시기적으로 IOM의 제의가 늦었음(후진국을 제외하고는 이미 억류국민의 국적국에서 다각적인 호송조치 마련)

  - IOM에 일단 의존할 경우 여타 개도국 국민의 철수를 위한 고통수단등 아국이 필요이상으로 지원하여야 하는 부담을 안을 가능성이 많음.

  - IOM 회원국이 아닌 이라크 정부가 IOM 에게 어떠한 대우를 베풀것인지도 미상(ICRC는 이라크의 국내 적십자사를 회원으로 포함하고 있음)

0007

aspects of immigration and ethnic affairs. **Programs:** Family Holiday; Youth. **Projects:** Combatting Prejudice in School.

**Publications:** (in English) • *Clearinghouse on Migration Issues Documentation and Abstract Service*, quarterly. • *Migration Action*, 3/year. • *Multicultural Australia Papers*, 10/year. • Also publishes bibliographies and monographs through the Clearing House on Migration Issues.

**Convention/Meeting:** annual.

★5291★ INFO-TURK/ATELIERS DU SOLEIL (Migration) (INFO-TURK)
38, rue des Eburons Phone: 2 2302783
B-1040 Brussels, Belgium Dogan Ozguden, Sec.
**Founded:** 1974. **Members:** 350. **Staff:** 8. **Budget:** $50,000. **Languages:** French, Turkish; *corresponds in English*. **Multinational.** Individuals concerned with the social welfare of Turks and other immigrants in Belgium. Defends the interests of underprivileged immigrants and refugees in Belgium with particular attention to Turkish immigrants. Provides cultural, educational, and social assistance to Turks. Strives to increase public awareness of the specific problems of Turkish immigrants in light of political conditions in Turkey. Works to defend human rights in Turkey. Operates Ateliers du Soleil, which are workshops designed to promote learning, basic skills, creativity, and artistic expression; organizes theatre productions, folk dance concerts, and other cultural events. Offers instruction in elementary Dutch, English, and French. Cooperates with democratic and humanitarian organizations. Maintains 5000 volume library of books and documents on Turkey and Turkish immigrants. **Telecommunications Services:** Fax, 2 2309542. **Committees:** Creativity Team; Editing Board; Educational Team; Graphical Works Team; Social Assistance Group. **Formerly:** (1985) Info-Turk.

**Publications:** *INFO-TURK* (bulletin, in English and French), monthly. • Also publishes books and pamphlets on Turkey and Turkish immigrants.

**Convention/Meeting:** annual.

★5292★ INFORMATION AND SUPPORT GROUP FOR IMMIGRANT WORKERS (Migration) (GISTI)
(Groupe d'Information et de Soutien des Travailleurs Immigres - GISTI)
46, rue de Montreuil Phone: 1 43670406
F-75011 Paris, France Patrick Mony, Contact
**Founded:** 1972. **Members:** 60. **Staff:** 4. **Budget:** 700,000 Fr. **Languages:** French; *corresponds in English*. **National.** Jurists, researchers, and social workers united to defend the rights of immigrants in France. Opposes and seeks to change the legislation of the present government concerning restrictions on: entry of immigrants into France; the rights of foreigners with a French spouse; social security benefits and family loans to immigrants; public education for foreign children; the granting of asylum to foreigners. Examines legislative texts and their application to administrative practices. Offers colloquia and training courses in the history of immigration laws and the rights of immigrants.

**Publications:** *Plein Droit* (in French), periodic. • Also publishes *Guide des Etrangers Face a l'Administration, Guide des Jeunes Etrangers en France*, information packets, and papers.

★5293★ INTERNATIONAL CATHOLIC MIGRATION COMMISSION (ICMC)
(Commission Internationale Catholique pour les Migrations - CICM)
37-39, rue de Vermont
Case Postale 96 Phone: 22 334150
CH-1211 Geneva 20, Switzerland Dr. Andre N. Van Chau, Sec.Gen.
**Founded:** 1951. **Languages:** French, German, Spanish; *corresponds in English*. **Multinational.** National Catholic affiliate agencies in 76 countries. Coordinates members' activities on behalf of migrants and refugees. Assists in refugee resettlement by providing health care and language or vocational training and living expenses for refugees ineligible for governmental assistance. Offers interest-free travel loans and pre-emigration services designed to ease culture shock. Serves as a conduit of funds between donor and recipient agencies. Maintains worldwide network of emigration processing offices that link first asylum and emigration countries with national Catholic offices in the United States, Canada, and Australia. Conducts refugee officer training program. **Telecommunications Services:** Fax, 22 347929. **Committees:** Catholic Committee for Intra-European Migration. **Also Known As:** Comision Catolica Internacional de Migracion; Commissione Cattolica Internazionale per le Migrazioni; Internationale Katholische Kommission fur Wanderungsfragen.

**Publications:** *Annual Report*. • *Migration News*, semiannual. • *Migrations*, semiannual. • *Newsletter*, quarterly. • Also publishes periodic papers (in German).

**Convention/Meeting:** annual.

★5294★ INTERNATIONAL ORGANIZATION FOR MIGRATION (IOM)
17, route des Morillons
Case Postale 71 Phone: 22 7179111
CH-1211 Geneva 19, Switzerland James N. Purcell, Dir.Gen.
**Founded:** 1951. **Staff:** 815. **Budget:** $128,000,000. **Languages:** French, Spanish; *corresponds in English*. **Multinational.** Representatives of governments of 35 nations and 17 observer states. Fosters orderly and planned migration of refugees, displaced persons, and other individuals to countries offering resettlement opportunities. Aids transfer of specialized human resources to promote economic, educational and social advancement of developing countries. Promotes technical cooperation. Holds biennial seminar. Maintains 6000 volume library. **Telecommunications Services:** Fax, 22 7986150; telexes, 415722. **Departments:** Latin American Programmes; Liaison and Research; Medical Services; Operations and Transport; Planning. **Programs:** Cultural; Language Training; National Migration; Refugee Migration; Resources in Developing Countries; Technical Cooperation in Planning Migration Programmes; Transfer of Qualified Human Resources in Developing Countries. **Also Known As:** Comite Intergubernamental para las Migraciones. **Formerly:** Intergovernmental Committee for European Migration.

**Publications:** *International Migration* (in English), quarterly. • *IOM Annual Report* (in English, French, and Spanish). • *IOM Latin American Migration Journal* (in English and Spanish), 3/year. • *Monthly Dispatch* (newsletter, in English, French, and Spanish). • Also publishes *IOM in Facts* and *IOM Historical Summary*.

**Convention/Meeting:** annual council session.

★5295★ INTERNATIONAL TRACING SERVICE (Missing Persons) (ITS)
(Internationaler Suchdienst - IS)
**Founded:** 1943. **Languages:** French, German; *corresponds in English*. **Multinational.** Operates under the auspices of the International Committee to the Red Cross (see separate entry). Makes available documentation on German and non-German victims of Nazi persecution. **Also Known As:** Service International de Recherches. Organization has declined revision and listing; description is reprinted from the previous edition.

**Publications:** *Annual Report*.

**Convention/Meeting:** annual.

★5296★ MISSING PERSONS INTERNATIONAL (MPI)
P.O. Box 1337 Phone: (818) 377-5857
Canyon Country, CA 91351, United States June Ramsay, Ph.D., Founder & Exec.Dir.
**Founded:** 1975. **Members:** 43,000. **Languages:** French, Spanish; *corresponds in English*. **Multinational.** Individuals in 34 countries who are searching for missing persons. Assists members' efforts to find adoptees, natural parents, adoptive parents, missing relatives, runaways, rape victims, kidnap victims, MIAs, POWs, and abandoned children. Organizes programs related to adoption problems including runaways, child and parent abuse, rape, foster homes, and diagnosis of inherited diseases. Provides advisory and reference services including literature-searching, abstracting, indexing, current-awareness, and analytic data; answers inquiries and makes referrals to other sources. Distributes publications and data compilations. Maintains extensive library of materials relevant to the identities of adoptees and family history. Bestows awards. Services are available to nonmembers for a fee. **Telecommunications Services:** Fax, (805)252-1239. **Formerly:** (1980) Searchers-International; (1984) Adoptee/Natural Parent Locators; (1986) Adoptee/Natural Parent Locators - International; (1988) Worldwide Searches.

**Publications:** *In Search of Identity* (newsletter), monthly. • *Missing Persons International - Associate Directory*, periodic. • *Missing Persons International - Referral Directory*, monthly.

**Convention/Meeting:** monthly.

★5297★ SOCIETY FOR THE ADVANCEMENT OF CHILDBIRTH (Natural Family Planning) (EFRAT)
(Agudah Le'eidud Hayeluda Beam Hayehudi - EFRAT)
P.O. Box 6325 Phone: 2 828507
Jerusalem 91062, Israel Prof. Avraham Amir, Chm.
**Founded:** 1963. **Staff:** 30. **Budget:** $60,000. **Regional Groups:** 4. **Languages:** Hebrew; *does not correspond in English*. **National.** Encourages childbearing among Jews in Israel and elsewhere; seeks to minimize the incidence of abortion among Jews. Operates charitable program; organizes lectures. **Convention/Meeting:** none.

**Publications:** *Yidion Efrat* (in Hebrew), quarterly. • Also publishes informational material.

0008

중근동과

# I O M 개 요

1. 현 황

가. 정식 명칭 : 국제 이민기구 (International Organization for Migration, ICM)

나. 설립 경위 : 1951년 유럽이민 운동을 위한 가칭 "정부간 위원회" 로 발족 (벨기에 브뤼셀)

다. 본 부 : 스위스 제네바

라. 회원국 및 옵저버 현황

o 회원국 (36 개국)

- 미주 (18) : 미국, 알젠틴, 볼리비아, 칠레, 콜롬비아, 엘살바돌, 코스타리카, 도미니카 (공), 에쿠아돌, 파나마, 니카라과, 파라과이, 페루, 우루과이, 베네수엘라, 혼두라스, 카나다, 과테말라

- 구주 (11) : 오스트리아, 벨지움, 룩셈부룩, 그리이스, 이태리, 서독, 덴마크, 네델란드, 폴투갈, 스위스, 노르웨이

- 중동 (2) : 이스라엘, 키프로스
- 아프리카 (1) : 케냐
- 아주 (3) : 태국, 한국, 필리핀
- 대양주 (1) : 오주

0009

o 옵저버 (14 개국)
- 미주 (4) : 벨리제, 과테말라, 멕시코
- 구주 (7) : 영국, 프랑스, 스페인, 스웨덴, 로마교황청, 산마리노, 말타
- 중동 (2) : 이집트, 터어키
- 아주 (1) : 일본
- 아프리카(1) : 우간다

2. 목 적

가. 수민국과 송출국의 특정 수요에 응해 질서있는 계획이주 (해외 취업 포함) 추진

o 관계 정부의 정책 및 법률, 이민 경향 및 문제점 연구 분석

o 2년에 1회 세미나 개최, 관련 정부, 국제기구, 이주 희망자들에게 권고 또는 조언

o 이주자 또는 난민들에게 수민국에서의 정착에 필요한 지식이나 언어등에 대한 훈련 또는 오리엔테이션 제공

나. 난민 정착 기회를 제공하는 국가에 대한 난민의 송출 및 정착 추진

o 정치적, 종교적, 윤리적 이유 때문에 조국을 떠나야만 하는 난민 지원

o 이주할 기회가 있는 난민이 경제적 어려움으로 이주를 못하는 경우가 없도록 원조

o 유엔난민 고등 판무관실 (UNHCR), 국제적십자위원회 (ICRC), 적십자 연맹 (LRCS) 등과 긴밀한 협조

o 가족 재결합 계획 추진

0010

다. 개도국의 경제, 교육, 사회적 발전을 도모하기 위한 전문 인력의 교류

o 국가발전에 필요한 특정분야 (정부기관, 대학, 전문기술학교, 기타 공공기관) 에 대한 선별적 고급 전문가 공급

o 유능한 고급인력의 모국 귀환 알선

3. 조 직

o 이사회 (연 1회 개최, 전회원국 대표와 옵저버로 구성)

o 집행위원회 (연 2회 개최, 1년 임기의 9개 회원국 대표로 구성)

o 소위원회 (예산재정위원회 및 수송협력 위원회)

o 사무국 (총장, 차장)

o 세미나 (2년마다 1회 개최)

4. 회원자격 및 의무

o 회원국 수에 대한 제한 규정 없음.

o 헌장 이행준수 및 행정운영 경비 분담

o 이사회의 2/3 다수결로 가입 결정

5. 재 정

o 행정운영비 : 합의된 배당비율 의거 전회원 분담

o 사업 운영

- 이민 송출국 및 수민국 기부금
- 특수사업을 위한 회원국 기부금
- 기타, 후원자 및 지원단체 기부금

0011

6. IOM 의 국제기구등과의 협조 현황

가. IOM 과 협력하는 국제기구

1) IOM 과 협력협정 체결 국제기구 (23) :

- U.N. High Commissioner for Refuggess (UNHCR),
- U.N. Disaster Relief Coordinater (UNDRO),
- Economic Commission for Latin America and the Caribbean (ECLAC)
- Economic Commission for Africa (ECA)
- Economic and Social Council for Asia and the Pacific (ESCAP)
- Latin American Economic System (SELA)
- U.N. Population Division
- U.N. Fund for Population Activities (UNFPA)
- U.N. Development Programme (UNDP)
- U.N. Volunteers Programme (UNV)
- U.N. Center for Human Rights
- U.N. Educational, Scientific and Cultural Organization (UNESCO)
- Food and Agriculture Organization of the U.N. (FAO)
- International Labour Organisation (ILO)
- World Health Organization (WHO)
- Organization of American States (OAS)
- Inter - American Development Bank (IDB)
- Commission of the Cartagena Agreement (Andean Pact)
- Organization for Economic Co-operation and Development (OECD)
- Council of Europe
- Commission of European Communities (CEC)
- Italo-Latin American Institute (IILA)
- Instituto de Cooperacion Iberoamericana (ICI).

0012

2) IOM 이 옵저버인 국제기구 (4) :

- Economic and Social Council (Ecosoc)
- U.N. Conference on Trade and Development (UNCTAD)
- U.N. Industrial Development Organization (UNIDO)
- International Maritime Organization (IMO)

나. IOM 과 협조하는 각급 지원기구 (23) :

- American Council for Nationalities Service
- International Council of Voluntary Agencies
- American Fund for Czechoslovak Refugees Inc.
- International Rescue Committee
- Buddhist Council for Refugee Rescue and Resettlement
- International Social Service
- CARE Inc.
- Lutheran World Federation
- Catholic Relief Services
- National Council of Young Men's Christian Associations
- Centro de Estudios'y Promocion Social
- Norwegian Refugee Council
- Comite national d'entraide franco-vietnamien, franco-cambodgien, franco-laotien
- Polish American Immigration and Relief Committee
- Food for the Hungry International
- Presiding Bishop's Fund for World Relief

0013

- Hebrew Immigrant Aid Society (HIAS Inc.)
- Tolstoy Foundation Inc.
- International Catholic Migration Commission
- United Ukrainian American Relief Committee
- International Council on Social Welfare
- World Council of Churches
- World Relief Refugee Services

7. 지역사무소 소재지 (39 개국)
   o 미주 (16) : 미국, 알젠틴, 볼리비아, 칠레, 콜롬비아, 코스타리카, 도미니카(공), 에쿠아돌, 엘살바돌, 니카라과, 파나마, 파라과이, 페루, 우루과이, 베네수엘라, 혼두라스
   o 구주 (9) : 오스트리아, 벨지움, 룩셈부룩, 그리스, 이태리, 서독, 폴부칼, 프랑스, 스페인, 영국
   o 중동 (2) : 키스로스, 수단
   o 아주 (9) : 홍콩, 인도네시아, 일본, 말레이시아, 파키스탄, 필리핀, 싱가폴, 호주, 태국
   o 아프리카(3): 케냐, 소말리아, 지부티

8. 아국과의 관계
   o 85.11.20 제 52차 총회시 업저버로 가입
   o 86.7.9 - 7.15 Kotteck 홍콩 주재 ICM 사무소장 방한
   o 86.12.7 - 12.10 Horst Habenicht ICM 기획부장
   o 88.11.29. 정회원으로 가입
     (년간 약 6만불의 분담금 지불)

0014

9. 90년 상반기 IOM 의 업무실적 (90. 1 - 6 월)

가. 난민 이주지원 : 122,337 명

- ㅇ 유럽 유출 난민 : 50,406 명
- ㅇ 중동, 아프리카 유출 난민 : 3,432 명
- ㅇ 동남아 유출 난민 : 61,144 명
- ㅇ 근동 유출 난민 : 1,853 명
- ㅇ 라틴 아메리카 유출 난민 : 5,455 명
- ㅇ 기 타 : 4 명

나. 해외이주 지원 : 4,422 명

- ㅇ 일반 이민 : 2,598 명
- ㅇ 개발 이민 : 1,824 명

0015

| 관리번호 | 90/1507 |
|---|---|

| | 분류번호 | 보존기간 |
|---|---|---|
| | | |

# 발 신 전 보

번 호 : WGV-1150 900829 1422 DP 종별 :

수 신 : 주 제네바 대사 . 총영사

발 신 : 장 관 (중근동)

제 목 : 이라크, 쿠웨이트 교민 철수

대 : GVW-1629

1. 이라크, 쿠웨이트 잔류 아국교민은 8. 29.현재 449명(공관 직원 포함)인바, 아국인의 경우에는 아직까지 이라크 당국의 출국허가를 받아 철수가 이루어지고 있으므로 현 단계에서는 IOM의 지원을 특별히 요청할 필요성은 없는 것으로 판단 됨.

2. 그러나, 향후 사태 전개에 따라 아국인 철수 및 보호를 위해 국제기구의 지원을 요청할 필요성이 발생할 수 있으므로 IOM, ICRC등 귀지 소재 국제기구의 관련 동향을 계속 파악 보고 바람. 끝.

(중동아프리카국장 이 두 복)

19 90. 12. 31.에 예고문에 의거 일반문서로 재 분류됨.

국제기구조약국장

| 앙고재 | 90년 8월 29일 | 중근동과 | 기안자 | | 과 장 | 심의관 | 국 장 | | 차 관 | 장 관 |
|---|---|---|---|---|---|---|---|---|---|---|
| | | | 조해용 | | 鄭 | | 전결 | | | |

| 보안통제 | 외신과통제 |
|---|---|
| 鄭 | |

0016

원 본

# 외 무 부

암호수신

종 별 :

번 호 : GVW-1645 일 시 : 90 0829 1200

수 신 : 장관(중근동,국기,영해)

발 신 : 주 제네바 대사

제 목 : 이라크 및 쿠웨이트 아국교민 안전철수

연:GVW-1629

1. 연호관련 IOM(국제이민 기구) PURCELL 사무총장은 별첨 본직앞 공한을 통해 걸프지역 국가에 있는 외국인 안전철수를 지원키 위한 계획(PROGRAMME)을 시행하기 위해 이미 동지역 IOM 조사단을 파견하였으며 쿠웨이트 및 이라크 지역에 외국인 수는 약 2 백만명으로 추산되며, 이들 수송키 위해서는 우선적 5 천만불의 경비가 소요된다고 하면서 회원국의 기여금 지원을 요청하여 왔으며, 아울러 중동지역 사태에 대한 IOM 의 관여문제를 검토하기 위해 집행위원회 회의를 9.4. 개최될 예정임을 통보하여 왔음.

2. IOM 의 외국인 안전수송계획 및 재정지원 요청에대한 검토의견 회시 바람.

3. 참고로 현재 이르크 및 쿠웨이트의 아국교민(근로자 포함) 잔류자 및 출국자수 통보 바람.

첨부: IOM 공한 1 부.(GVW(F)-0308). 끝

(대사 이상옥-국장)

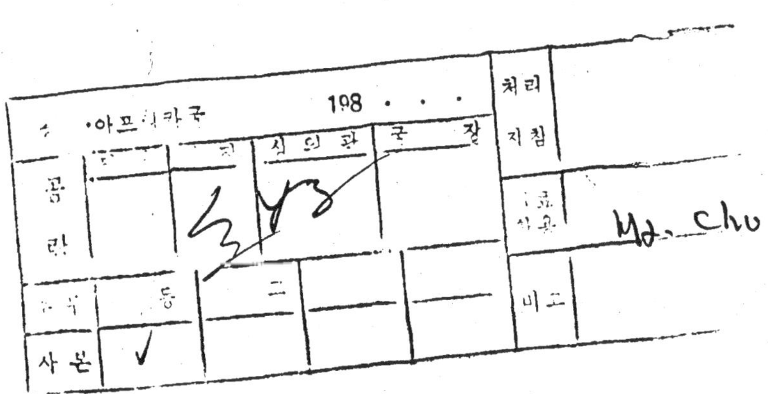

중아국 대책반 차관 1차보 2차보 국기국 통상국 영교국 청와대 안기부

PAGE 1

90.08.30 01:14

외신 2과 통제관 DO

0017

GVW(F)-0308 00820 1200 접수

INTERNATIONAL ORGANIZATION FOR MIGRATION

THE DIRECTOR GENERAL

GENEVA, SWITZERLAND

28 August 1990

Sir,

I have the honour to refer to the programme of return assistance which is being undertaken by the International Organization for Migration (IOM) on behalf of foreign nationals stranded in certain countries of the Middle East as a result of the situation in the region, and to submit a special appeal for necessary funding. The purpose of this emergency programme and the constitutional framework in which it will be implemented were described in the Aide Memoire attached to my letter of 24 August. In proposing to undertake this programme IOM recognizes the primary responsibility of States to ensure the safe return home of their endangered citizens but that such States may require IOM assistance in fulfilling this responsibility.

The objective of IOM's proposed programme is to provide sufficient assistance to affected States so as to assure that accelerated departure mechanisms are established and available for the safe return home of stranded foreign nationals. Already, more than 200,000 such persons have arrived in transit countries seeking return home, and additional thousands arrive each day (13,000 new arrivals were reported on Monday, 27 August). Out of necessity, several departure programmes have been created in recent days for specific populations. These programmes have been useful in meeting the most pressing needs of the selected populations and will continue to be important. For the immediate future,

H.E. Mr. Sang Ock Lee
Ambassador
Permanent Observer
The Office of the Permanent Observer
of the Republic of Korea to the United
Nations Office and Permanent Delegation
to the other international organizations
in Geneva
P.O. Box 566
1215 GENEVE 15

5-1

0018

However, priority attention must also be given to (1) initiating returns of nationals for whom no similar organized departure arrangements presently exist and (2) developing a consolidated framework and resource system for planning and executing all movements equitably and in as cost beneficial a manner as possible under present circumstances. These are the areas on which IOM will concentrate initially.

Although precise figures of foreign nationals at risk in Kuwait and Iraq are not available, best estimates are that there are some two to two and a half million persons, from a variety of States, in that category. While the borders of all five countries neighbouring Iraq are opened, the largest concentration to date of persons in transit seeking to return to their home countries has occurred in Jordan.

In order to determine immediate needs, IOM has dispatched an assessment team to the region. From Jordan, the team has identified several critically important departure needs relating to citizens of the Philippines and South Asia. IOM has already begun to make several urgent departure arrangements by shifting resources from other programmes which will not be needed until later in the year. These advanced resources must, of course, be paid back.

To undertake the proposed programmes, IOM must now issue an urgent appeal for resources both to (1) begin making travel arrangements for persons most in need and (2) set up necessary structures to administer these complicated arrangements. Because some of the responses which need to be initiated urgently cannot be delayed until assessment missions are completed, this appeal constitutes an initial, start-up effort, and calls for funds to initiate and continue vital travel arrangements. Once needs are better known, and depending upon the evolution of the situation, an additional or revised appeal may be considered.

With regard to funding required to make the most critical transportation arrangements, we estimate that some US$50 million will be required initially. We understand that some governments may wish to contribute specific air, sea, or land transport services. Such in-kind contributions will be welcomed to the degree they meet priority movement needs, but we urgently request that no less than 50 per cent of the initial US$50 million be contributed in cash.

We estimate that start-up resources required to establish implementing structures will amount to US$800,000. Actions are already underway to establish such a presence in Jordan, with the agreement of the national authorities. Other offices will be set up as needs dictate and new resources are made available. As IOM has no offices or staff in this region, mobilization of new implementing structures must proceed without delay.

0019

5-2

Further information regarding these requests is enclosed.

Analyses of the number of nationals in Kuwait and Iraq as well as those already present in Jordan, lead to this initial transportation estimate. The number of movements we will be able to accomplish will depend on several factors: (1) the availability of transportation capacity (already severely limited due to the crisis in the Gulf). (2) the increasing costs due to higher fuel prices and insurance rates, (3) the excessive costs of charter operations from the region due to the risks mentioned above. and (4) the more costly one-way nature of these movements.

In order to stretch resources, we will ask those individuals who have the ability to pay to do so. Similarly, we will request the home countries of persons moved to either reimburse the costs of the movements or contribute partially or in-kind toward their payment. But no person will be denied [illegible]

The role which IOM has agreed to assume with regard to transportation in this emergency was thoroughly discussed at a recent meeting of involved International Organizations. All agreed that transportation is an area where IOM has experience and expertise, and they pledged their support. It was also agreed that the involved International Organizations would stay in close contact during this emergency. This initial appeal is being issued directly by IOM because of the urgency of the situation and with the knowledge of other organizations. This practice will be followed also in subsequent appeals, if they become necessary.

I respectfully request your Government's immediate and favourable response to this urgent appeal.

Please accept, Sir, the assurance of my highest consideration.

James N Purcell Jr

James N. Purcell, Jr.

0020

5-3

GULF EMERGENCY PROGRAMME

SPECIAL APPEAL

TRANSPORTATION FUND

Estimate number I is based on the total number of persons in Iraq/Koweit, by nationality, on the assumption that the number that would initially require assistance and leave under the programme would be 10% of that total. In order to make an initial estimate, costs are based on air rates from Amman to the capital of the country of repatriation. The second estimates that the cost of transport could be reduced by half through concessional fares, charters and the use of ships. Charter options and transport by ship, as well as more accurate figures on the numbers of individuals involved, points of departure and destination of persons requiring assistance, will oblige a revision as soon as possible by the assessment team. The estimate also does not take into account the extent to which Governments listed will be able to fund movements directly.

| NATIONALITY | NUMBER | COST I | COST II |
|---|---|---|---|
| Egypt | 170,000 | 25,500,000 | 12,250,000 |
| India | 18,000 | 8,910,000 | 4,455,000 |
| Pakistan | 10,000 | 4,580,000 | 2,290.000 |
| Sri Lanka | 15,000 | 8,955,000 | 4,475,000 |
| Bangladesh | 7,500 | 4,402,500 | 2,201,250 |
| Philippines | 5,000 | 4,460,000 | 2,230,000 |
| Iran | 5,500 | 1,699,500 | 849,750 |
| Morocco | 3,600 | 2,311,200 | 1,155,600 |
| Yugoslavia | 730 | 259,150 | 129,575 |
| USSR | 920 | 556,600 | 278,300 |
| Thailand | 1,180 | 939,280 | 469,640 |
| Others | 5,000 | 3,000,000 | 1,500,000 |
| TOTAL | 242,430 | USD 65,583,230 | USD 32,791,615 |

In order to initiate repatriation transport assistance as rapidly as possible, and recognizing the great number of unknowns, IOM considers that an initial transportation fund of USD 50,000,000 will be necessary. In-kind transportation contributions up to 50 percent of this amount will be welcomed, to the degree that they meet priority transportation requirements.

5-4

0021

GULF EMERGENCY PROGRAMME

SPECIAL APPEAL

The following assumes an initial operation of four months, focussing on Jordan, with smaller operations in other countries (Turkey, Syria, Saudi Arabia and Iran) as the situation dictates. As the purpose of the operation is to repatriate persons who have fled from Iraq and Kuwait as rapidly and efficiently as possible, the location of operations will need to be flexible. Wherever possible, costs will be minimized by sharing existing facilities of cooperating International Organizations. All figures are in U.S. Dollars.

JORDAN

| Personnel | Per diem | Travel | Total | |
|---|---|---|---|---|
| 3 Officials | 31,200 | 4,800 | 36,000 | |
| 4 Operations Clerks | 46,240 | 6,400 | 52,640 | |
| Local Staff | | | 80,000 | |
| Communications | | | 30,000 | |
| Misc Equipment | | | 20,000 | |
| Vehicles | | | 15,000 | |
| Additional Travel | | | 40,000 | 273,640 |

SAUDI ARABIA/TURKEY/IRAN
SYRIA

| | | | | |
|---|---|---|---|---|
| 4 Officials | 76,800 | 9,800 | 86,600 | |
| 4 Ops Clerks | 76,800 | 9,800 | 86,600 | |
| Local staff | | | 60,000 | |
| Travel | | | 30,000 | |
| Misc. Office | | | 16,000 | |
| Communications | | | 20,000 | 299,200 |

HEADQUARTERS

| | | | | |
|---|---|---|---|---|
| 1 Official | | | 35,000 | |
| 1 Ops clerk | | | 15,000 | |
| 1 Accountant | | | 35,000 | |
| Communications | | | 30,000 | |
| Travel | | | 30,000 | 145,000 |
| | Sub-total | | | 717,840 |
| | Overhead/Contingency | | | 82,160 |
| | TOTAL | | | 800,000 |

5-5

0022

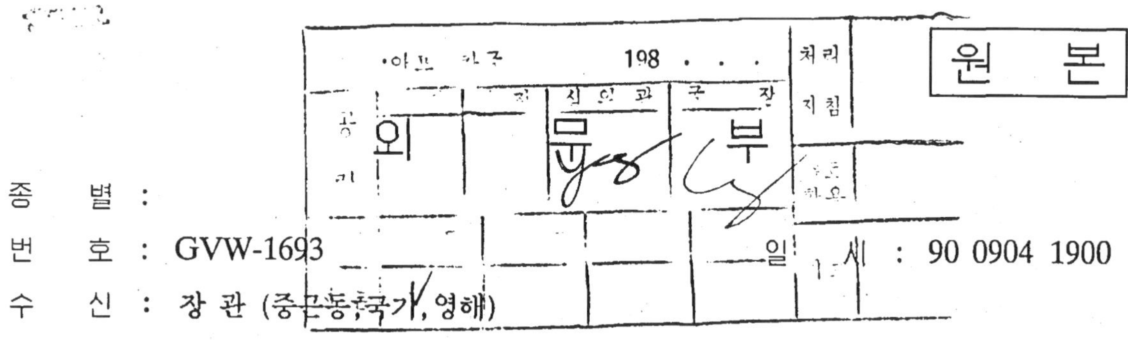


종 별 :

번 호 : GVW-1693 일 시 : 90 0904 1900

수 신 : 장 관 (중근동, 국기, 영해)

발 신 : 주 제네바 대사

제 목 : IOM 집행위원회 특별회의 개최

연: GVW-1645

1. 표제회의가 9.4.당지에서 IOM 집행위원국및 회원국 36개국 대표와 중동사태와관련된 32개국 대표가 특별빈객으로 참석한 가운데 STIGLICH 집행위의장 사회로 개최됨.(본직및 김종훈서기관 참석)

2. PURCELL IOM 사무총장은 중동사태와 관련한, IOM 의 그간의 활동을 보고하면서, IOM 실태조사단이 요르단에 파견되어 활동중이며, IOM 과 UNDRO 가 공동으로 9.3.부터 스리랑카인 및 방글라데시인 9천여명을 항공편으로 귀국 조치하고 있다고 밝힘.

동 사무총장은 금번사태 발발이전 이라크 및 쿠웨이트에 250만명의 외국인이 체류하고 있었으며 이들중 60퍼센트가 에집트인이며 20퍼센트가 아시아인이라고 말하고,특히 25만여명의 방글라데시, 파키스탄, 필리핀 및 스리랑카인이 긴박한 상황에 처해있어, IOM 및 UNDRO 가 동인들의 귀국을 최우선적으로 추진하고 있다고 말함.

동 사무총장은 자국민보호는 본국정부에 1차적책임이 있으나 국제기구도 이를 지원하지 않을수없는 형편임을 강조하고, 금번 IOM 활동에 2천3백만불의 추가예산이 소요된다고 말하면서, 각국 정부의 기여금 공여를 요청함.

3. 에집트, 방글라데시, 필리핀, 파키스탄 및 스리랑카대표등은 자국정부의 자국민 귀환조치를 설명하고 IOM 및 유엔산하기구의 지원을 요청하였으며, 미국, 벨지움, 이태리, 호주, 알젠틴, 화란대표등은 IOM의 금번활동을 평가하고 기여금 제공등 가능한 재정적 지원을 위해 노력하겠다고 말함.

한편 이날 회의에서 카나다대표는 동국정부가 IOM의 금번활동을 위해 1백만 카나다 달러를 기여하기로 결정하였다고 말하였으며, 스위스대표는 25만 서서프랑의

중아국 국기국 영교국 미주국 통상국 정책반 1차보 2차보 안기부

PAGE 1 90.09.05 08:38 FC

외신 1과 통제관

0023

기여결정을 밝힘. 또한 덴마크및 스웨덴대표는 금번사태와 관련한 유엔산하기구 활동지원을 위해 자국정부가 각기 450만불 및 850만불을 기여하기로 결정하였으며 동기여금중 일부가 IOM 활동에 사용될 것이라고 밝힘.

4. 이어 회의는 중동사태와 관련한 IOM활동에 관한 결의안(MC/ EX/ L129)을 만장일치로 채택한바, 동 결의안은 IOM 의 그간의 활동 및 향후계획을 승인하고, 이를 위해 사무총장이 IOM 특별기금 및 가능한 유가증권을 활용하도록 허가 하였으며, 회원국및 관련국가에 대해 기여금 제공을 요청하는 내용임.

5. 동 회의관련 문서 정파편 송부함.끝.

(대사 이상옥-국장)

7 9/10(화)신 사본 과사실

원 본

# 외 무 부

종 별 :

번 호 : GVW-1715　　　　　　일 시 : 90 0907 1600

수 신 : 장 관(국기, 영해, 중근동)

발 신 : 주 제네바 대사

제 목 : 중동사태관련 IOM 사무총장 서한

연: GVW-1093

이라크 및 쿠웨이트로부터의 외국인 철수에 따른 긴급재정지원 요청과 관련, 9.6. IOM 사무국은 당관앞 FAX 공한을 통해 동일자 PURCELL IOM사무총장의 장관앞 FAX 서한 사본을 당관에 송부하여왔는바, 동건 관련 본부방침이 정해지면 당관에도 통보 바람. 끝

(대사 이상옥-국장)

국기국　1차보　중아국　정문국　영교국　안기부　미주국　대책반

PAGE 1　　　　90.09.08 09:03 WG

외신 1과 통제관

0025

9/7(허) 신
중아, 영교국 협조PM
기 | 탄리 대신 명년
도 분담금 + α
지원 검토

↓ 0
↑ WOIMUBU K246510
WOIMUBU K24651
↓ 415722Y IOM CH

TO : HIS EXCELLENCY THE MINISTER FOR FOREIGN AFFAIRS
SEOUL, REPUBLIC OF KOREA TELEX 24 651

FROM : IOM, GENEVA

DATE : 6 SEPTEMBER L990

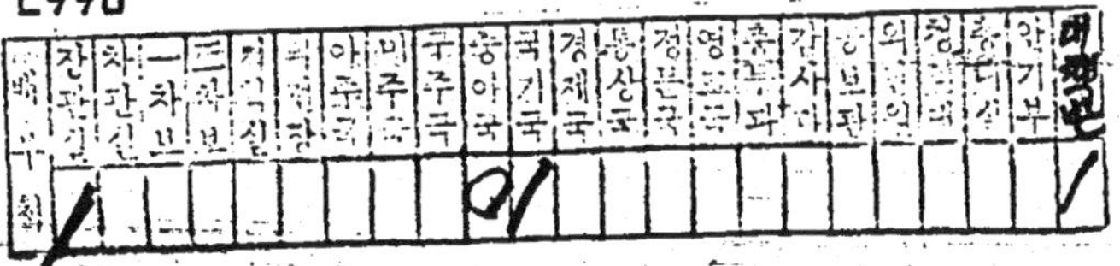

EXCELLENCY,

AS WE ARE ALL PAINFULLY AWARE, THE STREAM OF FOREIGN NATIONALS FLOWING OUT OF KUWAIT AND IRAQ HAS BECOME A FLOOD. THE ABILITY TO COPE WITH THIS CRISIS OF HUMANITY IN FLIGHT IS AT THE BREAKING POINT.

0026

THEIR COUNTRIES OF ORIGIN, BUT NEITHER AIRCRAFT SPACE AVAILABILITY NOR PRESENT FINANCIAL RESOURCES CAN HOPE EVEN TO KEEP PACE WITH THE DIRE NEEDS RESULTING FROM SOARING RATES OF ARRIVAL. MORE - MUCH MORE HAS TO BE DONE IMMEDIATELY TO INCREASE RAPID OUTWARD MOVEMENT FROM COUNTRIES WILLING TO PROVIDE TEMPORRY SAFE HAVEN BUT OVERWHELMED BY THE SHEER MASS OF HUMANITY IN NEED. ENERGETIC MEASURES MUST BE TAKEN AT ONCE, BEFORE HUMAN SUFFERING BECOMES HUMAN TRAGEDY.

THE INTERNATIONAL ORGANIZATION FOR MIGRATION (IOM) HAS BEEN REQUESTED BY UNDRO, THE UN AGENCY WHICH HAS BEEN CHARGED WITH THE CO-ORDINATION OF RELIEF EFFORTS ON BEHALF OF PERSONS DISPLACED AS A RESULT OF THE EVENTS IN KUWAIT, TO ASSUME THE LEAD ROLE FOR REPATRIATIONTRANSPORTATION. IN THAT CONTEXT, IOM HAS DRAWN UP A PLAN OF ACTION AND ALREADY APPEALED TO A NUMBER OF GOVERNMENTS ?INCLUDING YOUR OWN? IN LATE AUGUST FOR FINANCIAL CONTRIBUTIONS. THESE ACTIONS WERE FULLY ENDORSED BY THE IOM EXECUTIVE COMMITTEE, MEETING IN SPECIAL SESSION IN GENEVAON 4 SEPTEMBER, AND UNDERSCORED BY THE ADOPTION OF A RESOLUTION CALLING UPON MEMBER STATES AND OTHER INTERESTED STATES AND ENTITIES, INTER ALIA, ''TO PROVDE AS A MATTER OF URGENCY THE NECESSARY FINANCIAL AND LOGISTICAL ASSISTANCE NEEDED TO IMPLEMENT THIS PROGRAMME.''

THE PAST WEEK'S EXPERIENCE, COMBINED WITH FRESH INFORMATION RECEIVED SUBSEQUENT TO THE AFOREMENTIONED MEETING, INDICATE CLERLY THAT COMMERCIAL AIRCRAFT SPACE THROUGH REGULAR AIRPORT FACILITIES AND REPATRIATION BY AVAILABLE COMMERCIAL VESSELS WILL CONTINUE TO BE OUTSTRIPPED BY THE WAVES OF HUMAN BEINGS ARRIVING IN INCREASINGLY DESPERATE STRAITS. ADDITIONAL CAPACITY MUST BE FOUND NOW.

0027

IOM WILL CONTINUE TO SEEK CHARTER SPACE WITH THE SAME VIGOUR WE HAVE TO DATE. FOR T WE CONTINUE TO NEED FINA IAL CONTRIBUTIONS URGENTLY. BUT TIME IS OF THE ESSENCE, AND IMMEDIATE IN-KIND CONTRIBUTIONS OF THE AIRCRAFT AND SHIP CAPACITY NEEDED COULD SAVE ENOUGH OF THAT TIME TO AVERT EVEN GREATER SUFFERING. MORE AIRCRAFT AND SHIPS - NOW - ARE THE KEY. WE THEREFORE URGENTY APPEAL TO YOUR COUNTRY TO MAKE AVAILABLE IMMEDIATELY, AS AN IN-KIND CONTRIBUTION TO THIS INTERNATIONAL HUANITARIAN UNDERTAKING, COMMERCIAL OR MILITARY AIRCRAFT AND/OR SHIPS TO AUGMENT DEPARTURE SPACE AVAILABILITY.

AT THIS TIME, THE FOCUS OF OUR REPATRIATION EFFORTS IS ON JORDAN, WHERE CONDITIONS HAVE BECOME SO STRAINED THAT THE AUTHORITIES AND DONOR REPRESENTATIVES ON THE GROUND HAVE THEMSELVES STRESSED REPATRIATION TRANSPORTATION AS BEING THE TOP PRIORITY. ANY IN-KIND CONTRIBUTIONS RECEIVED IN RESPONSE TO THIS APPEAL WILL THEREFORE INITIALLY BE DIRECTED TO ALLEVIATING THE PRESSURE IN JORDAN WHOSE AUTHORITIES HAVE UNDERSCORED THE URGENT NEED FOR SUCH A FURTHER DISPLAY OF INTERNATIONAL SOLIDARITY. THEY HAVE ALSO INDICATED THEIR READINESS TO FACILITATE THE TECHNICAL ASPECTS OF SUCH AN UNDERTAKING.

IT IS MY STRONG HOPE THAT YOU WILL LOOK FAVOURABLY ON THIS REQUEST. GIVEN THE URGENCY OF THE NEED, WHICH CANNOT BE OVERSTATD, I WOULD GREATLY APPRECIATE YOUR GOVERNMENT'S RESPONSE AS SOON AS POSSIBLE.

ACCEPT, EXCELLENCY, THE ASSURANCE OF MY HIGHEST CONSIDERATION.

SIGNED, JAMES N. PURCELL, JR., DIRECTOR GENERAL, INTERNATIONAL ORGANIZATION FOR MIGRATION (IOM)

++0

↑ WOIMUBU K24651

↓ 415722Y IOM CH

0028

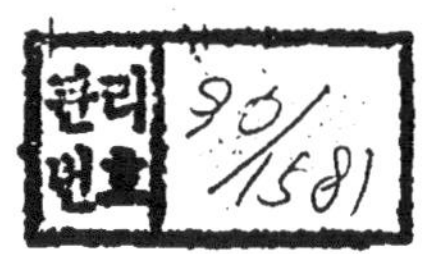

지급

| 분류기호 문서번호 | 중근동720-1581 | 협조문용지 (720-2327) | 결재 | 담당 | 과장 | 국장 |
|---|---|---|---|---|---|---|
| 시행일자 | 1990. 9. 8. | | | 조세영 | (서명) | (서명) |
| 수신 | 영사교민국장 | 발신 | 중동아프리카국장 | | | (서명) |
| 제목 | 국제이민 기구(IOM)의 지원요청 | | | | | |

1. 국제 이민 기구(IOM)는 별첨 장관 앞 텔렉스를 통하여 금번 페르시아만 사태로 인하여 인접국에 대피한 외국인들의 본국 귀환을 위하여 동기구 회원국인 아국이 상업용 또는 군용 비행기 및 선박을 제공하여 줄 것을 요청하여 온바, 국제이민기구 관련 업무는 귀국 소관으로 사료되어 이송하오니 검토 조치하여 주시기 바랍니다.

2. 상기와 관련, 금번 사태관련 국제사회의 노력에 적극 동참한다는 아국의 기본입장에 비추어 국제이민기구 측 요청에 대하여 가능한 범위내에서 성의를 표시하는 것이 바람직할 것으로 사료됨을 첨언합니다.

첨부 : 국제이민기구의 장관 앞 텔렉스 사본 1부. 끝.

1990.12.31.에 예고문에 의거 일반문서로 재분류

0029

↓ 0
↑ WOIMUBU K246510
WOIMUBU K24651
↓ 415722Y IOM CH

TO : HIS EXCELLENCY THE MINISTER FOR FOREIGN AFFAIRS
SEOUL, REPUBLIC OF KOREA TELEX 24 651

FROM : IOM, GENEVA

DATE : 6 SEPTEMBER L990

EXCELLENCY,

AS WE ARE ALL PAINFULLY AWARE, THE STREAM OF FOREIGN NATIONALS FLOWING OUT OF KUWAIT AND IRAQ HAS BECOME A FLOOD. THE ABILITY TO COPE WITH THIS CRISIS OF HUMANITY IN FLIGHT IS AT THE BREAKING POINT.

0030

THEIR COUNTRIES OF ORIGIN, BUT NEITHER AIRCRAFT SPACE AVAILABILITY NOR PRESENT FIN[illegible] RESOURCES CAN HOPE E[illegible] KEEP PACE WITH THE DIRE NEEDS RESUL[illegible]NG FROM SOARING RATES OF ARRIVAL. MORE - MUCH MORE HAS TO BE DONE IMMEDIATELY TO INCREASE RAPID OUTWARD MOVEMENT FROM COUNTRIES WILLING TO PROVIDE TEMPORRY SAFE HAVEN BUT OVERWHELMED BY THE SHEER MASS OF HUMANITY IN NEED. ENERGETIC MEASURES MUST BE TAKEN AT ONCE, BEFORE HUMAN SUFFERING BECOMES HUMAN TRAGEDY.

THE INTERNATIONAL ORGANIZATION FOR MIGRATION (IOM) HAS BEEN REQUESTED BY UNDRO, THE UN AGENCY WHICH HAS BEEN CHARGED WITH THE CO-ORDINATION OF RELIEF EFFORTS ON BEHALF OF PERSONS DISPLACED AS A RESULT OF THE EVENTS IN KUWAIT, TO ASSUME THE LEAD ROLE FOR REPATRIATIONTRANSPORTATION. IN THAT CONTEXT, IOM HAS DRAWN UP A PLAN OF ACTION AND ALREADY APPEALED TO A NUMBER OF GOVERNMENTS ?INCLUDING YOUR OWN? IN LATE AUGUST FOR FINANCIAL CONTRIBUTIONS. THESE ACTIONS WERE FULLY ENDORSED BY THE IOM EXECUTIVE COMMITTEE, MEETING IN SPECIAL SESSION IN GENEVAON 4 SEPTEMBER, AND UNDERSCORED BY THE ADOPTION OF A RESOLUTION CALLING UPON MEMBER STATES AND OTHER INTERESTED STATES AND ENTITIES, INTER ALIA, ''TO PROVDE AS A MATTER OF URGENCY THE NECESSARY FINANCIAL AND LOGISTICAL ASSISTANCE NEEDED TO IMPLEMENT THIS PROGRAMME.''

THE PAST WEEK'S EXPERIENCE, COMBINED WITH FRESH INFORMATION RECEIVED SUBSEQUENT TO THE AFOREMENTIONED MEETING, INDICATE CLERLY THAT COMMERCIAL AIRCRAFT SPACE THROUGH REGULAR AIRPORT FACILITIES AND REPATRIATION BY AVAILABLE COMMERCIAL VESSELS WILL CONTINUE TO BE OUTSTRIPPED BY THE WAVES OF HUMAN BEINGS ARRIVING IN INCREASINGLY DESPERATE STRAITS. ADDITIONAL CAPACITY MUST BE FOUND NOW.

0031

IOM WILL CONTINUE [illegible]EEK CHARTER SPACE WIT[illegible] SAME VIGOUR WE HAVE TO DATE. FOR TH[illegible] WE CONTINUE TO NEED FINA[illegible]IAL CONTRIBUTIONS URGENTLY. BUT TIME IS OF THE ESSENCE, AND IMMEDIATE IN-KIND CONTRIBUTIONS OF THE AIRCRAFT AND SHIP CAPACITY NEEDED COULD SAVE ENOUGH OF THAT TIME TO AVERT EVEN GREATER SUFFERING. MORE AIRCRAFT AND SHIPS -- NOW -- ARE THE KEY. WE THEREFORE URGENTY APPEAL TO YOUR COUNTRY TO MAKE AVAILABLE IMMEDIATELY, AS AN IN-KIND CONTRIBUTION TO THIS INTERNATIONAL HUANITARIAN UNDERTAKING, COMMERCIAL OR MILITARY AIRCRAFT AND/OR SHIPS TO AUGMENT DEPARTURE SPACE AVAILABILITY.

AT THIS TIME, THE FOCUS OF OUR REPATRIATION EFFORTS IS ON JORDAN, WHERE CONDITIONS HAVE BECOME SO STRAINED THAT THE AUTHORITIES AND DONOR REPRESENTATIVES ON THE GROUND HAVE THEMSELVES STRESSED REPATRIATION TRANSPORTATION AS BEING THE TOP PRIORITY. ANY IN-KIND CONTRIBUTIONS RECEIVED IN RESPONSE TO THIS APPEAL WILL THEREFORE INITIALLY BE DIRECTED TO ALLEVIATING THE PRESSURE IN JORDAN WHOSE AUTHORITIES HAVE UNDERSCORED THE URGENT NEED FOR SUCH A FURTHER DISPLAY OF INTERNATIONAL SOLIDARITY. THEY HAVE ALSO INDICATED THEIR READINESS TO FACILITATE THE TECHNICAL ASPECTS OF SUCH AN UNDERTAKING.

IT IS MY STRONG HOPE THAT YOU WILL LOOK FAVOURABLY ON THIS REQUEST. GIVEN THE URGENCY OF THE NEED, WHICH CANNOT BE OVERSTATD, I WOULD GREATLY APPRECIATE YOUR GOVERNMENT'S RESPONSE AS SOON AS POSSIBLE.

ACCEPT, EXCELLENCY, THE ASSURANCE OF MY HIGHEST CONSIDERATION.

SIGNED, JAMES N. PURCELL, JR., DIRECTOR GENERAL, INTERNATIONAL ORGANIZATION FOR MIGRATION (IOM)

++0

↑ WOIMUBU K24651

↓ 415722Y IOM CH

0032

| 분류기호 문서번호 | 영해 20810 - 326 | 협조문용지 ( ) | 결재 | 담 당 | 과 장 | 국 장 |
|---|---|---|---|---|---|---|
| 시행일자 | 1990. 9. 10. | | | | | |
| 수 신 | 수신처 참조 | 발 신 | 영사교민국장 (서명) | | | |
| 제 목 | 국제 이민기구 지원 | | | | | |

1. 국제 이민기구 (IOM) James N. Purcell 사무총장은 9. 6 자 장관 앞 팩시 서한을 통해 이라크 사태로 인한 난민 수송을 위해 아국이 상업용, 군용 ~~또는~~ 항공기 또는 선박을 제공해 줄 것을 요청해 왔읍니다.

2. IOM 은 이라크 사태 이후 방글라데시, 필리핀, 파키스탄인등 난민 수송을 위해 회원국에 특별 기여금 공여를 호소하였던 바, 미국, 벨지움, 이태리, 호주, 알젠틴, 화란 등이 재정적 지원을 약속하였고, 카나다는 100만 카나다불, 스위스는 25만 스위스 프랑의 기여금 공여를 결정했으며, 덴마크와 스웨덴은 금번 사태와 관련한 유엔 산하 기구 활동 기여금 (덴마크 : 450 만불, 스웨덴 : 850 만불) 중 일부를 IOM 활동에 사용토록 할 계획으로 있읍니다.

3. IOM 의 금번 활동이 비록 아국인 수송을 위한 것이

/ 계 속 ... 0033

1505 - 8 일 (1)
85. 9. 9 승인 "내가아낀 종이 한장 늘어나는 나라살림"
190㎜×268㎜(인쇄용지 2급 60g /㎡)
가 40-41 1987. 10. 13.

아닐지라도 인도적 및 국제협력적 차원에서 동 사무총장의 요청에

대해 가능한 지원 (특별 기여금 제공등) 을 검토코자 하는 바,

별첨 IOM 개요를 참고, 아국의 지원 필요성 여부, 지원범위 및

재원등에 관한 귀견을 회보하여 주시기 바랍니다. 끝.

수신처 : 기획관리실장, 국제기구조약국장, 중동아프리카국장

0034

중근동과

# I O M 개 요

================

1. 현 황

가. 정식 명칭 : 국제 이민기구 (International Organization for Migration, ICM)

나. 설립 경위 : 1951년 유럽이민 운동을 위한 가칭 "정부간 위원회" 로 발족 (벨기에 브뤼셀)

다. 본 부 : 스위스 제네바

라. 회원국 및 옵저버 현황

o 회원국 (36 개국)

- 미주 (18) : 미국, 알젠틴, 볼리비아, 칠레, 콜롬비아, 엘살바돌, 코스타리카, 도미니카 (공), 에쿠아돌, 파나마, 니카라과, 파라과이, 페루, 우루과이, 베네수엘라, 혼두라스, 카나다, 과테말라

- 구주 (11) : 오스트리아, 벨지움, 룩셈부륵, 그리이스, 이태리, 서독, 덴마크, 네델란드, 폴투칼, 스위스, 노르웨이

- 중동 (2) : 이스라엘, 키프로스
- 아프리카 (1) : 케냐
- 아주 (3) : 태국, 한국, 필리핀
- 대양주 (1) : 호주

0035

o 옵저버 (14 개국)
- 미주 (4) : 벨리제, 과테말라, 멕시코
- 구주 (7) : 영국, 프랑스, 스페인, 스웨덴, 로마교황청, 산마리노, 말타
- 중동 (2) : 이집트, 터어키
- 아주 (1) : 일본
- 아프리카(1) : 우간다

2. 목 적

가. 수민국과 송출국의 특정 수요에 응해 질서있는 계획이주 (해외 취업 포함) 추진

o 관계 정부의 정책 및 법률, 이민 경향 및 문제점 연구 분석
o 2년에 1회 세미나 개최, 관련 정부, 국제기구, 이주 희망자들에게 권고 또는 조언
o 이주자 또는 난민들에게 수민국에서의 정착에 필요한 지식이나 언어등에 대한 훈련 또는 오리엔테이션 제공

나. 난민 정착 기회를 제공하는 국가에 대한 난민의 송출 및 정착 추진

o 정치적, 종교적, 윤리적 이유 때문에 조국을 떠나야만 하는 난민 지원
o 이주할 기회가 있는 난민이 경제적 어려움으로 이주를 못하는 경우가 없도록 원조
o 유엔난민 고등 판무관실 (UNHCR), 국제적십자위원회 (ICRC), 적십자 연맹 (LRCS) 등과 긴밀한 협조
o 가족 재결합 계획 추진

0036

다. 개도국의 경제, 교육, 사회적 발전을 도모하기 위한 전문 인력의 교류

o 국가발전에 필요한 특정분야 (정부기관, 대학, 전문 기술학교, 기타 공공기관) 에 대한 선별적 고급 전문가 공급

o 유능한 고급인력의 모국 귀환 알선

3. 조 직

o 이사회 (연 1회 개최, 전회원국 대표와 옵저버로 구성)

o 집행위원회 (연 2회 개최, 1년 임기의 9개 회원국 대표로 구성)

o 소위원회 (예산재정위원회 및 수송협력 위원회)

o 사무국 (총장, 차장)

o 세미나 (2년마다 1회 개최)

4. 회원자격 및 의무

o 회원국 수에 대한 제한 규정 없음.

o 헌장 이행준수 및 행정운영 경비 분담

o 이사회의 2/3 다수결로 가입 결정

5. 재 정

o 행정운영비 : 합의된 배당비율 의거 전회원 분담

o 사업 운영

- 이민 송출국 및 수민국 기부금
- 특수사업을 위한 회원국 기부금
- 기타, 후원자 및 지원단체 기부금

0037

6. IOM 의 국제기구등과의 협조 현황

가. IOM 과 협력하는 국제기구

1) IOM 과 협력협정 체결 국제기구 (23) :

- U.N. High Commissioner for Refuggess (UNHCR),
- U.N. Disaster Relief Coordinater (UNDRO),
- Economic Commission for Latin America and the Caribbean (ECLAC)
- Economic Commission for Africa (ECA)
- Economic and Social Council for Asia and the Pacific (ESCAP)
- Latin American Economic System (SELA)
- U.N. Population Division
- U.N. Fund for Population Activities (UNFPA)
- U.N. Development Programme (UNDP)
- U.N. Volunteers Programme (UNV)
- U.N. Center for Human Rights
- U.N. Educational, Scientific and Cultural Organization (UNESCO)
- Food and Agriculture Organization of the U.N. (FAO)
- International Labour Organisation (ILO)
- World Health Organization (WHO)
- Organization of American States (OAS)
- Inter - American Development Bank (IDB)
- Commission of the Cartagena Agreement (Andean Pact)
- Organization for Economic Co-operation and Development (OECD)
- Council of Europe
- Commission of European Communities (CEC)
- Italo-Latin American Institute (IILA)
- Instituto de Cooperacion Iberoamericana (ICI)

0038

2) IOM 이 옵저버인 국제기구 (4) :

- Economic and Social Council (Ecosoc)
- U.N. Conference on Trade and Development (UNCTAD)
- U.N. Industrial Development Organization (UNIDO)
- International Maritime Organization (IMO)

나. IOM 과 협조하는 각급 지원기구 (23) :

- American Council for Nationalities Service
- International Council of Voluntary Agencies
- American Fund for Czechoslovak Refugees Inc.
- International Rescue Committee
- Buddhist Council for Refugee Rescue and Resettlement
- International Social Service
- CARE Inc.
- Lutheran World Federation
- Catholic Relief Services
- National Council of Young Men's Christian Associations
- Centro de Estudios'y Promocion Social
- Norwegian Refugee Council
- Comite national d'entraide franco-vietnamien, franco-cambodgien, franco-laotien
- Polish American Immigration and Relief Committee
- Food for the Hungry International
- Presiding Bishop's Fund for World Relief

0039

- Hebrew Immigrant Aid Society (HIAS Inc.)
- Tolstoy Foundation Inc.
- International Catholic Migration Commission
- United Ukrainian American Relief Committee
- International Council on Social Welfare
- World Council of Churches
- World Relief Refugee Services

7. 지역사무소 소재지 (39 개국)

o 미주 (16) : 미국, 알젠틴, 볼리비아, 칠레, 콜롬비아, 코스타리카, 도미니카(공), 에쿠아돌, 엘살바돌, 니카라과, 파나마, 파라과이, 페루, 우루과이, 베네수엘라, 혼두라스

o 구주 (9) : 오스트리아, 벨지움, 룩셈부룩, 그리스, 이태리, 서독, 폴루칼, 프랑스, 스페인, 영국

o 중동 (2) : 키스로스, 수단

o 아주 (9) : 홍콩, 인도네시아, 일본, 말레이시아, 파키스탄, 필리핀, 싱가폴, 호주, 태국

o 아프리카(3): 케냐, 소말리아, 지부티

8. 아국과의 관계

o 85.11.20 제 52차 총회시 업저버로 가입

o 86.7.9 - 7.15 Kotteck 홍콩 주재 ICM 사무소장 방한

o 86.12.7 - 12.10 Horst Habenicht ICM 기획부장

o 88.11.29. 정회원으로 가입
(년간 약 6만불의 분담금 지불)

0040

9. 90년 상반기 IOM 의 업무실적 (90. 1 - 6 월)

가. 난민 이주지원 : 122,337 명

- ○ 유럽 유출 난민 : 50,406 명
- ○ 중동, 아프리카 유출 난민 : 3,432 명
- ○ 동남아 유출 난민 : 61,144 명
- ○ 근동 유출 난민 : 1,853 명
- ○ 라틴 아메리카 유출 난민 : 5,455 명
- ○ 기 타 : 4 명

나. 해외이주 지원 : 4,422 명

- ○ 일반 이민 : 2,598 명
- ○ 개발 이민 : 1,824 명

0041

# I O M 개 요

1. 정식 명칭 : 국제 이민 기구(Int'l Organization for Migration : IOM)

2. 설립 및 성격 : 1951년 유럽 이민 지원을 위하여 설립된 정부간 기구

3. 본 부 : 스위스 제네바

4. 사무총장 : James N. Purcell

5. 회원국 및 옵서버 현황

   o 회원국 : 아국 포함 36개국

   o 옵서버 : 14개국

6. 주요 사업

   o 질서있는 계획 이주(해외 취업 포함)

   o 난민의 송출 및 정착

   o 개도국 발전을 위한 전문 인력 교류

7. 예 산 : 128 백만불 (90)

8. 90년 상반기 사업 실적

   o 난민 이주 지원 122,337 명

   o 해외 이주 지원 4,422 명

9. 아국과의 관계

   o 85년 옵서버 가입

   o 88년 정회원 가입

     ※ 연간 약 6만불의 분담금 지불

0042

| 분류기호 문서번호 | 국기20300-177 | 협 조 문 용 지 ( 2181-2 ) | 결재 | 담당 | 과장 | 국장 |
|---|---|---|---|---|---|---|
| 시행일자 | 1990.9.12. | | | 신용이 | | |
| 수 신 | 영사교민국장 | 발 신 | 국제기구조약국장 | (서 명) | | |
| 제 목 | 국제이민기구(IOM) 지원 | | | | | |

대 : 영해 20810-326

1. 대호 국제이민기구의 난민수송 지원 요청 관련, 당국은 동사업 참여가 인도적 차원과 국제~~사회 발전에 기여한다는~~ 협력 이라는 관점에서 지원 필요성에는 동의하나, 88.11. 아국의 동기구 가입후 가입 실익에 비해 과도한 분담금 지불의 문제점이 있음에 비추어 볼때 특별기여금 지출은 현실적으로 어려움이 있는 것으로 사료됩니다.

2. 그러나, 귀국에서 현재 동기구로부터의 탈퇴문제를 검토하고 있다면 명년도 기구 탈퇴를 전제로 이미 계상되어 있는 91년도 분담금과 기타 가용자금을 활용하여 지원금을 염출하는 방안을 고려할 수 있다고 봅니다. 끝

0043

국제 이민기구 (IOM) 의 난민 수송 협조 요청 대책

==================================================

90. 9. 13.

영 사 교 민 국

해 외 이 주 과

0044

1. 문제의 제기

ㅇ 이라크 사태로 야기된 외국인 난민 문제 해결을 위해 국제 이민기구는 아국에 특별기여금 또는 난민 수송을 위한 수송기 (항공기 또는 선박) 제공을 요청함.

2. 난민 현황

ㅇ 이라크 및 쿠웨이트내 체류중인 250 만명의 외국인중 일부가 요르단 및 터키에 피난 대피중임.

* 동 외국인중 60% 가 이집트인, 20%가 아시아인

ㅇ 특히 25만명의 방글라데시, 파키스탄, 필리핀 및 스리랑카인이 긴박한 상황에 처해 있음.

3. 국제 이민기구 (IOM) 요청 사항

ㅇ IOM 의 Purcell 사무총장은 8. 24 자 주 제네바대사 앞 서한을 통해 난민 수송을 위한 기여금 지원 요청

ㅇ 동 총장은 또한 9.6 자 외무부장관 앞 팩시 서한을 통해 난민 수송을 위한 항공기 또는 선박 제공을 요청함.

ㅇ IOM 홍콩 사무소장은 9.12 자 외무부 영사교민국장 앞 팩시 서한을 통해 난민 수송을 위한 IOM 의 역할과 관련, 아국의 조치에 필요한 협조 제공을 약속함.

0045

4. IOM의 난민 지원 요청에 대한 각국 반응

o 9.4. 제네바 개최 IOM 집행 위원회 특별 회의 개최

- 카나다 : IOM 활동을 위해 100만 카나다불 기여 결정
- 스위스 : 25만 스위스 프랑 기여 결정
- 덴마크 : 이라크 사태와 관련한 유엔 산하기구 활동 지원을 위해 기여하기로 결정한 450 만불중 일부를 IOM 활동에 사용되도록 조치
- 스웨덴 : 이라크 사태와 관련한 유엔 산하기구 활동 지원을 위해 기여하기로 결정한 850 만불중 일부를 IOM 활동에 사용되도록 조치

* IOM 측은 난민 수송을 위해 6,000 만불이 소요될 것으로 예상하고 있으며, 9.10 현재 3,500 만불 확보

5. 세계 각국 및 기구의 난민 지원 현황 (9.12. 주요르단대사 보고)

- 영 국 : 난민 수송 및 구호 경비 지원 2,200 만불
- 인 도 : 비행기 11편 (자국민 수송)
- EC 및 프랑스 : 비행기 5 편
- 뉴질랜드 : 비행기 3 편
- 이 태 리 : 쌀 40톤 (175 만불 상당)
- 미 국 : 식량 및 의약품 (100 만불 상당)
- 파키스탄 : 식량 및 의약품 30톤 (자국민용), 비행기 1편 (자국민용)
- 화란, 노르웨이 : 적십자 구호인력 지원

0046

6. 대　책

o IOM 의 이라크 난민 문제 해결을 위한 활동에 대해 현 난민 상황으로 보아 인도적 및 국제협력적 차원에서 어느정도 성의를 표시하는 것이 바람직한 것으로 판단됨.

o 필리핀, 스리랑카등 일부 국가에서 자국민 수송 지원을 요청하는 경우 지원 효과의 극대화를 위해 IOM 을 통해 지원하는 방안을 검토함이 좋을 듯함.

0047

## 협 조 문 용 지

| 분류기호 문서번호 | 국기20300- 177 | ( 2181-2 ) | 결재 | 담당 | 과장 | 국장 |
|---|---|---|---|---|---|---|
| 시행일자 | 1990.9.12. | | | | | |
| 수 신 | 영사교민국장 | 발 신 | 국제기구조약국장 (서명) | | | |
| 제 목 | 국제이민기구(IOM) 지원 | | | | | |

대 : 영해 20810-326

1. 대호 국제이민기구의 난민수송 지원 요청 관련, 당국은 동사업 참여가 인도적 차원과 국제 협력이라는 관점에서 지원 필요성에는 동의하나, 88.11. 아국의 동기구 가입후 가입 실익에 비해 과도한 분담금 지불의 문제점이 있음에 비추어 볼때 특별기여금 지출은 현실적으로 어려움이 있는 것으로 사료됩니다.

2. 그러나, 귀국에서 현재 동기구로부터의 탈퇴문제를 검토하고 있다면 명년도 기구 탈퇴를 전제로 이미 계상되어 있는 91년도 분담금과 기타 가용자금을 활용하여 지원금을 염출하는 방안을 고려할 수 있다고 봅니다. 끝

| 영사교민국 | 90.9.13. 인 | 담 당 | 계 장 | 과 장 | 관리관 | 국 장 |
|---|---|---|---|---|---|---|
| | | (서명) | | | | (서명) |

0048

| 관리 번호 | 90/1603 |
|---|---|

# 외 무 부

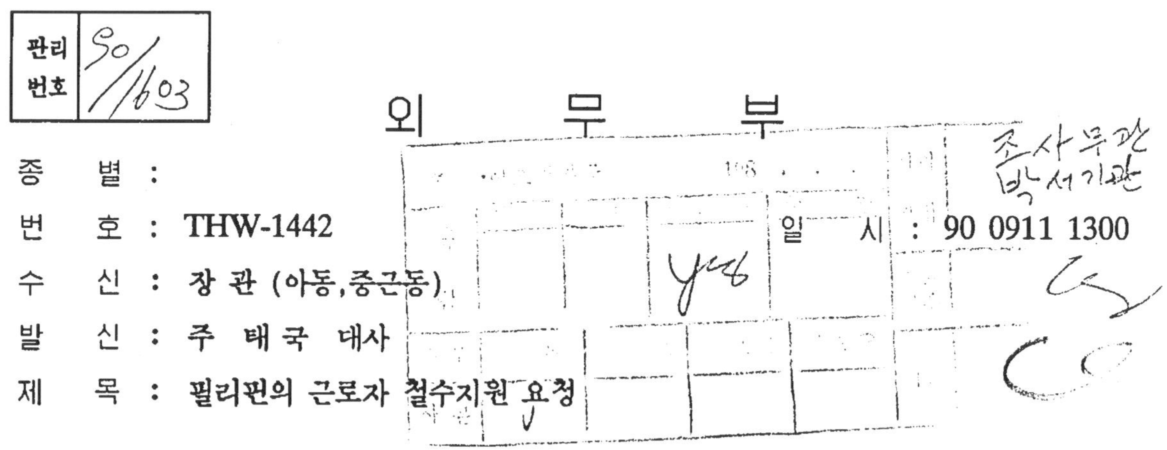

종 별 :

번 호 : THW-1442 일 시 : 90 0911 1300

수 신 : 장 관 (아동,중근동)

발 신 : 주 태국 대사

제 목 : 필리핀의 근로자 철수지원 요청

대 : WTH-1109

1. 대호건 정참사관이 9.10. MR.VARA-POJ 외무성 정책기획과장에 문의한바,동 과장 설명요지는 아래와 같으며 진전사항은 추보하겠음.

가. 9.6. 주필리핀대사관을 통하여 이락, 쿠웨이트로부터의 필리핀근로자 철수 지원 요청을 받았는바, 이에대해 같은 아세안 회원국으로서 필리핀측을 도와주겠다는 용의를 표명하였음. 다만, 동 지원요청 내용이 일반적인 요청이었기때문에 태국정부는 필리핀정부가 동 지원내역을 보다 구체적으로 요청해 주도록 대기중에 있음.

나. 필리핀측은 태국측이 태국 민간항공기를 암만에 파견하여 필리핀근로자를 만닐라로 수송하도록 주선하여 줄 경우 필요하다면 비용은 자담하겠다는 의향을 표명한 것으로 알고 있음.

다. 태국측으로서는 전세기 지원요청을 받을경우, 쿠웨이트 및 이락으로부터 약 7천여명의 태국 근로자를 지난주 태국 민간항공기를 이용, 방콕으로 수송완료한 경험이 있으므로 이러한 방법을 고려하는 것이 보다 용이할 것임.

라. 필리핀정부로 부터 구체적 지원요청을 받아 다음방침을 정하는대로 이를 당관에 알려주겠음.

2. 동 과장에 의하면 주쿠웨이트 태국대사관의 외교관들은 전원 인근국가로철수하였으며 주쿠웨이트대사관은 쿠웨이트 현지인들이 CARETAKER 로서 관리하고 있는 상태라고함을 참고로 보고함.

(대사 정 주년-국 장)

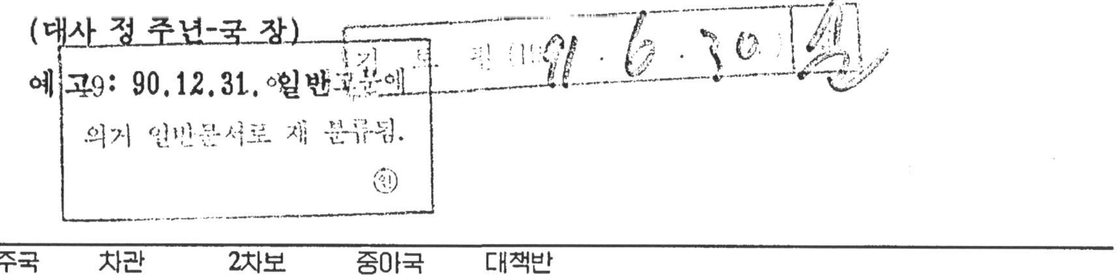

예고: 90.12.31. 일반

검토필(1990.12.31.)

일반문서로 재분류(91.6.30)

의거 일반문서로 재 분류됨.

아주국 차관 2차보 중아국 대책반

PAGE 1 90.09.11 17:10

외신 2과 통제관 BN

0049

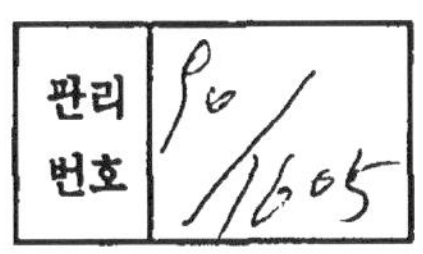

# 외 무 부

종 별 :

번 호 : MAW-1317 일 시 : 90 0911 1430

수 신 : 장관(아동,사본:주 말련 대사)

발 신 : 주 말련 대사 대리

제 목 : 필리핀 근로자 철수지원 요청

대:WMA-0661

연:MAW-1243

검토필(1990.12.31.)

9.11 오참사관은 ASMAN NAZIR 외무부 동남아 과장과 접촉 표제관련 진전사항을 문의한바, 동 과장은 주재국의 대 필리핀 지원입장에는 변함이 없으나 이락.쿠웨이트에는 필리핀외에도 다수국가들의 교민들이 철수치 못하고 있는 실정임을 감안, 이들의 철수를 위한 공동노력 가능성을 모색키 위해 한국을 비롯한 우방국들의 의사를 상금 타진중에 있으나 아직 구체적인 진전은 없다고함. 끝

(대사대리 김경준-국장)

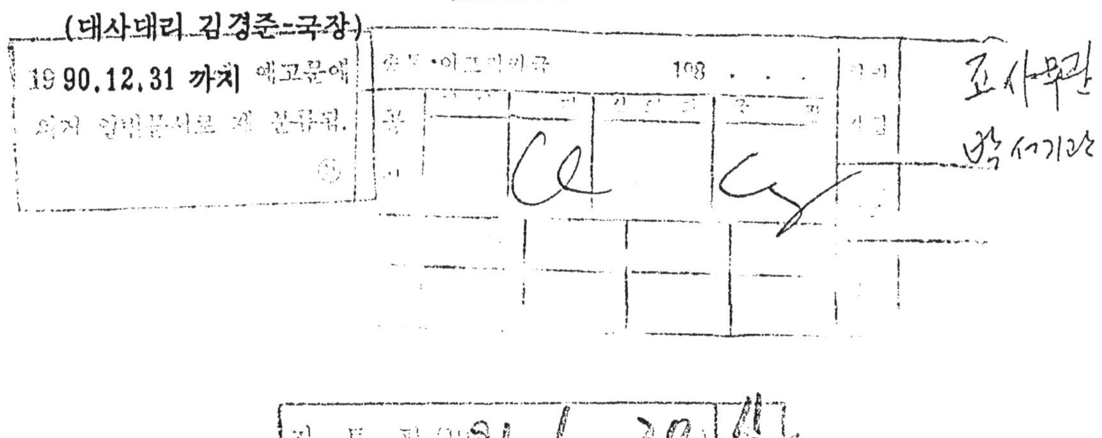

1990.12.31 까지 예고문에 의거 일반문서로 재분류됨.

검토필(1991.6.30.)

아주국 중아국 대책반

PAGE 1

90.09.11 17:07

외신 2과 통제관 BN

0050

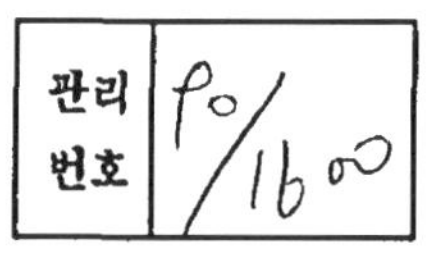

# 외 무 부

종 별 :

번 호 : AUW-0709 일 시 : 90 0911 1700

수 신 : 장관(아동,중근동,기협)

발 신 : 주 호주 대사

제 목 : 중동사태관련 대외원조

대:WAU-0629

연:AUW-0686,0688

1. 9.11 주재국은 중동사태로 인한 피난민을 위하여 연호 50 만 호주불 이외에 추가로 150 만 호주불을 IOM, UNICEF, 적십자등을 통해 원조키로 결정하였다고 발표함.

2. 대호관련 주재국은 동남아, 서남아 피난민 구호및 송환을 위한 전세기지원(군용, 민항기 파견)을 검토한바 있었으나 항공기 직접파견에는 시간이 소요되며 경비면에서 효율적이지 못하다는점을 감안, 피난민에게 조속히 혜택이 돌아갈수 있는 현금원조를 제공키로 하였다함을 참고로 첨언함. 끝.

(대사 이창수-과장)

예고:90.12.31.까지

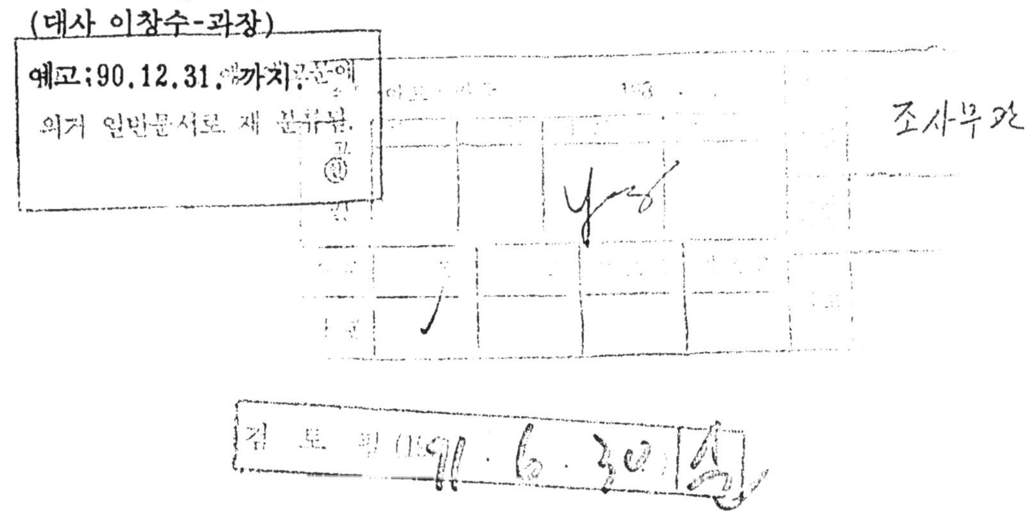

아주국 차관 1차보 2차보 중아국 경제국 청와대 안기부 대책반

PAGE 1

90.09.11 18:50

외신 2과 통제관 DO

0051

폐기
일반 검토중

페르샤만 사태 관련

필리핀, 사태지역 체류 자국근로자 철수지원 요청

90. 9.

외 무 부

0052

필리핀 정부는 9.4(화) 이라크 및 쿠웨이트 체류 자국근로자의 긴급 철수를 위해 아국을 포함한 아시아제국의 지원을 요청하여 온바 다음과 같이 보고 및 건의드립니다.

필리핀측 요청사항

o 망그라푸스 외무장관, 주비 아시아지역 아태 10개국 대사 초치, 이라크 및 쿠웨이트지역 체류 자국근로자 1만명의 긴급철수를 위한 지원을 요청해 옴
  - 한국, 일본, 호주, 인도, 태국, 인니, 싱가폴, 말련, 브루나이, 파키스탄
o 민간항공기(DC-10 또는 B-747)를 암만 또는 아부다비로 급파하여 필리핀 노동자들을 마닐라까지 수송 해줄 것을 요청
  - 필리핀의 어려운 경제사정을 감안, 무상원조 형식으로 지원 희망
  - 필리핀 근로자 집결 현황
    · 쿠웨이트: 4천명
    · 암　　만: 2천명
    · 이라크, 쿠웨이트 국경지대: 4-5천명
  * 필리핀측도 철수를 위해 자국 항공기 3대 매일운항 및 선박 2척 쿠웨이트 파송을 준비중임.

관련국 반응

o 일본, 호주: 민항기 파견은 고려치 않고 있으며 UNDRO, IOM 등 국제기구를 통해 필리핀에 한정치 않고 요르단 체재 외국난민 송환 및 구호를 위한 기금원조
o 아세안국: - 검토에 다소 시간 소요
  - 말련을 제외하고는 민항기 파견 불고려
o 인도, 파키스탄: 자국인 철수문제가 시급하여 필리핀 지원 불가

0053

건 의

o 필리핀측 요청사항을 아래 이유에서 긍정적으로 검토함

- 한국전 참전등 필리핀과의 전통적 우호관계 및 7.16 대규모 지진 피해복구 작업등 필리핀의 어려운 경제사정을 감안

- 아시아 지역내 우방국가의 요청을 적극적 자세로 수용함으로써, 우리의 대아시아 선린외교를 강화하는 계기로 활용

- 필요시, 페르샤만 사태와 관련한 우리측 지원 노력의 일환으로 대미 설명에 활용

o 단 우리측 민항 전세항공기 파견문제는 현재 가용한 유휴 항공기가 없는 상태이고 비경제적(필리핀-페르샤만지역 왕복의 2배소요)인 점을 감안, 약 500명 철수에 소요되는 경비 미불50만불을 무상으로 현금지원 할 것을 건의함.

- 소요예산은 예비비에서 충당

- 여타 서남아국가의 유사한 요청시 대응방안 사전준비 필요

0054

# 외 무 부

암호수신

종 별 :

번 호 : SKW-0435 일 시 : 90 0912 1700

수 신 : 장관(아서,중근동)

발 신 : 주 스리랑카 대사

제 목 : 스리랑카 난민 지원문제

주재국 HERAT 외무장관은 외무부 주요 간부를 배석시킨 가운데 금 9.12(금)1530 당지 주재 주요 선진국 대사들을 초치(본직도 참석), 금번 쿠웨이트 사태로 인하여 아직 본국으로 귀환되지 못하고 있는 스리랑카인 약 8 만 5 천명(주로농촌출신 가정부로 구성) 이 현지에서 극심한 어려움을 겪고 있는 실정을 설명하면서 그들의 조속한 본국 귀환을 위하여 선진 우방국들이 국제 이민기구(IOM) 와의 협조하에 항공기나 배의 차타 또는 기금 공여를 요청하는 브리핑이 있었음을 보고함.

(대사 김봉규-국장)

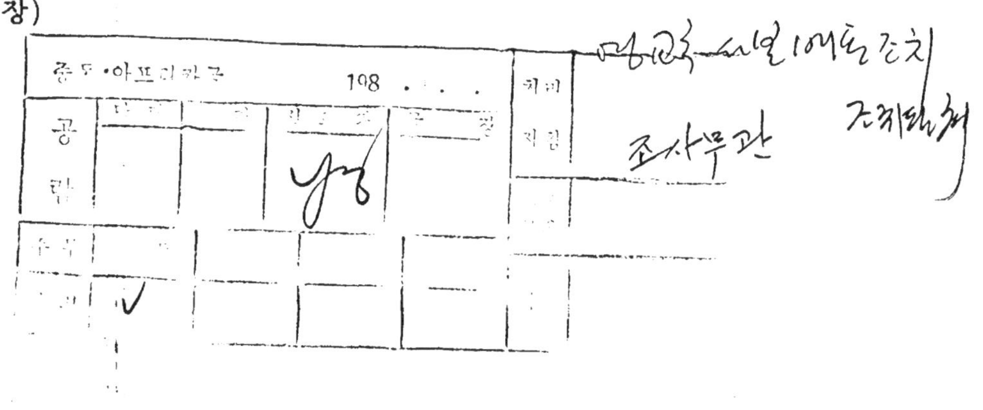

아주국 차관 1차보 2차보 중아국 청와대

PAGE 1

90.09.13 01:47

외신 2과 통제관 CW

0055

원 본

# 외 무 부

종 별 :

번 호 : DEW-0386 일 시 : 90 0912 1700

수 신 : 장 관(중근동,구이)

발 신 : 주 덴마크 대사

제 목 : 걸프만 난민원조

1. 주재국 언론보도에 의하면 당지 교회 대외원조단체인 FOLKEKIRKENS NOEDHJAELP 는 9.12.요르단내의 걸프만 사태 난민들을 위한 긴급구호물품을 공수할 예정이라 하며, 동 물품내용은분유 25톤, 담요 5천장, 건육 및 비스켓 각 6톤,텐트 250개와 다량의정수제등 이라함.

2. 덴마크 적십자사로 이미 걸프만 난민들에 대한긴급원조로 비행기 1대분의 식량을 지원한외에난민수용소 3개를 건설한 것으로 알려짐. 끝.

(대사 장선섭-국장)

| ·아프리카국 | | | 198 . . . | | 처리 지침 | 조사무관 박서기 |
|---|---|---|---|---|---|---|
| 공 람 | 담당 | 과장 | 심의관 | 국 장 | 자료 활용 | |
| | | | | | 비고 | |

중아국 구주국 미주국 통상국 대책반 1차보

PAGE 1 90.09.13 01:51 CT

외신 1과 통제관

0056

영해

# INTERNATIONAL ORGANIZATION FOR MIGRATION (IOM)

國 際 移 民 機 構

REGIONAL OFFICE FOR EAST ASIA

TELEPHONE: 3-322441-6
CABLES: PROMIGRANT HONG KONG
TELEX: 55566 HX
FAX: 3-881204

RM. 904, YAU MA TEI CARPARK BUILDING 9/F.
250, SHANGHAI STREET
KOWLOON, HONG KONG.

MAILING ADDRESS:
P. O. BOX 71509
KOWLOON CENTRAL POST OFFICE
HONG KONG.

**TELEFAX**

TO: DIRECTOR GENERAL
CONSULAR AFFAIRS AND OVERSEAS RESIDENTS
MINISTRY FOR FOREIGN AFFAIRS
SEOUL, KOREA

FM: INTERNATIONAL ORGANIZATION FOR MIGRATION - HONG KONG

DATE: 12TH SEPTEMBER 1990

MISC-184

ACCORDING TO COMMUNICATION RECEIVED FROM OUR HEADQUARTERS IN GENEVA, THE DIRECTOR GENERAL OF IOM HAD APPEALED TO YOUR GOVERNMENT FOR SUPPORT TO THE INTERNATIONAL EFFORTS, UNDERWAY TO RESOLVE THE PROBLEM OF FOREIGNERS STRANDED IN COUNTRIES NEIGHBOURING IRAQ. (FOR EASIER REFERENCE PLEASE FIND ENCLOSED COPY OF THAT LETTER, AS WELL AS COPY OF A DRAFT RESOLUTION WHICH MEANWHILE HAS BEEN APPROVED BY THE IOM EXECUTIVE COUNCIL.) - PURPOSE OF THIS MESSAGE IS TO LET YOU KNOW THAT THIS OFFICE IS READY TO HELP WITH PROVIDING ANY ADDITIONAL INFORMATION YOU MIGHT WISH TO OBTAIN IN RELATION WITH IOM'S ROLE IN THE CURRENT GULF CRISIS.

ALFRED V. KOTTEK
IOM REGIONAL REPRESENTATIVE
HONG KONG

CC: CONSULATE GENERAL OF THE REPUBLIC OF KOREA IN HONG KONG

| 영사교민국 | | 국 장 |
|---|---|---|

0057

HEADQUARTERS: GENEVA, SWITZERLAND

EXCELLENCY,

AS WE ARE ALL PAINFULLY AWARE, THE STREAM OF FOREIGN NATIONALS FLOWING OUT OF KUWAIT AND IRAQ HAS BECOME A FLOOD. THE ABILITY TO COPE WITH THIS CRISIS OF HUMANITY IN FLIGHT IS AT THE BREAKING POINT.

MUCH HAS BEEN DONE TO SPEED UP ONWARD MOVEMENT OF THE DISPLACED TO THEIR COUNTRIES OF ORIGIN, BUT NEITHER AIRCRAFT SPACE AVAILABILITY NOR PRESENT FINANCIAL RESOURCES CAN HOPE EVEN TO KEEP PACE WITH THE DIRE NEEDS RESULTING FROM SOARING RATES OF ARRIVAL. MORE - MUCH MORE - HAS TO BE DONE IMMEDIATELY TO INCREASE RAPID OUTWARD MOVEMENT FROM COUNTRIES WILLING TO PROVIDE TEMPORARY SAFE HAVEN BUT OVERWHELMED BY THE SHEER MASS OF HUMANITY IN NEED. ENERGETIC MEASURES MUST BE TAKEN AT ONCE, BEFORE HUMAN SUFFERING BECOMES HUMAN TRAGEDY.

THE INTERNATIONAL ORGANIZATION FOR MIGRATION (IOM) HAS BEEN REQUESTED BY UNDRO, THE UN AGENCY WHICH HAS BEEN CHARGED WITH THE CO-ORDINATION OF RELIEF EFFORTS ON BEHALF OF PERSONS DISPLACED AS A RESULT OF THE EVENTS IN KUWAIT, TO ASSUME THE LEAD ROLE FOR REPATRIATION TRANSPORTATION. IN THAT CONTEXT, IOM HAS DRAWN UP A PLAN OF ACTION AND ALREADY APPEALED TO A NUMBER OF GOVERNMENTS [INCLUDING YOUR OWN] IN LATE AUGUST FOR FINANCIAL CONTRIBUTIONS. THESE ACTIONS WERE FULLY ENDORSED BY THE IOM EXECUTIVE COMMITTEE, MEETING IN SPECIAL SESSION IN GENEVA ON 4 SEPTEMBER, AND UNDERSCORED BY THE ADOPTION OF A RESOLUTION CALLING UPON MEMBER STATES AND OTHER INTERESTED STATES AND ENTITIES, INTER ALIA, ''TO PROVIDE AS A MATTER OF URGENCY THE NECESSARY FINANCIAL AND LOGISTICAL ASSISTANCE NEEDED TO IMPLEMENT THIS PROGRAMME.''

0058

- 2 -

THE PAST WEEK'S EXPERIENCE, COMBINED WITH FRESH INFORMATION RECEIVED SUBSEQUENT TO THE AFOREMENTIONED MEETING, INDICATE CLEARLY THAT COMMERCIAL AIRCRAFT SPACE THROUGH REGULAR AIRPORT FACILITIES AND REPATRIATION BY AVAILABLE COMMERCIAL VESSELS WILL CONTINUE TO BE OUTSTRIPPED BY THE WAVES OF HUMAN BEINGS ARRIVING IN INCREASINGLY DESPERATE STRAITS. ADDITIONAL CAPACITY MUST BE FOUND NOW.

IOM WILL CONTINUE TO SEEK CHARTER SPACE WITH THE SAME VIGOUR WE HAVE TO DATE. FOR THIS WE CONTINUE TO NEED FINANCIAL CONTRIBUTIONS URGENTLY. BUT TIME IS OF THE ESSENCE, AND IMMEDIATE IN-KIND CONTRIBUTIONS OF THE AIRCRAFT AND SHIP CAPACITY NEEDED COULD SAVE ENOUGH OF THAT TIME TO AVERT EVEN GREATER SUFFERING. MORE AIRCRAFT AND SHIPS - NOW - ARE THE KEY. WE THEREFORE URGENTLY APPEAL TO YOUR COUNTRY TO MAKE AVAILABLE IMMEDIATELY, AS AN IN-KIND CONTRIBUTION TO THIS INTERNATIONAL HUMANITARIAN UNDERTAKING, COMMERCIAL OR MILITARY AIRCRAFT AND/OR SHIPS TO AUGMENT DEPARTURE SPACE AVAILABILITY.

AT THIS TIME, THE FOCUS OF OUR REPATRIATION EFFORTS IS ON JORDAN, WHERE CONDITIONS HAVE BECOME SO STRAINED THAT THE AUTHORITIES AND DONOR REPRESENTATIVES ON THE GROUND HAVE THEMSELVES STRESSED REPATRIATION TRANSPORTATION AS BEING THE TOP PRIORITY. ANY IN-KIND CONTRIBUTIONS RECEIVED IN RESPONSE TO THIS APPEAL WILL THEREFORE INITIALLY BE DIRECTED TO ALLEVIATING THE PRESSURE IN JORDAN WHOSE AUTHORITIES HAVE UNDERSCORED THE URGENT NEED FOR SUCH A FURTHER DISPLAY OF INTERNATIONAL SOLIDARITY. THEY HAVE ALSO INDICATED THEIR READINESS TO FACILITATE THE TECHNICAL ASPECTS OF SUCH AN UNDERTAKING.

IT IS MY STRONG HOPE THAT YOU WILL LOOK FAVOURABLY ON THIS REQUEST. GIVEN THE URGENCY OF THE NEED, WHICH CANNOT BE OVERSTATED, I WOULD GREATLY APPRECIATE YOUR GOVERNMENT'S RESPONSE AS SOON AS POSSIBLE.

ACCEPT, EXCELLENCY, THE ASSURANCE OF MY HIGHEST CONSIDERATION.

SIGNED, JAMES N. PURCELL, JR., DIRECTOR GENERAL, INTERNATIONAL ORGANIZATION FOR MIGRATION (IOM)

0059

# 이라크 및 쿠웨이트 아국인 철수 현황

(9.13. 현재)

| 구분 / 국명 | 소 속 | 철수 내역 | | | | | 비 고 (기철수 경비) |
|---|---|---|---|---|---|---|---|
| | | 귀국완료 | 제3국대피 | 요르단대기 | 미철수(잔류중) | 계 | |
| 이라크 | .현대건설등 진출 건설업체 | 398명 | 0 | 21명 | 252명 | 671명 | $ 433,000 |
| | .진출상사(은행포함) | 8 | 0 | 0 | 1 | 9 | |
| | .공관원 및 가족(KOTRA포함) | 24 | 0 | 0 | 11 | 35 | |
| | .기타(무의탁 교민 포함) | 3 | 3 | 0 | 1 | 7 | |
| 쿠웨이트 | .현대건설등 진출 건설업체 | 325 | 0 | 0 | 0 | 325 | $ 592,000 |
| | .진출상사(은행포함) | 38 | 0 | 0 | 0 | 38 | |
| | .공관원 및 가족 | 26 | 4 | 0 | 0 | 30 | |
| | .기타(무의탁 교민 포함) | 203 | 0 | 0 | 9 | 212 | |
| 소 계 | | 1,025명 | 7명 | 21명 | 274명 | 1,327명 | $1,025,000 |

0060

# 이라크 및 쿠웨이트 아국 업체 소속 삼국인 철수 현황

(9.13. 현재)

| 국명＼구분 | 소속 | 철수 내역 | | | | | 조치 내용 | 비고 (기지원 철수경비) |
|---|---|---|---|---|---|---|---|---|
| | | 국적 | 귀국완료 | 요르단대기 | 미철수 (잔류중) | 계 | | |
| 이라크 | 현대건설 | 방글라데쉬인 | 112명 | 128 명 | 210명 | 450명 | - 8.25-9.3, 112명 현대측 자사 부담, 귀국 조치<br>- 128명, 현대측 자사 부담 금명간 귀국 조치 예정 | $104,000 |
| | | 태국인 | 70 | 1 | 79 | 150 | - 8.21, 6명 현대측, 주 요르단 태국 대사관 인계, 귀국 조치<br>- 9.2-9.7, 65명 현대측 자사 부담, 귀국 조치<br>- 1명, 현대측 금명간 자사 부담 귀국 조치 예정 | |
| | 삼성종합건설 | 필리핀인<br>태국인 | 1<br>29 | | | 1<br>29 | - 8.19 필리핀인 1명, 태국인 29명 삼성측 자사 부담, 귀국 조치 | $ 35,000 |
| | 정우개발 | 방글라데쉬인 | 21 | 0 | 1 | 22 | - 8.24 21명 정우측 자사 부담 귀국 조치 | $ 15,000 |
| | 한양 | 방글라데쉬인 | 9 | 0 | 12 | 21 | - 8.25 9명 한양측 자사 부담 귀국 조치 | $ 7,000 |
| 쿠웨이트 | 현대건설 | 중국인 | 46 | | | 46 | - 8.17 46명 주 요르단 중국 대사관 인계, 귀국 조치 | |
| | | 인도인 | 14 | | | 14 | - 8.25 14명 주 이라크 인도 대사관 인계, 귀국 조치 | |
| | | 태국인 | 1,267 | | | 1,267 | - 8.21-8.25 1,267명 태국 정부 자국 특별기로 귀국 조치 | |
| 소계 | | | 1,569명 | 129명 | 302명 | 2,000명 | | $161,000 |

242

0061

# 교 민 철 수 현 황

(90.9.13. 08:00 현재)

〈이 라 크〉

o 철수 인원 총 457 명

o 잔류 인원 265 명

o 소속별 잔류 인원 내역

- 공관원(고용원 및 가족 포함) 11명
- 현대 건설 195
- 남광 토건 1
- 삼성 건설 39
- 정 우 2
- 한 양 15
- 삼성 물산 1
- 기 타 1

이라크 및 쿠웨이트
총 1,327명
. 이라크 722
- 쿠웨이트 605

※ 쿠웨이트 잔류희망교민 9명 제외 전원 철수

605
596

457
596
1053

0062

90. 9. 14 대책반장 주재
관계부처 국장회의시 제출,
동일 64차 이수교상이 전달

9/15 신
공관

# 국제 이민기구 (IOM) 의 난민 수송 협조 요청 대책

90. 9.

영 사 교 민 국

0063

## 1. 문제의 제기

o 이라크 사태로 야기된 외국인 난민 문제 해결을 위해 국제 이민기구는 아국에 특별기여금 또는 난민 수송을 위한 항공기 또는 선박 제공을 요청함.

## 2. 난민 현황

o 이라크 및 쿠웨이트내 체류중인 250 만명의 외국인중 일부가 요르단 및 터키에 피난 대피중임.

* 동 외국인중 60% 가 이집트인, 20% 가 아시아인

o 특히 25만명의 방글라데시, 파키스탄, 필리핀 및 스리랑카인이 긴박한 상황에 처해 있음.

## 3. 국제 이민기구 (IOM) 요청 사항

o IOM 의 Purcell 사무총장은 8.24 자 주제네바대사 앞 서한을 통해 난민 수송을 위한 특별 기여금 지원 요청

o 동 총장은 또한 9.6 자 외무부장관 앞 팩시 서한을 통해 난민 수송을 위한 항공기 또는 선박 제공을 요청함.

o IOM 홍콩 사무소장은 9.12 자 외무부 영사교민국장 앞 팩시 서한을 통해 난민 수송을 위한 IOM 의 역할과 관련, 아국의 조치에 필요한 협조 제공을 약속함.

0064

## 4. IOM의 난민 지원 요청에 대한 각국 반응

o 9.4. 제네바 개최 IOM 집행 위원회 특별 회의 개최시

- 카나다 : IOM 활동을 위해 100 만 카나다불 기여 결정
- 스위스 : 25 만 스위스 프랑 기여 결정
- 덴마크 : 이라크 사태와 관련한 유엔 산하기구 활동 지원을 위해 기여하기로 결정한 450 만불중 일부를 IOM 활동에 사용되도록 조치
- 스웨덴 : 이라크 사태와 관련한 유엔 산하기구 활동 지원을 위해 기여하기로 결정한 850 만불중 일부를 IOM 활동에 사용되도록 조치

* IOM 측은 난민 수송을 위해 6,000 만불이 소요될 것으로 예상하고 있으며, 9.10 현재 3,500 만불 확보

o 9.4. 필리핀 정부의 10개국 대사 초치 자국민 수송을 위한 지원 요청시

- 일본 : 유엔 재해 구호 본부 (UNDRO) 를 통해 IOM 에 1,200 만불 지원 결정

* 일본은 이라크의 쿠웨이트 침공사태 발발후 UNDRO 에 난민을 위한 식량 및 의료품 지원을 위해 800 만불 기제공

- 호주 : 200만 호주불 (160만 미불) 을 IOM, UNICEF, ICRC 등을 통해 지원키로 결정

0065

## 5. 세계 각국 및 기구의 난민 지원 현황 (9.12. 주요르단대사 보고)

- 영 국 : 난민 수송 및 구호 경비 지원 2,200 만불
- 인 도 : 비행기 11편 (자국민 수송)
- EC 및 프랑스 : 비행기 5 편
- 뉴질랜드 : 비행기 3 편
- 이 태 리 : 쌀 40톤 (175 만불 상당)
- 미 국 : 식량 및 의약품 (100 만불 상당)
- 파키스탄 : 식량 및 의약품 30 톤 (자국민용),
  비행기 1편 (자국민용)
- 화란, 노르웨이 : 적십자 구호 인력 지원

## 6. 아국의 아국인 및 외국인 철수 지원 현황

가. 아국인 철수 지원

o 이라크 및 쿠웨이트내 아국인 총 1,327 명중 9.13 현재 1,053 명 철수

- 이라크에 265 명, 쿠웨이트에 9명 잔류

o 2회 (8.21 및 8.25) 에 걸친 특별기 파견등 아국인 철수 경비 : 102 만 5 천불

- 아국인 철수 경비중 무의탁 교민 항공료 및 체류비 지원 (예비비) : 23 만 308 불

나. 외국인 철수 지원

o 9.13 현재 이라크내 아국 업체 고용 외국인 1,569 명에 대한 본국 지원 : 16만 1천불

- 현대건설 : 182 명, 10만 4천불
- 삼성 종합건설 : 30명, 3만 5천불
- 정우개발 : 21명, 1만 5천불
- 한 양 : 9명, 7 천불

0066

## 7. 대 책

o IOM 의 이라크 난민 문제 해결을 위한 활동에 대해 현 난민 상황으로 보아 인도적 및 국제협력적 차원에서 어느정도 성의를 표시하는 것이 바람직한 것으로 판단됨.

o 필리핀, 스리랑카등 일부 국가에서 자국민 수송 지원을 요청하는 경우 지원 효과의 극대화를 위해 IOM 을 통해 지원하는 것이 지원 효과의 극대화를 기할 수 있을 것으로 사료됨.

o 미, 영, 일, 호주등 지원예와 아국의 사정 (9.12 대홍수등) 을 고려, 50만불을 IOM 에 지원하되 대외 발표시 내외국인 철수 비용 118 만 6 천불을 포함, 홍보하는 것이 바람직함.

0067

한신전

원 본

암호수신

# 외 무 부

종 별 : 지 급

번 호 : GVW-1753 일 시 : 90 0914 1230

수 신 : 장관(영해,국기,중근동)

발 신 : 주 제네바 대사대리

제 목 : IOM 지원 요청

대: WGV-1207

1. IOM 사무총장의 이라크 및 쿠웨이트에서의 외국인 철수 지원 요청에 대한 각국의 기여금액(서약액 포함)은 9.13 현재 36.8 백만불이며 각국의 기여금 서약액수 아래와 같음. 그외에 아래 국가가 자국 적십자사등을 통해 수송기를 제공키로 하였다함.

가. 각국 기여금 서약 액수(단위:미불)

미국-10 백만불

일본-12 백만불

스웨덴-5.2 백만불

영국-3.8 백만불

핀란드-2.2 백만불

카나다-85 만불

호주-83 만불

노르웨이-95 만불

덴마크-25 만불

스위스-20 만불

나. 수송기 제공 국가

스위스, 일본, 스웨덴, 노르웨이, 프랑스, 벨지움, 뉴질랜드

2. 아국의 경우 현 상황으로서는, 대호 예산 및 국내 사정을 감안 진전상황을 일단 관망하는 것이 좋은 것으로 사료됨. 끝

(대사대리 박영우-국장)

영교국 중아국 국기국

PAGE 1

| 영사교민국 | 변인 | 담 당 | 계 장 | 과 장 | 관리관 | 국 장 |
|---|---|---|---|---|---|---|
| | | | | | | |

90.09.15 06:03

외신 2과 통제관 CW

0068

| 관리 번호 | 90/1260 |
|---|---|

원 본

# 외 무 부

종 별 :

번 호 : JOW-0437 일 시 : 90 0915 1630

수 신 : 장 관(중근동)

발 신 : 주 요르단 대사

제 목 : 주재국 난민처리 협조 요청 관련

연:JOW-0417

연호 주재국 난미처리 협조요청을 접수한지 1 주일이 경과한 반면 국내적으로는 홍수 피해등으로 당분간 동요청 수락회신을 기대할수없는 상황임을 감안 금9.15 본직은 외무성 OTHMAN 국제기구국장을 방문 금세기 초유의 아국 수해상황(외무장관의 기자회견 내용 주재국 신문게재)을 설명하고 현재로서는 아국정부 및 전국민이 동 복구에 여념이 없어 표제 요청에대한 아측의 조기 응신이 어려울것에 대해 이해를 구했던바, 동 국장은 아국의 최악의 홍수피해에 대해 금시초문이라고 하면서 조속한 시일내에 피해를 복구할수 있기를 기대한다고 말함

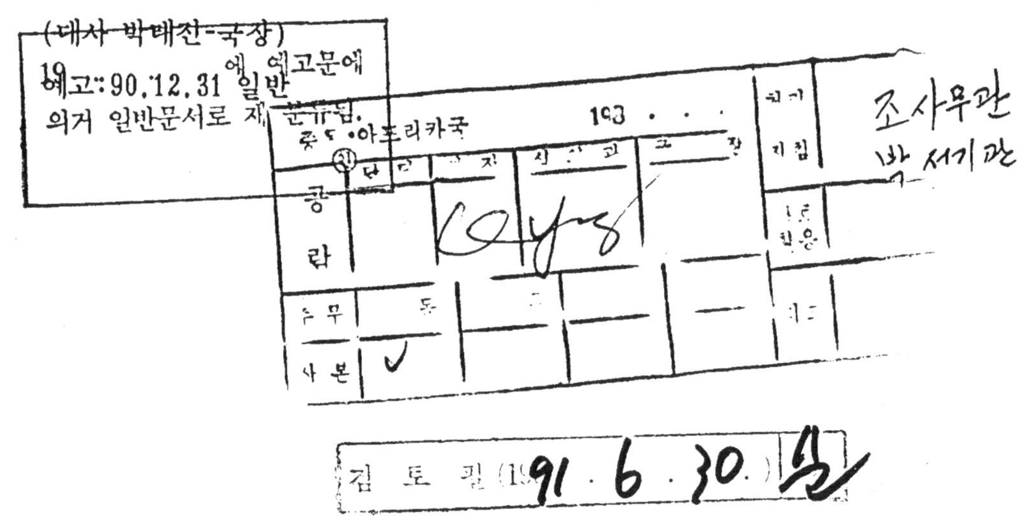


중아국 차관 1차보 2차보 청와대

PAGE 1

90.09.16 07:33

외신 2과 통제관 CF

0069

원 본

# 외 무 부

종 별 :

번 호 : JOW-0428 일 시 : 90 0919 1630

수 신 : 장 관(중근동,마그,영재,노동,기정)

발 신 : 주 요르단 대사

제 목 : 난민구호

1. 9.11. 현재 이라크.쿠웨이트로 부터 철수한 제 3국 난민에 대한 세계 각국및 기구의 원조 현황은 다음과 같음

-영국: 난민 수송및 구호경비 지원(22백만불)

-인도: 비행기 11편(자국민 수송)

- EC 및 프랑스: 비행기 5편

-뉴질랜드: 비행기 3편

-이태리: 쌀(1.75백만불 상당) 40톤

-미국: 식량및 의약품(1백만불 상당)

파키스탄: 식량및 의약품(30톤, 자국민용) 비행기 1편(자국민 수송)

-화란및 노르웨이: 적십자사 구호인력 지원

2.걸프사태 발생후 자국민 철수 및 구호와 관련 주재국을 방문한 주요 외국인사는 다음과 같음

-외상: 파키스탄, 방글라데시, 필리핀,인도

-기타 각료급: 인도 교통장관 및 국무장관, 영국 해외개발상, UNDP 사무총장,WFP 재난 구호책임자

-차관급: 태국 외무차관, 인도 상공차관

(대사 박태진-국장)

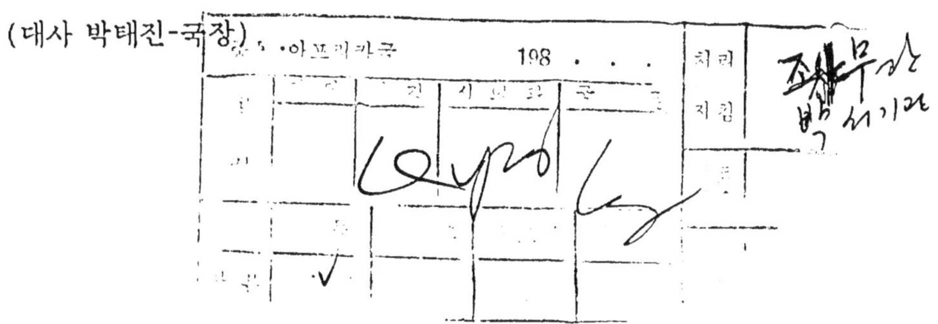

중아국 1차보 중아국 영교국 안기부 노동부 대책반 미주국 통상국 2차보

PAGE 1 90.09.12 05:25 DA

외신 1과 통제관

0070

한보현

# 주 제 네 바 대 표 부

제네(정) 20320- P76　　　　　　　　　　　　1990. 9.19

수신 : 장관

참조 : 영사교민국장

제목 : IOM 공한 및 자료송부

연 : GVW-1753

1. 연호 IOM 사무국은 별첨 공한을 통해 IOM의 걸프지역 외국인 수송 사업현황 및 동 사업에 대한 각국의 기여 현황을 통보하여 왔는바, 이를 송부합니다.

- 아　　　래 -

0 외국인 수송인원 : 19,463명(9.14. 현재)

0 각국기여 현황

- 기여금(37,4백만불) 및 수송비행기 제공(25,347,140불 상당)

2. IOM 사무국에서 발간하는 IOM Monthly Dispatch을 별첨 송부합니다.

첨부 : IOM 공한 및 Monthly Dispatch(NO. 139) 끝.

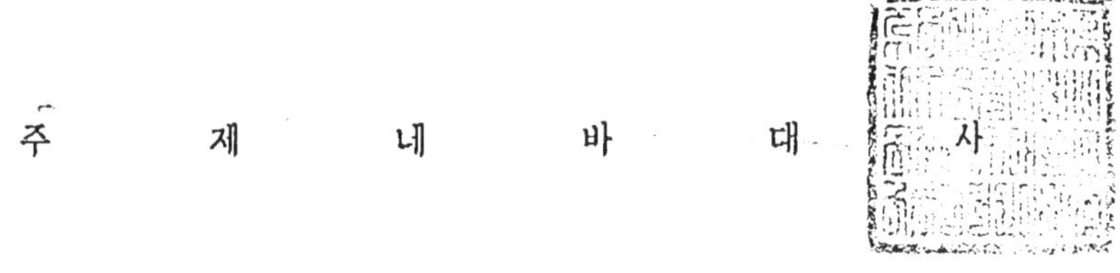

주 제 네 바 대 사

53023

0071

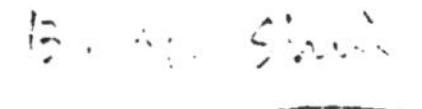

INTERNATIONAL ORGANIZATION FOR MIGRATION (IOM)
ORGANISATION INTERNATIONALE POUR LES MIGRATIONS (OIM)
ORGANIZACIÓN INTERNACIONAL PARA LAS MIGRACIONES (OIM)

Telephone: 717 91 11
Cable Address: Promigrant Geneva
Telex: 415 722
Telefax: 798 61 50

17, route des Morillons
P.O. Box 71
CH-1211 GENEVA 19
SWITZERLAND

INTERNATIONAL ORGANIZATION FOR MIGRATION

TO: THE PERMANENT MISSIONS OF:

ARGENTINA, AUSTRALIA, AUSTRIA, BANGLADESH, BELIZE, BOLIVIA, BRAZIL, BELGIUM, CANADA, CAPE VERDE, CHILE, CHINA, COLOMBIA, COSTA RICA, CYPRUS, DENMARK, DOMINICAN REP., ECUADOR, EGYPT, EL SALVADOR, FRANCE, FINLAND, GERMANY (FED. REP. OF), GHANA, GUINEA-BISSAU, GREECE, GUATEMALA, HOLY SEE, HONDURAS, INDIA, INDONESIA, IRAN, ISRAEL, ITALY, JAPAN, JORDAN, KENYA, KOREA (REP. OF), LUXEMBOURG, MEXICO, NETHERLANDS, NEW ZEALAND, NICARAGUA, NORWAY, PAKISTAN, PANAMA, PARAGUAY, PERU, PHILIPPINES, PORTUGAL, SAN MARINO, SAUDI ARABIA, SOMALIA, SPAIN, SRI LANKA, SWEDEN, SWITZERLAND, SYRIAN ARAB REP., THAILAND, TURKEY, UGANDA, U.S.S.R., UNITED KINGDOM, U.S.A., URUGUAY, VENEZUELA, YUGOSLAVIA, ZIMBABWE AND THE COMMISSION OF THE EUROPEAN COMMUNITIES

COPY TO UNDRO GENEVA

FROM: INTERNATIONAL ORGANIZATION FOR MIGRATION, GENEVA

DATE: 14.9.1990 jeh

SUBJECT: IOM'S GULF EMERGENCY PROGRAMME : UPDATED PLAN OF ACTION

PURSUANT TO THE REQUEST FORMULATED AT THE SPECIAL SESSION OF THE IOM EXECUTIVE COMMITTEE ON 4 SEPTEMBER, IOM'S PLAN OF ACTION (THE FIRST VERSION OF WHICH WAS DISTRIBUTED AT THE AFOREMENTIONED MEETING) HAS BEEN UPDATED TO REFLECT THE SITUATION AS AT 14 SEPTEMBER. A COPY OF THE UP-TO-DATE DOCUMENT IS ENCLOSED FOR YOUR INFORMATION. FURTHER COPIES ARE AVAILABLE FROM IOM HQS.

PURCELL

0072

INTERNATIONAL ORGANIZATION FOR MIGRATION (IOM)
ORGANISATION INTERNATIONALE POUR LES MIGRATIONS (OIM)
ORGANIZACIÓN INTERNACIONAL PARA LAS MIGRACIONES (OIM)

Telephone: 717 91 11
Cable Address: Promigrant Geneva
Telex: 415 722
Telefax: 798 61 50

17, route des Morillons
P.O. Box 71
CH-1211 GENEVA 19
SWITZERLAND

14 September 1990

PLAN OF ACTION - UPDATE ON OPERATIONS

The Plan of Action on repatriation of foreign nationals stranded in the Middle East as a result of the crisis in the region, presented on 4 September to the Special Session of the Executive Committee of the International Organization for Migration proposed an intervention by the international community to repatriate nationals of Bangladesh, Pakistan, the Philippines and Sri Lanka.

During the Special Session of the Executive Committee, the representatives of Egypt and India requested that their countries be included as well.

Including departures booked for today, 14 September, 19,463 persons have been repatriated from Jordan through IOM-coordinated operations. Most have been nationals of Bangladesh, Sri Lanka and the Philippines. IOM assistance to date to nationals of Pakistan has been limited, but discussions are underway with the Pakistan authorities concerning ways to supplement that Government's already considerable direct efforts. Similarly, at the request of the Government of India, IOM will soon be facilitating the first return movements of Indian nationals under international auspices. All together, commitments for 50,007 seats have been made thus far for movements under the international airlift from Jordan, corresponding to specific needs identified by the relevant authorities.

A request by the Turkish Government for international assistance to repatriate foreign nationals stranded in Turkey was submitted to UNDRO on Friday, 7 September. By Sunday, 9 September an IOM staff member had arrived in Ankara and on 12 September the first 800 persons were repatriated on 4 flights to Bangladesh. In all, 59 flights from Turkey to Dhaka have been contracted by IOM and the EC to carry 11,800 persons. Additional flights and destinations will be added as need arises.

Operations are carried out in close coordination with UNDRO, the affected countries and the European Communities. Arrangements with the EC foresee harmonization of capacity, exchange of information on case-load, available aircraft and charter conditions, co-operation in Amman, Jordan and Diyarbakir, Turkey on local transportation and check-in procedures as well as joint operation of certain flights.

0073

The Deputy Director General of IOM left for Egypt on 11 September to discuss with the relevant authorities IOM involvement in the repatriation effort.

An IOM team is presently in Teheran to assess in close coordination with UNDRO the needs of foreign nationals stranded in Iran.

Pledges for contributions - either to IOM or through UNDRO - have reached approximately US$ 37.1 million (exact figure subject to exchange fluctuations). In addition, the European Community has made its own arrangements to provide substantial amounts to the coordinated effort. Out of these funds, the EC has agreed to share the cost of two joint operations with a contribution of US$ 3,327,850.

Responses to an appeal to provide in-kind contributions to the effort, in particular through aircraft, are presently under evaluation. A first series of flights with a plane provided by New Zealand has been completed. Aircraft donated through the Norwegian, Spanish and Swedish Red Cross Societies as well as the Swiss Government are expected to go into operation soon.

Funds already committed by IOM towards the chartering of aircraft and ships amount to US$ 25,347,140. This figure does not include the amounts spent by the EC.

Most of the air companies contracted have to be paid before transportation commences. While generous pledges have been received, the cash outflow for transportation already carried out has put a heavy burden on IOM's liquidity.

A. TRANSPORTATION CONTRACTED

1. IOM/UNDRO-contracted capacity (excluding to Egypt) from:

| | | |
|---|---|---|
| Jordan | 37,307 persons | US$ 22,022,140 |
| Turkey | 5,000 persons | US$ 3,325,000 |

2. EC-contracted capacity (excluding Egypt)

| | |
|---|---|
| Jordan | 12,700 persons |
| Turkey | 6,800 persons |

---

B. PROJECTED INCOME

1. Contributions pledged for transportation:

| | | |
|---|---|---|
| AUSTRALIA | AUS$ 1 MILLION | |
| AUSTRIA | AS 3,000,000 | |
| CANADA | CAN$ 1 MILLION | |
| DENMARK | DKR. 1.5 MILLION | (+ unspecified amount through UNDRO) |
| FINLAND | FIM 8 MILLION | |
| ITALY | US$ 500,000 | (through UNDRO) |
| JAPAN | US$ 12 MILLION | (through UNDRO) |
| NORWAY | NKR. 5.5 MILLION | |
| SWEDEN | SKR. 30 MILLION | (through UNDRO) |
| SWITZERLAND | SFR 250,000 | |
| UNITED KINGDOM | UKL 2 MILLION | |
| UNITED STATES | US$ 10 MILLION | |

2. In-kind contribution:

| | | |
|---|---|---|
| NEW ZEALAND | 2 AIRCRAFT/TOTAL 5 ROTATIONS | 475 PERSONS |
| NORWAY RED CROSS | 1 AIRCRAFT/3 ROTATIONS | 273 PERSONS |
| SPANISH RED CROSS | 1 AIRCRAFT (250 SEATS) | AS LONG AS NEEDED |
| SWEDISH RED CROSS | 1 AIRCRAFT/10 ROTATIONS | 4,660 PERSONS |
| SWITZERLAND | 1 AIRCRAFT (190 SEATS) | UP TO 1 MONTH, MAX SFR 6 MILLION |

3. EC Contribution US$ 3,327,850 50% towards operation of 20 flights carrying 9,780 persons

0075

IOM - PLAN OF ACTION / UPDATE

Persons in need of international assistance in:

JORDAN

| Nationals of: | Number of persons Est. a/o 14 September 1990 | Movements Departed a/o 14.9.90 | Movements Booked to depart |
|---|---|---|---|
| Bangladesh | 9,799 | 14,043 | 5,718 |
| India | 12,477 | - | 12,000 |
| Pakistan | 700* | 323 | Under discussion with Pakistan authorities |
| Philippines | 5,124 | 1,520 | 6,589 |
| Sri Lanka | 6,891 | 3,577 | 6,237 |
| Total | 34,991 | 19,463 | 30,544 |

Total Int. Airlift 50,007

* Reflects only persons for whom the Government of Pakistan has requested IOM assistance.

IOM Geneva, 14 September 1990

0076

원 본

# 외 무 부

종 별 :

번 호 : GVW-1855 일 시 : 90 0924 1800

수 신 : 장관(미북,국기,영해)

발 신 : 주제네바대사

제 목 : 페만사태 관련 아측지원 방안

대: AM-0189

1. 대호에 따라 난민수송 지원을 위해 50만불을 기여할 예정임을 IOM에 공식 통보해도 가한지 회보바람.

2. 참고로 IOM당국이 작성한 9.18.현재 각국지원 현황표를 별첨 송부함.

첨부: 각국지원 현황표

( GVW(F)-0355). 끝

미주국 1차보 2차보 중아국 국기국 영교국 안기부

PAGE 1

90.09.25 07:57 BX

외신 1과 통제관

0077

GVW(F)-0355 00924 1800

주 UVW-1855 첨부.

GULF EMERGENCY PROGRAMME
PLEDGES AND RECEIPT FOR TRANSPORTATION
as at 18 September 1990

| 1. CASH CONTRIBUTIONS | PLEDGED | RECEIVED USD |
|---|---|---|
| AUSTRALIA | AUD 1,000,000.00 | 625,000.00 |
| AUSTRIA | * ATS 3,000,000.00 | |
| CANADA | CAD 1,000,000.00 | 884,955.75 |
| DENMARK | DKK 1,500,000.00 | |
| FINLAND | FIM 8,000,000.00 | |
| GERMANY | DEM 5,000,000.00 | |
| ITALY | * USD 500,000.00 | |
| JAPAN | * USD 12,000,000.00 | |
| NETHERLANDS | NLG 2,000,000.00 | |
| NORWAY | NOK 5,500,000.00 | 902,615.95 |
| SWEDEN | * SEK 30,000,000.00 | |
| SWITZERLAND | CHF 250,000.00 | |
| UNITED KINGDOM | GBP 2,000,000.00 | 3,720,600.00 |
| U.S.A. | USD 10,000,000.00 | 2,750,000.00 |
| EUROPEAN COMMUNITY ** | USD 3,327,850.00 | |
| 2. PRIVATE DONATIONS | | |
| US-AIM | USD 1,500.00 | 1,500.00 |
| TOTAL | USD 44,650,000.00 | 8,884,071.70 |
| 3. IN-KIND CONTRIBUTIONS | | |
| NEW ZEALAND | USD 151,300.00 1 Hercules 3 flights (210 pak-450,84 MNL-800) | |
| NORWAY | 1 Aircraft | |
| SPAIN (RED CROSS) | USD 1,250,000.00 1 Aircraft 10 flights (2500 DAC-500) | |
| SWEDEN (RED CROSS) | USD 2,330,000.00 1 Aircraft 10 flights (4660 DAC-500) | |
| SWITZERLAND | USD 4,615,000.00 1 Aircraft | |
| TOTAL IN KIND CONTRIBUTIONS | USD 8,356,300.00 | |

* Through UNDRO
** Earmarked to cover a 50% share of a series of 20 flights from Amman to Colombo and Manila

0078 ~~0125~~ ~~0126~~

| | 분류번호 | 보존기간 |
|---|---|---|
| | | |

# 발 신 전 보

WGV-1252 900925 1822 DY

번 호 : ~~재내바~~ 종별 : 지급

수 신 : 주 대사.총영사

발 신 : 장 관 (영해)

제 목 : IOM 지원

대 : GVW - 1855

연 : WGV - 1207

1. 대호, 정부는 IOM 의 난민 수송 지원 요청 문제를 신중히 검토한 결과, 금번 걸프만 사태로 야기된 난민의 인도적 측면을 고려하고 난민 수송을 위한 IOM 의 호소에 대한 각국의 긍정적 반응 및 필리핀, 스리랑카 등 일부 국가들이 자국 난민 수송을 위한 아국의 협조 요청등을 감안하여 50만불을 IOM 특별 기여금으로 출연키로 결정했음.
2. 이와 관련, 귀관은 상기 아국 정부의 결정 사항을 IOM 측에 적의 통보하고 특히, 아국의 경제여건, 최근의 홍수피해 및 아국이 그동안 난민 수송을 위해 총 127만 3천불 (아국인 귀국 수송비 : 102만 5천불, 아국 건설업체 고용 외국인 본국 수송비 : 24만 8천불) 을 기지출했음을 설명하여 금번 특별 기여금 출연 효과가 극대화 되도록 조치 바람.
3. 상기 특별기여금은 아국이 걸프만 사태에 직.간접으로 관련된 당사국에 대한 원조자금 (총 2억 2천만불) 에서 ~~의 일부로 충당~~ 지출될 것인 바, 따라서 50만불에 대한 송금은 동 원조자금에 대한 국회의 추경예산 처리가 이루어진 이후에나 가능할 것임을 참고 바람. 끝.

(차관 유 종 하)

미주국장

아중동국장

| 앙고재 | 년월일 | 과 | 기안자 | | 과 장 | | 국 장 | 제2차관보 | 차 관 | 장 관 |
|---|---|---|---|---|---|---|---|---|---|---|
| | | | | | | | | | | |

국제기구조약국장

대책반장

| 보안통제 | 외신과통제 |
|---|---|
| | |

0079

# 협조문용지

| 분류기호 문서번호 | 영해20810-347 | ( 2397, 2398 ) | 결재 | 담 당 | 과 장 | 국 장 |
|---|---|---|---|---|---|---|
| 시행일자 | 1990. 9. 27. | | | | | |
| 수 신 | 아 주 국 장 | 발신 | 영사교민국장 | (서명) | | |
| 제 목 | 걸프만 사태 관련 난민 수송 지원 | | | | | |

당국은 걸프만 사태와 관련, 난민 수송을 위해 특별 지원을 요청한 국제난민기구 (IOM) 에 별첨과 같이 50 만불을 특별 기여금으로 pledge 하도록 주제네바 대표부에 지시한 바 있으니, 필리핀, 스리랑카등 아시아 일부 국가들의 재정지원 요청에 대한 대책 수립시 참고하시기 바랍니다.

첨부 : 상기 전문 사본 1 부. 끝.

0080

PERMANENT MISSION OF THE REPUBLIC OF KOREA

GENEVA

27 September 1990

Sir,

With reference to your letters dated 24, 28 August and 6 September 1990 concerning the appeal for funding the IOM assistance in the return of foreign nationals stranded in the Gulf region, I have the honour to inform you that the Government of the Republic of Korea has decided to pledge five hundreds thousands US dollars (US$ 500,000) as the voluntary contribution in this regard.

Apart from the above contribution to the IOM, the Republic of Korea has already spent one million two hundreds seventy three thousands US dollars (US$ 1,273,000) on the repatriation of Korean and foreign nationals employed by the Korean companies in the Gulf area.

Moreover, the recent national economic situation and latest calamity caused by flood in my country has become financial constraints. Despite these difficulties, my country's commitment to the United Nations efforts in the region in general and its support for the much needed work by the IOM there in particular have led the Government to make the decision in favor of such special contribution subject to supplementary budget approval by the National Assembly.

Please accept, Sir, the renewed assurances of my highest consideration.

Sang Ock LEE
Ambassador

Mr. James N. PURCELL, Jr.
Director-General
International Organization
for Migration
17, route des Morillons
1211 Genève 19

0081

한실장

# 주 제 네 바 대 표 부

제네(정) 20320- 1031 1990. 9.28

수신 : 장관

참조 : 영사교민국장,미주국장,국제기구조약국장

제목 : 페르샤만 사태 관련 IOM 지원

대 : WGV-1252

1. 대호 당관은 IOM 사무총장앞 공한을 통해 IOM의 난민 수송지원 사업에 대한 아국의 50만불 기여금 출연 결정 사실을 통보하였는바, 참고로 상기 공한을 별첨 송부합니다.

2. 아울러 IOM 사무국에서 배포한 9.26 현재 IOM에 접수된 각국 기여현황 및 난민 수송지원 사업 현황자료를 별첨 송부합니다.

첨부 : 1. 상기 공한 사본 1부.
2. IOM 난민수송사업 현황 자료. 끝.

주 제 네 바 대

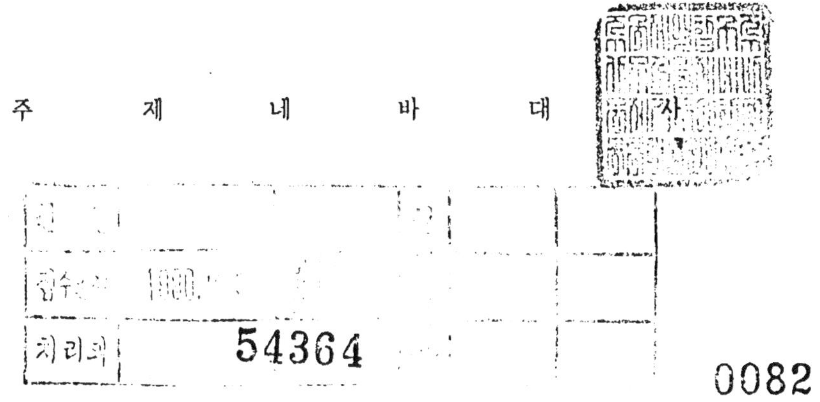


0082

**PERMANENT MISSION OF THE REPUBLIC OF KOREA**

**GENEVA**

27 September 1990

Sir,

With reference to your letters dated 24, 28 August and 6 September 1990 concerning the appeal for funding the IOM assistance in the return of foreign nationals stranded in the Gulf region, I have the honour to inform you that the Government of the Republic of Korea has decided to pledge five hundreds thousands US dollars (US$ 500,000) as the voluntary contribution in this regard.

Apart from the above contribution to the IOM, the Republic of Korea has already spent one million two hundreds seventy three thousands US dollars (US$ 1,273,000) on the repatriation of Korean and foreign nationals employed by the Korean companies in the Gulf area.

Moreover, the recent national economic situation and latest calamity caused by flood in my country has become financial constraints. Despite these difficulties, my country's commitment to the United Nations efforts in the region in general and its support for the much needed work by the IOM there in particular have led the Government to make the decision in favor of such special contribution subject to supplementary budget approval by the National Assembly.

Please accept, Sir, the renewed assurances of my highest consideration.

Sang Ock LEE
Ambassador

Mr. James N. PURCELL, Jr.
Director-General
International Organization
for Migration
17, route des Morillons
1211 Genève 19

0083

INTERNATIONAL ORGANIZATION FOR MIGRATION (IOM)
ORGANISATION INTERNATIONALE POUR LES MIGRATIONS (OIM)
ORGANIZACIÓN INTERNACIONAL PARA LAS MIGRACIONES (OIM)

Telephone: 717 91 11
Cable Address: Promigrant Geneva
Telex: 415 722
Telefax: 798 61 50

17, route des Morillons
P.O. Box 71
CH-1211 GENEVA 19
SWITZERLAND

INTERNATIONAL ORGANIZATION FOR MIGRATION

TO: THE PERMANENT MISSIONS OF:

ARGENTINA, AUSTRALIA, AUSTRIA, BANGLADESH, BELIZE, BOLIVIA, BRAZIL, BELGIUM, CANADA, CAPE VERDE, CHILE, CHINA, COLOMBIA, COSTA RICA, CYPRUS, DENMARK, DOMINICAN REP., ECUADOR, EGYPT, EL SALVADOR, FRANCE, FINLAND, GERMANY (FED. REP. OF), GHANA, GUINEA-BISSAU, GREECE, GUATEMALA, HOLY SEE, HONDURAS, INDIA, INDONESIA, IRAN, ISRAEL, ITALY, JAPAN, JORDAN, KENYA, KOREA (REP. OF), LUXEMBOURG, MEXICO, NETHERLANDS, NEW ZEALAND, NICARAGUA, NORWAY, PAKISTAN, PANAMA, PARAGUAY, PERU, PHILIPPINES, PORTUGAL, SAN MARINO, SAUDI ARABIA, SINGAPORE, SOMALIA, SPAIN, SRI LANKA, SWEDEN, SWITZERLAND, SYRIAN ARAB REP., THAILAND, TURKEY, UGANDA, U.S.S.R., UNITED KINGDOM, U.S.A., URUGUAY, VENEZUELA, YUGOSLAVIA, ZIMBABWE AND THE COMMISSION OF THE EUROPEAN COMMUNITIES

COPY TO UNDRO GENEVA AND PRINCE SADRUDDIN AGA KHAN, PERSONAL REPRESENTATIVE FOR HUMANITARIAN ASSISTANCE RELATING TO THE CRISIS BETWEEN IRAQ AND KUWAIT

FROM: INTERNATIONAL ORGANIZATION FOR MIGRATION, GENEVA

DATE: 27.9.1990 jeh

SUBJECT: IOM'S GULF EMERGENCY PROGRAMME : UPDATED PLAN OF ACTION

WITH REFERENCE TO OUR COMMUNICATION OF 21 SEPT 1990, PLEASE FIND ENCLOSED A FURTHER UPDATE OF THE IOM PLAN OF ACTION. COPIES ARE AVAILABLE FROM IOM HQS.

PURCELL

0084

INTERNATIONAL ORGANIZATION FOR MIGRATION (IOM)
ORGANISATION INTERNATIONALE POUR LES MIGRATIONS (OIM)
ORGANIZACIÓN INTERNACIONAL PARA LAS MIGRACIONES (OIM)

Telephone: 717 91 11
Cable Address: Promigrant Geneva
Telex: 415 722
Telefax: 798 61 50

17, route des Morillons
P.O. Box 71
CH - 1211 GENEVA 19
SWITZERLAND

PLAN OF ACTION - UPDATE OF OPERATIONS

Region-wide, 56,736 foreign residents of Kuwait and Iraq have returned to their home countries under IOM auspices since 3 September. In addition, firm IOM bookings exist for a further 25,541 passengers.

From Jordan, as of 26 September, IOM-arranged departures had reached 53,158, of whom the largest groups have been Bangladeshis (28,506), Sri Lankans (8,959) and Filipinos (6,528). In total, 154 international airlift charter flights left Amman between 3 and 26 September. Both figures include, in certain cases, transport arrangements initiated by the respective countries of nationality and supported logistically and financially by IOM. When combined with departures handled entirely by countries of nationality, outflow had thus begun to surpass slightly the rate of arrivals. However, reports reaching IOM as this update is being prepared indicate a new surge in arrivals. IOM consequently is in the process of adding departure capacity to increase offtake significantly in the next days.

As regards inland transport (viz. para. 12 of UNDRO Jordan sitrep No. 11 of 25 September), and in recognition of the burden shouldered by the Jordanian authorities in providing this vital link thus far, IOM will finance future bus transportation linked to IOM-co-ordinated repatriation flights.

Internationally-assisted repatriations from Turkey, including IOM and joint IOM-EC flights, have so far benefitted 2,635 Bangladeshis and 383 Pakistanis, or a total of 3,018 passengers on 13 charter and regular flights. IOM staff in Ankara, Diyarbakir and Habur continue to monitor needs and contract capacity accordingly, as well as to co-ordinate departures with local authorities.

One IOM official is currently in Teheran arranging air departures from that city as well as from Tabriz. Thus far, 146 persons have left Iran under IOM auspices; an additional 168 are currently being booked either on regular flights from Teheran to various destinations or on special charter flights from Tabriz to Dhaka.

In addition to the above, IOM continues to receive small numbers of requests for repatriation assistance from various locations throughout the Middle East. Arrangements are thus made through IOM Headquarters for individual and small-group movements on regularly scheduled air services or, if warranted, special charters such as the one which departed Riyadh for Colombo on 22 September with 414 persons aboard.

../..

0085

Estimates of the foreign populations remaining in Kuwait and Iraq and in need of internationally-assisted repatriation vary widely. Nevertheless, by all indications, potentially large numbers of nationals of many of the countries most affected thus far (e.g., Bangladesh, India, Pakistan, Philippines and Sri Lanka), as well as of certain other countries, still wish or need to repatriate. In the latter category, for example, the Socialist Republic of Vietnam has requested IOM assistance for the return of some 16,000 of its nationals at present in Iraq.

Given the ever more complex planning required to deal with diversifying points of departure and destination, as well as larger variations in caseloads and their impact on aircraft capacity requirements, close co-ordination and information sharing remain of the essence. Regular contacts between IOM and the EC, UNDRO, national authorities and the Office of Prince Sadruddin Aga Khan, at both Headquarters and field levels, have greatly facilitated an organized, quick response to repatriation transport needs to-date. IOM requests all concerned to continue providing whatever data they may have concerning requirements and contributions as early as possible in order to ensure orderly, planned and regular outflow commensurate with needs.

A breakdown of pledged contributions - which totalled US$ 47,448,000 in cash and US$ 8,356,300 in kind as at 26 September - is laid out in Annex I. Donors' efforts to transfer funds as expeditiously as possible have been, and will continue to be, highly appreciated. Annex II contains departure and booking statistics, broken down by country of transit and country of nationality. Annex III provides detailed information on individual flights paid for to date, including destination, passenger loads and price. It should be noted that Annex III reflects only actual payments of US$ 14,080,921 and does not include commitments, which surpass US$ 9 million.

27 September 1990

0086

GULF EMERGENCY PROGRAMME
PLEDGES AND RECEIPT FOR TRANSPORTATION
as at 26 September 1990

| *1. CASH CONTRIBUTIONS* | *PLEDGED* | *RECEIVED USD* |
|---|---|---|
| AUSTRALIA | AUD 1,000,000.00 | 831,982.69 |
| AUSTRIA | ATS 3,000,000.00 | |
| CANADA | CAD 2,000,000.00 | 1,769,911.50 |
| DENMARK | DKK 1,500,000.00 | 249,196.00 |
| FINLAND | FIM 8,000,000.00 | 2,162,735.00 |
| GERMANY | DEM 5,000,000.00 | |
| ITALY | 1) USD 500,000.00 | |
| JAPAN | 1) USD 12,000,000.00 | 8,640,000.00 |
| NETHERLANDS | NLG 2,000,000.00 | |
| NORWAY | NOK 15,500,000.00 | 902,615.95 |
| SWEDEN | 1) SEK 30,000,000.00 | |
| SWITZERLAND | CHF 250,000.00 | |
| UNITED KINGDOM | GBP 2,000,000.00 | 3,720,800.00 |
| U.S.A. | USD 10,250,000.00 | 10,050,000.00 |
| EUROPEAN COMMUNITY | 2) USD 3,327,850.00 | |
| *2. PRIVATE DONATIONS* | | |
| US-AIM | USD 1,500.00 | 1,500.00 |
| AUSTRALIAN CARE | AUD 75,000.00 | 62,500.00 |
| *TOTAL* | USD 47,448,000.00 | 28,391,241.14 |
| *3. IN-KIND CONTRIBUTIONS* | | |
| NEW ZEALAND | USD 161,300.00 1 Hercules 3 flights(210 pak-450.84 MNL-800) | |
| NORWAY | 1 Aircraft | |
| SPAIN (RED CROSS) | USD 1,250,000.00 1 Aircraft 10 flights (2500 DAC-500) | |
| SWEDEN (RED CROSS) | USD 2,330,000.00 1 Aircraft 10 flights (4660 DAC-500) | |
| SWITZERLAND | CHF 6,000,000.00 1 Aircraft | |
| *TOTAL IN KIND CONTRIBUTIONS* | USD 8,356,300.00 | |

1) through UNDRO
2) 50% of joint operations IOM/EEC of 20 flights (10 to Manila, 10 to Colombo)

0087

GULF EMERGENCY PROGRAMME
UTILIZED IN-KIND DONATIONS (FLIGHTS)
as at 23 September 1990

(departures from Amman, Jordan)

| SOURCE | NO. OF FLIGHTS | TOTAL FLIGHTS | DESTINATION | NO. OF PAX | TOTAL PAX | TOTAL COST ESTIMATE USD |
|---|---|---|---|---|---|---|
| NEW ZEALAND GOVERNMENT | 1 | | Dhaka | 111 | | |
| | 2 | | Manila | 176 | | |
| | 4 | | Karachi | 433 | | |
| | 1 | | Colombo | 121 | | |
| | 1 | | Bombay | 198 | | |
| | | 9 | | | 1,039 | |
| NORWAY GOVERNMENT | 2 | | Cairo | 176 | | |
| | | 2 | | | 176 | |
| SPANISH RED CROSS | 6 | | Karachi | 1,558 | | |
| | | 6 | | | 1,558 | |
| SWEDISH RED CROSS | 4 | | Bombay | 1,863 | | |
| | 6 | | Dhaka | 2,756 | | |
| | | 10 | | | 4,619 | |
| SWITZERLAND GOVERNMENT | 4 | | Dhaka | 784 | | |
| | 1 | | Bombay | 175 | | |
| | | 5 | | | 959 | |
| UNITED KINGDOM GOVERNMENT | 4 | | Bombay | 1,561 | | |
| | 1 | | Dhaka | 390 | | |
| | | 5 | | | 1,951 | |
| TOTALS = | | 37 | | | 10,302 | 6,064,720.00 |

0088

Annex II

IOM - PLAN OF ACTION/UPDATED

**JORDAN**

| Nationals of : | Movements | |
|---|---|---|
| | DEPARTED 3-26/9/1990 | BOOKED TO DEPART 27/9-10/10/1990 |
| Bangladesh | 28,506 | 4,392 |
| India | 6,481 | 5,597 |
| Pakistan | 2,778 | 0 |
| Philippines | 6,528 | 2,409 |
| Sri Lanka | 8,959 | 11,566 |
| Egypt | 176 | 91 |
| | 53,158 | 24,055 |

**TURKEY**

| Nationals of : | Movements | |
|---|---|---|
| | DEPARTED 3-26/9/1990 | BOOKED TO DEPART 27/9-10/10/1990 |
| Bangladesh | 2,635 | 900 |
| India | 0 | 0 |
| Pakistan | 383 | 400 |
| Philippines | 0 | 0 |
| Sri Lanka | 0 | 18 |
| Egypt | 0 | 0 |
| | 3,018 | 1,318 |

**IRAN**

| Nationals of : | Movements | |
|---|---|---|
| | DEPARTED 3-26/9/1990 | BOOKED TO DEPART 27/9-10/10/1990 |
| Bangladesh | 88 | 140 |
| India | 8 | 0 |
| Pakistan | 25 | 10 |
| Philippines | 0 | 12 |
| Sri Lanka | 25 | 6 |
| Egypt | 0 | 0 |
| | 146 | 168 |

0089

6894C /lw
27/9/90

Annex III

page 1

GULF EMERGENCY PROGRAMME
as at 26 September 1990

| AIRLINE COMPANY | ROUTING | CHARTER | DATE OF DEPARTURE | NO. OF PAX | TOTAL PAX | PAID USD | TOTAL PAYMENT |
|---|---|---|---|---|---|---|---|
| ROYAL JORDANIAN AIRLINE | Amman - Dhaka | MIRJ 23 043 | 08.09.90 | 230 | | 177,000.00 | |
| | | MIRJ 23 044 | 09.09.90 | 227 | | 177,000.00 | |
| | | MIRJ 23 045 | 11.09.90 | 231 | | 177,000.00 | |
| | | MIRJ 23 046 | 11.09.90 | 231 | | 177,000.00 | |
| | | MIRJ 23 047 | 12.09.90 | 232 | | 177,000.00 | |
| | | MIRJ 23 048 | 13.09.90 | 231 | | 177,000.00 | |
| | | MIRJ 23 203 | 22.09.90 | 277 | | 159,500.00 | |
| | | MIRJ 23 204 | 23.09.90 | 277 | | 159,500.00 | |
| | | MIRJ 23 205 | 24.09.90 | 276 | | 159,500.00 | |
| | | MIRJ 23 206 | 24.09.90 | 275 | | 159,500.00 | |
| | | MIRJ 23 207 | 24.09.90 | 276 | | 159,500.00 | |
| | Amman - Colombo | MIRJ 23 001 | 03.09.90 | 182 | | 137,500.00 | |
| | | MIRJ 23 002 | 04.09.90 | 184 | | 137,500.00 | |
| | | MIRJ 23 003 | 05.09.90 | 187 | | 137,500.00 | |
| | | MIRJ 23 004 | 05.09.90 | 182 | | 137,500.00 | |
| | | MIRJ 23 005 | 06.09.90 | 184 | | 137,500.00 | |
| | | MIRJ 23 006 | 07.09.90 | 183 | | 137,500.00 | |
| | | MIRJ 23 049 | 08.09.90 | 183 | | 137,500.00 | |
| | | MIRJ 23 050 | 09.09.90 | 183 | | 137,500.00 | |
| | | MIRJ 23 051 | 10.09.90 | 185 | | 137,500.00 | |
| | | MIRJ 23 052 | 10.09.90 | 188 | | 137,500.00 | |
| | | MIRJ 23 053 | 11.09.90 | 181 | | 137,500.00 | |

0090

| (continued ROYAL JORDANIAN AIRLINE) | (continued Amman - Colombo) | MIRJ 23 054 | 13.09.90 | 190 | | 137,500.00 | |
|---|---|---|---|---|---|---|---|
| | | MIRJ 23 091 | 13.09.90 | 183 | | 114,660.00 | |
| | | MIRJ 23 092 | 14.09.90 | 190 | | 114,660.00 | |
| | | MIRJ 23 093 | 15.09.90 | 182 | | 114,660.00 | |
| | | MIRJ 23 094 | 16.09.90 | 182 | | 114,660.00 | |
| | | MIRJ 23 095 | 16.09.90 | 182 | | 114,660.00 | |
| | | MIRJ 23 096 | 17.09.90 | 182 | | 114,660.00 | |
| | | MIRJ 23 097 | 18.09.90 | 182 | | 114,660.00 | |
| | | MIRJ 23 098 | 19.09.90 | 182 | | 114,660.00 | |
| | | MIRJ 23 099 | 19.09.90 | 275 | | 165,000.00 | |
| | | MIRJ 23 100 | 20.09.90 | 275 | | 165,000.00 | |
| | | MIRJ 23 101 | 20.09.90 | 275 | | 165,000.00 | |
| | | MIRJ 23 102 | 20.09.90 | 275 | | 165,000.00 | |
| | **Amman - Manila** | MIRJ 23 202 | 19.09.90 | 231 | | 184,800.00 | |
| | | | | | 7,771 | | 5,271,580.00 |

| *AIRLINE COMPANY* | *ROUTING* | *CHARTER* | *DATE OF DEPARTURE* | *NO. OF PAX* | *TOTAL PAX* | *PAID USD* | *TOTAL PAYMENT* |
|---|---|---|---|---|---|---|---|
| **TOWER AIR** | **Amman - Manila** | MIFF 23 074 | 11.09.90 | 480 | | 380,000.00 | |
| | | MIFF 23 075 | 13.09.90 | 479 | | 380,000.00 | |
| | | MIFF 23 076 | 14.09.90 | 487 | | 380,000.00 | |
| | | MIFF 23 077 | 15.09.90 | 477 | | 380,000.00 | |
| | | MIFF 23 078 | 17.09.90 | 486 | | 380,000.00 | |
| | | MIFF 23 079 | 19.09.90 | 481 | | 380,000.00 | |
| | | MIFF 23 080 | 20.09.90 | 477 | | 380,000.00 | |
| | | MIFF 23 081 | 22.09.90 | 474 | | 380,000.00 | |
| | | MIFF 23 082 | 23.09.90 | 484 | | 380,000.00 | |
| | | | | | 4,325 | | 3,420,000.00 |

0091

| AIRLINE COMPANY | ROUTING | CHARTER | DATE OF DEPARTURE | NO. OF PAX | TOTAL PAX | PAID USD | TOTAL PAYMENT |
|---|---|---|---|---|---|---|---|
| TURKISH AIRLINES | Diyarbakir Dhaka | MITK 23 500 | 12.09.90 | 201 | | 133,000.00 | |
| | | MITK 23 501 | 12.09.90 | 200 | | 133,000.00 | |
| | | MITK 23 502 | 12.09.90 | 201 | | 133,000.00 | |
| | | MITK 23 503 | 12.09.90 | 200 | | 133,000.00 | |
| | | MITK 23 504 | 13.09.90 | 200 | | 133,000.00 | |
| | | MITK 23 507 | 18.09.90 | 200 | | 133,000.00 | |
| | | MITK 23 508 | 19.09.90 | 200 | | 133,000.00 | |
| | | | 18.09.90 | 335 | | 217,750.00 | |
| | | | 19.09.90 | 335 | | 227,500.00 | |
| | | | 20.09.90 | 350 | | 227,500.00 | |
| | | | | | 2,422 | | 1,603,750.00 |

| AIRLINE COMPANY | ROUTING | CHARTER | DATE OF DEPARTURE | NO. OF PAX | TOTAL PAX | PAID USD | TOTAL PAYMENT |
|---|---|---|---|---|---|---|---|
| TATE AERO-SERVICES LTD. | Amman - Dhaka | MITA 23 007 | 04.09.90 | 165 | | 119,955.00 | |
| | | MITA 23 008 | 05.09.90 | 166 | | 119,955.00 | |
| | | MITA 23 009 | 06.09.90 | 165 | | 119,955.00 | |
| | | MITA 23 010 | 07.09.90 | 165 | | 119,955.00 | |
| | | MITA 23 011 | 08.09.90 | 165 | | 119,955.00 | |
| | | MITA 23 012 | 09.09.90 | 170 | | 119,955.00 | |
| | | MITA 23 013 | 09.09.90 | 167 | | 119,955.00 | |
| | | MITA 23 014 | 10.09.90 | 165 | | 119,955.00 | |
| | | MITA 23 057 | 10.09.90 | 300 | | 177,762.00 | |
| | | | | | 1,628 | | 1,137,402.00 |

| AIRLINE COMPANY | ROUTING | CHARTER | DATE OF DEPARTURE | NO. OF PAX | TOTAL PAX | PAID USD | TOTAL PAYMENT |
|---|---|---|---|---|---|---|---|
| SAUDI ARABIAN AIRLINES | Riyadh - Colombo | MISV 23 751 | 22.09.90 | 414 | | 106,666.00 | |
| | | | | | 414 | | 106,666.00 |

0092

| AIRLINE COMPANY | ROUTING | CHARTER | DATE OF DEPARTURE | NO. OF PAX | TOTAL PAX | PAID USD | TOTAL PAYMENT |
|---|---|---|---|---|---|---|---|
| EVER-GREEN INT. AIRLINES | Amman - Colombo | MIEZ 23 105 | 15.09.90 | 501 | | 285,570.00 | |
| | | Passenger tax | | | | 30,060.00 | |
| | | MIEZ 23 106 | 17.09.90 | 501 | | 285,570.00 | |
| | | Passenger tax | | | | 30,060.00 | |
| | | MIEZ 23 107 | 19.09.90 | 500 | | 285,570.00 | |
| | | Passenger tax | | | | 30,060.00 | |
| | | MIEZ 23 108 | 20.09.90 | 501 | | 285,570.00 | |
| | | Passenger tax | | | | 30,060.00 | |
| | | | | | 2,003 | | 1,262,520.00 |

| AIRLINE COMPANY | ROUTING | CHARTER | DATE OF DEPARTURE | NO. OF PAX | TOTAL PAX | PAID USD | TOTAL PAYMENT |
|---|---|---|---|---|---|---|---|
| OMEGA AIRLINES | Amman - Colombo | MIOM 23 113 | 14.09.90 | 180 | | 108,000.00 | |
| | | | | | 180 | | 108,000.00 |

| AIRLINE COMPANY | ROUTING | CHARTER | DATE OF DEPARTURE | NO. OF PAX | TOTAL PAX | PAID USD | TOTAL PAYMENT |
|---|---|---|---|---|---|---|---|
| PAKISTAN INT. AIRLINES | Teheran - Dhaka | MIPK 23 800 | 17.09.90 | 88 | | 53,815.00 | |
| | Teheran - Colombo | MIPK 23 800 | 17.09.90 | 25 | | 15,673.00 | |
| | Teheran - Karachi | MIPK 23 800 | 17.09.90 | 11 | | 4,315.00 | |
| | | | | | 124 | | 73,803.00 |

| AIRLINE COMPANY | ROUTING | CHARTER | DATE OF DEPARTURE | NO. OF PAX | TOTAL PAX | PAID USD | TOTAL PAYMENT |
|---|---|---|---|---|---|---|---|
| JAPAN AIRLINES | Amman - Manila | MIJL 23 128 | 23.09.90 | 272 | | 240,000.00 | |
| | | | | | 272 | | 240,000.00 |

| SHIPPING COMPANY | ROUTING | REF. | DATE OF DEPARTURE | NO. OF PAX | TOTAL PAX | PAID USD | TOTAL PAYMENT |
|---|---|---|---|---|---|---|---|
| ORIENT SHIPPING | Aqaba - Colombo | M/V SAINA E ARAB | 15.09.90 | 1,768 | | 707,200.00 | |
| | | | | | 1,768 | | 707,200.00 |

| Bus transport Amman, Jordan | 150,000.00 |
|---|---|

| GRAND TOTAL | | PAX | | USD |
|---|---|---|---|---|
| | | 20,907 | | 14,080,921.00 |

0093

원 본

# 외 무 부

종 별 :

번 호 : GVW-1963 일 시 : 90 1004 1200

수 신 : 장 관 (영해,국기,미북)

발 신 : 주 제네바 대사

제 목 : 페만사태 관련 IOM 지원

연: 제네(정) 20320-1031

IOM 사무국은 별첨 공한을 통해 IOM 의 난민 수송지원 사업에 대한 아국의 50만불 기여결정과 관련 기여금은 하기 IOM 구좌에 송금하여 줄것을 요청하였음.

0 은행명 및 주소: SOCIETE DE BANKUE SUISSE, 1211GENEVE 11, SUISSE

0 구좌번호 및 소유주: NO. 145. 718/6, INTERNATIONAL ORGANIZATION FOR MIGRATION

첨부: 상기 IOM 공한.끝 (GVW (F)-381)

(대사 이상옥-국장)

| 영사교민국 | 담 당 | 계 장 | 과 장 | 관리관 | 국 장 |
|---|---|---|---|---|---|
| | | | | | |

영교국 미주국 국기국

PAGE 1 90.10.05 01:02 FC

외신 1과 통제관

0094

GVW(기)-381 0/004 1200

INTERNATIONAL ORGANIZATION FOR MIGRATION GVW-1965 3214

THE DIRECTOR GENERAL

GENEVA. SWITZERLAND

1 October 1990

Sir,

I have the honour to acknowledge receipt of your letter dated 27 September 1990 informing me of the decision of your Government to make a voluntary contribution of US$ 500,000 to IOM's Gulf Emergency Programme.

I should like to take this opportunity to express our deep gratitude to your Government for this generous contribution, which will go far in alleviating the plight of many displaced persons.

Please have the funds transferred to: Société de Banque Suisse, 1211 Genève 11, for credit to our US dollar account No. 145.718/6, International Organization for Migration.

Please accept, Sir, the assurance of my highest consideration.

James N Purcell Jr

James N. Purcell, Jr.

S.E. Mr. Sang Ock Lee
Ambassador
Permanent Observer of the Republic
of Korea to the United Nations Office
in Geneva and Permanent Delegate to
other international organizations
in Geneva
20, route de Pré-Bois
1215 GENEVA 15

1-1

0095

1990-10-04 16:03 KOREAN MISSION GENEVA 2 022 791 0525 P.09

주 제 네 바 대 표 부

제네(정) 20320-1056 1990.10. 5

수신 : 장관

참조 : 영사교민국장

제목 : 페만사태 관련 IOM자료 송부

연 : GVW-1963

연호 IOM의 난민수송지원 사업과 관련 10.3 현재 아국을 포함한 각국 기여 현황 및 난민수송지원 사업현황 자료를 별첨 송부합니다.

첨부 : 상기 자료 1부. 끝.

주 제 네 바 대 사

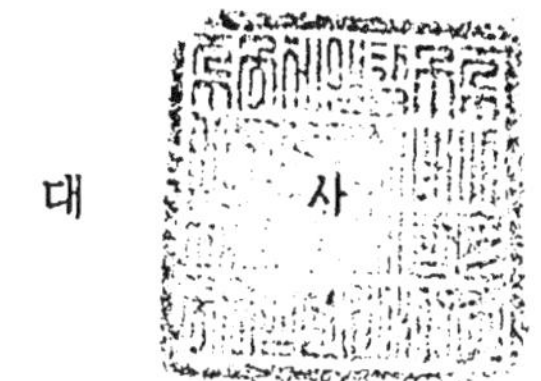

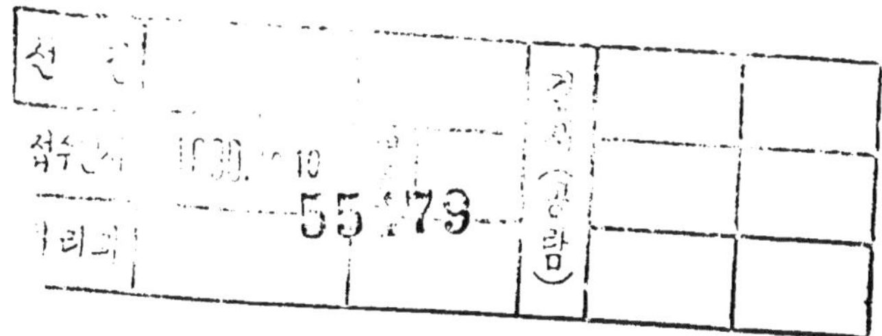

0096

INTERNATIONAL ORGANIZATION FOR MIGRATION (IOM)
ORGANISATION INTERNATIONALE POUR LES MIGRATIONS (OIM)
ORGANIZACIÓN INTERNACIONAL PARA LAS MIGRACIONES (OIM)

Telephone: 717 91 11
Cable Address: Promigrant Geneva
Telex: 415 722
Telefax: 798 61 50

17, route des Morillons
P.O. Box 71
CH-1211 GENEVA 19
SWITZERLAND

INTERNATIONAL ORGANIZATION FOR MIGRATION

TO: THE PERMANENT MISSIONS OF:

ARGENTINA, AUSTRALIA, AUSTRIA, BANGLADESH, BELIZE, BOLIVIA, BRAZIL, BELGIUM, CANADA, CAPE VERDE, CHILE, CHINA, COLOMBIA, COSTA RICA, CYPRUS, DENMARK, DOMINICAN REP., ECUADOR, EGYPT, EL SALVADOR, FRANCE, FINLAND, GERMANY, GHANA, GUINEA-BISSAU, GREECE, GUATEMALA, HOLY SEE, HONDURAS, INDIA, INDONESIA, IRAN, ISRAEL, ITALY, JAPAN, JORDAN, KENYA, KOREA (REP. OF), LUXEMBOURG, MEXICO, NETHERLANDS, NEW ZEALAND, NICARAGUA, NORWAY, PAKISTAN, PANAMA, PARAGUAY, PERU, PHILIPPINES, PORTUGAL, SAN MARINO, SAUDI ARABIA, SINGAPORE, SOMALIA, SPAIN, SRI LANKA, SWEDEN, SWITZERLAND, SYRIAN ARAB REP., THAILAND, TURKEY, UGANDA, U.S.S.R., UNITED KINGDOM, U.S.A., URUGUAY, VENEZUELA, YUGOSLAVIA, ZIMBABWE AND THE COMMISSION OF THE EUROPEAN COMMUNITIES

COPY TO UNDRO GENEVA AND PRINCE SADRUDDIN AGA KHAN, PERSONAL REPRESENTATIVE FOR HUMANITARIAN ASSISTANCE RELATING TO THE CRISIS BETWEEN IRAQ AND KUWAIT

FROM: INTERNATIONAL ORGANIZATION FOR MIGRATION, GENEVA

DATE: 04 OCTOBER 1990

SUBJECT: IOM'S GULF EMERGENCY PROGRAMME : UPDATED PLAN OF ACTION

WITH REFERENCE TO OUR COMMUNICATION OF 27 SEPT 1990, PLEASE FIND ENCLOSED A FURTHER UPDATE OF THE IOM PLAN OF ACTION. COPIES ARE AVAILABLE FROM IOM HQS.

PURCELL

0097

INTERNATIONAL ORGANIZATION FOR MIGRATION (IOM)
ORGANISATION INTERNATIONALE POUR LES MIGRATIONS (OIM)
ORGANIZACIÓN INTERNACIONAL PARA LAS MIGRACIONES (OIM)

Telephone: 717 91 11
Cable Address: Promigrant Geneva
Telex: 415 722
Telefax: 798 61 50

17, route des Morillons
P.O. Box 71
CH - 1211 GENEVA 19
SWITZERLAND

PLAN OF ACTION - UPDATE OF OPERATIONS

From 3 September to close of business 3 October, a total of 73,520 foreign residents of Iraq and Kuwait left Jordan, Turkey, Iran and Saudi Arabia for their home countries with repatriation assistance from IOM. Firm bookings have been made for a further 37,126 evacuees to depart between 4 and 15 October 1990, principally to Bangladesh, India, the Philippines and Sri Lanka. Daily adjustments are made to flight bookings and destinations in response to shifting requirements. This logistical process is further complicated by the wide variations in daily arrival rates - both in absolute numbers and in nationality composition - and lack of firm information concerning likely sizes and directions of future flows.

In Jordan, IOM has been endeavouring, as a bare minimum, to ensure that daily departures at least equal new arrivals; the ultimate goal, of course, is to reduce the transit population as rapidly as possible. If sudden large increases in arrivals, like those which occurred on several days last week, signal a new trend, they must be dealt with speedily through increased uplift in the following days. If, instead, they are isolated instances, overly increased uplift could outstrip departure processing capabilities and result in overcapacity or flight delays.

Working closely with the authorities of Jordan and the most affected countries of origin as well as UNDRO, the Office of the Secretary General's Personal Representive and the EC, IOM has responded to the best available needs assessment and has doubled daily offtake from Jordan since the last IOM update was issued. Up to and including 3 October, 69,236 persons had departed Jordan on 232 IOM-co-ordinated international repatriation flights. Further charters with a total capacity of 36,873 seats have been booked through 15 October. (A detailed breakdown by nationality of these totals, as well as of the departure/booking statistics in the following paragraphs, are contained in Annex II.

In view of the urgent cash requirements for inland transportation in Jordan, IOM has provided US$ 700,000 to the High Committee for Assistance to Transit Evacuees over the past week and plans to continue its support. The separate UNDRO appeal for this purpose, and the anticipated response, will greatly assist the financing of this vital link in the repatriation pipeline.

../..

0098

Total air departures from Turkey arranged by IOM or jointly by IOM with the EC reached 3,698 as of 3 October. As most new arrivals now are reported to be in possession of private vehicles, or will repatriate overland by bus, camp populations in need of air transport are dramatically reduced. Current plans therefore call for individual or small group repatriations on commercial flights from Ankara (66 firm bookings to date) rather than charters. IOM teams remain in place, however, to adjust plans as the need arises, and additional aircraft capacity could be made available almost immediately.

One IOM staff member remains in Iran to handle air departures from Teheran and Tabriz, which now total 172 IOM-arranged repatriations. Moreover, in Iran as well as in Turkey, IOM is responding to a formal request from the Government of Pakistan, whose bilateral efforts to repatriate its nationals in need have already been enormous, to assist them with overland repatriation.

IOM has also arranged the departure of 414 Sri Lankans from Saudi>Arabia, and continues to co-ordinate individual and small-group departures from other Middle Eastern locations.

Detailed information on IOM-chartered flights for which payment had been settled as of 3 October is contained in Annex III. It should be noted that these are payments only; the total thus does not reflect flights already carried out for which billing has not yet been processed, nor does it reflect commitments for future flights.

The logistical complexity and uncertainty of this repatriation scheme, as described in the first paragraphs of this update, have obvious ramifications for IOM's ability to project accurately and with some precision financial requirements. At present, IOM is drawing up a revised needs assessment and financial plan to be incorporated in an overall appeal to be issued shortly by the Office of the Personal Representative. As of 4 October, however, IOM estimates that announced contributions, which now total over US$ 60 million (cash and kind; see Annex I for details), should cover needs at present drawdown rates into the week of 8 October. Clearly, additional contributions will be needed shortly. Efforts by the international community, beginning now, to activate the processes required so quick response can be made once needs are more clearly determined will be of utmost assistance to IOM in meeting its obligations.

4 October 1990

0099

Annex I
page 1

GULF EMERGENCY PROGRAMME
PLEDGES AND RECEIPT FOR TRANSPORTATION
as at 3 October 1990

| *1. CASH CONTRIBUTIONS* | *PLEDGED* | *RECEIVED USD* |
|---|---|---|
| AUSTRALIA | 3) AUD 1,000,000.00 | 831,982.69 |
| AUSTRIA | 1) ATS 3,000,000.00 | |
| CANADA | CAD 5,000,000.00 | 1,769,911.50 |
| DENMARK | 3) DKK 1,500,000.00 | 249,196.00 |
| FINLAND | 3) FIM 8,000,000.00 | 2,162,735.00 |
| GERMANY | DEM 5,000,000.00 | |
| ITALY | 1) USD 500,000.00 | 485,000.00 |
| JAPAN | 1) USD 12,000,000.00 | 8,640,000.00 |
| KOREA | USD 500,000.00 | |
| NETHERLANDS | NLG 2,000,000.00 | |
| NORWAY | 3) NOK 15,500,000.00 | 2,556,110.00 |
| SWEDEN | 1) SEK 30,000,000.00 | |
| SWITZERLAND | 3) CHF 250,000.00 | 192,307.69 |
| UNITED KINGDOM | 3) GBP 2,000,000.00 | 3,720,800.00 |
| U.S.A. | 3) USD 10,250,000.00 | 10,050,000.00 |
| EUROPEAN COMMUNITY | 2) USD 3,327,850.00 | |
| *2. PRIVATE DONATIONS* | | |
| US-AIM | USD 1,500.00 | 1,500.00 |
| AUSTCARE | AUD 75,000.00 | 62,500.00 |
| *TOTAL* | USD 50,533,000.00 | 30,722,042.88 |

1) through UNDRO
2) 50% of joint operations IOM/EEC of 20 flights (10 to Manila, 10 to Colombo)
3) Paid in full

0100

# GULF EMERGENCY PROGRAMME
# UTILIZED IN-KIND DONATIONS (FLIGHTS)
## as at 30 September 1990

(departures from Amman, Jordan)

| SOURCE | NO. OF FLIGHTS | TOTAL FLIGHTS | DESTINATION | NO. OF PAX | TOTAL PAX | TOTAL COST ESTIMATE USD |
|---|---|---|---|---|---|---|
| NEW ZEALAND GOVERNMENT | 6 | | Dhaka | 700 | | |
| | 3 | | Manila | 257 | | |
| | 3 | | Karachi | 323 | | |
| | 1 | | Colombo | 121 | | |
| | 1 | | Bombay | 129 | | |
| | | 14 | | | 1,530 | |
| NORWAY GOVERNMENT | 2 | | Cairo | 176 | | |
| | | 2 | | | 176 | |
| SPANISH RED CROSS | 7 | | Karachi | 1,819 | | |
| | 2 | | Bombay | 478 | | |
| | 1 | | Colombo | 271 | | |
| | | 10 | | | 2,568 | |
| SWEDISH RED CROSS | 6 | | Bombay | 2,812 | | |
| | 6 | | Dhaka | 2,752 | | |
| | | 12 | | | 5,564 | |
| SWITZERLAND GOVERNMENT | 4 | | Dhaka | 784 | | |
| | 8 | | Bombay | 1,611 | | |
| | | 12 | | | 2,395 | |
| UNITED KINGDOM GOVERNMENT | 4 | | Bombay | 1,561 | | |
| | 3 | | Dhaka | 1,170 | | |
| | | 7 | | | 2,731 | |
| UNITED STATES GOVERNMENT | 1 | | Colombo | 120 | | |
| | 1 | | Dhaka | 122 | | |
| | 1 | | Manila | 119 | | |
| | | 3 | | | 361 | |
| LUTHERAN WORLD FEDERATION | 8 | | Dhaka | 2,014 | | |
| | | 8 | | | 2,014 | |
| TOTALS = | | 68 | | | 17,339 | 10,230,010.00 |

0101

Annex II

## IOM - PLAN OF ACTION/UPDATED

### JORDAN

| Nationals of : | Movements DEPARTED 3/9-3/10/1990 | BOOKED TO DEPART 4-15/10/1990 |
|---|---|---|
| Bangladesh | 33,906 | 5,594 |
| India | 11,682 | 5,802 |
| Mauritius | 2 | 1 |
| Nepal | 17 | 0 |
| Pakistan | 2,783 | 0 |
| Philippines | 8,111 | 2,456 |
| Sri Lanka | 12,438 | 23,020 |
| Egypt | 297 | 0 |
| | 69,236 | 36,873 |

### TURKEY

| Nationals of : | Movements DEPARTED 3/9-3/10/1990 | BOOKED TO DEPART 4-10/10/1990 |
|---|---|---|
| Bangladesh | 3,270 | 2 |
| India | 0 | 0 |
| Pakistan | 387 | 0 |
| Philippines | 0 | 0 |
| Sri Lanka | 41 | 64 |
| Egypt | 0 | 0 |
| | 3,698 | 66 |

### IRAN

| Nationals of : | Movements DEPARTED 3/9-3/10/1990 | BOOKED TO DEPART 4/10-10/10/1990 |
|---|---|---|
| Bangladesh | 88 | 178 |
| India | 8 | 5 |
| Pakistan | 40 | 0 |
| Philippines | 5 | 3 |
| Sri Lanka | 31 | 1 |
| Egypt | 0 | 0 |
| | 172 | 187 |

6894C
4/10/90

0102

GULF EMERGENCY PROGRAMME
PAYMENTS
as at 3 October 1990

| AIRLINE COMPANY | ROUTING | CHARTER | DATE OF DEPARTURE | NO. OF PAX | TOTAL PAX | PAID USD | TOTAL PAYMENT |
|---|---|---|---|---|---|---|---|
| ROYAL JORDANIAN AIRLINE | Amman - Dhaka | MIRJ 23 043 | 08.09.90 | 230 | | 177,000.00 | |
| | | MIRJ 23 044 | 09.09.90 | 227 | | 177,000.00 | |
| | | MIRJ 23 045 | 11.09.90 | 231 | | 177,000.00 | |
| | | MIRJ 23 046 | 11.09.90 | 231 | | 177,000.00 | |
| | | MIRJ 23 047 | 12.09.90 | 232 | | 177,000.00 | |
| | | MIRJ 23 048 | 13.09.90 | 231 | | 177,000.00 | |
| | | MIRJ 23 203 | 22.09.90 | 277 | | 159,500.00 | |
| | | MIRJ 23 204 | 23.09.90 | 277 | | 159,500.00 | |
| | | MIRJ 23 205 | 24.09.90 | 276 | | 159,500.00 | |
| | | MIRJ 23 206 | 25.09.90 | 275 | | 159,500.00 | |
| | | MIRJ 23 207 | 25.09.90 | 276 | | 159,500.00 | |
| | | MIRJ 23 208 | 26.09.90 | 275 | | 159,500.00 | |
| | | MIRJ 23 209 | 27.09.90 | 268 | | 159,500.00 | |
| | | MIRJ 23 210 | 28.09.90 | 280 | | 159,500.00 | |
| | | MIRJ 23 211 | 28.09.90 | 275 | | 159,500.00 | |
| | | MIRJ 23 212 | 29.09.90 | 275 | | 159,500.00 | |
| | | MIRJ 23 227 | 29.09.90 | 236 | | 159,500.00 | |
| | | MIRJ 23 228 | 30.09.90 | 237 | | 159,500.00 | |
| | | MIRJ 23 229 | 01.10.90 | 231 | | 159,500.00 | |
| | Amman - Colombo | MIRJ 23 001 | 03.09.90 | 182 | | 137,500.00 | |
| | | MIRJ 23 002 | 04.09.90 | 184 | | 137,500.00 | |
| | | MIRJ 23 003 | 05.09.90 | 187 | | 137,500.00 | |

0103

| | | | | | | | |
|---|---|---|---|---|---|---|---|
| (continued ROYAL JORDANIAN AIRLINE) | (continued Amman - Colombo) | MIRJ 23 004 | 05.09.90 | 182 | | 137,500.00 | |
| | | MIRJ 23 005 | 06.09.90 | 184 | | 137,500.00 | |
| | | MIRJ 23 006 | 07.09.90 | 183 | | 137,500.00 | |
| | | MIRJ 23 049 | 08.09.90 | 183 | | 137,500.00 | |
| | | MIRJ 23 050 | 09.09.90 | 183 | | 137,500.00 | |
| | | MIRJ 23 051 | 10.09.90 | 185 | | 137,500.00 | |
| | | MIRJ 23 052 | 10.09.90 | 188 | | 137,500.00 | |
| | | MIRJ 23 053 | 11.09.90 | 181 | | 137,500.00 | |
| | | MIRJ 23 054 | 13.09.90 | 190 | | 137,500.00 | |
| | | MIRJ 23 091 | 13.09.90 | 183 | | 114,660.00 | |
| | | MIRJ 23 092 | 14.09.90 | 190 | | 114,660.00 | |
| | | MIRJ 23 093 | 15.09.90 | 182 | | 114,660.00 | |
| | | MIRJ 23 094 | 16.09.90 | 182 | | 114,660.00 | |
| | | MIRJ 23 095 | 16.09.90 | 182 | | 114,660.00 | |
| | | MIRJ 23 096 | 17.09.90 | 182 | | 114,660.00 | |
| | | MIRJ 23 097 | 18.09.90 | 182 | | 114,660.00 | |
| | | MIRJ 23 098 | 19.09.90 | 182 | | 114,660.00 | |
| | | MIRJ 23 099 | 19.09.90 | 275 | | 165,000.00 | |
| | | MIRJ 23 100 | 20.09.90 | 275 | | 165,000.00 | |
| | | MIRJ 23 101 | 20.09.90 | 275 | | 165,000.00 | |
| | | MIRJ 23 102 | 20.09.90 | 275 | | 165,000.00 | |
| | | MIRJ 23 237 | 29.09.90 | 182 | | 92,820.00 | |
| | | MIRJ 23 238 | 30.09.90 | 178 | | 92,820.00 | |
| | | MIRJ23 239 | 01.10.90 | 182 | | 92,820.00 | |
| | | MIRJ 23 240 | 01.10.90 | 179 | | 92,820.00 | |
| | **Amman - Manila** | MIRJ 23 202 | 19.09.90 | 231 | | 184,800.00 | |
| | | | | | 10,569 | | 6,918,860.00 |

0104

| AIRLINE COMPANY | ROUTING | CHARTER | DATE OF DEPARTURE | NO. OF PAX | TOTAL PAX | PAID USD | TOTAL PAYMENT |
|---|---|---|---|---|---|---|---|
| TOWER AIR | Amman - Manila | MIFF 23 074 | 11.09.90 | 480 | | 380,000.00 | |
| | | MIFF 23 075 | 13.09.90 | 479 | | 380,000.00 | |
| | | MIFF 23 076 | 14.09.90 | 487 | | 380,000.00 | |
| | | MIFF 23 077 | 15.09.90 | 477 | | 380,000.00 | |
| | | MIFF 23 078 | 17.09.90 | 486 | | 380,000.00 | |
| | | MIFF 23 079 | 19.09.90 | 481 | | 380,000.00 | |
| | | MIFF 23 080 | 20.09.90 | 477 | | 380,000.00 | |
| | | MIFF 23 081 | 22.09.90 | 474 | | 380,000.00 | |
| | | MIFF 23 082 | 23.09.90 | 484 | | 380,000.00 | |
| | | MIFF 23 083 | 25.09.90 | 476 | | 380,000.00 | |
| | | MIFF 23 084 | 26.09.90 | 482 | | 380,000.00 | |
| | | MIFF 23 085 | 28.09.90 | 476 | | 380,000.00 | |
| | | MIFF 23 086 | 29.09.90 | 479 | | 380,000.00 | |
| | | | | | 6,238 | | 4,940,000.00 |

| AIRLINE COMPANY | ROUTING | CHARTER | DATE OF DEPARTURE | NO. OF PAX | TOTAL PAX | PAID USD | TOTAL PAYMENT |
|---|---|---|---|---|---|---|---|
| TURKISH AIRLINES | Diyarbakir Dhaka | MITK 23 500 | 12.09.90 | 201 | | 133,000.00 | |
| | | MITK 23 501 | 12.09.90 | 200 | | 133,000.00 | |
| | | MITK 23 502 | 12.09.90 | 201 | | 133,000.00 | |
| | | MITK 23 503 | 12.09.90 | 200 | | 133,000.00 | |
| | | MITK 23 504 | 13.09.90 | 200 | | 133,000.00 | |
| | | MITK 23 506 | 18.09.90 | 330 | | 217,750.00 | |
| | | MITK 23 507 | 18.09.90 | 200 | | 133,000.00 | |
| | | MITK 23 508 | 19.09.90 | 200 | | 133,000.00 | |
| | | MITK 23 509 | 21.09.90 | 201 | | 133,000.00 | |

0105

| AIRLINE COMPANY | ROUTING | CHARTER | DATE OF DEPARTURE | NO. OF PAX | TOTAL PAX | PAID USD | TOTAL PAYMENT |
|---|---|---|---|---|---|---|---|
| (continued TURKISH AIRLINES) | (continued Diyarbakir - Dhaka) | MITK 23 532 | 19.09.90 | 349 | | 227,500.00 | |
| | | MITK 23 533 | 20.09.90 | 350 | | 227,500.00 | |
| | | MITK 23 534 | 21.09.90 | 351 | | 227,500.00 | |
| | | MITK 23 535 | 22.09.90 | 280 | | 182,000.00 | |
| | Diyarbakir-Karachi | MITK 23 536 | 25.09.90 | 211 | | 80,000.00 | |
| | | MITK 23 537 | 27.09.90 | 211 | | 80,000.00 | |
| | | | | | 3,685 | | 2,306,250.00 |

| AIRLINE COMPANY | ROUTING | CHARTER | DATE OF DEPARTURE | NO. OF PAX | TOTAL PAX | PAID USD | TOTAL PAYMENT |
|---|---|---|---|---|---|---|---|
| TATE AERO-SERVICES LTD. | Amman - Dhaka | MITA 23 007 | 04.09.90 | 165 | | 119,955.00 | |
| | | MITA 23 008 | 05.09.90 | 166 | | 119,955.00 | |
| | | MITA 23 009 | 06.09.90 | 165 | | 119,955.00 | |
| | | MITA 23 010 | 07.09.90 | 165 | | 119,955.00 | |
| | | MITA 23 011 | 08.09.90 | 165 | | 119,955.00 | |
| | | MITA 23 012 | 09.09.90 | 170 | | 119,955.00 | |
| | | MITA 23 013 | 09.09.90 | 167 | | 119,955.00 | |
| | | MITA 23 014 | 10.09.90 | 165 | | 119,955.00 | |
| | | MITA 23 057 | 10.09.90 | 300 | | 177,762.00 | |
| | Amman - Colombo | RJ 1980/1 | 01.10.90 | 182 | | 108,472.00 | |
| | | RJ 1982/3 | 02.10.90 | 182 | | 108,472.00 | |
| | | RJ 1986/7 | 02.10.90 | 231 | | 137,676.00 | |
| | | RJ 1984/5 | 03.10.90 | 182 | | 108,472.00 | |
| | | RJ 1988/9 | 03.10.90 | 231 | | 137,676.00 | |
| | | | | | 2,636 | | 1,738,170.00 |

| AIRLINE COMPANY | ROUTING | CHARTER | DATE OF DEPARTURE | NO. OF PAX | TOTAL PAX | PAID USD | TOTAL PAYMENT |
|---|---|---|---|---|---|---|---|
| SAUDI ARABIAN AIRLINES | Riyadh - Colombo | MISV 23 751 | 22.09.90 | 414 | | 106,666.00 | |
| | | | | | 414 | | 106,666.00 |

0106

| AIRLINE COMPANY | ROUTING | CHARTER | DATE OF DEPARTURE | NO. OF PAX | TOTAL PAX | PAID USD | TOTAL PAYMENT |
|---|---|---|---|---|---|---|---|
| EVER-GREEN INT. AIRLINES | Amman - Colombo | MIEZ 23 105 | 15.09.90 | 501 | | 285,570.00 | |
| | | Passenger tax | | | | 30,060.00 | |
| | | MIEZ 23 106 | 17.09.90 | 501 | | 285,570.00 | |
| | | Passenger tax | | | | 30,060.00 | |
| | | MIEZ 23 107 | 19.09.90 | 500 | | 285,570.00 | |
| | | Passenger tax | | | | 30,060.00 | |
| | | MIEZ 23 108 | 20.09.90 | 501 | | 285,570.00 | |
| | | Passenger tax | | | | 30,060.00 | |
| | | | | | 2,003 | | 1,262,520.00 |

| AIRLINE COMPANY | ROUTING | CHARTER | DATE OF DEPARTURE | NO. OF PAX | TOTAL PAX | PAID USD | TOTAL PAYMENT |
|---|---|---|---|---|---|---|---|
| OMEGA AIRLINES | Amman - Colombo | MIOM 23 113 | 14.09.90 | 180 | | 108,000.00 | |
| | | | | | 180 | | 108,000.00 |

| AIRLINE COMPANY | ROUTING | CHARTER | DATE OF DEPARTURE | NO. OF PAX | TOTAL PAX | PAID USD | TOTAL PAYMENT |
|---|---|---|---|---|---|---|---|
| PAKISTAN INT. AIRLINES | Teheran - - Dhaka Colombo Karachi | MIPK 23 800 | 17.09.90 | 88<br>25<br>11 | | 86,230.00 | |
| | | | | | 124 | | 86,230.00 |

| AIRLINE COMPANY | ROUTING | CHARTER | DATE OF DEPARTURE | NO. OF PAX | TOTAL PAX | PAID USD | TOTAL PAYMENT |
|---|---|---|---|---|---|---|---|
| JAPAN AIRLINES | Amman - Manila | MIJL 23 126 | 23.09.90 | 272 | | 240,000.00 | |
| | | | | | 272 | | 240,000.00 |

| AIRLINE COMPANY | ROUTING | CHARTER | DATE OF DEPARTURE | NO. OF PAX | TOTAL PAX | PAID USD | TOTAL PAYMENT |
|---|---|---|---|---|---|---|---|
| NATIONAIR | Amman - Bombay | MINX 23 261 | 30.09.90 | 290 | | 126,000.00 | |
| | | MINX 23 262 | 01.10.90 | 269 | | 126,000.00 | |
| | | MINX 23 273 | 01.10.90 | 478 | | 228,200.00 | |
| | | | | | 1,037 | | 480,200.00 |

0107

Annex III
page 6

| AIRLINE COMPANY | ROUTING | CHARTER | DATE OF DEPARTURE | NO. OF PAX | TOTAL PAX | PAID USD | TOTAL PAYMENT |
|---|---|---|---|---|---|---|---|
| ALL NIPPON AIRWAYS | Amman - Manila | MINH 23 129 | 19.09.90 | 297 | | 237,600.00 | |
| | | | | | 297 | | 237,600.00 |

| SHIPPING COMPANY | ROUTING | REF. | DATE OF DEPARTURE | NO. OF PAX | TOTAL PAX | PAID USD | TOTAL PAYMENT |
|---|---|---|---|---|---|---|---|
| ORIENT SHIPPING | Aqaba - Colombo | M/V SAINAE ARAB | 15.09.90 | 1,768 | | 707,200.00 | |
| | | | | | 1,768 | | 707,200.00 |

| Bus transport Amman, Jordan | 700,000.00 |
|---|---|

| GRAND TOTAL | | PAX | | USD |
|---|---|---|---|---|
| | | 29,223 | | 19,831,696.00 |

Division of Banking

0108

한시녹화
영해

**INTERNATIONAL ORGANIZATION FOR MIGRATION (IOM)**

國 際 移 民 機 構

TELEPHONE: 3-322441-6
CABLES: PROMIGRANT HONG KONG
TELEX: 55566 HX
FAX: 3-881204

REGIONAL OFFICE FOR EAST ASIA
RM. 904, YAU MA TEI CARPARK BUILDING 9/F.
250, SHANGHAI STREET
KOWLOON, HONG KONG.

MAILING ADDRESS:
P. O. BOX 71509
KOWLOON CENTRAL POST OFFICE
HONG KONG.

FE-MISC-181

12th October 1990

Dear Sir,

**Gulf Crisis**

A special Session of the IOM Executive Committee was called on 4th of September 1990 in order to deal with the emergency situation which has developed in the Gulf.

At this Session IOM - in its role as lead agency of the international community for transport related matters - was asked to provide participating Governments with updated information in regard to the repatriation activities.

In pursuance of this request this Office is sending ..... copies of documents MC/EX/512, MC/EX/513, MC/EX/SR/393 as well as the latest report issued by IOM Geneva.

Sincerely yours,

Alfred V. Kottek
Regional Representative

Director-General,
Consular Affairs and Overseas Residents,
Ministry of Foreign Affairs,
77, Sejongro, Jongro-gu,
SEOUL
KOREA

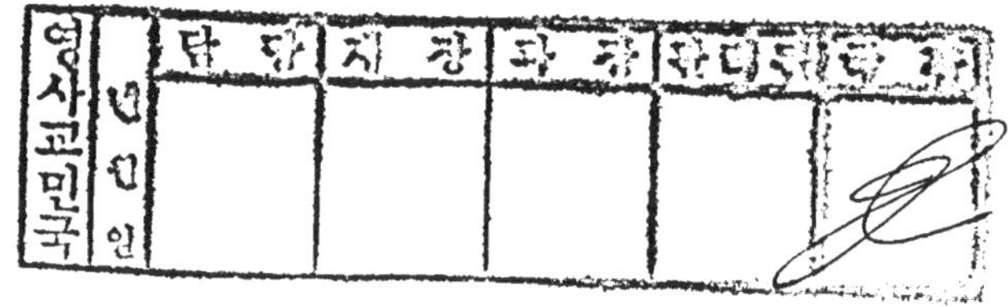


HEADQUARTERS: GENEVA, SWITZERLAND.

0109

INTERNATIONAL ORGANIZATION FOR MIGRATION (IOM)
ORGANISATION INTERNATIONALE POUR LES MIGRATIONS (OIM)
ORGANIZACIÓN INTERNACIONAL PARA LAS MIGRACIONES (OIM)

Telephone: 717 91 11
Cable Address: Promigrant Geneva
Telex: 415 722
Telefax: 798 61 50

17, route des Morillons
P.O. Box 71
CH-1211 GENEVA 19
SWITZERLAND

2/8

**PLAN OF ACTON - UPDATE OF OPERATIONS**

By close of business on 10 October 1990, 106,341 foreign residents of Iraq and Kuwait had left Jordan, Turkey, Iran and Saudi Arabia for their countries of origin through the IOM-co-ordinated international airlift. This region-wide total includes 42,501 Bangladeshis, 29,258 Sri Lankans, 19,778 Indians, 10,776 Filipinos, 3,700 Pakistanis, 297 Egyptians and 31 persons of various other nationalities who have received such assistance since 3 September. Detailed breakdowns by country of departure and country of nationality may be found in Annex II. It should again be noted that all statistics mentioned concern only those returns through the IOM-assisted international airlift. They do not take into account persons whose repatriation was arranged directly by their countries of origin, or under bilateral arrangements; for certain nationalities, such repatriations far exceed those handled under multilateral auspices.

In Jordan, IOM increased daily outbound movements during the past week in response to worrying growth in the transit population in the first days of October. By 10 October, confirmed IOM-assisted departures from Jordan had reached a total of 98,974 - of whom 29,738 were passengers on 99 charter flights between 4 and 10 October. The 100,000th person to leave Jordan under this five-week old emergency programme is departing today, 11 October, for the Philippines.

By allocating additional staff, chartering more aircraft capacity and utilizing all available departure facilities, IOM has increased outflow to such an extent that transit camp populations have fallen dramatically. From over 43,000 on 4 October when the last IOM update was issued, camp populations are expected to drop to a level of only some 1,000 persons by Friday, 12 October.

Firm bookings from Amman are more than adequate to cover expected needs over the next few days; they are reviewed regularly, however, and can be adapted to changing requirements almost immediately in case of need.

0110

In Turkey, comparatively few new arrivals require international assistance for repatriation by air. Consequently, no charter flights are booked at present. On the other hand, IOM continues to address the needs of individuals and small groups. To date, 6,582 persons have left Turkey through the IOM-co-ordinated international airlift which included flights arranged by IOM alone or jointly with the EC.

From Iran, a total of 371 persons - the vast majority Bangladeshis (263) - have now returned to their home countries with IOM assistance. These include one Aeroflot charter flight which left Teheran for Dhaka with 175 passengers on board on 6 October. An IOM staff member in Teheran continues to work closely with the Iranian authorities as well as the countries of origin and the United Nations to ensure that air repatriation requirements are met in a timely fashion.

Annex I contains an updated status of contributions. The efforts of donors to date to arrange speedy transfer of their pledges are appreciated. In order to avoid cashflow difficulties, it would be appreciated if payment of outstanding pledges could be made as soon as possible, since IOM's air and bus transportation commitments currently exceed actual cash in hand.

Annex III provides a detailed breakdown of invoices settled during the week of 4-10 October, followed by totals to date by segregated by airline and route. Corresponding detail concerning invoices settled during the period 3 September - 3 October 1990 were contained in the Plan of Action Update issued by IOM on 4 October. If required, additional copies of the latter may be obtained from IOM Headquarters upon request.

11 October 1990

0111

Annex I
Page 2

4/8

# GULF EMERGENCY PROGRAMME
## UTILIZED IN-KIND DONATIONS (FLIGHTS)
### as at 7 October 1990

(departures from Amman, Jordan)

| SOURCE | NO. OF FLIGHTS | TOTAL FLIGHTS | DESTINATION | NO. OF PAX | TOTAL PAX | TOTAL COST ESTIMATE USD |
|---|---|---|---|---|---|---|
| NEW ZEALAND GOVERNMENT | 6 | | Dhaka | 717 | | |
| | 3 | | Manila | 257 | | |
| | 3 | | Karachi | 323 | | |
| | 1 | | Colombo | 121 | | |
| | 1 | | Bombay | 129 | | |
| | | 14 | | | 1,547 | |
| NORWAY GOVERNMENT | 3 | | Cairo | 297 | | |
| | | 3 | | | 297 | |
| SPANISH RED CROSS | 8 | | Karachi | 2,089 | | |
| | 2 | | Bombay | 478 | | |
| | | 10 | | | 2,567 | |
| SWEDISH RED CROSS | 6 | | Bombay | 2,812 | | |
| | 6 | | Dhaka | 2,752 | | |
| | | 12 | | | 5,564 | |
| SWITZERLAND GOVERNMENT | 4 | | Dhaka | 784 | | |
| | 10 | | Bombay | 1,991 | | |
| | 4 | | Colombo | 704 | | |
| | | 18 | | | 3,479 | |
| UNITED KINGDOM GOVERNMENT | 4 | | Bombay | 1,561 | | |
| | 3 | | Dhaka | 1,170 | | |
| | | 7 | | | 2,731 | |
| UNITED STATES GOVERNMENT | 1 | | Colombo | 120 | | |
| | 1 | | Dhaka | 122 | | |
| | 1 | | Manila | 119 | | |
| | | 3 | | | 361 | |
| LUTHERAN WORLD FEDERATION | 8 | | Dhaka | 2,014 | | |
| | | 8 | | | 2,014 | |
| TOTALS = | | 75 | | | 18,560 | 10,950,400.00 |

0112

Annex I
Page 1

5/8

# GULF EMERGENCY PROGRAMME
## PLEDGES AND RECEIPT FOR TRANSPORTATION
as at 10 October 1990

| 1. CASH CONTRIBUTIONS | PLEDGED | RECEIVED USD |
|---|---|---|
| AUSTRALIA | 3) AUD 1,000,000.00 | 831,982.89 |
| AUSTRIA | 1) ATS 3,000,000.00 | |
| CANADA | CAD 5,000,000.00 | 1,769,911.50 |
| DENMARK | 3) DKK 1,500,000.00 | 249,196.00 |
| FINLAND | 3) FIM 8,000,000.00 | 2,162,735.00 |
| GERMANY | DEM 5,000,000.00 | |
| ITALY | 1) USD 500,000.00 | 485,000.00 |
| JAPAN | 1) USD 12,000,000.00 * | 8,640,000.00 |
| KOREA | USD 500,000.00 | |
| NETHERLANDS | NLG 2,000,000.00 | |
| NORWAY | 3) NOK 15,500,000.00 | 2,556,110.00 |
| SWEDEN | 1) SEK 30,000,000.00 | |
| SWITZERLAND | 3) CHF 250,000.00 | 192,307.69 |
| UNITED KINGDOM | 3) GBP 2,000,000.00 | 3,720,800.00 |
| U.S.A. | 3) USD 10,250,000.00 | 10,050,000.00 |
| EUROPEAN COMMUNITY | 2) USD 3,327,850.00 | |
| **2. PRIVATE DONATIONS** | | |
| US-AIM | USD 3,460.00 | 3,460.00 |
| AUSTCARE | AUD 75,000.00 | 62,500.00 |
| **TOTAL** | USD 50,534,960.00 | 30,724,002.88 |

1) through UNDRO
2) 50% of joint operations IOM/EEC of 20 flights (10 to Manila, 10 to Colombo)
3) Paid in full
* Paid in full USD 8,640,000.00 received in cash
USD 3,000,000.00 paid directly by UNDRO for transportation
USD 360,000.00 3% retained by UNDRO

0113

Annex II

6/8

# IOM - PLAN OF ACTION/UPDATE

## JORDAN

| Nationals of : | Movements DEPARTED 3/9-10/10/1990 | BOOKED TO DEPART 11-17/10/1990 |
|---|---|---|
| Bangladesh | 36,297 | 501 |
| India | 19,762 | 1,166 |
| Pakistan | 3,061 | 275 |
| Philippines | 10,768 | 1,463 |
| Sri Lanka | 28,758 | 5,496 |
| Egypt | 297 | 0 |
| Other | 31 | 2 |
| | 98,974 | 8,903 |

## TURKEY

| Nationals of : | Movements DEPARTED 3/9-10/10/1990 | BOOKED TO DEPART 11-21/10/1990 |
|---|---|---|
| Bangladesh | 5,941 | 30 |
| Pakistan | 589 | 0 |
| Sri Lanka | 52 | 60 |
| Sudan | 0 | 3 |
| | 6,582 | 93 |

## IRAN

| Nationals of : | Movements DEPARTED 3/9-10/10/1990 | BOOKED TO DEPART 11-21/10/1990 |
|---|---|---|
| Bangladesh | 263 | 2 |
| India | 16 | 4 |
| Pakistan | 50 | 0 |
| Philippines | 8 | 0 |
| Sri Lanka | 34 | 17 |
| | 371 | 23 |

6894C
11/10/90

0114

Annex III
Page 1

## GULF EMERGENCY PROGRAMME
## PAYMENTS

as at 10 October 1990

| AIRLINE COMPANY | ROUTING | CHARTER FLIGHTS | DATE OF DEPARTURE | NO.OF PAX | PAID USD | TOTAL PAYMENTS |
|---|---|---|---|---|---|---|
| ROYAL JORDANIAN | AMMAN-DHAKA | | | | | |
| | PAID THRU 3.10.90 | 19 | | 4,840 | 3,135,500.00 | |
| | | MIRJ23 230 | 02.10.90 | 278 | 159,500.00 | |
| | | MIRJ23 338 | 06.10.90 | 231 | 134,000.00 | |
| | AMMAN-COLOMBO | | | | | |
| | PAID THRU 3.10.90 | 28 | | 5,498 | 3,598,560.00 | |
| | | MIRJ23 300 | 02.10.90 | 183 | 92,800.00 | |
| | | MIRJ23 301 | 02.10.90 | 198 | 92,800.00 | |
| | | MIRJ23 322 | 06.10.90 | 183 | 92,820.00 | |
| | | MIRJ23 323 | 06.10.90 | 184 | 92,820.00 | |
| | | MIRJ23 324 | 06.10.90 | 182 | 92,820.00 | |
| | AMMAN-MANILA | | | | | |
| | PAID THRU 3.10.90 | 1 | | 231 | 184,800.00 | |
| | | MIRJ23 312 | 04.10.90 | 239 | 184,800.00 | |
| | | | | 12,247 | | 7,861,260.00 |
| TOWER AIR | AMMAN-MANILA | | | | | |
| | PAID THRU 3.10.90 | 13 | | 6,236 | 4,940,000.00 | |
| | | MIFF23 087 | 02.10.90 | 472 | 380,000.00 | |
| | | MIFF23 088 | 04.10.90 | 486 | 380,000.00 | |
| | | | | 7,194 | | 5,700,000.00 |
| TURKISH AIRLINES | DIYARBAKIR-DHAKA | 13 | | 3,263 | 2,146,250.00 | |
| | DIYARBAKIR-KARACHI | 2 | | 422 | 160,000.00 | |
| | PAID THRU 3.10.90 | | | 3,685 | | 2,306,250.00 |
| TATE AERO-SERVICES | AMMAN-DHAKA | 9 | | 1,628 | 1,137,402.00 | |
| | AMMAN-COLOMBO | 5 | | 1,008 | 600,768.00 | |
| | PAID THRU 3.10.90 | | | | | |
| | | MILZ23 340 | 06.10.90 | 151 | 77,010.00 | |
| | | MILZ23 341 | 07.10.90 | 152 | 77,010.00 | |
| | | | | 2,939 | | 1,892,190.00 |
| SAUDI ARABIAN AIRLINES | RIYADH-COLOMBO | | | | | |
| | PAID THRU 3.10.90 | 1 | | 414 | 106,666.00 | |
| | | MISV23 752 | 11.10.90 | 265 | 90,667.00 | |
| | | | | 679 | | 197,333.00 |
| EVERGREEN AIRLINES | AMMAN-COLOMBO | | | | | |
| | PAID THRU 3.10.90 | 4 | | 2,003 | 1,262,520.00 | |
| | | MIEZ23 111 | 05.10.90 | 500 | 309,330.00 | |
| | | MIEZ23 112 | 06.10.90 | 501 | 315,630.00 | |
| | | | | 3,004 | | 1,887,480.00 |
| OMEGA AIRLINES | AMMAN-COLOMBO PAID THRU 3.10.90 | 1 | | 180 | 108,000.00 | 108,000.00 |

0115

8/8.

| AIRLINE COMPANY | ROUTING | CHARTER FLIGHTS | DATE OF DEPARTURE | NO.OF PAX | PAID USD | TOTAL PAYMENTS |
|---|---|---|---|---|---|---|
| PAKISTAN AIRLINES | TEHERAN-DHAKA -COLOMBO -KARACHI PAID THRU 3.10.90 | 1 | | 124 | 86,230.00 | 86,230.00 |
| JAPAN AIRLINES | AMMAN-MANILA PAID THRU 3.10.90 | 1 | | 272 | 240,000.00 | |
| | | MIJL23 095 | 05.10.90 | 239 | 191,200.00 | |
| | | | | 511 | | 431,200.00 |
| NATIONAIR | AMMAN-BOMBAY PAID THRU 3.10.90 | 3 | | 1,037 | 480,200.00 | |
| | | MINX23 264 | 03.10.90 | 259 | 126,000.00 | |
| | | MINX23 265 | 04.10.90 | 265 | 126,000.00 | |
| | | MINX23 266 | 05.10.90 | 259 | 126,000.00 | |
| | | MINX23 267 | 06.10.90 | 258 | 126,000.00 | |
| | | MINX23 268 | 07.10.90 | 253 | 126,000.00 | |
| | | MINX23 274 | 02.10.90 | 487 | 228,200.00 | |
| | | MINX23 276 | 04.10.90 | 490 | 228,200.00 | |
| | AMMAN-COLOMBO | MINX23 277 | 06.10.90 | 477 | 266,700.00 | |
| | | MINX23 279 | 07.10.90 | 475 | 266,700.00 | |
| | | | | 4,260 | | 2,100,000.00 |
| ALL NIPPON AIRWAYS | AMMAN-MANILA PAID THRU 3.10.90 | 1 | | 297 | 237,600.00 | 237,600.00 |
| EGYPTAIR | AMMAN-MANILA | MIMS23 353 | 05.10.90 | 202 | 163,200.00 | |
| | | MIMS23 354 | 06.10.90 | 208 | 163,200.00 | |
| | | MIMS23 355 | 07.10.90 | 204 | 163,200.00 | |
| | | | | 614 | | 489,600.00 |
| GULF AIR | AMMAN-KARACHI | MIGF23 094 | 25.09.90 | 243 | 72,900.00 | 72,900.00 |
| TURKER TOURISM TRAVEL AG. | ANKARA-COLOMBO | MITK23 538 | 03.10.90 | 41 | 31,488.00 | 31,488.00 |
| TYCHE TRAVEL & TOURS | AMMAN-COLOMBO | MISU23 326 | 04.10.90 | 155 | 75,330.00 | |
| | | MISU23 327 | 05.10.90 | 174 | 84,564.00 | |
| | | MISU23 328 | 06.10.90 | 174 | 84,564.00 | |
| | | | | 503 | | 244,458.00 |
| ORIENT SHIPPING | AQABA-COLOMBO PAID THRU 3.10.90 | 1 | | 1,768 | 707,200.00 | 707,200.00 |
| Bus transport Amman, Jordan | | | | | | 1,132,837.50 |
| GRAND TOTAL | | | | 38,289 | | 25,486,026.50 |

0116

International Organization for Migration

17, route des Morillons P.O. Box 71 CH-1211 Geneva 19 (Switzerland) ☎ (022) 717 9111 Tx. 415 722 Fax 798 6150

# MONTHLY DISPATCH

12 October 1990
No. 140

IN THIS ISSUE :

*26 September: The "Safina I Arab" arrives in Colombo harbour.*



## IOM'S GULF EMERGENCY PROGRAMME

### FIRST SHIP CHARTERED BY IOM ARRIVES IN COLOMBO

On 16 September 1990, 1,768 Sri Lankan men and women set sail from Aqaba on board the first ship chartered by IOM in the framework of its operation to repatriate foreigners stranded in Jordan. After a voyage of ten days, they reached Colombo on 26 September.

Although some people had asked fellow Sri Lankans departing earlier to let their families know they were alive and in Jordan, nobody knew what to expect upon arrival. None of them had been able to tell their families that they were on their way home. None but one... a passenger handed to IOM's spokeswoman a piece of paper with a message to be telexed to his family. For a few days, IOM's spokeswoman felt uneasy as the telex could not get through to Sri Lanka. What if the message never reached the family? Finally, the telex operator gave the good news: the telex had got through.

However, thanks to the Sri Lankan authorities and an IOM official who flew to Colombo a few days before the ship was due to arrive, many families got the message as newspapers, radio and TV networks spread the news.

On their arrival, the passengers were welcomed by the wife of the President of Sri Lanka, the Minister of Labour and government officials, in the presence of the national media who reported on the event.

*A convoy in the desert*

... Their trip started in Amman, on 15 September 1990. Buses were due to appear at 4 a.m. in three different places in and around Amman to pick them up for a four-hour trip to Aqaba, where the "Safina I Arab", a Pakistani passenger ship, had just arrived. But at four, no buses were to be seen, and the people who had spent the night in the streets surrounding the Sri Lankan Consulate started to become anxious, fearing that their repatriation was delayed. The IOM staff on the spot - used to such delays - started their usual search for a person in charge at this time of day (or rather, night). It took four hours altogether to have the correct number of buses at the various camps, another three hours to board all 1,768 passengers. By 11 a.m., a long convoy of 41 buses started its trip south to the port of Aqaba.

Along the way across the desert, a few service stations provided some rest and shelter. Approximately one and a half hours after they departed, they stopped at one of these stations and, to the amazement of the personnel and the few customers present, some 1,800 people alighted from the buses and literally invaded the premises. Jordanian one-dinar notes were flying all over the place in exchange for bread, fruit, biscuits, water, cigarettes and plates of food.

*The last leg of their journey home*

Once the whole convoy had arrived in Aqaba, a long line of 41 buses could be seen waiting close to the pier. IOM staff monitored the boarding: two buses at a time were admitted on the pier as there were two access ramps for the passengers. The men got off the buses first to pick up their belongings and carry them to the ship, and the women followed with lighter bags.

At 11 p.m., everybody was on board. A dinner, composed of curry, rice and bread was ready for the passengers. The Safina I Arab actually set sail at 3 a.m. on 16th September, after the final administrative procedures had been completed.

0118

## THE "ANTONOV" EXPERIENCE

The last evacuation flight on the chartered Aeroflot Antonov - the biggest cargo plane in the world - took place on 19 September with 439 passengers on board. Altogether, 3,600 Bangladeshis were repatriated on the Antonov, in 8 flights from Amman to Dacca. The Antonov was one of the very first planes proposed for the international airlift at a time of great emergency in the repatriation process.

*Entering the Antonov's "mouth"*

A trip on the Antonov was quite an experience for both the passengers and the IOM escort team. As the capacity of the plane was close to 500, some time was needed first to call out the names of the passengers and then get these 500 individuals "seated" in an orderly way in a plane that does not have seats! At loading time, the Antonov looks like a monstrous whale with its jaws wide open. From inside the plane, the Antonov is like a huge tunnel with mattresses spread on its floor and layers of ropes fixed at each end for people to hold on to at take-off and landing. The sides of the plane were reserved for luggage, parcels, handbags and... eucalyptus plants that the people had somehow managed to carry with them. Between the luggage "compartment" and the mattresses, a narrow passage way was meant to let people circulate. However, most of the time, it was blocked with parcels.

On an average, it took some two hours for all the passengers to board the plane. They stood patiently in line and proceeded calmly towards the mouth of the plane, letting the crew direct their pace. The Soviet crew was particularly kind and helpful, not only directing the people to their "seats" but also helping carry the personal belongings on board. Remarkably, despite the uncomfortable conditions of their flight, it is only when they were on board the plane that the people started to smile: only then were they sure that home was within reach. It was quite a sight to see nearly 500 people sitting in irregular rows, with the knowledge that the journey would last for eight hours. And the IOM staff member who waved "goodbye" was rewarded with the sight of some 500 hands waving back.

*Soviet crew directing passengers to their seats.*

0119

DEPUTY DIRECTOR GENERAL DISCUSSES RETURNING MIGRANT SITUATION IN CAIRO

IOM's Deputy Director General, Ambassador Héctor Charry-Samper, on mission in Egypt from 10 to 21 September, met with members of the Government including the State Minister of Foreign Affairs, the Minister of Immigration and the Minister of Labour. Meetings were further held with UN agencies and representatives of the EC, ICRC and the League of the Red Cross and Red Crescent Societies. Discussions focussed on the present state of the repatriation process and the need for the international community's support. Besides the emergency situation, other aspects related to the repatriation were dealt with, including reinsertion problems in the country, possibilities of resettlement in third countries of some skilled professionals, promoting the creation of jobs through small and medium enterprises, supporting Egyptian technical cooperation for Africa, and language and vocational training courses.

UPDATE OF IOM'S OPERATIONS IN THE GULF

- From 3 September to 3 October, a total of 73,520 foreign residents of Iraq and Kuwait left Jordan, Turkey, Iran and Saudi Arabia for their home countries with repatriation assistance from IOM. They include mainly 37,624 Bangladeshis, 12,510 Sri Lankans, 11,690 Indians, 8,116 Filipinos and 3,210 Pakistanis. Firm bookings have been made for a further 37,126 evacuees to depart between 4 and 15 October 1990.

  Working closely with the authorities of Jordan and the most affected countries of origin as well as UNDRO, the Office of the Secretary General's Personal Representative and the EC, IOM has responded to the best available needs assessment and has doubled daily offtake from Jordan since the beginning of October, to reach 5 to 6,000 departures per day.

- In view of the urgent cash requirements for inland transportation in Jordan from the camp sites to the airport, IOM has provided US$ 700,000 to the Jordanian High Committee for Assistance to Transit Evacuees and plans to continue its support.

- The logistical complexity and uncertainty of this repatriation scheme have obvious ramifications for IOM's ability to project financial requirements accurately. At present, IOM is drawing up a revised needs assessment and financial plan to be incorporated in an overall appeal to be issued shortly by the Office of the Personal Representative. As of 4 October, however, IOM estimates that announced contributions, which now total over US$ 60 million in cash and kind, should cover needs at present drawdown rates into the week of 8 October.

- A special representative of the Director General arrived in Turkey on 9 September to assess the situation and discuss IOM's assistance in the repatriation process. He met with the President of Turkey who gave his full support to the repatriation programme. Since 11 September, a team of five IOM staff members are handling the evacuation process in close cooperation with the Turkish authorities, the embassies of the countries concerned and the national Red Crescent Society. So far, 6,582 repatriations have taken place, for the most part to Bangladesh.

- On 8 October 1990, a special contribution was pledged to IOM by Her Royal Highness, Princess Irene of Greece on behalf of the non-governmental organization, World in Harmony. The contribution is to cover the cost of one flight at an estimated amount of US$ 159,500.

# IOM IN THE PRESS

Evening Standard

MONDAY, 10 SEPTEMBER 1990 — 7

# Hold the rope and head for freedom

Refugees in Jordan: another half a million are still on the way from Iraq

from JOHN PASSMORE
Jordan, Monday

WHEN the Antonov joined the airlift, Regina Boucault started worrying about the image. Madame Boucault is one of those Frenchwomen who manages to maintain a certain chic even after 36 hours without sleep, and as head of public information for the International Organisation for Migration she is anxious that the repatriation of 100,000 Asians who fled to Jordan should be no less dignified.

The Antonov, however, is not an aeroplane designed to create an impression. It can transport 106 tons of rice from the World Food Programme stocks in Bangladesh and it can fly back with 450 Bangladeshis. The only trouble is that it treats both cargoes much the same.

The passengers troop into the cargo hold—about the size of gymnasium—and find no seats but a floor covered with mattresses. The cheerful Russian loadmasters with their orange overalls unzipped to reveal American T-shirts, stretch ropes down the length of the space.

The idea is that the passengers sit on the mattresses and hold onto the ropes. It means that when the lumbering, propeller-driven giant finally gets off the runway and begins to climb, the entire passenger complement does not end up in a heap in the tail.

"I was worried about the impression our organisation would give from this," said Madame Boucault. "People would say we sent Third World migrants back in Third World conditions.

"BUT then, when I looked into the plane and saw them all sitting in rows on the mattresses, I saw something I had not seen in all the time I have been here. I saw smiles on their faces."

This is the last stage of the long road home. After escaping from Iraq and Kuwait, it takes maybe two weeks to progress down the 200 miles ... the border to the Queen ... Airport.

... make the journey ... refugees from every war ... ory, with rumour and ... it sweeping through ranks like the dust ...

... man would want it. It is flat and dirty brown and scattered with sharp grey stones. Every day the sun hits it like a blow from a steam hammer.

This was where last week 50,000 people fought for water, where bread was distributed by being thrown into the crowd in a manner reminiscent of the farmyard and where soldiers beat the people back into line with their belts.

Things are better now. The numbers are down to only 25,000 in Shaalam Camp No 1 and they are almost all single men. They form queues half-a-mile long, shuffling forward in the dust to collect three pieces of unleavened bread and three tomatoes each day.

Brigadier Fawaz Sharif of the desert police stood and watched them, tapping his polished walking stick against the side of his polished shoe.

"It is easy for people to criticise but how am I to deal with a crowd like this. I have 15 men taken to hospital after being hit by stones. How would Great Britain have dealt with a crowd like this in India?"

The answer he wanted was: with the Lee Enfield .303 rifle.

"Exactly," said the briga- ...

... need of medical supplies any more. He could use some more antibiotics and more anti-scorpion serum but he said: "We can manage."

The secret was to move the people on down the line to new and expanded camps closer to the airport. But even that is fraught with difficulty.

When Naser Abed drove his bus into the camp and announced that he was taking passengers to Amman, it caused uproar.

Vishnu Mohan, who had lived for 12 years in Kuwait operating a complicated pipeline television camera and had been in Shaalam for two days, insisted: "He is asking 50 Kuwaiti dinars. How do we know he won't drive us two kilometres down the road and leave us. We paid our last driver 2500 Iraqi dinars to take us to Amman and we ended up here."

WITH exchange rates in as much of a mess as the rest of his life, it was not easy to work out what everybody's dinars are worth any more. But he made it sound a lot.

All the same Naser's bus filled up. Most of the passen- ...

... people picking their way between those trying to sleep.

Outside, the building is ringed with makeshift tents and everywhere there are piles of luggage tied with string.

There is, however, a better atmosphere. Prabudas Donapatti was as happy as a man could be in his position. He had been a cook for a wealthy Kuwaiti family and after three weeks he was cooking again—he had some water and a can of corned beef in a pot and his wife Laxmi was pushing hopelessly inadequate twigs into the flames underneath.

On the other side of the building 300 Bangladeshis sat on the ground, their knees under their chins, listening to a man with a megaphone reading out names.

If their name came up it meant the priority accorded the date on their exit stamp had finally been turned into a seat on a plane.

The man with the megaphone, Mohammad Gulamustapha, had himself reached the top of the list nearly a week ago but found his vocation as a volunteer with the International Organisation for Migration. He could even persuade the crowd to leave paths for people to walk through. "The Jordanians don't know how to deal with our people," he said.

The best news was that the bus ride to the airport was free. The embassies charter the buses and the people ...

---

STAMPA SERA

Cos'è e come funziona l'Oim di Ginevra

# Un radar umanitario per milioni di esuli

Profughi vietnamiti in viaggio verso la Malaysia: fra i compiti fondamentali dell'Oim c'è anche quello dell'assistenza

GINEVRA

A-POLITICA e umanitaria, sorta nel 1951 con compiti principalmente operativi e a quel tempo strutturata in Comitato, l'Organizzazione Internazionale per le Migrazioni (Oim) è punto di riferimento, nel mondo, per milioni di ... costrette a lasciare il ... Paese o a causa dell'in... (rifugiati) o perché al... di una vita un minimo ... di quella loro ... in patria (nazionali). ... è in Route des Morillons, un palazzo chiaro con i ... rossi, affondato nel ... erchi, aiuole, giardini. ... eriscono 52 Stati: 35 ... membri e 17 con lo ... osservatori. Fra i ..., Svizzera, Germania, ... tti i Paesi del Nord, Centro e Sud America, ... Thailandia, Fi..., Kenya. Fra i se... de, Belize, Egitto, ... rancia, Turchia ... sentanza dell'Or... sistono in una ...

... pure l'agricoltura, compresa la proposta di viaggi in alcune nazioni sudamericane per agricoltori che colà intendano acquistare terreni e trasferirsi stabilmente. Controlli medici, messa a punto di un'adeguata rete di trasporti e insegnamento delle lingue sono poi la base dei servizi.

In Afghanistan, per esempio, uno dei problemi è procurare degenza e terapie specialistiche in ospedali stranieri a quei feriti afghani che, in Pakistan, si trovino nell'impossibilità di essere adeguatamente curati. Nei campi profughi dell'Asia meridionale, l'urgenza si chiama anche educazione sanitaria: nozioni di base vengono regolarmente impartite, e corsi di addestramento sono previsti per un certo numero di ospiti, i quali dovranno poi vigilare sull'igiene e la salute dei campi.

Uffici sanitari dell'Oim esistono in pianta stabile in numerose località come la Thailandia, Hong-Kong, la Malaysia, Singapore, le Filippine e il Vietnam. E dovunque, nel mondo, il personale dell'Organizzazione può svolgere i tanti accertamenti igienico-sanitari che i diversi Stati richiedono prima di accogliere i migranti.

Per quanto riguarda l'opera di agevolazione dei viaggi, dalla fine dell'88 è entrata per esempio in funzione la linea aerea che collega direttamente la città di Ho-Chi Minh a Manila. Nell'... oltre 20.000 vietnamiti ... ti trasferiti in Aust... Stati Uniti e ... dotte ...

... immediatamente di mezzi di trasporto sono previste anche per le merci. In caso di terremoti o inondazioni o di altre catastrofi naturali, l'Oim agisce di stretto concerto con l'United Nations Disaster Relief Office (Undro) reperendo gli aerei per il trasporto urgente di materiale di soccorso nelle zone sinistrate.

Altro problema, per gli emigranti - rifugiati o nazionali che siano -, le lingue. Di concerto con i governi della nazione ospite, e non di rado con le sovvenzioni della Comunità Internazionale (per esempio il Consiglio d'Europa), l'Oim organizza corsi di francese, inglese, tedesco, spagnolo. Il Portogallo è il Paese a maggior percentuale di emigranti nazionali. Alto il numero degli stagionali, anche italiani. Per loro, l'anno scorso, a Roma, sono stati approntati 14 corsi di lingue; tra l'altro, per gli italiani che facciano domanda di lavorare in Germania, l'averne seguito almeno uno è titolo preferenziale. Imponente anche il settore documentazione e ricerca: in questi uffici di Ginevra è nato il progetto per il Museo mondiale delle Migrazioni, a Buenos Aires, e qui continuano ad apparire - in apposite pubblicazioni e riviste - i più moderni e approfonditi studi ... le sue con... nomi...

---

Dagbladet
OSLO

# MAT INN - FOLK UT

## Luftbro til Jordan

AMMAN (Dagbladet): Iblant finnes det små lyspunkter i elendighetens mørke. Historien om samarbeidet mellom ulike FN-organer som resulterte i at deres virksomhet ble samordnet til flyktningens beste, er et ... punkt.

CORDELIA EDVARDSON
I JORDAN

Da svensken Lars Björkmann, som arbeider ved FNs matvare-program i Roma, ble sendt til Amman for å organisere ristranspor-ten til flyktningene, fikk han en glimrende ide:

Rislageret befinner seg i Dakka i Bangladesh. Risen transporteres i verdens største fraktfly, en russisk Antonov 124. Hvorfor skulle dette flyet dra tomt hjem når det fantes tusenvis av flyktninger fra Kuwait som var strandet i Jordan og som ventet på transport hjem til Bangladesh? spurte han seg selv. De kunne risikere å vente svært lenge fordi fattige Bangladesh ba... re skal ha fire sivile fly og ikke har penger til å chartre noen.

### Sammenpakket

Björkmann tok kontakt med IOM (International Organization for Migration), det FN-organ som tar hånd om hjemtransporten av titusen-talls utslåtte flyktninger fra Kuwait, og hvis hjemland ikke selv kan ordne med hjemreise.

IOM syntes tanken ... [illegible] ... i Amman ved ... – flyktninger ... [illegible] ... med ti flygninger ... kan ta 450 perso... pakket på utlagt golvet, kan mellom ... flyktninger komm... gladesh.

Noen enkel ope... imidlertid ikke. Jor... ti og ineffektivitet ... lange forsinkelser og ... ner. Men det ordner ... slutt.

### Tilværelsen kn...

Et annet spørsmål ... hva disse menneske... hjem til. Millioner av ... fikk sin tilværelse knust ... gust i år da Saddam Hus... derte Kuwait. Det hand... bare om de hundretusen... tearbeidere fra verdens ... land som arbeidet i Kuwai... ti ganger så mange famil... lemmer levde av deres lønn... me i Bangladesh, Egypt, In... lippinene osv.

Lønna og sparepengene ... de fleste tilfeller fortsatt står ... i stengte kuwaitiske banker ... desuten er blitt verdiløse, ... også legge grunnlaget for et ... liv i hjemlandet. De betydde ... dannelse til barn eller småsesk... et hus som skulle bygges, en ... lapp som skulle kjøpes. Alt det ... forsvant som en luftspeiling i ... kenen melkom Kuwait og Amman ...

... hver gang. Her deles ...

---

THE JAPAN TIMES

# $12 million pledged for Asian refugees

The government will extend $12 million in additional aid to help Asian refugees fleeing Iraq to Jordan and other neighboring countries, the Foreign Ministry announced Friday.

Following a request from the United Nations' International Organization of Migration, the decision was reached in negotiations between the Foreign and Finance ministries and later approved at a regular Cabinet meeting.

The decision follows an Aug. 30 promise of $1 billion to U.S.-led multinational forces in the Gulf.

Japan has previously offered $10 million to help U.N.-led refugee relief activities in Jordan.

Since Iraq's Aug. 2 invasion of Kuwait, more than 270,000 Philippine, Bangladeshi and other Asian migrant workers in Iraq and Kuwait have taken refuge in neighboring Jordan, Turkey and Saudi Arabia in their efforts to return to their home countries.

Of these, 200,000 are reported to have returned to their homes at the expense of their governments or private funds.

Ministry officials said, however, that an estimated 70,000 Asian refugees are currently being forced to stay in camp... in desert areas in the nati... bordering Iraq and Kuwa...

The IOM has been rec...

... ing countries, via ... the United Nat... Relief Coordin... about $23.46 ... tional donat... refugees.

The gov... cision w... manita... cials e... Me... Wel... ma... J...

... doctors and other experts will leave for Saudi Arabia be... Sept. 19 and 20 to assist ... and others flowing in ...

... ssion of the ... oreign Affairs ... ian Minister ... the gov- ...

---

The Island

# IOM spends US dollars 7.5 m to bring 9,220 stranded Lankans

Mr. Yeyba Maroofi, Special Advisor to the International Organisation for Migration (IOM), on meeting President R. Premadasa at the Presidential Secretariat yesterday informed that the IOM had assisted in the transport of 9,220 persons up to September 21 from Amman to Colombo, 7,400 by air and 1,768 by ship.

In addition the IOM was committed up to September 27 to bring back a further 3,830 persons and was prepared to hel...

... move Sri Lankans out of Kuwait and back to Sri Lanka, using all means of transportation, land, sea and air.

The President stressed the need for material support to the returning migrant workers, specially in view of the loss of earnings which they had suffered and deprivation of support for their dependants. It was observed that the rehabilitation of such returning workers was within the terms of reference of IO...

0121

## ON IOM'S AGENDA

22-25 October 1990 IOM REGIONAL LATIN AMERICAN SEMINAR ON MIGRATION FOR DEVELOPMENT (La Paz, Bolivia).

As announced last month, IOM's Regional Latin American Seminar on "Migration for Development" will take place from 22 to 25 October 1990 in La Paz, Bolivia. Government representatives from 18 Latin American and Caribbean countries will participate, together with senior officials from IOM's Headquarters in Geneva and its representatives in each member country of the region. The event will be inaugurated by H.E. the President of Bolivia, Dr. Jaime Paz Zamora and by the Deputy Director General of IOM, Ambassador Héctor Charry-Samper. The inauguration ceremony will also be attended by representatives of embassies and international organizations accredited in Bolivia.

This seminar is to take place at a time of great changes and transformations in the world which have a bearing on the development of Latin America and the Caribbean. Present tendencies and projections on the migration process in this decade indicate that migration will play an increasingly active role in the development of countries.

As a forum for coordination and consultation between the Organization and its member governments, the Seminar will analyze migratory problems and their affects on the development process in the region. In this context, discussions will focus on the articulation which should exist between migration policy and development strategies at the national, sub-regional and regional levels.

Within the concept of Migration for Development, which considers international migration an important process of social and economic change, the Seminar will analyze such themes as the transfer of qualified human resources and their strategic role in the technological transformation of Latin American societies, the strengthening of national structures which administer migration aimed at development through technical cooperation provided by IOM, the role of migration in the processes of sub-regional and regional integration and the potential of the programme of migrants with capital to invest, in the context of the region's external debts.

The conclusions and recommendations of this Seminar will allow IOM to devise Migration for Development programmes which match the priority needs of the governments for the 1990s.

0122

| MIGRATION ACTIVITIES | Sept. 1989 | **Sept. 1990** | Cumulative Jan.-Sept. 1990 |
|---|---|---|---|
| REFUGEES departing from... | 28,964 | **18,112** | 165,622 |
| Europe | 11,826 | **1,947** | 57,183 |
| Middle East and Africa | 957 | **555** | 4,477 |
| South East Asia | 14,153 | **14,236*** | 92,950 |
| Near East | 567 | **426** | 2,611 |
| Latin America | 1,419 | **933** | 8,289 |
| Other | 42 | **15** | 112 |
| NATIONAL MIGRATION | 753 | **944** | 7,938 |
| Migrant workers | 250 | **392** | 4,469 |
| Migration for development | 503 | **552** | 3,469 |
| TOTAL | 29,717 | **19,056** | 173,560 |

Provisional figures

* Excluding 1,815 persons moved to the Refugee Processing Centre in Bataan, Philippines.

N.B. Repatriation movements under the Gulf Emergency Programme are not included in the above figures. They are given on page 4.

0123

사본 : 주네리 이주관

신

# 주 제 네 바 대 표 부

제네(정) 20320-1102　　　　　　　　　　　　　　1990.10.19

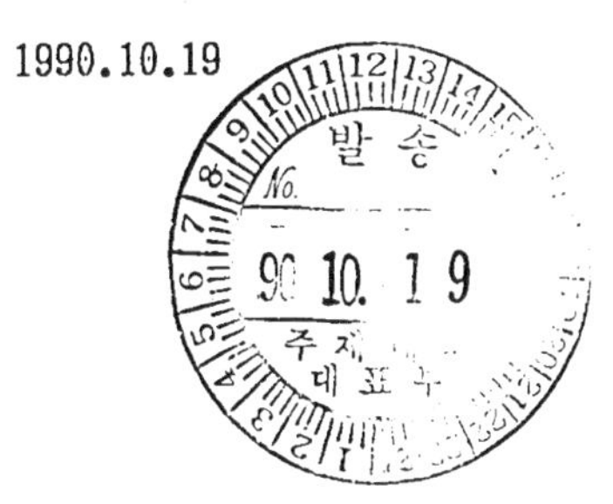

수신 : 장관

참조 : 국제기구조약국장 , 영사교민국장.

제목 : 페만사태 관련 IOM공한 송부

1. IOM 사무총장은 별첨 공한을 통해 페만사태 관련 IOM은 그동안 이라크.쿠웨이트 지역에서 약 122,000의 외국인 월수를 지원하였으나 아직 이라크.쿠웨이트 지역에 잔류하고 있는 약 4만명 외국인의 철수를 위해 IOM은 13,5백만불의 추가 재원이 필요하다고 하면서 추가 기여금 제공을 요청하여 왔는바, 이를 별첨 송부합니다.

2. 아울러 10.10 현재 IOM의 각국 기여금 서약 현황 및 외국인 철수지원 사업 현황 자료를 별첨 송부합니다.

첨부 : IOM 사무총장 공한 및 자료. 끝.

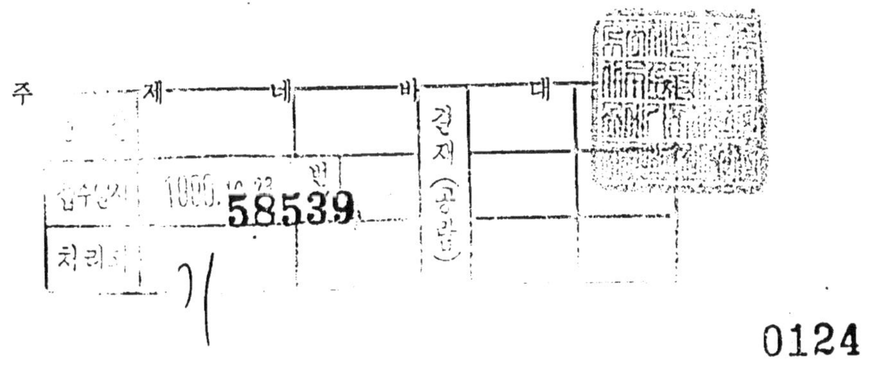

0124

INTERNATIONAL ORGANIZATION FOR MIGRATION

B. Al. Shin

THE DIRECTOR GENERAL

GENEVA, SWITZERLAND

18 October 1990

Sir,

Thanks to the quick and generous response of governments like your own, the International Organization for Migration (IOM) has, in the space of seven weeks, been able to co-ordinate the repatriation of over 122,000 foreign residents of Iraq and Kuwait in need of international assistance to return to their home countries. This massive airlift complements what countries - often among the world's poorest - have done directly to facilitate the return of their citizens. As a result, populations in transit camps have been rapidly reduced. The initial challenge has been met and human suffering, already too great, prevented from becoming overwhelming. In helping to meet that challenge, IOM has exhausted all the resources put at its disposal by the international community.

Yet the flow into transit countries continues - albeit currently in smaller numbers than before - and undoubtedly will continue for some time. If IOM is to continue to assist the innocent victims of this crisis, additional funding is urgently needed.

IOM's best assessment is that between 25,000 and 40,000 foreigners still in Iraq and Kuwait are likely to need international repatriation assistance in the short term. This figure, necessarily imprecise in view of the circumstances, is nevertheless the result of extensive contact with national and international sources; it includes only those who both wish to depart immediately and would be permitted to do so. Many more may have chosen not to leave, may not be permitted to leave, or may be unlocatable or unaware of departure possibilities. Moreover, it is quite distinct from the much larger number who might leave should the situation in Iraq and Kuwait further deteriorate.

./..

His Excellency
Mr. Sang Ock Lee
Ambassador
Permanent Observer of the Republic of Korea
to the United Nations Office and
Permanent Delegate to the other
international organizations in Geneva
20, route de Pré-Bois
1215 Geneva 15

0125

Based on the above estimate of 40,000 persons in need in the short term and taking into consideration their countries of destination, IOM calculates that some US$ 27 million would be required to cover international air transportation and related inland transport. On the assumption that the present understanding whereby the European Communities finance the repatriation of one-half of the caseload and IOM covers the remainder, IOM will need US$ 13.5 million to meet its commitment to the international community. And, above all, to those migrants whose suffering need no longer be described.

Early contributions are vital to the continuation of an international airlift which, thus far, has met the needs quickly and efficiently. It is my sincere hope that your Government will again be in a position to respond rapidly to this pressing humanitarian need.

Accept, Sir, the assurances of my highest consideration.

James N Purcell Jr

James N. Purcell, Jr.

0126

INTE‖‖ONAL ORGANIZATION FOR MIG[illegible]ION (IOM)
ORGANISATION INTERNATIONALE POUR LES MIGRATIONS (OIM)
ORGANIZACIÓN INTERNACIONAL PARA LAS MIGRACIONES (OIM)

B. M. Shin

Telephone: 717 91 11
Cable Address: Promigrant Geneva
Telex: 415 722
Telefax: 798 61 50

17, route des Morillons
P.O. Box 71
CH - 1211 GENEVA 19
SWITZERLAND

INTERNATIONAL ORGANIZATION FOR MIGRATION

TO: THE PERMANENT MISSIONS OF:

ARGENTINA, AUSTRALIA, AUSTRIA, BANGLADESH, BELIZE, BOLIVIA, BRAZIL, BELGIUM, CANADA, CAPE VERDE, CHILE, CHINA, COLOMBIA, COSTA RICA, CYPRUS, DENMARK, DOMINICAN REP., ECUADOR, EGYPT, EL SALVADOR, FRANCE, FINLAND, GERMANY, GHANA, GUINEA-BISSAU, GREECE, GUATEMALA, HOLY SEE, HONDURAS, INDIA, INDONESIA, IRAN, ISRAEL, ITALY, JAPAN, JORDAN, KENYA, KOREA (REP. OF), LUXEMBOURG, MEXICO, NETHERLANDS, NEW ZEALAND, NICARAGUA, NORWAY, PAKISTAN, PANAMA, PARAGUAY, PERU, PHILIPPINES, PORTUGAL, SAN MARINO, SAUDI ARABIA, SINGAPORE, SOMALIA, SPAIN, SRI LANKA, SWEDEN, SWITZERLAND, SYRIAN ARAB REP., THAILAND, TURKEY, UGANDA, U.S.S.R., UNITED KINGDOM, U.S.A., URUGUAY, VENEZUELA, YUGOSLAVIA, ZIMBABWE AND THE COMMISSION OF THE EUROPEAN COMMUNITIES

COPY TO UNDRO GENEVA AND PRINCE SADRUDDIN AGA KHAN, PERSONAL REPRESENTATIVE FOR HUMANITARIAN ASSISTANCE RELATING TO THE CRISIS BETWEEN IRAQ AND KUWAIT

FROM: INTERNATIONAL ORGANIZATION FOR MIGRATION, GENEVA

DATE: 18 OCTOBER 1990

SUBJECT: IOM'S GULF EMERGENCY PROGRAMME : UPDATED PLAN OF ACTION

WITH REFERENCE TO OUR COMMUNICATION OF 11 OCTOBER 1990, PLEASE FIND ENCLOSED A FURTHER UPDATE OF THE IOM PLAN OF ACTION. COPIES ARE AVAILABLE FROM IOM HQS.

PURCELL

0127

INTERNATIONAL ORGANIZATION FOR MIGRATION (IOM)
ORGANISATION INTERNATIONALE POUR LES MIGRATIONS (OIM)
ORGANIZACIÓN INTERNACIONAL PARA LAS MIGRACIONES (OIM)

Telephone: 717 91 11
Cable Address: Promigrant Geneva
Telex: 415 722
Telefax: 798 61 50

17, route des Morillons
P.O. Box 71
CH-1211 GENEVA 19
SWITZERLAND

PLAN OF ACTION - UPDATE OF OPERATIONS

Between 3 September and close of business 17 October, 122,307 foreign residents of Iraq and Kuwait returned to their countries of origin with international assistance co-ordinated by IOM. This region-wide total, reflecting departures from Jordan, Turkey, Iran and Saudi Arabia, includes 43,294 Bangladeshis, 39,167 Sri Lankans, 22,450 Indians, 13,044 Filipinos, 4,021 Pakistanis, 297 Egyptians and 34 persons of various other nationalities. A detailed breakdown, by country of departure and country of nationality, is contained in Annex II.

As regards Jordan, 15,659 persons left from Amman on IOM co-ordinated flights in the past week. While well below the peak of the previous week - a fact that staff strength has been adjusted to reflect - departures are scheduled to keep pace with arrivals. IOM Amman monitors the situation daily and remains able to adapt almost immediately to changing requirements.

By 17 October, total IOM-assisted departures from Jordan had reached 114,633. Confirmed bookings are held for a further 2,690 passengers to leave Amman through 21 October. The ground transport for persons leaving Jordan on IOM-assisted flights (i.e., flights chartered by or donated to IOM, or joint IOM/EC flights) is being covered by IOM as part of the overall repatriation travel.

Departures from Turkey under the IOM-coordinated airlift now total 6,612. From Iran, 383 persons have been repatriated under IOM auspices to date. Finally, a charter flight with 267 Sri Lankans aboard left Riyadh for Colombo on 11 October, bringing to 679 the number of persons repatriated by the Organization from Saudi Arabia to date.

Annex III contains detailed breakdown of invoices settled during the week of 11-17 October, as well as a totals to date segregated by airline and route. A full breakdown of the latter since the beginning of this special programme may be reconstructed by referring to the plan of action updates of 4 October and 11 October. Additional copies of the latter, if required, may be obtained from IOM Headquarters.

Annex I contains an updated list of contributions. Urgent payment of those still listed as pledges is requested in order to allow timely settlement of obligations. This is particularly pressing as IOM's commitments already exceed the total pledges by some US$ 500,000. Moreover, as outlined below, IOM is in urgent need of additional contributions now.

0128

Looking ahead, and recognizing the difficulties of obtaining precise data in present circumstances, IOM estimates that between 25,000 and 40,000 foreign residents of Iraq and Kuwait remain in need of international repatriation in the short term. This is defined as those who are known to desire repatriation and who are able to travel. Using best available information on nationalities and airfares, US$ 27 million will be needed to arrange their repatriation. Assuming that current arrangements continue, whereby IOM covers half of the cost of internationally-financed repatriations and the EC the other half, IOM will need US$ 13.5 million for this purpose. Details of this are contained in the consolidated needs document prepared by the Secretary General's Personal Representative, which will be the subject of discussion at the special meeting convened for Friday, 19 October in Geneva. An advance appeal for these funds was addressed to major donors by IOM today, 18 October.

18 October 1990

Annex I
Page 1

GULF EMERGENCY PROGRAMME
PLEDGES AND RECEIPT FOR TRANSPORTATION
as at 17 October 1990

| *1. CASH CONTRIBUTIONS* | *PLEDGED* | *RECEIVED USD* |
|---|---|---|
| AUSTRALIA | 3) AUD 1,000,000.00 | 831,982.69 |
| AUSTRIA | 1) ATS 3,000,000.00 | |
| CANADA | 3) CAD 5,000,000.00 | 4,401,490.45 |
| DENMARK | 3) DKK 1,500,000.00 | 249,196.00 |
| FINLAND | 3) FIM 8,000,000.00 | 2,162,735.00 |
| GERMANY | 3) DEM 5,000,000.00 | 3,205,128.05 |
| ITALY | 1) USD 500,000.00 | 485,000.00 |
| JAPAN | 1) USD 12,000,000.00 * | 8,640,000.00 |
| KOREA (REPUBLIC OF) | USD 500,000.00 | |
| NETHERLANDS | NLG 2,000,000.00 | |
| NORWAY | 3) NOK 15,500,000.00 | 2,556,110.00 |
| SWEDEN | 1) SEK 30,000,000.00 | |
| SWITZERLAND | 3) CHF 250,000.00 | 192,307.69 |
| UNITED KINGDOM | 3) GBP 2,000,000.00 | 3,720,800.00 |
| U.S.A. | 3) USD 10,250,000.00 | 10,050,000.00 |
| EUROPEAN COMMUNITY | 2) USD 3,327,850.00 | |
| *2. PRIVATE DONATIONS* | | |
| US-AIM | USD 3,460.00 | 3,460.00 |
| AUSTCARE | AUD 75,000.00 | 62,500.00 |
| WORLD IN HARMONY | USD 159,500.00 | 159,500.00 |
| *TOTAL* | USD 50,694,460.00 | 36,720,209.88 |

1) through UNDRO
2) 50% of joint operations IOM/EEC of 20 flights (10 to Manila, 10 to Colombo)
3) Paid in full
* Paid in full USD 8,640,000.00 received in cash
USD 3,000,000.00 paid directly by UNDRO for transportation
USD 360,000.00 3% retained by UNDRO

0130

## GULF EMERGENCY PROGRAMME
## UTILIZED IN-KIND DONATIONS (FLIGHTS)
**as at 15 October 1990**

(departures from Amman, Jordan)

| SOURCE | NO. OF FLIGHTS | TOTAL FLIGHTS | DESTINATION | NO. OF PAX | TOTAL PAX | TOTAL COST ESTIMATE USD |
|---|---|---|---|---|---|---|
| NEW ZEALAND GOVERNMENT | 6 | | Dhaka | 717 | | |
| | 3 | | Manila | 257 | | |
| | 3 | | Karachi | 323 | | |
| | 1 | | Colombo | 121 | | |
| | 1 | | Bombay | 129 | | |
| | | 14 | | | 1,547 | |
| NORWAY GOVERNMENT | 3 | | Cairo | 297 | | |
| | | 3 | | | 297 | |
| SPANISH RED CROSS | 8 | | Karachi | 2,089 | | |
| | 2 | | Bombay | 478 | | |
| | | 10 | | | 2,567 | |
| SWEDISH RED CROSS | 6 | | Bombay | 2,812 | | |
| | 6 | | Dhaka | 2,752 | | |
| | | 12 | | | 5,564 | |
| SWITZERLAND GOVERNMENT | 4 | | Dhaka | 784 | | |
| | 14 | | Bombay | 2,672 | | |
| | 7 | | Colombo | 1,206 | | |
| | | 25 | | | 4,662 | |
| UNITED KINGDOM GOVERNMENT | 4 | | Bombay | 1,561 | | |
| | 3 | | Dhaka | 1,170 | | |
| | | 7 | | | 2,731 | |
| UNITED STATES GOVERNMENT | 1 | | Colombo | 120 | | |
| | 1 | | Dhaka | 122 | | |
| | 1 | | Manila | 119 | | |
| | | 3 | | | 361 | |
| LUTHERAN WORLD FEDERATION | 8 | | Dhaka | 2,014 | | |
| | | 8 | | | 2,014 | |
| **TOTALS =** | | **82** | | | **19,743** | **11,648,370.00** |

0131

Annex II

IOM - PLAN OF ACTION/UPDATED

| Country | Nationals of: | Movements: DEPARTED 3/9-17/10/1990 | BOOKED TO DEPART 18-21/10/1990 |
|---|---|---|---|
| **JORDAN** | | | |
| | Bangladesh | 37,081 | 158 |
| | India | 22,436 | 1,134 |
| | Pakistan | 3,362 | 157 |
| | Philippines | 13,039 | 275 |
| | Sri Lanka | 38,386 | 2,392 |
| | Egypt | 297 | 0 |
| | Other | 32 | 0 |
| | | 114,633 | 4,116 |
| **TURKEY** | | | |
| | Bangladesh | 5,950 | 30 |
| | Pakistan | 589 | 0 |
| | Sri Lanka | 71 | 60 |
| | Sudan | 2 | 3 |
| | | 6,612 | 93 |
| **IRAN** | | | |
| | Bangladesh | 263 | 2 |
| | India | 14 | 4 |
| | Pakistan | 70 | 0 |
| | Philippines | 5 | 0 |
| | Sri Lanka | 31 | 3 |
| | | 383 | 9 |
| **SAUDI ARABIA** | | | |
| | Sri Lanka | 679 | 0 |

6894C
18/10/90

0132

Annex III
Page 1

GULF EMERGENCY PROGRAMME
PAYMENTS

as at 17 October 1990

| AIRLINE COMPANY | ROUTING | CHARTER FLIGHTS | DATE OF DEPARTURE | NO.OF PAX | PAID USD | TOTAL PAYMENTS |
|---|---|---|---|---|---|---|
| ROYAL JORDANIAN AIRLINE | AMMAN-DHAKA | | | | | |
| | PAID THRU 10.10.90 | 21 | | 5,349 | 3,429,000.00 | |
| | | MIRJ23 339 | 07.10.90 | 231 | 134,000.00 | |
| | | MIRJ23 363 | 08.10.90 | 240 | 159,500.00 | |
| | | MIRJ23 365 | 10.10.90 | 277 | 159,500.00 | |
| | AMMAN-COLOMBO | | | | | |
| | PAID THRU 10.10.90 | 33 | | 6,428 | 4,062,660.00 | |
| | | MIRJ23 321 | 05.10.90 | 182 | 92,820.00 | |
| | | MIRJ23 325 | 07.10.90 | 183 | 92,820.00 | |
| | | MIRJ23 387 | 10.10.90 | 181 | 92,820.00 | |
| | | MIRJ23 388 | 11.10.90 | 184 | 92,820.00 | |
| | | MIRJ23 437 | 10.10.90 | 182 | 92,820.00 | |
| | | MIRJ23 438 | 11.10.90 | 187 | 92,820.00 | |
| | | MIRJ23 439 | 11.10.90 | 182 | 92,820.00 | |
| | AMMAN-MANILA | | | | | |
| | PAID THRU 10.10.90 | 2 | | 470 | 369,600.00 | |
| | | MIRJ23 311 | 03.10.90 | 226 | 184,800.00 | |
| | | MIRJ23 313 | 08.10.90 | 231 | 184,800.00 | |
| | | MIRJ23 314 | 10.10.90 | 233 | 184,800.00 | |
| | | MIRJ23 315 | 11.10.90 | 231 | 184,800.00 | |
| | AMMAN-KARACHI | MIRJ23 362 | 07.10.90 | 278 | 110,000.00 | |
| | | | | 15,475 | | 9,813,200.00 |
| TOWER AIR | AMMAN-MANILA | | | | | |
| | PAID THRU 10.10.90 | 15 | | 7,194 | 5,700,000.00 | |
| | | MIFF23 361 | 11.10.90 | 489 | 380,000.00 | |
| | AMMAN-BOMBAY | MIFF23 357 | 07.10.90 | 483 | 220,000.00 | |
| | | MIFF23 358 | 08.10.90 | 484 | 220,000.00 | |
| | | MIFF23 359 | 09.10.90 | 483 | 220,000.00 | |
| | | MIFF23 360 | 10.10.90 | 481 | 220,000.00 | |
| | | | | 9,614 | | 6,960,000.00 |
| TURKISH AIRLINES | DIYARBAKIR-DHAKA | 13 | | 3,263 | 2,146,250.00 | |
| | DIYARBAKIR-KARACHI | 2 | | 422 | 160,000.00 | |
| | PAID THRU 10.10.90 | | | 3,685 | | 2,306,250.00 |

0133

Annex III
Page 2

| AIRLINE COMPANY | ROUTING | CHARTER FLIGHTS | DATE OF DEPARTURE | NO.OF PAX | PAID USD | TOTAL PAYMENTS |
|---|---|---|---|---|---|---|
| TATE AERO-SERVICES LTD. | AMMAN-DHAKA | 9 | | 1,628 | 1,137,402.00 | |
| | AMMAN-COLOMBO | 7 | | 1,311 | 754,788.00 | |
| | PAID THRU 10.10.90 | | | | | |
| | | MILZ23 342 | 08.10.90 | 151 | 77,010.00 | |
| | | MILZ23 343 | 09.10.90 | 151 | 77,010.00 | |
| | | MILZ23 344 | 09.10.90 | 151 | 77,010.00 | |
| | | MILZ23 408 | 10.10.90 | 151 | 77,010.00 | |
| | | MILZ23 409 | 10.10.90 | 151 | 77,010.00 | |
| | | MILZ23 410 | 10.10.90 | 151 | 77,010.00 | |
| | | MILZ23 411 | 11.10.90 | 151 | 77,010.00 | |
| | | MILZ23 417 | 15.10.90 | 157 | 80,070.00 | |
| | | MILZ23 418 | 15.10.90 | 156 | 80,070.00 | |
| | | | | 4,309 | | 2,591,400.00 |
| SAUDI ARABIAN AIRLINES | RIYADH-COLOMBO PAID THRU 10.10.90 | 2 | | 679 | 197,333.00 | 197,333.00 |
| EVERGREEN INT. AIRLINES | AMMAN-COLOMBO | | | | | |
| | PAID THRU 10.10.90 | 6 | | 3,004 | 1,887,480.00 | |
| | | MIEZ23 109 | 29.09.90 | 488 | 315,630.00 | |
| | | MIEZ23 110 | 01.10.90 | 500 | 315,630.00 | |
| | AMMAN-BOMBAY | MIEZ23 345 | 09.10.90 | 509 | 275,550.00 | |
| | | MIEZ23 346 | 10.10.90 | 500 | 275,550.00 | |
| | | MIEZ23 347 | 10.10.90 | 505 | 275,550.00 | |
| | | | | 5,506 | | 3,345,390.00 |
| OMEGA AIRLINES | AMMAN-COLOMBO PAID THRU 10.10.90 | 1 | | 180 | 108,000.00 | 108,000.00 |
| PAKISTAN INT. AIRLINES | TEHERAN-DHAKA -COLOMBO -KARACHI PAID THRU 10.10.90 | 1 | | 124 | 86,230.00 | 86,230.00 |
| JAPAN AIRLINES | AMMAN-MANILA PAID THRU 10.10.90 | 2 | | 511 | 431,200.00 | 431,200.00 |
| NATIONAIR | AMMAN-BOMBAY | | | | | |
| | PAID THRU 10.10.90 | 10 | | 3,308 | 1,566,600.00 | |
| | | MINX23 263 | 02.10.90 | 253 | 126,000.00 | |
| | | MINX23 269 | 08.10.90 | 254 | 126,000.00 | |
| | | MINX23 270 | 09.10.90 | 255 | 126,000.00 | |
| | | MINX23 271 | 10.10.90 | 252 | 126,000.00 | |
| | | MINX23 272 | 11.10.90 | 251 | 126,000.00 | |
| | | MINX23 275 | 03.10.90 | 480 | 228,200.00 | |
| | | MINX23 284 | 13.10.90 | 482 | 204,400.00 | |
| | | MINX23 285 | 14.10.90 | 480 | 204,400.00 | |
| | AMMAN-COLOMBO | | | | | |
| | PAID THRU 10.10.90 | 2 | | 4,260 | 453,400.00 | |
| | | MINX23 280 | 08.10.90 | 476 | 266,700.00 | |
| | | MINX23 281 | 10.10.90 | 476 | 266,700.00 | |
| | | MINX23 282 | 11.10.90 | 476 | 266,700.00 | |
| | AMMAN-DHAKA | MINX23 283 | 12.10.90 | 291 | 256,100.00 | |
| | | | | 8,686 | | 4,423,200.00 |

0134

| AIRLINE COMPANY | ROUTING | CHARTER FLIGHTS | DATE OF DEPARTURE | NO.OF PAX | PAID USD | TOTAL PAYMENTS |
|---|---|---|---|---|---|---|
| ALL NIPPON AIRWAYS | AMMAN-MANILA PAID THRU 10.10.90 | 1 | | 297 | 237,600.00 | 237,600.00 |
| EGYPTAIR | AMMAN-MANILA PAID THRU 10.10.90 | 3 | | 614 | 489,600.00 | |
| | | MIMS23 356 | 08.10.90 | 203 | 163,200.00 | |
| | | MIMS23 367 | 10.10.90 | 205 | 163,200.00 | |
| | | MIMS23 368 | 10.10.90 | 208 | 163,200.00 | |
| | | MIMS23 369 | 11.10.90 | 205 | 163,200.00 | |
| | | | | 1,435 | | 1,142,400.00 |
| GULF AIR | AMMAN-KARACHI | 1 | | 243 | 72,900.00 | 72,900.00 |
| TURKER TOURISM TRAVEL AG. | ANKARA-COLOMBO | 1 | | 41 | 31,488.00 | 31,488.00 |
| TYCHE TRAVEL & TOURS | AMMAN-COLOMBO PAID THRU 10.10.90 | 3 | | 503 | 244,458.00 | |
| | | MISU23 329 | 06.10.90 | 174 | 84,564.00 | |
| | | MISU23 330 | 07.10.90 | 174 | 84,564.00 | |
| | | | | 851 | | 413,586.00 |
| EMIRATES | AMMAN-BOMBAY | MIEK23 443 | 10.10.90 | 184 | 81,450.00 | |
| | | MIEK23 444 | 10.10.90 | 256 | 118,350.00 | |
| | AMMAN-COLOMBO | MIEK23 458 | 11.10.90 | 264 | 131,500.00 | |
| | | MIEK23 459 | 11.10.90 | 182 | 90,500.00 | |
| | | | | 886 | | 421,800.00 |
| WORLD AIRWAYS | AMMAN-COLOMBO | MIWO23 370 | 06.10.90 | 339 | 219,480.00 | |
| | | MIWO23 371 | 07.10.90 | 354 | 219,480.00 | |
| | | MIWO23 372 | 08.10.90 | 363 | 219,480.00 | |
| | | MIWO23 373 | 09.10.90 | 354 | 219,480.00 | |
| | | MIWO23 374 | 10.10.90 | 354 | 219,480.00 | |
| | | MIWO23 375 | 11.10.90 | 355 | 219,480.00 | |
| | | MIWO23 375 | 12.10.90 | 357 | 219,480.00 | |
| | | MIWO23 377 | 14.10.90 | 354 | 219,480.00 | |
| | | | | 2,830 | | 1,755,840.00 |
| ORIENT SHIPPING | AQABA-COLOMBO PAID THRU 10.10.90 | 1 | | 1,768 | 707,200.00 | 707,200.00 |
| Bus transport Amman, Jordan | | | | | | 1,740,862.50 |
| **GRAND TOTAL** | | | | **57,120** | | **36,785,879.50** |

0135

한사무관

원 본

# 외 무 부

종 별 :

번 호 : GVW-2741 일 시 : 90 1130 1800

수 신 : 장 관 (영해,미북,국기)

발 신 : 주 제네바 대사대리

제 목 : IOM 기여금

연: GVW-1963

1. 11.30(금) IOM SCHATZER 기여조정 담당관은 당관에 전화로 걸프지역사태 관련아국이 IOM에 서약한 기여금(50만불)을 언제 납부할수 있는지 문의하면서, 이미 납지한 기여금은 이미 소진되었고 외국인 귀환사업은 계속 진행되고 있으므로 기금 서약국에 대해 기여금 조속 납부를 요망하여 왔음.

2. 상기 IOM 기여금 납부시기 당관에 통보 바람.끝

(대사대리 박영우-국장)

| 영사교민국 | 년 월 일 | 담 당 | 계 장 | 과 장 | 관리관 | 국 장 |
|---|---|---|---|---|---|---|
| | | | | | | |

영교국 미주국 국기국

PAGE 1

90.12.01 07:46 FC

외신 1과 통제관

0136

| | 분류번호 | 보존기간 |
|---|---|---|
| | | |

# 발 신 전 보

번 호 : WGV-1629 901204 1013 FI 종별 :

수 신 : 주 제네바 대사. 총영사

발 신 : 장 관 (영해)

제 목 : IOM 지원

연 : WGV - 1207, 1252

대 : GVW - 1855, 1963, 2741

대호, IOM 의 중동 사태로 인한 난민들 수송 지원 관련, 아국 정부의 IOM 특별 기여금 50 만불 송금이 국회절차로 지연되고 있으나, 12월 중순 경에는 귀관에 송금할 예정이니 양지 바람. 끝.

(영사교민국장 허 리 훈)

| 보 안 통 제 | |
|---|---|

| 앙 고 재 | 90년 12월 3일 | 해외이주과 | 기안자 성 명 | | 과 장 | | 국 장 | | 차 관 | 장 관 |
|---|---|---|---|---|---|---|---|---|---|---|
| | | | | | | | 전결 | | | |

| 외신과통제 |
|---|
| |

0137

김창호

원 본

# 외 무 부

종 별 :

번 호 : GVW-2846 일 시 : 90 1221 1730

수 신 : 장 관 (영해)

발 신 : 주 제네바 대사

제 목 : 중동사태 관련 IOM 자발적 기여금

대: WGV-1629

대호 기여금(50만불)이 당관에 발송되었으면 통보바람.

금년도 당관앞 본부발송 최종 파편은 12.22(토)임을 참고바람.끝

(대사 이상옥-국장)

| 영사교민국 | 년 월 일 | 담 당 | 계 장 | 과 장 | 관리관 | 국 장 |
|---|---|---|---|---|---|---|
| | | | | | | |

영교국

PAGE 1

90.12.22 07:34 FC

외신 1과 통제관

0138

91-500

# 협조문용지

| 분류기호 문서번호 | 영해20810-106 | ( 2397, 2398 ) | 결재 | 담 당 | 과 장 | 국 장 |
|---|---|---|---|---|---|---|
| 시행일자 | 1990. 12. 24. | | | | | |
| 수 신 | 중동아프리카국장 | 발신 | 영사교민국장 (서명) | | | |
| 제 목 | IOM 기여금 | | | | | |

걸프만 사태와 관련, 정부 방침으로 기결정된 IOM 특별 기여금 50만불을 현재 송금 수속중임을 통보하니, 업무에 참고하시기 바랍니다. 끝.

19 91. 6. 30 예고문에 의거 일반

0139

| | 분류번호 | 보존기간 |
|---|---|---|
| | | |

# 발 신 전 보

번 호 : WGV-1704 901226 1116 FK 종별 :

수 신 : 주 제네바 대사. 총영사

발 신 : 장 관 (영해)

제 목 : IOM 지원

연 : WGV - 1629

대 : GVW - 2846

연호 IOM 특별 기여금은 현재 송금 수속중에 있는바, 수령 즉시 IOM 에 적의 전달하고 결과 보고 바람. 끝.

(영사교민국장 허 리 훈)

| 보안 통제 | |
|---|---|

| 앙 고 재 | 90년 12월 26일 | 해외이주과 | 기안자 성명 김창곤 | | 과장 | | 국장 | | 차관 | 장관 |
|---|---|---|---|---|---|---|---|---|---|---|

| 외신과통제 |
|---|
| |

0140

관리번호

원 본

# 외 무 부

종 별 :

번 호 : GVW-0041 일 시 : 91 0108 1730

수 신 : 장 관 (영해,국기,미북)

발 신 : 주 제네바 대사대리

제 목 : IOM 기여금 납부

대: WGV-1740

대호, 1.8 당관 신부남 서기관은 중동사태 관련 아국의 IOM 특별기여금 50만불을IOM 사무국에 전달하였음.끝.

(대사대리 박영우-국장)

| 영사교민국 | 년 월 일 | 담 당 | 계 장 | 과 장 | 심의관 | 국 장 |
|---|---|---|---|---|---|---|
| | | | | | | |

영교국 미주국 국기국

PAGE 1

91.01.09 07:42 FC

외신 1과 통제관

0141

# 長 官 님 報 告 事 項

| 報 告 畢 |
| --- |
| |

1991. 1. 14.
領 事 僑 民 局
海 外 移 住 課

## 題 目 : IOM 事務次長, 長官님 禮訪 申請

1. 姓　　名 : Charry - Samper ( 콜롬비아 人 )

2. 訪韓 豫定日 : 1991. 2. 3 - 6

3. 訪 韓 目 的 :

o 韓. IOM 間 移民 協力 增進 協議

※ Charry-Samper 事務次長은 '91.1 月末 泰國, 필리핀, 인도네시아 訪問 機會에 訪韓 希望 表明

4. 韓. IOM 間 協力 現況

o 1988.11.29. IOM 에 正會員國으로 加入한 以來 年間 約 7萬弗의 分擔金 支拂

o 我國은 걸프만 事態 關聯 難民 輸送을 爲해 50萬弗의 特別 寄與金 支援 ('91. 1. 8 傳達)

5. 韓. IOM 間 懸案

o IOM 은 移民情報 提供 및 秩序있는 移民 推進보다는 難民 輸送 業務 置重으로 我國이 받는 實質的인 受惠 無

o 現在 IOM 正會員國 脫退 및 옵서버國 잔류 方案 檢討中

0142

참고 자료

# 국제 이민기구 개요

1. 연 혁 :

- 1951.12. 브랏셀에서 정부간 이민기구 (Intergovernmental Committee for Migration) 로 발족
- 1989.11. 국제 이민기구 (International Orgamization for Migration) 로 명칭 변경

2. 회원국 및 옵저버국 현황

- 회 원 국 : 39 개국
- 옵저버국 : 26 개국

3. 구 성

- 이 사 회 : 39개국 회원국 대표로 구성, IOM 의 정책, 기획, 재정에 대한 최종 결정
- 집행위원회 : 이사회에서 선출된 10 개국으로 구성, 이사회 업무 준비 및 예산, 재정 소위원회와 수송 조정 소위원회의 보고를 기초로 권고안 수립
- 사 무 국 : 이사회 및 집행위원회가 제정한 규칙과 규정에 따라 기구의 행정 및 집행기능을 수행

※ 사무총장은 James Purcell (미국), 사무차장은 Hector Charry-Samper (콜롬비아)

0143

4. 아국과의 관계

o 1988. 11. 29 정회원으로 가입

o 분 담 금

- 1991 년 : 100,580 서서프랑 (행정 예산 총액의 0.47 %)

- 1990 년 : 90,000 서서프랑

- 1989 년 : 84,000 서서프랑

o 91.1.8 페르샤만 사태 관련, 특별 기여금 50만불 제공

5. IOM 업무 실적 ( 90. 1 - 11 )

o 난민 이주 : 197,715 명

o 일반 이주 : 10,031 명

0144

원 본

# 외 무 부

종 별 :

번 호 : GVW-0097 일 시 : 91 0117 1100

수 신 : 장관(영해,국기,미북)

발 신 : 주제네바대사대리

제 목 : IOM 사무총장 공한

1. 1.16(수) PURCELL IOM 사무총장은 걸프지역 난민철수와 관련 별첨 공한을 아국 외무장관께 전달하여 줄것을 요청하여 왔는바, 이를 FAX 송부함.

2. 동 공한에서 IOM 은 걸프지역에서 분쟁발생시 난민 수송책임을 UN 으로부터위임 받아 걸프지역에서 난민을 수송하고 구호물자를 반입하기 위한 민간 및 군용 비행기의 공급원을 조사하고 있다고 하면서, 아국 정부에대해 민간 및 군용 비행기의동원 가능성을 고려하여 줄 것을 요청하고, 동원이 가능할 경우 수송기의 탑재능력및 동원에 필요한 사전 소요시간도 알려줄 것을 요청함. 끝.

첨부: IOM사무총장 공한( GVW(F)-0022). 끝.

(대사대리 박영우-국장)

| 영사교민국 | 년 월 일 | 담 당 | 계 장 | 과 장 | 심의관 | 국 장 |
|---|---|---|---|---|---|---|
| | | | | | | |

영교국 장관 차관 1차보 2차보 미주국 중아국 중아국 국기국
청와대 총리실 안기부 대책반

PAGE 1 91.01.18 02:11 CG

외신 1과 통제관

0145

1991-01-17 17:09 KOREAN MISSION GENEVA 2 022 791 0525 P.01

GVW(F)-0022 10117 1100 2/2

"GVW-91 첨부"

INTERNATIONAL ORGANIZATION FOR MIGRATION

THE DIRECTOR GENERAL

GENEVA, SWITZERLAND

EXCELLENCY,

THE UNITED NATIONS HAS AGAIN ENTRUSTED THE INTERNATIONAL ORGANIZATION FOR MIGRATION (IOM) WITH THE RESPONSIBILITY FOR THE TRANSPORTATION OF DISPLACED PERSONS IN THE EVENT OF AN OUTBREAK OF HOSTILITIES IN THE PERSIAN GULF REGION AND A MASSIVE INFLUX INTO COUNTRIES NEIGHBOURING IRAQ AND KUWAIT.

UNLIKE THE SITUATION PREVAILING FROM SEPTEMBER 1990 - WHEN THE INTERNATIONAL COMMUNITY UNDERTOOK AN EMERGENCY EVACUATION PROGRAMME IN THE GULF - UNTIL NOW, IOM ANTICIPATES THAT COMMERCIAL AIRCRAFT FOR THIS FURTHER REPATRIATION EFFORT, IF ONE NEEDS TO BE MOUNTED, WILL BE SCARCE. CONSEQUENTLY, IOM HAS UNDERTAKEN TO CANVASS POTENTIAL SOURCES OF CIVILIAN OR MILITARY AIRCRAFT IN ORDER TO DETERMINE AVAILABILITY OF CAPACITY ON SHORT NOTICE TO TRANSPORT EVACUEES OUT OF THE REGION IF NECESSARY, AS WELL AS TO TRANSPORT RELIEF SUPPLIES IN. WE WOULD ALSO APPRECIATE RECEIVING INDICATIONS AS TO WHETHER GOVERNMENTS COULD MAKE SHIPS AVAILABLE, FOR SAILINGS FROM SYRIA TO EGYPT AND SUDAN, SHOULD LARGE-SCALE EVACUATION OF NATIONALS OF THESE COUNTRIES BE REQUIRED.

I SHOULD STRESS THAT THIS INFORMATION IS BEING REQUESTED AT THIS STAGE AS A CONTINGENCY MEASURE, AND STILL VERY MUCH IN THE HOPE THAT NO SUCH EVACUATION WILL BE REQUIRED. HOWEVER, IN VIEW OF PRESENT CIRCUMSTANCES, I BELIEVE IT IS PRUDENT TO BEGIN COLLECTING AND CENTRALIZING SUCH DATA AS INPUT FOR IOM'S OWN PLANNING, AND AS A RESOURCE WHICH CAN BE SHARED WITH OTHER MEMBERS OF THE UNITED NATIONS/IOM EMERGENCY TEAM AS NEEDED.

WHILE AT THIS STAGE NO INDICATION OF PROSPECTIVE NUMBERS OF PERSONS TO BE EVACUATED CAN BE GIVEN, UPLIFT POINTS FORESEEN ARE IRAN, JORDAN, SYRIA AND TURKEY.

I WOULD URGE YOUR GOVERNMENT TO CONSIDER THE POSSIBILITY OF PROVIDING IOM WITH CAPACITY ON CIVILIAN OR MILITARY AIRCRAFT AND, IF THIS IS POSSIBLE, PROVIDING US WITH DETAILS AS TO LIKELY CAPACITY AND LEAD-TIME REQUIRED FOR REQUESTS TO BE ACTED UPON. AS REGARDS CARGO CAPACITY, ANY SIMILAR INFORMATION PROVIDED WILL, AS INDICATED ABOVE, BE SHARED WITH UNDRO AND OTHER MEMBERS OF THE EMERGENCY TEAM CONSTITUTED BY THE INTERNATIONAL COMMUNITY.

FOR REPLIES AND ALSO IN CASE FURTHER INFORMATION IS REQUIRED THE PERSON TO BE CONTACTED AT IOM HQS IS:

MR. GERHARD SLIWIK
CHIEF, DIVISION OF TRANSPORT AND LOGISTICS
DEPARTMENT OF OPERATIONS
INTERNATIONAL ORGANIZATION FOR MIGRATION (IOM)
17, ROUTE DES MORILLONS
1211 GENEVA 19 - SWITZERLAND

| | | | |
|---|---|---|---|
| PHONE | 717.9111 | TELEX | 415.722 ICEM CH |
| SITA | GVAICCR | FAX | 798.61.50 |

YOUR URGENT ATTENTION TO THIS REQUEST WOULD BE HIGHLY APPRECIATED.

ACCEPT, EXCELLENCY, THE ASSURANCE OF MY HIGHEST CONSIDERATION.

James N. Purcell, Jr.

JAMES N. PURCELL, JR.

1-1

0146

TOTAL P.01

원 본

# 외 무 부

종 별 :

번 호 : GVW-0097 일 시 : 91 0117 1100

수 신 : 장관(영해,국기,미북)

발 신 : 주제네바대사대리

제 목 : IOM 사무총장 공한

1. 1.16(수) PURCELL IOM 사무총장은 걸프지역 난민철수와 관련 별첨 공한을 아국 외무장관께 전달하여 줄것을 요청하여 왔는바, 이를 FAX 송부함.

2. 동 공한에서 IOM 은 걸프지역에서 분쟁발생시 난민 수송책임을 UN 으로 부터위임 받아 걸프지역에서 난민을 수송하고 구호물자를 반입하기 위한 민간 및 군용 비행기의 공급원을 조사하고 있다고 하면서, 아국 정부에대해 민간 및 군용 비행기의동원 가능성을 고려하여 줄 것을 요청하고, 동원이 가능할 경우 수송기의 탑재능력및 동원에 필요한 사전 소요시간도 알려줄 것을 요청함. 끝.

첨부: IOM사무총장 공한( GVW(F)-0022). 끝.

(대사대리 박영우-국장)

| 영사교민국 | 년월일 | 담 당 | 과 장 | 심의관 | 국 장 |
|---|---|---|---|---|---|
| | | | | | |

영교국 장관 차관 1차보 2차보 미주국 중아국 중아국 국기국
청와대 총리실 안기부 대책반

PAGE 1 91.01.18 02:11 CG
외신 1과 통제관

0147

91-01-17 17:03 KOREAN MISSION GENEVA 2 022 791 0525 P.01

GVW(HI)-0017 10117 1100 2/2

INTERNATIONAL ORGANIZATION FOR MIGRATION "GVW-91 첨부"

THE DIRECTOR GENERAL

GENEVA, SWITZERLAND

EXCELLENCY,

THE UNITED NATIONS HAS AGAIN ENTRUSTED THE INTERNATIONAL ORGANIZATION FOR MIGRATION (IOM) WITH THE RESPONSIBILITY FOR THE TRANSPORTATION OF DISPLACED PERSONS IN THE EVENT OF AN OUTBREAK OF HOSTILITIES IN THE PERSIAN GULF REGION AND A MASSIVE INFLUX INTO COUNTRIES NEIGHBOURING IRAQ AND KUWAIT.

UNLIKE THE SITUATION PREVAILING FROM SEPTEMBER 1990 - WHEN THE INTERNATIONAL COMMUNITY UNDERTOOK AN EMERGENCY EVACUATION PROGRAMME IN THE GULF - UNTIL NOW, IOM ANTICIPATES THAT COMMERCIAL AIRCRAFT FOR THIS FURTHER REPATRIATION EFFORT, IF ONE NEEDS TO BE MOUNTED, WILL BE SCARCE. CONSEQUENTLY, IOM HAS UNDERTAKEN TO CANVASS POTENTIAL SOURCES OF CIVILIAN OR MILITARY AIRCRAFT IN ORDER TO DETERMINE AVAILABILITY OF CAPACITY ON SHORT NOTICE TO TRANSPORT EVACUEES OUT OF THE REGION IF NECESSARY, AS WELL AS TO TRANSPORT RELIEF SUPPLIES IN. WE WOULD ALSO APPRECIATE RECEIVING INDICATIONS AS TO WHETHER GOVERNMENTS COULD MAKE SHIPS AVAILABLE, FOR SAILINGS FROM SYRIA TO EGYPT AND SUDAN, SHOULD LARGE-SCALE EVACUATION OF NATIONALS OF THESE COUNTRIES BE REQUIRED.

I SHOULD STRESS THAT THIS INFORMATION IS BEING REQUESTED AT THIS STAGE AS A CONTINGENCY MEASURE, AND STILL VERY MUCH IN THE HOPE THAT NO SUCH EVACUATION WILL BE REQUIRED. HOWEVER, IN VIEW OF PRESENT CIRCUMSTANCES, I BELIEVE IT IS PRUDENT TO BEGIN COLLECTING AND CENTRALIZING SUCH DATA AS INPUT FOR IOM'S OWN PLANNING, AND AS A RESOURCE WHICH CAN BE SHARED WITH OTHER MEMBERS OF THE UNITED NATIONS/IOM EMERGENCY TEAM AS NEEDED.

WHILE AT THIS STAGE NO INDICATION OF PROSPECTIVE NUMBERS OF PERSONS TO BE EVACUATED CAN BE GIVEN, UPLIFT POINTS FORESEEN ARE IRAN, JORDAN, SYRIA AND TURKEY.

I WOULD URGE YOUR GOVERNMENT TO CONSIDER THE POSSIBILITY OF PROVIDING IOM WITH CAPACITY ON CIVILIAN OR MILITARY AIRCRAFT AND, IF THIS IS POSSIBLE, PROVIDING US WITH DETAILS AS TO LIKELY CAPACITY AND LEAD-TIME REQUIRED FOR REQUESTS TO BE ACTED UPON. AS REGARDS CARGO CAPACITY, ANY SIMILAR INFORMATION PROVIDED WILL, AS INDICATED ABOVE, BE SHARED WITH UNDRO AND OTHER MEMBERS OF THE EMERGENCY TEAM CONSTITUTED BY THE INTERNATIONAL COMMUNITY.

FOR REPLIES AND ALSO IN CASE FURTHER INFORMATION IS REQUIRED THE PERSON TO BE CONTACTED AT IOM HQS IS:

MR. GERHARD SLIWIK
CHIEF, DIVISION OF TRANSPORT AND LOGISTICS
DEPARTMENT OF OPERATIONS
INTERNATIONAL ORGANIZATION FOR MIGRATION (IOM)
17, ROUTE DES MORILLONS
1211 GENEVA 19 - SWITZERLAND

| PHONE | 717.9111 | TELEX | 415.722 ICEM CH |
|---|---|---|---|
| SITA | GVAICCR | FAX | 798.61.50 |

YOUR URGENT ATTENTION TO THIS REQUEST WOULD BE HIGHLY APPRECIATED.

ACCEPT, EXCELLENCY, THE ASSURANCE OF MY HIGHEST CONSIDERATION.

James N. Purcell, Jr.

JAMES N. PURCELL, JR.

1-1

0148

TOTAL P.01

# 협조문용지

| 분류기호<br>문서번호 | 영해20810-21 | ( 2397, 2398 ) | 결재 | 담 당 | 과 장 | 국 장 |
|---|---|---|---|---|---|---|
| 시행일자 | 1991. 1. 24. | | | | | |
| 수 신 | 걸프사태 비상대책 본부장 | 발신 | 영사교민국장 | | | (서명) |
| 제 목 | 난민 수송 항공기 제공 요청 | | | | | |

1. 국제 이민기구 (IOM) Purcell 사무총장은 걸프 사태와 관련, 장관님 앞 공한을 통해 난민 수송을 위한 항공기 제공 고려를 요청해 온 바, 걸프사태에 관한 종합적 추가지원 검토시 동 IOM 의 요청 사항을 의안으로 제기하여 주시기 바랍니다.

2. 아국은 금번 걸프전쟁 발발 이전인 90. 12월 난민의 인도적 측면 및 국제협력적 차원에서 50만불을 특별 기여금으로 제공한 바 있음을 참고로 첨언합니다.

첨부 : 1. IOM 의 요청 공한 사본 1 부.

2. 장관님 보고사항 사본 1 부. 끝.

0149

| 분류기호<br>문서번호 | 영해20810-<br>41 | 협조문용지<br>( 2397, 2398 ) | 결<br><br>재 | 담 당 | 과 장 | 국 장 |
|---|---|---|---|---|---|---|
| 시행일자 | 1991. 1. 24. | | | | | |
| 수 신 | 걸프사태 비상대책 본부장 | 발신 | 영사교민국장 (서명) | | | |
| 제 목 | 난민 수송 항공기 제공 요청 | | | | | |

1. 국제 이민기구 (IOM) Purcell 사무총장은 걸프 사태와 관련, 장관님 앞 공한을 통해 난민 수송을 위한 항공기 제공 고려를 요청해 온 바, 걸프사태에 관한 종합적 추가지원 검토시 동 IOM 의 요청 사항을 의안으로 제기하여 주시기 바랍니다.

2. 아국은 금번 걸프전쟁 발발 이전인 90. 12월 난민의 인도적 측면 및 국제협력적 차원에서 50만불을 특별 기여금으로 제공한 바 있음을 참고로 첨언합니다.

첨부 : 1. IOM 의 요청 공한 사본 1 부.

2. 장관님 보고사항 사본 1 부. 끝.

0150

# 國際 移民機構 (IOM), 難民 輸送用 民間 또는 軍用 航空機 提供 要請

| 앙고재 | 담당 | 과장 | 국장 | 차관보 | 차관 | 장관 |
|---|---|---|---|---|---|---|

1991. 1. 18.

領 事 僑 民 局

海 外 移 住 課

0151

# 國際 移民機構 (IOM), 難民 輸送用 民間 또는 軍用 航空機 提供 要請

## 1. 問題의 提起

o Purcell 國際移民機構 (IOM) 事務總長은 1.16 걸프地域 難民 輸送을 爲한 支援 要請 公翰을 駐제네바 代表部를 通해 外務部長官께 傳達해 줄것을 要望

## 2. 支援 要請 事項

o 걸프地域 難民輸送 및 救護物資 搬入을 爲한 民間 및 軍用 航空機의 提供 考慮 要請

o 提供可能 境遇 同 航空機의 搭載能力 및 提供 可能時期 通報 要請

## 3. IOM 概要

o IOM 은 移民 및 難民 事業 推進 目的으로 1951年 發足, 現在 39個 會員國 및 26個 옵서버國으로 構成

o 我國은 1988.11月 正會員國으로 加入, 年間 7-8 萬弗의 分擔金 支拂

o 我國은 특히 금번 걸프만 事態 關聯, 難民 輸送 支援을 爲해 難民의 人道的 側面 및 國際協力的 次元에서 50萬弗 特別 寄與金 提供 (91.1.8)

0152

## 4. 檢討 意見

- 政府는 금번 걸프灣 事態 關聯, 總 2億 2,000 萬弗 支援 및 軍 醫療團 派遣 (豫程)

- 政府는 특히 中東地域 殘留 我國 勤勞者 및 僑民 (約 5,000 餘名) 의 安全 및 輸送에 一次的 關心

- 따라서 現在 外國人 難民 輸送을 爲한 民間 또는 軍用 航空機 提供은 豫算 事情上 難望

## 5. 對　　策

- 걸프灣 事態 關聯 政府次元 綜合的 追加 支援 檢討時 議題로 提起.　끝.

0153

# 長 官 님 報 告 事 項

1991. 1. 18.
領事僑民局
海外移住課

## 題 目 : 國際 移民機構 (IOM), 難民 輸送用 民間 또는 軍用 航空機 提供 要請

### 1. 問題의 提起

- Purcell 國際移民機構 (IOM) 事務總長은 1.16 걸프地域 難民 輸送을 爲한 支援 要請 公翰을 駐제네바 代表部를 通해 外務部長官께 傳達해 줄것을 要望

### 2. 支援 要請 事項

- 걸프地域 難民輸送 및 救護物資 搬入을 爲한 民間 및 軍用 航空機의 提供 考慮 要請
- 提供可能 境遇 同 航空機의 搭載能力 및 提供 可能時期 通報 要請

### 3. IOM 槪要

- IOM 은 移民 및 難民 事業 推進 目的으로 1951年 發足, 現在 39個 會員國 및 26個 옵서버國으로 構成
- 我國은 1988.11月 正會員國으로 加入, 年間 7-8 萬弗의 分擔金 支拂
- 我國은 특히 금번 걸프灣 事態 關聯, 難民 輸送 支援을 爲해 難民의 人道的 側面 및 國際協力的 次元에서 50萬弗 特別 寄與金 提供 (91.1.8)

0154

## 4. 檢討 意見

- ○ 政府는 금번 걸프灣 事態 關聯, 總 2億 2,000 萬弗 支援 및 軍 醫療團 派遣 (豫程)
- ○ 政府는 특히 中東地域 殘留 我國 勤勞者 및 僑民 (約 5,000 餘名) 의 安全 및 輸送에 一次的 關心
- ○ 따라서 現在 外國人 難民 輸送을 爲한 民間 또는 軍用 航空機 提供은 豫算 事情上 難望

## 5. 對 策

- ○ 걸프灣 事態 關聯 政府次元 綜合的 追加 支援 檢討時 議題로 提起. 끝.

0155

원 본

암호수신

# 외 무 부

종 별 :

번 호 : GVW-0123 일 시 : 91 0121 1800

수 신 : 장관(영해)

발 신 : 주 제네바 대사대리

제 목 : IOM 지원 요청

대: WGV-0096

연: GVW-0097

1. 걸프지역 난민수송을 위한 IOM 의 수송기 제공 요청과 관련, 1.21. 당관 신부남서기관은 SLIWIK IOM 수송.지원과장에게 대호 아국입장을 전달함.

2. 동인은 아국의 즉각적인 반응에 감사한다고 하면서 걸프지역에서 전쟁발발후 예상외로 쿠웨이트 및 이락 주변국가로의 난민 유입은 요르단으로의 소규모 난민 유입외에는 없으나 IOM 은 인접국가로의 대규모 난민 유입에 대비중에 있다함. 한편 현재 IOM 의 수송기 제공 요청에 긍정적인 반응을 보인 국가는 스위스와 일본 2 개국이라함.

동건 진전상황 있을시 추보 하겠음. 끝.

(대사대리 박영우-장관)

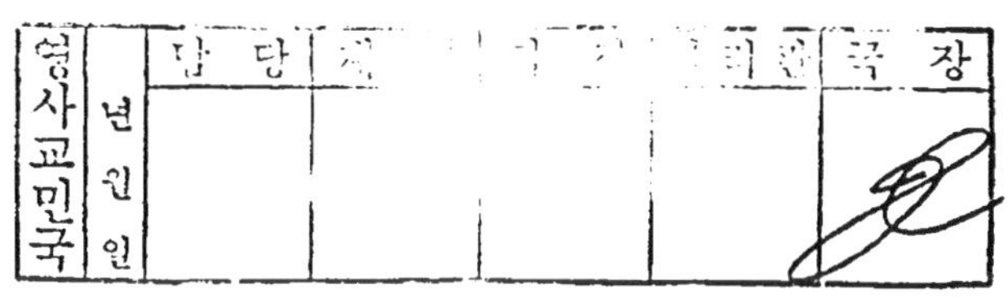

영교국 장관 차관 1차보 2차보 중아국 청와대 총리실 안기부

PAGE 1 91.01.22 17:55

외신 2과 통제관 DO

0156

| | 분류번호 | 보존기간 |
|---|---|---|
| | | |

# 발 신 전 보

번 호 : WGV-0096 910119 1103 DP 종별 : 암호 송신

수 신 : 주 제네바 대사 대리

발 신 : 장 관 (영해)

제 목 : IOM 지원 요청

대 : GVW - 0097

1. 대호, 걸프만 지역 난민 수송을 위한 IOM 의 민간 및 군용 항공기 제공 요청 관련, 정부는 현재 중동지역 잔류 아국 근로자와 교민의 안전 및 수송에 최우선 순위를 두고 있어 외국인 난민 수송을 위한 민간 또는 군용 항공기 제공은 ~~예산 사정상~~ 어려운 실정에 있음.

2. 다만, 난민의 인도적 측면 및 국제협력적 차원을 고려 걸프만 사태 관련 종합적 추가 지원 검토시 의제로 제기 관계부처와 협의코자 하는 바, ~~최종 방침에 대해서는 추후 통보 예정이니~~ IOM 에 대해 일단 상기 아국 입장을 적의 전달하는 한편, IOM 의 난민 수송 계획을 ~~타진~~ 참고로 보고 바람. 끝.

(영사교민국장 허리훈)

제2차관보:

| 보 안 통 제 | |
|---|---|

| 앙 고 재 | 91년 1월 19일 | 해외이주과 | 기안자 성 명 | | 과 장 | | 국 장 | | 차 관 | 장 관 |
|---|---|---|---|---|---|---|---|---|---|---|
| | | | | | | | 전결 | | | |

외신과통제

0157

주종휘

원 본

# 외 무 부

종 별 :

번 호 : GVW-0220 일 시 : 91 0201 1630

수 신 : 장관(영해,국기)

발 신 : 주 제네바 대사대리

제 목 : IOM 걸프지역 지원

IOM 은 1.31 자 전회원국 공관앞 공한을통해 IOM 의 걸프지역 난민 수송 사업 현황을알려왔는바, 동 공한에 의하면 일본과 불란서가수송기를 제공키로 하였고, 미국이 750,000 미불,스위스가 500,000 스위스 프랑, 카나다가 500,000 카나다불을 각각기여금으로 서약하였으며, 91.1.8-30 간IOM 이 지원한 난민 총 인원은 7,183 명이라함. 상기 공한 금파편 송부함. 끝

(대사대리 박영우-국장)

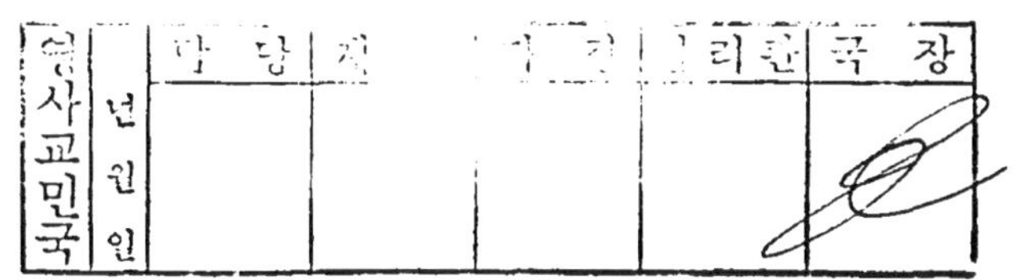

영교국 1차보 중아국 국기국 안기부 2차보

PAGE 1

91.02.02 03:44 BX

외신 1과 통제관

0158

주공철

# 주 제 네 바 대 표 부

제네(정) 20320-132　　　　　　　　　　　　　　1991. 2. 1

수신 : 장관

참조 : 영사교민국장

제목 : IOM 걸프지역 지원

연 : GVW-0220

1. IOM은 1.31자 전회원국 공관앞 공한을 통해 90. 9. - 1.15 및 90.1.15이후 현재까지의 걸프지역 난민 수송사업 관련 각국의 대 IOM 기여금 현황 및 IOM이 지원한 외국인 철수 인원 현황 자료를 전달하여 왔는바, 이를 별첨 송부합니다.

2. 참고로 90. 9월이후 각국의 대 IOM 기여금 총액은 80,998,406미불(아국 50만불 포함)이며 IOM이 지원한 외국인 철수인원 162,600명이라함을 첨언합니다.

첨부 : 상기 자료 각 1부. 끝.

주 제 네 바 대 사

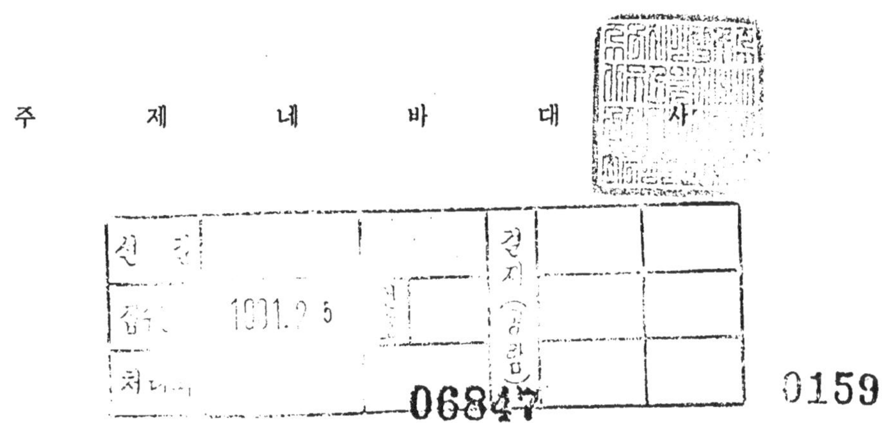


0159

INTERNATIONAL ORGANIZATION FOR MIGRATION (IOM)
ORGANISATION INTERNATIONALE POUR LES MIGRATIONS (OIM)
ORGANIZACIÓN INTERNACIONAL PARA LAS MIGRACIONES (OIM)

Telephone: 717 91 11
Cable Address: Promigrant Geneva
Telex: 415 722
Telefax: 798 61 50

17, route des Morillons
P.O. Box 71
CH - 1211 GENEVA 19
SWITZERLAND

TO: THE PERMANENT MISSIONS OF:

ARGENTINA, AUSTRALIA, AUSTRIA, BANGLADESH, BELIZE, BOLIVIA, BRAZIL, BELGIUM, CANADA, CAPE VERDE, CHILE, CHINA, COLOMBIA, COSTA RICA, CYPRUS, DENMARK, DOMINICAN REP., ECUADOR, EGYPT, EL SALVADOR, FINLAND, FRANCE, GERMANY, GHANA, GUINEA-BISSAU, GREECE, GUATEMALA, HOLY SEE, HONDURAS, HUNGARY, INDIA, INDONESIA, IRAN, ISRAEL, ITALY, JAPAN, JORDAN, KENYA, KOREA (REP. OF), LUXEMBOURG, MEXICO, NETHERLANDS, NEW ZEALAND, NICARAGUA, NORWAY, PAKISTAN, PANAMA, PARAGUAY, PERU, PHILIPPINES, PORTUGAL, SAN MARINO, SAUDI ARABIA, SINGAPORE, SOMALIA, SPAIN, SRI LANKA, SUDAN, SWEDEN, SWITZERLAND, SYRIAN ARAB REP., THAILAND, TURKEY, UGANDA, U.S.S.R., UNITED KINGDOM, U.S.A., URUGUAY, VENEZUELA, VIETNAM, YEMEN (REP OF), YUGOSLAVIA, ZAMBIA, ZIMBABWE AND THE COMMISSION OF THE EUROPEAN COMMUNITIES

COPY TO: - OFFICE OF THE PERSONAL REPRESENTATIVE OF THE U.N. SECRETARY GENERAL FOR HUMANITARIAN ASSISTANCE RELATING TO THE CRISIS BETWEEN IRAQ AND KUWAIT
- UNDRO, UNDP, UNHCR, UNICEF, WFP, WHO, IBRD, ICRC.

FROM : INTERNATIONAL ORGANIZATION FOR MIGRATION, GENEVA

DATE : 31 JANUARY 1991

SUBJECT: **IOM'S GEP II. UPDATED PLAN OF ACTION NO. 1**

0160

INTERNATIONAL ORGANIZATION FOR MIGRATION (IOM)
ORGANISATION INTERNATIONALE POUR LES MIGRATIONS (OIM)
ORGANIZACIÓN INTERNACIONAL PARA LAS MIGRACIONES (OIM)

Telephone: 717 91 11
Cable Address: Promigrant Geneva
Telex: 415 722
Telefax: 798 61 50

17, route des Morillons
P.O. Box 71
CH-1211 GENEVA 19
SWITZERLAND

**REGIONAL HUMANITARIAN PLAN OF ACTION**
**UPDATE OF IOM OPERATIONS AS AT 30 JANUARY 1991**

On 11 January 1991, the United Nations launched a consolidated Regional Humanitarian Plan of Action to assist persons who might flee Iraq and Kuwait in the event of hostilities. This co-ordinated, multi-agency effort addressed, among other needs, internal and international evacuation transportation, for which IOM was designated the responsible international agency. IOM's estimated financial requirements, both for immediate action and in the event of large-scale movements of persons into Iran, Jordan, Syria and Turkey, were incorporated in the consolidated Plan (see Annex I for the status as at 30 January of pledges and payments toward IOM's needs under the Plan).

One of IOM's first actions under the Plan was to reinforce or reactivate the operational presence established in Iran, Jordan and Turkey for the previous phase of the international evacuation effort. An evaluation of needs in Syria was also a priority, and an operational presence was established there on 14 January. As at 30 January, IOM has deployed 24 international staff in the aforementioned countries; in each case, they are fully integrated into the U.N./IOM emergency team and are assisted by locally-recruited employees. In addition, for operational reasons, IOM has reinforced its presence in Egypt to handle the increasing number of of evacuations, essentially in transit, being arranged through that country.

In operational terms, one of IOM's first concerns was to plan in the face of a rapid drop in scheduled commercial air service to and from the region. This, combined with skyrocketing insurance costs and security considerations, made it clear that evacuations on the scale of those IOM had been carrying out since September 1990* on regular or charter aircraft would be increasingly difficult to arrange. As this also affected agencies charged with setting up adequate infrastructure to deal with any influx and with pre-positioning relief supplies, the Director General appealed to governments on 17 January 1991 to evaluate what commercial or military aircraft they might be able to make available to overcome this difficulty. While focusing on passenger aircraft, the Director General offered for IOM to act as a focal point for information on availability of cargo planes as well, with such information to be shared with all agencies involved at their regular Geneva co-ordinating meetings. To date, the Governments of France and Japan have made offers of aircraft in response to this request.

* For the sake of convenience, internationally-assisted evacuations handled by IOM from 3/9/1990 - 16/1/91 are referred to as Gulf Emergency Programme (GEP) I; those pursuant to the Regional Humanitarian Plan of Action and covered by this report are referred to as GEP II.

0161

As regards evacuations arranged by IOM since mid-January, these have totalled 7,183 region-wide as at 30 January. This includes 7,080 persons assisted in their departure from Jordan; 79 evacuees from Syria and 24 from Saudi Arabia. A full breakdown, by country of departure and country of nationality, is contained in Annex II.

It should be noted that unlike IOM's earlier activities, evacuations under GEP II not only entail responsibility for inland transport in all cases but increasingly concern movements by a combination of land, sea and/or air routes. As one example, IOM's arrangements for the repatriation of the first group of Vietnamese nationals assisted under GEP II involved bus transport within Jordan from camps to Aqaba, a ferry crossing from Aqaba to Nuweibe (Egypt), connection with a waiting bus convoy for the leg Nuweibe/Cairo, and departure from Cairo Airport on Japanese-donated planes for the flight to Viet Nam.

As concerns financing, by 30 January cash pledges had been received equivalent to US$ 8,453,713 (See Annex I). At this early stage of operations under GEP II, insufficient invoices are in hand to provide a meaningful statement of settlement of expenditures similar to the third Annex to IOM's GEP I plan of action. Such an Annex will, however, be included in future GEP II updates.

31 January 1991

0162

ANNEX I

## REGIONAL HUMANITARIAN PLAN OF ACTION RELATING TO THE CRISIS BETWEEN IRAQ AND KUWAIT (GEP II)

## PLEDGES AND RECEIPTS FOR TRANSPORTATION as at 30 January 1991

| *1. CASH CONTRIBUTIONS* | *PLEDGED* | *RECEIVED USD* |
|---|---|---|
| AUSTRIA | 1) USD 310,000.00 | |
| CANADA | CAD 500,000.00 | 431,034.00 |
| | 1) USD 151,496.00 | |
| JAPAN | 1) USD 5,000,000.00 | 5,000,000.00 |
| SWEDEN | 1) USD 1,066,083.00 | 1,066,083.00 |
| SWITZERLAND | CHF 500,000.00 | |
| UNITED KINGDOM | 1) USD 351,400.00 | |
| U.S.A. | USD 750,000.00 | |
| ***TOTAL*** | USD 8,453,713.00 | 6,497,117.00 |
| ***2. IN-KIND CONTRIBUTIONS*** | ***PLEDGED*** | ***EST. VALUE*** |
| FRANCE | Flights to evacuate 7 - 10,000 persons | up to approx. FRF 10 Million |
| ***TOTAL IN KIND CONTRIBUTIONS*** | | USD 1,984,000.00 |

1) Through UNDRO

0163

Annex II

GULF EMERGENCY PROGRAMME - PHASE II

IOM - PLAN OF ACTION

| Country | Nationals of: | Movements | |
|---|---|---|---|
| | | DEPARTED 18-30/01/91 | BOOKED TO DEPART 31/01-02/02/91 |
| JORDAN | | | |
| | Bangladesh | 0 | 75 |
| | Egypt | 4,138 | 0 |
| | India | 0 | 454 |
| | Pakistan | 0 | 30 |
| | Sri Lanka | 0 | 43 |
| | Sudan | 1,291 | 834 |
| | Vietnam | 963 | 0 |
| | Yemen | 569 | 0 |
| | Other | 119 | 0 |
| | | 7,080 | 1,436 |
| IRAN | | | |
| | Bangladesh | 0 | 2 |
| | Yemen | 0 | 11 |
| | | 0 | 13 |
| SYRIA | | | |
| | Somalia | 0 | 10 |
| | Sudan | 79 | 62 |
| | Others | 0 | 3 |
| | | 79 | 75 |
| SAUDI ARABIA | | | |
| | Pakistan | 24 | 0 |

7368C
31/1/91

0164

INTERNATIONAL ORGANIZATION FOR MIGRATION (IOM)
ORGANISATION INTERNATIONALE POUR LES MIGRATIONS (OIM)
ORGANIZACIÓN INTERNACIONAL PARA LAS MIGRACIONES (OIM)

Telephone: 717 91 11
Cable Address: Promigrant Geneva
Telex: 415 722
Telefax: 798 61 50

17, route des Morillons
P.O. Box 71
CH-1211 GENEVA 19
SWITZERLAND

TO: THE PERMANENT MISSIONS OF:

ARGENTINA, AUSTRALIA, AUSTRIA, BANGLADESH, BELIZE, BOLIVIA, BRAZIL, BELGIUM, CANADA, CAPE VERDE, CHILE, CHINA, COLOMBIA, COSTA RICA, CYPRUS, DENMARK, DOMINICAN REP., ECUADOR, EGYPT, EL SALVADOR, FRANCE, FINLAND, GERMANY, GHANA, GUINEA-BISSAU, GREECE, GUATEMALA, HOLY SEE, HONDURAS, INDIA, INDONESIA, IRAN, ISRAEL, ITALY, JAPAN, JORDAN, KENYA, KOREA (REP. OF), LUXEMBOURG, MEXICO, NETHERLANDS, NEW ZEALAND, NICARAGUA, NORWAY, PAKISTAN, PANAMA, PARAGUAY, PERU, PHILIPPINES, PORTUGAL, SAN MARINO, SAUDI ARABIA, SINGAPORE, SOMALIA, SPAIN, SRI LANKA, SUDAN, SWEDEN, SWITZERLAND, SYRIAN ARAB REP., THAILAND, TURKEY, UGANDA, U.S.S.R., UNITED KINGDOM, U.S.A., URUGUAY, VENEZUELA, VIETNAM, YUGOSLAVIA, ZIMBABWE AND THE COMMISSION OF THE EUROPEAN COMMUNITIES

COPY TO:
- SADRUDDIN AGA KHAN, PERSONAL REPRESENTATIVE OF THE U.N. SECRETARY GENERAL FOR HUMANITARIAN ASSISTANCE RELATING TO THE CRISIS BETWEEN IRAQ AND KUWAIT
- UNDRO GENEVA
- INTERNATIONAL BANK FOR RECONSTRUCTION AND DEVELOPMENT
- INTERNATIONAL COMMITTEE OF THE RED CROSS

FROM : INTERNATIONAL ORGANIZATION FOR MIGRATION, GENEVA

DATE : 31 JANUARY 1991

SUBJECT: IOM'S GULF EMERGENCY PROGRAMME : UPDATED PLAN OF ACTION

Since the Gulf Emergency Programme (GEP) began in September 1990, IOM has regularly updated its Plan of Action for the information of governments and organizations concerned. The latest update, reflecting the situation as at 15 January 1991, was issued on 17 January 1991.

Today's update adjusts, where necessary, previously-reported statistics concerning persons already evacuated or scheduled for evacuation by mid-January. It also reflects current information on contributions and settlement of obligations related to the aforementioned movements. As nearly all such obligations have now been met, **this will be the last update on IOM's GEP.** A final, audited financial statement will be submitted at the earliest possible opportunity.

On 11 January 1991, a consolidated Regional Humanitarian Plan of Action was launched. This co-ordinated, multi-agency approach to potential humanitarian relief needs in the event of large-scale outflow from Iraq and Kuwait included, as part of the overall United Nations-led effort, IOM's responsibility and plans for the transport of persons. **IOM will begin, as of today, a new and separate series of weekly updates on its activities under this consolidated Plan of Action. Entitled, for the sake of simplicity: <u>IOM's GEP II: Updated Plan of Action</u>, the first number will be sent to all recipients of this report automatically under separate cover.** Future updates will be numbered for easier reference.

0165

ANNEX I
Page 1

**GULF EMERGENCY PROGRAMME**
**PLEDGES AND RECEIPT FOR TRANSPORTATION**
**as at 31 January 1991**

| *1. CASH CONTRIBUTIONS* | *PLEDGED* | *RECEIVED USD* |
|---|---|---|
| AUSTRALIA | 3) AUD 1,250,000.00 | 1,028,833.08 |
| AUSTRIA | 1) ATS 3,000,000.00 | 234,521.00 |
| CANADA | 3) CAD 6,000,000.00 | 5,278,683.43 |
| DENMARK | 3) DKK 1,500,000.00 | 249,196.00 |
| FINLAND | 3) FIM 13,000,000.00 | 3,562,903.02 |
| | 8) USD 1,586,189.00 | 1,586,189.00 |
| GERMANY | 3) DEM 15,800,000.00 | 10,357,445.93 |
| ITALY | 1) USD 840,000.00 | 825,000.00 |
| JAPAN | 9) USD 9,920,000.00 | 9,920,000.00 |
| KOREA (REPUBLIC OF) | 3) USD 500,000.00 | 500,000.00 |
| LUXEMBOURG | 3) LUF 10,000,000.00 | 320,512.82 |
| NETHERLANDS | 3) NLG 2,000,000.00 | 1,174,225.74 |
| NORWAY | 3) NOK 24,500,000.00 | 4,096,414.64 |
| SWEDEN | 1) SEK 30,000,000.00 | 5,143,615.00 |
| SWITZERLAND | 3) CHF 250,000.00 | 192,307.69 |
| UNITED KINGDOM | 3) GBP 2,000,000.00 | 3,720,800.00 |
| U.S.A. | 3) USD 11,117,000.00 | 11,117,000.00 |
| EUROPEAN COMMUNITY | 2) USD 3,178,225.00 | 3,178,225.00 |
| | 4) USD 108,000.00 | 108,000.00 |
| | 5) ECU 3,000,000.00 | 2,388,684.50 |
| | 6) USD 97,625.00 | 97,625.00 |
| | 7) ECU 2,000,000.00 | |
| ICRC | 3) USD 300,000.00 | 300,000.00 |
| *2. PRIVATE DONATIONS* | | |
| US-AIM | USD 16,105.00 | 16,105.00 |
| AUSTCARE | AUD 75,000.00 | 62,500.00 |
| WORLD IN HARMONY | USD 159,500.00 | 159,500.00 |
| *TOTAL* | USD 69,967,019.00 | 65,618,286.85 |

1) through UNDRO (3% retained by UNDRO)
2) 50% of joint operations IOM/EEC of 20 flights (10 to Manila, 10 to Colombo)
3) Paid in full
4) For repatriation of approx. 540 Sudanese Nationals stranded in Jordan
5) For air Transportation ex. Jordan
6) For air Transportation Amman to Bombay
7) For air Transportation ex. Jordan and Turkey before 21 January 1991
Pledge reduced by ECU 2,000,000.00
8) Through UNDRO (3% retained by UNDRO) Include USD 272,480.00 for post return and reintegration assistance to persons displaced from Irak and Kuwait
9) Adjusted to reflect actual pledge/receipt/expenditure attributable solely to IOM. The remainder of the previously-reported contribution of USD 12.5 million was allocated to UNDRO and is reflected in its reporting and accounting.

0166

## GULF EMERGENCY PROGRAMME
## UTILIZED IN-KIND DONATIONS (FLIGHTS)
## as at 31 January 1991

(departures from Amman, Jordan)

| | *NO. OF FLIGHTS* | *TOTAL FLIGHTS* | *DESTINATION* | *NO. OF PAX* | *TOTAL PAX* | *USD TOTAL COST ESTIMATE If IOM had contracted equivalent space* |
|---|---|---|---|---|---|---|
| NEW ZEALAND | 5 | | Dhaka | 590 | | |
| GOVERNMENT | 3 | | Manila | 257 | | |
| | 4 | | Karachi | 450 | | |
| | 1 | | Colombo | 121 | | |
| | 1 | | Bombay | 129 | | |
| | | 14 | | | 1,547 | 907,856.00 |
| NORWAY | 3 | | Cairo | 297 | | |
| GOVERNMENT | | 3 | | | 297 | 74,250.00 |
| SPANISH | 8 | | Karachi | 2,103 | | |
| RED CROSS | 2 | | Bombay | 478 | | |
| | | 10 | | | 2,581 | 1,103,140.00 |
| SWEDISH | 6 | | Bombay | 2,812 | | |
| RED CROSS | 9 | | Dhaka | 4,138 | | |
| | 9 | | Colombo | 4,174 | | |
| | | 24 | | | 11,124 | 6,488,340.00 |
| SWITZERLAND | 4 | | Dhaka | 681 | | |
| GOVERNMENT | 14 | | Bombay | 2,775 | | |
| | 7 | | Colombo | 1,206 | | |
| | | 25 | | | 4,662 | 2,453,250.00 |
| UNITED | 4 | | Bombay | 1,561 | | |
| KINGDOM | 3 | | Dhaka | 1,170 | | |
| GOVERNMENT | | 7 | | | 2,731 | 1,455,160.00 |
| UNITED | 1 | | Colombo | 120 | | |
| STATES | 1 | | Dhaka | 122 | | |
| GOVERNMENT | 1 | | Manila | 119 | | |
| | | 3 | | | 361 | 249,792.00 |
| LUTHERAN | 8 | | Dhaka | 2,014 | | |
| WORLD | | | | | | |
| FEDERATION | | 8 | | | 2,014 | 1,268,820.00 |
| ICRC | 2 | | Bombay | 611 | | |
| | | 2 | | | 611 | 281,060.00 |
| SINGAPORE | 1 | | Colombo | 70 | | |
| GOVERNMENT | | 1 | | | 70 | 43,400.00 |
| BRUNEI | 1 | | Colombo | 70 | | |
| GOVERNMENT | | 1 | | | 70 | 43,400.00 |
| Taxes and fees applicable prior to waiver dates | | | | | | 1,011,652.00 |
| **TOTALS =** | | **98** | | | **26,068** | **15,380,120.00** |

NOTE: Above based on per seat costs as follows:
CMB 620, DAC 630, MNL 828, BOM 460, CAI 250, KHI 420

0167

Annex II

IOM - PLAN OF ACTION/UPDATED

| Country | Nationals of: | Movements DEPARTED 3/9/90-16/1/91 |
|---|---|---|
| JORDAN | | |
| | Bangladesh | 37,664 |
| | India | 29,594 |
| | Pakistan | 4,232 |
| | Philippines | 14,809 |
| | Sri Lanka | 42,404 |
| | Egypt | 301 |
| | Sudan | 6,720 |
| | Vietnam | 4,110 |
| | Other | 198 |
| | | 140,032 |
| TURKEY | | |
| | Bangladesh | 5,906 |
| | Pakistan | 591 |
| | Sri Lanka | 292 |
| | Sudan | 6 |
| | Vietnam | 1,085 |
| | Philippines | 9 |
| | | 7,889 |
| IRAQ | Sri Lanka | 4,678 |
| | Vietnam | 7,616 |
| | Philippines | 882 |
| | | 13,176 |
| IRAN | | |
| | Bangladesh | 269 |
| | India | 21 |
| | Pakistan | 74 |
| | Philippines | 7 |
| | Sri Lanka | 51 |
| | Other | 15 |
| | | 437 |
| SAUDI ARABIA | | |
| | Sri Lanka | 679 |
| OTHER | | |
| | Philippines | 281 |
| | Other | 106 |
| | | 387 |

0168

6894C

# GULF EMERGENCY PROGRAMME
## PAYMENTS
## as at 31 January 1991

| AIRLINE COMPANY | ROUTING | CHARTER | DATE OF DEPARTURE | NO. OF PAX | TOTAL PAX | PAID USD | TOTAL PAYMENT |
|---|---|---|---|---|---|---|---|
| ROYAL JORDANIAN AIRLINE | Amman - Dhaka | MIRJ 23 043 | 08.09.90 | 230 | | 177,000.00 | |
| | | MIRJ 23 044 | 09.09.90 | 227 | | 177,000.00 | |
| | | MIRJ 23 045 | 11.09.90 | 231 | | 177,000.00 | |
| | | MIRJ 23 046 | 11.09.90 | 231 | | 177,000.00 | |
| | | MIRJ 23 047 | 12.09.90 | 232 | | 177,000.00 | |
| | | MIRJ 23 048 | 13.09.90 | 231 | | 177,000.00 | |
| | | MIRJ 23 203 | 22.09.90 | 277 | | 159,500.00 | |
| | | MIRJ 23 204 | 23.09.90 | 277 | | 159,500.00 | |
| | | MIRJ 23 205 | 24.09.90 | 276 | | 159,500.00 | |
| | | MIRJ 23 206 | 25.09.90 | 275 | | 159,500.00 | |
| | | MIRJ 23 207 | 25.09.90 | 276 | | 159,500.00 | |
| | | MIRJ 23 208 | 26.09.90 | 275 | | 159,500.00 | |
| | | MIRJ 23 209 | 27.09.90 | 268 | | 159,500.00 | |
| | | MIRJ 23 210 | 28.09.90 | 280 | | 159,500.00 | |
| | | MIRJ 23 211 | 28.09.90 | 275 | | 159,500.00 | |
| | | MIRJ 23 212 | 29.09.90 | 275 | | 159,500.00 | |
| | | MIRJ 23 227 | 29.09.90 | 236 | | 134,000.00 | |
| | | MIRJ 23 228 | 30.09.90 | 237 | | 134,000.00 | |
| | | MIRJ 23 229 | 01.10.90 | 231 | | 134,000.00 | |
| | | MIRJ 23 230 | 02.10.90 | 278 | | 159,500.00 | |
| | | MIRJ 23 231 | 03.10.90 | 275 | | 159,500.00 | |
| | | MIRJ 23 232 | 04.10.90 | 276 | | 159,500.00 | |
| | | MIRJ 23 233 | 04.10.90 | 275 | | 159,500.00 | |
| | | MIRJ 23 234 | 04.10.90 | 275 | | 159,500.00 | |
| | | MIRJ 23 235 | 06.10.90 | 275 | | 159,500.00 | |
| | | MIRJ 23 236 | 07.10.90 | 276 | | 159,500.00 | |
| | | MIRJ 23 338 | 06.10.90 | 231 | | 134,000.00 | |
| | | MIRJ 23 339 | 07.10.90 | 231 | | 134,000.00 | |
| | | MIRJ 23 363 | 08.10.90 | 240 | | 159,500.00 | |
| | | MIRJ 23 364 | 09.10.90 | 275 | | 159,500.00 | |
| | | MIRJ 23 365 | 10.10.90 | 277 | | 159,500.00 | |
| | | PF 0/71310 | 21.10.90 | 46 | | 17,480.00 | |
| | | PF 0/71316 | 21.10.90 | 26 | | 8,495.00 | |
| | | PF 0/71324 | 31.10.90 | 10 | | 5,568.50 | |
| | | PF 0/71343 | 07.11.90 | 14 | | 5,320.00 | |
| | | PF 0/71358 | 14.11.90 | 12 | | 4,560.00 | |
| | | PF 0/71367 | 21.11.90 | 14 | | 5,320.00 | |
| | | PF 0/71379 | 25.11.90 | 8 | | 3,040.00 | |
| | | PF 0/71384 | 05.12.90 | 103 | | 39,140.00 | |
| | | PF 0/71398 | 09.12.90 | 17 | | 6,460.00 | |
| | | PF 0/71405 | 12.12.90 | 9 | | 3,420.00 | |
| | | PF 0/71411 | 18.12.90 | 5 | | 1,900.00 | |
| | | PF 0/71426 | 25.12.90 | 2 | | 760.00 | |
| | | PF 1/71502 | 01.01.91 | 5 | | 1,900.00 | |
| | | PF 1/71509 | 09.01.91 | 7 | | 2,660.00 | |
| | | PF 1/71522 | 12.01.91 | 7 | 8,309 | 2,660.00 | 5,030,683.50 |
| | Amman - Colombo | MIRJ 23 001 | 03.09.90 | 182 | | 137,500.00 | |
| | | MIRJ 23 002 | 04.09.90 | 184 | | 137,500.00 | |

0169

| | | | |
|---|---|---|---|
| MIRJ 23 003 | 05.09.90 | 187 | 137,500.00 |
| MIRJ 23 004 | 05.09.90 | 182 | 137,500.00 |
| MIRJ 23 005 | 06.09.90 | 184 | 137,500.00 |
| MIRJ 23 006 | 07.09.90 | 183 | 137,500.00 |
| MIRJ 23 049 | 08.09.90 | 183 | 137,500.00 |
| MIRJ 23 050 | 09.09.90 | 183 | 137,500.00 |
| MIRJ 23 051 | 10.09.90 | 185 | 137,500.00 |
| MIRJ 23 052 | 10.09.90 | 188 | 137,500.00 |
| MIRJ 23 053 | 11.09.90 | 181 | 137,500.00 |
| MIRJ 23 054 | 13.09.90 | 190 | 137,500.00 |
| MIRJ 23 091 | 13.09.90 | 183 | 114,660.00 |
| MIRJ 23 092 | 14.09.90 | 190 | 114,660.00 |
| MIRJ 23 093 | 15.09.90 | 182 | 114,660.00 |
| MIRJ 23 094 | 16.09.90 | 182 | 114,660.00 |
| MIRJ 23 095 | 16.09.90 | 182 | 114,660.00 |
| MIRJ 23 096 | 17.09.90 | 182 | 114,660.00 |
| MIRJ 23 097 | 18.09.90 | 182 | 114,660.00 |
| MIRJ 23 098 | 19.09.90 | 182 | 114,660.00 |
| MIRJ 23 099 | 19.09.90 | 275 | 165,000.00 |
| MIRJ 23 100 | 20.09.90 | 275 | 165,000.00 |
| MIRJ 23 101 | 20.09.90 | 275 | 165,000.00 |
| MIRJ 23 102 | 20.09.90 | 275 | 165,000.00 |
| MIRJ 23 237 | 29.09.90 | 182 | 92,820.00 |
| MIRJ 23 238 | 30.09.90 | 178 | 92,820.00 |
| MIRJ 23 239 | 01.10.90 | 182 | 92,820.00 |
| MIRJ 23 240 | 01.10.90 | 179 | 92,820.00 |
| MIRJ 23 300 | 02.10.90 | 183 | 92,820.00 |
| MIRJ 23 301 | 02.10.90 | 198 | 92,820.00 |
| MIRJ 23 302 | 03.10.90 | 182 | 92,820.00 |
| MIRJ 23 303 | 04.10.90 | 183 | 92,820.00 |
| MIRJ 23 304 | 04.10.90 | 183 | 92,820.00 |
| MIRJ 23 305 | 05.10.90 | 181 | 92,820.00 |
| MIRJ 23 321 | 05.10.90 | 182 | 92,820.00 |
| MIRJ 23 322 | 06.10.90 | 183 | 92,820.00 |
| MIRJ 23 323 | 06.10.90 | 184 | 92,820.00 |
| MIRJ 23 324 | 06.10.90 | 182 | 92,820.00 |
| MIRJ 23 325 | 07.10.90 | 183 | 92,820.00 |
| MIRJ 23 384 | 08.10.90 | 180 | 92,820.00 |
| MIRJ 23 385 | 09.10.90 | 182 | 92,820.00 |
| MIRJ 23 386 | 09.10.90 | 231 | 117,810.00 |
| MIRJ 23 387 | 10.10.90 | 181 | 92,820.00 |
| MIRJ 23 388 | 11.10.90 | 184 | 92,820.00 |
| MIRJ 23 435 | 08.10.90 | 181 | 92,820.00 |
| MIRJ 23 436 | 09.10.90 | 182 | 92,820.00 |
| MIRJ 23 437 | 10.10.90 | 182 | 92,820.00 |
| MIRJ 23 438 | 11.10.90 | 187 | 92,820.00 |
| MIRJ 23 439 | 11.10.90 | 182 | 92,820.00 |
| MIRJ 23 441 | 09.10.90 | 179 | 92,820.00 |
| MIRJ 23 442 | 09.10.90 | 182 | 92,820.00 |
| MIRJ 23 455 | 09.10.90 | 182 | 92,820.00 |
| MIRJ 23 456 | 11.10.90 | 275 | 140,250.00 |
| MIRJ 23 466 | 17.10.90 | 277 | 140,250.00 |
| MIRJ 23 467 | 17.10.90 | 277 | 117,800.00 |
| PF 0/71349 | 11.11.90 | 12 | 4,572.00 |

| | | | | | | |
|---|---|---|---|---|---|---|
| | PF 0/71353 | 13.11.90 | 19 | | 7,239.00 | |
| | PF 0/71359 | 16.11.90 | 24 | | 9,144.00 | |
| | PF 0/71363 | 18.11.90 | 10 | | 3,810.00 | |
| | PF 0/71368 | 21.11.90 | 15 | | 5,715.00 | |
| | PF 0/71375 | 25.11.90 | 26 | | 9,906.00 | |
| | PF 0/71380 | 26.11.90 | 19 | | 7,239.00 | |
| | PF 0/71382 | 28.11.90 | 23 | | 8,763.00 | |
| | PF 0/71386 | 30.11.90 | 20 | | 7,620.00 | |
| | PF 0/71391 | 03.12.90 | 6 | | 2,286.00 | |
| | PF 0/71396 | 07.12.90 | 11 | | 4,361.00 | |
| | PF 0/71402 | 12.12.90 | 20 | | 7,620.00 | |
| | PF 0/71404 | 10.12.90 | 4 | | 1,524.00 | |
| | PF 0/71406 | 13.12.90 | 30 | | 11,430.00 | |
| | PF 0/71407 | 15.12.90 | 65 | | 24,765.00 | |
| | PF 0/71413 | 17.12.90 | 5 | | 1,905.00 | |
| | PF 0/71414 | 20.12.90 | 40 | | 15,240.00 | |
| | PF 0/71419 | 21.12.90 | 3 | | 990.60 | |
| | PF 0/71422 | 23.12.90 | 8 | | 3,048.00 | |
| | PF 0/71430 | 26.12.90 | 10 | | 3,810.00 | |
| | PF 0/71432 | 29.12.90 | 19 | | 7,239.00 | |
| | PF 0/71437 | 31.12.90 | 10 | | 3,810.00 | |
| | PF 1/71506 | 03.01.91 | 9 | | 3,429.00 | |
| | PF 1/71512 | 06.01.91 | 10 | | 3,024.20 | |
| | PF 1/71516 | 09.01.91 | 9 | | 3,429.00 | |
| | PF 1/71517 | 08.01.91 | 3 | 11,196 | 1,080.00 | 6,412,528.80 |
| **Amman - Manila** | MIRJ 23 202 | 19.09.90 | 231 | | 184,800.00 | |
| | MIRJ 23 311 | 03.10.90 | 226 | | 184,800.00 | |
| | MIRJ 23 312 | 04.10.90 | 239 | | 184,800.00 | |
| | MIRJ 23 313 | 08.10.90 | 231 | | 184,800.00 | |
| | MIRJ 23 314 | 10.10.90 | 233 | | 184,800.00 | |
| | MIRJ 23 315 | 11.10.90 | 231 | | 184,800.00 | |
| | MIRJ 23 318 | 15.10.90 | 231 | | 184,800.00 | |
| | MIRJ 23 320 | 18.10.90 | 275 | | 220,000.00 | |
| | MIRJ 23 475 | 06.11.90 | 275 | | 165,000.00 | |
| | PF 0/71313 | 24.10.90 | 84 | | 45,024.00 | |
| | PF 0/71314 | 25.10.90 | 40 | | 21,440.00 | |
| | PF 0/71321 | 21.10.90 | 61 | | 32,696.00 | |
| | PF 0/71323 | 31.10.90 | 151 | | 79,882.50 | |
| | PF 0/71350 | 11.11.90 | 159 | | 84,456.10 | |
| | PF 0/71354 | 14.11.90 | 41 | | 21,815.20 | |
| | PF 0/71366 | 21.11.90 | 18 | | 9,648.00 | |
| | PF 0/71376 | 25.11.90 | 8 | | 4,288.00 | |
| | PF 0/71385 | 28.11.90 | 14 | | 7,343.20 | |
| | PF 0/71395 | 05.12.90 | 11 | | 5,449.70 | |
| | PF 0/71423 | 23.12.90 | 5 | | 2,680.00 | |
| | PF 0/71427 | 26.12.90 | 4 | | 1,697.70 | |
| | PF 0/71435 | 30.12.90 | 5 | | 2,680.00 | |
| | PF 350/43 | 31.10.90 | 2 | | 1,072.00 | |
| | PF 1/71503 | 02.01.91 | 51 | | 26,253.60 | |
| | PF 1/71504 | 03.01.91 | 81 | 2,907 | 43,416.00 | 2,068,442.00 |
| **Amman - Karachi** | MIRJ 23 317 | 14.10.90 | 148 | | 72,800.00 | |
| | MIRJ 23 362 | 07.10.90 | 278 | | 110,000.00 | |
| | MIRJ 23 366 | 11.10.90 | 281 | | 110,000.00 | |
| | PF 0/71319 | 26.10.90 | 69 | | 22,096.80 | |

0171

| | | | | | | |
|---|---|---|---|---|---|---|
| | PF 0/71334 | 02.11.90 | 7 | | 2,268.00 | |
| | PF 0/71346 | 11.11.90 | 76 | | 23,938.70 | |
| | PF 0/71360 | 16.11.90 | 42 | | 13,608.00 | |
| | PF 0/71365 | 19.11.90 | 20 | | 5,276.10 | |
| | PF 0/71372 | 21.11.90 | 7 | | 2,268.00 | |
| | PF 0/71377 | 28.11.90 | 31 | | 10,044.00 | |
| | PF 0/71397 | 07.12.90 | 19 | | 6,156.00 | |
| | PF 0/71410 | 16.12.90 | 16 | | 5,184.00 | |
| | PF 0/71420 | 23.12.90 | 21 | | 6,526.20 | |
| | PF 0/71424 | 24.12.90 | 3 | | 972.00 | |
| | PF 0/71433 | 28.12.90 | 1 | | 324.00 | |
| | PF 0/71436 | 31.12.90 | 81 | | 25,558.70 | |
| | PF 1/71505 | 04.01.91 | 3 | | 972.00 | |
| | PF 1/71523 | 12.01.91 | 10 | 1,113 | 3,240.00 | 421,232.50 |
| **Amman - Bombay** | MIRJ 23 389 | 12.10.90 | 232 | | 103,950.00 | |
| | MIRJ 23 440 | 12.10.90 | 183 | | 81,900.00 | |
| | MIRJ 23 465 | 16.10.90 | 181 | | 81,900.00 | |
| | MIRJ 23 474 | 02.11.90 | 278 | | 97,625.00 | |
| | MIRJ 23 476 | 08.11.90 | 268 | | 96,560.00 | |
| | MIRJ 23 477 | 08.11.90 | 184 | | 63,900.00 | |
| | MIRJ 23 478 | 09.11.90 | 280 | | 96,560.00 | |
| | MIRJ 23 479 | 10.11.90 | 246 | | 87,330.00 | |
| | MIRJ 23 480 | 12.11.90 | 278 | | 97,625.00 | |
| | MIRJ 23 481 | 13.11.90 | 276 | | 97,625.00 | |
| | MIRJ 23 482 | 12.11.90 | 294 | | 97,625.00 | |
| | MIRJ 23 483 | 14.11.90 | 276 | | 97,625.00 | |
| | MIRJ 23 484 | 13.11.90 | 233 | | 82,000.00 | |
| | MIRJ 23 485 | 15.11.90 | 282 | | 97,625.00 | |
| | MIRJ 23 486 | 15.11.90 | 234 | | 82,000.00 | |
| | MIRJ 23 487 | 15.11.90 | 282 | | 97,625.00 | |
| | MIRJ 23 488 | 15.11.90 | 188 | | 63,900.00 | |
| | MIRJ 23 489 | 16.11.90 | 285 | | 97,625.00 | |
| | MIRJ 23 490 | 16.11.90 | 184 | | 63,900.00 | |
| | MIRJ 23 491 | 16.11.90 | 194 | | 63,900.00 | |
| | MIRJ 23 492 | 19.11.90 | 182 | | 63,545.00 | |
| | MIRJ 23 493 | 19.11.90 | 188 | | 63,900.00 | |
| | MIRJ 23 494 | 20.11.90 | 274 | | 96,560.00 | |
| | MIRJ 23 495 | 21.11.90 | 281 | | 97,625.00 | |
| | MIRJ 23 496 | 21.11.90 | 242 | | 82,000.00 | |
| | MIRJ 23 497 | 22.11.90 | 292 | | 97,625.00 | |
| | MIRJ 23 498 | 24.11.90 | 185 | | 63,545.00 | |
| | PF 0/71317 | 25.10.90 | 127 | | 47,700.40 | |
| | PF 0/71320 | 27.10.90 | 32 | | 11,919.60 | |
| | PF 0/71327 | 29.10.90 | 74 | | 27,526.80 | |
| | PF 0/71328 | 31.10.90 | 19 | | 7,353.00 | |
| | PF 0/71333 | 03.11.90 | 71 | | 26,935.20 | |
| | PF 0/71341 | 07.11.90 | 16 | | 5,882.40 | |
| | PF 0/71344 | 07.11.90 | 42 | | 14,412.60 | |
| | PF 0/71374 | 24.11.90 | 12 | | 4,489.20 | |
| | PF 0/71387 | 29.11.90 | 12 | | 4,064.80 | |
| | PF 0/71394 | 04.12.90 | 10 | | 3,650.00 | |
| | PF 0/71399 | 09.12.90 | 12 | | 3,942.00 | |
| | PF 0/71403 | 12.12.90 | 7 | | 2,409.00 | |
| | PF 0/71408 | 15.12.90 | 19 | | 6,935.00 | |

| Route | Reference | Date | Pax | Total pax | Amount | Total amount |
|---|---|---|---|---|---|---|
| | PF 0/71418 | 22.12.90 | 17 | | 6,120.00 | |
| | PF 0/71425 | 24.12.90 | 6 | | 2,160.00 | |
| | PF 0/71428 | 26.12.90 | 19 | | 6,696.00 | |
| | PF 1/71507 | 03.01.91 | 1 | | 360.00 | |
| | PF 1/71510 | 06.01.91 | 5 | 7,003 | 1,656.00 | 2,497,812.00 |
| Amman - Santiago | PF 0/71306 | 26.10.90 | 1 | | 1,924.50 | |
| | | | | 1 | | 1,924.50 |
| Amman - Mauritius | PF 0/71315 | 23.10.90 | 3 | | 3,372.45 | |
| | | | | 3 | | 3,372.45 |
| Amman - Abu Dhabi | PF 0/71318 | 24.10.90 | 3 | | 561.60 | |
| | | | | 3 | | 561.60 |
| Amman - Ad. Abeba | PF 0/71336 | 04.11.90 | 1 | | 449.60 | |
| | | | | 1 | | 449.60 |
| Amman - London | PF 0/71381 | 26.11.90 | 2 | | 492.00 | |
| | | | | 2 | | 492.00 |
| Amman - Khartoum | MIRJ 23 499 | 10.12.90 | 275 | | 53,625.00 | |
| | MIRJ 23 908 | 11.12.90 | 276 | | 53,625.00 | |
| | MIRJ 23 910 | 13.12.90 | 263 | | 53,430.00 | |
| | MIRJ 23 914 | 23.12.90 | 231 | | 45,045.00 | |
| | MIRJ 23 918 | 31.12.90 | 233 | | 45,045.00 | |
| | MIRJ 23 007 | 04.01.91 | 183 | | 35,490.00 | |
| | MIRJ 23 008 | 04.01.91 | 187 | | 35,295.00 | |
| | MIRJ 23 014 | 07.01.91 | 188 | | 35,490.00 | |
| | PF 0/71370 | 21.11.90 | 1 | 1,837 | 422.50 | 357,467.50 |
| Amman - Tripoli | PF 0/71331 | 03.11.90 | 1 | | 161.50 | |
| | | | | 1 | | 161.50 |
| Amman - S. Antonio | PF 0/71393 | 07.12.90 | 1 | | 718.40 | |
| | | | | 1 | | 718.40 |
| Amman - Bangkok | PF 350/44 | 31.10.90 | 1 | | 457.50 | |
| | | | | 1 | | 457.50 |
| Amman - Geneva | PF 350/75 | 02.12.90 | 1 | | 529.80 | |
| | | | | 1 | | 529.80 |
| Amman - New Delhi | PF 0/71415 | 21.12.90 | 53 | | 18,550.00 | |
| | | | | 53 | | 18,550.00 |
| Amman - Mogadishu | PF 0/71390 | 02.12.90 | 2 | | 1,171.70 | |
| | | | | 2 | | 1,171.70 |
| Amman - Djibouti | PF 0/71417 | 23.12.90 | 1 | | 350.70 | |
| | | | | 1 | | 350.70 |
| Amman - Hanoi | MIRJ 23 001 | 02.01.91 | 273 | | 177,450.00 | |
| | MIRJ 23 002 | 02.01.91 | 229 | | 148,850.00 | |
| | MIRJ 23 003 | 03.01.91 | 229 | | 148,850.00 | |
| | MIRJ 23 004 | 04.01.91 | 273 | | 177,450.00 | |
| | MIRJ 23 009 | 04.01.91 | 229 | | 148,850.00 | |
| | MIRJ 23 010 | 05.01.91 | 229 | | 148,850.00 | |
| | MIRJ 23 011 | 06.01.91 | 229 | | 148,850.00 | |
| | MIRJ 23 012 | 06.01.91 | 229 | | 148,850.00 | |
| | MIRJ 23 013 | 06.01.91 | 229 | | 148,850.00 | |
| | MIRJ 23 015 | 07.01.91 | 229 | | 148,850.00 | |
| | MIRJ 23 016 | 08.01.91 | 273 | | 177,450.00 | |
| | MIRJ 23 017 | 08.01.91 | 229 | 2,880 | 148,850.00 | 1,872,000.00 |
| Amman - New Delhi | PF 1/71519 | 09.01.91 | 3 | | 1,050.00 | |
| | | | | 3 | | 1,050.00 |
| Escort cost | | | | | 1,327.19 | |
| | | | | 35,318 | | 18,691,283.24 |

0173

| AIRLINE COMPANY | ROUTING | CHARTER | DATE OF DEPARTURE | NO. OF PAX | TOTAL PAX | PAID USD | TOTAL PAYMENT |
|---|---|---|---|---|---|---|---|
| TOWER AIR | Amman - Manila | MIFF 23 074 | 11.09.90 | 480 | | 380,000.00 | |
| | | MIFF 23 075 | 13.09.90 | 477 | | 380,000.00 | |
| | | MIFF 23 076 | 14.09.90 | 487 | | 380,000.00 | |
| | | MIFF 23 077 | 15.09.90 | 477 | | 380,000.00 | |
| | | MIFF 23 078 | 17.09.90 | 486 | | 380,000.00 | |
| | | MIFF 23 079 | 19.09.90 | 481 | | 380,000.00 | |
| | | MIFF 23 080 | 20.09.90 | 477 | | 380,000.00 | |
| | | MIFF 23 081 | 22.09.90 | 474 | | 380,000.00 | |
| | | MIFF 23 082 | 23.09.90 | 484 | | 380,000.00 | |
| | | MIFF 23 083 | 25.09.90 | 476 | | 380,000.00 | |
| | | MIFF 23 084 | 26.09.90 | 482 | | 380,000.00 | |
| | | MIFF 23 085 | 28.09.90 | 476 | | 380,000.00 | |
| | | MIFF 23 086 | 29.09.90 | 479 | | 380,000.00 | |
| | | MIFF 23 087 | 02.10.90 | 472 | | 380,000.00 | |
| | | MIFF 23 088 | 04.10.90 | 486 | | 380,000.00 | |
| | | MIFF 23 361 | 11.10.90 | 489 | 7,683 | 380,000.00 | 6,080,000.00 |
| | Amman - Bombay | MIFF 23 357 | 07.10.90 | 483 | | 220,000.00 | |
| | | MIFF 23 358 | 08.10.90 | 484 | | 220,000.00 | |
| | | MIFF 23 359 | 09.10.90 | 483 | | 220,000.00 | |
| | | MIFF 23 360 | 10.10.90 | 481 | 1,931 | 220,000.00 | 880,000.00 |
| | | | | | 9,614 | | 6,960,000.00 |

| AIRLINE COMPANY | ROUTING | CHARTER | DATE OF DEPARTURE | NO. OF PAX | TOTAL PAX | PAID USD | TOTAL PAYMENT |
|---|---|---|---|---|---|---|---|
| TURKISH AIRLINES | Diyarbakir - Dhaka | MITK 23 500 | 12.09.90 | 201 | | 133,000.00 | |
| | | MITK 23 501 | 12.09.90 | 200 | | 133,000.00 | |
| | | MITK 23 502 | 12.09.90 | 201 | | 133,000.00 | |
| | | MITK 23 503 | 12.09.90 | 200 | | 133,000.00 | |
| | | MITK 23 504 | 13.09.90 | 200 | | 133,000.00 | |
| | | MITK 23 506 | 18.09.90 | 330 | | 217,750.00 | |
| | | MITK 23 507 | 18.09.90 | 200 | | 133,000.00 | |
| | | MITK 23 508 | 19.09.90 | 200 | | 133,000.00 | |
| | | MITK 23 509 | 21.09.90 | 201 | | 133,000.00 | |
| | | MITK 23 532 | 19.09.90 | 349 | | 227,500.00 | |
| | | MITK 23 533 | 20.09.90 | 350 | | 227,500.00 | |
| | | MITK 23 534 | 21.09.90 | 351 | | 227,500.00 | |
| | | MITK 23 535 | 22.09.90 | 280 | 3,263 | 182,000.00 | 2,146,250.00 |
| | Diyarbakir- Karachi | MITK 23 536 | 25.09.90 | 211 | | 80,000.00 | |
| | | MITK 23 537 | 27.09.90 | 211 | 422 | 80,000.00 | 160,000.00 |
| | Diyarbakir- Hanoi | MITK 23 565 | 25.10.90 | 202 | | 150,000.00 | |
| | | MITK 23 566 | 26.10.90 | 200 | | 150,000.00 | |
| | | MITK 23 567 | 27.10.90 | 93 | 495 | 150,000.00 | 450,000.00 |
| | | | | | 4,180 | | 2,756,250.00 |

| AIRLINE COMPANY | ROUTING | CHARTER | DATE OF DEPARTURE | NO. OF PAX | TOTAL PAX | PAID USD | TOTAL PAYMENT |
|---|---|---|---|---|---|---|---|
| TATE AERO - SERVICES | Amman - Dhaka | MITA 23 007 | 04.09.90 | 165 | | 119,955.00 | |
| | | MITA 23 008 | 05.09.90 | 166 | | 119,955.00 | |
| | | MITA 23 009 | 06.09.90 | 165 | | 119,955.00 | |
| | | MITA 23 010 | 07.09.90 | 165 | | 119,955.00 | |

| | | | | | | | |
|---|---|---|---|---|---|---|---|
| | | MITA 23 011 | 08.09.90 | 165 | | 119,955.00 | |
| | | MITA 23 012 | 09.09.90 | 170 | | 119,955.00 | |
| | | MITA 23 013 | 09.09.90 | 167 | | 119,955.00 | |
| | | MITA 23 014 | 10.09.90 | 165 | | 119,955.00 | |
| | | MITA 23 057 | 10.09.90 | 265 | | 177,762.00 | |
| | | MILZ 23 422 | 19.10.90 | 155 | 1,748 | 99,659.00 | 1,237,061.00 |
| | Amman - Colombo | RJ 1980/1 | 01.10.90 | 182 | | 108,472.00 | |
| | | RJ 1982/3 | 02.10.90 | 182 | | 108,472.00 | |
| | | RJ 1986/7 | 02.10.90 | 231 | | 137,676.00 | |
| | | RJ 1984/5 | 03.10.90 | 182 | | 108,472.00 | |
| | | RJ 1988/9 | 03.10.90 | 231 | | 137,676.00 | |
| | | MILZ 23 340 | 06.10.90 | 151 | | 77,010.00 | |
| | | MILZ 23 341 | 07.10.90 | 152 | | 77,010.00 | |
| | | MILZ 23 342 | 08.10.90 | 151 | | 77,010.00 | |
| | | MILZ 23 343 | 09.10.90 | 151 | | 77,010.00 | |
| | | MILZ 23 344 | 09.10.90 | 151 | | 77,010.00 | |
| | | MILZ 23 408 | 10.10.90 | 151 | | 77,010.00 | |
| | | MILZ 23 409 | 10.10.90 | 151 | | 77,010.00 | |
| | | MILZ 23 410 | 10.10.90 | 151 | | 77,010.00 | |
| | | MILZ 23 411 | 11.10.90 | 151 | | 77,010.00 | |
| | | MILZ 23 412 | 11.10.90 | 151 | | 77,010.00 | |
| | | MILZ 23 413 | 12.10.90 | 151 | | 77,010.00 | |
| | | MILZ 23 414 | 12.10.90 | 151 | | 77,010.00 | |
| | | MILZ 23 415 | 13.10.90 | 151 | | 77,010.00 | |
| | | MILZ 23 416 | 13.10.90 | 152 | | 77,010.00 | |
| | | MILZ 23 417 | 15.10.90 | 157 | | 80,070.00 | |
| | | MILZ 23 418 | 15.10.90 | 156 | | 80,070.00 | |
| | | MILZ 23 419 | 16.10.90 | 157 | | 80,070.00 | |
| | | MILZ 23 420 | 16.10.90 | 161 | | 82,110.00 | |
| | | MILZ 23 421 | 17.10.90 | 157 | | 80,070.00 | |
| | | MILZ 23 425 | 22.10.90 | 161 | | 82,110.00 | |
| | | MILZ 23 426 | 22.10.90 | 162 | 4,235 | 82,110.00 | 2,245,518.00 |
| | Amman - Bombay | MILZ 23 424 | 21.10.90 | 152 | | 79,373.00 | |
| | | | | | 152 | | 79,373.00 |
| | Amman - Karachi | MILZ 23 423 | 19.10.90 | 163 | | 71,967.00 | |
| | | | | | 163 | | 71,967.00 |
| | | | | | 6,298 | | 3,633,919.00 |

| AIRLINE COMPANY | ROUTING | CHARTER | DATE OF DEPARTURE | NO. OF PAX | TOTAL PAX | PAID USD | TOTAL PAYMENT |
|---|---|---|---|---|---|---|---|
| SAUDI ARAB AIRLINES | Riyadh - Colombo | MISV 23 751 | 22.09.90 | 414 | | 106,666.00 | |
| | | MISV 23 752 | 11.10.90 | 265 | | 90,667.00 | |
| | | | | | 679 | | 197,333.00 |

| AIRLINE COMPANY | ROUTING | CHARTER | DATE OF DEPARTURE | NO. OF PAX | TOTAL PAX | PAID USD | TOTAL PAYMENT |
|---|---|---|---|---|---|---|---|
| EVER-GREEN INT. AIRLINES | Amman - Colombo | MIEZ 23 105 | 15.09.90 | 501 | | 315,630.00 | |
| | | MIEZ 23 106 | 17.09.90 | 494 | | 315,630.00 | |
| | | MIEZ 23 107 | 19.09.90 | 500 | | 315,630.00 | |
| | | MIEZ 23 108 | 20.09.90 | 501 | | 315,630.00 | |
| | | MIEZ 23 109 | 29.09.90 | 488 | | 315,630.00 | |
| | | MIEZ 23 110 | 01.10.90 | 500 | | 315,630.00 | |
| | | MIEZ 23 111 | 05.10.90 | 500 | | 309,330.00 | |

0175

| | | | | | | | |
|---|---|---|---|---|---|---|---|
| | | MIEZ 23 112 | 06.10.90 | 501 | | 315,630.00 | |
| | | MIEZ 23 348 | 17.10.90 | 500 | 4,485 | 285,570.00 | 2,804,310.00 |
| | Amman - Bombay | MIEZ 23 345 | 09.10.90 | 509 | | 275,550.00 | |
| | | MIEZ 23 346 | 10.10.90 | 500 | | 275,550.00 | |
| | | MIEZ 23 347 | 10.10.90 | 505 | 1,514 | 275,550.00 | 826,650.00 |
| | Depositioning | | | | | 65,469.05 | |
| | | | | | 5,999 | | 3,630,960.00 |

| AIRLINE COMPANY | ROUTING | CHARTER | DATE OF DEPARTURE | NO. OF PAX | TOTAL PAX | PAID USD | TOTAL PAYMENT |
|---|---|---|---|---|---|---|---|
| OMEGA AIRLINES | Amman - Colombo | MIOM 23 113 | 14.09.90 | 180 | | 108,000.00 | |
| | | | | | 180 | | 108,000.00 |

| AIRLINE COMPANY | ROUTING | CHARTER | DATE OF DEPARTURE | NO. OF PAX | TOTAL PAX | PAID USD | TOTAL PAYMENT |
|---|---|---|---|---|---|---|---|
| PAKISTAN INT. AIRLINES | Teheran - | MIPK 23 800 | 17.09.90 | | | | |
| | - Dhaka | | | 88 | | | |
| | Colombo | | | 25 | | | |
| | Karachi | | | 11 | | | |
| | | | | | 124 | 86,230.00 | 86,230.00 |
| | Teheran - Karachi | PF 0/70095 | 24.09.90 | 11 | | 2,579.22 | |
| | | PF 0/70099 | 01.10.90 | 10 | | 4,176.92 | |
| | | PF 0/70155 | 15.10.90 | 5 | | 1,097.03 | |
| | | PF 0/70162 | 29.10.90 | 5 | | 1,296.41 | |
| | | PF 0/70164 | 05.11.90 | 1 | | 433.48 | |
| | | PF 0/70173 | 03.12.90 | 2 | 34 | 1,738.50 | 11,321.56 |
| | Teheran - Lahore | PF 0/70156 | 15.10.90 | 5 | | 1,801.67 | |
| | | PF 0/70170 | 26.11.90 | 6 | 11 | 2,388.19 | 4,189.86 |
| | Teheran - Colombo | PF 0/70158 | 22.10.90 | 2 | | 1,380.34 | |
| | | PF 0/70154 | 15.10.90 | 3 | | 2,021.62 | |
| | | PF 0/70165 | 05.11.90 | 5 | | 3,462.65 | |
| | | PF 0/70167 | 26.11.90 | 1 | | 693.70 | |
| | | PF 0/70168 | 19.11.90 | 1 | | 347.24 | |
| | | PF 0/70171 | 26.11.90 | 1 | | 693.70 | |
| | | | | | 13 | | 8,599.25 |
| | Teheran - Manila | PF 0/70152B | 08.10.90 | 3 | | 1,361.52 | |
| | | | | | 3 | | 1,361.52 |
| | Teheran - Bangkok | PF 0/70160 | 29.10.90 | 3 | | 1,505.19 | |
| | | | | | 3 | | 1,505.19 |
| | Teheran - Islamabad | PF 0/70163 | 29.10.90 | 1 | | 526.98 | |
| | | | | | 1 | | 526.98 |
| | Teheran - Dhaka | PF 0/70166 | 05.11.90 | 6 | | 4,052.58 | |
| | | | | | 6 | | 4,052.58 |
| | Teheran - | PF 0/70093 | 01.10.90 | | | | |
| | Bangkok | | | 5 | | 3,403.08 | |
| | Colombo | | | 1 | | 624.62 | |
| | Karachi | | | 5 | 11 | 1,290.77 | 5,318.47 |
| | | | | | 206 | | 123,105.41 |

| AIRLINE COMPANY | ROUTING | CHARTER | DATE OF DEPARTURE | NO. OF PAX | TOTAL PAX | PAID USD | TOTAL PAYMENT |
|---|---|---|---|---|---|---|---|
| JAPAN AIRLINES | Amman - Manila | MIJL 23 128 | 23.09.90 | 272 | | 240,000.00 | |
| | | MIJL 23 095 | 05.10.90 | 239 | | 191,200.00 | |
| | | | | | 511 | | 431,200.00 |

| AIRLINE COMPANY | ROUTING | CHARTER | DATE OF DEPARTURE | NO. OF PAX | TOTAL PAX | PAID USD | TOTAL PAYMENT |
|---|---|---|---|---|---|---|---|
| NATIONAIR | Amman - Bombay | MINX 23 261 | 30.09.90 | 290 | | 126,000.00 | |
| | | MINX 23 262 | 01.10.90 | 269 | | 126,000.00 | |
| | | MINX 23 263 | 02.10.90 | 253 | | 126,000.00 | |
| | | MINX 23 264 | 03.10.90 | 259 | | 126,000.00 | |
| | | MINX 23 265 | 04.10.90 | 265 | | 126,000.00 | |
| | | MINX 23 266 | 05.10.90 | 259 | | 126,000.00 | |
| | | MINX 23 267 | 06.10.90 | 258 | | 126,000.00 | |
| | | MINX 23 268 | 07.10.90 | 253 | | 126,000.00 | |
| | | MINX 23 269 | 08.10.90 | 254 | | 126,000.00 | |
| | | MINX 23 270 | 09.10.90 | 255 | | 126,000.00 | |
| | | MINX 23 271 | 10.10.90 | 252 | | 126,000.00 | |
| | | MINX 23 272 | 11.10.90 | 251 | | 126,000.00 | |
| | | MINX 23 273 | 01.10.90 | 478 | | 228,200.00 | |
| | | MINX 23 274 | 02.10.90 | 487 | | 228,200.00 | |
| | | MINX 23 275 | 03.10.90 | 480 | | 228,200.00 | |
| | | MINX 23 276 | 04.10.90 | 490 | | 228,200.00 | |
| | | MINX 23 284 | 13.10.90 | 482 | | 204,400.00 | |
| | | MINX 23 285 | 14.10.90 | 480 | | 204,400.00 | |
| | | MINX 23 287 | 21.10.90 | 449 | 6,464 | 204,400.00 | 3,038,000.00 |
| | Amman - Colombo | MINX 23 277 | 06.10.90 | 477 | | 266,700.00 | |
| | | MINX 23 278 | 06.10.90 | 479 | | 266,700.00 | |
| | | MINX 23 279 | 07.10.90 | 475 | | 266,700.00 | |
| | | MINX 23 280 | 08.10.90 | 476 | | 266,700.00 | |
| | | MINX 23 281 | 10.10.90 | 476 | | 266,700.00 | |
| | | MINX 23 282 | 11.10.90 | 476 | | 266,700.00 | |
| | | MINX 23 286 | 19.10.90 | 476 | 3,335 | 242,900.00 | 1,843,100.00 |
| | Amman - Dhaka | MINX 23 283 | 12.10.90 | 291 | 291 | 256,100.00 | 256,100.00 |
| | Refund of Royalties | | | | | -92,120.00 | |
| | Cancellation fee (5 rotations) | | | | | 107,143.00 | |
| | | | | | 10,090 | | 5,152,223.00 |

| AIRLINE COMPANY | ROUTING | CHARTER | DATE OF DEPARTURE | NO. OF PAX | TOTAL PAX | PAID USD | TOTAL PAYMENT |
|---|---|---|---|---|---|---|---|
| ALL NIPPON AIRWAYS | Amman - Manila | MINH 23 129 | 19.09.90 | 297 | | 237,600.00 | |
| | | | | | 297 | | 237,600.00 |

| AIRLINE COMPANY | ROUTING | CHARTER | DATE OF DEPARTURE | NO. OF PAX | TOTAL PAX | PAID USD | TOTAL PAYMENT |
|---|---|---|---|---|---|---|---|
| EGYPTAIR | Amman - Manila | MIMS 23 353 | 05.10.90 | 202 | | 163,200.00 | |
| | | MIMS 23 354 | 06.10.90 | 208 | | 163,200.00 | |
| | | MIMS 23 355 | 07.10.90 | 204 | | 163,200.00 | |
| | | MIMS 23 356 | 08.10.90 | 203 | | 163,200.00 | |
| | | MIMS 23 367 | 10.10.90 | 206 | | 164,000.00 | |
| | | MIMS 23 368 | 10.10.90 | 209 | | 164,000.00 | |

0177

| | | MIMS 23 369 | 11.10.90 | 206 | | 164,000.00 | |
|---|---|---|---|---|---|---|---|
| | | | | | 1,438 | | 1,144,800.00 |

| AIRLINE COMPANY | ROUTING | CHARTER | DATE OF DEPARTURE | NO. OF PAX | TOTAL PAX | PAID USD | TOTAL PAYMENT |
|---|---|---|---|---|---|---|---|
| **GULF AIR** | **Amman -** | MIGF 23 094 | 25.09.90 | 243 | | 72,900.00 | |
| | **Karachi** | | | | 243 | | 72,900.00 |
| | **Amman -** | PF 0/71348 | 13.11.90 | 56 | | 20,577.00 | |
| | **Dhaka** | PF 0/71335 | 05.11.90 | 74 | | 25,954.00 | |
| | | PF 0/71400 | 10.12.90 | 31 | 161 | 11,780.00 | 58,311.00 |
| | **Amman -** | PF 0/71338 | 08.11.90 | 60 | | 22,860.00 | |
| | **Colombo** | PF 0/71342 | 09.11.90 | 13 | 73 | 4,953.00 | 27,813.00 |
| | **Amman -** | PF 0/71362 | 16.11.90 | 67 | | 35,912.00 | |
| | **Manila** | | | | 67 | | 35,912.00 |
| | | | | | 544 | | 194,936.00 |

| AIRLINE COMPANY | ROUTING | CHARTER | DATE OF DEPARTURE | NO. OF PAX | TOTAL PAX | PAID USD | TOTAL PAYMENT |
|---|---|---|---|---|---|---|---|
| **TURKER TOURISM TRAVEL AG.** | **Ankara - Colombo** | MITK 23 538 | 03.10.90 | 41 | | 31,488.00 | |
| | | MITK 23 539 | 06.10.90 | 47 | | 32,286.00 | |
| | | MITK 23 540 | 08.10.90 | 2 | | 1,300.00 | |
| | | MITK 23 541 | 08.10.90 | 11 | | 7,920.00 | |
| | | MITK 23 556 | 14.10.90 | 19 | | 12,090.00 | |
| | | MITK 23 557 | 14.10.90 | 9 | | 5,940.00 | |
| | | PF 0/74809 | 22.10.90 | 32 | | 23,088.00 | |
| | | PF 0/74811 | 29.10.90 | 21 | | 15,480.00 | |
| | | PF 0/74812 | 03.11.90 | 30 | | 21,672.00 | |
| | | PF 0/74815 | 12.11.90 | 21 | | 15,264.00 | |
| | | PF 0/74818 | 19.11.90 | 23 | | 16,704.00 | |
| | | PF 0/74821 | 26.11.90 | 3 | | 2,160.00 | |
| | | PF 0/74823 | 03.12.90 | 4 | | 2,904.00 | |
| | | PF 0/74824 | 08.12.90 | 15 | | 10,848.00 | |
| | | PF 0/74827 | 15.12.90 | 7 | | 5,040.00 | |
| | | PF 0/74828 | 24.12.90 | 10 | | 7,224.00 | |
| | | PF 0/74830 | 31.12.90 | 8 | | 5,760.00 | |
| | | PF 1/71854 | 12.01.91 | 2 | 305 | 1,488.00 | 218,656.00 |
| | **Ankara -** | PF 0/74822 | 23.10.90 | 9 | | 1,620.00 | |
| | **Manila** | | | | 9 | | 1,620.00 |
| | **Ankara -** | PF 0/74810 | 14.10.90 | 2 | | 1,142.00 | |
| | **Khartoum** | PF 0/74813 | 03.11.90 | 2 | | 1,164.00 | |
| | | PF 0/74826 | 16.12.90 | 2 | 6 | 1,106.00 | 3,412.00 |
| | **Ankara -** | PF 0/74819 | 14.10.90 | 2 | | 1,431.00 | |
| | **Afghan.** | | | | 2 | | 1,431.00 |
| | **Ankara -** | PF 0/74814 | 04.11.90 | 1 | | 835.00 | |
| | **Dhaka** | PF 0/74816 | 11.11.90 | 2 | 3 | 1,669.00 | 2,504.00 |
| | **Ankara -** | PF 0/74825 | 03.12.90 | 2 | | 1,264.00 | |
| | **Islamabad** | | | | 2 | | 1,264.00 |
| | **Ankara -** | Staff Travel | 12.12.90 | 1 | | 166.00 | |
| | **Diy-Ank** | | | | 1 | | 166.00 |
| | **Ankara -** | PF 1/71501 | 15.01.91 | 1 | | 80.00 | |
| | **Istanbul** | | | | 1 | | 80.00 |
| | **Istanbul -** | PF 1/71853 | 12.01.91 | 1 | | 640.00 | |
| | **Colombo** | | | | 1 | | 640.00 |
| | | | | | 330 | | 229,773.00 |

0178

| AIRLINE COMPANY | ROUTING | CHARTER | DATE OF DEPARTURE | NO. OF PAX | TOTAL PAX | PAID USD | TOTAL PAYMENT |
|---|---|---|---|---|---|---|---|
| TYCHE TRAVEL & TOURS | Amman - Colombo | MISU 23 326 | 04.10.90 | 155 | | 75,330.00 | |
| | | MISU 23 327 | 05.10.90 | 174 | | 84,564.00 | |
| | | MISU 23 328 | 06.10.90 | 174 | | 84,564.00 | |
| | | MISU 23 329 | 07.10.90 | 174 | | 84,564.00 | |
| | | MISU 23 330 | 07.10.90 | 174 | 851 | 84,564.00 | 413,586.00 |
| | Amman - Hanoi | MISU 23 030 | 15.01.91 | 300 | | 238,500.00 | |
| | | MISU 23 031 | 17.01.91 | 310 | 610 | 246,450.00 | 484,950.00 |
| | | | | | 1,461 | | 898,536.00 |

| AIRLINE COMPANY | ROUTING | CHARTER | DATE OF DEPARTURE | NO. OF PAX | TOTAL PAX | PAID USD | TOTAL PAYMENT |
|---|---|---|---|---|---|---|---|
| EMIRATES | Amman - Bombay | MIEK 23 443 | 10.10.90 | 184 | | 81,450.00 | |
| | | MIEK 23 444 | 10.10.90 | 256 | | 118,350.00 | |
| | | PF 0/70153 | 13.10.90 | 1 | | 548.55 | |
| | | PF 0/70157 | 20.10.90 | 4 | 445 | 2,218.96 | 202,567.51 |
| | Amman - Colombo | MIEK 23 458 | 11.10.90 | 264 | | 131,500.00 | |
| | | MIEK 23 459 | 11.10.90 | 182 | 446 | 90,500.00 | 222,000.00 |
| | | | | | 891 | | 424,567.51 |

| AIRLINE COMPANY | ROUTING | CHARTER | DATE OF DEPARTURE | NO. OF PAX | TOTAL PAX | PAID USD | TOTAL PAYMENT |
|---|---|---|---|---|---|---|---|
| WORLD AIRWAYS | Amman - Colombo | MIWO 23 370 | 06.10.90 | 339 | | 219,480.00 | |
| | | MIWO 23 371 | 07.10.90 | 354 | | 219,480.00 | |
| | | MIWO 23 372 | 08.10.90 | 363 | | 219,480.00 | |
| | | MIWO 23 373 | 09.10.90 | 354 | | 219,480.00 | |
| | | MIWO 23 374 | 10.10.90 | 354 | | 219,480.00 | |
| | | MIWO 23 375 | 11.10.90 | 355 | | 219,480.00 | |
| | | MIWO 23 376 | 13.10.90 | 357 | | 219,480.00 | |
| | | MIWO 23 377 | 14.10.90 | 354 | | 219,480.00 | |
| | | MIWO 23 379 | 17.10.90 | 359 | | 219,480.00 | |
| | | MIWO 23 380 | 18.10.90 | 356 | | 219,480.00 | |
| | | MIWO 23 381 | 19.10.90 | 355 | | 219,480.00 | |
| | | MIWO 23 382 | 20.10.90 | 355 | | 219,480.00 | |
| | | MIWO 23 383 | 21.10.90 | 355 | 4,610 | 219,480.00 | 2,853,240.00 |
| | Amman - Bombay | MIWO 23 378 | 15.10.90 | 354 | | 201,072.00 | |
| | | | | | 354 | | 201,072.00 |
| | | | | | 4,964 | | 3,054,312.00 |

| AIRLINE COMPANY | ROUTING | CHARTER | DATE OF DEPARTURE | NO. OF PAX | TOTAL PAX | PAID USD | TOTAL PAYMENT |
|---|---|---|---|---|---|---|---|
| AEROFLOT | Teheran - Dhaka | MISU 23 501 | 06.10.90 | 175 | | 81,667.00 | |
| | | | | | | | |
| | | | | | 175 | | 81,667.00 |

| AIRLINE COMPANY | ROUTING | CHARTER | DATE OF DEPARTURE | NO. OF PAX | TOTAL PAX | PAID USD | TOTAL PAYMENT |
|---|---|---|---|---|---|---|---|
| ZA'TARAH & CO | Cairo - Manila | PF 0/71308 | 23.10.90 | 37 | | 19,610.00 | |
| | | PF 0/74941 | 14.12.90 | 5 | 42 | 1,425.00 | 21,035.00 |
| | Amman - Manila | PF 0/71309 | 22.10.90 | 57 | | 28,720.00 | |
| | | PF 0/71322 | 29.10.90 | 61 | | 32,330.00 | |

0179

| | | | | | | | |
|---|---|---|---|---|---|---|---|
| | | PF 0/71332 | 02.11.90 | 123 | | 63,635.00 | |
| | | PF 0/71347 | 08.11.90 | 55 | | 28,190.00 | |
| | | PF 0/71361 | 15.11.90 | 40 | | 19,810.00 | |
| | | PF 0/71388 | 29.11.90 | 15 | | 7,420.00 | |
| | | PF 0/71401 | 10.12.90 | 4 | | 2,120.00 | |
| | | PF 0/71409 | 17.12.90 | 7 | | 3,710.00 | |
| | | PF 0/71416 | 20.12.90 | 8 | | 4,240.00 | |
| | | PF 0/71431 | 27.12.90 | 9 | | 4,770.00 | |
| | | PF 1/71513 | 07.01.91 | 7 | | 3,280.00 | |
| | | PF 1/71515 | 14.01.91 | 15 | 401 | 7,520.00 | 205,745.00 |
| | Amman - Djibouti | PF 0/71325 | 31.10.90 | 18 | | 9,562.50 | |
| | | PF 0/71337 | 07.11.90 | 1 | | 485.00 | |
| | | PF 0/71352 | 14.11.90 | 2 | 21 | 970.00 | 11,017.50 |
| | Amman - Cairo | PF 0/71357 | 14.11.90 | 4 | | 178.00 | |
| | | | | | 4 | | 178.00 |
| | Amman - Banjul | PF 0/71355 | 15.11.90 | 1 | | 955.00 | |
| | | | | | 1 | | 955.00 |
| | Amman - Paris | PF 0/71364 | 17.11.90 | 8 | | 2,407.00 | |
| | | | | | 8 | | 2,407.00 |
| | Amman - Khartoum | PF 0/71329 | 31.10.90 | 1 | | 225.00 | |
| | | PF 0/71340 | 14.11.90 | 1 | | 225.00 | |
| | | PF 1/71514 | 09.01.91 | 1 | 3 | 225.00 | 675.00 |
| | Amman - San Paolo | PF 0/71369 | 29.11.90 | 5 | | 3,118.50 | |
| | | | | | 5 | | 3,118.50 |
| | Amman - Kinshasa | PF 0/71326 | 01.11.90 | 1 | | 885.00 | |
| | | | | | 1 | | 885.00 |
| | Amman - Mogadishu | PF 0/71330 | 02.11.90 | 3 | | 1,845.00 | |
| | | PF 0/71356 | 16.11.90 | 6 | | 3,540.00 | |
| | | PF 0/71371 | 21.11.90 | 11 | 20 | 5,310.00 | 10,695.00 |
| | Amman - Hanoi | MIMS 23 022 | 09.01.91 | 208 | | 153,750.00 | |
| | | MIMS 23 023 | 10.01.91 | 205 | | 153,750.00 | |
| | | MIMS 23 029 | 12.01.91 | 207 | 620 | 153,750.00 | 461,250.00 |
| | Amman - Bombay | PF 1/71520 | 11.01.91 | 21 | | 7,455.00 | |
| | | | | | 21 | | 7,455.00 |
| | Damascus-Manila | PF 0/71373 | 26.11.90 | 9 | | 6,660.00 | |
| | | PF 0/71421 | 24.12.90 | 1 | | 740.00 | |
| | | PF 0/74940 | 13.12.90 | 4 | | 2,960.00 | |
| | | PF 0/74957 | 20.12.90 | 3 | 17 | 2,220.00 | 12,580.00 |
| | | | | | 1,164 | | 737,996.00 |

| AIRLINE COMPANY | ROUTING | CHARTER | DATE OF DEPARTURE | NO. OF PAX | TOTAL PAX | PAID USD | TOTAL PAYMENT |
|---|---|---|---|---|---|---|---|
| INTER. FREIGHT SERVICES | Basrah - Colombo | MIIA 23 753 | 27.10.90 | 427 | | 234,952.00 | |
| | | MIIA 23 754 | 28.10.90 | 441 | | 235,290.00 | |
| | | MIIA 23 755 | 29.10.90 | 441 | | 234,216.00 | |
| | | MIIA 23 756 | 31.10.90 | 437 | | 233,426.00 | |
| | | MIIA 23 757 | 03.11.90 | 440 | | 233,480.00 | |
| | | MIIA 23 758 | 05.11.90 | 441 | | 233,660.00 | |
| | | MIIA 23 759 | 07.11.90 | 442 | | 233,622.00 | |
| | | MIIA 23 760 | 10.11.90 | 443 | | 233,738.00 | |
| | | MIIA 23 761 | 13.11.90 | 440 | | 233,660.00 | |
| | | MIIA 23 762 | 18.11.90 | 297 | | 229,942.00 | |
| | | MIIA 23 763 | 27.11.90 | 430 | 4,679 | 228,442.00 | 2,564,428.00 |

| | | | | | | | |
|---|---|---|---|---|---|---|---|
| | **Basrah - Manila** | MIIA 23 906 | 01.12.90 | 437 | | 282,295.00 | |
| | | MIIA 23 907 | 12.12.90 | 445 | 882 | 282,295.00 | 564,590.00 |
| | **Baghdad - Hanoi** | MIIA 23 700 | 18.11.90 | 168 | | 143,698.00 | |
| | | MIIA 23 701 | 19.11.90 | 173 | | 143,671.00 | |
| | | MIIA 23 702 | 20.11.90 | 177 | | 146,048.00 | |
| | | MIIA 23 703 | 21.11.90 | 177 | | 146,048.00 | |
| | | MIIA 23 704 | 22.11.90 | 177 | | 146,048.00 | |
| | | MIIA 23 705 | 23.11.90 | 177 | | 146,048.00 | |
| | | MIIA 23 706 | 24.11.90 | 177 | | 146,048.00 | |
| | | MIIA 23 707 | 25.11.90 | 176 | | 146,021.00 | |
| | | MIIA 23 708 | 26.11.90 | 176 | | 146,021.00 | |
| | | MIIA 23 709 | 27.11.90 | 140 | | 115,948.00 | |
| | | MIIA 23 710 | 27.11.90 | 177 | | 144,975.00 | |
| | | MIIA 23 711 | 28.11.90 | 430 | | 351,016.00 | |
| | | MIIA 23 712 | 28.11.90 | 177 | | 150,886.00 | |
| | | MIIA 23 713 | 29.11.90 | 440 | | 356,328.00 | |
| | | MIIA 23 714 | 01.12.90 | 440 | | 356,328.00 | |
| | | MIIA 23 715 | 01.12.90 | 177 | | 144,975.00 | |
| | | MIIA 23 716 | 02.12.90 | 440 | | 356,328.00 | |
| | | MIIA 23 717 | 03.12.90 | 440 | | 356,328.00 | |
| | | MIIA 23 718 | 04.12.90 | 430 | | 356,126.00 | |
| | | MIIA 23 719 | 05.12.90 | 435 | | 356,227.00 | |
| | | MIIA 23 720 | 06.12.90 | 440 | | 356,328.00 | |
| | | MIIA 23 721 | 08.12.90 | 435 | | 356,126.00 | |
| | | MIIA 23 722 | 09.12.90 | 440 | | 356,328.00 | |
| | | MIIA 23 723 | 23.12.90 | 170 | | 144,834.00 | |
| | | MIIA 23 724 | 24.12.90 | 175 | | 144,935.00 | |
| | | MIIA 23 725 | 27.12.90 | 178 | | 144,935.00 | |
| | | MIIA 23 726 | 28.12.90 | 175 | 7,317 | 144,935.00 | 6,003,537.00 |
| | IRAK Inland Ground Transportation | | | | | 52,222.00 | |
| | | | | | 12,878 | | 9,184,777.00 |

| *AIRLINE COMPANY* | *ROUTING* | *CHARTER* | *DATE OF DEPARTURE* | *NO. OF PAX* | ***TOTAL PAX*** | *PAID USD* | ***TOTAL PAYMENT*** |
|---|---|---|---|---|---|---|---|
| **SUDAN AIRWAYS** | **Amman - Khartoum** | MISD 23 468 | 31.10.90 | 198 | | 37,000.00 | |
| | | MISD 23 469 | 02.11.90 | 190 | | 37,000.00 | |
| | | MISD 23 470 | 06.11.90 | 198 | | 37,000.00 | |
| | | MISD 23 471 | 09.11.90 | 195 | | 37,000.00 | |
| | | MISD 23 472 | 13.11.90 | 205 | | 37,000.00 | |
| | | MISD 23 473 | 16.11.90 | 188 | | 37,000.00 | |
| | | MISD 23 900 | 20.11.90 | 171 | | 34,200.00 | |
| | | MISD 23 901 | 23.11.90 | 178 | | 34,000.00 | |
| | | MISD 23 902 | 27.11.90 | 188 | | 37,000.00 | |
| | | MISD 23 903 | 30.11.90 | 191 | | 36,600.00 | |
| | | MISD 23 904 | 05.12.90 | 187 | | 37,000.00 | |
| | | MISD 23 905 | 07.12.90 | 186 | | 37,000.00 | |
| | | MISD 23 909 | 12.12.90 | 152 | | 30,400.00 | |
| | | MISD 23 911 | 14.12.90 | 95 | | 19,000.00 | |
| | | MISD 23 912 | 19.12.90 | 158 | | 31,400.00 | |
| | | MISD 23 913 | 21.12.90 | 183 | | 36,200.00 | |
| | | MISD 23 915 | 25.12.90 | 160 | | 31,200.00 | |
| | | MISD 23 916 | 28.12.90 | 190 | | 37,000.00 | |
| | | MISD 23 917 | 29.12.90 | 183 | | 36,600.00 | |

0181

| AIRLINE COMPANY | ROUTING | CHARTER | DATE OF DEPARTURE | NO. OF PAX | TOTAL PAX | PAID USD | TOTAL PAYMENT |
|---|---|---|---|---|---|---|---|
| | | MISD 23 005 | 04.01.91 | 193 | | 38,600.00 | |
| | | MISD 23 006 | 04.01.91 | 184 | | 36,600.00 | |
| | | MISD 23 019 | 08.01.91 | 174 | | 34,000.00 | |
| | | MISD 23 024 | 11.01.91 | 188 | | 45,880.00 | |
| | | MISD 23 025 | 12.01.91 | 185 | | 45,880.00 | |
| | | MISD 23 026 | 12.01.91 | 185 | | 45,880.00 | |
| | | MISD 23 027 | 14.01.91 | 185 | | 45,880.00 | |
| | | MISD 23 028 | 13.01.91 | 186 | | 45,880.00 | |
| | | | | | 4,876 | | 998,200.00 |

| AIRLINE COMPANY | ROUTING | CHARTER | DATE OF DEPARTURE | NO. OF PAX | TOTAL PAX | PAID USD | TOTAL PAYMENT |
|---|---|---|---|---|---|---|---|
| **IRAN AIR** | **Teheran - Bombay** | PF 0/70096 | 27.09.90 | 6 | | 2,883.85 | |
| | | PF 0/70100 | 04.10.90 | 5 | | 2,363.85 | |
| | | PF 0/70152 | 10.10.90 | 3 | 14 | 1,512.30 | 6,760.00 |
| | **Teheran - Karachi** | PF 0/70176 | 15.12.90 | 6 | | 2,640.16 | |
| | | | | | 6 | | 2,640.16 |
| | | | | | 20 | | 9,400.16 |

| AIRLINE COMPANY | ROUTING | CHARTER | DATE OF DEPARTURE | NO. OF PAX | TOTAL PAX | PAID USD | TOTAL PAYMENT |
|---|---|---|---|---|---|---|---|
| **MARTINAIR HOLLAND** | **Cancellation fee** | | | | | 540,935.67 | |
| | | | | | | | 540,935.67 |

| AIRLINE COMPANY | ROUTING | CHARTER | DATE OF DEPARTURE | NO. OF PAX | TOTAL PAX | PAID USD | TOTAL PAYMENT |
|---|---|---|---|---|---|---|---|
| **AIR FRANCE** | **Damascus-Djibouti** | PF 0/74902 | 27.09.90 | 2 | | 2,223.08 | |
| | | | | | 2 | | 2,223.08 |

| AIRLINE COMPANY | ROUTING | CHARTER | DATE OF DEPARTURE | NO. OF PAX | TOTAL PAX | PAID USD | TOTAL PAYMENT |
|---|---|---|---|---|---|---|---|
| **MAHASNI TRAVEL TOURISM AGENCY** | **Damascus-Colombo** | PF 0/74905 | 29.10.90 | 1 | | 742.00 | |
| | | PF 0/74907 | 05.11.90 | 1 | | 742.00 | |
| | | | | | 2 | | 1,484.00 |
| | **Damascus-Khartoum** | PF 0/74903 | 23.10.90 | 1 | | 328.75 | |
| | | PF 0/74906 | 07.11.90 | 18 | | 5,786.00 | |
| | | PF 0/74908 | 14.11.90 | 5 | | 1,019.25 | |
| | | PF 0/74910 | 21.11.90 | 1 | | 328.75 | |
| | | PF 0/74912 | 21.11.90 | 1 | | 328.75 | |
| | | PF 0/74915 | 21.11.90 | 3 | | 986.25 | |
| | | PF 0/74917 | 28.11.90 | 2 | | 657.50 | |
| | | PF 0/74918 | 28.11.90 | 1 | | 328.75 | |
| | | PF 0/74919 | 28.11.90 | 1 | | 328.75 | |
| | | PF 0/74921 | 28.11.90 | 4 | | 854.90 | |
| | | PF 0/74922 | 28.11.90 | 1 | | 328.75 | |
| | | PF 0/74924 | 05.12.90 | 1 | | 328.75 | |
| | | PF 0/74925 | 05.12.90 | 1 | | 328.75 | |
| | | PF 0/74926 | 19.12.90 | 1 | | 328.75 | |
| | | PF 0/74927 | 12.12.90 | 1 | | 328.75 | |
| | | PF 0/74928 | 05.12.90 | 2 | | 657.50 | |
| | | PF 0/74932 | 05.11.90 | 1 | | 328.75 | |

0182

| AIRLINE COMPANY | ROUTING | CHARTER | DATE OF DEPARTURE | NO. OF PAX | TOTAL PAX | PAID USD | TOTAL PAYMENT |
|---|---|---|---|---|---|---|---|
| | | PF 0/74933 | 05.12.90 | 1 | | 328.75 | |
| | | PF 0/74934 | 05.12.90 | 1 | | 328.75 | |
| | | PF 0/74935 | 05.12.90 | 3 | | 986.25 | |
| | | PF 0/74936 | 12.12.90 | 3 | | 986.25 | |
| | | PF 0/74937 | 12.12.90 | 2 | | 657.50 | |
| | | PF 0/74938 | 12.12.90 | 3 | | 986.25 | |
| | | PF 0/74939 | 19.12.90 | 1 | | 328.75 | |
| | | PF 0/74942 | 26.12.90 | 1 | | 328.75 | |
| | | PF 0/74943 | 26.12.90 | 1 | | 328.75 | |
| | | PF 0/74945 | 12.12.90 | 1 | | 328.75 | |
| | | PF 0/74946 | 19.12.90 | 1 | | 328.75 | |
| | | PF 0/74948 | 19.12.90 | 1 | | 328.75 | |
| | | PF 0/74949 | 19.12.90 | 4 | | 1,315.00 | |
| | | PF 0/74950 | 19.12.90 | 1 | | 328.75 | |
| | | PF 0/74953 | 19.12.90 | 1 | | 328.75 | |
| | | PF 1/71651 | 01.01.91 | 1 | | 348.50 | |
| | | PF 1/71652 | 01.01.91 | 4 | | 767.00 | |
| | | PF 1/71653 | 01.01.91 | 1 | | 348.50 | |
| | | PF 1/71654 | 01.01.91 | 1 | | 348.50 | |
| | | PF 1/71655 | 01.01.91 | 1 | | 348.50 | |
| | | PF 1/71656 | 01.01.91 | 1 | | 348.50 | |
| | | PF 1/71657 | 01.01.91 | 1 | | 348.50 | |
| | | PF 1/71659 | 08.01.91 | 3 | | 1,045.50 | |
| | | PF 1/71660 | 08.01.91 | 2 | | 697.00 | |
| | | PF 1/71661 | 08.01.91 | 3 | | 1,045.50 | |
| | | PF 1/71662 | 08.01.91 | 3 | | 1,045.50 | |
| | | PF 1/71663 | 01.01.91 | 1 | | 348.50 | |
| | | PF 1/71664 | 01.01.91 | 1 | | 348.50 | |
| | | PF 1/71665 | 08.01.91 | 1 | | 348.50 | |
| | | PF 1/71666 | 08.01.91 | 7 | | 2,439.50 | |
| | | | | | 101 | | 31,972.90 |
| | **Damascus-** | PF 0/74909 | 24.11.90 | 1 | | 613.65 | |
| | **Istanbul** | | | | 1 | | 613.65 |
| | **Damascus-** | PF 0/74923 | 04.12.90 | 1 | | 613.75 | |
| | **Bombay** | | | | 1 | | 613.75 |
| | **Damascus-** | PF 0/74904 | 06.11.90 | 2 | | 339.00 | |
| | **Cairo** | | | | 2 | | 339.00 |
| | | | | | 107 | | 35,023.30 |

| *AIRLINE COMPANY* | *ROUTING* | *CHARTER* | *DATE OF DEPARTURE* | *NO. OF PAX* | ***TOTAL PAX*** | *PAID USD* | ***TOTAL PAYMENT*** |
|---|---|---|---|---|---|---|---|
| **FINE-MINISTER** | **Handling fee** | | | | | 1,976.00 | |
| | | | | | | | 1,976.00 |

| *AIRLINE COMPANY* | *ROUTING* | *CHARTER* | *DATE OF DEPARTURE* | *NO. OF PAX* | ***TOTAL PAX*** | *PAID USD* | ***TOTAL PAYMENT*** |
|---|---|---|---|---|---|---|---|
| **THAI AIRWAYS INT'L LTD.** | **Ankara - Manila** | PF 0/74822 | 23.11.90 | 9 | | 5,314.96 | |
| | | | | | 9 | | 5,314.96 |

0183

| AIRLINE COMPANY | ROUTING | CHARTER | DATE OF DEPARTURE | NO. OF PAX | TOTAL PAX | PAID USD | TOTAL PAYMENT |
|---|---|---|---|---|---|---|---|
| ELWAN TRAVEL AG. | Amman - Manila | PF 1/71508 | 04.01.91 | 49 | | 26,509.00 | |
| | | | | | 49 | | 26,509.00 |

| AIRLINE COMPANY | ROUTING | CHARTER | DATE OF DEPARTURE | NO. OF PAX | TOTAL PAX | PAID USD | TOTAL PAYMENT |
|---|---|---|---|---|---|---|---|
| JORDAN INT. TRAVEL & TOURS | Amman - Karachi | PF 0/71339 | 07.11.90 | 122 | | 35,507.00 | |
| | | PF 1/71528 | 14.01.91 | 38 | | 13,536.00 | |
| | | | | | 160 | | 49,043.00 |

| SHIPPING COMPANY | ROUTING | REFERENCE | DATE OF DEPARTURE | NO. OF PAX | TOTAL PAX | PAID USD | TOTAL PAYMENT |
|---|---|---|---|---|---|---|---|
| ORIENT SHIPPING | Aqaba - Colombo | M/V SAINA E ARAB | 15.09.90 | 1,768 | | 707,200.00 | |
| | | | | | 1,768 | | 707,200.00 |

| Jordan Inland Ground Transportation | 4,203,800.00 | 4,203,800.00 |
|---|---|---|

| GRAND TOTAL | | PAX | | USD |
|---|---|---|---|---|
| | | 104,208 | | 64,518,332.38 |

Division of Banking

0184

# IOM 事務次長 面談時 長官님 말씀 要旨

2-3-6 방한

## 1. 人事 말씀

- 금번 東南亞 (泰國, 필리핀, 印尼) 訪問 機會에 韓國을 訪問한 것을 歡迎함.
- 本人이 알기로는 事務次長의 금번 訪韓이 세번째인 것으로 기억됨
  첫번째는 1975年 콜롬비아 下院 外務委員長으로서,
  두번째는 1987年 駐 제네바 代表部 콜롬비아 大使로서, 그리고
  이번에는 IOM 事務次長으로서 訪韓한 것으로 알고 있음.
- 서울과 제네바는 氣候 與件은 비슷하나 8時間의 時差로 다소 疲勞하지는
  않은 지 ?

## 2. 걸프事態 關聯 歡談

- 금번 걸프 戰爭은 東西間 데탕트 時代를 맞아 世界 모두가 平和를
  갈구하는 時期에 發生한 不幸한 事態임.
- 現在 戰勢는 美國이 主導하는 多國籍軍에 有利하게 展開되고 있는
  것으로 보이지만 이라크 軍의 抵抗이 意外로 頑强하고 특히 이라크가
  포로를 "人間 防牌"로 活用하고 있는 等 앞으로의 戰爭 向方이 憂慮됨.
- 금번 걸프 事態로 惹起된 難民 處理를 위해 IOM 이 多角的인 解決
  努力을 하고 있는 것으로 알고 있음. 我國은 지난 8月 2次에 걸쳐
  民間 航空機를 동원 我國人을 撤收한 바 있으며, 今年 1月 다시
  3次에 걸쳐 民間 航空機로 我國 僑民 및 勤勞者들 撤收하였음.
- 한편 IOM 의 難民 輸送 支援 要請과 關聯, 昨年 12月 難民의 人道的
  側面과 國際協力的 次元에서 50萬弗을 特別 寄與金으로 提供한 바 있음.
  금번 難民 輸送을 爲한 航空機 支援 要請은 我國 豫算 形便上 어려우나
  걸프灣 事態에 관한 綜合的인 檢討時 關係機關과 協議할 計劃임.

0185

## 3. IOM 과의 協力 問題

- 我國은 IOM 과의 協力을 通한 秩序있는 移民을 推進하고자 1988. 11月 加入했음.
- IOM 이 그동안 國際難民 處理 및 秩序있는 移民 推進 業務에 많은 寄與를 해온 것으로 알고 있으며, 앞으로 我國과도 IOM 과의 移民협력이 보다 强化되기를 期待함.

## 4. 맺음 말씀

- 本人이 駐 제네바 大使로 在職時 事務次長께서 여러모로 協調하여 주신데 대해 늘 고맙게 생각하고 있음.
- 금번 訪韓이 韓國을 보다 理解하는데 有益한 機會가 되기를 바라며, 滯韓中 不便한 点이 있을시 連絡주시면 必要한 協調를 하겠음.

0186

# Charry-Samper 國際移民機構 (IOM) 事務次長 人的事項

○ 姓　　名 : 엑또르 차리 삼페르 (Hector Charry Samper)

○ 生年月日 : 1933年生 (~~54~~ 58 歲)

○ 主要 經歷 :

- 60 - 62　　下院 外務委員長
- 62 - 63　　法務長官
- 63 - 67　　駐 아르헨티나 大使
- 70 - 73　　駐 베네수엘라 및 트리니다드 토바고 大使
- 74 - 76　　下院 外務委員長
- 78 - 79　　ILO 執行理事會 議長
- 83　　人種 差別 撤廢 世界 會議 議長
- 86　　유엔 人權委員會 議長
- 87　　UNHCR 執行委員會 議長
- 89.1 - 現在　　國際 移民機構 (IOM) 事務次長

○ 其他 活動 : 憲法 및 國際法 敎授, 辯護士 (著書 多數)

○ 家族 事項 : 夫人 및 1 女

0187

참고 자료

# 국제 이민기구 개요

1. 연　　혁 :

   o 1951.12. 브뤼셀에서 구주 정부간 이민위원회 (ICEM) 로 발족

   o 1980 정부간 이민위원회 (ICM) 으로 변경

   o 1989.11. 국제 이민기구 (International Orgamization for Migration) 로 명칭 변경

2. 회원국 및 옵저버국 현황

   o 회 원 국 : 39 개국

   o 옵저버국 : 25 개국

3. 구　　성

   o 이 사 회 : 39개국 회원국 대표로 구성, IOM 의 정책, 기획, 재정에 대한 최종 결정

   o 집행위원회 : 이사회에서 선출된 10 개국으로 구성, 이사회 업무 준비 및 예산, 재정 소위원회와 수송 조정 소위원회의 보고를 기초로 권고안 수립

   o 사 무 국 : 이사회 및 집행위원회가 제정한 규칙과 규정에 따라 기구의 행정 및 집행기능을 수행

※ 사무총장은 James Purcell (미국), 사무차장은 Hector Charry-Samper ( 콜롬비아 )

0188

4. IOM 주요 이주사업

- o Return of Talent Programme : 개도국의 우수 두뇌 유출 방지 위해 선진국에서 습득한 기술 및 경험을 가진 전문인력을 국적국 또는 인근 지역국으로 입국토록 하는 사업
- o Selective Migration Programme : 개도국에서 경제개발 위해 필요한 고급인력을 IOM 이 선진국에서 모집, 적격자를 선발하여 해당 개도국에 장기적으로 체류토록 하는 사업
- o Integrated Experts Programme : 구주지역 전문 인력을 중장기간 중남미 개도국에 파견하여 전문 기술 및 경험을 개도국에 전수케 하는 것이 목적
- o Horizontal Cooperation in the Freld of Qualified Human Resourees : 역내 전문인력 이주 및 정부내 전문가의 교환을 통해 역내 개도국 발전에 기여함을 목적으로 IOM 은 역내 전문인력 이주 및 교환의 중개 역할을 함.

5. 아국과의 관계

- o 1988.11.29 정회원으로 가입
- o 분 담 금
  - 1991 년 : 100,580 서서프랑 (행정 예산 총액의 0.47%)
  - 1990 년 : 90,000 서서프랑
  - 1989 년 : 84,000 서서프랑
- o 91.1.8. 페르샤만 사태 관련, 특별 기여금 50만불 제공

6. IOM 업무 실적 (90.1 - 11)

- o 난민 이주 : 197,715 명
- o 일반 이주 : 10,031 명

※ Gulf 만 사태 난민 수송을 위한 지원 현황 첨부

0189

# Gulf 만 사태 난민 수송을 위한 지원 현황

1990. 12. 19. 현재

| 1. State | 약 속 금 액 | 지 불 액 |
|---|---|---|
| Australia | AUD 1,250,000.00 | 1,028,833.08 |
| Austria | ATS 3,000,000.00 | 234,521.00 |
| Canada | CAD 6,000,000.00 | 5,278,683.43 |
| Denmark | DKK 1,500,000.00 | 249,196.00 |
| Finland | FLM 13,000,000.00 | 3,562,903.02 |
| Germany | DEM 15,800,000.00 | 10,357,445.93 |
| Italy | USD 840,000.00 | 825,000.00 |
| Japan | USD 12,500,000.00 | 12,500,000.00 |
| Korea | USD 500,000.00 | 91.1.8 제공 |
| Luxemburg | LUF 10,000,000.00 | |
| Netherlands | NLG 2,000,000.00 | 1,174,225.74 |
| Norway | NOK 24,500,000.00 | 4,096,414.64 |
| Sweden | SFK 30,000,000.00 | 5,143,615.00 |
| Switzerland | CHF 250,000.00 | 192,307.69 |
| United Kingdom | GBP 2,000,000.00 | 3,720,800.00 |
| U.S.A. | USD 11,117,000.00 | 11,117,000.00 |
| European Community | USD 3,178,225.00<br>USD 108,000.00<br>ECU 3,000,000.00<br>USD 97,625.00<br>ECU 4,000,000.00<br>USD 300,000.00 | 3,178,225.00<br><br>1,105,204.00<br><br><br>300,000.00 |
| 2. Private donations | | |
| US - AIM | USD 15,275.00 | 15,275.00 |
| Austcare | AUS 75,000.00 | 62,500.00 |
| World in Harmony | USD 159,500.00 | 159,500.00 |
| TOTAL | USD 73,680,000.00 | 64,601,649.53 |

0190

o IOM Gulf 만 난민 본국 송환 활동

| 난 민 국 적 | 인 원 수 |
|---|---|
| 스 리 랑 카 | 47,807 |
| 방 글 라 데 쉬 | 43,756 |
| 인 도 | 29,385 |
| 필 리 핀 | 15,294 |
| 파 키 스 탄 | 4,699 |
| 베 트 남 | 6,389 |
| 수 단 | 2,124 |
| 이 집 트 | 301 |
| 기 타 | 137 |
| 총 계 | 149,892 |

o 난민 출발지별 현황

| 출 발 지 | 인 원 수 |
|---|---|
| 요 르 단 | 130,250 |
| 터 어 키 | 7,841 |
| 이 란 | 958 |
| 이 라 크 | 10,419 |
| 기 타 | 424 |
| 총 계 | 149,892 |

0191

| 정 리 보 존 문 서 목 록 | | | | | |
|---|---|---|---|---|---|
| 기록물종류 | 일반공문서철 | 등록번호 | 2019040008 | 등록일자 | 2019-04-04 |
| 분류번호 | 721.1 | 국가코드 | XF | 보존기간 | 영구 |
| 명 칭 | 걸프사태 : 외국인 수송 및 난민 지원, 1990-91. 전3권 | | | | |
| 생 산 과 | 중근동과/해외이주과/국제기구과 | 생산년도 | 1990~1991 | 담당그룹 | |
| 권 차 명 | V.2 ICRC(국제적십자사) 지원 | | | | |
| 내용목차 | * 1990.12.28 3만불 지원 통보<br>1991.3.25 3만불 지원 | | | | |

0001

| 관리번호 | 90/778 |
|---|---|

원 본

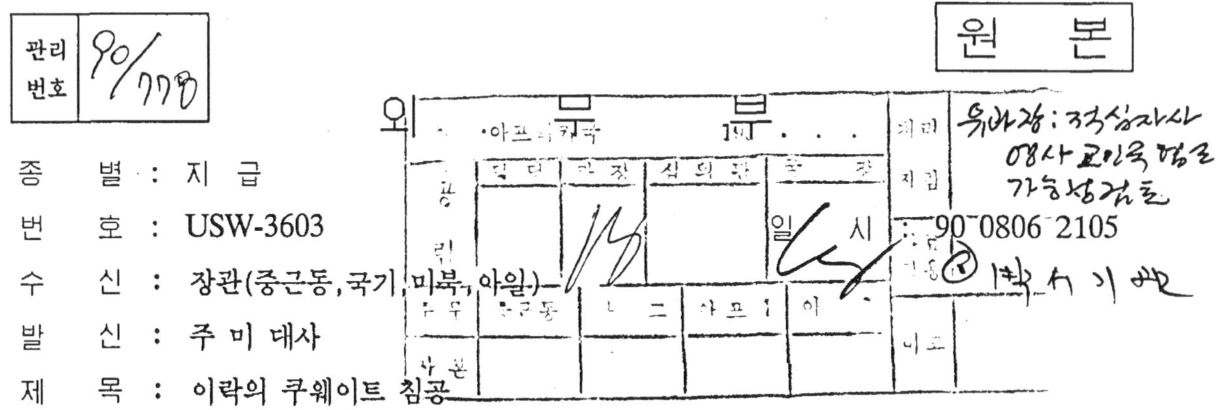

종 별 : 지 급

번 호 : USW-3603

수 신 : 장관(중근동,국기,미북,아일)

발 신 : 주 미 대사

제 목 : 이락의 쿠웨이트 침공

금 8.6 당관 유명환 참사관은 당지 일본 대사관 KIMURA 공사로부터, 쿠웨이트 사태 관련 미측의 EC 회원국, 소련, 일본과 공동 추진 코자 하는 국제 적십자 위 를 통한 자국민 철수 계획에 관한 금일 오전 미 국무부 브리핑 내용을 청취한바 동 관련 사항 요지 아래임.

1. 브리핑 실시자국무부 근동국 MACK 부차관보, 국제기구조약국 WOLF 부차관보, 동아태국 ANDERSON 부차관보

2. 브리핑 참석국 EC (현 의장국인 이태리는 대표 자격으로 참석), 소련, 일본

3. 브리핑 내용

가. 이라크 및 쿠웨이트내 미국인 안전 여부

-이라크 거주 외국인들은 대부분 국적별로 분리 수용중이라하는바 주간에는비교적 자유롭게 행동할수 있다함. 또한 이락 정부로부터 동국내 거주 미국인의 안전에 대해서는 보장을 받고 있음.

-주 쿠웨이트 미국 대사관과의 통신망이 두절됨에 따라 쿠웨이트 거주 미국인의 안전 여부에 관한 상세 정보를 입수치 못하고 있는 형편인바 이락 정부는 미측의 안전 여부 확인 요청에 대해 쿠웨이트 임시 정부와 접촉하라는 답변만을 하고있음.

나. 미측 제안 요지

-전술한바와같이 쿠웨이트 거주 미국인의 안전 여부를 확인할수도 없고, 상황이 계속 악화됨에 따라, 미측은 제네바 소재 국제 적십자 위 를 접촉, 우선 쿠웨이트가 법적으로 전쟁 상태에 있으므로 전시에 있어서의 민간인의 보호에 관한 협약등 제네바 협약이 적용되어야함을 지적하고 국제적시자위 의 협조를 요청하여둔바 있음.

-미측은 금일 브리핑 참석국들과 공동으로 국제 적십자위 에 대해 쿠웨이트로부터의 자국민 철수에 대한 협조를 요청하것을 제안함(철수 경로는 대부분

중아국 장관 차관 1차보 2차보 아주국 미주국 국기국 정문국
청와대 안기부

PAGE 1 90.08.07 11:29
외신 2과 통제관 DH

0002

공로이나, 육상 호송 철수도 가능)

4. 기타 일본측 언급사항

-미측은 금일 브리핑 참석국들에 대해 명일중으로 상기 공동 제안에의 참여여부를 회답해 줄것을 요청했다함.

-또한 미측은 동 공동 제안 참여국 확대를 전혀 고려치 않고 있고, 일본측도 국무부나 외무성 본부와의 사전 협의 없이 한일 우호 관계에 비추어 전기 미측 브리핑 내용을 당관에 통보한것이라함.

(대사 박동진-국장)

예고:90.12.31 일반

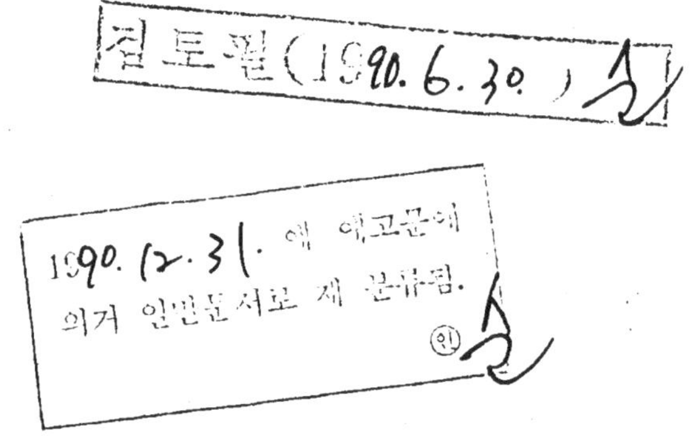


PAGE 2

0003

관리번호 90/841

재검

| 분류기호 문서번호 | 중근동 720-1069 | 기 안 용 지 | 시 행 상 특별취급 | |
|---|---|---|---|---|
| 보존기간 | 영구.준영구 10. 5. 3. 1 | 장 관 | | |
| 수 신 처 보존기간 | | | | |
| 시행일자 | 1990. 8. 7. | | | |

| 보조기관 | | 협조기관 | | 문서통제 |
|---|---|---|---|---|
| 국 장 | 전결 | | | 검열 1990. 8. 8 통제관 |
| 심의관 | | | | |
| 과 장 | 鄭 | | | |
| 기안책임자 | 박 종 순 | | | 발 송 인 |

| 경 유 수 신 참 조 | 대한적십자사 | 발신명의 | | 발송 1990 8. 08 외무부 |
|---|---|---|---|---|

| 제 목 | 이라크 및 쿠웨이트 아국 교민 안전 철수 |
|---|---|

1. 8.2. 이라크의 쿠웨이트 침공으로 이라크가 쿠웨이트를 완전 점령함에 따라 미국의 군사 개입 검토 및 UN의 대 이라크 재재등이 예상 돼 향후 급박한 상황으로의 전개가 전망됨에따라 아국으로서는 이라크 및 쿠웨이트 아국교민 (도합 1269명)의 긴급 안전 철수 문제가 제기되고 있습니다.

2. 주미 아국대사는 동 쿠웨이트 사태와 관련, 미측의 EC회원국, 소련, 일본과의 공동 추진으로 국제 적십자위를 통한 자국민 철수 계획에 관한 8.6. 미국무부 브리핑 내용 및 이와 관련한 미측 제안을 아래와 같이

1990.12.31에 예고문에 의거 일반문서로 재분류됨.

0004

보고하여 왔는바, 동 상황을 감안 귀사가 국제 적십자와 접촉, 아국 교민의

안전 철수에 협조를 요청, 동 협조 가능성을 타진하여 그 결과를 지급

회보하여 주시기 바랍니다.

- 아 래 -

가. 브리핑 내용

o 이라크 및 쿠웨이트내 미국인 안전 여부

- 이라크 거주 외국인들은 대부분 국적별 분리 수용중

- 이라크 정부로 부터의 국내 거주 미국인 안전에 대한 보장

- 미측의 재 쿠웨이트 미국인 안전 여부 확인 요청에 대해

이라크는 쿠웨이트 임시정부와 접촉하라고 답변

나. 미측 제안 요지

o 쿠웨이트 거주 미국인 안전 여부 확인 불가 및 사태 악화로,

미측은 제네바 소재 국제 적십자 위를 접촉, 쿠웨이트가 법적

으로 전쟁상태에 있으므로, 전시 민간인 보호에 관한 협약등

제네바 협약 적용을 지적, 국제 적십자 위의 협조를 요청해 둠

o 미측은 EC 회원국, 소련 및 일본과 공동으로 국제 적십자위에

대해 쿠웨이트로 부터의 자국민 철수에 협조 요청할 것을 제안함

다. 특기사항

o 미측은 금일중 상기 국가들의 동 공동 제안 참여 여부에 대해

회답을 요청함 끝

예고 : 90. 12. 31. 일반

0005

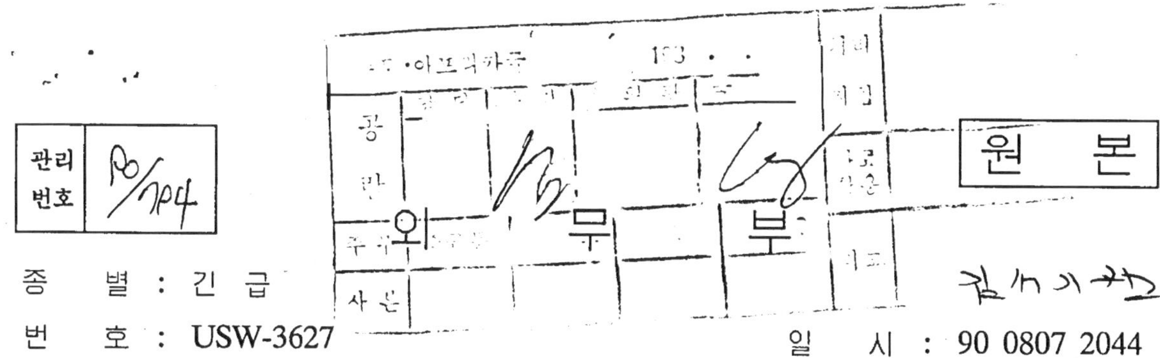


종 별 : 긴 급

번 호 : USW-3627　　　　일 시 : 90 0807 2044

수 신 : 장관(중근동,국기, 미북,아일,구일)

발 신 : 주 미 대사

제 목 : 중동사태 관련 외국인 철수

연 USW-3603

금 8.7 당관 유명환 참사관은 당지 일본대사관 니시다 참사관으로 부터 연호관련 금일 오후 국무부에서 실시된 관계국간 회의 결과및 금번 중동 사태 관련평가등을 청취하였는바, 동요지 하기 보고함(임성남 서기관 배석)

1. 국무부 회의결과

가. 참석국 미.일, 소, 캐나다, EC 회원국(영, 불, 서독, 이태리, 덴마크, 스위스등))

나. 참석자 미측은 국무부 근동국 MACK 부차관보, 국제기구 조약국 WOLF 부차관보, 여타국은 공사 또는 참사관

다. 협의 내용

1)미측은 회의 모두에, ICRC 가 이락 정부를 접촉, 현재 DE FACTO DETAINEE라 할수있는 이락 및 쿠웨이트 거주 외국인들이 철수할수 있도록 필요한 조치를 취해줄것을 요청하는 JOINT DEMARCHE 초안을 제시함.

2)금일 회의 참석자 전원이 상기 미측안에 기본적으로 동의를 표시하였으며, 제네바 주재 해당국 대사에게 ICRC 를 접촉, 동 DEMARCHE 를 공식 전달토록 훈령할것에 합의함.

3)한편 일본측은 금일 회의석상에서, 비록 이라크의 후원하에 수립된 쿠웨이트 임시 정부의 구성 각료등이 불명확하기는 하나, ICRC 가 쿠웨이트 임시정부도 접촉, 전기 외국인 철수관련 협조 요청을 전달할것을 제안함 (일본측으로서는이락보다는 쿠웨이트내의 상황이 보다 더 불안정하므로 여사한 접촉이 필요할것으로 생각하기는 하나, 일본 정부가 나서서 정부간 접촉을 시도하는경우 여사한접촉이 쿠웨이트 임시 정부에 대한 승인으로 비춰질수 있으므로 ICRC 를 통한 간접 접촉이 바람직할것으로

| 중아국 | 장관 | 차관 | 1차보 | 2차보 | 아주국 | 미주국 | 구주국 | 국기국 |
|---|---|---|---|---|---|---|---|---|
| 정문국 | 정와대 | 안기부 | | | | | | |

PAGE 1　　　　90.08.08 11:16

외신 2과 통제관 BN

0006

판단했다함)

4)미국등 회의 참석국들이 일본측 제안에 동의를 표함에 따라 전기 구상도 실시키로 합의함.

5)또한 영국측은 ICRC 를 통한 JOINT DEMRCHE 외에 금일 회의 참석국이 각각 주이락 대사나 대사 대리등 고위급 외교 채널을 통해 이락 정부에 대해 외국인 철수 관련 협조 요청을 공식 전달할것을 제안함.

6)미국측은 외교 채널을 통한 전기 DEMARCHE 및 ICRC 를 통한 JOINT DEMARCHE 가 DUAL-TRACK APPROACH 로서 효과적일것이라고 언급한후 이를 적극 지지함. 여타 참석국도 기본적으로 지지 입장을 표하였으나, 단, 소련측은 본국 정부의 승인을 받은후 동참키로함.

2. 금번 중동 사태 관련 평가

가. 쿠웨이트내 상황이 악화 일로에 있다는 점에 인식을 같이 하였으며, 특히 음료수 및 식품 품귀 현상이 심화될 경우 일종의 PANIC 상태가 도래할것으로 봄.(따라서 외국인 철수 조치가 신속하게 이루어져야 한다는점을 미측은 거듭 강조함)

나. 니시다 참사관는 사견임을 전제로, 상기 영국측 제안에 미측이 즉각적인 동의를 표한점을 감안할때, 미.영간에는 금번 중동 사태 관련 긴밀한 협의가 이루어지고 있는것으로 본다고 언급한후, 특히 미측은 최후의 수단인 무력 사용 이전에 명분을 찾기 위해 실현 가능한 모든 조치(대이락 공개 규탄, 경제 제재, ICRC 등을 통한 국제적 압력 행사등)를 취하기 위해 노력하고 있는것으로 보인다고 언급함.

다. 또한 동 참사관은 이락및 쿠웨이트 거주 미국인이 일종의 볼모로 잡혀있는 현 상황하에서는 미국의 군사 행동이 어려울것으로 예측된다고하고 특히 사우디로서는 자국 영토를 관통하는 이락 송유관을 폐쇄하는 경우, 이를 구실로한 이락의 침공이 예상되므로 여사한 폐쇄 조치를 즉각 취하지 못하고 있는것으로 본다고 말함.

(대사 박동진-국장)

예고 90.12.31 일반

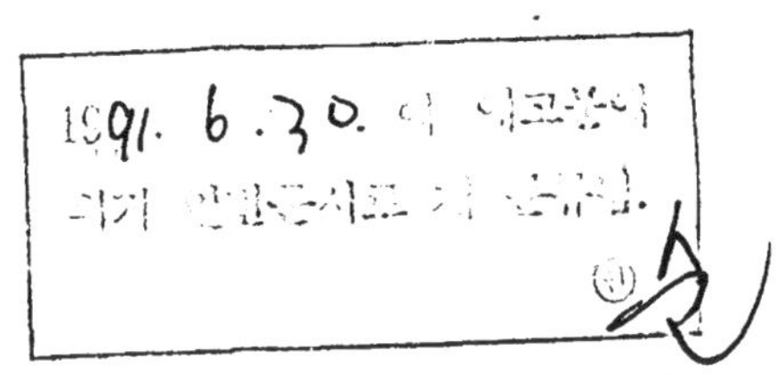


PAGE 2

0007

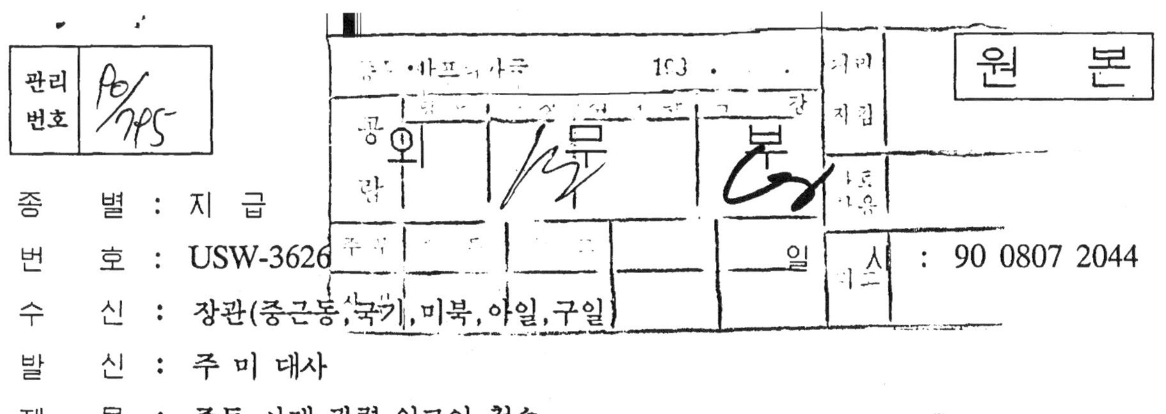

| 관리 번호 | 90/785 |
|---|---|

원 본

종 별 : 지 급

번 호 : USW-3626

일 시 : 90 0807 2044

수 신 : 장관(중근동,국기,미북,아일,구일)

발 신 : 주 미 대사

제 목 : 중동 사태 관련 외국인 철수

연 USW-3627

연호 1. 다. 항 미측 JOINT DEMARCHE 초안을 별첨 타전함.

첨부 미측 초안

(대사 박동진-국장)

90.12.31 일반

별첨

TOALL MEETING PARTICIPANTS

FROM JOHN WOLF, DEPARTMENT OF STATE

BELOW IS SOME PROPOSED LANGUAGE FOR THE JOINT DEMARCHE TO THE ICRC FORYOUR CONSIDERATION BEFORE TODAY'S MEETING.

--THE RECENT IRAQI INVASION OF KUWAIT IS OF ENORMOUS CONCERN TO OUR GOVERNMENTS, AND INDEED, TO THE INTIRE WORLD. CENTRAL TO THIS CONCERN IS THEFATE OF THE MANY FOREIGN NATIONALS CURRENTLY LIVING AND WORKING IN KUWAIT. THEIR SAFETY MUST NOT BE DEPENDENT ON THE RESOLUTION OF THE POLITICAL/MILITARY CRISIS.

--THE ICRC'S UNIQUE HUMANITARIAN ROLE IN THE WORLD AND RESPONSIBILITIES UNDER THE FOURTH GENEVA COVENTION LEAD US TO TURN TO THE ICRC FOR ASSISTANCE IN THE PROTECTION OF OUR NATIONALS AND ALL NON-COMBATANTS CAUGHT UP IN THE CURRENT CRISIS. WE TODAY FORMALLY REQUEST THE ICRC TO ACT ON OUR BEHALF TO HELP FACILITATE THE IMMEDIATE DEPARTURE FROM KUWAIT OF FOREIGN NATIONALS WHO SO DESIRE. WE WILL, OF COURSE, PROVIDE ANY LOGISTICAL SUPPORT FOR THIS EFFORT THAT YOU FEEL NECESSARY.

중아국 아주국 미주국 구주국 국기국

PAGE 1

90.08.08 11:20

외신 2과 통제관 BN

0008

-IRAQ, AS A SIGNATORY TO THE FOURTH CONVENTION, CANNOT DENY ITS RESPONSIBILITY BOTH TO PROTECT NON-COMBATANTS AND TO ALLOW THEM TO DEPART, IF THEY SO DESIRE. IF YOU BELIEVE IT WOULD BE HELPFUL, WE ARE PREPARED, AS A GROUP, TO MAKE THIS POINT TO IRAQ DIRECTLY. IN DOING SO, WE WILL UNEQUIVOCALLY REJECT ANY ARGUMENT THAT IRAQ IS NOT AN OCCUPYING POWER. WE WILL INSISTTHAT EFFORTS TO PROTECT NONCOMBATANTS BEGIN IMMEDIATELY.

--WE WOULD HOPE YOU COULD SHARE WITH US YOUR THOUGHTS ON HOW THE ICRC COULD PROCEED IN ACCOMPLISHING THE IMMEDIATE DEPARTURE OF OUR NATIONALS, AND ON WHAT OUR GOVERNMENT AND THE UN CAN DO TO ASSIST THE ICRC.END

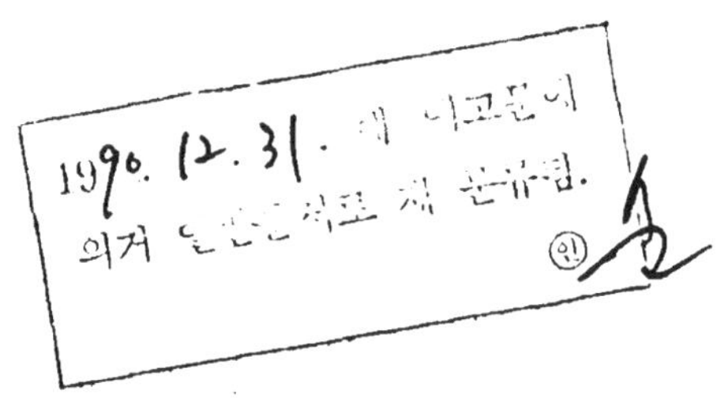

PAGE 2

0009

# 국제적십자 위원회(ICRC)

90.8.9. 국제기구과

1. 연혁

   1863년 국제 부상병 구호위원회(International Committee for the Relief of the Wounded)로 발족하여, 1875년 현 명칭으로 개칭

2. 소재지 : 스위스 제네바

3. 회 원 : 순수 민간기구로 스위스 국민 25인이 회원이며, ICRC에 의하여 승인된 적십자사는 전세계 143개임

4. 기능

   o 국제전, 내전 및 국내 분쟁시 중립기구로서의 역할을 수행하며, 적십자 기본원리를 수호하고, 제네바 협약의 적용 및 동 협약상 위임된 임무를 수행.
   o 부상자 보호, 원조 및 그들의 정신적 안정, 존엄성, 가족권, 종교적 신념등에 관여
   o 고문, 잔혹행위, 약식 처형, 집단 학살, 추방, 인질, 약탈, 민간재산의 무자비한 파괴행위 방지
   o 무력 분쟁의 희생자인 피난민 구호 활동 참가
   o 정치범 수용상태의 국제적 기준 부합여부 확인
   o 전쟁포로나 민간인 수용자 방문 및 감시자 없는 상태에서의 동 수용자 면담
   o 제네바와 직접 연결된 16개 방송국을 통한 전세계적 라디오 통신망 제공

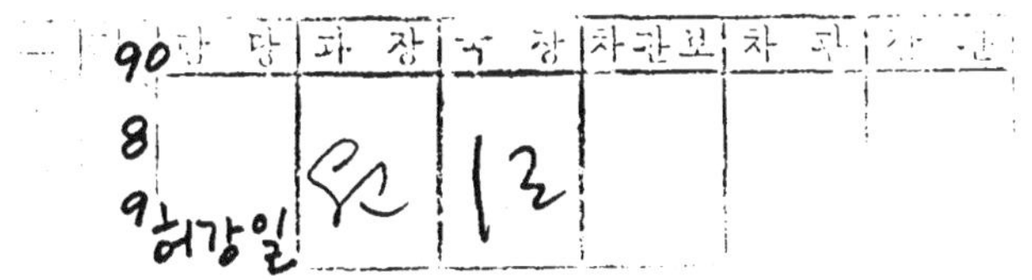

0010

5. 조직 : 총회(25인), 집행위원회(7인) 및 사무국

- o Medical Division : 분쟁지역에서의 의료수요를 측정하여 의료 서비스를 제공하고 전범 및 정치범으로 수감되어 있는 자들을 방문하는 일을 담당.
- o Relief Division : 분쟁지역 물자구입 사정, 물자비축 사정 및 물자수요를 측정하여 필요한 기본물자와 구호 자금을 모집하고, 이의 공정한 배분을 담당

6. 아국과의 관계 : 1955년 대한 적십자사가 ICRC에 의하여 승인되었으며, 그간 아국은 ICRC를 통한 국제구호 사업에 적극 참여하여 왔음(구체 사업내용 별첨)

7. 참고

ICRC와 유사한 기구로 LRCS(적십자사 연맹)가 있으며, ICRC가 전쟁이나 내전등으로 인한 피난민, 정치범등의 주로 정치적인 국제 구호문제에 관여하는 반면, LRCS는 지진, 폭풍등으로 인한 자연재해등의 비정치적 구호 활동에 주로 관여하고 있음. 끝

0011

[illegible] 및 발전계획 지원 ( 1989. 1.1일 ~ 12. 31)

| [illegible]명 | 금액(한화) | 내 용 | 일자 | 비고 |
|---|---|---|---|---|
| 말레이시아 | US$1,000(686,500) | Sungei Besi 캠프 지원용 | 1. 9 | 직송 |
| 네팔 | US$5,000(3,432,500) | 발전계획 지원 | 1. 23 | " |
| 소련 | US$31,856(21,885,072) | 소련 아르메니아 지진 복구계획 지원 | 2. 7 | 연맹 |
| 버마 | US$5,000(3,379,000) | 화재 이재민 구호 | 3. 16 | 연맹 |
| 인도 | US$10,000(6,701,000) | 보필가스 이재민 구호 | 4. 15 | " |
| | US$17,567(11,770,000)상당 | 인도적십자 혈액원 지원용 혈액백 | 8. 20 | 직송 |
| 싱가포르 | US$5,000(3,445,500) | 청소년적십자 캠프 지원 | 5. 10 | 연맹 |
| 세네갈 | US$3,000(2,008,800) | 세네갈 모리타니아 충돌 이재민 구호 | 6. 19 | " |
| [illegible]국 | US$10,000(6,727,000) | 홍수 이재민 구호 | 9. 7 | " |
| 미국 | US$20,000(13,484,000) | 캘리포니아 지진 이재민 구호 | 10. 31 | " |
| 알제리아 | US$10,000(6,761,000) | 지진 이재민 구호 | 11. 24 | " |
| 헝가리 | US$10,000(6,806,000) | 헝가리계 루마니아 난민 구호 | 12. 28 | 직송 |
| 계 | US$128,423(87,086,372) | | | |

3. 국제분담금 납부 현황 ( 1989년도)

| 구 분 | 금액(한화) | 납부일자 |
|---|---|---|
| 적십자사연맹 분담금 | SFrs. 141,960([illegible]9,634,556) | 3. 16 |
| 적십자국제위원회 기여금 | SFrs. [illegible],146(22,817,760) | 9. 30 |
| 계 | SFrs. [illegible],106(82,452,316) | |

0012

1990년도 7. 23일 현재 No. year month day ( )

| 일자 | 국명 | 금액 | 한화 | 내용 | 비고 |
|---|---|---|---|---|---|
| | | (적십자연맹) RC US$ 20,000 | 82,032,000 | 루마니아 유혈사태 | ICRC |
| | | US$ 100,000 | (계약로) | 이재민 구호 | |
| 2.9 | 영국 | US$ 10,000 | 6,918,000 | 강풍 이재민 구호 | " |
| 2.16 | 트리니다드토바고 | US$ 5,000 | 3,466,000 | 트리니다드토바고 경유 라이베리아 난민 구호 | 연맹 |
| 3.6 | 서사모아 | US$ 5,000 | 3,498,000 | 태풍 OFA 이재민 구호 | 연맹 |
| 3.6 | 파키스탄 | US$ 2,000 | | 아프간 난민 구호 사업中 장애자 치료 및 재활사업 | 직접 지원 |
| 4.6 | 이디오피아 | US$ 5,000 | 3,565,000 | 기근 이재민 구호 | 연맹 |
| 5.18 | 베트남 | US$ 10,000 | 7,088,000 | 베트남 RC 본사 건물 보수 지원 | 직송 |
| 5.26 | 알리위낭 연수원 | US$ 5,000 | 3,545,000 | 알리위낭 연수원 재정 지원 | " |
| 7.5 | 이란 | US$ 20,000 | 14,374,000 | 지진피해 이재민 구호 | 연맹 |
| 7.13 | " | US$ 30,000 | 21,591,000 | " (담요 10,000장) | " |
| 7.1 | " (외무 지원) | US$ 175,000 | (현품) 의료품 | " (6개 컨테이너) | 직송 |
| 7.4 | " | US$ 88,000 | (현품) 모포 | " (9개 ") | " |
| 7.8 | " | US$ 40,000 | ( " ) 의료품 | " (생필품) | " |
| 7.1 | 중국(연변조선족) | US$ 10,000 | 7,183,000 | 발전 계획 지원 (잔액: 28,000불.) | " |
| 7.23 | 필리핀 | US$ 10,000 | 7,184,000 | 지진 이재민 구호 (잔액: 18,000불) | 연맹 |

국제구호

0013

AUG 09 '90 10:51 KOREA RED CROSS (744-0235)

戰時에 있어서의 民間人의 保護에 관한
1949年 8月12日字 제네바 協約(第4協約)

90.8.8. 국제기구과

제4조 본 협약에 의하여 보호되는 자는 ....... 충돌 당사국 또는 점령국의 권력내에 있는 자로서 동 충돌 당사국 또는 점령국의 국민이 아닌 자이다. .......

제14조 ...... 이익보호국 및 국제적십자 위원회는 이러한 병원. 안전지대 및 지구의 설정 및 승인을 용이하게 하기 위하여 주선을 제공하도록 초청된다

제35조 충돌이 개시될 때 또는 그것의 진행기간중에 충돌 당사국의 영역으로부터 퇴거하기를 희망하는 모든 피보호자들은 그 퇴거가 그 나라의 국가적 이익에 반하지 않는 한, 그 영역으로부터 퇴거할 권리를 가진다. .......

| 담 당 | 과 장 | 국 장 | 차관보 | 차 관 | 장 관 |
|---|---|---|---|---|---|
| 허강일 | | | | | |

0014

## (6) 戰時에 있어서의 民間人의 保護에 관한 1949年 8月 12日字 제네바 協約(第4協約)

署 名 1949年 8月 12日
發 效 1950年 10月 21日
大韓民國 1966年 8月 16日 發效(조약 제218호)

戰時에 있어서의 民間人의 保護에 관한 協約을 制定할 目的으로 1949年 4月 21日부터 同年 8月 12日까지 제네바에서 開催된 外交官會議에 參加한 諸政府의 下記 署名 全權委員은 다음과 같이 合意하였다.

(全權委員名略)

### 第1篇 總 則

第1條
第2條 } 第1協約第1條─第3條와 同文
第3條

**第4條** 本協約에 의하여 保護되는 者는 武力衝突 또는 占領의 경우에 있어서 特定時點에 그 形式의 如何에 관계없이 衝突當事國 또는 占領國의 權力內에 있는 者로서 同衝突當事國 또는 占領國의 國民이 아닌 者이다.

本協約의 拘束을 받지 않는 國家의 國民은 本協約의 保護를 받지 못한다. 交戰國領域內에 있는 中立國의 國民 또는 共同交戰國의 國民은 그들의 本國이 그들을 權力下에 두고있는 國家內에 通常的인 外交代表를 駐在시키고 있는 期間동안은 被保護者로 看做되지 아니한다.

단, 第2篇의 諸規定은 第13條에서 規定한 바와 같이 그 適用範圍에 있어 보다 廣範하다.

陸戰에 있어서의 軍隊의 負傷者 및 病者의 狀態改善에 관한 1949年 8月 12日字 제네바協約, 海上에 있어서의 軍隊의 負傷者, 病者 및 遭難者의 狀態改善에 관한 1949年 8月 12日字 제네바協約 또는 포로의 待遇에 관한 1949年 8月 12日字 제네바協約에 의하여 保護를 받는 者는 本協約이 意味하는 被保護者로 考慮되지 아니한다.

**第5條** 衝突當事國의 領域內에서 被保護人이 個人으로서 衝突當事國의 安全을 害하는 活動을 하였다는 嫌疑 또는 그러한 活動에 從事하고 있다는 事實을 當該紛爭當事國에 確認하였을 경우에는, 그러한 個人은 同人을 위하여 行使된다면 그러한 衝突當事國의 安全에 有害한 協約上의 諸權利와 特權을 要請할 수 없다.

占領地域內에서 被保護人이 占領國의 間諜으로 抑留되고 있는 동안 그러한 者는 絶對的인 軍事上의 安全이 要求하는 경우에 있어서는 本協約에 基한 通信의 自由를 喪失한 것으로 간주된다.

그러나 어느 경우에 있어서도 그러한 者는 人道的인 待遇를 받아야 하며, 訴追의 경우에 있어서는 本協約에서 規定한 公平한 正式裁判을 받을 權利를 剝奪당하지 아니한다. 또한 그러한 者는 衝突當事者 또는 占領國의 安全이 許하는 早速한 時日內에 本協約에 基한 完全한 權利와 特權을 許與받아야 한다.

**第6條** 本協約은 第2條에 言及된 衝突 또는 占領의 開始時부터 適用된다.

衝突當事國의 領域內에 있어서는 本協約의 適用은 軍事行動의 一般的 終了와 同時에 停止된다.

占領地域의 경우에 있어서는 本協約의 適用은 軍事行動의 一般的 終了 1年後에 停止된다. 단, 占領國은 占領期間中 同地域內에서 政府機能을 行使하는 限度에 있어 本協約 第1條로부터 第12條, 第27條, 第29條부터 第34條, 第47條, 第49條, 第51條, 第52條, 第53條, 第59條, 第61條에서 第77條 및 第143條의 諸規定의 拘束을 받는다.

그러한 期間後에 釋放, 送還 또는 定着을 받을 被保護人은 그동안 本協約에 의한 利益을 계속 享有한다.

**第7條** 第11條, 第14條, 第15條, 第17條, 第36條, 第108條, 第109條, 第132條, 第133條 및 第149條에서 明文으로 規定한 協定에 부가하여 締約國은 別途의 規定을 設定함이 適當하다고 認定하는 모든 關係事項에 관하여 其他 特別協定을 締結할 수 있다. 어떠한 特別協定이라도 本協約에서 정하는 被保護人의 地位에 不利한 영향을 미치거나 또는 本協約이 그들 被保護人에게 부여하는 權利를 制限하여서는 아니된다.

被保護人은 本協約의 適用을 받는 동안 前記 諸協約의 利益을 계속 享有한다. 단, 반대의 明文規定이 上述한 또는 追後의 諸協定에 包含되었거나, 또는 被保護人에 관한 보다 有利한 措置가 衝突當事國의 一方 또는 他方에 의하여 취하여졌을 경우에는 例外로 한다.

**第8條** 被保護人은 어떠한 경우에 있어서도 本協約 및 前條에 言及된 特別協定(그러한 協定이 있는 경우)에 의하여 保障된 權利를 部分的으로나 또는 全體的으로도 拋棄할 수 없다.

**第9條** 第3協約 第8條와 同文

**第10條** 本協約의 諸規定은 國際赤十字委員會 또는 其他의 公平한 人道的機關이 關係衝突當事國의 同意를 얻어 民間人의 保護 및 그 救濟를 위하여 취하는 人道的 活動을 妨害하는 것은 아니다.

**第11條** 締約國은 언제라도 公平과 有效性에 관한 모든 保障을 提供하는 機關에 대하여 本協約에 의하여 利益保護國에 주어진 職務를 委任할 것에 同意할 수 있다.

本協約에 의하여 保護되는 者가 理由如何를 불문하고 利益保護國 또는 前項에 規定된 機關의 活動에 의한 利益을 받지 못하는 경우, 또는 利益이 中斷된 경우에는 抑留國은 中立國 또는 그러한 機關에 대하여 衝突當事國에 의하여 指定된 利益이 本協約에 基하여 遂行하는 機能을 引受하도록 要求하여야 한다.

이에 따라 保護가 마련되지 않았을 경우에는 抑留國은 本條의 規定에 따라 本協約에 의하여 利益保護國이 遂行하는 人道的인 機能을 擔當하도록 國際赤十字委員會와 같은 人道的인 機關의 用役의 提供을 要求하거나 또는 받아들여야 한다.

前記의 目的을 위하여 關係國에 의하여 招請된 또는 스스로 申請한 中立國 또는 機關은 本協約에 의하여 保護되는 者가 所屬하는 衝突當事國에 대하여 責任感을 가지고 行動하도록 要求되며, 또한 當該機能을 引受하여 公平하게 遂行할 地位에 있다는 充分한 保障을 提供하도록 要求된다.

前記 諸規定은 軍事的인 理由, 특히 그 領域의 全部 또는 많은 部分이 占領되어 他國 또는 그 同盟國과의 交涉의 自由를 一時的으로라도 制限당한 國家를 當事者로 하는 國家間의 特別協定에 의하여 損傷되어서는 안된다.

本協約에 있어서 利益保護國이란 本條의 의미에서 機關이란 말의 代身으로 適用된다.

本條의 規定은 占領地域內에 있는



0015

中立國의 國民 또는 그 本國이 正常的인 外交代表를 駐在시키지 않고 있는 交戰國의 領域內에 있는 中立國의 國民에 대하여 適用된다.

**第12條** 被保護者의 利益을 위하여 合當하다고 認定되는 경우, 특히 本協約의 適用 또는 解釋에 관하여 衝突當事國間에 意見의 相違가 있는 경우에는 利益保護國은 이러한 意見의 相違를 解決하기 위하여 周旋에 나서야 한다.

이 目的을 위하여 各利益保護國은 1當事國의 招請 또는 自國의 發意로 可能하면 適當히 選定된 中立領域內에서 衝突當事國 代表의, 그리고 특히 被保護人에 대하여 責任을 지고 있는 當局의 會議開催를 提議할 수 있다. 衝突當事國은 이 目的을 위하여 그들에게 提示된 提案을 實施할 義務를 진다. 利益保護國은 必要한 경우에는 衝突當事國의 同意를 위하여 中立國에 속하는 者 또는 國際赤十字委員會에 의하여 委任된 者로서 그러한 會議에 參席토록 招請될 者의 名單을 提議할 수 있다.

## 第2編 戰爭의 特定結果에 대한 住民의 一般的 保護

**第13條** 第2編의 規定은 특히 人種, 國籍, 宗敎 또는 政治的 意見에 根據한 不利한 差別을 받음이 없이 衝突當事國의 住民 全體에 適用되며, 또 戰爭에 의하여 發生되는 苦痛을 輕減함을 目的으로 한다.

**第14條** 平時에 있어서 締約國, 그리고 敵對行爲의 勃發後에 있어서 敵對行爲의 當事國은 各者의 領域內에, 그리고 必要한 경우에는 占領地域內에 負傷者, 病者, 老人, 15歲 未滿의 兒童, 姙産婦 및 7歲未滿의 幼兒의 母를 戰爭의 영향으로부터 保護하기 위하여 組織되는 病院, 安全地帶 및 地區를 設定할 수 있다.

關係國은 敵對行爲의 勃發時 및 敵對行爲의 계속기간 중 그들이 設定한 地帶 및 地區를 相互承認하는 데 관한 協定을 締結할 수 있다. 關係國은 이 目的을 위하여 必要하다고 認定되는 修正을 가하여 本協定에 附屬된 協定案의 規定을 適用할 수 있다.

利益保護國 및 國際赤十字委員會는 이러한 病院·安全地帶 및 地區의 設定 및 承認을 容易하게 하기 위하여 周旋을 提供하도록 招請된다.

**第15條** 어느 衝突當事國의 一方은 直接으로 또는 中立國 또는 人道的인 機構를 통하여 戰爭이 계속되고 있는 地域內에 下記者를 差別없이 戰爭의 영향으로부터 保護하기 위한 中立地帶를 設置할 것을 相對方 當事國에 提議할 수 있다.

ⓐ 負傷者 또는 病者(戰鬪員, 非戰鬪員 不問)

ⓑ 敵對行爲에 參加하지 아니하고 그 地域에 居住하는 동안 어떠한 軍事的 性質을 가진 事業도 遂行하지 아니하는 民間人

關係國이 提案한 中立地帶의 地理的 位置管理, 食糧供給 및 監視에 관하여 合意하였을 경우에는 衝突當事國의 代表者는 文書에 의한 協定을 締結, 署名하여야 한다. 同協定은 地帶中立化의 時期와 存續期間을 確定해 두어야 한다.

**第16條** 負傷者, 病者, 虛弱者 및 姙産婦는 特別한 保護 및 尊重의 대상이 되어야 한다.

軍事的인 事情이 許諾하는 限, 各衝突當事國은 死亡者 및 負傷者를 搜索하고 遭難者 및 기타 重大한 危險에 處한 者를 救助하고 掠奪 및 虐待로부터 이들을 保護하기 위하여 취하여지는 措置에 便益을 提供하여야 한다.

**第17條** 衝突當事國은 攻擊 또는 包圍된 地域으로부터의 負傷者·病者·虛弱者·老人·兒童 및 姙産婦의 撤收 및 同地域으로 向하는 宗敎要員·醫務要員 및 醫療器材의 通過를 위한 地域的 協定을 締結하도록 努力하여야 한다.

**第18條** 負傷者, 病者, 虛弱者 및 姙産婦를 看護하기 위하여 設立된 民間病院은 어떠한 경우에도 攻擊의 對象이 되어서는 아니되며, 항상 衝突當事國에 의하여 尊重되고 保護되어야 한다.

衝突當事國은 모든 民間病院에 대하여 그 病院이 民間病院이라는 것과 그 病院이 使用하는 建物이 第19條의 規定에 따라 病院으로서의 保護를 剝奪당할 만한 目的으로 使用되고 있지 않다는 것을 提示하는 證明書를 發給하여야 한다.

民間病院은 國家의 許可가 있는 경우에 限하여 陸戰에 있어서의 軍隊의 負傷者 및 病者의 狀態改善에 관한 1949年 8月 12日字 제네바協約 第38條에 規定된 標識에 의하여 表示되어야 한다.

衝突當事國은 軍事上의 事情이 許하는 限 敵對行爲의 可能性을 除去하기 위하여 敵의 陸·空·海軍에게 民間病院을 明白히 보일 수 있도록 明確한 標識를 부착하는 必要한 措置를 취하여야 한다.

病院이 軍事目標物에 近接해 있음으로써 露出된 危險에 비추어 그러한 病院은 可能한 限, 그러한 目標物로부터 멀어져 位置할 것이 要望된다.

**第19條** 民間病院이 享有할 수 있는 保護는 그러한 病院이 그 人道的인 任務를 벗어나 敵에게 有害行爲를 하도록 使用된 경우를 除外하고는 消滅되어서는 아니된다. 단, 그 保護는 모든 適當한 경우에 合理的인 期限을 정한 警告를 發하고, 그 警告가 無視된 後가 아니면 消滅될 수 없다.

負傷者 또는 病者인 軍隊의 構成員이 이들 病院에서 看護되고 있는 事實 또는 이들 戰鬪員으로부터 받아둔 小武器 및 彈藥이 存在하나, 아직 正當한 機關에 引渡되지 않고 있는 事實은 敵에게 有害한 行爲로 認定되지 아니한다.

**第20條** 民間人 負傷者 및 病者, 虛弱者 및 姙産婦의 搜索·撤收·輸送 및 看護에 從事하는 者를 包含하여 民間病院의 運營 및 管理에 正規로 또는 全的으로 從事하는 者는 尊重되고 保護되어야 한다.

占領地域 또는 軍事作戰地域內에서 上述한 者는 所持者의 寫眞을 添附하고, 責任있는 當局의 스탬프를 捺印하여 그들의 身分을 證明하는 證明書 및 任務遂行中 左腕에 달아야 할 捺印된 防水性腕章에 의하여 識別될 수 있도록 하여야 한다. 이 腕章은 國家에 의하여 交付되어야 하며, 아울러 陸戰에 있어서의 軍隊의 負傷者 및 病者의 狀態改善에 관한 1949年 8月 12日字 제네바協約 第38條에 정한 標識를 달아야 한다.

民間病院의 運營 및 管理에 從事하는 其他의 職員도 그들이 雇傭되는 동안 本條에 規定된 바에 따라, 그리고 本條에 規定된 條件下에서 尊重되고 保護되며, 腕章을 使用할 權利가 있다. 身分證明書에는 그들이 從事하는 任務를 記載하여야 한다.

各病院의 事務所는 恒常 그 職員의 最近名簿를 自國 또는 占領軍의 權限있는 當國의 使用에 供할 수 있도록 備置하여야 한다.

**第21條** 民間人 負傷者 및 病者, 虛弱者 및 姙産婦를 輸送하는 陸上의 護送車輛隊 또는 病院列車 또는 海上의 特殊船舶은 第18條에서 規定된 病院과 同一하게 尊重 및 保護되어야 하며, 아울러 國家의 同意를 얻어 陸戰에 있어서의 軍隊의 負傷者 및 病者의 狀態改善에 관한 1949年 8月 12日字 제네바協約의 第38條에서 規定한 特殊標識를 揭示하여 表示하여야 한다.

**第22條** 民間人 負傷者 및 病者·虛弱者 및 姙産婦의 撤收 또는 醫務要員 및 醫療機構의 輸送을 위하여 全的으로 使用되는 航空機는 모든 關係衝突當事國間에 特別히 合意된 高度, 時



0016

刻 및 航路에 따라 飛行하고 있는 동안은 攻擊되어서는 아니되고 尊重되어야 한다.

이들 航空機는 陸戰에 있어서의 軍隊의 負傷者 및 病者의 狀態改善에 관한 1949年 8月 12日字 제네바協約 第38條에서 定하는 特殊標識로 表示되어야 한다.

別途의 合意가 없는 限, 敵 또는 敵占領領域上의 飛行은 禁止된다.

그러한 航空機는 모든 着陸要求에 服從하여야 한다. 이러한 要求에 의하여 着陸하는 경우에는 同航空機는 그 乘客과 함께 調査가 있을 때에는 調査를 받은 後에 飛行을 계속할 수 있다.

**第23條** 各締約國은 他方締約國, 비록 敵國일지라도 民間人에게만 向하는 醫療品 및 病院用品, 그리고 宗敎上의 儀式을 위하여 必要로 하는 物品等 모든 託送品의 自由通過를 許容하여야 한다. 各締約國은 15歲未滿의 兒童, 姙産婦에게 送付되는 不可缺한 食料品, 被服 및 營養劑 등 모든 託送品의 自由通過를 許可하여야 한다.

締約國은 다음과 같은 경우를 憂慮할 重大한 理由가 있다고 認定하는 경우를 除外하고는 前項에서 말한 託送品의 自由通過를 許可할 義務를 진다.

ⓐ 託送品이 그 行先地에 到着하지 못할 憂慮가 있는 경우
ⓑ 管理가 有效하게 實施되지 못할 憂慮가 있는 경우
ⓒ 敵이 當該託送品이 없으면 自身이 供給 또는 生産하지 않으면 안 될 物品의 代身으로 그 託送品을 充當하거나, 또는 當該託送品이 없었더라면 그러한 物品의 生産에 必要한 原料, 用役 또는 設備를 使用치 않게 됨으로써 敵의 軍事力 또는 經濟에 대하여 明白히 利益을 주게 될 憂慮가 있는 경우

本條 第①項에서 言及한 託送品의 通過를 許可하는 國家는 그 託送品의 利益을 받는 者에 대한 分配가 現地에 있어서의 利益保護國의 監督下에 행하여질 것을 그 許可의 條件으로 할 수 있다.

前記의 託送品은 可能한 限 迅速히 輸送되어야 하며, 또한 託送品의 自由通過를 許可하는 國家는 그 通過를 許可하는 데 관한 技術的 條件을 정할 權利를 갖는다.

**第24條** 衝突當事國은 戰爭의 結果로 孤兒가 되었거나 또는 自己家族들로부터 離散된 15歲未滿의 兒童이 遺棄되지 않도록, 그리고 모든 경우에 있어 그들의 扶養, 宗敎生活 및 敎育이 容易하게 保障됨을 確保하기 위한 必要한 措置를 취하여야 한다. 그들의 敎育은 可能한 限 類似한 文化的 傳統을 가진 者들에게 委託되어야 한다.

衝突當事國은 第①項에 言及된 諸原則이 遵守되리라는 適當한 保障이 있는 경우에는 利益保護國의 同意를 얻어(만일 그러한 利益保護國이 있는 경우) 衝突이 계속되고 있는 동안 前記 兒童들의 中立國內 收容에 대하여 便宜를 提供하여야 한다.

衝突當事國은 또한 12歲未滿의 모든 兒童들에게 名札의 佩用 또는 其他의 方法으로 그들의 身元을 識別케 할 수 있도록 하여야 한다.

**第25條** 衝突當事國의 領域 또는 그 占領地域內에 있는 모든 者에 대하여는 그들의 家族이 있는 場所의 如何를 不問하고 嚴密한 私的性格을 가진 消息을 그들 家族들과 相互傳達할 수 있도록 하여야 한다. 이러한 書信은 迅速히, 그리고 不當하게 遲滯함이 없이 傳達되어야 한다.

만일 어떤 事情에 의하여 通常郵便으로는 自己家族과의 書信交換이 困難 또는 不可能하게 되었을 경우에는 關係衝突當事國은 第140條에 規定된 中央被保護者情報局과 같은 中立的인 仲介機關에 依賴하여야 하며, 그러한 仲介機關과 協議하여 특히 各國赤十字社의 協力을 얻어 가장 좋은 條件下에서 그들의 任務遂行을 確保하기 위한 方法을 決定하여야 한다.

만약 衝突當事國이 家族通信을 制限할 必要가 있다고 認定하는 경우에는 그러한 制限을 自由로이 選擇된 25개의 單語가 들어갈 수 있는 標準書式의 强制使用과 同書式에 의한 書信의 回數를 月 1回로 制限하는 것에 局限되어야 한다.

**第26條** 各衝突當事國은 戰爭 때문에 離散된 家族들이 相互連絡을 回復하고 될 수 있으면, 再會하려는 目的으로서 행하는 照會에 대하여 便宜를 提供하여야 한다. 各衝突當事國은 특히 이러한 事業에 從事하는 團體가 自國에서 용인될 수 있고, 또한 그러한 團體가 自國의 安全保障規則에 따르는 限, 同團體의 事業을 奬勵하여야 한다.

## 第3編 被保護者의 地位 및 待遇

### 第1部 衝突當事國의 領域 및 占領地域內에 공통되는 規則

**第27條** 被保護者들은 모든 경우에 있어서 그들의 身體·名譽·家族으로서 가지는 諸權利, 信仰 및 宗敎上의 行事, 風俗 및 慣習을 尊重받을 權利를 가진다. 그들은 항상 人道的으로 待遇되어야 하며, 특히 모든 暴行 또는 脅迫, 侮辱 및 公衆의 好奇心으로부터 保護되어야 한다.

婦女子들은 그들의 名譽에 대한 侵害, 특히 强姦, 强制賣淫 또는 其他 모든 形態의 외설 행위로부터 特別히 保護되어야 한다.

被保護者를 그 權力下에 두고 있는 衝突當事國은 健康狀態, 年齡, 宗敎 또는 性別에 관한 規定을 侵害함이 없이, 특히 人種, 宗敎 또는 政治的 意見을 根據로 하는 不利한 差別을 둠이 없이 모든 被保護者들을 同一한 考慮下에 待遇하여야 한다.

그러나 衝突當事國은 被保護者에 관하여 戰爭의 結果로 必要케 된 統制 및 安全措置를 취할 수 있다.

**第28條** 被保護者의 所在地는 軍事行動으로부터 보호되는 地點 또는 地域으로 利用되어서는 아니된다.

**第29條** 被保護者를 權力下에 두고 있는 衝突當事國은 招來될지도 모르는 個人的 責任에 관계없이 自國의 機關이 그러한 被保護者에게 부여하는 待遇에 대하여 責任을 진다.

**第30條** 被保護者는 利益保護國, 國際赤十字委員會, 그들이 在留하는 國家의 赤十字會 또는 被保護者들을 援助하는 기타 團體에 대하여 申請할 수 있는 모든 便宜를 가진다.

前記의 諸團體는 軍事上 또는 安全上의 考慮에 의하여 정하여지는 制限의 範圍內에 이 目的을 위한 諸般便宜를 當局으로부터 提供받아야 한다.

抑留國 또는 占領國은 利益保護國 및 國際赤十字委員會의 代表에 의한 第143條에 規定하는 訪問以外에 被保護者들에게 대한 精神的 援助 또는 物質的 救護의 提供을 目的으로 하는 其他 團體의 代表者에 의한 被保護者 訪問에 대하여도 可能한 限 많은 便宜를 提供하여야 한다.

**第31條** 被保護者 또는 第三者로부터 특히 情報를 얻기 위하여 被保護者들에게 肉體的 또는 精神的 强制를 가하여서는 아니된다.

**第32條** 締約國은 그 權力下에 두고 있는 被保護者들에게 肉體的 苦痛을 주거나 또는 그들을 虐殺하는 것과 같은 性格을 가진 措置를 취함을 禁止할 것에 특히 同意한다. 이러한 禁止는 被保護者들의 殺害·拷問·肉體的 刑罰·身體의 切斷, 그들의 治療上 必要치 않은 醫學的 또는 科學的 實驗에 適用될 뿐 아니라 그것이 民間機關에 의하여 행하여지거나 또는 軍事的 機關에 의하여 행하여지거나를 막론하고, 其他의 모든 殘忍한 措置에도 適用된다.



0017

**第33條** 被保護者는 그 自身이 행하지 않은 違反行爲로 인하여 處罰되어서는 아니된다. 團體罰 및 모든 脅迫 또는 恐嚇에 의한 措置는 禁止된다.

掠奪은 禁止된다.

被保護者 및 그들의 財産에 대한 報復은 禁止된다.

**第34條** 人質은 禁止된다.

## 第2部 衝突當事國의 領域에 있는 外國人

**第35條** 衝突이 開始될 때 또는 그것의 進行期間中에 衝突當事國의 領域으로부터 退去하기를 希望하는 모든 被保護者들은 그 退去가 그 나라의 國家的 利益에 反하지 않는 限, 그 領域으로부터 退去할 權利를 가진다. 그들의 退去申請에 대하여는 正規로 制定된 節次에 따라 決定하여야 하며, 同決定은 可能한 限 迅速히 행하여져야 한다. 退去를 許可받은 被保護者들은 旅行에 必要한 金錢을 所持하고 또한 適當한 量의 個人用品을 携帶할 수 있다.

當該領域으로부터의 退去를 拒否당한 者들은 再審査를 위하여 抑留國이 指定하는 法院 또는 行政廳에서 同拒否에 대하여 可能한 限 迅速히 再審査를 받을 權利를 가진다.

利益保護國의 代表의 要請이 있을 때는 當該領域으로부터의 退去許可申請에 대한 拒否理由 및 退去를 拒否당한 者들의 姓名을 可能한 限 迅速히 그들에게 通告하여야 한다.

**第36條** 前條에 의하여 許可되는 退去는 安全, 衛生, 保健 및 食糧에 관하여 滿足할 만한 條件下에서 遂行되어야 한다. 그것에 관한 모든 費用은 抑留國 領域의 出國地點으로부터는 그들의 行先地가 되는 國家가 負擔하고, 中立國으로 退去할 경우에는 恩澤을 받는 者의 所屬國이 負擔하여야 한다. 그 移動에 관한 實施細目은 必要할 때에는 關係國間의 特別協定으로서 정할 수 있다.

前項의 規定은 衝突當事國이 敵의 權力下에 있는 自由國民의 交換 및 送還에 관하여 特別協定을 締結하는 것을 妨害하지 아니한다.

**第37條** 訴訟係屬中에 拘禁되어 있거나 또는 自由刑에 服役하고 있는 被保護者들은 拘禁되어 있는 동안 人道的으로 待遇되어야 한다.

이들이 釋放되는 即時로 前記 各條의 規定에 따라 그 領域으로부터 退去를 要求할 수 있다.

**第38條** 被保護者의 地位는 本協約 특히 第27條 및 第41條에 의하여 認定되는 特別措置를 例外로 하고 原則的으로 平時에 있어서의 外國人에 관한 規定에 의하여 계속 規律되어야 한다. 어떠한 경우에 있어서도 被保護者들에게 대하여는 다음과 같은 諸權利를 부여하여야 한다.

① 被保護者들은 그들 個人 또는 集團에게 送付되는 救護品을 받을 수 있을 것

② 被保護者는 그 健康狀態로 보아 必要한 경우에는 關係國의 國民들과 同等한 程度로 醫療上의 看護 및 入院治療를 받을 것

③ 被保護者는 自己가 信奉하는 宗敎를 믿을 수 있고, 또 同一한 宗派에 속하는 聖職者들로부터 宗敎上의 援助를 받을 것

④ 被保護者가 戰爭의 危險에 直面하고 있는 地區에 居住하고 있을 경우에는 關係國의 國民과 同一한 程度로 그 地區로부터의 移轉을 許容받을 것

⑤ 15歲未滿의 兒童, 妊産婦 및 7歲未滿의 幼兒를 가진 婦人은 그들에게 相當하는 關係國의 國民과 同等한 待遇에 의한 恩澤을 받을 것

**第39條** 戰爭으로 인하여 有給職業을 喪失한 被保護者들에 대하여는 有給職業을 구할 機會를 부여하여야 한다. 그러한 機會는 安全上의 考慮 및 第40條의 規定에 따를 것을 條件으로 하고 被保護者가 滯留하는 國家의 國民이 享有하는 것과 同等한 것이어야 한다.

衝突當事國이 어떤 被保護者에 대하여 統制措置를 適用한 結果로 그 自身의 生活維持를 不可能케 하였을 경우, 특히 安全上의 理由에 의하여 被保護者가 適當한 條件으로 有給職業에 就業함을 妨害받았을 경우에는 그 衝突當事國은 그 被保護者 및 그의 扶養을 받는 者들의 生活을 保障하여야 한다.

被保護者들은 어떠한 경우에 있어서도 本國, 利益保護國 또는 第30條에서 言及한 救護團體로부터 手當을 支給받을 수 없다.

**第40條** 被保護者는 그가 滯留하는 衝突當事國의 國民과 同等한 程度 이상으로는 勞動을 强制받지 아니한다.

被保護者가 敵國의 國民일 경우에는 人間으로서의 食糧·住居·被服·輸送 및 健康을 確保하기 위하여 正常的으로 必要한 勞動으로서 軍事行動의 遂行에 直接關係가 없는 것 이외에는 그들에게 强要할 수 없다.

前②項에서 言及한 경우에 있어서 勞動을 强制당한 被保護者로 특히 賃金, 勞動時間, 被服 및 器具, 豫備的作業訓練, 그리고 業務上의 災害 및 疾病에 대한 補償에 관하여 그들이 滯留하는 國家의 勞動者들과 同一한 條件 및 保護의 恩澤을 받는다.

前記의 規定이 違反될 경우에는 被保護者는 第30條에 의하여 異議申請의 權利行使를 許容받는다.

**第41條** 被保護者를 그 權力下에 두고 있는 國家는 本協約에서 말하는 統制措置가 不適當하다고 認定하는 경우에 있어서도 第42條 및 第43條의 規定에 의한 住居指定 또는 抑留보다 더 苛酷한 統制措置를 取하여서는 아니된다.

住居를 指定하는 決定에 의하여 從來의 住居로부터 他場所로 移動할 것을 要求받은 者에 대하여 第39條 第②項의 規定을 適用함에 있어 抑留國은 可能한 限, 本協約 第3編 第4部에서 정하는 福祉의 基準에 따라야 한다.

**第42條** 被保護者의 抑留 또는 住居指定은 抑留國의 安全保障上 이를 絶對必要로 하는 경우에 限하여 命할 수 있다.

만일 어떤 者가 利益保護國의 代表를 통하여 自發的으로 抑留를 요구하고, 또한 그의 事情이 抑留를 必要로 할 때에는 그 者를 權力下에 두고 있는 國家는 그를 抑留하여야 한다.

**第43條** 被保護者로 抑留되었거나 또는 住居指定을 받은 者는 再審査를 위하여 抑留國이 指定하는 適當한 法院 또는 行政機關에서 可能한 限, 迅速히 그러한 處分에 대하여 再審査를 받을 權利를 가진다. 抑留 또는 住居指定이 계속된 경우에는 最初의 決定을 有利하게 變更시키기 위하여 定期的으로, 그리고 最少限 年 2回 各事件의 審査를 행하여야 한다.

抑留國은 關係被保護者의 反對가 없는 限 抑留되었거나 住居指定을 받은 者 또는 住居指定으로부터 放免된 者들의 姓名을 可能한 限, 迅速히 利益保護國에 通告하여야 한다. 本條 第①項에서 言及한 法院 또는 行政機關의 決定은 同一한 條件下에서 可能한 限 迅速히 利益保護國에 通告되어야 한다.

**第44條** 抑留國이 本協約에서 말하는 統制措置를 適用함에 있어 事實上 어떠한 政府의 保護도 받지 않고 있는 亡命者를 다만 그들이 法律上 敵國의 國籍을 가지고 있다는 理由만으로써 適性의 外國人으로 取扱하여서는 아니된다.

**第45條** 被保護者들은 本協約의 締約國이외의 國家에 移送되어서는 아니된다. 이 規定은 敵對行爲의 終了 후에 있어서의 被保護者들의 送還 또는 居住國에의 歸還을 妨害하는 것은 아니다.



0018

抑留國은 當該締約國이 本協約을 適用할 意思 및 能力을 가지고 있음을 確認한 후에만 被保護者들을 本協約의 締約國에 移送할 수 있다.

被保護者들이 그러한 事情下에서 移送되었을 경우 被保護者들을 받아들인 國家는 被保護者들이 그 保護下에 있는 동안 本協約을 適用할 責任을 진다. 그러나 被保護者들을 받아들인 國家가 어떤 重要한 點들에 대하여 本協約의 規定을 施行치 않았을 경우에는 被保護者들을 移送한 國家는 利益保護國의 通告에 따라 그들의 狀態를 改善하기 위하여 有效한 措置를 취하거나, 또는 被保護者의 返還을 要請하여야 한다. 그러한 要請은 받아들여져야 한다.

被保護者들은 어떠한 경우에라도 그들의 政治的 意見 또는 宗敎的 信仰 때문에 迫害를 받을 憂慮가 있는 國家에 移送되어서는 아니된다.

本條의 規定은 敵對行爲의 開始前에 締結된 犯罪人引渡條約에 따라 普通의 刑法上의 犯罪行爲 때문에 訴追되고 있는 被保護者들의 引渡를 妨害하지 아니한다.

**第46條** 被保護者에 대하여 취하여진 制限的 措置는 아직 廢止되고 있지않는 限, 敵對行爲의 終了 후에 可能한 限 早速히 廢止되어야 한다.

被保護者들의 財産에 관하여 취하여진 制限的 措置는 抑留國의 法令에 따라 敵對行爲의 終了後에 可能한 限 早速히 廢止되어야 한다.

## 第3部 占領地域

**第47條** 占領地域에 있는 被保護者들은 어떠한 경우 및 어떠한 方法으로도 占領의 結果로 同地域의 制度 또는 政治上에 招來되는 모든 變化, 占領地域 當局과 占領國間에 締結되는 모든 協定 또는 占領國에 의한 占領地域의 全部 또는 一部의 倂合에 의하여 本協約의 諸恩澤을 剝奪당하여서는 아니된다.

**第48條** 領域은 占領당한 國家의 國民이 아닌 被保護者들은 第35條의 規定이 따를 것을 條件으로 하고, 그 領域을 退去할 權利를 行使할 수 있다. 이에 관한 決定은 同條에 의하여 占領國이 制定하는 節次에 따라 행하여야 한다.

**第49條** 被保護者들을 占領地域으로부터 占領國의 領域 또는 被占領 與否를 不問하고 他國의 領域으로 個人的 또는 集團的으로 强制移送 또는 追放하는 것은 그 理由如何를 不問하고 禁止된다.

그러나 占領國은 住民의 安全 또는 軍事上의 理由 때문에 必要한 경우에는 一定한 區域의 全部 또는 一部의 撤去를 實施할 수 있다. 그러한 撤去는 物的理由로 인하여 不可避한 경우를 除外하고는 被保護者들을 占領地域의 境界 밖으로 移動시키는 것이어서는 아니된다. 이렇게 하여 撤去당한 者들은 當該地區에서의 敵對行爲가 終了되는 즉시로 各者의 家庭으로 送還되어야 한다.

前記의 移動 또는 撤去를 實施하는 占領國은 可能한 限 被保護者들을 받아들일 適當한 施設을 設備할 것과 同移動이 衛生, 保健, 安全 및 給食에 대하여 滿足할 만한 條件下에서 행하여질 것과 同一家族의 構成員들이 離散하지 않을 것을 確保하여야 한다.

移動 및 撤去를 實施할 때에는 즉시 利益保護國에 이를 通告하여야 한다.

占領國은 住民의 安全 또는 緊急한 軍事上의 理由 때문에 必要한 경우를 除外하고는 被保護者들을 戰爭의 危險을 많이 받고 있는 地區에 抑留하여서는 아니된다.

占領國은 自國의 民間人 住民의 一部를 自己의 占領地域으로 追放하거나 또는 移動시켜서는 아니된다.

**第50條** 占領國은 國家 또는 現地當局의 協力下에 兒童들의 監護 및 敎育에 專用된 모든 施設의 適當한 運營에 대하여 便宜를 提供하여야 한다.

占領國은 兒童들의 身元確認 및 親子關係의 登錄을 容易케 하기 위하여 必要한 措置를 취하여야 한다. 占領國은 어떠한 경우에라도 兒童들의 身分上의 地位를 變更시키거나 또는 그들을 自國에 從屬하는 團體 또는 機構에 編入시켜서는 아니된다.

現地의 施設이 適當치 않을 경우에는 占領國은 戰爭의 結果로 孤兒가 되었거나 또는 自己의 父母와 離別하고 또한 親族 또는 友人에 의하여 適當한 監護를 받을 수 없는 兒童들의 扶養 및 敎育이 可能한 限, 그 兒童들과 同一한 國籍, 言語 및 宗敎를 가진 者들에 의하여 행하여지도록 措置를 취하여야 한다.

第136條에 따라 設置되는 情報局의 한 特別課는 身元이 不明한 兒童들의 身元을 判明하기 위하여 必要한 모든 措置를 취할 責任을 진다. 그들의 父母 또는 親族들에 관한 詳細한 정보를 入手하는 대로 항상 記錄하여야 한다.

占領國의 15歲未滿의 兒童, 妊産婦 및 7歲未滿의 幼兒를 가진 婦人들을 위하여 占領前에 採擇된 食糧, 醫療上의 看護 및 戰爭의 영향으로부터의 保護에 관한 有利한 措置의 適用을 妨害하여서는 아니된다.

**第51條** 占領國은 被保護者들에게 대하여 自國의 軍隊 또는 補助部隊에 勤務할 것을 强要하여서는 아니된다. 自發的 志願을 시키는 것을 目
된다.
的으로 하는 壓力 또는 宣傳은 禁止

占領國은 被保護者들이 18歲 이상이고, 또한 다만 占領軍의 需要, 公益事業 또는 被占領國住民의 衣·食·住, 輸送 또는 健康 때문에 必要한 勞動을 위해서가 아니면 被保護者들에게 勞動을 强要할 수 없다. 被保護者들은 軍事行動에의 參加義務를 지게 强要받지 아니한다. 占領國은 被保護者들에 대하여 그들이 强制勞動을 하고 있는 施設의 安全을 强制手段을 使用하여 確保하도록 强要하여서는 아니된다.

勞動은 勞務를 徵發당한 者들이 滯留하는 占領地域內에서만 행하여져야 한다. 그러한 者들은 可能한 限 從前의 勤務場所에서 일을 계속하도록 하여야 한다. 勞動者들에게 대하여는 公正한 賃金을 支拂하여야 하며, 勞動은 勞動者들의 肉體的·知的 能力에 符合하는 것이어야 한다. 被占領國內에서 施行되고 있는 것으로 勞動條件 및 보호에 관한 法令 특히 賃金, 勞動時間, 設備, 豫備的 作業訓練, 그리고 業務上의 災害 및 疾病에 대한 補償에 관한 法令은 本條에서 말하는 勞動에 從事하는 被保護者들에게 適用된다.

勞務의 徵發은 어떠한 경우에라도 軍事的 또는 準軍事的 性格을 가진 組織內에 勞動者들을 動員하는 것이 되어서는 아니된다.

**第52條** 어떠한 契約, 協定 또는 規則이라도 勞動者의 自進與否 및 그의 滯留場所 如何를 不問하고 利益保護國의 介入을 要請하기 위하여 同國代表들에게 申請하는 勞動者의 權利를 侵害하여서는 아니된다.

勞動者들로 하여금 占領國을 위해 일하게 하기 위하여 占領地域內에서 失業을 發生시키거나, 또는 勞動者들에게 부여되는 機會를 制限함을 目的으로 하는 모든 措置는 禁止된다.

**第53條** 個人的인 것이거나 또는 集團的인 것임을 불문하고 私人, 國家, 其他의 公共當局, 社會團體 또는 協同團體에 속하는 不動産 또는 動産의 占領軍에 의한 破壞는 그것이 軍事行動에 의하여 絶對必要하게 된 경우를 除外하고는 일체 禁止된다.

**第54條** 占領國은 占領地域內에 있는 公務員 또는 法官들이 良心에 따라



0019

되는 그러한 勞動에 從事하는 것을 自己의 職務遂行을 忌避한 경우에라도 그 公務員 또는 法官의 身分을 變更시키거나, 또는 어떠한 方法으로 그들에게 制裁를 加하거나, 또는 强制的 또는 差別的 措置를 취하여서는 아니된다.

이와 같은 禁止는 第51條 第②項의 適用을 妨害하지 아니한다. 同禁止는 公務員들을 그들의 職責으로부터 解任시키는 占領國의 權利에 대하여 영향을 미치지 아니한다.

**第55條** 占領國은 利用可能한 모든 手段으로써 住民의 食糧 및 醫療品의 供給을 確保할 義務를 진다. 특히 占領國은 占領地域의 資源이 不充分할 경우에는 必要한 食糧, 醫療品 및 기타의 物品들을 輸入하여야 한다.

占領國은 占領軍 및 行政要員들의 使用에 充當할 경우와 民間人住民들의 需要를 考慮한 경우를 除外하고는 占領地域內에 있는 食糧物品 또는 醫療品을 徵發하여서는 아니된다. 占領國은 다른 諸國際條約에 대한 公正한 對價의 支拂을 確保키 위하여 必要한 措置를 취하여야 한다.

保護國은 緊急한 軍事上의 要求에 의하여 一時的 制限이 必要하게 될 경우를 除外하고 언제라도 占領地域에 있어서의 食糧 및 醫療品의 供給狀態를 自由로이 調査할 수 있다.

**第56條** 占領國은 利用可能한 모든 手段을 다하여 國家 및 現地當局의 協力下에 占領地域에 있어서의 醫療上 및 病院의 施設과 用役, 그리고 公衆保健 및 衛生을 確保하고 또한 維持할 義務를 진다. 占領國은 특히 傳染病 및 流行病의 蔓延을 防止하기 위하여 必要한 豫防的 措置를 採擇하여 이를 實施하여야 한다.

占領地域內에 새로운 病院들이 設立되고, 또한 被占領國의 權限있는 機關이 그 地域內에서 活動하고 있지 아니할 경우에는 占領當局은 必要한 경우 第18條에 規定된 承認을 그들에 부여하여야 한다. 또한 占領當局은 유사한 事情下에서는 第20條 및 第21條의 規定에 따라 病院職員 및 輸送車輛에 대하여도 承認을 부여하여야 한다.

占領國은 保健 및 衛生措置를 採擇하고, 또 이를 實施함에 있어서는 占領地域住民들의 道德的 및 倫理的 感情을 考慮하여야 한다.

**第57條** 占領國은 軍隊의 負傷者 및 病者들을 看護하기 위하여 緊急한 必要가 있을 경우에 한하여, 그리고 患者들의 看護 및 治療와 民間人住民들의 入院要求를 위하여 適當한 措置가 適當한 때에 취하여진 것을 條件으로 하고 民間人病院들을 一時的으로 徵發할 수 있다.

民間人病院의 器材 및 貯藏品들은 그것들이 民間人住民들의 需要에 必要하게 되는 限 徵發할 수 없다.

**第58條** 占領國은 聖職者들에게 대하여 그들과 同一한 宗派에 속하는 者들에게 宗敎上의 援助를 부여하는 것을 許容하여야 한다.

또한 占領國은 宗敎上의 必要에 所要되는 圖書 및 資料 등을 受領하고 占領地域內의 配布를 促進하여야 한다.

**第59條** 占領地域住民의 全部 또는 一部에 대한 物資의 供給이 不充分할 경우에는 占領國은 同住民들을 위한 救護計劃에 同意하여야 하며, 또한 使用可能한 모든 手段을 다하여 同計劃이 實施될 수 있도록 便宜를 提供하여야 한다.

國家 또는 國際赤十字委員會와 같은 公正한 人道的 機構에 의하여 實施되는 前記의 計劃은 특히 食糧, 醫療品 및 衣類의 送付를 內容으로 하는 것이어야 한다.

모든 締約國은 이러한 送品들의 自由通過를 許可하고, 또한 그것들의 保護를 保障하여야 한다.

그러나 敵國에 의하여 占領되고 있는 地域으로 가는 送品의 自由通過를



許可하는 國家는 送品들을 檢査하고 指定된 時刻 및 經路에 의한 通過를 規律하며, 그 送品들이 窮乏한 住民들의 救護를 위하여 使用된 것이고 占領國의 利益을 위하여 使用된 것이 아니라는 것을 保護國을 통하여 充分히 確認할 權利를 가진다.

**第60條** 救護品은 第55條, 第56條 및 第59條에 의거한 占領國의 責任을 免除하지는 아니한다. 占領國은 緊急한 必要가 있고 그것이 占領國住民의 利益을 위한 것이며, 또한 利益保護國의 同意를 얻은 경우를 除外하고는 어떠한 方法으로도 救濟品의 指定된 用途를 變更시켜서는 아니된다.

**第61條** 前記의 諸條에서 말한 救護品의 分配는 利益保護國의 協力 및 監督下에서 행하여져야 한다. 이 任務는 또한 占領國과 保護國間의 協定에 의하여 中立國, 國際赤十字委員會 또는 其他의 公正한 人道的 團體에 委任될 수 있다.

그러한 救護品은 占領地域의 經濟를 위하여 必要하지 않은 한, 그 地域內에서 모든 賦課金, 稅金 또는 關稅를 免除받는다. 占領國은 이러한 救護品들이 迅速히 分配될 수 있도록 便宜를 提供하여야 한다.

모든 締約國은 占領地域으로 가는 그러한 救護品들의 無償通過 또는 輸送을 許可하도록 努力하여야 한다.

**第62條** 占領地域에 있는 被保護者들은 緊急한 安全上의 理由에 따를 것을 條件으로 하고 個人앞으로 보내온 救護品의 受領을 許容받아야 한다.

**第63條** 占領國이 緊急한 安全上의 理由 때문에 취하는 一時的 및 例外的인 諸措置에 따를 것을 條件으로 하고,

ⓐ 承認된 各國赤十字社는 赤十字國際會議에 의하여 制定된 赤十字原則에 따라 그들의 活動을 遂行할 수 있다. 그 밖의 救護團體들은 同一한 條件下에서 人道的 活動의 繼續을 許容받는다.

ⓑ 占領國은 이러한 團體들의 職員 및 組織에 대하여 前記의 活動을 妨害하게 될 變更을 要求하여서는 아니된다.

이와 같은 原則들은 重要한 公益事業의 維持, 救護品의 分配 및 救護事業의 組織化에 의하여 民間人住民들의 生活條件을 確保함을 目的으로 이미 存在하거나, 또는 將次 設立될 非軍事的 性格을 가진 特別團體의 活動 및 職員에 대하여도 適用된다.

**第64條** 被占領國의 刑罰法令은 그것이 占領國의 安全을 威脅하거나, 또는 本協約의 適用에 障碍가 되는 경우에 占領國이 이를 廢止 또는 停止시키는 경우를 除外하고는 계속하여 效力을 가진다. 占領地域의 法院은 本協約의 適用의 障害를 考慮하고, 또한 裁判의 效果的인 施行을 保障할 必要에 따를 것을 條件으로 하여 前記의 法令에서 規定하는 모든 犯罪行爲에 대하여 任務를 계속 遂行하여야 한다.

그러나 占領國은 占領地域의 住民으로 하여금 自國이 本協約에 의거한 諸義務를 履行하고 當該地域의 秩序있는 統治를 維持하며, 占領國의 安全, 占領軍 또는 占領行政機關의 構成員 및 그의 財産의 安全과, 그리고 그들이 使用하는 施設 및 通信線의 安全을 確保할 수 있도록 하기 위하여 絶對 必要한 諸規定에 服從시킬 수 있다.

**第65條** 占領國이 制定한 刑罰規定은 住民들이 使用하는 言語로 公布하고, 또한 住民들에게 周知시킨 후가 아니면 效力은 소급되지 아니한다.

**第66條** 第64條 第②項에 의거하여 占領國이 公布한 刑罰規定에 違反하는 行爲가 있을 경우에는 占領國은 正當하게 構成되고, 非政治的인 占領國의 軍事裁判所에 被疑者들을 引渡할 수 있다. 단, 同軍事裁判所는 被占領國內에서 開廷되어야 한다. 上訴法院은 될 수 있는 대로 被占領國內에서 開廷되어야 한다.

0020

**第67條** 法院은 犯罪行爲前에 施行되어 있고, 또한 法의 一般原則, 특히 刑罰은 犯罪行爲에 相應하는 것이어야 한다는 原則에 合致되는 法律의 規定만을 適用하여야 한다. 法院은 被告人이 占領國의 國民이 아니라는 事實을 考慮에 넣어야 한다.

**第68條** 占領國을 害할 意思만을 가지고 행한 犯罪行爲로서 占領軍 또는 占領行政機關構成員들의 生命 또는 身體에 危害를 가하지 않고 重大한 集團的 危險을 發生시키지 않으며 또한 占領軍 또는 占領行政機關의 財產이나 그들이 使用하는 施設에 대하여 重大한 損害를 주지 않은 犯罪를 범한 被保護者들은 抑留 또는 단순한 拘禁에 處한다. 단, 그 抑留 또는 拘禁期間은 犯罪行爲에 相應하는 것이어야 한다. 뿐만 아니라 抑留 또는 拘禁은 그러한 犯罪行爲에 관하여 被保護者들로부터 自由를 剝奪하기 위하여 취하여지는 唯一한 措置로 되어야 한다. 本協約 第96條에 規定된 法院은 自由裁量에 의하여 拘禁刑을 同一한 期間의 抑留刑으로 變更할 수 있다.

第64條 및 第65條에 따라 占領國이 公布하는 刑罰規定은 被保護者들이 間諜으로서 犯한 行爲와 占領軍의 軍事施設에 대하여 행한 重大한 怠業 또는 1人 또는 그 이상의 者들을 死亡케 한 故意的인 犯罪行爲 때문에 有罪가 된 경우에는 그 被保護者들에게 대하여 死刑을 科할 수 있다. 단, 占領開始前에 施行되던 占領地域의 法令에 의하여 그러한 犯罪行爲에 死刑을 科할 수 있는 경우에 限한다.

死刑은 法院이 被告人이 占領國의 國民이 아니고 同國에 대하여 忠誠義務를 지지 아니한다는 事實을 特別히 留意한 후가 아니면, 被保護者들에게 言渡되어서는 아니된다.

死刑은 어떠한 경우에라도 犯罪行爲時에 18歲未滿인 被保護者들에게 言渡되어서는 아니된다.

**第69條** 모든 경우에 있어서 犯罪行爲로 起訴된 被保護者가 裁判이 있을 때까지 拘束된 期間은 그에게 言渡되는 拘禁刑의 期間에 通算되어야 한다.

**第70條** 被保護者들은 戰爭法規 및 慣習에 違反한 경우를 除外하고는 占領前이나 또는 占領이 一時的으로 中斷된 동안에 犯한 行爲 또는 表明한 意見 때문에 占領國에 의하여 逮捕 또는 起訴되거나 有罪로 되어서는 아니된다.

敵對行爲의 開始 전에 被占領國의 領域內에 亡命한 占領國의 國民은 敵對行爲의 開始 후에 행한 犯罪行爲로 인하거나 또는 敵對行爲의 開始 전에 행한 普通法上의 犯罪行爲로서 被占領國의 法令에 의하면, 平和時에도 犯罪人引渡가 행하여지게 된 犯罪行爲로 인한 경우를 除外하고는 逮捕되거나 起訴되거나 有罪로 되거나 또는 占領地域으로부터 追放되어서는 아니된다.

**第71條** 占領國의 管轄法院은 正式裁判을 행한 후가 아니면 判決을 言渡하여서는 아니된다.

占領國에 의하여 起訴된 被告人은 自己에게 대한 公訴事實의 詳細한 內容을 즉시 그들이 理解할 수 있는 言語의 書面으로 通告받고, 또한 可能한 限 迅速히 裁判에 回附되어야 한다. 保護國은 死刑 또는 2年 이상의 拘禁刑에 該當하는 公訴事實에 관하여 占領國이 被保護者들을 상대로 開始한 모든 司法節次를 通告받아야 한다. 利益保護國은 또한 언제라도 그러한 司法節次의 狀況에 관한 情報를 入手할 수 있어야 한다. 뿐만아니라 利益保護國은 그 要請에 따라 前記의 司法節次 및 被保護者들을 상대로 占領國이 開始한 기타 모든 司法節次의 詳細한 內容을 通告받을 權利를 가진다.

前記 第②項에 規定된 利益保護國에 대한 通告書는 즉시로 送付되어야 하며, 또한 어떠한 경우에라도 第1回 公判期日의 3週日 전에 到着되어야 한다. 裁判開廷時에 本條의 規定이 完全히 遵守되고 있다는 證據가 提出되지 않는 限, 裁判이 開始되어서는 아니된다. 通告書에는 다음 事項들을 記載하여야 한다.

ⓐ 被告人의 身元
ⓑ 居住 또는 抑留의 場所
ⓒ 公訴事實의 明細(訴追의 根據가 되는 刑罰規定의 記載를 包含)
ⓓ 事件을 審理하는 法院
ⓔ 第1回 公判의 場所 및 日字

**第72條** 被告人은 自己防禦를 위하여 必要한 證據를 提出할 權利를 가지고 특히 證人召喚을 要求할 수 있다. 被告人은 自己가 選任한 資格있는 辯護人의 援助를 받을 權利를 가지며, 그 辯護人은 自由로이 被告人을 訪問할 수 있고 또한 辯護準備를 위하여 必要한 諸便宜를 享有하여야 한다.

被告人이 辯護人을 選任치 못하였을 경우에는 保護國은 被告人에게 辯護人을 提供할 수 있다. 被告人이 重大한 犯罪로 訴追되고 있고, 또한 利益保護國이 活動하고 있지 않을 경우에는 占領國은 被告人의 同意를 얻어 辯護人을 提供하여야 한다.

被告人은 通譯官의 援助를 받을 權利를 自己意思로 抛棄하지 않는 限, 豫備的 迅問中 및 裁判中에 있어서 通譯官의 援助를 받아야 한다. 被告人은 언제라도 通譯官을 忌避하고 또한 그의 交替를 要求할 權利를 가진다.

**第73條** 有罪判決을 받은 者는 法院이 適用하는 法令에서 規定하는 上訴의 權利를 가진다. 그에게 대하여는 上訴 또는 請願의 權利 및 이것을 行使할 수 있는 期間에 관하여 完全히 通告하여야 한다.

本第3部에서 規定되는 刑事節次는 그것이 適用可能한 限, 上訴가 있을 경우 이에 準用하여야 한다. 法院이 適用하는 法令이 上訴에 관하여 規定하고 있지 않을 경우에는 有罪判決을 받은 者는 事實認證 및 判決에 대하여 占領國의 權限있는 當局에 請願할 權利를 가진다.

**第74條** 利益保護國의 代表는 그 裁判이 例外的으로 占領國의 安全을 위하여 非公開的으로 進行되지 않는 限, 모든 被保護者의 裁判에 立會할 權利를 가진다. 裁判이 非公開的으로 開廷될 경우에는 占領國은 그것을 利益保護國에 通告하여야 한다. 利益保護國에는 裁判의 日字 및 場所에 관한 通告書를 送付하여야 한다.

死刑 또는 2年 이상의 拘禁刑이 言渡된 모든 判決은 理由를 첨부하여 可能한 限, 迅速히 利益保護國에 通告되어야 한다. 그 通告書에는 第71條에 의거하여 행하여지는 通告와의 關係와 拘禁刑인 경우에는 刑의 執行場所를 記載하여야 한다. 前述한 判決 이외의 判決記錄은 法院이 保管하고, 또한 利益保護國代表들의 열람에 提供하여야 한다. 死刑 또는 2年 이상의 拘禁刑이 言渡된 判決의 경우에 있어서 許容되는 上訴期間은 利益保護國이 判決通告書를 接受한 때로부터 起算된다.

**第75條** 死刑判決을 받은 者들은 어떠한 경우에라도 特赦 또는 死刑의 執行停止를 請願할 權利를 剝奪당하여서는 아니된다.

어떠한 死刑判決이라도 死刑을 確定하는 終局判決이나 特赦 또는 死刑의 執行停止를 拒否하는 決定의 通告書를 利益保護國이 接受한 日字로부터 最少限 6個月의 期間이 經過하기 전에 執行되어서는 아니된다.

占領國 또는 占領軍의 安全에 대하여 組織的 威脅이 된 重大하고 緊急한 事情이 있을 경우에는 前項에 規定된 6個月의 死刑停止期間은 個個의 事件에 대하여 短縮될 수 있다. 단, 이것은 항시 利益保護國이 同期間의 短縮에 대하여 通告를 받을 것과 또한 死刑判決에 관하여 權限있는 占領當局에 意見을 提示할 充分한 時間 및



0021

機會를 부여받을 것을 條件으로 한다.

**第76條** 犯罪行爲로 起訴된 被保護者들은 被占領國에서 拘禁되어야 하며, 有罪判決을 받았을 경우에는 被占領國內에서 刑에 服役하여야 한다. 그들은 可能한 限 다른 被拘禁者들로부터 分離되어야 하며, 또한 良好한 健康을 維持하기에 充分하고 또한 最少限 被占領國의 刑務所에서 부여되는 것과 同一한 食糧 및 衛生條件을 享有하여야 한다.

그들은 그들의 健康狀態가 必要로 하는 醫療를 받아야 한다.

그들은 또한 그들이 要求하는 宗敎上의 援助를 받을 權利를 가진다.

婦女子들은 分離된 場所에 拘禁되어야 하며, 또한 女性의 直接監視下에 두어야 한다.

未成年者들에게 대한 特別待遇에 관하여는 適當히 考慮하여야 한다.

拘禁當하고 있는 被抑留者들은 第143條의 規定에 따라 利益保護國 및 國際赤十字委員會代表들의 訪問을 받을 權利를 가진다.

그러한 者들은 每月 最少限 1個의 救護品 小包를 받을 權利를 가진다.

**第77條** 占領地域內의 法院에 의하여 犯罪行爲의 訴追를 받았거나 또는 有罪判決을 받은 被保護者들은 占領이 終了될 때에 關係記錄과 더불어 釋放된 地域의 當局에 引渡되어야 한다.

**第78條** 占領國은 安全保障上의 絶對的 理由로 被保護者들에 관한 安全措置를 취할 必要가 있다고 認定한 경우에라도 住居指定 또는 抑留이상의 措置를 취할 수 없다.

그러한 住居指定 또는 抑留에 관한 決定은 占領國이 本協約規定에 따라 정하는 일정한 節次에 좇아서 행하여야 한다. 이 節次는 關係當事者의 訴請權을 包含하여야 한다. 訴請에 대하여는 可能한 限 迅速한 決定이 있어야 한다. 住居指定 또는 抑留의 決定이 確認되었을 경우에는 同決定은 占領國이 設置한 權限있는 機關에 의하여 必要하다면 每 6個月마다 定期的으로 審査를 받아야 한다.

住居指定의 處分을 받고 自己故鄕을 떠날 것을 要求받은 被保護者들은 本協約 第39條의 完全한 恩澤을 享有한다.

## 第4部 被抑留者의 待遇에 관한 規定

### 第1章 總 則

**第79條** 衝突當事國은 第41條·第42條·第43條·第68條 및 第78條의 規定에 의한 경우를 제외하고는 被保護者들을 抑留하여서는 아니된다.

**第80條** 被抑留者들은 私法上의 行爲能力을 保有하고 또 그것에 따르는 權利로서 그들의 地位와 矛盾되지 않는 權利를 行使하여야 한다.

**第81條** 被保護者들을 抑留하는 衝突當事國은 그들을 無償으로 扶養하고, 또한 그들의 健康狀態에 必要한 醫療를 그들에게 提供하여야 한다.

前記의 費用支拂에 充當하기 위하여 被抑留者들의 手當·俸給 또는 債權額에서 控除하여서는 아니된다.

被抑留者들의 扶養을 받는 者들이 生活을 維持하기 위한 適當한 手段을 가지고 있지 않거나 또는 生計를 營爲할 수 없을 경우에는, 抑留國은 그들의 生活을 支援하여 주어야 한다.

**第82條** 抑留國은 被抑留者들을 可能한 限 그들의 國籍·言語 및 慣習에 따라 收容하여야 한다. 同一한 國籍을 가진 被抑留者들은 言語의 差異만으로써 分離되어서는 아니된다.

同一한 家族의 構成員 특히 父母와 子女들은 職業上 또는 健康上의 理由나 本部 第9章의 規定을 施行키 위하여 一時的 別居가 必要하게 될 경우를 除外하고는 抑留期間中 收容所內의 同一한 場所에서 함께 留宿시켜야 한다. 被抑留者들은 그들의 監護를 받지 않고 放置되고 있는 自己의 子女들이 自己와 함께 收容되도록 要請할 수 있다.

同一한 家族의 構成員인 被抑留者들은 可能한 限 同一建物內에 收容되어야 하며, 또한 다른 抑留者들로부터 分離된 收容施設과 正常的인 家庭生活을 營爲하기 위한 諸便宜를 그들에게 提供하여야 한다.

### 第2章 抑留場所

**第83條** 抑留國은 戰爭의 危險을 많이 받고 있는 地區에 抑留場所를 設置하여서는 아니된다.

抑留國은 抑留場所의 地理的 位置에 관한 모든 有益한 情報를 利益保護國의 仲介를 통하여 敵國에 提供하여야 한다.

抑留收容所는 軍事上 事情이 許諾한 때에는 언제라도 晝間에 空中으로부터 明確히 識別될 수 있도록 IC라는 文字로 表示하여야 한다. 그러나 關係諸國은 其他의 標識方法에 대하여도 合意할 수 있다. 抑留收容所가 아닌 場所에는 그러한 標識를 使用하여서는 안 된다.

**第84條** 被抑留者들은 捕虜 및 다른 어떤 理由로 自由를 剝奪당한 者들로부터 分離 收容되고 또한 따로 管理되어야 한다.

**第85條** 抑留國은 被保護者들의 抑留開始時부터 그들에게 衛生上 및 保健上의 모든 保障을 주고, 또한 氣候의 苛酷 및 戰爭의 영향에 대한 有效한 保護를 주는 建物 또는 區劃內에 收容하는 것을 確保키 위하여 必要하고 可能한 모든 措置를 취하여야 한다. 어떠한 경우에라도 永久的인 抑留場所는 非衛生的인 地域이나 또는 氣候가 被抑留者들에게 有害한 地域에 設置되어서는 아니된다. 被保護者들이 一時的으로 抑留되고 있는 地域이 非衛生的인 곳이거나 또는 그 地域의 氣候가 그들의 健康에 有害한 경우에는 當該被保護者들은 事情이 許容하는 限, 迅速히 보다 適當한 곳으로 移動되어야 한다.

建物들은 濕氣를 完全히 防止하고 充分한 暖房裝置를 가져야 하며, 특히 日沒時로부터 消燈時까지의 사이에는 燈을 켜야 한다. 寢室은 充分한 넓이를 가지고 또한 換氣가 잘되어야 한다. 被抑留者들에게는 氣候와 그들의 年齡·性別 및 健康狀態를 考慮하여 適當한 寢具 및 充分한 毛布를 주어야 한다.

被抑留者들에게 대하여는 衛生規則에 合致되고 또한 항상 淸潔狀態가 維持되어온 衛生設備를 그들의 使用을 위하여 提供하여야 한다. 그들에게 대하여는 各者의 日常的인 身體淸潔 및 세탁을 위하여 充分한 물과 비누를 提供하여야 한다. 그들에게 대하여는 이것을 위하여 必要한 設備및 便宜를 提供하여야 한다. 그들에게 대하여는 또한 샤워 또는 浴湯을 利用시켜야 한다. 그들에게는 세탁 및 淸掃를 위하여 必要한 時間을 提供하여야 한다.

例外的이고 또한 一時的 措置로서 어떤 家族의 構成員이 아닌 女子被抑留者들을 男子들과 同一한 抑留場所內에 收容할 必要가 있을 경우에는 그러한 女子抑留者들이 使用할 分離된 寢室과 衛生設備를 提供하여야 한다.

**第86條** 抑留國은 宗派의 如何를 不問하고 被抑留者들이 宗敎的 儀式을 擧行하기 위하여 適當한 場所를 自由로이 使用할 수 있도록 하여야 한다.

**第87條** 다른 適當한 便宜를 利用할 수 있는 경우를 除外하고 各抑留場所는 賣店을 設置하여야 한다. 賣店의 目的은 被抑留者들이 個人的 福祉및 慰安을 增進할 食料品 및 日用品을 現地 市場價格보다 高額이 아닌 價格으로 購入할 수 있도록 하는 것이어야 한다.

賣店이 獲得한 利益金은 各抑留場所에 設定되는 福祉基金 구좌의 貸邊



0022

에 記入하고, 또한 그 抑留場所에 속하는 被抑留者들의 利益을 위하여 管理되어야 한다. 第88條에 規定된 被抑留者委員會는 賣店 및 前記基金의 運營을 監視할 權利를 가진다.

抑留場所가 閉鎖된 경우에는 福祉基金의 殘額은 同一한 國籍을 가진 被抑留者들을 위한 抑留場所의 福祉基金에 移讓되어야 한다. 만일 그러한 抑留場所가 存在치 않을 경우에는 同殘額은 抑留國의 權力內에 계속 殘留하는 모든 被抑留者들의 利益을 위하여 管理되는 中央福祉基金에 移讓되어야 한다. 全國的 釋放의 경우에는 關係國間에 反對의 協定이 없는 限, 前記利益金을 抑留國에 남겨두어야 한다.

**第88條** 空襲, 기타의 戰爭危險을 받고 있는 모든 抑留場所에는 必要한 保護를 確保하기 위하여 適當한 數 및 構造의 待避所를 設置하여야 한다. 警報가 있을 경우에는 被抑留者들은 前記의 危險으로부터 宿舍를 防護하기 위하여 殘存하는 者를 제외하고 可能한 限 迅速히 待避所에 들어갈 수 있다. 住民들을 위하여 취하는 防護措置는 被抑留者들에게도 適用되어야 한다.

抑留場所에는 火災의 危險에 對備하여 適切한 모든 豫防措置를 취하여야 한다.

## 第3章 食糧 및 被服

**第89條** 被抑留者들을 위한 日常的인 食糧配給은 그것의 分量 및 種類에 있어서 그들의 良好한 健康狀態를 維持하고 또한 營養不足을 防止하기에 充分한 것이어야 한다. 또한 被抑留者들의 食性도 考慮하여야 한다.

被抑留者들에 대하여는 또한 그들이 別途로 所有하는 모든 飮食物을 스스로 調理할 수 있는 手段을 부여하여야 한다.

被抑留者들에 대하여는 充分한 飮料水를 供給하여야 한다.

吸煙을 許容하여야 한다.

勞動을 하는 被抑留者들에게 대하여는 그들이 從事하는 勞動의 種類에 따라 食糧을 增配하여야 한다.

姙産婦와 15歲未滿의 兒童들에게 대하여는 그들의 生理的 必要에 따라 食糧을 增配하여야 한다.

**第90條** 被抑留者들이 抑留되었을 경우에는 必要한 被服, 신발, 및 벌의 內衣를 準備하고, 또한 그 후에라도 必要하다면 새로운 補給을 調達받을 수 있도록 그들에게 모든 便宜를 提供하여야 한다. 만일 被抑留者들이 氣候條件에 相應한 充分한 衣類를 所持하지 못하고 또한 아무런 衣類調達도 받을 수 없을 경우에는, 抑留國은 그들에게 衣類를 無償으로 供給하여야 한다.

抑留國이 被抑留者들에게 供給하는 衣類와 그 衣類에 첨부되는 外部的 標識는 侮辱的인 것이거나, 또는 被抑留者들을 嘲笑의 대상이 되게 하는 것이어서는 아니된다.

勞動者들에게 대하여는 勞動의 性格上 必要할 경우에는 作業服을 包含하는 適當한 勞動用具를 提供하여야 한다.

## 第4章 衛生 및 醫療

**第91條** 各收容所에는 資格있는 醫師의 指揮下에 두고 또한 被抑留者들이 必要한 治療와 適當한 食事를 받을 수 있는 適當한 診療所를 設置하여야 한다. 傳染病 및 精神病에 걸린 患者들을 위하여 隔離病室을 設置하여야 한다.

姙産婦 및 重患의 被抑留者 또는 特別治療나 外科手術이나 入院을 요하는 狀態에 있는 被抑留者들은 適當한 治療를 받을 수 있는 施設에 收容되어야 하며, 또한 一般住民들이 받는 것보다 못지않은 治療를 받도록 하여야 한다.



被抑留者들은 그들의 希望에 따라 自國의 國籍을 가진 醫療要員의 治療를 받아야 한다.

被抑留者들이 診療를 받기 위하여 醫療當局에 出頭하는 것을 妨害할 수 없다. 抑留國의 醫療當局은 要請이 있을 경우에는 治療를 받은 各被抑留者에게 그의 疾病 또는 負傷의 性質, 그리고 治療의 期間 및 種類를 記載한 公式證明書를 發給하여야 한다. 同證明書의 寫本 1通은 第140條에 規定되는 中央被保護者情報局에 送付하여야 한다.

被抑留者들의 良好한 健康狀態를 維持하기 위하여 必要한 모든 器具, 특히 供給을 包含하는 器具는 被抑留者들에게 대하여 無料이어야 한다.

**第92條** 被抑留者들의 身體檢査는 最少限 月 1回씩 행하여야 한다. 同檢査는 특히 被抑留者들의 健康·營養 및 清潔의 一般的 狀態를 管理하고, 또한 傳染病 특히 結核, 말라리아 및 性病을 檢出함을 目的으로 하여야 한다. 同檢査는 특히 各被抑留者의 體重測定 및 最小限 每年 1回의 X線에 의한 檢診을 包含하여야 한다.

## 第5章 宗敎的·知的 및 肉體的 活動

**第93條** 被抑留者들은 抑留當局이 制定하는 日常的 規律에 服從할 것을 條件으로 自己의 宗敎義務(宗敎儀式에의 參席 包含)를 履行함에 있어서 完全한 自由를 享有한다.

抑留되고 있는 聖職者들은 同一한 宗派에 속하는 被抑留者들에게 대하여 自己의 聖職을 自由로이 행하도록 許容받아야 한다. 이를 위하여 抑留國은 同一한 言語를 使用하거나 同一한 宗派에 속하는 被保護者들이 있는 各種의 收容所에 이러한 聖職者들이 公平히 配置되는 것을 確保하여야 한다. 聖職者들의 數가 너무 적을 경우에는 抑留國은 그들에게 一場所에서 他場所로 巡回하는 데 必要한 諸便宜(輸送手段包含)를 提供하여야 하며, 또한 入院中에 있는 被抑留者들을 訪問하는 것을 許容하여야 한다. 聖職者들은 自己의 聖職에 관한 事項에 대하여 抑留國의 宗敎當局 및 可能한 限 自己의 宗派에 속하는 國際的 宗敎團體들과 通信連絡을 할 自由를 가진다. 그러한 通信連絡은 第107條에서 말한 割當數의 一部로 認定되어서는 아니된다. 그러나 이 通信連絡은 第112條의 規定에 따라 행하여야 한다.

被抑留者들이 自己의 意思에 따라 自己宗派에 속하는 聖職者들의 援助를 받지 못하거나 또는 聖職者들의 數가 너무 적을 경우에는 같은 敎理의 地方宗敎當局은 抑留國과 合意하여 被抑留者들의 敎理에 맞는 聖職者를 任命하여야 하며, 만일 그러한 措置가 宗派的 見地에서 可能하다면 同一한 宗派에 속하는 聖職者나 資格있는 一般信徒를 任命할 수 있다. 後者는 自己가 引受한 聖職에 대하여 부여된 諸便宜를 享有한다. 이와 같이 하여 任命된 者들은 抑留國이 紀律및 安全을 위하여 設定한 모든 規則에 服從하여야 한다.

**第94條** 抑留國은 抑留者들에게 知的, 敎育的 및 娛樂的 活動과 運動競技를 奬勵하여야 한다. 但, 그러한 諸活動 및 運動競技에의 參加與否는 被抑留者들의 自由에 맡겨야 한다. 抑留國은 특히 適當한 場所를 提供하여 被抑留者들의 諸活動 및 運動競技의 實行을 確保하기 위한 모든 可能한 措置를 취하여야 한다.

被抑留者들에게 대하여는 그들의 研究의 계속 또는 새로운 研究課題의 着手를 위한 可能한 모든 便宜를 提供하여야 한다. 兒童 및 靑少年들의 敎育은 必히 確保되어야 하며, 그들에게는 學校가 收容所內에 있거나 또는 收容所外에 있거나를 不問하고 通學을 許容하여야 한다.

0023

被抑留者들에게 대하여는 體操, 運動, 屋外競技를 위한 機會를 부여하여야 한다. 이를 위하여 모든 收容所內에 充分한 空地를 確保하여야 한다. 兒童 및 青少年들을 위하여 特別한 運動場을 確保하여야 한다.

**第95條** 抑留國은 被抑留者가 希望하지 아니하는 限, 그들을 勞動者로서 使用하여서는 아니된다. 抑留되지 않은 被保護者에게 强制的으로 課하여진 本協約 第40條 또는 第51條의 違反이 될 勞動 및 品位를 損傷케 하거나, 또는 屈辱的 性質을 가진 勞動은 어떠한 경우에도 禁止된다.

被抑留者는 6週間의 勞動期間後에는 8日前의 豫告에 의하여 언제든지 勞動을 中止할 수 있다.

前記의 規定은 抑留國이 抑留되어 있는 醫師, 齒科醫師, 기타의 醫務要員을 同一한 收容所에 抑留되어 있는 者를 위하여 그 職業的 能力에 따라 使用하거나, 또는 抑留者를 收容所의 管理와 維持를 위한 勞動에 使用하거나 이들을 炊事場, 기타 家事에 使用하거나, 또는 空襲이나 기타의 戰爭危險에 대한 被抑留者의 保護와 관련있는 任務에 從事하도록 要求하는 權利를 害하지 아니한다. 다만, 被抑留者에 대하여는 醫務官이 그의 身體에 不適當하다고 認定하는 일을 하도록 要求하여서는 아니된다.

抑留國은 모든 勞動條件, 醫療 및 賃金의 支拂에 대하여 勞動에 使用되는 모든 被抑留者가 職業上의 災害및 疾病에 대한 補償을 받을 것을 確保하는 데 대하여 全責任을 진다. 前記의 勞動條件 및 補償을 정하는 基準은 國內法令 및 現行慣習에 따라야 한다. 이 基準은 어떠한 경우에도 同一한 地方의 同一한 性質의 勞動에 있어서 認定되는 基準보다 不利하여서는 아니된다. 勞動에 대한 賃金은 被抑留者의 生活을 無償으로 維持하며, 또한 被抑留者가 그의 健康狀態를 위하여 必要로 하는 醫療를 供給하여야 한 抑留國의 義務에 대하여 適當한 考慮를 한 後 被抑留者와 抑留國 또한 경우에 따라서는 抑留 이외의 使用者間의 特別協定에 의하여 公平하게 決定되어야 한다. 本條 第③項에 言及된 部類에 항상 明示된 被抑留者에 대한 勞動條件과 職業上의 災害와 疾病에 대한 補償範圍는 同一地方의 同一性質의 勞動이 適用되는 範圍보다 不利한 것이어서는 아니된다.

**第96條** 모든 勞動分遣隊는 收容所의 一部가 되며 그에 從屬한다. 抑留國의 權限 있는 當局 및 收容所長은 當該 勞動分遣隊에서의 本協約規定의 遵守에 관하여 責任을 진다. 收容所長은 그 收容所에 所屬하는 勞動分遣隊의 最新名單을 保管하고, 또한 그 收容所를 訪問할 수 있는 利益保護國, 國際赤十字委員會 또는 기타의 人道的 團體의 代表에게 그 名單을 送付하여야 한다.

## 第6章 個人財產 및 金錢關係

**第97條** 被抑留者에게는 個人用品의 所持가 許容되어야 한다. 被抑留者가 所持하는 金錢, 手票, 證券 등 有價物은 所定의 節次에 의한 경우를 除外하고는 押收할 수 없다. 押收한 物件에 대하여는 詳細한 領收證을 發給하여야 한다.

前記의 金錢은 第98條에 정하는 바에 따라 各被抑留者의 計定에 이를 記入하여야 한다. 그 金錢은 所有者가 抑留되어 있는 地域에 施行되고 있는 法令이 要求하는 경우, 또는 被抑留者가 同意한 경우를 除外하고는 다른 通貨로 交換할 수 없다.

특히 個人的 또는 情緒的 價値만을 가지는 物品은 이를 押收하여서는 아니된다.

女子被抑留者는 女子 이외의 者가 搜索하여서는 아니된다.

被抑留者가 釋放되거나 또는 送還된 때에는 抑留中에 押收 당한 모든 物品, 金錢 기타의 有價物을 返還하고, 또한 第98條에 따라 가졌던 計定의 貸邊殘高를 現金으로 支拂하여야 한다. 다만, 抑留國이 施行中의 法令에 의하여 留置하는 物品 또는 金額은 除外한다. 被抑留者의 財產이 이와같이 留置되고 있는 경우에는 詳細한 受領證을 그 所有者에게 發給하여야 한다.

被抑留者가 所持하는 家族에 관한 文書 또는 身分證明書를 押收함에 있어서 受領證을 發給하여야 한다. 被抑留者에 대하여는 항상 身分證明書를 携帶시켜야 한다. 抑留當局은 身分證明書를 所持하고 있지 아니하는 被抑留者에 대하여는 特別證明書를 發給하여야 하며, 그 特別證明書는 抑留의 終了時까지 身分證明書를 代身한다.

被抑留者는 物品을 購入하기 위하여 現金이나 購買券으로서 일정한 金額을 携帶할 수 있다.

**第98條** 모든 被抑留者는 담배, 化粧品등의 物品을 購入하는 데 充分한 手當을 定期的으로 支拂받아야 한다. 그 手當의 支拂은 외상 또는 購入券의 形式으로 행할 수 있다.

被抑留者는 또한 自己의 本國, 利益保護國, 被抑留者를 援助하는 團體 또는 自己의 家族으로부터 手當을 支給받고, 또한 抑留國의 法令에 따라 그들의 財產으로부터 생기는 所得을 받을 수 있다. 被抑留者의 本國이 支拂하는 手當額은 被抑留者의 種類(虛弱者, 病者, 妊產婦 등)에 대하여 同一한 것이라야 하며, 또한 本協約 第27條에서 禁止한 바와 같이 被抑留者에게 差別을 두어 被抑留者의 本國이 割當하거나 抑留國이 分配하여서는 아니된다.

抑留國은 各被抑留者에 대하여 正規의 計定을 開設하여야 하며, 또한 本條에 規定한 手當, 被抑留者가 受領한 送金 및 被抑留者로부터 押收한 金額으로서 그가 抑留되어 있는 國家에서 施行되고 있는 法令에 따라 使用할 수 있는 것은 그 計定의 貸邊에 이를 記入하여야 한다. 被抑留者는 그 家族 및 기타 被扶養者에 送金하기 위하여 그 國家에서 施行되고 있는 法令과 矛盾되지 아니하는 모든 便宜를 許與받아야 한다. 被抑留者는 抑留國이 정하는 制限內에서 自己의 計定으로부터 그 個人的 經費를 위하여 必要한 額을 引出할 수 있다. 被抑留者는 언제나 自己의 計定을 調査하고, 또한 그 寫本을 받는 데 適當한 便宜를 許與받아야 한다. 計定의 證明書는 請求가 있을 때에는 利益保護國에 提供하여야 하며, 또한 被抑留者가 移動된 때에도 被抑留者에게 수반시켜야 한다.

## 第7章 管理 및 紀律

**第99條** 各收容所는 抑留國의 正規軍隊 또는 正規行政廳에서 選定된 責任 있는 將校나 公務員의 指揮下에 두어야 한다. 收容所를 指揮하는 將校나 公務員은 自國의 公用語(公用語가 2 이상일 때에는 그 중의 1)로써 쓰여진 本協約의 謄本을 所持하고, 또한 本協約의 適用에 대하여 責任을 져야 한다. 被抑留者를 監督하는 職員은 本協約의 諸規定과 그 適用을 確保하기 위하여 취하여진 行政措置에 관하여 敎育을 받아야 한다.

本協約 및 本協約에 의하여 締結되는 特別協定의 本文은 被抑留者가 理解하는 言語로써 收容所內部에 揭示되거나, 또는 被抑留委員會에 所持시켜야 한다.

各種의 規則·命令·通告 및 公示는 被抑留者에게 이를 通知하고, 또한 被抑留者가 理解하는 言語로써 收容所內部에 이를 揭示하여야 한다.

被抑留者에 대하여 個人的으로 發하는 命令도 當該被抑留者가 理解하는 言語로써 행하여야 한다.

**第100條** 收容所에서의 紀律制度는 人



0024

道의 原則에 合致되는 것이라야 하며 또한 어떠한 경우에도 被抑留者에 대하여 그 健康에 危險한 肉體的 疲勞를 주고 또는 肉體的이거나 精神的인 苦痛을 수반하는 規定을 包含하여서는 아니된다. 文身에 의한 識別標識 또는 身體에 대한 記號 또는 標識의 押印에 의한 識別은 禁止된다.

특히 長時間에 걸친 不動姿勢와 點呼, 懲戒를 위한 訓練, 軍事訓練과 演習 또는 食糧의 減配는 禁止한다.

**第101條** 被抑留者는 그를 그 權限內에 둔 當局에 대하여 抑留條件에 관한 請願을 提起할 權利를 가진다.

被抑留者는 또한 抑留條件에 관하여 異議를 提起하려는 事項에 대하여 利益保護國代表의 注意를 喚起시키기 위하여 被抑留者委員會를 통하거나, 또는 必要하다고 認定하는 때에는 直接 利益保護國代表에게 申請할 權利를 無制限으로 가진다.

이러한 請願과 異議는 즉시 變更을 加함이 없이 傳達되어야 하며, 그 理由가 없다고 認定되는 경우에도 處罰의 理由가 되어서는 아니된다.

被抑留者委員會는 利益保護國의 代表에게 收容所의 狀態 및 被抑留者의 要求에 관한 定期的 報告를 할 수 있다.

**第102條** 被抑留者는 모든 收容所에서, 抑留國, 利益保護國, 國際赤十字委員會 및 被抑留者를 援助하는 기타의 團體에 대하여 被抑留者를 代表하는 權限을 부여받는 被抑留者委員會의 委員을 6個月마다 自由로이 秘密投票로써 選擇하여야 한다. 同被抑留者委員會의 委員은 再選될 수 있다.

이와 같이 選出된 被抑留者는 그의 當選에 대하여 抑留當局의 承認을 얻은 後 그 任務에 着手한다. 承認의 拒否 또는 免職의 理由는 關係利益保護國에 通告하여야 한다.

**第103條** 被抑留者委員會는 被抑留者의 肉體的·精神的 및 知的 福祉를 위하여 貢獻하여야 한다.

특히 被抑留者가 그 相互間에 扶助하는 制度를 組織할 것을 決定한 경우에는 이 組織은 本協約의 他規定에 의하여 被抑留者委員會에 委任되는 特別한 任務와는 別途로 被抑留者委員會의 權限에 속하는 것으로 한다.

**第104條** 被抑留者委員會의 委員에 대하여는 그 任務遂行이 다른 勞動으로 인하여 한층 困難하여질 때에는 그 다른 勞動을 强制하여서는 아니된다.

被抑留者委員會의 委員은 그가 必要로 하는 補助者를 被抑留者 중에서 指名할 수 있다. 被抑留者委員에 대하여는 모든 物質的 便宜, 특히 그 任務達成에 必要한 어느 程度의 行動의 自由(勞動分遣隊의 訪問, 補給品의 受領)을 許與하여야 한다.

被抑留者委員會의 委員에 대하여는 抑留國當局, 利益保護國 및 國際赤十字委員會 및 그들의 代表 또는 被抑留者를 援助하는 團體와 郵便 및 電信으로 通信하기 위한 便宜를 許與하여야 한다. 勞動分遣隊의 被抑留者委員會委員은 本收容所의 被抑留者委員會와 通信하기 위하여 同一한 便宜를 享有한다. 이 通信은 制限하여서는 아니되며, 또한 第107條에 정하는 割當數의 一部를 構成하는 것으로 認定되지 아니한다.

移動되는 被抑留者委員會의 委員에 대하여는 그 事務를 後任者에게 引繼하기 위한 充分한 時間를 부여하여야 한다.

## 第 8 章　外部와의 關係

**第105條** 抑留國은 被保護者를 抑留하였을 때에는 즉시 被保護者의 本國및 利益保護國에 대하여 本章의 規定을 實施하기 위하여 취하는 措置를 通知하여야 한다. 抑留國은 그 措置가 후에 變更되었을 때에는 그 變更에 관하여도 同一하게 關係當局에 通知하여야 한다.

**第106條** 各被抑留者에 대하여는 그가 抑留된 즉시 또는 收容所에 到着한後 늦어도 1週 이내에, 그리고 疾病에 걸렸거나 他收容所 또는 病院에 移動되었을 경우에도 1週日 이내에 그 家族과 第140條에 정하는 中央被抑留者情報局에 抑留된 事實, 住所 및 健康狀態를 通知하는 葉書를 직접 送付할 수 있도록 하여야 하며, 또한 그 葉書는 可能한 限 本協約에 附屬된 樣式과 同一한 것이어야 한다. 그 葉書는 可能한 限 早速히 送付되어야 하며 어떠한 경우에도 遲延되어서는 아니된다.

**第107條** 被抑留者에 대하여는 便紙 및 葉書의 受發을 許容하여야 한다. 抑留國이 各被抑留者가 發送하는 便紙 및 葉書의 數를 制限할 必要가 있다고 認定할 경우에는 그 數는 每月 便紙 2通 및 葉書 4通보다 적어서는 아니된다. 그러한 便紙와 葉書는 可能한 限 本協約에 附屬된 樣式과 同一한 樣式으로 作成하여야 한다. 被抑留者에게 送付된 通信이 制限되어야 할 경우에는 그 制限은 普通 抑留國의 要請에 따라 被抑留者의 本國만이 命할 수 있다. 이러한 便紙 및 葉書는 適當한 期間內에 發送되어야 하며, 懲戒事由로서 遲延 또는 留置되어서는 아니된다.

長期間에 걸쳐 家族으로부터 消息을 듣지 못한 被抑留者 또는 家族과의 사이에 普通郵便經路를 통하여 消息을 주고 받을 수 없는 被抑留者 및 家族으로부터 심히 遠距離에 있는 被抑留者에 대하여는 電報를 發信할 것이 許可되어야 한다. 그 料金은 被抑留者가 處分할 수 있는 通貨로써 支拂되어야 한다. 被抑留者는 緊急하다고 認定되는 경우에도 이 規定에 의한 恩澤을 받아야 한다.

被抑留者의 通信은 原則的으로 母國語로 적어야 한다. 衝突當事國은 기타의 言語로써 通信을 許可할 수 있다.

**第108條** 被抑留者에 대하여는 특히 食糧, 被服, 醫療品, 書籍 및 被抑留者의 必要를 充足시키는 宗敎, 敎育 또는 娛樂用物品을 內容으로 하는 個人 또는 集團的 荷物을 郵便 또는 기타의 方法에 의하여 受領할 것을 許可하여야 한다. 그 荷物은 抑留國에 대하여 本協約에서 抑留國에 課하여진 義務를 免하는 것은 아니다.

軍事上의 必要로서 이러한 荷物의 數量을 制限하여야 할 경우에는 利益保護國, 國際赤十字委員會 또는 被抑留者에게 援助를 提供하는 기타 團體로서 荷物의 傳達責任을 지는 機關에 그 制限에 관한 通告를 하여야 한다.

個人 또는 集團에게 보내는 荷物의 送付에 관한 條件은 必要하다면 關係國間의 特別協定의 對象으로 하여야 한다. 關係國은 어떠한 경우에도 被抑留者의 救濟品受領을 遲延시켜서는 아니된다. 圖書는 被服 또는 食糧이든 荷物 속에 넣어서는 아니된다. 醫療救濟品은 原則的으로 集團的 荷物로서 送付되어야 한다.

**第109條** 集團的 救濟品의 受領 및 分配條件에 관하여 衝突當事國間에 特別協定이 없는 경우에는 本協約에 附屬하는 集團的 救濟에 관한 規則을 適用하여야 한다.

前記의 特別協定은 어떠한 경우에도 被抑留者委員會가 被抑留者에게 보내어진 集團的 救濟品을 保有, 分配 및 受取人의 利益이 되도록 處分하는 權利를 制限하여서는 아니된다.

또한 이러한 特別協定은 利益保護國, 國際赤十字委員會 또는 被抑留者에게 援助를 提供하는 기타의 團體로서 集團的 荷物의 傳達責任을 맡은 機關의 代表가 受取人에 대한 當該荷物의 分配를 監督할 權利를 制限하여서는 아니된다.

**第110條** 被抑留者를 위한 모든 救濟品은 輸入稅, 關稅 및 手數料, 기타의 課徵을 免除받는다.

他國으로부터 被抑留者에게 보내어



0025

지거나 또는 被抑留者가 發送하는 모든 物品(小包郵便으로 發送하는 救濟小包를 包含한다) 및 郵便에 의한 送金은 直接으로 送付되거나 또는 第136條에서 정하는 被保護者情報局 또는 第140條에서 정하는 中央被保護者情報局을 통하여 送付되거나를 不問하고 發送國, 受取國 및 仲介國에 있어서 郵便料金을 免除받는다. 이를 위하여 특히 抑留所 또는 普通 刑務所內에 留置되는 敵國의 民間人을 위한 1947年의 萬國郵便協約 및 萬國郵便聯合의 諸協定으로 정하는 免除는 本協約에 의하여 保護되는 기타의 被抑留者에게도 許與된다. 그러나 前記協定의 非署名國도 同一한 條件으로 料金의 免除를 許與하여야 한다.

被抑留者에게 보내어진 救濟品이 重量, 기타의 理由에 의하여 郵便으로써 送付할 수 없을 경우에는 그 輸送費는 抑留國의 管理下에 있는 모든 領域에 있어서는 抑留國이 負擔하여야 한다. 本協定의 其他의 締約國은 各己의 領域에 있어서의 輸送費를 負擔하여야 한다.

이러한 救濟品의 輸送에 관련되는 費用으로서 前各項에서 規定되지 아니한 것은 發送人이 이를 負擔하여야 한다.

締約國은 被抑留者가 發信하거나 受信하는 電報料金을 可能한 限 減額하도록 努力하여야 한다.

**第111條** 軍事行動 때문에 關係國이 第106條, 第107條, 第108條 및 第113條에서 정하는 郵便 및 救濟品의 輸送을 確保하는 義務를 遂行하지 못하는 경우에는 關係利益保護國, 國際赤十字委員會 또는 衝突當事國이 正式으로 承認한 기타의 團體가 正當한 輸送手段(鐵道, 自動車, 船舶, 航空機 등)에 의하여 그 郵便 및 救濟品의 傳達을 確保할 수 있다. 이를 위하여 締約國은 그들에게 이러한 輸送手段을 提供하여, 특히 必要한 安導券을 부여함으로써 同輸送手段의 運行을 許可하도록 努力하여야 한다.

이러한 輸送手段은 다음의 것을 輸送하기 위하여서도 使用할 수 있다.

ⓐ 第140條에 規定된 中央被保護者情報局과 第136條에 規定된 各國의 被保護者情報局과의 사이에서 交換되는 通信, 名簿 및 報告書

ⓑ 利益保護國, 國際赤十字委員會 또는 被抑留者를 援助하는 團體가 그 代表 또는 衝突當事國과의 사이에 交換되는 被抑留者에 관한 通信 및 報告書

前記의 規定은 衝突當事國이 希望하는 경우에 다른 輸送手段에 관하여 約定을 맺을 權利를 制限하지 않으며 또한 安導券을 相互合意한 條件에 따라 그 輸送手段에 부여하는 것을 妨害하는 것은 아니다.

輸送手段의 使用에 要하는 費用은 그것에 의하여 恩澤을 받는 者들이 속하는 衝突當事國이 荷物의 重要性에 비례하여 負擔하여야 한다.

**第112條** 被抑留者가 送付하는 書信의 檢閱은 可能한 限 迅速하게 이를 행하여야 한다.

被抑留者에게 送付되는 荷物의 檢査는 그 속에 든 物品을 損傷할 念慮가 있는 條件下에서 행하여져서는 아니된다. 同檢査는 受取人이 正當히 委任한 被抑留者의 立會下에서 행하여야 한다. 被抑留者에게 個人的 또는 集團的으로 가는 荷物의 引渡는 檢査의 困難을 理由로 遲延되어서는 아니된다.

衝突當事國이 命하는 通信의 禁止는 그것이 軍事的 理由에 의하거나 政治的 理由에 의하거나를 不問하고 一時的이어야 하며, 또한 禁止期間은 可能한 限 짧아야 한다.

**第113條** 抑留國은 被抑留者에게 보내어지거나 또는 被抑留者가 發送하는 遺言狀, 委任狀, 其他의 文書가 利益保護國 또는 第140條에 規定된 中央被保護者情報局을 통하여, 또는 기타 必要한 方法으로 傳達되도록 모든 適當한 便宜를 提供하여야 한다.

抑留國은 어떠한 경우에라도 前記한 文書의 妥當하고 適法한 樣式에 의한 作成 및 認證에 대하여 被抑留者에게 便宜를 提供하여야 한다. 특히 抑留國은 被抑留者가 辯護士와 相談하는 것을 許容하여야 한다.

**第114條** 抑留國은 被抑留者에 대하여 抑留條件 및 適用法令에 違反하지 아니하는 限, 그 財産을 管理할 수 있도록 모든 便宜를 提供하여야 한다. 이를 위하여 抑留國은 緊急한 경우에 있어서 事情이 許容한다면, 被抑留者가 收容所로부터 外出함을 許容하여야 한다.

**第115條** 被抑留者가 訴訟의 當事國가 되는 모든 경우에 있어서 抑留國은 本人이 希望한다면, 그의 抑留事實을 그 法院에 通告하여야 하며 또한 法的 制限範圍內에서 被抑留者의 事件에 관한 豫審과 實施 또는 法院判決의 執行에 관하여 그의 抑留事由가 不利한 條件을 구성하지 않도록 모든 必要한 措置를 취하여야 한다.

**第116條** 各被抑留者는 定期的이며 可能한 限 頻繁한 訪問, 특히 그의 親族의 訪問을 받는 것을 許容받아야 한다.

各被抑留者는 緊急한 경우, 특히 親族의 死亡이나 重病時에는 可能한 限 歸家가 許可되어야 한다.

## 第 9 章 刑罰 및 懲戒罰

**第117條** 被抑留者가 抑留되어 있는 領域內에서 施行되고 있는 法令은 本章의 規定에 따를 것을 條件으로 抑留중에 違反行爲를 犯한 被抑留者에게 계속 適用된다.

一般的인 法律, 規則 또는 命令이 被抑留者가 행한 일정한 行爲에 대하여 處罰한 것을 規定하고 있는 경우에 있어서, 被抑留者가 행한 同一한 行爲에 대하여는 處罰하지 않도록 되어 있을 때에는 그 行爲에 대하여는 懲戒處罰만을 課하여야 한다.

被抑留者를 同一한 行爲 또는 同一한 犯罪事實에 관하여 二重處罰할 수 없다.

**第118條** 法院 또는 當局은 刑의 宣告를 행함에 있어서 被告人이 抑留國의 國民이 아니라는 事實을 可能한限 考慮하여야 한다. 法院 또는 當局은 被抑留者가 訴追받은 違反行爲에 관하여 規定된 刑罰을 自由로이 輕減할 수 있으며, 또한 이를 위하여 所定의 最輕刑罰을 반드시 適用할 義務는 지지 않는다.

日光이 비치지 아니하는 場所에서의 禁錮 및 일반적으로 모든 種類의 殘虐한 行爲를 禁止한다.

懲戒罰 또는 刑罰에 服役한 被抑留者는 기타 被抑留者와 相異한 待遇를 받지 아니한다.

被抑留者의 懲戒나 裁判 이전의 留置期間은 被抑留者에게 宣告하는 拘束의 懲戒罰 또는 刑罰에 通算하여야 한다.

被抑留者委員會는 同委員會가 代表하는 被抑留者에 대하여 취하여지는 모든 訴訟節次 및 그 結果에 관하여 通知를 받아야 한다.

**第119條** 被抑留者에 대하여 課할 수 있는 懲戒罰은 다음과 같다.

① 30日 이내의 期間에 限하여 第95條의 規定에 따라 被抑留者가 받은 賃金의 100분의 50 이하의 罰金

② 本協約에 規定된 待遇 이외에 許可되고 있는 特權의 停止

③ 收容所의 維持에 관한 1日 2時間 이내의 勞動

④ 拘禁

懲戒罰은 어떠한 경우에도 非人道的인 것, 殘虐한 것, 또는 被抑留者의 健康을 害하는 것이어서는 아니된다. 被抑留者의 年齡·性別 및 健康狀態를 考慮하여야 한다.

하나의 處罰期間은 被抑留者가 處罰받을 경우에 있어서 동시에 두 개 이상의 紀律違反行爲에 대하여 問責



0026

당한다 할지라도 이러한 違反行爲間의 關聯有無를 不問하고 最大限 連續 30日을 超過하여서는 아니된다.

**第120條** 逃走의 旣遂 또는 未遂 후에 逮捕된 被抑留者에 대하여는 그 行爲가 反復하여 행하여졌느냐의 與否를 不問하고 懲戒罰만을 課할 수 있다.

第118條 第③項의 規定에 불구하고 逃走의 旣遂 또는 未遂의 結果로서 處罰된 被抑留者는 특별한 監視下에 둘 수 있다. 그 監視는 被抑留者의 健康을 害하여서는 아니되고 收容所內에서 행하여져야 하며, 또한 本協約에 의하여 被抑留者에게 부여되는 어떠한 保護라도 排除하는 것이 되어서는 아니된다.

逃走의 旣遂 또는 未遂를 幇助하거나 敎唆한 被抑留者에 대하여는 그 行爲에 대하여 懲戒罰만을 課하여야 한다.

**第121條** 逃走의 旣遂 또는 未遂는 그 行爲가 反復하여 행하여진 경우라도 被抑留者가 逃走 중에 행한 犯罪行爲에 관하여 訴追되어 있을 때에 刑을 加重하는 情狀으로 認定되어서는 아니된다.

衝突當事國은 被抑留者의 違反行爲에 관하여 懲戒罰을 課하느냐 또는 刑罰을 課하느냐를 決定함에 있어서는 主務當局이 寬大히 處理하도록 하여야 한다.

**第122條** 紀律에 대한 犯罪를 構成하는 行爲는 즉시로 調査하여야 한다. 이 規定은 특히 逃走의 旣遂 또는 未遂에 대하여 適用한다. 再次 逮捕된 被抑留者는 主務當局에 可能한 限 迅速히 引渡되어야 한다.

紀律에 대한 犯罪가 있는 경우 未決拘禁期間은 모두 被抑留者에 대하여 最少限度로 하여야 하며 14日을 超過하여서는 아니된다. 그 期間은 어떠한 경우에도 拘禁刑에 이를 通算하여야 한다.

第124條 및 第125條의 規定은 紀律에 대한 犯罪로 인한 未決囚인 被抑留者에게 適用된다.

**第123條** 懲戒罰은 收容所長 또는 그를 代理하거나 그 懲戒權을 委任받은 責任있는 將校나 公務員만이 課할 수 있다. 단, 이것은 法院 및 上級當局의 權限을 侵害하는 것이어서는 아니된다.

立件된 被抑留者에 대하여는 懲戒判定 전에 그가 立件된 犯罪에 관한 正確한 內容을 通告하고, 또한 當該被抑留者가 自己의 行爲를 解明하고 辯護할 機會를 부여하여야 한다. 그 被抑留者에 대하여 특히 證人을 召喚하고 必要할 때에는 資格있는 通譯人에게 通譯시키는 것을 許諾하여야 한다. 判定은 當該被抑留者 및 被抑留者委員會의 委員의 立會下에서 宣告되어야 한다.

懲戒의 判定으로부터 執行까지의 期間은 1個月을 超過하여서는 아니된다.

어떤 被抑留者에게 중복하여 懲戒의 決定이 있었을 경우에는, 그중 어느 懲戒罰의 期間이 10日 이상일 때에는 그 執行까지에는 적어도 3日의 여유를 부여하여야 한다.

懲戒의 記錄은 收容所長이 保存하고, 利益保護國의 代表者의 閱覽에 供하여야 한다.

**第124條** 被抑留者는 어떠한 경우에도 懲戒施設(矯導所, 營倉, 徒刑場 ·등)에 移動시켜서 懲戒罰에 處하여서는 아니된다.

被抑留者를 懲戒罰에 處하는 場所는 衛生上의 要件과 合致하여야 하며 특히 適切한 寢具가 마련되어야 한다. 懲戒罰에 服하는 被抑留者는 그들로 하여금 淸潔한 狀態로 保持할 수 있도록 해주어야 한다.

懲戒罰에 服하는 女子被抑留者는 男子被抑留者와 隔離된 場所에 拘禁하고 또한 女子의 直接 監視下에 두어야 한다.

**第125條** 懲戒罰에 服하는 被抑留者에 대하여는 要請이 있으면 1日에 적어도 2時間 運動하고, 또한 屋外에 있을 수 있도록 許容하여야 한다.

그 被抑留者에 대하여는 要請이 있으면 每日 檢診을 받을 수 있도록 許容하여야 한다. 그 被抑留者는 그의 健康狀態에 따라 必要로 하는 治療를 받을 수 있으며, 必要한 경우에는 收容所의 醫務室 또는 病院에 移動되어야 한다.

그러한 被抑留者에 대하여는 읽고, 쓰고, 書信을 受發하는 일을 許容하여야 한다. 단, 小包의 受領이나 金錢의 支拂은 그들의 處罰이 終了될 때까지 保留할 수 있으며, 그동안 被抑留者委員會에 委託되어야 한다. 被抑留者委員會는 그 荷物 중에 腐敗하기 쉬운 物品을 醫務室에 引渡한다.

懲戒罰에 服하는 被抑留者로부터는 本協約 第107條 및 第143條의 規定의 恩澤을 剝奪할 수 없다.

**第126條** 第71條로부터 第76條까지의 規定은 抑留國의 領域內에 있는 被抑留者에 대한 訴訟節次에 類推하여 適用하여야 한다.

## 第10章 被抑留者의 移動

**第127條** 被抑留者의 移動은 항상 人道的으로 행하여져야 한다. 그 移動은 原則的으로 鐵道, 기타의 輸送手段에 의하여 적어도 抑留國 軍隊의 移動條件과 同等한 條件으로 행하여져야 한다. 例外的인 措置로서 徒步로 移動하지 않으면 아니되는 경우에는 被抑留者의 健康狀態가 그 移動에 適合하지 못할 때에는 그 移動을 행하여서는 아니되며, 또한 어떠한 경우에도 被抑留者를 過度하게 疲勞하게 해서는 아니된다.

抑留國는 移動 중인 被抑留者에 대하여 그 健康을 維持하는 데 충분한 飮料水와 食糧을 補給해야 하며, 必要한 被服, 適當한 宿舍 및 必要한 醫療를 供與하여야 한다. 抑留國은 移動中인 被抑留者의 安全을 確保하기 위하여 모든 適當한 豫備措置를 취하여야 한다. 抑留國은 移動되는 被抑留者의 完全한 名簿를 그 出發 전에 作成하여야 한다.

病者, 負傷者 또는 虛弱者인 被抑留者와 妊産婦는 移動이 그의 健康에 심히 害로울 때에는 移動하여서는 아니된다. 단, 그의 安全을 위하여 絶對로 移動이 必要한 경우는 例外로 한다.

戰線이 收容所에 接近하였을 경우에는 그 收容所의 被抑留者를 充分히 安全한 條件으로 移動시킬 수 있을 때와 被抑留者를 現地에 두면 移動하는 경우보다 한층 더 큰 危險에 直面케 될 때를 除外하고 移動시켜서는 아니된다.

抑留國은 被抑留者의 移動을 決定함에 있어서 被抑留者 自身의 利益을 考慮하여야 하며, 특히 그 者의 送還 또는 家庭에의 復歸를 한층 困難케 하는 것이어서는 아니된다.

**第128條** 移動하는 경우에는 被抑留者에 대하여 그 出發 및 새로운 郵便住所를 正式으로 通知하여야 한다.

이러한 通知는 被抑留者가 짐을 꾸리고 또한 家族에게 通知할 수 있는 時間的 여유를 두고 행하여져야 한다. 被抑留者에 대하여는 그 個人用品 및 受領한 通信과 小包의 携帶를 許容하여야 한다. 이러한 小荷物의 重量은 移動條件에 의하여 必要할 때에는 制限할 수 있다. 그러나 어떠한 경우에도 被抑留者 1人에 대하여 25kg 未滿으로 制限하여서는 아니된다.

舊收容所에 보내어진 通信 및 小包는 遲滯없이 被抑留者에게 送達되어야 한다.

收容所長은 被抑留者委員會와 協議하여 被抑留者의 共有物 및 第②項에 따라 課하여지는 制限에 의하여 被抑留者가 携帶할 수 없는 荷物의 輸送을 確保하기 위하여 必要한 措置를 취하여야 한다.



0027

## 第11章 死 亡

**第129條** 被抑留者의 遺言狀은 完全하게 保管하기 위하여 責任있는 當局이 受理할 것이며, 被抑留者가 死亡한 경우에는 當該被抑留者가 生前에 指定한 者에게 遲滯없이 送付하여야 한다.

被抑留者의 死亡은 모든 경우에 있어서 醫師가 確認하여야 한다. 그 死亡에 관하여는 死因 및 死亡時의 狀態를 記載한 死亡證明書를 作成하여야 한다.

正式死亡記錄은 正當하게 登錄하여 收容所가 있는 領域內에서 實施되는 節次에 따라서 作成하여야 하며, 그 認證謄本은 利益保護國 및 第140條에 規定된 中央被保護者情報局에 遲滯없이 送付하여야 한다.

**第130條** 抑留當局은 抑留되어 있는 동안 被抑留者를 可能한 限, 그가 속하는 宗敎儀式에 따라 鄭重히 埋葬하고 그 墳墓를 尊重할 것이며, 適切히 維持하고 언제라도 識別할 수 있는 標識를 하도록 하여야 한다.

死亡한 被抑留者는 不可避한 事情으로 共同의 墳墓를 使用할 必要가 있는 경우를 除外하고는 個個의 墳墓에 埋葬하여야 한다. 그 屍體는 衛生上 絶對로 必要한 경우, 死者의 宗敎에 의한 경우 또는 本人의 明示的 希望에 의한 경우에 한하여 火葬할 수 있다. 火葬한 경우에는 被抑留者의 死亡證明書에 火葬의 事實 및 理由를 記載하여야 한다. 그 遺骨은 安全한 保管을 위하여 抑留當局이 保管하며, 그의 親族의 要請이 있으면 可能한限 迅速히 그 者에게 引渡하여야 한다.

抑留國은 事情이 許諾하는 限, 迅速히 그리고 늦어도 敵對行爲의 終了時까지 第136條에 規定한 被保護者情報局을 통하여 死亡한 被抑留者를 識別하는 데 必要한 모든 明細 및 그 墓의 正確한 場所를 記載하여야 한다.

**第131條** 어떤 被抑留者의 死亡 또는 重大한 傷害가 衛兵, 기타의 被抑留者 또는 其他人에 의하여 惹起되었거나 또는 惹起된 嫌疑가 있을 경우, 또는 被抑留者의 原因不明의 死亡에 관하여 抑留國은 즉시로 正式調査를 행하여야 한다.

前記의 事項에 관한 通知는 즉시 利益保護國에 부여하여야 한다. 證人으로부터 얻은 供述을 包含하는 報告書를 作成하여 前記利益保護國에 送付하여야 한다.

調査에 의하여 1人 또는 2人 이상의 者가 罪를 犯하였다고 認定될 때에는, 抑留國은 責任을 追窮당한 者를 訴追하는 데 必要한 모든 措置를 취하여야 한다.

## 第12章 釋放, 送還 및 中立國內에서의 入院

**第132條** 抑留國은 各被抑留者의 抑留事由가 解除된 때에는 즉시 釋放하여야 한다.

各衝突當事國은 또한 敵對行爲의 期間中 特定種類의 被抑留者, 특히 兒童, 妊産婦, 幼兒 및 兒童의 母親, 負傷者 및 病者 또는 長期間 拘留되어 있던 被抑留者의 釋放, 送還, 居住地에의 復歸 또는 中立國에서의 入院을 위한 協定을 締結하도록 努力하여야 한다.

**第133條** 抑留는 敵對行爲의 終了후 可能한 限 早速히 이를 終止시켜야 한다.

衝突當事國의 領域內에 있는 被抑留者로서 懲戒罰만을 課할 수 없는 違反 중인 者는 그 節次가 終了할 때까지, 또는 事情에 따라 刑의 執行이 終了할 때까지 계속 留置할 수 있다. 이미 自由刑의 判決을 받은 被抑留者에 관하여도 同一하다.

抑留國 및 關係國은 離散된 被抑留者를 搜索하기 위하여 敵對行爲 또는 地域의 占領終了後에 協定으로서 委員會를 設置할 수 있다.

**第134條** 締約國은 敵對行爲 또는 占領이 終了에 있어서 모든 被抑留者가 그의 最後居住地에 復歸함을 確保하고, 또한 그의 送還이 容易하게 하기 위하여 努力하여야 한다.

**第135條** 釋放된 被抑留者가 抑留될 때에 居住하고 있던 場所에 復歸하기 위한 費用과 抑留國이 그들을 旅行中 또는 公海上에서 抑留하였을 경우에는 그들이 旅行을 完了하거나 또는 그 出發地點에 復歸하기 위한 費用은 抑留國이 負擔하여야 한다.

抑留國은 抑留前에 自國內에 恒久的인 居所를 가지고 있던 者에 대하여 그 領域內에 居住함을 許可하지 아니하는 경우에는 그 被抑留者의 送還費用을 支拂하여야 한다. 그러나 被抑留者가 自己自身의 責任으로나 또는 本國政府에 대한 忠誠心의 發路로서 歸國을 希望하는 경우에는, 抑留國은 自國領域의 出國地點 이후의 旅行費用을 支拂할 必要가 없다. 抑留國은 自己自身의 要請으로 抑留된 被抑留者의 送還費用을 支拂할 必要가 없다.

被抑留者가 第45條에 따라 移送된 경우에는 被抑留者의 移送을 행하는 國家 및 그들을 받아들이는 國家는 自國이 負擔하는 費用의 割當에 관하여 合意하여야 한다.

前記의 規定은 衝突當事國이 敵國의 手中에 있는 自國民의 交換 및 送還에 관하여 特別協定을 締結함을 妨害하지 아니한다.

## 第5部 被保護者情報局 및 中央被保護者情報局

**第136條** 各衝突當事國은 衝突의 開始 및 占領의 모든 경우에 있어서 그 權限內에 있는 被保護者에 관한 情報의 受領 및 傳達에 대한 責任을 지는 公的인 情報局을 設置하여야 한다.

各衝突當事國은 2週 이상 拘禁하였거나 住居를 指定하였거나, 또는 抑留한 모든 被保護者에 대하여 취한 措置에 관하여 自國의 被保護者情報局에 可及的 속히 通報하여야 한다. 또한 抑留國은 關係各部處로 하여금 被保護者에 관한 모든 移動(예컨대 移動, 釋放, 送還, 逃走, 入院, 出生, 死亡 등)에 관한 情報를 迅速히 前記被保護者情報局에 提供하도록 要求하여야 한다.

**第137條** 各國의 被保護者情報局은 利益保護國 및 第140條에 規定한 中央被保護者情報局을 통하여, 被保護者의 本國 또는 그들이 居住하였던 國家에 대하여 被保護者에 관한 情報를 迅速한 方法으로서 즉시 通知하여야 한다.

被保護者情報局은 被保護者에 관하여 受領하는 모든 照會에 回答하여야 한다. 被保護者情報局은 被保護者에 관한 情報를 傳達하여야 한다. 단, 그 傳達이 本人 또는 그 親族에게 害로운 경우에는 그러하지 아니하다. 이러한 경우라도 그 情報는 中央被保護者情報局에는 傳達하여야 하며, 同情報局은 그 事情에 관하여 通知를 받았을 때에는 第140條에 規定된 必要한 措置를 취하여야 한다.

被保護者情報局의 모든 通知書는 署名 또는 捺印에 의하여 認證되어야 한다.

**第138條** 被保護者情報局이 受領하고 傳達하는 情報는 被保護者의 身元을 正確히 識別하고, 또한 親族에게 迅速히 認知시킬 수 있게 하는 性質의 것이어야 한다. 各被保護者에 관한 情報는 적어도 姓名, 出生地 및 生年月日, 國籍, 最後居住地, 特徵, 父親의 姓名 및 母親의 結婚前의 姓, 本人에 관하여 취하여진 措置의 日字·場所 및 性質, 被保護者에 대한 通信을 送付할 住所 및 通知를 받은 者의 姓名과 住所를 包含하는 것이라야 한다.

이와 同一하게 重病 또는 重傷者인 被抑留者의 健康狀態에 관한 情報도



0028

定期的으로 可能하면 每週 提供하여야 한다.

**第139條** 各國의 被保護者情報局은 또한 第136條에 規定된 被保護者 또는 逃走하거나 死亡한 被保護者가 남긴 모든 個人的인 有價物의 收集에 관하여 責任을 지며, 또한 그 有價物을 直接으로 또는 必要한 경우에는 中央被保護者情報局을 통하여 關係者에게 送付하여야 한다. 被保護者情報局은 그 有價物을 封印袋에 넣어서 送付하여야 하며, 그 封印袋에는 有價物을 所持하고 있던 者를 識別하기 위하여 明確하고도 完全한 明細書 및 內容의 完全한 目錄을 添附하여야 한다. 이러한 모든 有價物의 受領 및 發送에 관하여는 詳細한 記錄을 남겨 두어야 한다.

**第140條** 被保護者(특히 被抑留者)에 관한 中央被保護者情報局은 中立國에 이를 設置하여야 한다. 國際赤十字委員會는 必要하다고 認定한 경우에는 關係國에 대하여 中央被保護者情報局을 組織한 것을 提議하여야 하며, 中央被保護者情報局은 捕虜의 待遇에 관한 1949年 8月 12日字 제네바協約 第123條에 規定된 中央捕虜情報局과 同一한 것으로 할 수 있다.

中央被保護者情報局의 任務는 第136條에 規定된 모든 種類의 情報로서 公的 또는 私的의 經路로 入手할 수 있는 것을 收集하고, 또한 關係者의 出生國 및 그들이 住所를 가진 國家에 情報를 可能한 限 迅速히 傳達하는 것이어야 한다. 단, 그 情報의 傳達이 그 情報와 關係있는 者나 그의 近親者에게 有害로운 경우에는 그러하지 아니하다. 中央被保護者情報局은 이 傳達에 관하여는 衝突當事國으로부터 適切한 便宜를 提供받아야 한다.

締約國 특히 그 國民이 中央被保護者情報局의 用役의 惠澤을 입은 國家는 中央被保護者情報局에 必要한 財政的 援助를 提供하여야 한다.

前記의 規定은 國際赤十字委員會 또는 第142條에 規定한 救濟團體의 人道的 活動을 制限하는 것으로 解釋하여서는 아니된다.

**第141條** 各國의 被保護者情報局 및 中央被保護者情報局은 모든 郵便料金의 免除 및 第110條에 規定한 免除를 받으며, 또한 可能한 限 電報料金의 免除 또는 적어도 相當한 減額을 받아야 한다.

## 第4篇 協約의 實施

### 第1部 總 則

**第142條** 抑留國이 自國의 安全을 保障하거나, 또는 기타 合理的인 必要에 對處하기 위하여 緊要하다고 認定하는 措置에 따를 것을 條件으로 宗敎團體, 救濟團體, 기타 被保護者를 援助하는 團體의 代表者 및 正當하게 委任받은 代理人들은 被保護者의 訪問, 그리고 그 出處의 如何를 不問하고 敎育, 娛樂 또는 宗敎目的을 가지는 救濟品과 物資를 分配하고 收容所內에서 餘暇를 利用하도록 援助하는 데 必要한 便宜를 抑留國으로부터 提供받아야 한다. 前記의 團體나 機關은 抑留國의 領域內에나 기타의 어떠한 國家內에도 設置할 수 있으며, 또한 國際的 性格을 가질 수 있다.

抑留國은 代表들이 自國領域內에서 抑留國의 監督下에 任務를 遂行할 것이 許容되고 있는 團體 또는 組織의 數를 制限할 수 있다. 단, 그 制限은 모든 被保護者에 대한 充分한 救濟를 效果的으로 施行하는 것을 妨害하여서는 아니된다.

이 分野에 있어서의 國際赤十字委員會의 特別한 地位는 항상 認定되고 尊重되어야 한다.

**第143條** 利益保護國의 代表者나 使節團은 被保護者가 있는 모든 場所, 특히 收容, 拘禁 및 勞動의 場所를 訪問할 수 있도록 許可되어야 한다.

利益保護國의 代表나 使節團은 被保護者가 使用하는 모든 施設에 出入할 수 있으며, 또한 立會人이 없이 直接으로 또는 通譯人을 통하여 被保護者와 會見할 수 있다.

이러한 訪問은 絶對的인 軍事上의 必要를 理由로 하는 例外的이고 一時的인 措置로서 행하여지는 경우를 除外하고는 禁止되지 아니한다. 그 訪問의 期間 및 回數는 이를 制限하여서는 아니된다.

利益保護國의 代表와 使節團은 訪問하고자 하는 場所를 自由로이 選定할 수 있다. 抑留國이나 占領國, 利益保護國 및 必要한 경우 訪問을 받는 者의 本國은 被抑留者의 同國人이 訪問에 參加하는 것을 合意할 수 있다.

國際赤十字委員會의 代表도 同一한 特權을 享有한다. 그 代表의 任命은 當該代表가 그의 任務를 遂行하는 領域을 管轄하는 國家의 承認을 받아야 한다.

**第144條** 締約國은 戰, 平時를 막론하고 本協約의 本文을 可及的 廣範圍하게 自國內에 普及시킬 것이며, 특히 軍敎育計劃, 可能하면 民間敎育計劃에도 本協約에 관한 學習을 包含시킴으로써 本協約의 原則을 全軍隊와 國民에게 習得시킬 것을 約定한다.

戰時에 있어서 被保護者에 대하여 責任을 지는 民間當局, 軍當局, 警察當局 및 기타 當局은 本協約의 本文을 所持하고, 또한 本協約의 規定에 대하여 特別한 敎育을 받아야 한다.

**第145條** 第1協約 第48條와 同文

**第146條** 第1協約 第49條와 同文

**第147條** 前條에서 말하는 重大한 違反行爲란 本協約이 保護하는 사람 또는 財産에 대하여 행하여지는 다음의 行爲를 意味한다. 즉, 故意的인 殺人, 身體 또는 健康을 크게 害치거나 苦痛을 주는 拷問이나 非人道的 待遇(生物學的 實驗을 包含), 被保護者를 不法으로 追放, 移送 또는 拘禁하는 것, 被保護者를 敵國의 軍隊에 服務하도록 强要하는 것, 本協約에 規定된 公正한 正規裁判을 받을 權利를 剝奪하는 것, 人質로 잡는 것 또는 軍事上의 必要에 따라 正當化되지 아니하는 不法 및 恣意的인 財産의 廣範한 破壞 또는 徵發

**第148條** 第1協約 第51條와 同文

**第149條** 第1協約 第52條와 同文

### 第2部 最終規定

**第150條** 第1協約 第55條와 同文

**第151條** 오늘 날짜의 本協約은 1949年 4月 21日 제네바에서 開催된 會議에 代表를 派遣한 國家에 대하여 1950年 2月 12日까지 그 署名을 위하여 開放된다.

**第152條** 第1協約 第57條와 同文

**第153條** 第1協約 第58條와 同文

**第154條** 本協約의 締約國으로서 1899年 7月 29日 또는 1907年 10月 18日의 陸戰法規 및 慣例에 관한 헤이그協約에 의하여 拘束받고 있는 國家間의 關係에 있어서는 本協約은 헤이그協約 附屬規則 第2章을 補完한다.

**第155條**
**第156條** 第1協約 第60條～第62條와 同文
**第157條**

**第158條** 各締約國은 本協約에서 自由로이 脫退할 수 있다.

脫退는 書面으로 스위스聯邦政府에 通告하여야 하며, 스위스聯邦政府는 그 通告를 모든 締約國政府에 傳達하여야 한다.

脫退는 스위스聯邦政府에 通告한 1年후에 發效한다. 단, 脫退國이 脫退를 通告한 當時에 戰爭에 介入하고 있는 경우에는 講和條約締結時까지 또한 本協約에 의하여 保護되는 者의 釋放·送還 및 居住地의 設定에 관련되는 事務가 終了될 때까지는 發效하지 아니한다.

脫退는 脫退하는 國家에 대하여서만 效力을 發生한다. 脫退는 文明人



0029

間에 確立된 慣行, 人道의 法則 및 大衆的 良心에 基因한 國際法의 原則에 따라 衝突當事國이 계속 履行하여야 할 義務를 害하여서는 아니된다.

第159條 第1協約 第64條와 同文

(署名省略)

## (7) 1949년 8월 12일자 제네바제협약에 대한 추가 및 국제적 무력충돌의 희생자 보호에 관한 의정서(제1의정서)

| | |
|---|---|
| 採 擇 | 1977年 6月 8日(제네바) |
| 發 效 | 1978年 12月 7日 |
| 大韓民國 | 1982年 7月 15日 發效(조약 제778호) |

### 전 문

체약당사국은,

제국민간에 평화가 지배하도록 하기 위한 그들의 진지한 희망을 선언하고,

모든 국가는 국제연합헌장에 따라 국제관계에 있어서 국가의 주권, 영토보존, 정치적 독립에 대하여 또는 국제연합의 목적과 불일치하는 여하한 방법으로 무력의 위협 또는 사용을 하지 않을 의무를 가진다는 것을 상기하고,

무력충돌의 희생자를 보호하는 제규정을 재확인하고 발전시키며 동 규정의 적용을 강화하기 위한 제조치를 보충할 필요가 있음을 믿고,

본 의정서 및 1949년 8월 12일자 제네바협약의 어느 규정도 국제연합헌장과 배치되는 여하한 침략행위 또는 무력행사를 합법화하거나 용인하는 것으로 해석될 수 없다는 확신을 표명하고,

나아가서 1949년 8월 12일자 제네바협약 및 본 의정서의 규정은 무력충돌의 성격이나 원인 또는 충돌당사국에 의하여 주장되거나 충돌당사국에 기인하는 이유에 근거한 어떠한 불리한 차별도 없이 이들 약정에 의하여 보호되는 모든 자에게 어떠한 상황하에서도 완전히 적용됨을 재확인하며,

다음과 같이 합의하였다.

### 제1편 총 칙

제1조 [일반원칙 및 적용범위] ① 체약당사국은 모든 경우에 있어서 본 의정서를 존중할 것과 본 의정서의 존중을 보장할 것을 약정한다.

② 본 의정서 또는 다른 국제협정의 적용을 받지 아니하는 경우에는 민간인 및 전투원은 확립된 관습, 인도원칙 및 공공양심의 명령으로부터 연원하는 국제법원칙의 보호와 권한하에 놓인다.

③ 전쟁희생자 보호를 위한 1949년 8월 12일자 제네바 제협약을 보완하는 본 의정서는 이들 협약의 공통조항인 제2조에 규정된 사태에 적용한다.

④ 전항에서 말하는 사태는 유엔헌장 및 "유엔헌장에 따른 국가간 우호관계와 협력에 관한 국제법원칙의 선언"에 의하여 보장된 민족자결권을 행사하기 위하여 식민통치, 외국의 점령 및 인종차별권에 대항하여 투쟁하는 무력충돌을 포함한다.

제2조 [정 의] 본 의정서의 목적을 위하여

① "제1협약", "제2협약", "제3협약" 및 "제4협약"이라 함은 각각 육전에 있어서의 군대의 부상자 및 병자의 상태개선에 관한 1949년 8월 12일자 제네바협약, 해상에 있어서의 군대의 부상자, 병자 및 난선자의 상태개선에 관한 1949년 8월 12일자 제네바협약, 포로의 대우에 관한 1949년 8월 12일자 제네바협약, 전시에 있어서의 민간인의 보호에 관한 1949년 8월 12일자 제네바협약을 의미하며, "제협약"이라 함은 전쟁희생자 보호를 위한 1949년 8월 12일자 제네바 4개협약을 의미한다.

② "무력충돌에 적용되는 국제법의 규칙"이라 함은 충돌당사국이 당사자인 국제협정에 명시된 전시에 적용되는 규칙과 전시에 적용가능한 국제법의 일반적으로 인정된 원칙 및 규칙을 의미한다.

③ "이익보호국"이라 함은 충돌당사국에 의하여 지정되고 적대당사국에 의하여 수락되었으며 제협약과 본 의정서에 따라 이익보호국에 부여된 기능을 수행할 것에 동의한 중립국 또는 충돌 비당사국을 의미한다.

④ "대리기관"이라 함은 제5조에 따라 이익보호국을 대신하여 활동하는 기구를 의미한다.

제3조 [적용의 개시 및 종료] 항시 적용되는 규정을 침해함이 없이,

① 제협약 및 본 의정서는 본 의정서 제1조에 규정된 사태가 개시될 때로부터 적용된다.

② 제협약 및 본 의정서의 적용은 충돌당사국의 영역내에서는 군사작전의 일반적인 종료시, 점령지역의 경우에는 점령의 종료시에 끝난다. 단, 양경우에 있어서 최종석방, 송환, 복귀가 그 후에 행하여지는 자는 예외로 한다. 이러한 자들은 그들의 최종석방, 송환, 복귀시까지 본 의정서 및 제협약의 관련규정으로부터 계속 혜택을 향유한다.

제4조 [충돌당사국의 법적지위] 제협약과 본 의정서의 적용 및 그에 규정된 협정의 체결은 충돌당사국의 법적지위에 영향을 주지 아니한다. 영토의 점령 또는 제협약 및 본 의정서의 적용은 문제지역의 법적지위에 영향을 주지 아니한다.

제5조 [이익보호국 및 그 대리기관의 지명] ① 충돌당사국은 충돌이 개시된 때부터 하기 조항에 따라 특히 이익보호국의 지명과 수락을 포함한 이익보호국제도의 적용에 의하여 협약과 본 의정서의 감시와 실시를 확보할 의무가 있다. 이러한 이익보호국은 충돌당사국의 이익을 보장할 의무를 진다.

② 제1조에 규정된 사태가 개시된날로부터 각 충돌당사국은 지체없이 제협약 및 본 의정서의 적용을 목적으로 이익보호국을 지정하여야 하며, 지체없이 그리고 동일한 목적을 위하여 적대국에 의하여 지명되고 자국에 의하여 수락된 이익보호국의 활동을 허용하여야 한다.

③ 본 의정서 1조에 규정된 사례가 개시된 때로부터 이익보호국이 지명되고 수락되지 않은 경우에는 기타 공정한 인도적 단체가 행동할 권리를 침해함이 없이 국제적십자위원회가 충돌당사국이 동의하는 이익보호국의 지체없는 지명을 목적으로 주선을 제공한다. 이 목적을 위하여 국제적십자위원회는 각 당사국에게 그 당사국이 적대당사국과의 관계에서 자국을 위하여 이익보호국으로 행동함을 수락할 수 있다고 생각하는 최소한 5개국의 명단을 제공할 것과 각 적대당사국에게 상대당사국의 이익보호국으로 수락할 수 있는 최소한 5개국의 명단을 제공할 것을 요청할 수 있다. 이들 명단은 요청을 접수한 때부터 2주일이내에 통보되어야 한다. 국제적십자위원회는 동 명단들을 비교하고 양측 명단에 기재된 후보국가에 대한 합의를 모색한다.

④ 전항의 규정에도 불구하고 이익보



0030

| 관리 번호 | 90/386 |
|---|---|

| | 분류번호 | 보존기간 |
|---|---|---|
| | | |

# 발 신 전 보

번 호 : WGV-1024 900808 0836 AQ 종별 :

수 신 : 주 제네바 대사. 총영사

발 신 : 장 관 (중근동)

제 목 : 이라크 및 쿠웨이트 아국 교민 안전 철수

1. 이라크의 쿠웨이트 침공에 의해 쿠웨이트를 완전 점령함에 따라 미국의 군사 개입 검토 및 UN의 대 이라크 제재 등이 예상돼, 긴박한 상황이 전개됨에 따라 아국으로서는 이라크 및 쿠웨이트 아국교민(도합 1269명)의 안전 철수 문제가 제기되고 있음.

2. 주미 아국 대사는 동 사태 관련, 미측의 EC 회원국, 소련, 일본과의 공동 추진으로 국제 적십자위를 통한 자국민 철수 계획에 관한 8.6. 미국 브리핑 내용 및 관련 제안 요지를 별첨 전문과 같이 보고하여 왔음.

3. 따라서, 이와같은 급박한 상황을 감안, 국제적십자측과 긴급 교섭, ~~동 적십자측의 긴밀한 협조로~~ 아국 교민의 안전 철수에 동 적십자측의 긴밀한 협조 가능성을 타진하고, 그 결과를 지급 보고 바람. 끝.

첨부 : 동 전문사본

(중동아국장 이 두 복)

예 고 : 90. 12. 31. 일반

1990. 12. 31. 에 예고문에 의거 일반문서로 재 분류됨.

| 보안 통제 | |
|---|---|

| 앙고재 | 90년 8월 7일 | 중근동과 | 기안자 성명 | | 과 장 | | 국 장 | | 차 관 | 장 관 |
|---|---|---|---|---|---|---|---|---|---|---|
| | | | 박종순 | | | | 전결 | | | |

| 외신과통제 |
|---|
| |

0031

| 관리 번호 | 90/7707 |
|---|---|

원 본

# 외 무 부

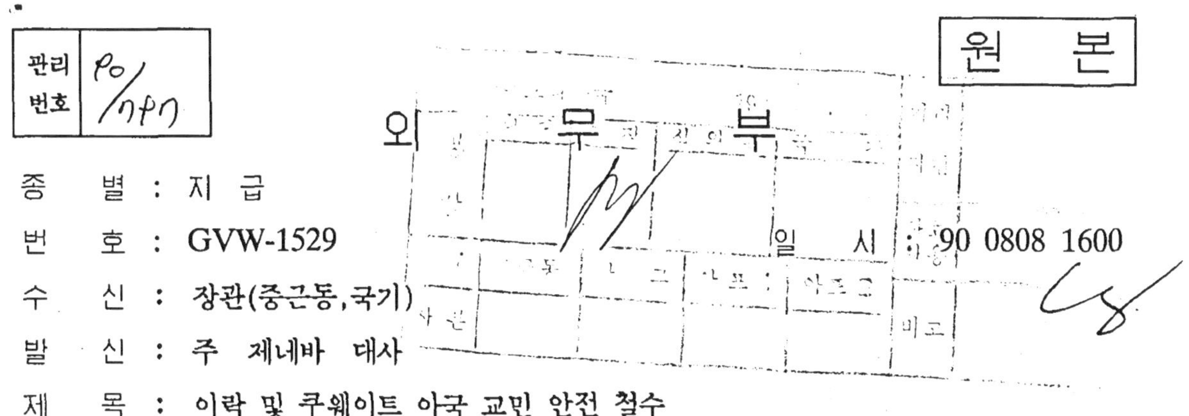

종 별 : 지 급

번 호 : GVW-1529 일 시 : 90 0808 1600

수 신 : 장관(중근동,국기)

발 신 : 주 제네바 대사

제 목 : 이락 및 쿠웨이트 아국 교민 안전 철수

대: WGV-1024

대호 관련 이량 참사관은 금 8.8(수) 오전 ICRC 의 이란. 이락 담당 과장 MR. DELAPRAZ 를 면담하여 표제 문제에 대해 ICRC 측의 협조를 요청한바, 동인의 언급요지 아래 보고함.(김종일 서기관 배석)

1. 본건 관련 이미 제네바 주재 미국, 이태리, 영국, 불란서 및 서독 대표부로 부터의 접촉이 있었음.

2. ICRC 가 우선적으로 해야 할 일은 쿠에이트에 ICRC 구호팀을 주재시키는 것인바, 현재로서는 쿠웨이트에 ICRC 구호팀이 주재하고 있지 않음.

3. ICRC 는 이미 6 개월 전부터 쿠웨이트 정부와 ICRC 팀 주재에 관한 협정 체결 교섭을 진행, 최근 서명단계에 왔으나 협정이 서명되기 전에 이락이 쿠웨이트를 침공하였음.

이에 따라 ICRC 는 최근 이락 정부에 바그다드 주재 ICRC 팀 (이란, 이락전발발 이후 이란 포로 보호 목적으로 주재) 을 쿠웨이트에 파견할수 있도록 협조해 줄것을 요청한바 (동 팀의 이동 경로는 바그다드 - 바스라 -쿠웨이트), 이락은 우선 쿠웨이트 신정부와 직접 접촉하라고 하여 쿠웨이트 신정부와 접촉토록 노력하였으나 접촉치 못하여 ( 또한 바그다드 주재 쿠웨이트 대사관도 8.7 폐쇄되어 접촉 불능), ICRC 는 명 8.9(목) 이락정부에 대해 동팀의 쿠웨븐트 파견 협조를 재 요청할 예정임.

4. 현재로서 ICRC 는 한국등 관계국가들의 관심을 TAKE NOTE 하고 ICRC 팀이 쿠웨이트에 파견되어 ICRC 의 구체적 활동이 개시될때 동 국가들과 세부적 협력 방안에 대해 협의 하겠음.

5. 이락주재 한국 교민 철수 문제는 한국과 이락간 외교관계가 단절댄 것은 아니므로 바그다드 주재 한국 총영사가 이락 정부와 동 문제를 교섭해야 할것임.

중아국 차관 1차보 2차보 국기국 영교국 청와대 안기부

PAGE 1

90.08.09 01:50

외신 2과 통제관 DH

0032

6. 일개 국가 또는 다수국가가 공동으로 이락 또는 쿠웨이트 신정부와 민간인 철수에 관한 합의를 하게 되더라도 철수 대상은 누구이며 철수 수단 (예: 미,영의 항공기 또는 함정등) 은 무엇으로 할것인가등의 문제가 남게될 것인바, 현재로서 ICRC 성격상 ICRC 가 특정국가를 대변하여 이러한 문제에 대해 이락정부와 협의할 입장은 아니므로 ICRC 로서는 ICRC 팀을 쿠웨이트에 파견 시킨이후세부적 철수 방안에 대해 관계국과 협력할수 있을 것임.

7. ICRC 팀이 일단 쿠웨이트에 파견 되면 1-2 일후에 ICRC 활동계획이 나오게 될 것인바, 이 단계가 되면 한국측과 신속히 접촉, 세부 협력 방안에 관해 긴밀히 협의토록 하겠음. 끝

(대사 이상옥-차관)

예고: 90.12.31. 일반

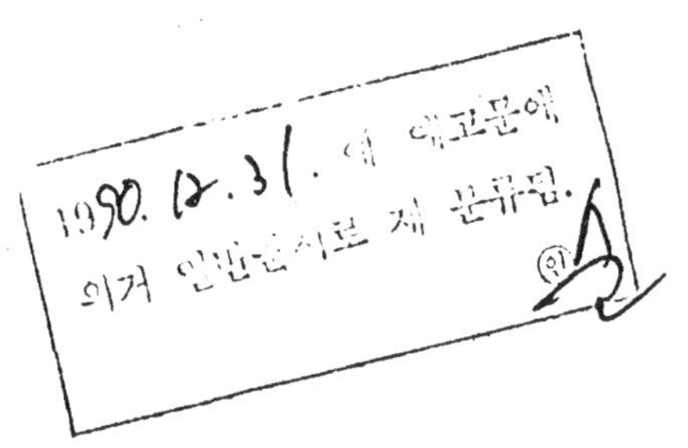


PAGE 2

0033

| 관리<br>번호 | 90/798 |
|---|---|

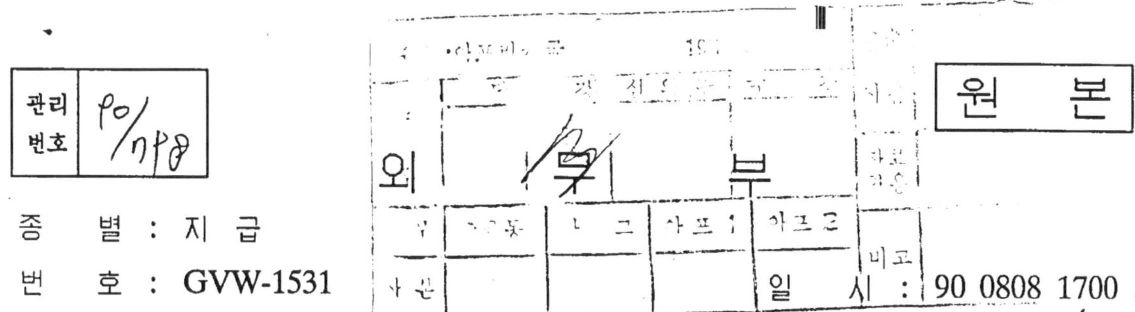

원 본

종 별 : 지 급

번 호 : GVW-1531　　　일 시 : 90 0808 1700

수 신 : 장관(중근동,국기) 사본:주미대사(본부중계요):본부중계필

발 신 : 주 제네바 대사

제 목 : 이락크 및 쿠웨이트 아국 교민 안전 철수

연: GVW-1529

1. 연호 관련 금 8.8(수) 당지 미국 대표부는 쿠웨이트 거주 외국인의 신변 안전 및 철수에 관하여 미국, 이태리(이씨 의장국), 일본등 대사가 16:30 미국 대표부에서 회합을 갖고 17:00 에는 ICRC 를 공동 방문하여 동건에 대한 ICRC의 협조를 공식 요청할 계획임을 알리고 아측도 이에 참여해 주도록 요청해 왔음.

2. 이에 대하여 당관은 본국정부로 부터의 훈령에 의하여 이미 오전에 ICRC 와 접촉하여 협조를 요청한바 있음을 알리고, 관련국가들과 공동으로 협조 요청 (JOINT DEMARCHE) 하는 것은 본국정부와 먼저 협의해야 겠다고 말한바, 미 대표부측은 한국이 이미 개별적으로 협조 요청을 하였다면 굳이 공동으로 하지 않아도 좋을 것이라고 언급하였음을 참고로 보고함.

3. 한편 ICRC 에 대한 공동 협조 요청 관련 미국 대표부가 본부로 부터 접수한 훈령 (TALKING POINTS) 사본을 당관에도 보내왔으므로 이를 아래 송부하니 참고 바람.

- 아래 -

- THE RECENT IRAQI INVASION OF KUWAIT IS OF ENORMOUS CONCERN TO OUR GOVERNMENTS, AND INDEED, TO THE ENTIRE WORLD. CENTRAL TO THIS CONCERN IS THEFATE OF THE MANY FOREIGN NATIONALS CURRENTLY LIVING AND WORKING IN KUWAIT. THEIR SAFETY MUST NOT BE DEPENDENT ON THE RESOLUTION OF THE POLITICAL/MILITARY CRISIS.

- THE ICRC'S UNIQUE HUMANITARIAN ROLE IN THE WORLD AND RESPONSIBILITIES UNDER THE FOURTH GENEVA CONVENTION LEAD US TO TURN TO THE ICRC FOR ASSISTANCE IN THE PROTECTION OF OUR NATIONALS AND ALL NON-COMBATANTS CAUGHT UP IN THE CURRENT CRISIS. WE TODAY FORMALLY REQUEST THE ICRC TO ACT ON OUR BEHALF TO

중아국　차관　1차보　2차보　국기국　청와대　안기부

PAGE 1　　　90.08.09 01:54

외신 2과 통제관 DH

0034

HELP FACILITATE THE IMMEDIATE DEPARTURE PROM KUWAIT OF FOREIGN NATIONALS WHO SO DESIRE. WE WILL, OF COURSE, PROVIDE ANY LOGISTICAL SUPPORT FOR THIS EFFORT THAT YOU FEEL NECESSARY.

- IRAQ, AS A SIGNATORY TO THE FOURTH CONVENTION, CANNOT DENY ITS RESPONSIBILITY BOTH TO PROTECT NON-COMBATANTS AND TO ALLOW THEM TO DEPART, IF THEY SO DESIRE. IF YOU BELIEVE IT WOULD BE HELPFUL, WE ARE PREPARED, AS A GROUP, TO MAKE THIS POINT TO IRAQ DIRECTLY. IN DOING SO, WE WILL UNEQUIVOCALLY REJECT ANY ARGUMENT THAT IRAQ IS NOT AN OCCUPYING POWER. WE WILL INSIST THAT EFFORTS TO PROTECT NON-COMBATANTS BEGIN IMMEDIATELY.

- WE WOULD HOPE YOU COULD SHARE WITH US YOUR THOUGHTS ON HOW THE ICRC COULD PROCEED IN ACCOMPLISHING THE IMMEDIATE DEPARTURE OF OUR NATIONALS, AND ON WHAT OUR GOVERNMENT AND THE UN CAN DO TO ASSIST THE ICRC. 끝

(대사 이상옥-차관)

예고: 90.12.31. 일반

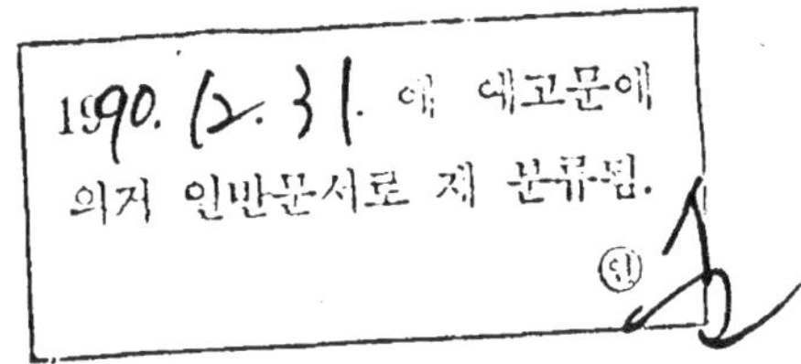
1990. 12. 31. 에 예고문에
의거 일반문서로 재 분류됨.

PAGE 2

0035

| 관리번호 | 90/838 |
|---|---|

원 본

# 외 무 부

종 별 :

번 호 : GVW-1544 일 시 : 90 0809 1900

수 신 : 장 관(중근동,국기)(사본:주미대사(본부중계필)

발 신 : 주 제네바 대사

제 목 : 쿠웨이트 거주 외국인 안전 철수

연: GVW-1531

연호 관련 당지 미국 대표부에 알아본 바를 아래 보고함.

1. 8.8(수) 오후 미국, 이태리 (EC), 일본등 대사와 쏘련 차석 대사 및 스위스 대사대리가 국제적십자 위원회 (ICRC) 를 공동 방문하여 쿠웨이트내 외국인들의 안전 철수를 위하여 ICRC 측의 협조를 요청한바, ICRC 측은 이라크 주재 ICRC 대표의 쿠웨이트 파견을 이라크에 요청중 이라고 하였으며, 이라크의 쿠웨이트 합병조치에 대하여 반대입장을 표명하는등 매우 호의적인 태도를 보였다고 함.

2. 상기 면담시 ICRC 측에서는 SOMARUGA 총재, KARTASH 부총재, GNAEDINGER 중동지역 담당, GROSSRIEDER 운영 담당 차석등이 참석하였음.

3. 한편 공동 보조와 관련 미국, 이태리 등은 로마에서도 이라크측과 교섭중이라 함. 끝

(대사 이상옥-차관)

예고 90.12.31. 일반

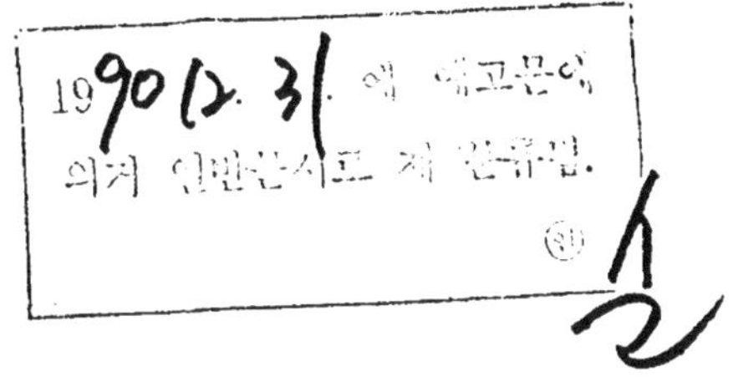


| 중동아프리카국 | 190 . . . | 처리지침 |
|---|---|---|
| 공람 | | 자료활용 |
| | | 비고 |

중아국 차관 1차보 2차보 국기국 안기부

PAGE 1 90.08.10 04:13

외신 2과 통제관 DL

0036

| 관리번호 | 90/p2f |
|---|---|

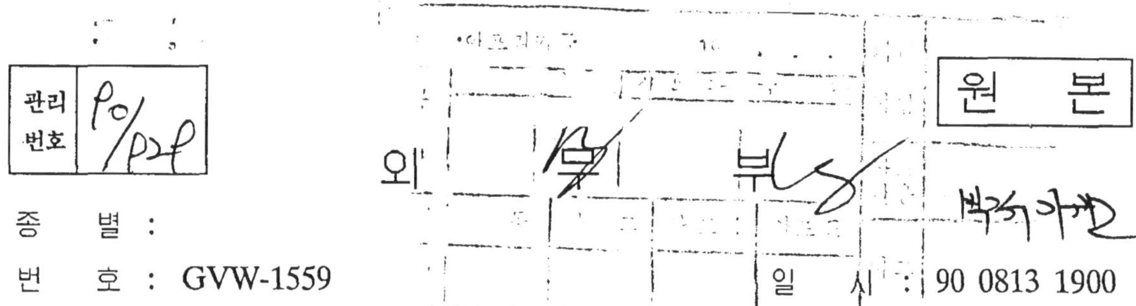

원 본

외 무 부

종 별 :

번 호 : GVW-1559 일 시 : 90 0813 1900

수 신 : 장관(중근동,국기)

발 신 : 주 제네바 대사

제 목 : 쿠웨이트 거주 외국인 안전 철수

연: GVW-1529, 1544

1. 당관 이량 참사관은 금 8.13(월) 국제 적십자 위원회(ICRC)의 DELAPRAZ 이란, 이락 담당과장과 접촉, 이라크 주재 ICRC 팀의 쿠웨이트 파견관련 그간 ICRC 측이 이락크측과 교섭한 경과에 관해 알아 보았는바, DELAPRAZ 과장은 8.12(일) 바그다드에서 이라크 측과 접촉이 있었고 8.14(화) 재접촉 할 예정인바, 아직 구체적 결과는 없다고 말하였다함.

2. DELAPRAZ 과장은 미국 및 스칸디나비아 국가들로 부터 쿠웨이트 거주 동국인 명단을 받았다고 하면서 아국도 쿠웨이트 거주 아국인 명단을 ICRC 에 제출해 주면 ICRC 활동에 도움이 될것이라고 말하였음.

3. 한편 당지 미국 대표부가 금일 당관에 알려온바에 의하면 지난주 8.10(금) 또 한차례 ICRC 측과 협의를 가졌다고 하면서 ICRC 측에 표명한 관련국의 공동 입장을 알려 왔는바, 참고로 별첨 송부함.

첨부: 관련국 공동 입장(BACKGROUND PAPER) 사본 1 부, 끝

(대사 이상옥-차관)

예고 90.12.31. 일반

BACK GROUND PAPER FOR ICRC DEMARCHE 8/10/90

- A MULTI-NATIONAL DEMARCHE TO THE IRAQI MINISTRY OF FOREIGN AFFAIRS IN BAGHDAD AUGUST 9 FAILED TO SECURE IRAQI APPROVAL FOR THE(208)DEPARTURE FROM IRAQ AND KUWAIT OF FOREIGN NATIONALS.

- INSTEAD, THE IRAQI MFA TOLD THE EC REPRESENTATIVES THAT ALL IRAQI LAND AND AIR FRONTIERS ARE CLOSED TO ALL PERSONS EXCEPT DIPLOMATS. THE OFFICIAL ALSO SAID THAT NO CHARTER PLANES OR SPECIAL LAND CONVOYS WOULD BE PERMITTED.

중아국 장관 차관 1차보 2차보 국기국 정문국 청와대 안기부

PAGE 1 90.08.14 10:01

외신 2과 통제관 CW

0037

- THE DEMARCHE, MADE BY THE EUROPEAN COMMUITY, HAD THE FULL SUPPORT OFAUSTRALIA, AUSTRIA, CANADA, FINLAND, THE GERMAN DEMOCRATIC REPUBLIC, JAPAN NEW ZEALAND, NORWAY, SWEDEN, SWITZERLAND, TURKEY AND THE UNITED STATES OF AMERICA.

- THE IRAQI MFA UNDERSECRETARY ALSO NOTIFIED OUR EMBASSY IN BAGHDAD SEPARATELY AUGUST 9 THAT IRAQI AND KUWAITI AIR AND LAND BORDERS ARE CLOSED TO ALL FOREIGNERS EXCEPT DIPLOMATS:

- IN ADDITION, THE IRAQIS IN KUWAIT SPECIFED TO THE DIPLOMATIC COMMUNITY THERE TAHT NON-DIPLOMATIC AMERICANS, CANADIANS, BRITISH AND OTHER WESTERN EUROPEANS WOULD NOT BE ALLOWED TO LEAVE KUWAIT. EMBASSY STAFF OF THERSECOUNTRIES ARE REQUIRED TO APPLY FOR PERMISSION TO LEAVE KUWAIT SEVEN DAYSPRIOR TO THEIR PLANNED DEPARTURE DATE:

- THE IRAQIS INFORMED ALL NATIONS WITH EMBASSIES IN KUWAIT AUGUST 9 THAT THESE MISSIONS' OFFICIAL STATUS IS "NULL AND VOID." THE GOI INSTRUCTED ALL STATES WITH REPRESENTATIVES IN KUWAIT TO TRANSFER ALL FUNCTIONS TO BAGHDAD NO LATER THAN AUGUST 24:

- DESPITE EARLIER ASSURANCES THAT ITS DEPARTURE WOULD BE PERMITTED, A CONVOY INCLUDING TEN U.S. GOVERNMENT DEPENDENTS WAS TURNED BACK BY IRAQI AUTHORITIES AUGUST 9 ON ITS WAY FROM BAGHDAD TO THE JORDANIAN BORDER:

- THERE HAVE BEEN ISOLATED REPORTS OF AMERICANS AND OTHER FOREIGNERS SUCCEEDING IN CROSSING THE KUWAITI BORDER INTO SAUDI ARABIA. HOWEVER, THESECASES ARE FAR OUTNUMBERED BY INCIDENTS IN WHICH FOREIGNERS HAVE BEEN PREVENTED FROM LEAVING:

- A CONVOY INCLUDING A LARGE NUMBER OF AMERICANS WAS TURNED BACK OUTSIDE KUWAIT CITY AUGUST 8. SMALLER GROUPS HAVE REPORTEDLY BEEN TURNED BACK BY IRAQI FORCES AT CHECKPOINTS CLOSE TO THE BORDER:

- IN ANOTHER INCIDENT, BUSES CARRYING STRANDED PASSENGERS FROM A SWISSAIR FLIGHT WERE NOT ALLOWED TO PROCEED TO THE BORDER:

- THERE ARE 117 U.S. GOVERNMENT PERSONNEL AND DEPENDENTS IN KUWAIT ANDAPPROXIMATELY 3000 PRIVATE U.S. CITIZENS IN THE COUNTRY:

- AMONG THE PRIVATE U.S. POPULATION, THERE ARE 750 ADULTS, 750 CHILDREN RESIDEING IN U.S. HOUSEHOLDS, AND 1500 MINORS LIVING WITH THEIR KUWAITI RELATIVES.

- SINCE OUR LAST DEMARCHE ON AUGUST 8, THE SITUATION HAS DETERIORATED.IRAQ HAS DECLARED ITS ANNEXATION OF KUWAIT:

- THIS ACTION HAS BEEN UNANIOMOUSLY REJECTED BY THE UN SECURITY COUNCIL AND DENOUNCED BY THE WORLD COMMUNITY:

- THE SITUATION IN KUWAIT IS LIKELY TO BECOME EVEN MORE DIFFICULT AFTER AUGUST 24. SHOULD IRAQ MOVE TO IMPEMENT ITS ORDER THAT ALL FOREIGN MISSIONS IN KUWAIT CLOSE AND TRANSFER OPERATIONS TO BAGHDAD, COMPLIANCE WOULD MEAN THAT OUR NATIONALS WOULD BE WITHOUT DIRECT REPRESENTATION IN KUWAIT:

- IRAQ IS RESPONSIBLE, AS A SIGNATORY TO THE FOURTH GENEVE CONVENTION,FOR THE SAFETY OF FOREIGN NATIONALS IN IRAQ. THIS RESPONSIBILITY INCLUDESRESPECT FOR THE FREEDOM OF FOREIGN NATIONALS TO DEPART IF THEY SO CHOOSE:

- AS WE AGREED AT OUR LAST MEETING, ITALY, REPRESENTING THE EC AND TENADDITIONAL COUNTRIES, MADE A DEMARCHE TO THE IRAQI GOVERNMENT MAKING THE POINTS ABOVE. THIS DEMARCHE WAS REJECTED. WE BELIEVE IT IS TIME FOR THE ICRC TO GO DIRECTLY TO THE GOVERNMENT OF IRAQ AND, IN THE MOST FORCIBLE TERMS, ASSERT ITS RIGHT TO ASSIST FOREIGN NATIONALS:

- THE DEFACTO IRAQI ANNEXATION MAY, IN FACT, MAKE IT EASIER FOR THE ICRC. IT IS NO LONGER NECESSARY FOR THE ICRC TO FIND A COMPETENT AUTHORITY IN KUWAIT. IT CAN SPEAK DIRECTLY TO THE GOVERNMENT OF IRAQ, WITH WHICH IT ALREADY ENJOYS A WORKING RELATIONSHIP:

- THE GOVERNMENTS HERE REPRESENTED PLACE THE UTMOST IMPORTANCE ON THE SAFETY OF OUR NATIONALS AND OF ALL FOREIGN NATIONALS CAUGHT UP IN THIS CONFLICT. THE ICRC, AS A NEUTRAL BODY ENJOYING TREMENDOUS INTERNATIONAL PRESTIGE, HAS THE BEST HOPE OF SECURING THEIR SAFETY AND EVENTUAL DEPARTURE. WEBELIEVE IT IS TIME FOR THE ICRC TO EXERT ITSELF TO THE FULLEST.

END



PAGE 3

0039

| 관리 번호 | 90/1455 |
|---|---|

| 분류번호 | 보존기간 |
|---|---|
| | |

# 발 신 전 보

번 호 : WGV-1060 900816 0920 FC 종별 :

수 신 : 주 제네바 대사. 총영사

발 신 : 장 관 (중근동)

제 목 : 이라크 및 쿠웨이트 아국교민 안전철수

대 : GVW - 1559

연 : WGV - 1024

1. 표제 철수관련, 그간 주이라크 아국대사의 이라크 정부측과의 교섭으로 이라크 당국이 아국인의 요르단 경유 출국허용을 결정함에 따라 현재 주이라크 및 쿠웨이트 아국대사의 진두 지휘아래 아국인의 요르단경유 철수가 별다른 차질없이 안전하게 잘 진행되고 있음.

2. 따라서, 현재로서는 국제적십자위의 협조없이도 동 철수가 순조로이 이루어 지고 있음을 감안, 향후 진전상황을 좀더 관망한후, 추후 국제적십자위 협조 필요성 있을시 대호 아국인 명단을 송부예정 임. 참고로 국제적십자위에 상기 철수상황을 설명하고, 접촉을 계속 유지하기 바람. 끝.

예고 : 1990. 12. 31

(중동아프리카국장 이두복)

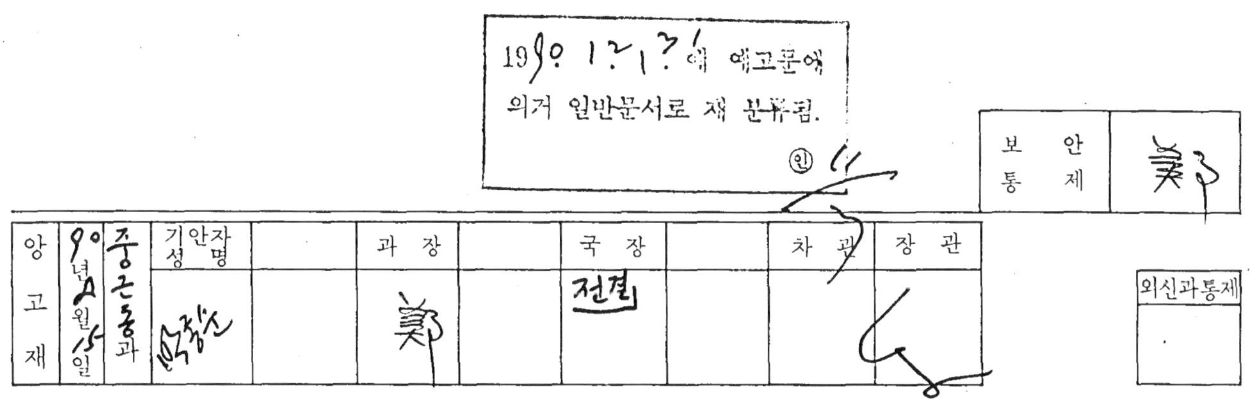
1990. 12. 31.에 예고문에 의거 일반문서로 재분류됨.

| 보안 통제 | |
|---|---|

| 앙 고 재 | 90년 8월 15일 | 중근동과 | 기안자 성명 | | 과 장 | | 국 장 | | 차 관 | 장 관 |
|---|---|---|---|---|---|---|---|---|---|---|
| | | | | | | | 전결 | | | |

외신과통제

0040

THE REPUBLIC OF KOREA NATIONAL RED CROSS

Total number of pages 2 following this page.
IF YOU DO NOT RECEIVE ALL PAGES, PLEASE CONTACT US ASAP.
Telephone : (02)755-9301 Telex : ROKNRC K28585
Telefax : (02)774-0735, 752-7410

To : 박 종 순 서기관님 FAX) 720-2686
From : 고 영 기 국제과장
Date : 90. 8. 16.
Subject: 중동 사태에 관한 국제 적십자 위원회 답신

---

오늘 받은 국제 적십자 위원회 TLX를 송부하오니
업무에 참고하시길 바랍니다.

0041

P.1

AUG 16 '90 16:56 KOREA RED CROSS (744-0735)

.K28585
.X CCR CH

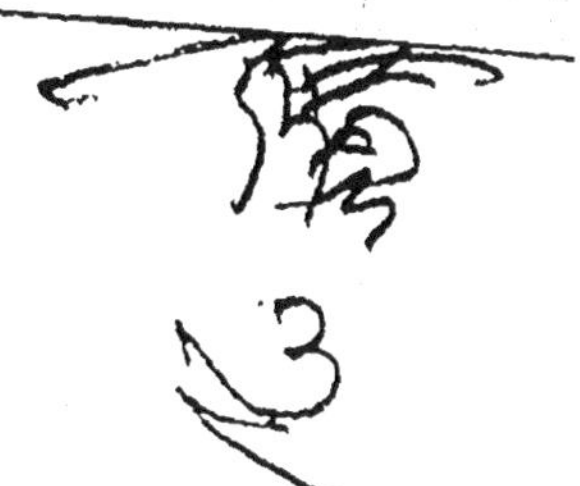

GENEVE DATE 15.08.90

IE KOREAN RED CROSS.

. MR. SANG-HYUP KIM - PRESIDENT OF KOREAN RED CROSS.

I REFERENCE TO YOUR MESSAGE ADDRESSED TO PRESIDENT SOMMARUGA
.UGUST 10, 1990, WE WOULD LIKE TO INFORM YOU THAT THE PERMA
T MISSION OF KOREA IN GENEVA CONTACTED ICRC ON THE 8TH AUGUST
JT THE KOREAN CITIZENS IN KUWAIT. WE REMAIN IN CONTACT WITH
A/M MISSION.

.NKING YOU FOR THE PRECISE INFORMATION YOU SENT US, WE HOPE TO
SOON ABLE TO DEAL WITH HUMANITARIAN PROBLEMS IN KUWAIT.

ST WISHES

ANNICHINI/DELAPRAZ ICRC MIDDLE EAST DESK

CC : CHRONO - LAN - OP/AS - TAFIRA - TAFAR

+++
ROKNRC K28585
414226X CCR CH

0042

P.2

AUG 16 '90 16:53 KOREA RED CROSS (744-0735)

RE: IRAQ/KUWAIT

PRIMO

ON 2 AUGUST 1990, IMMEDIATELY AFTER THE PRESENT CRISIS IN THE GULF BEGAN, THE ICRC REMINDED THE GOVERNMENTS OF IRAQ AND KUWAIT OF THEIR OBLIGATIONS UNDER THE FOUR GENEVA CONVENTIONS OF 1949 AND ASKED TO BE ALLOWED TO SEND A MISSION TO THE REGION.

SECUNDO

THE ICRC HAS KEPT IN CLOSE TOUCH WITH ITS USUAL CONTACTS IN THE REGION THROUGH ITS STAFF ALREADY WORKING IN THE MIDDLE EAST AND ITS REGIONAL DELEGATE FOR THE ARABIAN PENINSULA, WHO WAS DISPAT CHED TO SAUDI ARABIA ON 7 AUGUST 1990.

TERTIO

THE REPRESENTATIVES OF MANY GOVERNMENTS HAVE APPROACHED THE ICRC AND INFORMED IT OF THEIR CONCERN ABOUT THEIR NATIONALS IN KUWAIT AND IRAQ. THE ICRC HAS BEEN RECEIVING INDIVIDUAL TRACING REQUESTS AT ITS HEADQUARTERS IN GENEVA AND ITS VARIOUS DELEGATIONS.

QUARTO

WITH REGARD TO FOREIGN NATIONALS WISHING TO LEAVE THE REGION, THE ICRC HAS ADVISED GOVERNMENTS WHICH HAVE DIPLOMATIC RELATIONS WITH IRAQ TO USE THOSE CHANNELS FIRST. IT HAS INFORMED THEM OF ITS WILLINGNESS TO ASSIST WITH TRAVEL ARRANGEMENTS IF AN AGREEMENT IS REACHED OR IF ITS SERVICES ARE ESSENTIAL TO CARRY OUT THE EVACUA TIONS.

QUINTO

AT PRESENT THE ICRC IS CONCENTRATING ITS EFFORTS ON THE POSSIBI LITY OF SENDING ITS DELEGATES TO KUWAIT TO ASSESS THE GENERAL NEEDS FOR HUMANITARIAN ASSISTANCE AND IN PARTICULAR TO FIND A SOLUTION FOR EXCHANGES OF FAMILY MESSAGES.

SEXTO

THE ICRC WILL INFORM THE NATIONAL SOCIETIES AS SOON AS IT IS ABLE TO FOLLOW UP THE NUMEROUS TRACING REQUESTS SENT TO IT. THE NATIO NAL SOCIETIES CONCERNED ARE THEREFORE KINDLY REQUESTED NOT TO FORWARD ANY OF THEIR REQUESTS TO THE ICRC FOR THE TIME BEING.

SEPTIMO

THE ICRC WILL INFORM THE NATIONAL SOCIETIES AS SOON AS IT IS ABLE TO OPERATE IN KUWAIT ITSELF.

WITH BEST REGARDS

ANGELO GNAEDINGER
DELEGATE GENERAL FOR THE
MIDDLE EAST AND NORTH AFRICA

INFORMATION TO NATIONAL SOCIETIES
(PRESS DIVISION)

+++
++++

ROKNRC K28585
414226X CCR CH
14-08-90 15:37

0043

ROKNRC K28585
414226X CCR CH

1990.8.16.

TELEX

CICR GENEVE     DATE 15.08.90

TO THE KOREAN RED CROSS.

ATTN. MR. SANG-HYUP KIM - PRESIDENT OF KOREAN RED CROSS.

WITH REFERENCE TO YOUR MESSAGE ADDRESSED TO PRESIDENT SOMMARUGA ON AUGUST 10, 1990, WE WOULD LIKE TO INFORM YOU THAT THE PERMANENT MISSION OF KOREA IN GENEVA CONTACTED ICRC ON THE 8TH AUGUST ABOUT THE KOREAN CITIZENS IN KUWAIT. WE REMAIN IN CONTACT WITH THE A/M MISSION.

THANKING YOU FOR THE PRECISE INFORMATION YOU SENT US, WE HOPE TO BE SOON ABLE TO DEAL WITH HUMANITARIAN PROBLEMS IN KUWAIT.

BEST WISHES

L. ANNICHINI/DELAPRAZ ICRC MIDDLE EAST DESK

CC : CHRONO - LAN - OP/AS - TAFIRA - TAFAR

+++
ROKNRC K28585
414226X CCR CH

0044

P.3

AUG 16 '90 16:58 KOREA RED CROSS (744-0735)

AUG 18 '90 10:09 KOR RED CROSS (744-0735) P.1

중근동과 ― 박종선 서기관 귀하

TO THE INFORMATION SERVICES OF NATIONAL RED CROSS AND RED CRESCENT SOCIETIES
41/SN
14 AUGUST 1990

RE: IRAQ/KUWAIT

PRIMO

ON 2 AUGUST 1990, IMMEDIATELY AFTER THE PRESENT CRISIS IN THE GULF BEGAN, THE ICRC REMINDED THE GOVERNMENTS OF IRAQ AND KUWAIT OF THEIR OBLIGATIONS UNDER THE FOUR GENEVA CONVENTIONS OF 1949 AND ASKED TO BE ALLOWED TO SEND A MISSION TO THE REGION.

SECUNDO

THE ICRC HAS KEPT IN CLOSE TOUCH WITH ITS USUAL CONTACTS IN THE REGION THROUGH ITS STAFF ALREADY WORKING IN THE MIDDLE EAST AND ITS REGIONAL DELEGATE FOR THE ARABIAN PENINSULA, WHO WAS DISPAT CHED TO SAUDI ARABIA ON 7 AUGUST 1990.

TERTIO

THE REPRESENTATIVES OF MANY GOVERNMENTS HAVE APPROACHED THE ICRC AND INFORMED IT OF THEIR CONCERN ABOUT THEIR NATIONALS IN KUWAIT AND IRAQ. THE ICRC HAS BEEN RECEIVING INDIVIDUAL TRACING REQUESTS AT ITS HEADQUARTERS IN GENEVA AND ITS VARIOUS DELEGATIONS.

QUARTO

WITH REGARD TO FOREIGN NATIONALS WISHING TO LEAVE THE REGION, THE ICRC HAS ADVISED GOVERNMENTS WHICH HAVE DIPLOMATIC RELATIONS WITH IRAQ TO USE THOSE CHANNELS FIRST. IT HAS INFORMED THEM OF ITS WILLINGNESS TO ASSIST WITH TRAVEL ARRANGEMENTS IF AN AGREEMENT IS REACHED OR IF ITS SERVICES ARE ESSENTIAL TO CARRY OUT THE EVACUA TIONS.

QUINTO

AT PRESENT THE ICRC IS CONCENTRATING ITS EFFORTS ON THE POSSIBI LITY OF SENDING ITS DELEGATES TO KUWAIT TO ASSESS THE GENERAL NEEDS FOR HUMANITARIAN ASSISTANCE AND IN PARTICULAR TO FIND A SOLUTION FOR EXCHANGES OF FAMILY MESSAGES.

SEXTO

THE ICRC WILL INFORM THE NATIONAL SOCIETIES AS SOON AS IT IS ABLE TO FOLLOW UP THE NUMEROUS TRACING REQUESTS SENT TO IT. THE NATIO NAL SOCIETIES CONCERNED ARE THEREFORE KINDLY REQUESTED NOT TO FORWARD ANY OF THEIR REQUESTS TO THE ICRC FOR THE TIME BEING.

SEPTIMO

THE ICRC WILL INFORM THE NATIONAL SOCIETIES AS SOON AS IT IS ABLE TO OPERATE IN KUWAIT ITSELF.

WITH BEST REGARDS

ANGELO GNAEDINGER
DELEGATE GENERAL FOR THE
MIDDLE EAST AND NORTH AFRICA

INFORMATION TO NATIONAL SOCIETIES
(PRESS DIVISION)

0045

+++
++++
ROKNRC K28585
414226X CCR CH
14-08-90 15:37

AUG 31 '90 09:46 KOREA RED CROSS (744-0735) P.1

MEMO-TELEX CH
414226Z CCR CH
CI
STORED MSG REF 52221

POSSIBLE DUPLICATE MESSAGE

중근동과 박서기관 귀하.

CICR GENEVE, 28.8.90

TLX TO ALL RED CROSS SOCIETIES

ATTN: TRACING DEPARTMENTS
REFY: ANXIOUS FOR NEWS FOR KOWEIT
OUR TLX DATED 14.8.90 SIGNED GIROD

PRIMO
FOLLOWING OUR TLX A/M WE INFORM YOU THAT ICRC IS PURSUING NEGOCIATIONS WITH THE CONCERNED AUTHORITIES IN ORDER TO SEND DELEGATES TO KOWEIT TO EVALUATE HUMANITARIAN NEEDS AND ANSWER FAMILY REQUESTS.

SECUNDO
AT THIS POINT WE ASK YOU NOT TO SEND THE ANXIOUS FOR NEWS. WE SUGGEST YOU STOCK THEM IN YOUR OFFICE TILL FURTHER NOTICE WITH FOLLOWING INFORMATION:

- COMPLETE NAME OF SOUGHT PERSON
- DATE OF BIRTH
- NATIONALITY
- COMPLETE ADDRESS WITH TEL. NO.
- NAMES OTHER PERSONS WHO COULD PROVIDE INFORMATION
- RELATIONSHIP BETWEEN ENQUIRER AND SOUGHT PERSON

TERTIO
DESK IN CHARGE OF THESE REQUESTS IS: SO/ACR/IR RESP. MASSIMO CATALDI AND LUCIENNE ANNICHINI.

QUARTO
WE THANK YOU FOR YOUR ATTENTION REGARDING THESE RECOMMENDATIONS AND WILL NOT FAIL TO KEEP YOU INFORMED OF ANY NEW DEVELOPMENTS.

RGS.

M. CATALDI
IRAN/IRAQ DESK
CENTRAL TRACING AGENCY

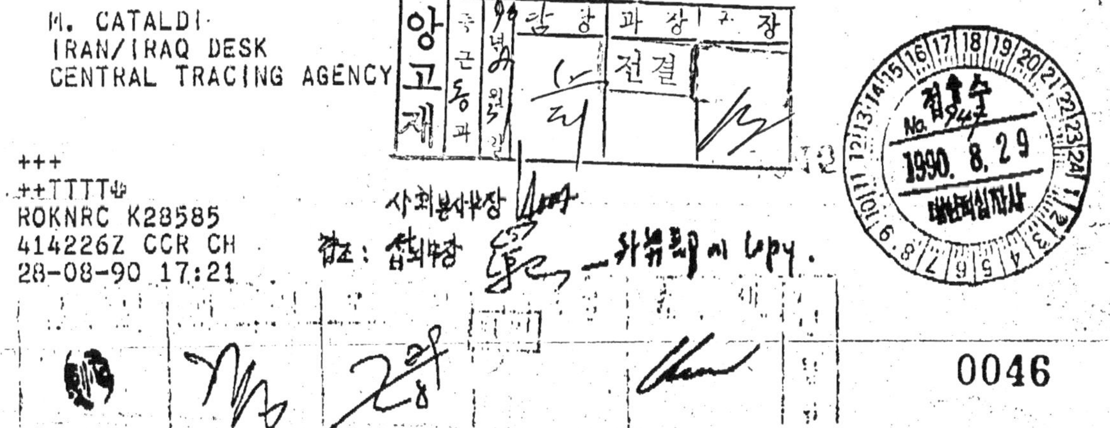


+++
++TTTT
ROKNRC K28585
414226Z CCR CH
28-08-90 17:21

해외공관 보고 김

| 관리 번호 | Po-1922 |
|---|---|

# 외 무 부

종 별 : 지 급

번 호 : USW-4094 일 시 : 90 0910 1853

수 신 : 장관(중근동,미북,국기) 사본:주제네바대사-중계필

발 신 : 주 미 대사

제 목 : 걸프사태관련 국무부 브리핑(난민 공수 문제등)

금 9.10 당관 이승관 공사는 국무부 DAVID MACK 중근동 담당 부차관보가 실시한 표제 브리핑에 참석하였는바, 동브리핑 요지 하기 보고함.(당관 임성남 2 등서기관 배석)

1. 난민 공수문제

가. 요르단 및 터키 국경 부근에 수용되어 있는 외국인 난민들은 현재 각종물자 부족으로 인하여 심한 고통을 겪고있음.

나. 제네바 소재 INTERNATIONAL ORGANIZATION FOR MIGRATION(IOM)에 따르면전기 난민들의 본국 공수를 위해서는 약 6 천만불이 소요될것으로 예상된다하며, 현재 이중 약 3 천 5 백만불이 확보된 상태라함.

다. 또한 IOM 측에 따르면, 동공수를 위해 동원가능한 비행기의 절대부족으로인해 곤란을 겪고 있다하는바, 금일 브리핑 참석자들이 본국정부에 난민수송을위한 자국 국적기 동원등을 건의해 준다면 도움이 될것임.

2. 주쿠웨이트 대사관 유지 문제

가. 금주말 현재 22 개 국가(오지리, 벨지움, 캐나다, 체코, 프랑스, 희랍,이태리, 화란, 폴란드, 스페인, 스위스, 영국, 서독, 방글라데쉬, 필리핀, 스리랑카, 이집트, 시리아, UAE, 브라질, 베네주엘라, 나이지리아)가 주쿠웨이트 대사관을 계속 유지하고 있는것으로 파악되고 있음.

나. 현재 주쿠웨이트 미국대사관에는 10 명 미만의 외교관이 잔류중임.(주이락 미국 대사관에도 10 명 미만의 외교관이 잔류중인바, 주쿠웨이트 대사관으로부터 바그다드로 철수후 이락측으로부터 출국허가를 받지 못한 미외교관 51 명도 함께 체류중임)

3. 외국인 부녀자 및 아동 출국문제

| 중아국 | 장관 | 차관 | 1차보 | 2차보 | 미주국 | 국기국 | 정문국 | 청와대 |
|---|---|---|---|---|---|---|---|---|
| 안기부 | 대책반 | | | | | | | |

PAGE 1

90.09.11 08:37

외신 2과 통제관 CW

0047

가. 이락 및 쿠웨이트에 억류되었던 외국인 부녀자및 어린이들의 이락 출국은 비교적 순조롭게 진행되었는바, 이락측도 어느정도는 협조적인 자세를 취했음.

(예:출국 대상자에 대한 쿠웨이트로부터 바그다드 까지의 교통편제공 및 출국 절차 간소화등)

나. 그러나 일부 외국인은 아직도 행방이 확인되지 않고 있으며, 자국 외교관접촉도 허용되지 않고 있음.)이락내에서 미국인의 경우는 약 80 명이 여사한 인질 상태에 처해 있음.)

다. 현재 쿠웨이트에는 약 1,400 명의 미국인이, 이락에는 약 320 명의 미국인이 계속 출국 불허상태임.(대부분 아랍계 미국인임.)

4. 외국인 출국문제 관련 ICRC 활용방안

가. 이란-이락 전쟁당시 ICRC 가 여러가지 긍정적 역할을 수행했던 점을 감안, 미측으로서는 ICRC 가 외국인 출국문제 관련 이락측과 접촉시 이락측이 호의적인 반응을 보일것으로 기대했으나, 이락측은 고위급 면담 주선에 소극적 반응을 보이는등 ICRC 를 REBUFF 하는듯한 반응을 보였음.

나. 현재 미측으로서는 제네바 주재 이락대사가 훗세인 대통령의 BROTHER-IN-LAW 로서 국내적으로 상당한 영향력이 있는점을 감안, 제네바주재 외교단을 통해 동대사와 접촉토록 주제네바 미국대사에게 훈령하는 방안을 내부적으로 검토중임.

(대사 박동진-국장)

예고:90.12.31 일반

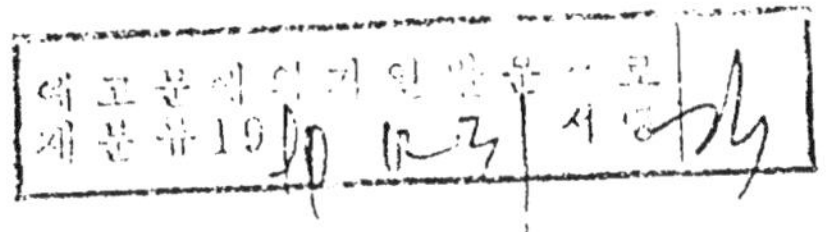

PAGE 2

0048

SEP 11 '90 15:40 NATION[illegible] BS 752)7410 P.1

THE REPUBLIC OF KOREA NATIONAL RED CROSS

Total number of pages ____ following this page.
IF YOU DO NOT RECEIVE ALL PAGES, PLEASE CONTACT US ASAP.
Telephone : (02)755-9301 Telex : ROKNRC K28585
Telefax : (02)774-0735, 752-7410

To : 박종순 서기관님 720-2686
From : 고영기 국제과장
Date : 90.9.11
Subject: 적십자국제위원회에서 보내온 텔렉스전문

---

방금 전화 통화에서 말씀드린대로 적십자국제위원회에서 받은 텔렉스 사본 송부해 드립니다. 업무에 참고하시기 바랍니다.

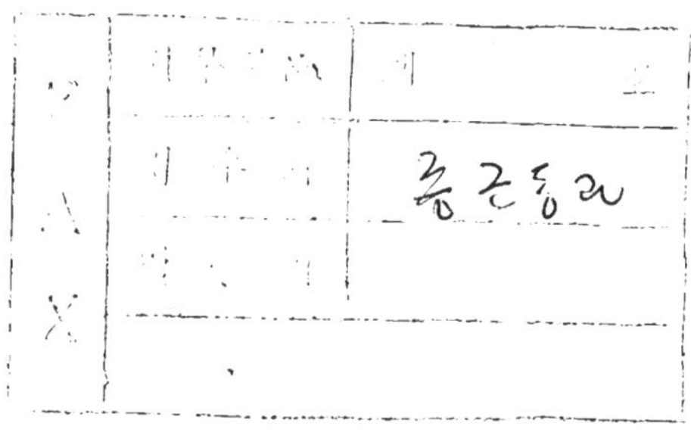

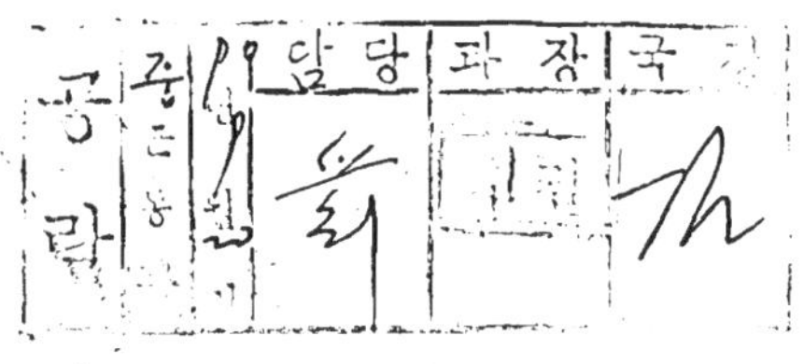

0049

ROKNRC K28585
ROKNRC K28585
MEMO-TELEX CH
414226A CCR CH
CI
STORED MSG REF 58543

TO THE INFORMATION SOCIETIES OF NATIONAL RED CROSS AND RED CRESCENT SOCIETIES
94/SN
7 SEPTEMBER 1990

MAIN POINTS OF ICRC PRESIDENT'S PRESS CONFERENCE
7 SEPTEMBER 1990

INTRODUCTION

ON HIS RETURN FROM A MISSION WHICH TOOK HIM TO AMMAN (1 DAY), BAGHDAD (3 DAYS) AND TEHRAN (2 DAYS), MR. CORNELIO SOMMARUGA SPOKE TO THE INTERNATIONAL PRESS AT ICRC HEADQUARTERS IN GENEVA.

THIS MISSION, AIMED AT MOBILIZING A COMPREHENSIVE HUMANITARIAN RESPONSE TO THE GULF CRISIS, WAS CONDUCTED WITHIN THE FRAMEWORK OF THE ICRC'S MANDATE UNDER THE THIRD (PRISONERS OF WAR) AND FOURTH (CIVILIAN POPULATION) GENEVA CONVENTIONS.

I) OBJECTIVES OF THE MISSION

A) TO BRING PROTECTION AND ASSISTANCE IN IRAQ AND KUWAIT TO

- FOREIGN CIVILIANS AUTHORIZED TO LEAVE THE TWO COUNTRIES
- FOREIGN CIVILIANS NOT AUTHORIZED TO LEAVE THE TWO COUNTRIES
- IRAQI AND KUWAITI CIVILIANS
- ANY KUWAITI PRISONERS OF WAR.

B) TO ENHANCE CO-ORDINATION AND STEP UP THE ICRC OPERATION IN JORDAN TO ASSIST FOREIGN NATIONALS IN TRANSIT.

C) TO BRING ASSISTANCE TO FOREIGN NATIONALS IN TRANSIT ON THE IRANIAN AND TURKISH BORDERS.

D) TO DISCUSS THE REPATRIATION OF IRANIAN AND IRAQI PRISONERS OF WAR.

II) PERSONS SEEN

- AMMAN: CROWN PRINCE HASSAN, ACTING HEAD OF STATE OF THE HASHEMITE KINGDOM OF JORDAN.
- BAGHDAD: MR. TARIQ AZIZ, IRAQI MINISTER OF FOREIGN AFFAIRS (TWO 3-HOUR MEETINGS).
- TEHRAN: MR. HASSAN EBRAHIM HABIBI, VICE-PRESIDENT, AND DR. ALI AKBAR VELAYATI, MINISTER OF FOREIGN AFFAIRS OF THE ISLAMIC REPUBLIC OF IRAN.

IN ALL THREE CAPITALS MR. SOMMARUGA ALSO HAD TALKS WITH LEADERS OF THE RESPECTIVE RED CRESCENT SOCIETIES.

WHILE IN AMMAN, THE ICRC PRESIDENT HAD A MEETING WITH MR. JAVIER PEREZ DE CUELLAR, UNITED NATIONS SECRETARY-GENERAL.



0050

- 2 -

III) MATTERS OF HUMANITARIAN CONCERN

A) JORDAN: REVIEW OF THE ICRC OPERATION LAUNCHED ON THE IRAQI/JORDANIAN BORDER ON 18 AUGUST. (REF. COM/SN NOS. 47, 50, 52)

B) IRAQ/KUWAIT: FOREIGN NATIONALS WITH THE MEANS TO LEAVE THE COUNTRY BUT NOT AUTHORIZED TO DO SO.

THE ICRC IS DETERMINED TO FIND A WAY TO ENSURE THAT THESE PEOPLE ARE VISITED AND GIVEN THE POSSIBILITY TO RECEIVE AND SEND RED CROSS MESSAGES.

C) IRAQ/KUWAIT: FOREIGN NATIONALS AUTHORIZED TO LEAVE THE TWO COUNTRIES BUT WITHOUT THE MEANS TO DO SO. HUNDREDS OF THOUSANDS OF PEOPLE IN THIS SITUATION ARE ESPECIALLY HARD HIT BY RATIONING, LACK OF TRANSPORT AND LACK OF CONTACT WITH THEIR DIPLOMATIC REPRESENTATIVES.

THE ICRC IS DETERMINED TO ASSIST THEM IN ARRANGING FOR THEIR DEPARTURE AND TO ISSUE THEM WITH TRAVEL DOCUMENTS.

✓ NO AGREEMENT WAS REACHED ON POINTS B) AND C) ABOVE AND THE ICRC IS AS YET UNABLE TO DISCHARGE ITS HUMANITARIAN MANDATE IN THESE AREAS.

D) IRAN/IRAQ BORDER: THE ICRC OFFERED ITS SERVICES TO ASSIST PEOPLE IN TRANSIT, IN CO-ORDINATION WITH OTHER HUMANITARIAN ORGANIZATIONS. CONSULTATIONS ON THIS SUBJECT BEGAN TODAY IN TEHRAN.

E) CIVILIAN POPULATION IN KUWAIT AND IRAQ: THE EFFECTS OF RATIONING ARE BEGINNING TO BE FELT AND THERE IS DISCRIMINATION AGAINST SOME GROUPS. THE ICRC IS READY TO ACT AS A NEUTRAL HUMANITARIAN INTERMEDIARY FOR THESE GROUPS IN CO-ORDINATION WITH THE UN. HOWEVER, IT WILL NOT BE TAKING ACTION IN THIS RESPECT OWING TO THE REJECTION OF A COMPREHENSIVE HUMANITARIAN SOLUTION.

THE PRESIDENT RECALLED THE ICRC'S APPEAL OF 2 AUGUST 1990 TO ALL PARTIES TO RESPECT THE GENEVA CONVENTIONS AND AGAIN STRESSED THE NEED TO ALLOW THE ICRC TO WORK IN ACCORDANCE WITH ITS HUMANITARIAN MANDATE.

IV) REPATRIATION OF IRANIAN AND IRAQI PRISONERS OF WAR

THE REPATRIATION OPERATION IS PROCEEDING SMOOTHLY AND OVER 54,000 IRANIAN AND IRAQI POWS HAVE BEEN REPATRIATED TO DATE.

THE ICRC PRESIDENT EXPRESSED DEEP REGRET THAT AFTER SEVERAL DAYS OF NEGOTIATIONS CONDUCTED WITH AN OPEN MIND, AND DESPITE THE SATISFACTORY INTERMEDIATE RESULTS, NO AGREEMENT ON A COMPREHENSIVE HUMANITARIAN OPERATION COULD BE SIGNED WITH THE IRAQI GOVERNMENT.

THE ICRC WILL CONTINUE ITS ACTIVITIES IN JORDAN AND IRAN AND WILL FOCUS ITS EFFORTS ON OBTAINING THE AUTHORIZATIONS IT NEEDS TO BE ABLE TO WORK IN KUWAIT AND IRAQ.

BEST REGARDS
JETTE SOERENSEN
INFORMATION TO NATIONAL SOCIETIES (PRESS DIVISION)

+++
++++
ROKNRC K28585
414226A CCR CH
07-09-90 23:18

9/8

0051

# 국제적십자 위원회(ICRC)

90.10.24. 국제기구과

1. 연혁

   1863년 국제 부상병 구호위원회(International Committee for the Relief of the Wounded)로 발족하여, 1875년 현 명칭으로 개칭

2. 소재지 : 스위스 제네바

3. 회 원 : 순수 민간기구로 스위스 국민 25인이 회원이며, ICRC에 의하여 승인된 적십자사는 전세계 143개임

4. 총 재 : Cornelio Sommaruga

5. 기능

   o 국제전, 내전 및 국내 분쟁시 중립기구로서의 역할을 수행하며, 적십자 기본원리를 수호하고, 제네바 협약의 적용 및 동 협약상 위임된 임무를 수행.
   o 부상자 보호, 원조 및 그들의 정신적 안정, 존엄성, 가족권, 종교적 신념등에 관여
   o 고문, 잔혹행위, 약식 처형, 집단 학살, 추방, 인질, 약탈, 민간재산의 무자비한 파괴행위 방지
   o 무력 분쟁의 희생자인 피난민 구호 활동 참가
   o 정치범 수용상태의 국제적 기준 부합여부 확인
   o 전쟁포로나 민간인 수용자 방문 및 감시자 없는 상태에서의 동 수용자 면담
   o 제네바와 직접 연결된 16개 방송국을 통한 전세계적 라디오 통신망 제공

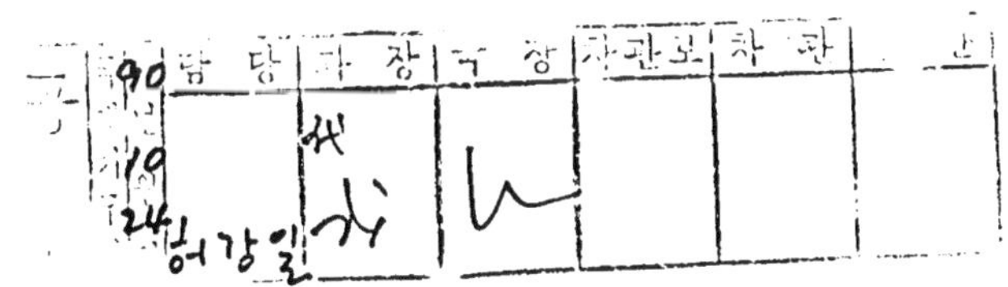

0052

6. 조직 : 총회(25인), 집행위원회(7인) 및 사무국

o Medical Division : 분쟁지역에서의 의료수요를 측정하여 의료 서비스를 제공하고 전범 및 정치범으로 수감되어 있는 자들을 방문하는 일을 담당.

o Relief Division : 분쟁지역 물자구입 사정, 물자비축 사정 및 물자수요를 측정하여 필요한 기본물자와 구호 자금을 모집하고, 이의 공정한 배분을 담당

7. 아국과의 관계

가. 가입

- 1955, 대한적십자사 ICRC에 의하여 승인
- 1966, 제네바 협약 가입
- 1982, 제네바 협약 추가의정서 가입

나. 기여금 관계

- 아국의 타국제기구 분담율은 0.22%인데 비해 ICRC 기여금율은 0.5%로 타국제기구에 비해 높은 비율의 기여금을 납부해 왔음
- 아국의 ICRC 기여금 현황

| 86 | 87 | 88 | 89 | 90 | 91(예상) |
|---|---|---|---|---|---|
| 10만5천$ | 12만5천$ | 15만$ | 15만$ | 15만$ | 15만$ |

* ICRC 총재는 수차(89.3월, 10월, 12월)에 걸친 외무장관앞 서한을 통해 20만$의 기여금을 요청. Sommaruga 총재는 90.12.14자 외무장관앞 서한에서 1991년도 아국 기여금으로 25만$을 요청.

8. 북한과의 관계

- 1956, 북적 승인
- 1961, 제네바 협약 가입

0053

9. 참고

가. ICRC와 유사한 기구로 LRCS(적십자사 연맹)가 있으며, ICRC가 전쟁이나 내전등으로 인한 피난민, 정치범등의 주로 정치적인 국제 구호문제에 관여하는 반면, LRCS는 지진, 폭풍등으로 인한 자연재해 등의 비정치적 구호 활동에 주로 관여하고 있음. 아측은 자연재해가 있을때 LRCS에 구호금품을 전달하여 왔으며, 정기적인 기여금은 납부치 않음.

나. Peter Küng

- 연 령 : 현 49세
- 국 적 : 스위스
- 현직책 : ICRC 홍콩 주재 지역사무소 책임자
  (Head, ICRC Regional Delegation in Hong Kong)
- 지금까지 16차례 방한한적 있으며, 3차례에 걸친 방북 경험도 있음(87.8, 88.3, 89.9월). 끝

0054

12/12 오(허)

# 주 제 네 바 대 표 부

제네(정) 20358-1292 1990.12. 7

수신 : 장관

참조 : 국제기구조약국장

제목 : ICRC 특별예산 사업

3기

90 12. 7

연 : GVW-1855(89. 10.12)

1. 당지 국제적십자위원회(ICRC)의 Kornevall 재정부장은 12.5 당관 이량참사관을 오찬에 초청, ICRC 특별예산사업에 관한 별첨 자료를 전달하면서 아국이 동 특별예산사업에 기여금을 공여해 줄 것을 요청하였읍니다. (ICRC의 Dominice 담당관 및 당관 김종일서기관 참석)

2. Kornevall 재정부장은 ICRC 특별예산 사업은 약 10여년전 부터 시작되어 4개지역(아시아, 아프리카, 중동 및 남미)을 대상으로 한 구호사업을 전개해 오고 있으며 지금까지 24개 국가가 특별예산 사업에 기여금을 공여하였음을 설명하면서, ICRC는 특별예산사업 참여 대상국을 확대하기 위해 한국, 브라질, 멕시코등을 접촉하고 있는바, 아국이 이를 적극 검토해 줄 것을 요청하였읍니다.

3. ICRC 특별예산사업에 소요되는 경비는 90년도의 경우 약 3.6억 서서프랑이며 기여금 공여국은 기여금 사용용도 및 사용처를 지정할 수 있다하는바, 아국의 ICRC 특별예산사업에 대한 기여금 공여 가능 여부를 검토하여 주시기 바랍니다.

첨부 : 1. 90년도 ICRC 특별예산 사업 관계 자료 1부.
2. 각국의 90년도 ICRC 기여금 공여 현황 1부. 끝.

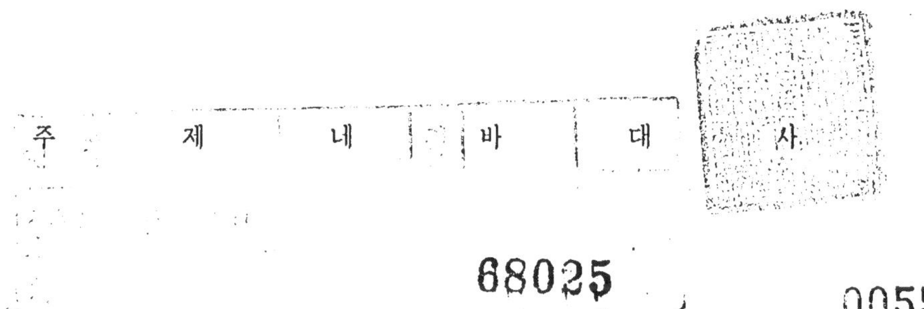


68025

0055

(별첨 2)

SO/REX/as
05 Dec. 1990

CONTRIBUTIONS
DES GOUVERNEMENTS
AUX BUDGETS DU CICR EN 1990

(en francs suisses)

(Pour BS montants reçus)
(Pour BT montants annoncés et reçus)

D1/BOBE1990.GVT

| ** | PAYS | BUDGET SIEGE | | | BUDGETS TERRAIN | | * ex-aequo |
|---|---|---|---|---|---|---|---|
| | | CONTRIBUTIONS REGULIERES | AUTRES CONTRIBUTIONS | TOTAL | en espèces | GRAND TOTAL | RANG |
| 1 | AFRIQUE DU SUD | | | | | | |
| 2 | ALBANIE | 500 | | 500 | | 500 | 66 |
| 3 | ALLEMAGNE, RDA | 5,000 | | 5,000 | | 5,000 | 55 |
| 4 | ALLEMAGNE, RFA | 970,750 | | 970,750 | 12,532,238 | 13,502,988 | 5 |
| 5 | ANGOLA | 21,905 | | 21,905 | | 21,905 | 42 |
| 6 | ARABIE SEOUDITE | | | | 745,000 | 745,000 | 18 |
| 7 | ARGENTINE | | | | | | |
| 8 | AUSTRALIE | 590,375 | | 590,375 | 1,997,878 | 2,588,253 | 14 |
| 9 | AUTRICHE | 181,056 | | 181,056 | 724,091 | 905,147 | 17 |
| 10 | BAHAMAS | 8,951 | | 8,951 | | 8,951 | 50 |
| 11 | BELGIQUE | 409,394 | 20,261 | 429,655 | | 429,655 | 19 |
| 12 | BELIZE | 7,492 | | 7,492 | | 7,492 | 51 |
| 13 | BIELORUSSIE | 6,000 | | 6,000 | | 6,000 | 54 |
| 14 | BIRMANIE | 14,600 | | 14,600 | | 14,600 | 45 |
| 15 | BOLIVIE | 6,442 | | 6,442 | | 6,442 | 53 |
| 16 | BOTSWANA | | | | | | |
| 17 | BRESIL | | | | | | |
| 18 | BULGARIE | | | | | | |
| 19 | BURKINA FASO | 18,144 | | 18,144 | | 18,144 | 43 |
| 20 | CAMEROUN | | | | | | |
| 20 | CANADA | 1,519,192 | | 1,519,192 | 8,784,428 | 10,303,620 | 8 |
| 21 | CAP-VERT | | 1,000 | 1,000 | | 1,000 | 64 |
| 22 | CHINE | 360,000 | | 360,000 | | 360,000 | 20 |
| 23 | CHYPRE | | | | | | |
| 24 | COLOMBIE | 120,155 | | 120,155 | | 120,155 | 29 |
| 25 | COREE, REP. | 205,500 | | 205,500 | | 205,500 | 25 |
| 26 | COSTA RICA | 30,400 | | 30,400 | | 30,400 | 35 |
| 27 | CUBA | | | | | | |
| 28 | DANEMARK | 1,118,693 | | 1,118,693 | 8,028,100 | 9,146,793 | 9 |
| 29 | DJIBOUTI | | | | | | |
| 30 | DOMINIQUE | 4,780 | | 4,780 | | 4,780 | 56 |
| 31 | EGYPTE | 83,850 | | 83,850 | | 83,850 | 32 |
| 32 | EQUATEUR | 3,671 | | 3,671 | | 3,671 | 59 |
| 33 | ESPAGNE | 1,101,231 | | 1,101,231 | | 1,101,231 | 16 |
| 34 | ETATS-UNIS | 9,019,838 | | 9,019,838 | 42,078,837 | 51,098,675 | 2 |
| 35 | FIDJI | | | | | | |
| 36 | FINLANDE | 932,905 | | 932,905 | 10,771,208 | 11,704,113 | 7 |
| 37 | FRANCE | 1,315,000 | | 1,315,000 | 3,280,000 | 4,595,000 | 12 |
| 38 | GRECE | | | | | | |
| 39 | GUINEE REP | 7,259 | | 7,259 | | 7,259 | 52 |
| 40 | HONGRIE | 10,000 | | 10,000 | | 10,000 | 48* |
| 41 | INDE | 23,780 | | 23,780 | | 23,780 | 40 |
| 42 | INDONESIE | | | | | | |
| | | 18,096,863 | 21,261 | 18,118,124 | 88,941,780 | 107,059,904 | |

0056

(Pour BS montants annoncés)
(Pour BT montants annoncés et reçus)

D1/BOBE1990.GVT

| RANG | PAYS | BUDGET SIEGE: CONTRIBUTIONS REGULIERES | BUDGET SIEGE: AUTRES CONTRIBUTIONS | BUDGET SIEGE: TOTAL | BUDGETS TERRAIN en espèces | GRAND TOTAL | * ex-aequo RANG |
|---|---|---|---|---|---|---|---|
| 43 | IRAK | 48,100 | | 48,100 | | 48,100 | 34 |
| 44 | IRLANDE | 178,320 | | 178,320 | 134,400 | 312,720 | 22 |
| 45 | ISLANDE | | | | | | |
| 46 | ISRAEL | | | | | | |
| 47 | ITALIE | 2,785,000 | | 2,785,000 | 11,663,557 | 14,448,557 | 4 |
| 48 | JAMAIQUE | 2,820 | | 2,820 | | 2,820 | 61 |
| 49 | JAPON | | | | 7,851,720 | 7,851,720 | 10 |
| 50 | JORDAN | 58,050 | | 58,050 | | 58,050 | 33 |
| 51 | LIBAN | | | | | | |
| 52 | LIBYE | | | | | | |
| 53 | LIECHTENSTEIN | 100,000 | | 100,000 | | 100,000 | 30* |
| 54 | LUXEMBOURG | 15,000 | | 15,000 | 1,506,344 | 1,521,344 | 15 |
| 55 | MALAISIE | 28,760 | | 28,760 | | 28,760 | 36 |
| 56 | MALI | | | | | | |
| 57 | MALTE | 2,720 | | 2,720 | | 2,720 | 62 |
| 58 | MAROC | 28,200 | | 28,200 | | 28,200 | 37 |
| 59 | MAURICE | | | | | | |
| 60 | MEXIQUE | 150,000 | | 150,000 | | 150,000 | 27 |
| 61 | MONACO | 29,500 | | 29,500 | 261,000 | 290,500 | 23 |
| 62 | MONGOLIE | | | | | | |
| 63 | NIGERIA | | | | | | |
| 64 | NORVEGE | | | | 3,400,975 | 3,400,975 | 13 |
| 65 | NOUVELLE-ZELANDE | 160,700 | | 160,700 | 79,859 | 240,559 | 24 |
| 66 | OMAN | | | | | | |
| 67 | PAYS-BAS | 732,882 | | 732,882 | 5,546,000 | 6,278,882 | 11 |
| 68 | PHILIPPINES | 24,399 | | 24,399 | | 24,399 | 38 |
| 69 | POLOGNE | | | | | | |
| 70 | PORTUGAL | 175,000 | | 175,000 | 171,000 | 346,000 | 21 |
| 71 | QATAR | | | | | | |
| 72 | ROYAUME-UNI | 685,260 | | 685,260 | 12,569,600 | 13,254,860 | 6 |
| 73 | RWANDA | | | | | | |
| 74 | SAINT-MARIN | 12,900 | | 12,900 | | 12,900 | 46 |
| 75 | SEYCHELLES | 14,792 | | 14,792 | | 14,792 | 44 |
| 76 | SINGAPOUR | | | | | | |
| 77 | SRI LANKA | 2,960 | | 2,960 | | 2,960 | 60 |
| 78 | SAINTE-LUCIE | 677 | | 677 | | 677 | 65 |
| 79 | ST VINCENT& GREN. | 4,560 | | 4,560 | | 4,560 | 57 |
| 80 | SOUDAN | 3,863 | | 3,863 | | 3,863 | 58 |
| 81 | SUEDE | 1,350,000 | | 1,350,000 | 27,758,253 | 29,108,253 | 3 |
| 82 | SUISSE | 50,000,000 | | 50,000,000 | 20,225,990 | 70,225,990 | 1 |
| 83 | TCHECOSLOVAQUIE | 100,000 | | 100,000 | | 100,000 | 30* |
| 84 | THAILANDE | 22,055 | | 22,055 | | 22,055 | 41 |
| 85 | TONGA | 12,161 | | 12,161 | | 12,161 | 47 |
| 86 | TRINIDAD & TOBAGO | 1,333 | | 1,333 | | 1,333 | 63 |
| 87 | TUNISIE | 10,000 | | 10,000 | | 10,000 | 48* |
| 88 | TURQUIE | 131,183 | | 131,183 | | 131,183 | 28 |
| 89 | UKRAINE | 24,000 | | 24,000 | | 24,000 | 39 |
| 90 | URSS | 170,000 | | 170,000 | | 170,000 | 26 |
| 91 | VENEZUELA | | | | | | |
| 92 | VIET-NAM | | | | | | |
| 93 | YEMEN, REP. ARABE | | | | | | |
| 94 | YOUGOSLAVIE | | | | | | |
| 95 | ZIMBABWE | | | | | | |
| | | 75,162,058 | 21,261 | 75,183,319 | 180,110,478 | 255,293,797 | |

0057

12/11 오
여유 분담금 있을시
거불 요망

# Peter Kung, ICRC 홍콩주재 대표 서한 요지

90.12.10.
국제기구과

1. 지난번 면담시 보여준 관심과 협조에 감사함.

2. 중국에서처럼 한반도에서도 남.북 이산가족이 재회할 수 있는 기회가 있도록 ICRC가 노력하겠음.

3. 한국 정부가 ICRC 분담금 증액건에 대하여 현재 검토중이나, 1991년도 예산은 이미 확정되었기 때문에 1992년도까지는 분담금 증액이 어려울 것이라는 귀하의 답변을 이해하나, ICRC의 긴급 원조사업에 자금이 필요한바, 1991년도 귀부의 타부서 예산이나 타부 예산을 사용하여 특별 분담금으로 지원하여 주기를 희망함.

| 공람 | 국제기구과 | 90년 12월 일 | 담당 | 과장 | 국장 | 차관보 | 차관 | 장관 |
|---|---|---|---|---|---|---|---|---|
| | | | 허강일 | | | | | |

0058

INTERNATIONAL COMMITTEE OF THE RED CROSS
REGIONAL DELEGATION (EAST ASIA)
紅十字國際委員會東亞地區代表辦事處

12/6 오
서남연합 면담 확인후
국장 보고

Mr. MOON Dong-Suk
Director General
International Organisations Bureau
Ministry of Foreign Affairs
Sejong-Ro 77
Seoul
Republic of Korea

Hong Kong, 2 November 1990

Dear Mr. Moon,

Let me thank you for your time and for the interest you expressed in our activities and problems. Indeed, without the full co-operation and support of governments and national Red Cross societies, the International Committee of the Red Cross (ICRC) would not be able to succeed in its difficult and often delicate task.

I was particularly happy to brief you on the efforts of our organisation in establishing contacts between separated family members in the region. Let's hope our contribution to realise a communication between the millions of separated family members on both sides of the Korean demarcation line will soon be as successful as in neighbouring China: Since the abolishing of Martial Law in Taiwan in 1987, the ICRC has received more than 120,000 family tracing cases and has successfully acted as an intermediary between the Red Cross in Taiwan and the China Red Cross Society in the Mainland.

2/...

0059

23/F SHUN HO TOWER 24-30 ICE HOUSE STREET CENTRAL HONG KONG TELEPHONE (852) 523 4433 FAX (852) 524 4566 TELEX 66766 ICRC HX

As far as our worldwide activities in favour of security detainees are concerned, it was the first time that I was given the opportunity to clarify the point of view of our institution to a high ranking official of your Government. I trust that this information has contributed to a better understanding of the usefulness of such activities and to dispel any possible misunderstandings.

We also have been discussing the financial support of your Government to the ICRC. I was happy to hear that you are studying an improvement, possibly substantial, in your contribution. However, you have pointed out that such an increase would not be possible before 1992, as next year's budget is already finalized. We hope that some of the ICRC actions described in our Emergency Appeal will attract your Government's particular interest, so that existing funds from other F. M. departments and possibly other ministries could be used already in 1991 for a specially "earmarked" contribution.

Again we express our appreciation for your sympathy and support and I hope to have the pleasure of meeting you again sometime at the beginning of next year.

Yours sincerely,

With my best regards

Peter Küng
Head of Delegation

cc: - Mr. KIM Sang-Hyup, President,
R.o. Korea Red Cross Society

- Amb. PARK Sang-Yong,
Ministry of Foreign Affairs, R.o. Korea

- ICRC, Geneva

0060

# 발 신 전 보

번 호 : WGV-1657 901213 1653 DZ 종별 :

수 신 : 주 제네바 대사. 총영사

발 신 : 장 관 (국기)

제 목 : ICRC 특별 예산사업

대 : 제네(정) 20358-1292(90.12.7)

1. 대호건 검토에 참고코자 하니 ICRC가 그간 Gulf만 사태와 관련하여 행한 난민구호 및 원조활동등 인도적 사업에 대하여 파악, 보고바람.

2. 92년도 이후의 기여금 납부 업무에 참고코자 하니, ICRC 기여금 납부 국가들중 아국과 같이 정부가 기여금을 납부하는 경우 이외에, 국내 적십자사등 관련 민간단체가 납부하는 경우가 있는지를 파악, 보고바람. 끝

(국제기구조약국장 문동석)

| 보안 통제 | Ri |
|---|---|

| 앙 고 재 | 90년 12월 13일 | 국기과 | 기안자 성명 | | 과 장 | | 국 장 | | 차 관 | 장 관 |
|---|---|---|---|---|---|---|---|---|---|---|
| | | | 허강일 | | Ri | | 전결 | | | h |

| 외신과통제 |
|---|
| |

0061

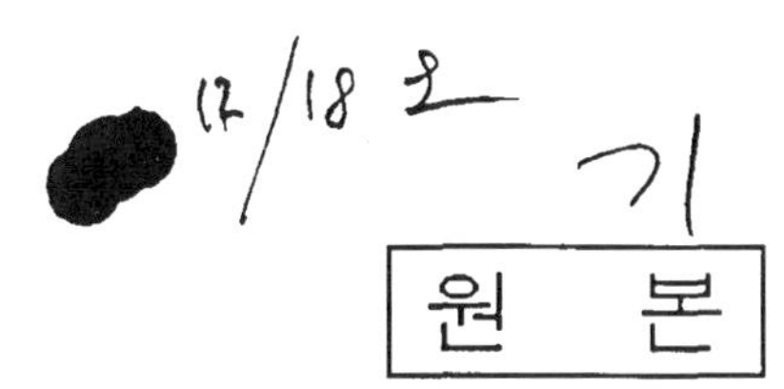

원 본

# 외 무 부

종 별 :

번 호 : GVW-2810 일 시 : 90 1217 1230

수 신 : 장관(국기) (사본: 대한적십자사)

발 신 : 주 제네바 대사

제 목 : ICRC 기여금

1. ICRC SOMMARUGA 총재는 12.14(금) 당지 주재 각국대사들을 초청, ICRC 의 91년주요사업 및 예산에 관해 설명하고 각국의 적극적인 기여금 공여를 요청하였음.(본직 참석)

2. 상기 관련 SOMMARUGA 총재는 12.14 자 외무장관앞 서한을 당관에 송부, 동 서한에서 91년 ICRC 예산 소요내역 (약 98 백만 서서프랑, 미화 약 80백만불 상당) 을설명하고 아국 정부가 91년도 기여금으로 25만 미불을 공영해 줄 것을 요청하였는 바, 동 서한 파편 송부 예정임. 끝

(대사 이상옥-국장)

국기국

PAGE 1

90.12.18 00:53 CG

외신 1과 통제관

0062

# 발 신 전 보

| | 분류번호 | 보존기간 |
|---|---|---|
| | | |

번 호 : WGV-1684 901220 1814 DY 종별 :

수 신 : 주 제네바 대사. 총영사

발 신 : 장 관 (국기)

제 목 : ICRC 특별예산 사업 지원

연 : WGV-1657

표제건 검토에 참고코자 하니 연호 1항에 관하여 우선 지급 보고바람.

(국제기구조약국장 문동석)

| 보 안 통 제 | |
|---|---|

| 앙 고 재 | 90년 12월 20일 | 국기과 | 기안자 성 명 | | 과 장 | | 국 장 | | 차 관 | 장 관 |
|---|---|---|---|---|---|---|---|---|---|---|
| | | | 허강일 | | | | 전결 | | | |

| 외신과통제 |
|---|
| |

0063

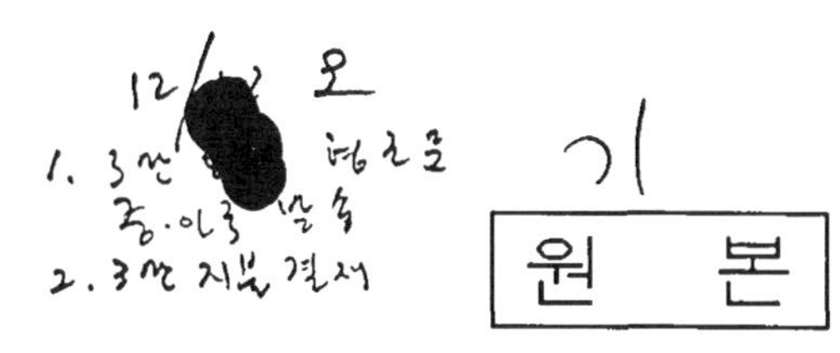

원 본

# 외 무 부

종 별 : 지 급

번 호 : GVW-2842 일 시 : 90 1221 1100

수 신 : 장관(국기)

발 신 : 주 제네바대사

제 목 : ICRC 특별예산사업 지원

대: WGV-1657

연: 제네(정) 20358-1078(90.10.10)

대호, ICRC 측에 파악한 바를 아래 보고함.

1. ICRC 가 걸프사태와 관련하여 행한 인도적사업

0 ICRC 는 8.2 걸프사태 발생 직후부터 전시희생자 보호등 구호활동 목적의 ICRC대표단 (DELEGATION) 을 쿠웨이트에 주재시키기 위해 이라크를 방문, 교섭을 하였으나 이라크 측의부정적 태도로 상금 ICRC 대표단 주재가 실현되지 못하고 있는바, ICRC는 계속 이라크측과 접촉하고 있다함.

0 다만 ICRC 는 걸프에서의 전쟁반발시 난민수용을 위한 3만명 수용규모의 캠프를 요르단 AZRAK 지역에 설치해 놓고 있다하며, 또한 전쟁발발시 응급 조치를 위한 취사도구, 의료용품등 물자들을 제네바 및 사이프러스에비축중이라고 함.

0 ICRC 걸프사태 관련 ICRC 활동에 소요될 경비를 1,300 만 서서프랑으로 추산되고 있으며 현재 각국정부 및 적십자사 또는 개인으로부터 약 985만 서서프랑의 기여금이 기납부 또는 납부 약속되어 있다고 함.

(동 자료 별첨)

2. ICRC 기여금

0 ICRC 에 대한 기여금은 각국정부뿐만 아니라 각국 적십자사에서도 자발적으로 납부하고 있음.

0 각국 적십자사로 부터의 기여금 납부액은 각국정부로 부터의 기여금 납부액과 비교할수 없을 정도로 적은 액수이나 상징적 의미가 크다함.

0 각국정부 및 각국 적십자사의 기여금 납부 현황상세는 연호 송부한 89년 ICRC 활동 보고서 참조바람.

국기국

PAGE 1

90.12.22 06:19 DA

외신 1과 통제관

0064

첨부: 걸프사태 관련 ICRC 에 대한 기여금 납부현황.
(GVW(F)-0597)
끝.
(대사 이상옥-국장)

GVW(F)-05P7 0/221 1100
"GVW-2842 첨부"

10-Dec-90 SO/REX

LIST OF CONTRIBUTIONS FOR IRAK/KOWEIT OPERATION (Cash appeal SFR. 9,504,000)

| DONOR | TYPE | APPEAL | ACTION | PLEDGE | FC | AMOUNT | RECEIPT | SFR |
|---|---|---|---|---|---|---|---|---|
| Australia | GVT | MENA | Irak/Koweit | 03-Sep-90 | A$ | 250,000.00 | 13-Sep-90 | 263,192.25 |
| Austria | GVT | MENA | Irak/Koweit | 13-Sep-90 | ATS | 4,600,000.00 | 26-Oct-90 | 535,090.71 |
| Canada | GVT | MENA | Irak/Koweit | 29-Aug-90 | CAD | 300,000.00 | 24-Sep-90 | 341,491.20 |
| Denmark | GVT | MENA | Irak/Koweit | 24-Aug-90 | DKK | 2,000,000.00 | 24-Sep-90 | 435,000.00 |
| Finland | GVT | MENA | Irak/Koweit | 28-Aug-90 | FIM | 250,000.00 | 09-Oct-90 | 87,609.25 |
| Germany | GVT | MENA | Irak/Koweit | 20-Sep-90 | DM | 1,500,000.00 | 15-Oct-90 | 1,243,500.00 |
| Ireland | GVT | MENA | Irak/Koweit | 12-Sep-90 | IEP | 60,000.00 | 18-Oct-90 | 134,400.00 |
| Japan | GVT | MENA | Irak/Koweit | 29-Aug-90 | USD | 2,000,000.00 | 11-Sep-90 | 2,580,000.00 |
| Norway | GVT | MENA | Irak/Koweit | 31-Aug-90 | NOK | 1,600,000.00 | 13-Sep-90 | 342,400.00 |
| Sweden | GVT | MENA | Irak/Koweit | 24-Aug-90 | SEK | 2,700,000.00 | 27-Nov-90 | 615,600.00 |
| Switzerland | GVT | MENA | Irak/Koweit | 23-Oct-90 | SFR | 1,000,000.00 | 13-Nov-90 | 1,000,000.00 |
| Switzerland | GVT | MENA | Irak/Koweit | 29-Nov-90 | SFR | 127,000.00 | 29-Nov-90 | 127,000.00 |
| United Kingdom | GVT | MENA | Irak/Koweit | 24-Aug-90 | UK₤ | 500,000.00 | 13-Sep-90 | 1,232,500.00 |
| United States | GVT | MENA | Irak/Koweit | 25-Aug-90 | USD | 300,000.00 | 10-Oct-90 | 387,000.00 |
| Australie | NS | MENA | Irak/Koweit | 20-Sep-90 | A$ | 9,690.05 | 21-Sep-90 | 10,492.39 |
| Brazil | NS | MENA | Irak/Koweit | 04-Sep-90 | USD | 3,000.00 | 24-Sep-90 | 3,900.00 |
| Canada | NS | MENA | Irak/Koweit | 24-Aug-90 | CAD | 10,000.00 | 03-Sep-90 | 11,069.29 |
| Finland | NS | MENA | Irak/Koweit | 28-Aug-90 | FIM | 250,000.00 | 10-Oct-90 | 87,625.00 |
| Ireland | NS | MENA | Irak/Koweit | 05-Oct-90 | IEP | 5,500.00 | 18-Oct-90 | 12,320.00 |
| Italy | NS | MENA | Irak/Koweit | 01-Sep-90 | LIT | 25,000,000.00 | - | 27,500.00 |
| Japan | NS | MENA | Irak/Koweit | 30-Aug-90 | YEN | 4,000,000.00 | 03-Sep-90 | 36,000.00 |
| Liechtenstein | NS | MENA | Irak/Koweit | 04-Oct-90 | SFR | 70,000.00 | 15-Oct-90 | 70,000.00 |
| Monaco | NS | MENA | Irak/Koweit | 07-Nov-90 | FF | 40,000.00 | 12-Nov-90 | 10,080.00 |
| Netherlands | NS | MENA | Irak/Koweit | 27-Nov-90 | SFR | 100,000.00 | - | 100,000.00 |
| United Kingdom | NS | MENA | Irak/Koweit | 24-Aug-90 | GBP | 25,000.00 | 04-Sep-90 | 61,625.00 |
| United States | NS | MENA | Irak/Koweit | 02-Sep-90 | U$ | 25,000.00 | 10-Sep-90 | 32,250.00 |
| Canton Appenzell | P | MENA | Irak/Koweit | 13-Sep-90 | SFR | 30,000.00 | 21-Sep-90 | 30,000.00 |
| Mairie Cologny | P | MENA | Irak/Koweit | 05-Oct-90 | SFR | 10,000.00 | 05-Oct-90 | 10,000.00 |
| Mme Zangger | P | MENA | Irak/Koweit | 08-Oct-90 | SFR | 10,000.00 | 08-Oct-90 | 10,000.00 |
| Pater Tanner | P | MENA | Irak/Koweit | 01-Oct-90 | SFR | 5,000.00 | 01-Oct-90 | 5,000.00 |
| Mme Amrein | P | MENA | Irak/Koweit | 30-Aug-90 | SFR | 100.00 | 30-Aug-90 | 100.00 |
| Drogerie Fassbind | P | MENA | Irak/Koweit | 30-Sep-90 | SFR | 100.00 | 30-Sep-90 | 100.00 |
| Ref Pfarramt | P | MENA | Irak/Koweit | 08-Nov-90 | SFR | 4,000.00 | 08-Nov-90 | 4,000.00 |
| R. T. Gustafson | P | MENA | Irak/Koweit | 14-Nov-90 | U$ | 248.70 | 27-Nov-90 | 248.70 |
| Dr. Ochsner | P | MENA | Irak/Koweit | 30-Aug-90 | SFR | 200.00 | 30-Aug-90 | 200.00 |
| TOTAL | | | | | | | | 9,847,293.79 |

1-1

Estimated expenditure 12.970.000

0066

(원본)

TOTAL P.02

| 분류기호<br>문서번호 | 국기 20350-<br>206 | 협 조 문 용 지<br>( 2181-2 ) | 결<br>재 | 담당 | 과장 | 국장 |
|---|---|---|---|---|---|---|
| | | | | 오영주 | | |
| 시행일자 | 1990. 12. 22. | | | | | |
| 수 신 | 중동아프리카국장 | 발 신 | 국제기구조약국장 | | | (서 명) |
| 제 목 | 걸프만 사태관련 지원예산 요청 | | | | | |

대 : 마그 20005-162

1\. 국제적십자위원회(ICRC)는 각국의 기여금 공여로 아시아, 아프리카 중동 및 남미 4개지역을 대상으로 구호 사업을 전개하고 있으며, 특히 걸프만 사태 발발이후에는 동지역에 총 1,300만 서서프랑이 소요되는 난민 수용 및 의료시설등을 위한 특별사업계획을 수립하고 각국정부 및 개인등으로 부터 이미 985만 서서프랑을 기접수하였다 합니다.

2\. 상기관련 ICRC는 아국도 동 특별사업 예산의 일부를 기여금 형식으로 지원해 줄것을 요청해온바, 아국의 걸프만사태 지원의 일환으로 국제적십자위원회 측에 3만불 지원을 추진하고자 하니 걸프만 사태 아국 지원금 소요내역으로 반영하여 주시기 바랍니다.

첨부 : 상기 주제네바 대표부 공한 사본. 끝

0067

| 분류기호 문서번호 | 국기20350- 제6 | 협조문용지 ( 2181-2 ) | 결재 | 담당 | 과장 | 국장 |
|---|---|---|---|---|---|---|
| 시행일자 | 1990. 12. 22. | | | | | |
| 수 신 | 중동아프리카국장 | 발 신 | 국제기구조약국장 (서명) | | | |
| 제 목 | 걸프만 사태관련 지원예산 요청 | | | | | |

대 : 마그 20005-162

1. 국제적십자위원회(ICRC)는 각국의 기여금 공여로 아시아, 아프리카 중동 및 남미 4개지역을 대상으로 구호 사업을 전개하고 있으며, 특히 걸프만 사태 발발이후에는 동지역에 총 1,300만 서서프랑이 소요되는 난민 수용 및 의료시설등을 위한 특별사업계획을 수립하고 각국정부 및 개인등으로 부터 이미 985만 서서프랑을 기접수하였다 합니다.

2. 상기관련 ICRC는 아국도 동 특별사업 예산의 일부를 기여금 형식으로 지원해 줄것을 요청해온바, 아국의 걸프만사태 지원의 일환으로 국제적십자위원회 측에 3만불 지원을 추진하고자 하니 걸프만 사태 아국 지원금 소요내역으로 반영하여 주시기 바랍니다.

첨부 : 상기 주제네바 대표부 공한 사본. 끝

0068

| 분류기호 문서번호 | 국기 20300- | 기 안 용 지 (전화 : 720-4050 ) | 시 행 상 특별취급 | |
|---|---|---|---|---|
| 보존기간 | 영구 . 준영구. 10. 5 . 3 . 1. | 차 관 | 장 관 | |
| 수 신 처 보존기간 | | 전결 | | |
| 시행일자 | 90.12.22. | | | |

| 보조기관 | 국장 | | 협조기관 | 기획관리실장 | 문 서 통 제 |
|---|---|---|---|---|---|
| | 과장 | | | 미주국장 | |
| | | | | 중동아프리카국장 | |
| 기안책임자 | | 오영주 | | 총무과장 | 발 송 인 |

| 경 유 수 신 참 조 | 건 의 | 발신명의 | | |
|---|---|---|---|---|
| 제 목 | 걸프만 사태관련 국제 적십자 위원회 특별예산 사업지원 | | | |

1. 국제적십자 위원회(ICRC)는 각국의 기여금 공여로 아시아, 아프리카, 중동 및 남미 4개지역을 대상으로 구호사업을 전개하고 있으며, 특히 걸프만 사태 발발이후에는 동지역에 총 1,300만 서서프랑이 소요되는 난민 수용 및 의료시설등을 위한 특별사업 계획을 수립하고 각국 정부 및 개인등으로부터 985만 서서프랑을 기접수하였다 합니다.

/계 속/

0069

2. 상기관련, ICRC는 아국도 동 특별사업 예산의 일부를 기여금 형식으로 지원해 줄것을 요청해온바, 아국의 걸프만 사태 지원의 일환으로 국제적십자 위원회측에 아래와 같이 사업비를 지원할 것을 건의하오니 재가하여 주시기 바랍니다.

- 아 래 -

1. 사업비 지원액 : $30,000

2. 사업비 송금처 : 주제네바 대표부

3. 예 산 항 목 : 정무활동 해외 경상이전비

첨부 : 상기 주제네바 대표부 공한 사본.

0070

| | 분류번호 | 보존기간 |
|---|---|---|
| | | |

# 발 신 전 보

번 호 : WGV-1742 901228 1103 FC 종별 :

수 신 : 주 제네바 대사. ~~총영사~~

발 신 : 장 관 (국기)

제 목 : ICRC 특별 예산사업 지원

연 : WGV-1657

대 : GVW-2842

1. 본부는 걸프만사태 지원금(병목)으로 ICRC측에 3만 미불을 지원키로 결정하였으니 동 사실을 ICRC측에 통보바람.

2. 지원금은 금년내 집행 완료한다는 방침하에 동 지원금을 본부에서 ICRC 사무국에 직송 조치하고자 하니 ICRC 관련부서의 송금구좌 번호를 파악, 지급 보고바람. 끝

(국제기구조약국장 문동석)

| 보안통제 | |
|---|---|

| 앙 고 재 | 90년 12월 날 일 | 국기과 | 기안자 성명 | | 과 장 | | 국 장 | | 차 관 | 장 관 |
|---|---|---|---|---|---|---|---|---|---|---|
| | | | | | | | | | | |

| 외신과통제 |
|---|
| |

0071

63

# 기 안 용 지

| 분류기호 문서번호 | 국기 20347- | (전화 : 720-4050 ) | 시 행 상 특별취급 | |
|---|---|---|---|---|
| 보존기간 | 영구 . 준영구. 10. 5 . 3 . 1. | 장 관 | | |
| 수 신 처 보존기간 | | | | |
| 시행일자 | 90.12.28. | | | |

| 보조기관 | 국장 | 전 결 | 협조기관 | | 문 서 통 제 |
|---|---|---|---|---|---|
| | 과장 | | | | 1990.12.29 |
| | | | | | |
| 기안책임자 | | 오영주 | | | 발 송 인 |

| 경 유 수 신 참 조 | 대한적십자사 총재 | 발신명의 | | 1990.12.29 |
|---|---|---|---|---|
| 제 목 | 국제적십자위원회(ICRC) 특별예산 사업 지원 | | | |

1. 국제적십자위원회는 각국의 기여금 공여로 아시아. 아프리카, 중동. 및 남미 4개지역을 대상으로 구호사업을 전개하고 있음을 알려오면서, 동 특별예산 사업에 우리나라도 기여금을 공여해줄 것을 요청하여 왔습니다.

2. 상기 요청 관련, 당부는 ICRC가 ~~국제적십자위원회가 특히~~ 걸프만 사태 발발이후 걸프만 ~~동~~지역에 총 1,300만 서서프랑이 소요되는 난민 수용 및

/계 속/

0072

의료시설등을 위한 특별사업 계획을 수립하고 각국으로부터 기금을

접수하고 있음을 감안하여, 우리나라의 걸프만사태 지원금 명목으로

ICRC의 특별예산 사업에 3만 미불을 지원키로 결정하였음을 알려드리니,

귀사 업무에 참고하시기 바랍니다. 끝

0073

| 분류기호<br>문서번호 | 국기20300-<br>283 | 협 조 문 용 지<br><br>( 2181-2 ) | 결<br><br>재 | 담당 | 과장 | 국장 |
|---|---|---|---|---|---|---|
| | | | | 오여극 | 역 | |
| 시행일자 | 1990. 12. 29. | | | | | |
| 수 신 | 총무과장 | 발 신 | 국제기구조약국장 (서 명) | | | |
| 제 목 | 특별지원금 지급 의뢰 | | | | | |

별첨과 같이 재가를 득한 걸프만사태 관련 국제적십자 위원회(ICRC) 특별사업에 대한 지원금 송금을 아래와 같이 의뢰하오니 필요한 조치를 취하여 주시기 바랍니다.

\- 아 래 -

1. 사업비 지원액 : $30,000(ICRC 사무국)

2. 송금처

o 송금은행 : SOCIETE DE BANQUE SUISSE, CASE POSTALE
2011 GENEVA. 11

o 구좌번호 : 129.986.4.

3. 예산항목 : 정무활동 해외 경상이전

첨부 : 재가문서 사본 1부. 끝

0074

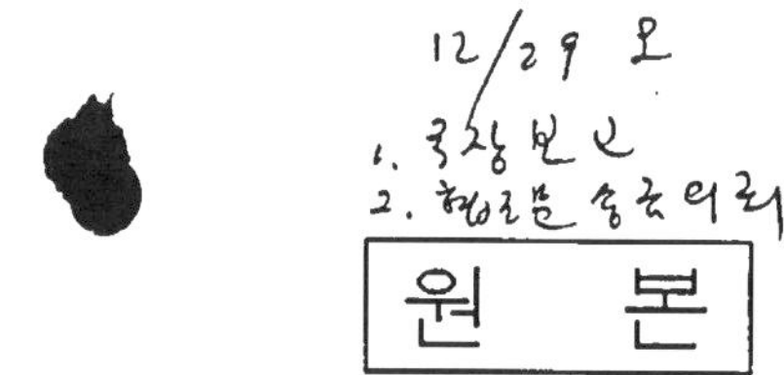
원 본

# 외 무 부

종 별 :

번 호 : GVW-2867 일 시 : 90 1228 1430

수 신 : 장 관 (국기)

발 신 : 주 제네바 대사대리

제 목 : ICRC 특별예산 사업지원

대: WGV-1742

1. 대호, 12.28(금) 당관은 아국이 걸프만사태 지원금 명목으로 3만미불을 지원키로 하였음을 ICRC 측에 통보함.

2. ICRC 측 구좌번호는 다음과 같음

- SOCIETE DE BANQUE SUISSE, CASE POSTALE 2011 GENEVA 11, ACCOUNT NO: 129.986.4. 끝.

(대사대리 박영우-국장)

국기국

PAGE 1

90.12.29 07:45 FC

외신 1과 통제관

0075

Seoul, 29 December 1990

Mr. Cornelio Sommaruga
President
International Committee of
the Red Cross, Geneva

Excellency,

I would like to acknowledge receipt of your letter dated 14 December 1990.

We understand that the world situation calls for increasing role of ICRC in undertaking its humanitarian works. We are sympathetic to your appeal to our country, a State party to the Geneva Convention, to augment our contribution to the ICRC's 1991 headquaters budget from US $150,000 of current year to US $250,000. However, I am obliged to tell you that, according to national budget planning procedures, our contribution to all international organizations including ICRC for 1991 has already been fixed as we face the fiscal year 1991 beginning January 1.

Nontheless, I am pleased to inform you that our government has decided to contribute US $30,000 toward special budget program of ICRC. The amount will ~~have~~ be~~en~~ remitted directly to the account of ICRC by the end of 1990.

As to the increase ~~of~~ in regular contribution of the Republic of Korea to the ICRC headquaters budget, I should say that your appeal will be given due consideration when budget planning begins for the ~~following~~ year 1992.

Please accept, Excellency, my highest esteem.

Chong Ha YOO
Acting Minister of
Foreign Affairs

CC : Peter Kung
Head of Regional Delegation(East Asia)
International Committee of the Red Cross
23/F Shun Ho Tower 24-30
Ice House St. Central Hong Kong

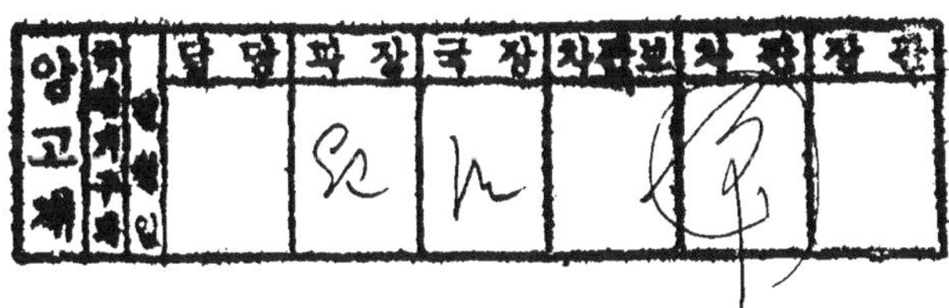

0076

650

| 분류기호 문서번호 | 국기20347- | 기 안 용 지 (전화 : ) | 시 행 상 특별취급 | |
|---|---|---|---|---|
| 보존기간 | 영구·준영구. 10. 5. 3. 1. | 장 관 | | |
| 수 신 처 보존기간 | | | | |
| 시행일자 | 91. 1. 7. | | | |

| 보조기관 | 국장 | 전 결 | 협조기관 | | 문 서 통 제 |
|---|---|---|---|---|---|
| | 과장 | | | | 1991. 1. 08 |
| 기안책임자 | 오영주 | | | | 발 송 인 |

| 경 유 수 신 참 조 | 주제네바대사대리 | 발신명의 | |
|---|---|---|---|
| 제 목 | ICRC 총재 서한에 대한 답신 | | |

연 : WGV -1742(90.12.28)

ICRC 총재의 아국 기여금 증액을 요청하는 90.12.14자 장관앞 서한에 대하여 별첨 내용의 차관명의 답신을 발송하였는바 업무에 참고하시기 바랍니다.

첨부 : 상기 서한 1부. 끝

0077

1505-25(2-1) 일(1)갑 190㎜×268㎜ 인쇄용지 2급 60g/㎡
85. 9. 9. 승인 "내가아낀 종이 한장 늘어나는 나라살림" 가 40-41 1989. 11. 14

MINISTRY OF FOREIGN AFFAIRS
REPUBLIC OF KOREA

Seoul, 29 December 1990

Mr. Cornelio Sommaruga
President
International Committee of
the Red Cross, Geneva

Excellency,

I would like to acknowledge receipt of your letter dated 14 December 1990.

We understand that the world situation calls for increasing role of ICRC in undertaking its humanitarian works. We are sympathetic to your appeal to our country, a State party to the Geneva Convention, to augment our contribution to the ICRC's 1991 headquaters budget from US $150,000 of current year to US $250,000. However, I am obliged to tell you that, according to national budget planning procedures, our contribution to all international organizations including ICRC for 1991 has already been fixed as we face the fiscal year 1991 beginning January 1.

Nontheless, I am pleased to inform you that our government has decided to contribute US $30,000 toward special budget program of ICRC. The amount will be remitted directly to the account of ICRC by the end of 1990.

As to the increase in regular contribution of the Republic of Korea to the ICRC headquaters budget, I should say that your appeal will be given due consideration when budget planning begins for the year 1992.

Please accept, Excellency, my highest esteem.

Chong Ha Yoo
Acting Minister of
Foreign Affairs

CC : Peter Kung
Head of Regional Delegation(East Asia)
International Committee of the Red Cross
23/F Shun Ho Tower 24-30
Ice House St. Central Hong Kong

0078

기

원 본

# 외 무 부

종 별 :

번 호 : GVW-0084 일 시 : 91 0115 1600

수 신 : 장 관 (국기,중근동)

발 신 : 주 제네바 대사대리

제 목 : 페만사태관련 ICRC 활동 계획

당지 국제적십자 위원회(ICRC)는 페만에서의 전쟁발발에 대비한 ICRC 의 준비상황 및 향후 활동계획에 관한 자료를 당관에 보내왔기 별첨 송부함.

첨부: 상기 자료(GVW(F)-17). 끝

(대사대리 박영우-국장)

국기국 중아국

PAGE 1 91.01.16 02:59 FC

외신 1과 통제관

0079

8

GVW(91)-0017 10115 1800
GVW-84 관련

UPDATE NO. 1 (1991) ON ICRC ACTIVITIES IN THE GULF
7 JANUARY 1991

## ICRC PREPAREDNESS FOR POSSIBLE NEEDS IN THE GULF

### BACKGROUND

AS TENSIONS MOUNT IN THE GULF WITH THE APPROACHING 15 JANUARY DEADLINE ESTABLISHED BY UN SECURITY COUNCIL RESOLUTION No. 678 OF 29 NOVEMBER 1990, THE ICRC IS PREPARING FOR POSSIBLE HUMANITARIAN INTERVENTION. IN SPITE OF REPEATED EFFORTS AT NEGOTIATION WITH IRAQI AUTHORITIES, THE ICRC HAS STILL NOT BEEN PERMITTED TO PROVIDE HUMANITARIAN PROTECTION AND ASSISTANCE FOR THE CIVILIAN POPULATION IN KUWAIT.

### ICRC MEASURES TAKEN FOR PREPAREDNESS IN THE GULF

WHILE HOPEFUL FOR A PEACEFUL SOLUTION OF THE GULF CRISIS, THE ICRC HAS NEVERTHELESS TAKEN STEPS TO PREPARE FOR RAPID INTERVENTION IN THE EVENT OF INTERNATIONAL ARMED CONFLICT.

ICRC DIPLOMATIC ACTIVITY INTENSIFIED AFTER THE ADOPTION OF RESOLUTION No. 678:

1) ON 11 DECEMBER, ICRC DIRECTOR OF OPERATIONS MR. JEAN DE COURTEN VISITED BAGHDAD AND HAD DISCUSSIONS WITH HIGH-RANKING IRAQI OFFICIALS REGARDING THE POSSIBILITY OF ICRC ACTIVITIES IN KUWAIT.

2) THE ICRC SENT A MEMORANDUM TO ALL 164 STATES PARTY TO THE GENEVA CONVENTIONS ON 14 DECEMBER, REMINDING THEM OF THEIR OBLIGATION TO RESPECT THE PROVISIONS OF INTERNATIONAL HUMANITARIAN LAW APPLICABLE IN ARMED CONFLICTS.

3) ALSO ON 14 DECEMBER, ICRC PRESIDENT CORNELIO SOMMARUGA ADDRESSED AMBASSADORS AND REPRESENTATIVES OF STATES PARTY TO THE GENEVA CONVENTIONS AT ICRC HEADQUARTERS IN GENEVA. THE ICRC PRESIDENT ONCE AGAIN REMINDED THE STATES OF THEIR OBLIGATIONS UNDER THE GENEVA CONVENTIONS AND THE TWO ADDITIONAL PROTOCOLS, AND MENTIONED THE APPLICABILITY OF INTERNATIONAL HUMANITARIAN LAW IN THE EVENT OF ARMED CONFLICT BETWEEN STATES. MR. SOMMARUGA WENT ON TO INFORM THE REPRESENTATIVES OF MEASURES TAKEN BY THE ICRC TO FULFIL THE MANDATE ENTRUSTED TO IT BY THE INTERNATIONAL COMMUNITY.

10-1

0080

4) A SECOND MEMORANDUM WAS SENT BY THE ICRC TO STATES WHICH COULD BECOME INVOLVED IN A CONFLICT IN THE REGION. THIS MEMORANDUM REITERATES THE BASIC PROVISIONS OF THE GENEVA CONVENTIONS REGARDING RESPECT FOR THE CIVILIAN POPULATION, TREATMENT OF PRISONERS AND THE WOUNDED, AND BASIC RULES OF CONDUCT FOR COMBATANTS. THE MEMORANDUM ALSO EXPLAINED PROCEDURES RELATED TO THE WORK OF THE CENTRAL TRACING AGENCY.

APART FROM THE DIPLOMATIC ACTIVITY DESCRIBED ABOVE, THE ICRC HAS TAKEN A NUMBER OF PRACTICAL STEPS TO ENSURE ITS PREPAREDNESS:

1) A PERMANENT TASK FORCE FOR THE GULF REGION HAS BEEN ESTABLISHED AT ICRC HEADQUARTERS. IT IS HEADED BY MR. PETER FUCHS, AND IT INCLUDES THE VARIOUS SERVICES AT HEADQUARTERS. THE TASK FORCE'S OBJECTIVE IS TO CO-ORDINATE AND DIRECT ICRC PREPARATIONS FOR IMMEDIATE ACTION IN THE EVENT OF AN OUTBREAK OF HOSTILITIES IN THE REGION.

2) THE ICRC HAS ORGANIZED MOBILE TEAMS. MORE THAN 50 DELEGATES FROM ICRC HEADQUARTERS IN GENEVA HAVE BEEN PUT ON STANDBY FOR IMMEDIATE DEPARTURE.

3) EQUIPMENT AND MATERIAL ASSISTANCE HAS ALSO BEEN MOBILIZED. IN CYPRUS AND IN EUROPE, THE ICRC HAS STORED MATERIAL FOR THE RAPID CONSTRUCTION OF A CAMP FOR 30,000 PEOPLE AND OF TRANSIT CAMPS EACH WITH A CAPACITY OF 5,000. LOGISTICAL MEANS AND MEDICAL MATERIAL HAVE BEEN PREPARED IN GENEVA. ICRC HEADQUARTERS HAS PREPARED SPECIAL TELECOMMUNICATIONS EQUIPMENT FOR IMMEDIATE DEPLOYMENT.

4) THE ICRC HAS ADDED PERSONNEL TO ALL DELEGATIONS IN THE REGION. SECURITY RISKS ARE CONSTANTLY BEING EVALUATED, AND ICRC STAFF HAS BEEN GIVEN THE MATERIAL AND TRAINING NECESSARY TO ENSURE THEIR SAFETY.

5) THE ICRC HAS PREPARED FOR CIRCULATION A SPECIAL DOCUMENT ON TRACING PROCEDURES FOR THE NATIONAL SOCIETIES OF COUNTRIES CONCERNED.

ICRC PLAN OF ACTION

AT THIS POINT, IT IS NOT POSSIBLE TO PRESENT A PRECISE OVERALL PLAN OF ACTION. NEVERTHELESS, IN THE EVENT OF A LARGE SCALE ICRC MEDICAL AND RELIEF OPERATION IN THE MIDDLE EAST, THE ICRC WILL CALL UPON NATIONAL SOCIETIES FOR PERSONNEL, LOGISTICS, MATERIAL AND FINANCIAL ASSISTANCE.

10-2

0081

THE ICRC WOULD APPRECIATE COMMUNICATION AS SOON AS POSSIBLE FROM THE NATIONAL SOCIETIES CONCERNING THE PERSONNEL, LOGISTICS, MATERIAL AND FINANCIAL ASSISTANCE THEY COULD PROVIDE IN THE EVENT OF ARMED CONFLICT IN THE GULF REGION. INFORMATION SHOULD REACH ICRC HEADQUARTERS BEFORE 10 JANUARY. THE MOBILIZATION WILL BE ORGANIZED AND CO-ORDINATED BY THE ICRC ACCORDING TO NEEDS AS THEY ARISE.

THE LEAGUE OF RED CROSS AND RED CRESCENT SOCIETIES HAS BEEN INFORMED OF THE ICRC's INTENTIONS. THE ICRC AND THE LEAGUE WILL CO-ORDINATE THE PLANNING OF THE HUMAN RESOURCES PROVIDED BY THE NATIONAL SOCIETIES. THE ICRC WILL KEEP NATIONAL SOCIETIES INFORMED OF FUTURE DEVELOPMENTS THROUGH REGULAR UPDATES. FOR FURTHER INFORMATION, PLEASE CONTACT SO/REX.

BEST REGARDS,

CHRISTIAN KORNEVALL
SO/REX, ICRC, GENEVA

10-3

0082

UPDATE NO. 2 ON ICRC ACTIVITIES IN THE GULF
11 JANUARY 1991

**ICRC PREPAREDNESS FOR POSSIBLE NEEDS IN THE GULF**

IN VIEW OF THE APPROACHING 15 JANUARY DEADLINE AND THE PRESENT STALEMATE IN DIPLOMATIC NEGOTIATIONS BETWEEN THE PARTIES CONCERNED WITH THE GULF CRISIS, THE ICRC HAS TAKEN FURTHER MEASURES TOWARD PREPARING THE ORGANIZATION FOR PROMPT INTERVENTION IN THE EVENT OF ARMED CONFLICT IN THE GULF REGION.

ICRC PERSONNEL PRESENT IN THE REGION

SEVENTY-SEVEN ICRC DELEGATES ALREADY IN THE REGION ARE PREPARED TO INTERVENE IF THE NEED ARISES. EXPATRIATE STAFF ARE LOCATED IN THE FOLLOWING PLACES: SAUDI ARABIA, EGYPT, IRAN, IRAQ, ISRAEL AND THE TERRITORIES OCCUPIED BY ISRAEL, JORDAN, LEBANON AND SYRIA.

MORE THAN 50 DELEGATES FROM GENEVA HAVE BEEN TRAINED AND BRIEFED ON THE SITUATION. ON 13 JANUARY, SOME OF THESE DELEGATES WILL LEAVE FOR IRAN AND BAHRAIN. OTHERS ARE PREPARED TO LEAVE FOR RIYADH AND OTHER DESTINATIONS ON SHORT NOTICE.

SPECIAL ICRC MISSIONS TO IRAN AND TURKEY WERE CARRIED OUT TO DISCUSS SETTING UP PROTECTION AND ASSISTANCE PROGRAMMES FOR POTENTIAL DISPLACED PERSONS WITH THE CONCERNED AUTHORITIES. AN AGREEMENT HAS BEEN REACHED REGARDING ICRC PREPARATIONS.

PREPARING FOR PROTECTION AND TRACING ACTIVITIES

ICRC REPRESENTATIVES ARE MEETING WITH OFFICIALS IN THE CAPITAL CITIES OF ALL PARTIES LIKELY TO BE INVOLVED IN ARMED CONFLICT IN THE GULF IN ORDER TO BRIEF THE MILITARY PERSONNEL OF THE RESPECTIVE PARTIES ON THE PROVISIONS OF INTERNATIONAL HUMANITARIAN LAW APPLICABLE IN INTERNATIONAL ARMED CONFLICT AND ON STANDARD ICRC PROCEDURES FOR TRACING ACTIVITIES.

RELIEF ASSISTANCE FOR DISPLACED PERSONS

IN THE EVENT OF ARMED CONFLICT AND SUBSEQUENT MASSIVE DISPLACEMENT OF PEOPLE FROM THE COMBAT AREA, THE ICRC WOULD SET UP TRANSIT/RECEPTION CAMPS IN THE COUNTRIES AFFECTED BY CONFLICT AND ALONG THEIR BORDERS. FOR PLANNING PURPOSES, THE ICRC HAS WORKED OUT A STANDARD CAMP MODULE TO SHELTER APPROXIMATELY 30 - 40,000 DISPLACED PERSONS. EACH CAMP MODULE WILL BE FULLY EQUIPPED WITH PROVISIONS FOR SHELTER IN DESERT CONDITIONS, SANITATION FACILITIES AND WATER SUPPLY.

ro-4

0083

AT THIS POINT, THE ICRC CONSIDERS IT REALISTIC TO PLAN FOR EIGHT SUCH CAMPS WHICH COULD PROVIDE SHELTER FOR UP TO 300,000 DISPLACED PERSONS. THIS PLAN INCLUDES EXISTING FACILITIES AND THE POTENTIAL CAPACITY INDICATED BY THE RED CRESCENT SOCIETIES OF THE REGION. THUS, THE ICRC, WITH THE ACTIVE PARTICIPATION OF NATIONAL SOCIETIES, SHOULD BE PREPARED TO MOBILIZE ALL MATERIAL AND PERSONNEL REQUIRED TO CONSTRUCT AND MANAGE 4 - 5 SUCH CAMP MODULES ON SHORT NOTICE.

BASED ON PREVIOUS EXPERIENCE EACH CAMP MODULE MUST INCLUDE THE FOLLOWING ITEMS:

FIELD INSTALLATIONS

1500 TENTS AND GROUND SHEETS (30 M2)
10 ADMINISTRATIVE TENTS (60 M2)
300 LATRINE UNITS
700 GARBAGE DRUMS

WATER TANKS WITH TOTAL CAPACITY OF 400,000 L
30 WATER DISTRIBUTION UNITS WITH TAPS
WATER SUPPLY EQUIPMENT SUCH AS PIPES, TAPS, GATES, ETC.

6000 KEROSENE STOVES EQUIPPED WITH WIND SHIELDS
ELECTRICAL INSTALLATIONS WITH GENERATORS, WIRES, POLES AND LAMPS

60,000 BLANKETS
6,000 KITCHEN SETS
1,500 JERRYCANS
20,000 CANDLES
5 MT OF SOAP

LOGISTICAL MEANS:

10 TOYOTA LAND CRUISERS
2 AMBULANCES
1 RUB HALL (240 M2)
500 PALLETS
OFFICE MATERIALS

PERSONNEL FOR EACH MODULE

10 EXPATRIATES INCLUDING A CAMP MANAGER AND PEOPLE RESPONSIBLE FOR ADMINISTRATION, WAREHOUSING, SANITATION, RECEPTION, MAINTENANCE, ETC.

SPECIFICATIONS NOT NOTED ABOVE CAN BE FOUND IN THE ICRC HANDBOOK FOR DONORS.

10-5

0084

NATIONAL SOCIETIES ARE REQUESTED TO INFORM THE ICRC RELIEF DIVISION REGARDING STOCK AVAILABILITY AND DELIVERY DELAYS.

PREPARATIONS FOR EMERGENCY MEDICAL ACTIVITIES

ICRC PREPARATIONS FOR EMERGENCY MEDICAL ACTIVITIES WILL BE GIVEN IN UPDATE NO. 3 WHICH WILL FOLLOW SHORTLY.

PERSONNEL

NATIONAL SOCIETIES ARE REQUESTED TO INDICATE HOW MANY PERSONS WOULD BE AVAILABLE.

PRECAUTIONARY MEASURES ARE BEING TAKEN BY THE ICRC TO ENSURE THE SAFETY OF PERSONNEL. SPECIFIC INSTRUCTIONS ON SAFETY AND PERSON SECURITY WILL BE GIVEN PRIOR TO DEPARTURE.

NATIONAL SOCIETIES RESPONSE

THE ICRC WISHES TO THANK THE NATIONAL SOCIETIES WHICH HAVE ALREADY INDICATED WHAT KIND OF ASSISTANCE THEY COULD PROVIDE IN THE CASE OF AN EMERGENCY SITUATION. FOR THE TIME BEING, REQUESTED PERSONNEL AND ASSISTANCE SHOULD BE PREPARED BUT NOT PUT ON STANDBY NOR DISPATCHED UNTIL NATIONAL SOCIETIES RECEIVE NOTICE FROM THE ICRC.

CO-ORDINATION

A MEETING WILL BE HELD THIS AFTERNOON BETWEEN THE DIRECTORS OF OPERATIONS OF THE ICRC AND THE LEAGUE TO DISCUSS PLANS FOR CO-ORDINATION.

FOR FURTHER INFORMATION PLEASE CONTACT SO/REX, MR. CH. KORNEVALL OR MR. A. BLAETTLER. FOR QUESTIONS RELATED TO RELIEF PLEASE CONTACT OP/SEC, MR. A. LENDORFF OR MS. M. HOCK.

BEST REGARDS,

CHRISTIAN KORNEVALL
SO/REX, ICRC, GENEVA

10-6

0085

UPDATE NO. 3 (1991) ON ICRC ACTIVITIES IN THE GULF
13 JANUARY 1991

ICRC PREPAREDNESS FOR POSSIBLE NEEDS IN THE GULF

WHILE STILL HOPING FOR SUCCESSFUL DIPLOMATIC DEVELOPMENTS IN THE REGION, THE ICRC IS STEPPING UP ITS PREPAREDNESS FOR POSSIBLE NEEDS IN CASE OF ARMED CONFLICT.

ICRC PRESENCE IN THE REGION

ON JANUARY 13, TWO ICRC TEAMS LEFT FOR IRAN AND BAHRAIN TO PREPARE LOGISTICS FOR POSSIBLE ICRC INTERVENTION.

RELIEF ASSISTANCE

A DC-9 AND A KING-AIR B200 HAVE BEEN PUT ON STANDBY AND ALL RELEVANT SPECIFICATIONS OF THESE TWO AIRCRAFT SUCH AS RED CROSS CALL SIGN, OWNERSHIP, REGISTRATION NUMBERS, MARKINGS AND SPECIFIC SSR RADAR CODES FOR ICRC AIRCRAFT HAVE BEEN NOTIFIED TO ALL PARTIES CONCERNED IN THE REGION.

PREPARATIONS FOR EMERGENCY MEDICAL ACTIVITIES

AS INDICATED IN UPDATE No. 2, PLEASE FIND BELOW DETAILS OF THE BASIC FRAMEWORK FOR THE ICRC OPERATION TO COVER THE INITIAL MEDICAL EMERGENCY PHASE AND DETAILS OF PERSONNEL REQUIREMENTS.

IN ADDITION TO MEDICAL PROGRAMMES RELATED TO THE ICRC'S PROTECTION ACTIVITIES ON BEHALF OF POW'S AND DETAINEES, THE ICRC FORESEES BEING INVOLVED IN TWO OTHER AREAS OF MEDICAL ACTIVITY:

0086

1) THE SETTING UP OF 10 SURGICAL HOSPITAL MODULES WITH A TOTAL CAPACITY OF 1000 BEDS TO CARE FOR WAR-WOUNDED COMBATANTS AND CIVILIANS.

2) THE SETTING UP OF MEDICAL FACILITIES TO CARE FOR THE DISPLACED POPULATIONS IN TRANSIT/RECEPTION CAMPS IN THE COUNTRIES AFFECTED BY CONFLICT AND ALONG THEIR BORDERS.

1) SURGICAL HOSPITAL MODULES

THE ICRC PLANS AT THIS STAGE TO PREPARE FIVE ICRC FIELD HOSPITAL MODULES WITH A CAPACITY OF 100 BEDS EACH AND FIVE ICRC MEDICAL TEAMS TO WORK IN EXISTING HOSPITAL FACILITIES IN THE REGION ALSO COVERING APPROXIMATELY 100 BEDS EACH.

FOR EACH 100 BED MODULE, ASSUMING OPERATION 24 HRS A DAY IN 3 SHIFTS, THE PERSONNEL REQUIREMENTS ARE THE FOLLOWING:

1 MEDICAL COORDINATOR
3 SURGEONS
3 ANAESTHETISTS
3 O.T. NURSES
1 MEDICAL ADMINISTRATOR/PHARMACIST
1 LAB. TECHNICIAN/BLOOD BANK SPECIALIST
1 PHYSIOTHERAPIST
1 X-RAY TECHNICIAN
1 SANITATION ENGINEER/TECHNICIAN
1 GENERAL TECHNICIAN/CONSTRUCTOR/ELECTRICIAN
1 HEAD NURSE
75 SURGICAL WARD NURSES (1 NURSE FOR 4 BEDS X 3 SHIFTS)

PLEASE NOTE THAT SUPPORT PERSONNEL SUCH AS CLERKS, ADMINISTRATIVE PERSONNEL, COOKS, CLEANERS, STRETCHER BEARERS, ETC. ARE NOT INCLUDED IN THESE FIGURES.

10-8

0087

2) MEDICAL FACILITIES IN TRANSIT/RECEPTION CAMPS.

FOR EACH OF THE 8 TRANSIT/RECEPTION CAMP MODULE DESCRIBED IN UPDATE No. 2, 2 DISPENSARY/CLINIC MODULES WILL BE REQUIRED, OPERATING 2 SHIFTS PER DAY. PERSONNEL REQUIRED FOR EACH MODULE IS AS FOLLOWS:

2 PHYSICIANS (GENERAL PRACTITIONERS)
12 NURSES
1 OR 2 GENERAL TECHNICIANS
1 OR 2 INTERPRETERS

PERSONNEL FOR THE BUILDING/INSTALLATION OF HOSPITALS, PERSONNEL FOR OVERALL COORDINATION AND POSSIBLY NEEDED FIRST-AID AND TRIAGE TEAMS HAVE NOT BEEN INCLUDED IN THE ABOVE CALCULATIONS.

THE ICRC IS PREPARING TO SET UP A MEDICAL COORDINATION UNIT IN GENEVA AND IN THE FIELD.

TO ENSURE HOMOGENEITY OF TEAMS, IT IS DESIRABLE THAT PARTICIPATING NATIONAL SOCIETIES ATTEMPT TO SET UP COMPLETE MODULES.

MATERIAL NEEDS WITH SPECIFICATIONS FOR THE SURGICAL HOSPITALS AS WELL AS FOR THE DISPENSARY MODULES WILL BE GIVEN IN UPDATE No. 4 WHICH WILL FOLLOW SHORTLY.

NATIONAL SOCIETIES' RESPONSE

THE ICRC THANKS THE NATIONAL SOCIETIES FOR INFORMING US ON THEIR READINESS. AS STRESSED IN UPDATE No. 2, NATIONAL SOCIETIES ARE REQUESTED TO PREPARE AS FAR AS POSSIBLE BOTH PERSONNEL AND MATERIAL ASSISTANCE, BUT NOT YET TO PUT THESE ON STANDBY NOR TO DISPATCH THEM UNTIL RECEIVING A DIRECT REQUEST FROM THE ICRC TO DO SO.

10 - P

0088

IT SHOULD BE BORNE IN MIND THAT INITIALLY ACCOMMODATION AND FOOD SUPPLY FOR ARRIVING TEAMS WOULD BE PROBLEMATIC OR EVEN NON-EXISTENT. PERSONNEL SHOULD THEREFORE BE EQUIPPED WITH NECESSARY PROVISIONS OF FOOD AND PERSONAL BELONGINGS SUCH AS SLEEPING BAGS AND PERSONAL HYGIENE ARTICLES, ETC.

THE ICRC ASSUMES THE RESPONSIBILITY OF ENSURING THE SAFETY OF PERSONNEL. SPECIFIC SAFETY INSTRUCTIONS AND THE NECESSARY MATERIAL FOR PERSONAL SECURITY WILL BE GIVEN PRIOR TO DEPARTURE.

COORDINATION

AS MENTIONED IN UPDATE NO. 2 CONSULTATIONS ARE GOING ON BETWEEN THE ICRC AND THE LEAGUE OF RED CROSS AND RED CRESCENT SOCIETIES. THE COORDINATION OF INTERNATIONAL RED CROSS AND RED CRESCENT ACTIVITIES WILL BE ASSUMED ON THE BASIS OF THE AGREEMENT SIGNED BY THE ICRC AND THE LEAGUE OF RED CROSS AND RED CRESCENT SOCIETIES ON OCTOBER 20, 1989.

FINANCE

THE ICRC WILL LAUNCH A FORMAL APPEAL TO THE INTERNATIONAL COMMUNITY FOR FINANCIAL SUPPORT FOR ITS OPERATION IN THE GULF REGION IN THE EVENT OF CONFLICT BREAKING OUT.

FOR FURTHER INFORMATION, PLEASE CONTACT SO/REX, WHILE FOR INFORMATION SPECIFICALLY RELATED TO MEDICAL MATTERS, PLEASE CONTACT ICRC OP/MED DR. R.RUSSBACH OR DR. J.C. MULLI.

BEST REGARDS

CHRISTIAN KORNEVALL
SO/REX, ICRC GENEVA

10-10

0089

TOTAL P.09

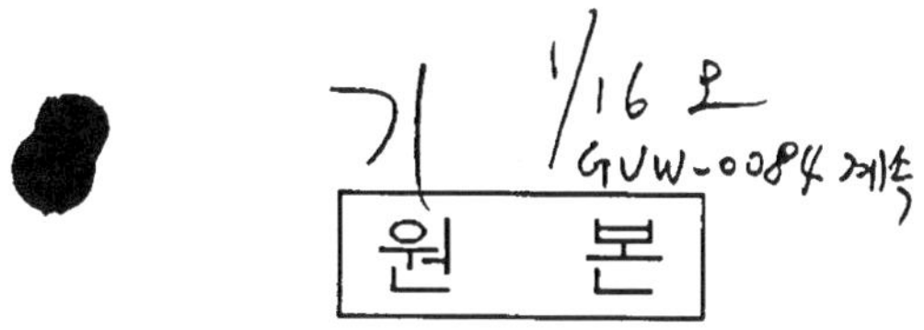

# 외 무 부

종 별 :

번 호 : GVW-0086 일 시 : 91 0115 1900

수 신 : 장 관(국기,중근동)

발 신 : 주 제네바 대사대리

제 목 : 페만사태 관련 ICRC 활동계획

연: GVW-0084

연호, 표제관련 ICRC 추가 자료를 별첨송부함.

첨부: 상기 자료.

( GVW(F)-0018). 끝.

(대사대리 박영우-국장)

국기국 중아국 1차보 2차보 정문국 안기부 미주국

PAGE 1

91.01.16 09:32 WG

외신 1과 통제관

0090

GVW(Fl)-0018 10115 1800

* UPDATE NO. 4 ON ICRC ACTIVITIES IN THE GULF
* 15 JANUARY 1991

"GVW-86 첨부"

* ICRC PREPAREDNESS FOR POSSIBLE NEEDS IN THE GULF

* AS INDICATED IN UPDATE NO. 3, PLEASE FIND BELOW DETAILS REGARDING
* MEDICAL MATERIAL AND MEDICINES REQUIRED BY THE ICRC IN PREPARATION
* FOR POSSIBLE EMERGENCY MEDICAL INTERVENTION IN THE EVENT OF ARMED
* CONFLICT IN THE GULF.

* PREPARATIONS FOR EMERGENCY MEDICAL ACTIVITIES

* THE BASIC MEDICAL MATERIALS AND MEDICINES REQUIRED FOR EMERGENCY
* MEDICAL INTERVENTION FALL INTO FIVE CATEGORIES:

* 1) BASIC MEDICAL MATERIAL FOR FIVE ICRC FIELD HOSPITAL MODULES
* WITH A CAPACITY OF 100 BEDS EACH.

* 2) BASIC MEDICAL MATERIAL FOR FIVE ICRC MEDICAL TEAMS TO WORK IN
* EXISTING HOSPITAL FACILITIES IN THE REGION, ALSO WITH THE
* CAPACITY FOR 100 BEDS EACH.

* 3) DISPOSABLE MEDICAL MATERIAL AND MEDICINES FOR CATEGORIES 1 AND
* 2 FOR 100 IN-PATIENTS FOR A PERIOD OF ONE MONTH (ASSUMING
* OPERATION AT FULL CAPACITY).

* 4) MEDICAL MATERIAL NEEDED IN TRANSIT/RECEPTION CAMP MODULES
* FOR DISPLACED PERSONS (TWO DISPENSARIES FOR EVERY 40,000
* DISPLACED PERSONS FOR A PERIOD OF ONE MONTH).

* 5) MEDICAL MATERIAL NEEDED TO ASSIST OTHER EXISTING MEDICAL
* STRUCTURES SUCH AS DISPENSARIES, FIRST AID POSTS, TRIAGE
* CENTRES AND HOSPITALS.

* NATIONAL SOCIETIES' RESPONSE

* THE ICRC THANKS THE NATIONAL SOCIETIES FOR INFORMATION REGARDING
* THE KIND OF ASSISTANCE THEY ARE ABLE TO PROVIDE IN CASE OF EMER-
* GENCY AND THE DELIVERY TIMES. ONCE AGAIN, NATIONAL SOCIETY PER-
* SONNEL AND ASSISTANCE SHOULD BE PREPARED BUT NOT PUT ON STANDBY
* NOR DISPATCHED UNTIL FURTHER NOTICE FROM THE ICRC.

* AN APPENDIX OF 8 PAGES IS ATTACHED FOR NATIONAL SOCIETIES' INFOR-
* MATION GIVING TECHNICAL DETAILS FOR REQUESTED MEDICAL MATERIAL
* AND MEDICINES.

* FOR FURTHER INFORMATION PLEASE CONTACT SO/REX OR OP/MED.
* BEST REGARDS,

* CHRISTIAN KORNEVALL
* SO/REX, ICRC, GENEVA

* NNNN

* 
415519 KOGE CH
* 414226V CCR CH

1-1

TOTAL P.01

0091

| 분류기호 문서번호 | 국기 20335- | 협조문용지 ( 2181-2 ) | 결 재 | 담당 | 과장 | 국장 |
|---|---|---|---|---|---|---|
| 시행일자 | 1991. 1. 17. | | | | | |
| 수 신 | 중근동과장 | 발 신 | 국제기구과장 (서 명) | | | |
| 제 목 | 걸프만사태 관련 국제적십자사(ICRC) 구호 계획 | | | | | |

1. GVW-0084, GVW-0086(91.1.15) 관련입니다.

2. 주제네바 대표부가 송부한 페르시아만 전쟁 발발에 대비한 국제적십자사 (ICRC)의 활동계획에 관한 자료에 의하면, ICRC는 전쟁지역 난민 수용을 위해서 총 300,000명 수용 가능한 Camp 및 야전병원을 설치할 계획이라 합니다.

3. 아국 교포가 걸프만 전쟁지역에 상금 잔류하고 있음을 감안하여 유사시 상기 ICRC 설치 Camp로 피난하는 방법도 고려할 수 있다고 사료하는바, 귀과의 걸프만사태 대응처리시 참고하시기 바랍니다. 끝

0092

| 분류기호 문서번호 | 국기20335- 11 | 협조문용지 ( 2181-2 ) | 결 재 | 담당 | 과장 | 국장 |
|---|---|---|---|---|---|---|
| 시행일자 | 1991. 1. 17. | | | | | |
| 수 신 | 중근동과장 | 발 신 | 국제기구과장 (서 명) | | | |
| 제 목 | 걸프만사태 관련 국제적십자사(ICRC) 구호 계획 | | | | | |

1. GVW-0084, GVW-0086(91.1.15) 관련입니다.

2. 주제네바 대표부가 송부한 페르시아만 전쟁 발발에 대비한 국제적십자사(ICRC)의 활동계획에 관한 자료에 의하면, ICRC는 전쟁지역 난민 수용을 위해서 총 300,000명 수용 가능한 Camp 및 야전병원을 설치할 계획이라 합니다.

3. 아국 고포가 걸프만 전쟁지역에 상금 잔류하고 있음을 감안하여 유사시 상기 ICRC 설치 Camp로 피난하는 방법도 고려할 수 있다고 사료하는바, 귀과의 걸프만사태 대응처리시 참고하시기 바랍니다. 끝

0093

<u>페르시아만 사태관련 ICRC 활동계획 및 아국 지원방안 검토</u>

1. 페르시아만 사태에 대비한 ICRC의 활동 현황

o Task Force 구성 :

페만의 전쟁 발발시 즉각 구호활동을 전개하기 위한 구체적 계획 수립을 위해 ICRC 본부에 Task Force 구성

o 구호반 구성 :

전쟁 발발시 구호활동에 즉각 동원될 수 있는 전문인력 약130여명을 페만 인근국에 배치

o 구호물자 동원 :

- 30,000명을 수용할 수 있는 Camp와 5,000명 수용의 임시 Camp를 건설할 수 있는 물자를 기 확보함
- 전쟁 발발시 30,000 수용 가능한 Camp 8개를 건설할 계획이며 이에 필요한 의약품, 텐트, 담요등의 물자 수요를 구체적으로 파악, 각국 적십자위원회에 지원 요청
- 5명의 의료진과 100개의 침상을 갖춘 야전병원 5동을 설치할 계획임.
- 구호물자 및 인원 수송을 위해 DC-9, King-Air B 200등 2대의 비행기를 대기중임.

o 각국 적십자 위원회에 대한 지원 요청

- ICRC는 상기 계획에 의거 각 적십자 위원회에 인원 및 물자의 지원을 요청하고, 전쟁 발발로 구체적인 요청이 있을때까지 인원 및 물자를 동원, 대기할 것을 당부

| 공람 | 국제기구과 | 6월 일 | 담 당 | 과 장 | 국 장 | 차관보 | 차 관 | 장 관 |
|---|---|---|---|---|---|---|---|---|
| | | | 오영주 | (서명) | (서명) | | | |

0094

2. 아국 지원현황

o 정부차원

- 외무부는 페르시아만 사태 지원금중 $30,000을 ICRC의 페르시아만 활동 지원금으로 지원(90.12)

o 대한적십자사

- ICRC 요청에 의거 전쟁 발발시 의료품을 지원할 예정

3. 검토의견

o 정부가 ICRC 구호사업에 직접 개입한 사례

- 아르메니아 지진사태($600,000 지원) 및 루마니아 자유화시위 ($200,000 및 의료품 지원)때 북방외교의 일환(당시 양국과 미수교 상태)으로 정부가 직접 개입하여 한적을 통해 ICRC에 지원한 바 있음.

o 하기 이유로 걸프만사태에 관련한 정부 차원의 ICRC 지원건은 당분간 관망하는 것이 바람직함.

- 현재 ICRC가 각국 적십자사를 상대로 지원을 요청하고 있는점. (한적은 상기 요청에 따라, 전쟁 발발시 의료품 지원을 계획중에 있음)

- 이미 $30,000을 아국 명의로 지원한점

o 전쟁 발발이후 사태 진전에 따라 아국정부도 참여할 필요가 있는 국제적 지인 움직임이 있을 경우 인도적 견지에서 주요 우방국과 보조를 맞추는 지원사업을 전개할 수 있음. 끝

0095

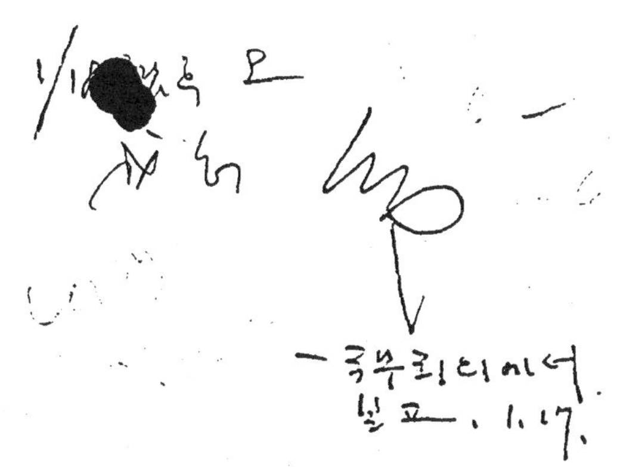

# 「페」灣事態 特別對策委員會 運營方案

사본: 관계국
기획관리실
미주국
영사교민국
국제경제국
국제기구국
통상국

1991. 1. 17

國務總理 行政調整室

0096

## 1. 페灣事態 特別對策 委員會

가. 構　　成

o 委員長 : 國務總理
o 委員(20) : 경제기획원, 통일원, 외무, 내무, 재무, 국방,
　　법무, 상공, 동자, 건설, 보사, 노동, 교통,
　　환경처, 공보처 장관, 안기부장, 비상기획위원장,
　　경제수석비서관, 서울특별시장, 행정조정실장(간사)

나. 機　　能

o 汎政府次元의 「페」灣事態 特別對策 樹立
o 部處別 重要對策 推進狀況 点檢.調整

다. 運　　營

o 戰爭 展開狀況에 따라 수시개최

## 2. 페灣事態 特別對策 實務委員會

가. 構　　成

o 委員長 : 國務總理 行政調整室長
o 委　員(20) : 경제기획원, 통일원, 외무, 내무, 재무, 국방,
　　법무, 상공, 동자, 건설, 보사, 노동, 교통,
　　환경처, 공보처 차관, 안기부제2차장, 비상기획
　　위원회 부위원장, 청와대 경제비서관,
　　서울특별시 부시장, 국무총리실 제2조정관(간사)

나. 機　　能

o 部處別 特別對策 推進狀況 点檢
o 特別對策 推進過程上 問題点 實務協議 調整
o 外交.安保, 經濟, 社會紀綱, 弘報 등 4個分野別 對策班
　構成.運營

0097

다. 分野別 對策班의 主要業務

< 外交.安保分野 >

o 外交網 非常體制 稼動 및 僑民 保護.撤收 措置
o 早期警報 및 戰場監視活動 增加
o 指揮統制體制 定期的 点檢
o 긴밀한 韓·美 情報交流體制 維持

< 經濟 分野 >

o 1段階 에너지 消費節約 對策 實施
o 2段階 에너지 消費節約 細部推進對策의 段階的 實施
o 주요 生必品 買占賣惜 단속반 稼動 및 政府備蓄物資 放出
o 주요 生必品 및 工産品 最高價格制 實施 檢討
o 輸出貨物 船積 圓滑化 및 主要 原資材 確保對策 實施

< 社會紀綱 確立 分野 >

o 社會雰圍氣 鎭靜을 위한 社會 주체별 行動指針 發表 및 國民協調 당부
o 不動産 投機, 料金 不當引上, 買占·賣惜등 經濟事犯 集中團束
o 公職紀綱 確立 및 公明選擧 對策 推進

< 弘報 對策 分野 >

o TV·新聞등 매스콤, 班常會를 통한 國民弘報 實施
o 페灣事態의 敎訓, 정부의 對應策의 主要 內容, 國民각자가 할 일 等
o 國務總理의 각계 指導層 人士와의 懇談會 開催
  - 國民運動 團體長, 言論界, 宗敎界, 經濟界 등
o 國務總理의 前方部隊 視察·激勵 및 弘報
o 狀況展開 및 政府의 對備 態勢에 대한 記者 會見
  - 安保狀況 및 對應姿勢 弘報

0098

3. 페灣事態 綜合狀況室 運營

가. 構　成

ㅇ 室　長 : 국무총리실 제2행정조정관
(부실장 : 경과심의관)

ㅇ 班員(20) : 총리실 과장 5명(분과반장), 사무관 5명,
관계부처 파견 공무원 10명 (사무관급)

* 派遣勤務者 차출에 대한 關係部處의 協調必要

나. 機　能

ㅇ 페灣事態 動向 및 關係部處 特別對策 推進狀況 点檢

ㅇ 主要狀況 수시보고

다. 運　營

ㅇ 傘下에 5個 분과반을 構成하여 分野別 推進狀況 點檢
- 綜合, 外交.安保, 經濟, 社會紀綱, 弘報 等

ㅇ 狀況 終了時까지 常時運營

0099

〈參考〉「페」灣 事態 非常對應 體制圖

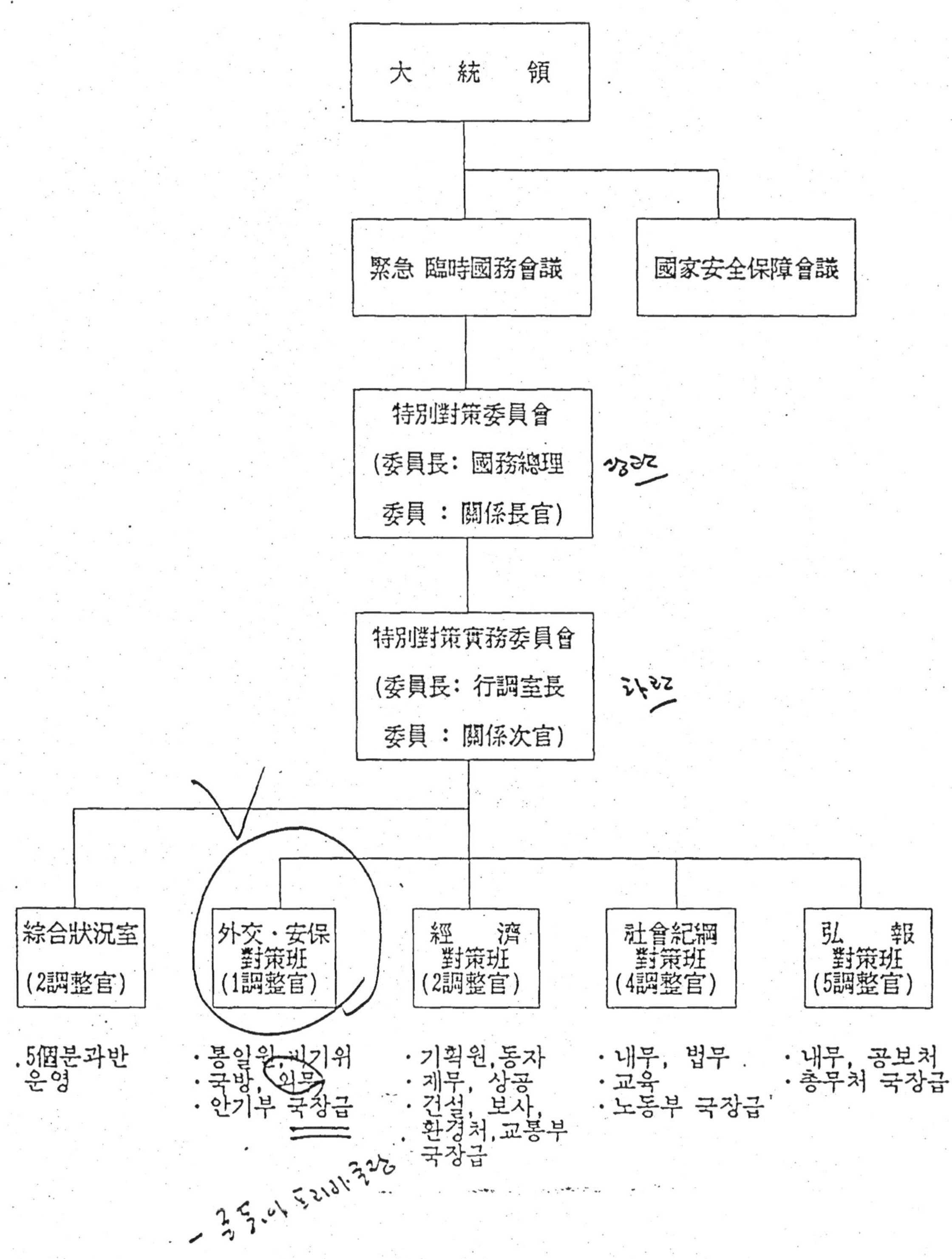


0100

# ※ 非常對應 機構 構成方案

## 페灣事態 特別對策 委員會

o 委員長 : 國務總理

o 위　원(19) : 경제기획원, 통일원, 외무, 내무, 재무, 국방, 법무, 상공, 동자, 건설, 보사, 노동, 교통, 공보처 장관, 안기부장, 비상기획위원장, 경제수석 비서관, 서울특별시장, 행정조정실장(간사)

## 페灣事態 特別對策 實務委員會

o 委員長 : 國務總理 行政調整室長

o 위　원(19) : 경제기획원, 통일원, 외무, 내무, 재무, 국방, 법무, 상공, 동자, 건설, 보사, 노동, 교통, 공보처 차관, 안기부제2차장, 비상기획위원회 부위원장, 청와대 경제비서관, 서울특별시 부시장, 국무총리실 제2조정관(간사)

※ 종합상황실 및 4개 분과대책반(외교 · 안보, 경제, 사회기강, 홍보) 구성 · 운영

## 페灣事態 綜合狀況室

o 構成(19)

- 실　장 : 국무총리실 제2행정조정관 (부실장 : 2행조실 담당 심의관)
- 반원(17) : 총리실 과장 5명(분과반장), 사무관 5명,
  관계부처 파견 공무원 7명(사무관급 5, 여직원 2)

o 運營

- 산하에 5個 분과반 構成하여 分野別 推進狀況 點檢
  · 종합, 외교안보, 경제, 사회기강, 홍보
- 戰爭勃發 前에는 總理室 職員만으로 運營(分科班別 每日 1回 會議開催)
- 戰爭勃發 後에는 綜合狀況室 別途確保 · 派遣勤務
- 「페」灣 動向 및 關係部處 推進狀況 日日 點檢 · 報告

- 3 -

0101

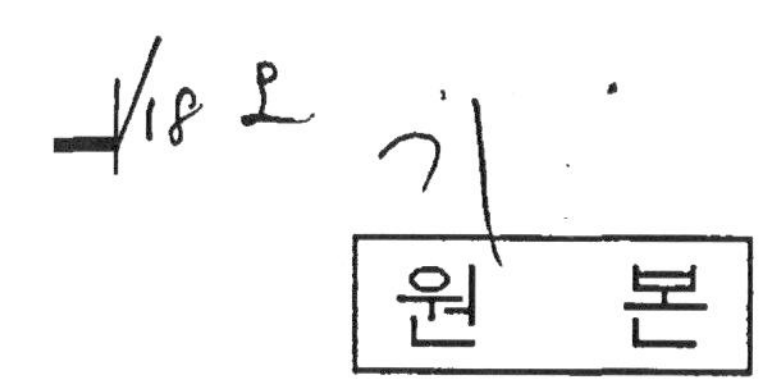

# 외 무 부

종 별 :

번 호 : GVW-0105 일 시 : 91 0117 1810

수 신 : 장관(국기,중근동)

발 신 : 주제네바대사대리

제 목 : 페만 전쟁발발 관련 ICRC 활동

1. 당지 국제적십자위원회( ICRC) 는 1.17 페만에서의 전쟁발발 관련 별첨 I 텔렉스를 통하여 ICRC 가 국제적십자연맹(LRCS) 의 협조를 얻어 취하고 있는 활동에대해설명하면서 각국이 동 활동수행에 필요한 현금을 지원해 줄 것을 요청해 왔으니 참고바람.

2. 표제관련 ICRC 추가자료 ( NO.5A 및 6)를 별첨 II 송부함.

첨부:상기 자료( GVW(F)-0024). 끝

(대사대리 박영우-국장)

| 국기국 | 장관 | 차관 | 1차보 | 2차보 | 중아국 | 중아국 | 정문국 | 청와대 |
|---|---|---|---|---|---|---|---|---|
| 총리실 | 안기부 | 대책반 | | | | | | |

PAGE 1

91.01.18 04:26 CG

외신 1과 통제관

0102

GVW(F)-0024

INTERNATIONAL COMMITTEE OF THE RED CROSS, GENEVA

"GVW-0105 첨부"

(별첨 1)

SPECIAL EMERGENCY APPEAL
FOR THE INTERNATIONAL ACTION
OF THE RED CROSS AND RED CRESCENT
FOR VICTIMS OF WAR IN THE GULF

17 JANUARY 1991

BACKGROUND

* GULF WAR: INTENSE MILITARY FIGHTING FLARED UP IN THE EARLY MORN
* ING HOURS ON 17 JANUARY 1991.

ICRC MANDATE APPLIES

* EXTREMELY CONCERNED ABOUT THE TRAGIC HUMANITARIAN CONSEQUEN
* CES OF THE HOSTILITIES IN THE GULF REGION, THE ICRC SENT OUT A
* NOTE VERBALE ON 17 JANUARY TO THE PARTIES CONCERNED TO REMIND
* THEM OF THE PRINCIPLES AND RULES OF INTERNATIONAL HUMANITARIAN
* LAW, MORE SPECIFICALLY THE GENEVA CONVENTIONS OF 12 AUGUST 1949
* FOR THE PROTECTION OF WAR VICTIMS.

* THIS NOTE VERBALE MADE REFERENCE TO PRINCIPLES AND RULES ON THE
* FOLLOWING SUBJECTS: RESPECT FOR THE CIVILIAN POPULATION, CARE FOR
* WOUNDED, SICK AND SHIPWRECKED MEMBERS OF THE ARMED FORCES,
* RESPECT AND PROTECTION FOR MEDICAL PERSONNEL AND ESTABLISHMENTS,
* HUMANE TREATMENT OF COMBATANTS WHO HAVE LAID DOWN THEIR ARMS, AND
* THE PROHIBITION OF THE USE OF CHEMICAL, BACTERIOLOGICAL, OR
* NUCLEAR WEAPONS. DETAILS OF THESE PRINCIPLES WERE SET OUT IN A
* MEMORANDUM, DATED 30 NOVEMBER 1990, SENT TO THE PARTIES CON
* CERNED.

* BY VIRTUE OF THE MANDATE CONFERRED UPON THE ICRC BY THE INTERNA
* TIONAL COMMUNITY THROUGH THE GENEVA CONVENTIONS OF 1949 AND THE
* TWO ADDITIONAL PROTOCOLS, THE ICRC HAS THE RIGHT AND THE OBLIGA
* TION TO INTERVENE IN THE GULF REGION ON BEHALF OF THE VICTIMS OF
* THIS INTERNATIONAL ARMED CONFLICT AND THE ICRC HAS OFFERED ITS
* SERVICES TO ALL PARTIES CONCERNED AS A NEUTRAL AND INDEPENDENT
* INTERMEDIARY.

CO-ORDINATION

* IN ACCORDANCE WITH THE AGREEMENT BETWEEN THE ICRC AND THE LEAGUE
* OF RED CROSS AND RED CRESCENT SOCIETIES, IN SITUATIONS OF INTER
* NATIONAL OR OTHER CONFLICT, THE ICRC, BY VIRTUE OF THE ROLE OF A
* SPECIFICALLY NEUTRAL AND INDEPENDENT INSTITUTION AND INTERMEDIARY
* CONFERRED UPON IT BY THE GENEVA CONVENTIONS AND THE STATUTES OF
* THE MOVEMENT, SHALL ASSUME THE GENERAL DIRECTION OF INTERNATIONAL
* RED CROSS AND RED CRESCENT ACTIONS.

* THE ICRC, IN CONSULTATION WITH THE LEAGUE, IS ESTABLISHING A GEN
* ERAL PLAN OF ACTION WHICH WILL INCLUDE LEAGUE PROGRAMMES AS THEY
* RELATE TO THE EFFECTS OF THE CONFLICT.

* THE ICRC HAS SET UP A TASK FORCE WHICH INCLUDES THE LEAGUE. WHEN
* EVER NEEDED THE NATIONAL SOCIETIES CONCERNED WILL BE ASSOCIATED.

* A MEMORANDUM OF UNDERSTANDING WAS SIGNED BETWEEN THE ICRC AND THE
* LEAGUE ON 16 JANUARY 1991.

7-1

0103

* ACTIVITIES FOR VICTIMS IN THE GULF

* ICRC EXPATRIATE STAFF ALREADY PRESENT IN THE DELEGATIONS IN THE
* REGION, HAVE BEEN REINFORCED OVER THE LAST FEW DAYS BY 15 DELE
* GATES SENT FROM GENEVA. DELEGATES ARE CURRENTLY LOCATED IN:
*

| | |
|---|---|
| SAUDI ARABIA | 5 |
| BAHRAIN | 2 |
| EGYPT | 1 |
| IRAN | 11 |
| IRAQ | 7 |
| ISRAEL AND THE TERRITORIES OCCUPIED BY ISRAEL | 45 |
| JORDAN | 9 |
| LEBANON | 7 |
| SYRIA | 2 |
| TURKEY | 1 |

* FORTY DELEGATES ARE READY TO LEAVE GENEVA IMMEDIATELY. FIFTY
* ADDITIONAL DELEGATES ARE ON STANDBY IN GENEVA, READY TO LEAVE ON
* SHORT NOTICE. THEY INCLUDE MEDICAL PERSONNEL AND SPECIALISTS IN
* PROTECTION AND TRACING, SANITATION, RELIEF, LOGISTICS AND COM-
* MUNICATIONS.

* THE LEAGUE HAS BEEN SUPPORTING THE JORDAN NATIONAL RED CRESCENT
* SOCIETY IN RUNNING THE TWO CAMPS AT AZRAQ AND THE EGYPTIAN AND
* YEMEN RED CRESCENT SOCIETIES WITH THEIR PROGRAMMES FOR RETURNEES.
* THE LEAGUE HAS ALSO APPEALED FOR ASSISTANCE TO INCREASE THE PRE
* PAREDNESS OF THE TURKISH RED CRESCENT SOCIETY AND THE KUWAIT RED
* CRESCENT SOCIETY (BASED IN BAHRAIN). IT HAS RECEIVED A SIMILAR
* REQUEST FROM THE SYRIAN ARAB RED CRESCENT SOCIETY. THE CONTINUA
* TION AND DEVELOPMENT OF THESE ACTIONS ARE INCLUDED IN THIS
* APPEAL.

* SEVERAL NATIONAL SOCIETIES HAVE ALREADY TAKEN STEPS TO MOBILI
* ZE PERSONNEL AND MATERIAL IN SUPPORT OF THE INTERNATIONAL ACTION
* OF THE RED CROSS AND RED CRESCENT FOR VICTIMS OF WAR IN THE GULF.

* OPERATIONAL OBJECTIVES FOR THE INTERNATIONAL
* ACTION OF THE RED CROSS AND RED CRESCENT

0104

* THE OBJECTIVES FOR INTERVENTION:

* 1. ENSURE PROTECTION AND ASSISTANCE FOR THE WOUNDED AND THE
* SHIPWRECKED. THE ICRC IS PREPARED TO PROVIDE EMERGENCY MEDICAL
* CARE WHERE NEEDS ARE NOT COVERED BY THE PARTIES INVOLVED.

* 2. PROTECT AND ASSIST ALL THOSE CAPTURED OR DETAINED AS A RESULT
* OF THE CONFLICT.

* 3. PROTECT AND ASSIST CIVILIANS IN THE CONFLICT REGION.

* 4. PROTECT AND ASSIST CIVILIANS FLEEING THE CONFLICT REGION.

* 5. ASSIST CIVILIANS WHO HAVE FLED THE CONFLICT REGION TO NEIGH
* BOURING COUNTRIES.

SPECIAL EMERGENCY APPEAL
FOR THE INTERNATIONAL ACTION OF
THE RED CROSS AND RED CRESCENT
FOR VICTIMS OF THE WAR IN THE GULF

SFR. 141 MILLION

* THIS AMOUNT INCLUDES DONATIONS IN KIND AND SERVICES. NATIONAL
* SOCIETIES ARE KINDLY REQUESTED TO SUPPORT THE OPERATIONS IN THE
* GULF WITH PERSONNEL AND DONATIONS IN KIND.

* A DETAILED BUDGET WILL BE PRESENTED TO DONORS ACCORDING TO STAN
* DARD ICRC BUDGET PROCEDURES AS SOON AS POSSIBLE.

* ICRC REPORTING ON OPERATIONS IN THE GULF REGION WILL FOLLOW THE
* STANDARD ICRC REPORTING SYSTEM FOR DONORS: UPDATES, SITREPS,
* ANNUAL REPORT AND AUDITOR'S REPORT.

EMERGENCY OPERATIONAL ACTIVITIES

* THE ABOVE AMOUNT IS BASED ON FIRST AVAILABLE INFORMATION AND ON
* ESTIMATES OF THE NEEDS TO BE COVERED BY RED CROSS AND RED CRES
* CENT OPERATIONS:

* 1. PROTECTION AND TRACING ACTIVITIES FOR POSSIBLY TENS OF THOU SANDS OF PRISONERS OF WAR AND DETAINEES AND MILLIONS OF DISPLACED CIVILIANS. ICRC PROTECTION ACTIVITIES FOR PRISON ERS OF WAR AND DETAINEES INCLUDE PRISON VISITS, REGISTERING OF PRISONERS AND EMERGENCY ASSISTANCE. TRACING ACTIVITIES INCLUDE: HANDLING TRACING REQUESTS, SENDING 'ANXIOUS FOR NEWS' MESSAGES, FAMILY MESSAGES AND REUNITING FAMILIES.

* 2. MEDICAL ACTIVITIES INCLUDING FIELD HOSPITALS WITH CAPACITY TOTALLING 1,000 BEDS, PUBLIC HEALTH SERVICES FOR CIVILIANS, SANITATION AND WATER SUPPLY IN THE INITIAL EMERGENCY PHASE. FOR DETAILS SEE ICRC UPDATES NO. 3 AND 4.

* 3. RELIEF ACTIVITIES DURING THIS PHASE INCLUDE ESTABLISHING CAMPS FOR DISPLACED PERSONS WITHIN AND OUTSIDE CONFLICT AREAS WHICH PROVIDE SHELTER, FOOD, SANITATION AND MEDICAL FIRST AID FOR APPROXIMATELY 300,000 DISPLACED PERSONS. FOR DETAILS SEE ICRC UPDATE NO. 2.

* 4. LOGISTICS, COMMUNICATIONS AND TRANSPORT INCLUDING TWO AIR PLANES ALREADY CHARTERED. FOR DETAILS SEE UPDATE NO. 3.

7-3

0105

* DONORS' RESPONSE

* IN VIEW OF THIS EMERGENCY SITUATION, DONORS ARE KINDLY ASKED TO
* RESPOND WITH PROMPT AND GENEROUS CASH CONTRIBUTIONS TO COVER THE
* COSTS OF THE INTERNATIONAL ACTION OF THE RED CROSS AND RED CRESCENT
* RELATED TO THE GULF CONFLICT.

* FOR FURTHER INFORMATION PLEASE CONTACT SO/REX.

* BEST REGARDS,

* JEAN DE COURTEN
* DIRECTOR OF OPERATIONS
* INTERNATIONAL COMMITTEE OF THE RED CROSS, GENEVA

* ++++
415519 KOGE CH
* 414226X CCR CH
* 17-01-91 10:33

7-4

0106

(별첨 2)

* ICRC UPDATE NO. 5A ON INTERNATIONAL RED CROSS AND RED CRESCENT
* ACTION IN THE GULF
* 17 JANUARY 1991

* RELIEF CAMP MODULES

* THE ICRC WISHES TO CONFIRM THE PLANS FOR EIGHT RELIEF CAMP
* MODULES DESCRIBED IN UPDATE NO. 2.

* EACH CAMP MODULES WILL HAVE TWO DISPENSARY MODULES ATTACHED.
* THE CAMP MODULES WILL BE OPERATED IN THE FOLLOWING MANNER:

| MODULE | NATIONAL SOCIETY - LEAD AGENT | DEGREE OF PREPAREDNESS |
|---|---|---|
| MODULE 1 | DUTCH RED CROSS (WITH SUPPORT FROM BELGIUM AND LUXEMBOURG) | ALERT |
| MODULE 2 | GERMAN RED CROSS | ALERT |
| MODULE 3 | DANISH RED CROSS (WITH SUPPORT FROM NORWAY FINLAND, SWEDEN AND ICELAND) | STANDBY |
| MODULE 4 | ICRC I/JORDAN RC/LEAGUE (STAFF FROM VARIOUS NS) | OPERATIONAL IN AZRAQ |
| MODULE 5 | ICRC II | READY FOR DISPATCH |
| MODULE 6 | ICRC III (WITH SUPPORT FROM VARIOUS NS) | IN PREPARATION |
| MODULE 7 | TO BE ANNOUNCED | PLANNING STAGE |
| MODULE 8 | TO BE ANNOUNCED | PLANNING STAGE |

* THE ICRC REQUESTS REPRESENTATIVES FROM THE LEAD AGENTS OF THE
* ABOVE MENTIONED NATIONAL SOCIETIES TO BE IN GENEVA ON 18 JANUARY
* 1991, BETWEEN 10H-15H. YOU WILL BE INFORMED OF PLANS AS THEY ARE
* FINALIZED.

* UPDATE NO. 5B WITH TECHNICAL INSTRUCTIONS HAS BEEN SENT TO
* THE NATIONAL SOCIETIES CONCERNED.

* FOR FURTHER INFORMATION CONTACT SO/REX OR OP/SEC, (A. LENDORFF).

* BEST REGARDS,

* CHRISTIAN KORNEVALL
* INTERNATIONAL COMMITTEE OF THE RED CROSS, GENEVA

* +++
* ++++
415519 KOGE CH
* 414224 CICR CH
* 17-01-91 14:36

7-5

0107

* ICRC UPDATE NO. 6 ON INTERNATIONAL RED CROSS AND RED CRESCENT
* ACTION IN THE GULF
* 17 JANUARY 1991

* FIELD HOSPITALS AND MEDICAL TEAMS

* THE ICRC CONFIRMS PLANS FOR FIVE ICRC FIELD HOSPITAL MODULES
* WITH A CAPACITY FOR 100 BEDS EACH AND FIVE ICRC MEDICAL TEAMS TO
* WORK IN EXISTING HOSPITAL FACILITIES IN THE REGION ALSO COVERING
* APPROXIMATELY 100 BEDS EACH, FOR TOTAL COVERAGE OF ABOUT 1,000
* BEDS. FOR DETAILS SEE ICRC UPDATES NO. 3 AND 4.

* PERSONNEL

* THE FIELD HOSPITAL MODULES AND MEDICAL TEAMS WILL BE OPERATED IN
* THE FOLLOWING MANNER:

| * TEAM | NATIONAL SOCIETY+ - LEAD AGENT | DEGREE OF PREPAREDNESS |
|---|---|---|
| * TEAM I | FINNISH RC I | ALERT |
| * TEAM II | DANISH I AND JAPANESE RC | ALERT |
| * TEAM III | NORWEGIAN RC | STANDBY |
| * TEAM IV | AUSTRIAN RC | STANDBY |
| * TEAM V | SWEDISH RC | STANDBY |
| * TEAM VI | DUTCH RC | STANDBY |
| * TEAM VII | FINNISH RC II AND OTHERS | IN PREPARATION |
| * TEAM VIII | DANISH RC II AND OTHERS | IN PREPARATION |
| * TEAM IX | MIXED NS PERSONNEL | PLANNING STAGE |
| * TEAM X | MIXED NS PERSONNEL | PLANNING STAGE |

* OTHER NATIONAL SOCIETIES WILL PROVIDE PERSONNEL TO WORK WITH
* THE ABOVE TEAMS.

* DEFINITION OF DEGREE OF PREPAREDNESS TERMS:

* ICRC DEFINITIONS FOR DEGREES OF PREPAREDNESS ARE AS FOLLOWS:

* ALERT = READY TO DEPART IN 24 HOURS

* STANDBY = HAVE PEOPLE READY TO DEPART AT SHORT NOTICE,
* CONTRACT IN ORDER

* IN PREPARATION = INFORM AND BRIEF PEOPLE, PREPARE MATERIALS,
* CONTRACTS PREPARED, SEND INFORMATION TO ICRC

* PLANNING STAGE = MATCH TEAMS, SEND INFORMATION TO ICRC
* HOSPITALS

* 5 MEDICAL TEAMS WITH FIELD HOSPITAL MODULES: 1 NORCROSS ALERT
* 3 NORCROSS STANDBY
* 1 FINCROSS STANDBY

* 5 MEDICAL TEAMS ARE PLANNED FOR WORK IN EXISTING HOSPITAL
* FACILITIES.

1-6 0108

* DISPENSARIES

* THE DEGREE OF PREPAREDNESS FOR DISPENSARY UNITS IS THE SAME AS
* THAT FOR CAMP MODULES, INDICATED IN UPDATE NO. 5A.

* THE ICRC REQUESTS REPRESENTATIVES FROM THE LEAD AGENTS OF THE
* ABOVE MENTIONED TEAMS TO BE IN GENEVA ON 19 JANUARY 1991, FOR
* BRIEFINGS WHICH WILL BE HELD FROM 10H - 17H.

* FOR FURTHER ORGANIZATIONAL INFORMATION PLEASE CONTACT SO/REX.

* CONTACT OP/MED ONLY FOR SPECIFIC MEDICAL/TECHNICAL QUESTIONS.

* BEST REGARDS,

* CHRISTIAN KORNEVALL
* SO/REX, INTERNATIONAL COMMITTEE OF THE RED CROSS, GENEVA

* ++
* ++
41[illegible]19 KOGE CH
* 41[illegible]26A CCR CH
* 17[illegible]1-91 17:32

0109

1-1

TOTAL P.07

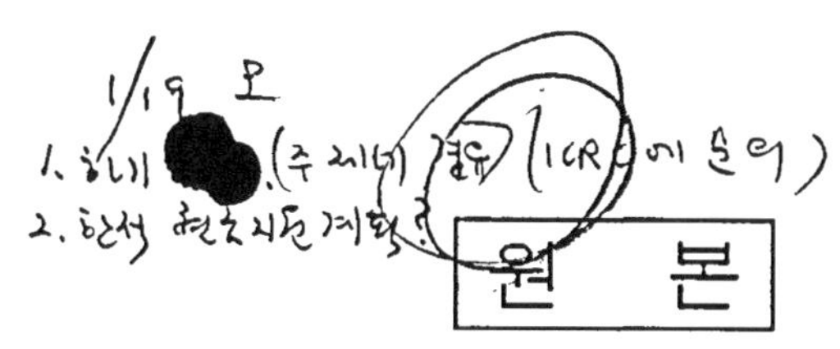

원 본

# 외 무 부

종 별 :

번 호 : GVW-0111 일 시 : 91 0118 1630

수 신 : 장 관 (국기,중근동)

발 신 : 주 제네바 대사대리

제 목 : 페만전쟁관련 ICRC 활동

연: GVW-0105

연호, 표제관련 ICRC 추가자료(NO 7)를 별첨 송부함.

첨부: 상기자료(GVW(F)-0026). 끝

(대사대리 박영우-국장)

국기국 중아국

PAGE 1

91.01.19 03:40 FC

외신 1과 통제관

0110

KOREAN MISSION GENEVA 022 791 0525 P.01

GVW(F)-0626 10118 1630

ICRC UPDATE NO. 7 ON INTERNATIONAL RED CROSS AND RED CRESCENT ACTION IN THE GULF
17 JANUARY 1991

"GVW-111 첨부"

## GENERAL

MILITARY ACTIVITY IN THE AREA IS CONTINUING BY AIR AND ON THE GROUND. NO ACCURATE PICTURE OF HUMANITARIAN NEEDS OF WOUNDED, SHIPWRECKED, PRISONERS OF WAR OR CIVILIANS CAN BE GIVEN AT THIS TIME.

OUR DELEGATION IN BAGHDAD IS IN PLACE, AND IS TRYING TO MAKE SUR VEYS OF THE SITUATION.

ALL OTHER DELEGATIONS IN THE REGION HAVE CONTACTED THE RELEVANT GOVERNMENTS AND NATIONAL SOCIETIES TO STEP UP THEIR PREPAREDNESS FOR EVENTUAL ACTION FOR THE VICTIMS OF THE WAR.

## APPLICATION OF THE ICRC MANDATE

THIS MORNING A NOTE VERBALE WAS SUBMITTED TO ALL PARTIES TO THE CONFLICT TO REMIND THEM OF THEIR OBLIGATIONS UNDER THE GENEVA CONVENTIONS OF 12 AUGUST 1949. AT 4:30 A.M. GENEVA TIME, IN A PRESS CONFERENCE, ICRC PRESIDENT SOMMARUGA SOLEMNLY APPEALED FOR THE OBSERVATION OF THE INTERNATIONAL HUMANITARIAN LAW FOR THE PROTECTION OF VICTIMS OF THE CONFLICT.

## COORDINATION

THE REPRESENTATIVES OF THE LEAGUE WERE INTEGRATED INTO THE ICRC SPECIAL TASK FORCE FOR THE GULF CONFLICT.

## INTERNATIONAL RED CROSS AND RED CRESCENT ACTIVITIES

PROTECTION AND TRACING: THE CENTRAL TRACING AGENCY HAS ESTAB LISHED CONTACT WITH THE ARMED FORCES ENGAGED IN THE CONFLICT AND WITH THEIR NATIONAL INFORMATION BUREAUX TO ASSIST PERSONS PRO TECTED BY THE GENEVA CONVENTIONS.

NATIONAL RED CROSS AND RED CRESCENT SOCIETIES AND ICRC DELEGATES THROUGHOUT THE WORLD HAVE BEEN INFORMED OF THE MEASURES TAKEN SO THAT FAMILIES CAN BE INFORMED ABOUT WHAT HAS BECOME OF RELATIVE
S
WHO ARE IN COUNTRIES WHERE COMMUNICATIONS WITH THE OUTSIDE WORLD HAVE BEEN CUT OFF BY THE FIGHTING.

WHERE POSSIBLE, THE ICRC DELEGATIONS AND THE NATIONAL RED CROSS AND RED CRESCENT SOCIETIES WILL WORK TOGETHER TO PROVIDE A MAIL SERVICE FOR ANY DISPLACED PERSONS OR REFUGEES WHO WISH TO REAS SURE THEIR RELATIVES THAT THEY ARE SAFE.

MEDICAL: ICRC UPDATE NO. 6 SET THE STRUCTURE AND ORGANIZATION OF MEDICAL PREPAREDNESS.

TEAM LEADERS OF SURGICAL UNITS HAVE BEEN CALLED IN FOR SPECIAL BRIEFINGS.

3-1

0111

* NATIONAL SOCIETIES CONFIRMED THAT THEY ARE PREPARED TO RESPOND T
* O
* REQUEST MADE BY THE ABOVE-MENTIONED UPDATE NO. 6.

* A JAPANESE SURGICAL TEAM IS ON ALERT AT GENEVA HEADQUARTERS.

* MEDICAL SHIPMENTS WILL LEAVE SATURDAY FOR BAHRAIN AND TEHERAN.

* THE IRAQI RED CRESCENT HAS APPROACHED THE ICRC IN BAGHDAD
* REQUESTING MEDICAL SUPPLIES.

* RELIEF: NATIONAL SOCIETIES HAVE CONFIRMED THAT THEY ARE PREPARE
* D
* ACCORDING TO THE NEEDS DEFINED IN UPDATE NO. 5A.

* THE NORDIC CAMP MODULE (DANCROSS) HAS BEEN UPGRADED TO ALERT
* STATUS.

* SURVEYS WERE CARRIED OUT FOR THE ESTABLISHMENT OF A CAMP NEAR TH
* E
* IRAN/IRAQ BORDER.

* THE SYRIAN GOVERNMENT HAS REQUESTED THE ICRC TO PROVIDE IMMEDIAT
* E
* CAMP FACILITIES FOR 30-40,000 DISPLACED PERSONS NEAR THE
* SYRIAN/IRAQ BORDER. THE DUTCH RED CROSS MODULE HAS BEEN MOBILIZE
* D
* FOR THIS CAMP.

* THE SYRIAN ARAB RED CRESCENT HAS REQUESTED THE LEAGUE FOR SUPPOR
* T
* FOR THEIR DISPLACED PERSON CENTRES ALONG THE JORDANIAN/SYRIAN
* BORDER. SUBSEQUENTLY, THE LEAGUE WILL COORDINATE WITH THE SYRIAN
* ARAB RED CRESCENT.

* STEPS ARE BEING TAKEN TO SUPPORT THE REQUEST OF THE JORDANIAN RE
* D
* CRESCENT FOR THE UPGRADING OF THE EXISTING FACILITIES AT AZRAK 1
* AND PARTICULARLY AZRAK 2 CAMP. ICRC TRANSIT 1/28 AT THE
* IRAQI/JORDANIAN BORDER IS OPERATIONAL.

* AN ICRC FLIGHT IS SCHEDULED FOR SATURDAY 19 JANUARY TO CARRY
* RELIEF GOODS FROM EUROPE TO TEHERAN FOR THE ESTABLISHMENT OF
* CAMPS FOR DISPLACED PERSONS.

* ANOTHER ICRC AIRCRAFT WITH MAINLY MEDICAL SUPPLIES AND
* ICRC/LEAGUE PERSONNEL ON BOARD WILL ARRIVE ON SATURDAY 19 JANUAR
* Y
* IN BAHRAIN.

3-2

0112

* PERSONNEL

* ICRC DELEGATES WERE TRAINED, ON FRIDAY/SATURDAY, JANUARY 18/19
* ADDITIONAL TEAMS WILL LEAVE FOR BAHRAIN, SAUDI ARABIA, JORDAN AN
* D
* IRAN.

* SUBJECT TO AVAILABILITY OF TRANSPORT, THE LEAGUE IS IMMEDIATELY
* SENDING LEAGUE DELEGATES TO LIASE WITH THE JORDANIAN RED CRESCEN
* T
* SOCIETY AND THE SYRIAN ARAB RED CRESCENT SOCIETY IN PREPARATION
* FOR POSSIBLE MOVEMENTS OF LARGE NUMBERS OF PERSONS. A LEAGUE
* DELEGATE WILL ALSO GO TO BAHRAIN TO LIASE WITH THE BAHRAIN RED
* CRESCENT AND THE KUWAITI RED CRESCENT IN THEIR DISASTER PREPARED
* NESS.

* NATIONAL SOCIETIES HAVE MOBILIZED STAFF TO MEET THE ICRC NEEDS
* FOR MEDICAL AND RELIEF PERSONNEL REQUESTED.

* FINANCE

* THE ICRC LAUNCHED ITS APPEAL FOR SFR. 141 MILLION FOR RED CROSS
* AND RED CRESCENT ACTIVITIES FOR VICTIMS OF THE GULF WAR ON 17
* JANUARY. WE KINDLY ASK DONORS TO ANNOUNCE THEIR CASH CONTRIBU
* TIONS.

* FOR FURTHER INFORMATION, PLEASE CONTACT SO/REX.

* BEST REGARDS,

* CHRISTIAN KORNEVALL
* SO/REX, INTERNATIONAL COMMITTEE OF THE RED CROSS, GENEVA

* +++

* ++++

3-3

TOTAL P.03 0113

1/23 오

# 주 제 네 바 대 표 부

제네(정) 20358-84 　　　　　　　　　　　　1991. 1.18

수신 : 장관

참조 : 국제기구조약국장,중동아프리카국장

제목 : 페만전쟁 관련 ICRC 보도자료

1.17 페르샤만에서의 전쟁발발관련, 동 전쟁관련 국가들에 대해 전쟁희생자에 관한 1949년 제네바의정서 규정을 준수할 것을 촉구하는 내용의 국제적십자위원회(ICRC) 보도자료를 별첨 송부하오니 참고 하시기 바랍니다.

첨부 : 동 보도자료(NO. 1658) 1부. 끝.

주 제 네 바 대

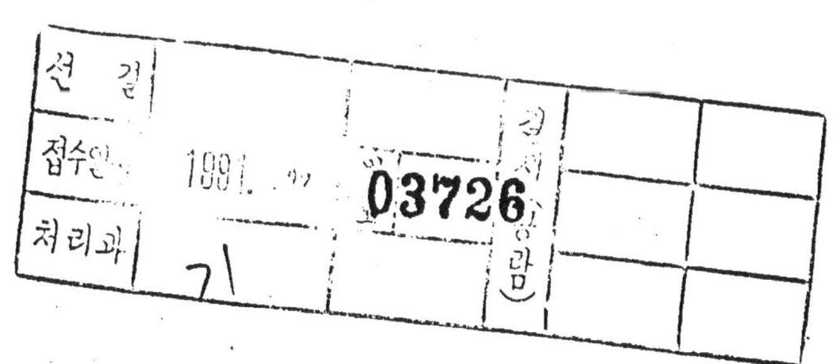

0114

COMITÉ INTERNATIONAL DE LA CROIX-ROUGE

DÉPARTEMENT DE LA COMMUNICATION
19, avenue da la Paix · CH-1202 GENÈVE
Tél. 734 60 01 · Télex 414 226 · Téléfax (022) 734 82 80

COMMUNIQUÉ DE PRESSE

Communiqué de presse No. 1658
17 janvier 1991

**GUERRE DU GOLFE : LE CICR RAPPELLE AUX ETATS LEURS OBLIGATIONS**

Genève (CICR) - A l'heure où la région du Golfe s'embrase, le Comité international de la Croix-Rouge (CICR) rappelle solennellement à toutes les Parties au conflit les engagements qu'elles ont pris en tant que signataires des Conventions de Genève de 1949 pour la protection des victimes de la guerre.

Un tel engagement de la part des Etats impliqués est particulièrement requis et attendu dans un contexte où des développements dramatiques pour la population civile peuvent être redoutés; en effet, les hostilités se déroulent dans un environnement rendant très périlleuse une réelle protection des civils exposés aux actes de guerre.

Compte tenu de ces circonstances, le CICR a insisté auprès des Etats impliqués, dans une note verbale remise ce jour, sur l'absolue nécessité de prendre, dans la conduite des hostilités, toutes les précautions visant à épargner les populations civiles. Il a par ailleurs rappelé que les militaires blessés, malades ou naufragés doivent être secourus et que les combattants mis hors de combat doivent être traités avec humanité. Quant au personnel et aux installations sanitaires, ils doivent en tout temps être respectés et protégés.

De plus, le CICR réitère aux Parties l'interdiction, réglée par le droit international humanitaire, d'utiliser des armes chimiques et bactériologiques et leur enjoint de ne pas avoir recours à l'arme atomique, incompatible avec ce droit. De manière générale, les armes de destruction massive frappant sans discrimination causent des ravages irréparables au sein de la population civile, qui doit être tenue à l'écart des combats.

Le **Comité international de la Croix-Rouge** (CICR) est, avec la Ligue des Sociétés de la Croix-Rouge et du Croissant-Rouge et les Sociétés nationales de la Croix-Rouge et du Croissant-Rouge reconnues, l'une des trois composantes du Mouvement international de la Croix-Rouge et du Croissant-Rouge. Institution humanitaire indépendante, le CICR est l'organe fondateur de la Croix-Rouge. Intermédiaire neutre en cas de conflits armés et de troubles, il s'efforce d'assurer, de sa propre initiative ou en se fondant sur les Conventions de Genève, protection et assistance aux victimes de guerres internationales et civiles, des troubles et tensions internes, apportant ainsi sa contribution à la paix dans le monde.

0115

Le CICR confirme qu'il est prêt à s'acquitter des tâches qui lui sont dévolues par les Conventions de Genève et par les Statuts du Mouvement international de la Croix-Rouge et du Croissant-Rouge, et il rappelle qu'il se met à la disposition des Parties intéressées en sa qualité d'intermédiaire neutre et indépendant. A cette fin, l'institution humanitaire doit plus particulièrement être mise en mesure d'accéder aux victimes du conflit telles que les prisonniers de guerre et les civils nécessitant protection et assistance. En outre, elle peut être appelée à remplir toute autre tâche requérant l'intervention d'un intermédiaire neutre ou que son droit d'initiative humanitaire, reconnu par la communauté des Etats, lui ferait proposer.

Enfin, le Comité international de la Croix-Rouge en appelle à toutes les Parties impliquées pour que soient créées les conditions nécessaires à la solution du conflit par le dialogue et non par les armes.

++++

0116

| 분류번호 | 보존기간 |
|---|---|
| | |

# 발 신 전 보

번 호 : WGV-0098 910119 1414 DP 종별 :

수 신 : 주 제네바 //대사. /총영사 대사대리

발 신 : 장 관 (국기)

제 목 : 페만전쟁 관련 ICRC 활동

대 : GVW-0111

1. 91.1.18 현재 이라크에 잔류중인 현대건설 근로자 22명의 소재 및 생사 여부가 확인되지 않고 있는바, 본부는 CNN TV 및 이라크 인근 국가를 통해 소재 파악등을 문의하고 있으나 진전이 없는 상황임.

2. 대호 자료에 의하면 ICRC가 동지역 난민들의 소재등을 파악하여 가족에게 알려주는 조치를 취할 것이라는바, ICRC 관계자에게 상기 현대건설 근로자들의 소재 및 안전여부를 파악해 줄것을 요청하고, 결과 보고바람.

3. 현대 본사측은 전쟁 발발시 아라크 잔류 근로자는 (바그다드 남서쪽 25Km Al Shaab 지역, 이라크사업본부 C주소: House No 98, G4QaQ 7, Mahallaal 910, Hai Al-Ryadh, Bagdad Tel: 443-4835 443-7141) 또는 바그다드 동북쪽 60Km 지점 BAQUBA 소재 현대건설 하청농장에 피신하도록 사전 지시한 바 있다 하며, 동 근로자와의 교신(이라크 공사비 국장 통해)은 1.16부터 두절되었다 함을 참고바람.

4. 상기 근로자 22명 영문 성명은 다음과 같음.

/계 속/

중동아프리카국장 [signature]

| 보 안 통 제 | [signature] |
|---|---|

| 앙 고 재 | 91 년 1 월 19 일 | 국기과 | 기안자 성명 | 과 장 | 국 장 | 차 관 | 장 관 |
|---|---|---|---|---|---|---|---|
| | | | 오영주 | [signature] | 전결 | | [signature] |

외신과통제

0117

| | | | |
|---|---|---|---|
| 1) | Kim Chong Hoon | 2) | Kim Kyu Moon |
| 3) | Kim Hyo Suk | 4) | Moon Dong Lak |
| 5) | Baek Chong Ho | 6) | Kim Moo Woong |
| 7) | Park Hyo Choong | 8) | Lee Chil Sung |
| 9) | Kim Han Taek | 10) | Lim Chin Soo |
| 11) | Yang Dong soo | 12) | Cho Sung Chul |
| 13) | Lim Poong Ho | 14) | Kim Myung Kyun |
| 15) | Chung Woon Boong | 16) | Kim Bong Kil |
| 17) | Lee Young Il | 18) | Lee Hyong Kyu |
| 19) | Park Chun Soo | 20) | Lee Man Ho |
| 21) | Lee Kyung Ryoil | 22) | Lee Young Chul. 끝 |

(국제기구조약국장 문동석)

0118

91. 1. 19. <조선>. 18면

# 通信두절…「現代」22명 所在불명

◇18일 오후 서울 종로구 계동 현대그룹사옥 6층 현대건설 이라크 대책본부사무실에서 직원들이 이라크 잔류근로자 가족들의 문의전화를 받는등 바쁘게 움직이고 있다. 〈사진=金桂昊기자〉

## 이라크서 16일 최종交信

### 회사、연락재개총력…가족들"애간장"

### 제3国 근로자 84명도 함께 있는듯

이라크에 남아있는 현대건설 직원및 근로자 22명의 소재와 생사여부가 전쟁 발발 이틀째인 18일까지 전혀확인되지않고 있어 회사관계자들과 가족들이 애태우고 있다.

현대건설측은전쟁이시작되기 전날인16일 저녁 이들22명이 한곳에 집결한 것을 확인, 철수를 지시했으나 17일 공습이 시작된이후 통신이끊겨 이들이 어떤 상황에 처해있는지 알 수 없다고말했다.

현대건설측은 이에따라 17일밤 자체통신시설을 갖추고 바그다드에 머물고 있는 미국CNN TV에 잔류근로자들의 소재파악을 부탁하는 한편, 요르단 바레인 이란 사우디아라비아등 인접 중동국가의 한국공관과 지사등을 통해 연락을 시도하고 있다.

현대건설측은 그러나 이날 오후까지 CNN 측으로부터 아무런 연락도 받지 못했으며, 인접국으로부터도 별다른 정보를얻지못했다고말했다.

현대건설 서울본사 대책본부(본부장 河五文전무·51)는 잔류근로자들이 바그다드에서 북쪽으로 30㎞쯤 떨어진 압샵의 이라크 사업본부(본부장 金鍾勳이사·50)에 아직까지 남아있을 가능성이 가장 큰 것으로 보고있다.

이러한 추정은 16일 저녁 서울 본사와의 마지막연락당시 근로자들이 모두 이곳에 집결해 있었고 이란국경까지의 거리가 2백㎞, 요르단국경까지가 6백㎞여서 어느쪽으로든 철수를 시작했다면 이미 도착했어야 한다는 판단에 따른 것이다.

일부관계자들은 바그다드에서 동북쪽으로 70㎞쯤 떨어진 바쿠바의 현대건설하청업체농장에 대피해있을 가능성도 있을것으로 보고 있다.

그러나 압샵의 본부건물이 이란-이라크8년전쟁속에서 한번의 공습도 받지 않을 정도로 안전한 곳에 있는데다 방공호등 대피시설이 마련돼 있어 위험을 무릅쓰고 바쿠바로 옮겼을 가능성은 희박한 것으로 보인다.

대책본부는 상황이 호전될 경우 이들이 거리가 비교적 가까운 이란쪽의 철수경로를 택할 것으로 보고 李在鎬해외업부본부이사(59)와 현대종합상사 테헤란지사직원 2명을 이란국경 코스라비에보내 이라크잔류근로자들을 기다리고 있다고 말했다.

현대건설측은 지난해 8월초 이라크의 쿠웨이트침공이후 8백여명의 현지근로자들의 철수를 서둘러왔으나 이라크측이 공사의 중요성을들어 책임자및 하자보수요원들을 잔류시켜달라고 요청, 개전까지 22명이 남게된것이라고 말했다.

회사측은 이들 근로자들은 지난 16일 이라크정부로부터 출국비자를 발급받아 언제든지 출국할수 있다고 말했다.

그러나 이라크여성과 결혼한 朴然重씨(36)와 李英哲씨(44)등 2명은 출국을 포기한 것으로 알려졌다. 현대건설은 전쟁발발이후 잔류직원및 근로자들의 가족에게 전화를 걸거나 직원들을집으로 직접 보내 안심시키고있다.

대책본부는 현대와 근로계약을 맺고 경비원등으로 일하던 방글라데시인등 제3국인은 모두 84명이라고 밝히고 이들도 압샵에서 현대 근로자들과 함께 지내고 있는 것으로 보인다고 말했다.

〈李東翰기자〉

0119

1/21 오 기

원 본

# 외 무 부

종 별 :

번 호 : GVW-0118 일 시 : 91 0119 2100

수 신 : 장관(국기)

발 신 : 주 제네바대사대리

제 목 : 페만전쟁 관련 ICRC 활동

대: WGV-0098

1. 금 1.19(토) 당관 김종일 서기관은 ICRC 의 TRACING 담당관 (MRS.CAGNEUX)과 접촉, 대호상황을 설명하고 ICRC 가 이라크 잔류 현대건설 근로자 22명의 소재및 안전여부를 파악해 줄것을 요청하였음. (동 22명 명단도 전달함)

2. CAGNEUX 담당관은 현지사정을 감안할때 상기 근로자들의 소재를 추적하기는어려울것으로 보이나 바그다드 주재 ICRC 대표단과 연락을 취하여 필요한 조치를하도록 하겠다고 말하였는바, 진전사항 추보 예정임.

끝.

(대사대리 박영우-국장)

| 국기국 | 장관 | 차관 | 1차보 | 2차보 | 미주국 | 중아국 | 정문국 | 청와대 |
|---|---|---|---|---|---|---|---|---|
| 총리실 | 안기부 | 대책반 | | | | | | |

상황실

PAGE 1

91.01.20 08:15 DA

외신 1과 통제관

0120

| 분류기호 문서번호 | 마그20005-9 | 협 조 문 용 지 ( ) | 결재 | 심의관 | 과 장 | 국 장 |
|---|---|---|---|---|---|---|
| | | | | 담 당 | | |
| 시행일자 | 1991. 1.21. | | | | | |
| 수 신 | 국제기구조약국장 | 발 신 | 중동아프리카국장(서명) | | | |
| 제 목 | 걸프사태 관련 지원(국제적십자사) | | | | | |

1. 대한적십자사는 걸프사태 관련 국제적십자사에 대한 지원문제를 검토하여 줄것을 요청하여 왔는바, 적의 처리하여 주시기 바랍니다.

2. 걸프사태 관련 기금중에서 지난번 국제적십자사에 지원한 3만불도 계획외 사업이었음에 비추어 동기금에서의 추가지원은 고려하지 않음이 좋겠습니다.

첨 부 : 대한적십자사의 관련공문 1부. 끝.

0121

1505-8일(1)
85. 9. 9 승인 "내가아낀 종이 한장 늘어나는 나라살림"

190㎜×268㎜(인쇄용지 2급 60g/㎡)
가 40-41 1990. 7. 9.

1/23 오

· 정부 ■■ 기지원 · 인적 ■■ 요청 기 [handwritten annotations]

| 분류기호 문서번호 | 마그20005-9 | 협 조 문 용 지 ( ) | 결재 | 심의관 담 당 | 과 장 | 국 장 |
|---|---|---|---|---|---|---|
| 시행일자 | 1991. 1.21. | | | | | |
| 수 신 | 국제기구조약국장 | 발 신 | 중동아프리카국장 (서명) | | | |
| 제 목 | 걸프사태 관련 지원(국제적십자사) | | | | | |

1. 대한적십자사는 걸프사태 관련 국제적십자사에 대한 지원문제를 검토하여 줄것을 요청하여 왔는바, 적의 처리하여 주시기 바랍니다.

2. 걸프사태 관련 기금중에서 지난번 국제적십자사에 지원한 3만불도 계획외 사업이었음에 비추어 동기금에서의 추가지원은 고려하지 않음이 좋겠습니다.

첨 부 : 대한적십자사의 관련공문 1부. 끝.

0122

1505 - 8 일 (1) 190㎜×268㎜(인쇄용지 2급 60g / ㎡)
85. 9. 9 승인 "내가아낀 종이 한장 늘어나는 나라살림" 가 40-41 1990. 7. 9.

# 대 한 적 십 자 사

(755－9301)

한적섭 91 - 204　　　　　　　　　　　1991. 1. 19

수신　외무부장관

참조　중동 아프리카국장

제목　페르시아만 전쟁희생자 지원에따른 의견 문의

1.　지난 1. 17 다국적군의 이라크 공격으로 시작된 페르시아만 전쟁으로 인해 수많은 부상자와 이재민이 발생할 것으로 예상되는 가운데, 적십자 국제위원회(ICRC)는 전쟁 희생자들을 구호하기 위해 SFrs. 141,000,000의 국제지원을 세계 각국에 호소하고 있습니다.

2.　본건과 관련하여 대한적십자사를 통한 정부의 지원 가능성을 신중히 검토하여 주실것을 귀부에 요청하오니 별첨된 서류를 참고 하신후 귀부의 의견을 회시하여 주시기 바랍니다.

첨부　:　적십자국제위원회 국제구호 호소 문서(사본)
　　　　적십자국제위원회 페르시아만 상황보고서 1-7호(사본)

총　　　재　　　김　　　상　　　협

1991. 1. 19　1755

0123

1/23 오

기

원 본

# 외 무 부

→ 일반문서로 재분류

종 별 :

번 호 : GVW-0121 일 시 : 91 0121 1700

수 신 : 장 관(국기,중근동)

발 신 : 주 제네바 대사대리

제 목 : 걸프 전쟁 관련 ICRC 활동

연: GVW-0111

연호, 표제관련 ICRC 추가 자료 (NO. 8,9 및10)를 별첨 송부함.

첨부: 상기 자료.끝

(GVW(F)-28)

(대사대리 박영우-국장)

| 국기국 | 장관 | 차관 | 1차보 | 2차보 | 중아국 | 정문국 | 청와대 | 총리실 |
|---|---|---|---|---|---|---|---|---|
| 안기부 | | | | | | | | |

PAGE 1

91.01.22 16:07 WG

외신 1과 통제관

0124

1/23 오
기

| 관리 번호 | 91-24 |
|---|---|

# 외 무 부

종 별 : 긴 급

번 호 : GVW-0130 일 시 : 91 0122 1700

수 신 : 장관(중근동,국기)

발 신 : 주 제네바 대사대리

제 목 : 쿠웨이트 잔류 아국교민 소재 파악

대: WGV-0112

연: GVW-1529(90.8.8)

1. 금 1.22(화) 당관 김종일 서기관은 ICRC 의 TRACING 담당관(MRS.CAGNEUX)과 접촉, 대호 상황을 설명하고 ICRC 가 쿠웨이트 잔류 아국인 교민 9 명의 소재 및 안전여부를 파악해 줄것을 요청하였음.(동 9 명 명단도 전달)

2. 이에대해 CAGNEUX 담당관은 상금 쿠웨이트에는 ICRC DELEGATION 이 주재하고 있지 않으므로(상세는 연호 참조), ICRC 로서도 별다른 조치를 취할 수 없는 상황이라고 말하면서, ICRC 로서는 일단 상기 9 명의 명단을 접수하되 ICRC DELEGATION 이 쿠웨이트에 주재한 이후에야 동인들의 소재파악을 위한 활동을 할수 있을 것이라고 말하였음.

3. 당관 김서기관이 ICRC DELEGATION 이 언제쯤 쿠웨이트에 주재할 수 있을것으로 전망하느냐고 질문한데 대해, CAGNEUX 담당관은 현재로서는 어떠한 전망도 할수 없다고 답변하였는바, 본건 진전 있는대로 추보 예정임.

4. 한편 IOM 은 걸프사태 이후 쿠웨이트, 이라크 주변국가에서 외국인 철수를 지원하여 왔으며 쿠웨이트, 이라크에는 IOM 직원이 주재하고 있지않아 상기 아국교민 소재 파악은 불가능하다고 함. 끝.

(대사대리 박영우-국장)

예고:91.6.30 일반

일반문서로 재분류(1991 . 6 .30 .)

중아국 장관 차관 1차보 2차보 국기국

PAGE 1

91.01.23 08:41

외신 2과 통제관 BW

0125

91. 1. 23. 〈조선〉. 23면

## 적십자사 걸프戰난민 구호

# 20萬弗 지원키로

대한적십자사는 걸프전쟁이 장기화할 조짐을 보이고 있고 미국등 다국적군과 이라크군과의 충돌로 사상자가 속출함에 따라 국제적십자사를 통해 부상자치료 및 난민구호활동에 적극 참여키로 했다.

대한적십자사는 이에따라 구호자금지원을 공식 요청해온 국제적십자위원회(ICRC)에 답신을 보내는 한편 총20만달러규모의 구호기금 마련에 들어갔다.

22일 대한적십자사 관계자에 따르면, 지난17일 걸프전쟁 발발직후 스위스제네바에 본부를 둔 국제적십자위원회로부터 긴급호소전문을 접수했으며, 전문은 대한적십자사가 현지에서의 구호사업에 착수한 국제적십자위원회의 활동에 적극동참해 줄 것을 공식요청했다는 것이다. 대한적십자사는 이 전문을 입수한 직후 긴급회의를 열어 국제적십자위원회의 요청에 응하기로 결정, 20만달러규모의 구호자금과 의약품을 지원해주기로 했다.

적십자사측은 현재 중동에 진출해있는 건설업체등과 정부보조금등으로 구호자금을 마련하는 방안을 검토중인것으로 알려졌다.

0126

281J

# 기 안 용 지

| 분류기호 문서번호 | 국기20335- | (전화 : 720-4050 ) | 시 행 상 특별취급 | |
|---|---|---|---|---|
| 보존기간 | 영구 . 준영구. 10. 5 . 3 . 1. | 장 관 | | |
| 수 신 처 보존기간 | | | | |
| 시행일자 | 91. 1. 24. | | | |

| 보조기관 | | 협조기관 | | 문서통제 |
|---|---|---|---|---|
| 국장 | 전 결 | | 중동·아프리카국장 | 1991. 1. 24 |
| 과장 | | | | |
| 기안책임자 | 오영주 | | | 발 송 인 |

| 경 유 수 신 참 조 | 대한적십자사총재 | 발신명의 | | 1991. 1. 24 |
|---|---|---|---|---|
| 제 목 | 걸프사태 관련 ICRC 지원에 대한 의견 회신 | | | |

1. 귀사 공문 91-204(91.1.19) 및 당부 공문 국기 20347-63893(90.12.28) 관련입니다.

2. 상기 당부 공문으로 통보하였듯이, 정부는 국제적십자사(ICRC)의 요청에 의거, 걸프사태 관련한 ICRC 사업에 정부의 걸프 지원금중 3만 미불을 기지원한바 있는 바, 정부예산으로 ~~귀사가 요청한 정부의~~ 추가 지원은 불가함을 알려드리니 참고하시기 바랍니다. 끝

0127

원 본

암호수신

# 외 무 부

종 별 :

번 호 : GVW-0173　　　　일 시 : 91 0125 1900

수 신 : 장관(국기,중근동)

발 신 : 주 제네바 대사대리

제 목 : 이라크 잔류교민 소재파악

대: WGV-0098

연: GVW-0118

대호, 이라크 잔류 현대건설 근로자 22 명의 소재 파악 관련 금 1.25(금) 당관 김종일 서기관이 ICRC 의 TRACING 담당관 (MRS.CAGNEUX) 에게 진전사항을 문의한바, ICRC 는 1.21(월) 동 22 명 명단을 ICRC 자체 체널을 통하여 바그다드주재 ICRC DELEGATION 에 발송조치 하였다고 말하고 바그다드주재 DELEGATION 으로 부터 회답이 있는대로 결과를 알려주겠다고 말하였기 중간 보고함. 끝

(대사대리 박영우-국장)

국기국　중아국

PAGE 1　　　　91.01.26　07:26

외신 2과　통제관 BT

0128

# 외 무 부

종 별 :

번 호 : IRW-0075 일 시 : 91 0125 2240

수 신 : 장관(비상대책본부장,중근동,노동부,건설부,기정)

발 신 : 주 이란 대사

제 목 : 현대 근로자 철수

1.기보고한 9인의 현대 근로자들은 전원 건강하며 명단은 하기와 같음.

김종훈, 김무웅, 임동호, 백정호, 문동남, 김효석, 김봉길, 임진두, 김명균.

또한 28인의 방글라데시 근로자도 현재 박타란에 체재중임.

2.잔류 현대 직원 13인은 이라크내에 안전하게 있으며, 이중 현지인과 결혼한 2인을 제외한 12인도 곧 대피할 것이라고 함.

3.당관에서 파견된 홍충웅 영사는 금 1.25.21:00 이란으로 대피한 9인의 현대직원과 면담할 예정이며, 이란측으로 부터 이들 9명의 신병을 인수할 예정임.

잔류 현대 직원에 관한 상세한 상황은 21:00 면담후 상세히 보고 하겠음.

끝.

(대사 정경일-국장)

노동부 503-9771 기송필 1.26 08시
(이의용 사무관)

건설부에도 Fax 송부필

| 대책반 | 장관 | 치관 | 1차보 | 2차보 | 미주국 | 중아국 | 청와대 | 총리실 |
|---|---|---|---|---|---|---|---|---|
| 안기부 | 건설부 | 노동부 | | | | | | |

PAGE 1 91.01.26 04:37 DA

외신 1과 통제관

0129

91.1.26. <한국경제>. 19면

## 現代建設 잔류근로자 22명중

# 9명 이란도착

이라크에 잔류중인 現代建設소속 근로자 22명가운데 9명이 25일하오(한국시간) 이라크를 탈출해 이란의 국경도시인 코스라비에 도착했다고 외무부가 이날 밝혔다.

외무부는 이라크를 탈출한 근로자 9명의 인적사항과 나머지 근로자 13명의 안전여부는 이들의 신병을 인수한후에야 알수있다고 밝혔다.

0130

| | 분류번호 | 보존기간 |
|---|---|---|
| | | |

# 발 신 전 보

번 호 : WGV-0134 910126 1023 AO 종별 :

수 신 : 주 제네바 ~~대사. 총영사~~ 대사대리

발 신 : 장 관 (국기)

제 목 : 이라크 잔류교민 소재 파악

대 : GVW-0173

하기사실을 ICRC측에 통보바람.

1. 대호 현대 근로자 22인중 9인은 이미 이란으로 대피하여 주이란 아국 대사관에서 이들 9인의 신병을 이란측으로부터 곧 인수할 예정이며, 동 명단은 아래와 같음.
(김종훈, 김무웅, 임동호, 백정호, 문동남, 김효석, 김봉길, 임진두, 김명균)

2. 이라크 잔류 현대직원 13인은 이라크내에 안전하게 있으며, 이중 현지인과 결혼한 2인을 제외한 11인도 곧 대피할 예정이라 하며, 이들 잔류 현대직원들에 대한 상세한 상황은 주이란 대사관에서 상기 9인의 신병 인도후 추보 예정인바, 보고 접수하는 대로 귀관 통보 예정임. 끝

(국제기구조약국장 문동석)

중동아프리카국장:

| 보 안 통 제 | |
|---|---|

| 앙 고 재 | 91년 1월 26일 | 국기과 | 기안자 성명 | 과 장 | 국 장 | 차 관 | 장 관 |
|---|---|---|---|---|---|---|---|
| | | | 허강일 | | 전결 | | |

| 외신과통제 |
|---|
| |

0131

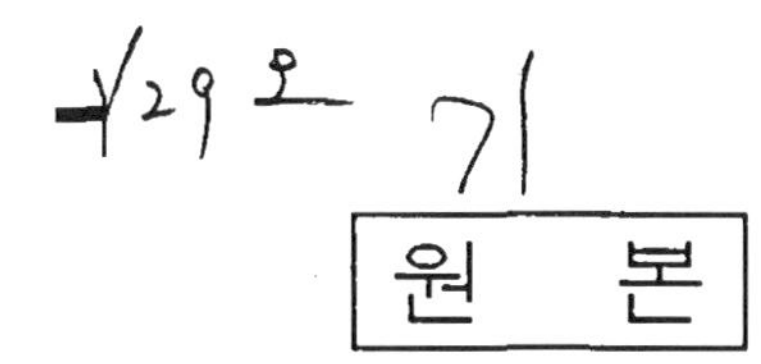

# 외 무 부

종 별 :

번 호 : GVW-0185 일 시 : 91 0128 1730

수 신 : 장관(국기,중근동)

발 신 : 주 제네바 대사대리

제 목 : 이락크 잔류 교민 소재 파악

대호, 현대 건설 직원 9명의 이란으로의 대피사실을 동명단과 함께 금 1.28(월)ICRC 측에 통보함.

끝

(대사대리 박영우-국장)

| 국기국 | 장관 | 차관 | 1차보 | 2차보 | 미주국 | 중아국 | 청와대 | 총리실 |
|---|---|---|---|---|---|---|---|---|
| 안기부 | 대책반 | | | | | | | |

PAGE 1

91.01.29 06:35 DA

외신 1과 통제관

0132

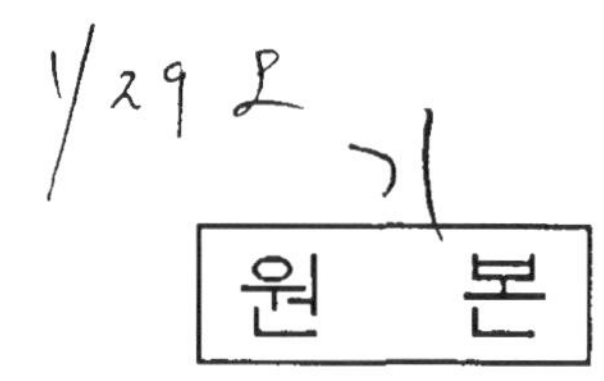

# 외 무 부

종 별 :

번 호 : GVW-0186 일 시 : 91 0128 1730

수 신 : 장 관 (국기,중근동)

발 신 : 주 제네바 대사대리

제 목 : 걸프전 관련 ICRC 활동

연: GVW-0121

연호 표제 관련 ICRC 추가 자료 ( NO. 11 및12) 를 별첨 송부함.

첨부: 상기자료 끝

( GVW(F)-38)

( 대사대리 박영우-국장)

| 국기국 | 장관 | 차관 | 1차보 | 2차보 | 중아국 | 정문국 | 청와대 | 총리실 |
|---|---|---|---|---|---|---|---|---|
| 안기부 | | | | | | | | |

PAGE 1

91.01.29 09:31 DA

외신 1과 통제관

0133

Gvw(기)-0038 10128 1230
Gvw-186 첨부

UPDATE No. 11 ON INTERNATIONAL RED CROSS AND RED CRESCENT ACTION IN THE GULF
22 JANUARY 1991

SUMMARY OF INTERNATIONAL RED CROSS AND RED CRESCENT ACTION IN THE GULF TO DATE

INTRODUCTION

THE FOLLOWING IS AN UP TO DATE SUMMARY OF INTERNATIONAL RED CROSS AND RED CRESCENT ACTION IN THE GULF SINCE THE INTENSIFICATION OF HOSTILITIES IN THE GULF REGION.

THE ICRC HAS OFFERED ITS SERVICES

SINCE THE BEGINNING OF THE GULF CRISIS, THE ICRC REGULARLY REMINDED THE GOVERNMENTS INVOLVED OF THEIR OBLIGATION TO RESPECT THE PROVISIONS OF THE GENEVA CONVENTIONS OF 12 AUGUST 1949.

WHEN HOSTILITIES FLARED UP ON 17 JANUARY, THE ICRC SENT A NOTE VERBALE TO THE PARTIES CONCERNED TO RECALL THE PRINCIPLES AND RULES OF INTERNATIONAL HUMANITARIAN LAW AND TO OFFER ITS SERVICES TO ALL PARTIES TO PROVIDE PROTECTION AND ASSISTANCE TO THE VICTIMS OF THE CONFLICT, AND TO ACT IN THE HUMANITARIAN FIELD AS A NEUTRAL INTERMEDIARY BETWEEN THE BELLIGERENTS.

THIS OFFER OF SERVICES HAS BEEN FAVOURABLY RECEIVED AND THE ICRC MAINTAINS CLOSE CONTACT WITH THE PARTIES CONCERNED WITH THE AIM OF ENSURING THE RESPECT OF THE PRISONERS OF WAR AND THE CIVILIAN POPULATION, AS WELL AS RESPECT FOR THE ESSENTIAL RULES ON THE CONDUCT OF HOSTILITIES.

INTERNATIONAL RED CROSS AND RED CRESCENT READY TO ACT

A PERMANENT TASK FORCE, WHICH INCLUDES THE LEAGUE, WAS SET UP AT ICRC HEADQUARTERS IN GENEVA TO CO-ORDINATE AND DIRECT RED CROSS AND RED CRESCENT PREPARATIONS FOR IMMEDIATE ACTION.

OVER THE LAST WEEK, MOST OF THE MATERIAL NEEDED FOR THE INTERNATIONAL RED CROSS AND RED CRESCENT ACTION IN THE GULF WAS MOBILIZED. "ADVANCED PREPAREDNESS POSTS" ARE BEING ESTABLISHED IN AMMAN, BAHRAIN, DAMASCUS AND BAKHTARAN (IRAN).

PROTECTION AND TRACING ACTIVITIES

THE ICRC HAS FREQUENT CONTACT WITH THE APPROPRIATE GOVERNMENTS TO RECALL THEIR OBLIGATION TO ABIDE BY ALL PROVISIONS OF THE GENEVA CONVENTIONS, IN PARTICULAR THOSE CONCERNING CIVILIANS, PRISONERS OF WAR, MEMBERS OF THE ARMED FORCES MISSING IN ACTION AND DISPERSED FAMILIES.

7-1

0134

THE CENTRAL TRACING AGENCY ESTABLISHED CONTACT WITH THE GOVERNMENTS INVOLVED IN THE CONFLICT AND THE RESPECTIVE NATIONAL INFORMATION BUREAUX IN ORDER TO RECEIVE ALL INFORMATION REGARDING CIVILIAN INTERNEES AND THE MISSING IN ACTION.

THE ICRC HAS JUST RESUMED OPERATIONAL CONTACT WITH ITS DELEGATION IN IRAQ. THE CENTRAL TRACING AGENCY EXPECTS TO FORWARD REQUESTS FOR FAMILY NEWS REGISTERED SINCE 17 JANUARY TO THE ICRC DELEGATION IN BAGHDAD WITHIN THE NEXT FEW DAYS.

## MEDICAL ACTIVITIES

PREPARATIONS FOR SETTING UP FIVE COMPLETE FIELD HOSPITAL MODULES, INCLUDING MEDICAL TEAMS, AND FIVE ADDITIONAL MEDICAL TEAMS TO WORK IN EXISTING HOSPITAL FACILITIES IN THE GULF REGION, ARE NEARLY FINALIZED. FOR DETAILS ON PLANS SEE UPDATES No. 3, 4, AND 6.

BAHRAIN: 3.5 TONNES OF MEDICINES AND MEDICAL SUPPLIES WERE DISPATCHED ON 19 JANUARY.

IRAN: 1 WHO BASIC KIT (FOR DISPENSARY SERVING 10,000 PERSONS FOR 3 MONTHS), AS WELL AS ABOUT 29 TONNES OF MEDICINES AND MEDICAL SUPPLIES AND MATERIAL FOR ONE FIELD HOSPITAL DESTINED FOR IRAQ WAS SENT ON 21 JANUARY.

JORDAN: MEDICAL/SURGICAL PERSONNEL FROM THE DANISH AND FINNISH RC ARRIVED ON 22 JANUARY. MATERIAL FOR ADDITIONAL CAMP DISPENSARIES, AS WELL AS A FIELD HOSPITAL AND ABOUT 18 TONNES OF MEDICINES AND MEDICAL SUPPLIES DESTINED FOR IRAQ WILL BE SENT ON 23 JANUARY.

SYRIA: 1 WHO BASIC KIT, MATERIAL FOR 1 CAMP DISPENSARY AND A JAPANESE MEDICAL/SURGICAL TEAM WERE DISPATCHED ON 21 JANUARY.

## RELIEF ACTIVITIES

PREPARATIONS TO ESTABLISH TRANSIT CAMPS AND CAMP MODULES TO SHELTER UP TO 300,000 PERSONS DISPLACED IN THE REGION CONTINUED. FOR DETAILS SEE UPDATES No. 2, 5A AND 5B.

ACCORDING TO THE STRATEGY DEVELOPED FOR THIS ACTION, ONE THIRD OF THE RELIEF MATERIALS DESTINED FOR USE IN THE GULF REGION ARE BEING DISPATCHED TO "ADVANCED PREPAREDNESS POSTS" IN AMMAN, BAHRAIN, DAMASCUS AND BAKHTARAN (IRAN). FOR MAXIMUM FLEXIBILITY, TWO THIRDS OF THE MATERIAL REMAINS IN EUROPE OR CYPRUS ON STANDBY, TO BE DISPATCHED WHEREVER NEEDED.

IRAN: MATERIAL WAS MOBILIZED FOR VARIOUS CAMPSITES WITH A TOTAL CAPACITY FOR 10,000 PERSONS. THIS MEANS THAT, ONE FIFTH OF THE MATERIAL PLANNED (CAPACITY 50,000) WAS SENT 21 JANUARY, THE REST OF THE MATERIAL IS READY FOR DISPATCH FROM EUROPE AND CYPRUS.

0135

7-2

JORDAN: AN ICRC TRANSIT CAMP, TRANSIT 1/28, ON THE JORDANIAN/IRAQI BORDER WITH A CAPACITY FOR 5,000 PERSONS IS FULLY OPERATIONAL.

THE AZRAQ 1 CAMP, MANAGED BY THE LEAGUE AND THE JORDAN NATIONAL RED CRESCENT SOCIETY, IS FULLY OPERATIONAL WITH THE CAPACITY FOR 30,000 PERSONS. THE AZRAQ 2 CAMP IS BEING UP-GRADED UNDER LEAGUE CO-ORDINATION.

SYRIA: MATERIAL LEFT 22 JANUARY ON TWO FLIGHTS FROM GENEVA AND LARNACA FOR THE CONSTRUCTION OF AN ICRC TRANSIT CAMP ON THE SYRIAN/IRAQI BORDER. THE EXACT LOCATION IS YET UNDETERMINED.

MATERIAL WAS MOBILIZED ON 17 JANUARY FOR A COMPLETE CAMP MODULE WHICH WILL BE MANAGED BY THE NETHERLANDS RED CROSS WITH DIRECT SUPPORT FROM THE BELGIAN AND LUXEMBOURG RC. MATERIAL ASSISTANCE FROM OTHER NATIONAL SOCIETIES WAS ALSO MOBILIZED. THE FIRST FLIGHTS LEFT 21 AND 22 JANUARY FOR DAMASCUS.

THE SYRIAN RED CRESCENT PLANS TO USE FOUR TRAINING CENTRES, EACH WITH THE CAPACITY FOR 10,000 PERSONS, FOR THE SHELTER OF REFUGEES.

TURKEY: THE TURKISH RED CRESCENT SOCIETY, WITH ASSISTANCE FROM BOTH THE ICRC AND THE LEAGUE, IS RE-INFORCING ITS MATERIAL RESOURCES.

OTHER CAMP MODULES: MATERIAL IS MOBILIZED OR IN PREPARATION FOR FOUR ADDITIONAL CAMP MODULES. THESE CAMPS WILL BE SET UP BY THE GERMAN RED CROSS, THE DANISH RED CROSS (WITH SUPPORT FROM OTHER NORDIC RC SOCIETIES) AND THE ICRC.

OUTSTANDING NEEDS FOR RELIEF ACTIVITIES:

THE ICRC SEEKS ADDITIONAL SUPPORT TO OBTAIN ALL NECESSARY MATERIAL AND LOGISTICAL MEANS FOR UP TO EIGHT CAMP MODULES AS OUTLINED IN UPDATE No. 2.

THE MATERIALS LISTED BELOW INDICATES FIRST PRIORITY COMPLETION OF SEVEN CAMP MODULES. CONTRIBUTIONS FOR ITEMS UNDER PRIORITY 2 WOULD BE USED FOR AN EIGHTH CAMP MODULE.

| ITEM | PRIORITY 1 | PRIORITY 2 |
|---|---|---|
| TENTS AND GROUND SHEETS, 30 M2 | 1,225 | 1,500 |
| TENTS AND GROUND SHEETS, 60 M2 | 24 | 10 |
| TENTS AND GROUND SHEETS, 120 M2 | -- | -- |
| RUBB/WAREHOUSE | 2 | 1 |
| BLANKETS | 54,000 | 60,000 |
| KITCHEN SETS | 4,810 | 6,000 |
| STOVES | 6,538 | 6,000 |
| 4X4 VEHICLES FOR PERSONNEL TRANSPORT | 10 | 10 |
| GENERATORS, 25 KVA | 1 | - |

0136

7-2

| GENERATORS, 60 KVA | 3 | 1 |
|---|---|---|
| GENERATORS, 15 KVA | - | - |

PLEASE SENT ALL PLEDGES TO ICRC RELIEF DIVISION (MRS. HOCK).

RESOURCES WILL BE ALLOCATED BY THE TASK FORCE FOR LEAGUE CO-ORDINATED PROGRAMMES FOR THE RED CRESCENT SOCIETIES OF KUWAIT, SYRIA, TURKEY AND YEMEN, AND/OR FOR THE SPECIAL ICRC FIELD REQUESTS EXPECTED IN THE NEAR FUTURE.

PERSONNEL: 139 PRESENT IN THE REGION

INTERNATIONAL RED CROSS AND RED CRESCENT PERSONNEL ARE PRESENT IN THE FOLLOWING COUNTRIES IN THE GULF REGION:

| COUNTRY | ICRC | LEAGUE | NATIONAL SOCIETY |
|---|---|---|---|
| BAHRAIN | 8 | 1 | -- |
| EGYPT | 1 | 1 | -- |
| IRAN | 22 | 1 | -- |
| IRAQ | 4 | -- | -- |
| ISRAEL AND THE TERRITORIES OCCUPIED BY ISRAEL | 45 | -- | -- |
| JORDAN | 13 | 3 | 8 |
| LEBANON | 7 | -- | -- |
| SAUDI ARABIA | 5 | -- | -- |
| SYRIA | 11 | 1 | 13 |
| YEMEN | -- | 2 | -- |
| TURKEY | 1 | -- | -- |

FINANCE

A SPECIAL APPEAL FOR SFR. 141 MILLION WAS SENT OUT ON 17 JANUARY FOR CONTRIBUTIONS IN CASH AND KIND FOR THIS ACTION. THE ICRC THANKS DONORS WHO HAVE ALREADY CONTRIBUTED TO THIS INTERNATIONAL RED CROSS AND RED CRESCENT ACTION AND URGES GOVERNMENTS AND NATIONAL SOCIETIES WHO HAVE NOT YET INDICATED THEIR CASH CONTRIBUTIONS TO DO SO AS SOON AS POSSIBLE.

FOR FURTHER INFORMATION PLEASE CONTACT SO/REX.

BEST REGARDS,

CHRISTIAN KORNEVALL
SO/REX, ICRC, GENEVA

0137

7-4

* UPDATE NO. 12 ON INTERNATIONAL RED CROSS AND RED CRESCENT ACTION
* IN THE MIDDLE EAST
* 27 JANUARY 1991

* INTRODUCTION

* MILITARY OPERATIONS, MOSTLY AIRBORNE, CONTINUED IN THE REGION.
* THE OIL SPILL IN KUWAIT IS A MAJOR ECOLOGICAL CONCERN.

* ICRC VISITED THE FIRST POWS AND CIVILIAN INTERNEES RESULTING
* FROM THE CONFLICT. ON 27 JANUARY ICRC ASSISTED 5,000 CIVILIANS
* BLOCKED AT THE JORDANIAN/IRAQI BORDER. MORE MATERIAL AND PERSON
* NEL WAS SENT TO THE REGION.

* PROTECTION AND TRACING

* PRISONERS OF WAR, MISSING IN ACTION AND CIVILIAN INTERNEES

* IN ACCORDANCE WITH THE THIRD GENEVA CONVENTION OF 12 AUGUST 1949:

* THE ICRC WAS NOTIFIED BY THE UNITED STATES NATIONAL INFORMATION
* BUREAU OF THE CAPTURE OF 42 MEMBERS OF THE IRAQI ARMED FORCES.

* THE ICRC SUBMITTED 24 REQUESTS ON MEMBERS OF THE ALLIED FORCES
* REPORTED MISSING IN ACTION TO THE IRAQI AUTHORITIES.

* ON 21 JANUARY 1991, ICRC DELEGATES VISITED TWO IRAQI POWS HELD BY
* THE BRITISH ARMED FORCES IN THE UNITED KINGDOM. ON 24 JANUARY,
* SEVEN IRAQI POWS HELD BY THE UNITED STATES ARMED FORCES WERE
* VISITED IN SAUDI ARABIA.

* IN ACCORDANCE WITH THE FOURTH GENEVA CONVENTION OF 12 AUGUST
* 1949:

* BETWEEN 21 AND 24 JANUARY, ICRC DELEGATES VISITED 61 IRAQI CIV
* ILIAN INTERNEES HELD BY THE BRITISH AUTHORITIES IN THE UNITED
* KINGDOM. THE ICRC ALSO HAD ACCESS TO EIGHT NON-IRAQI CIVILIANS
* INTERNED IN CONNECTION WITH THE CONFLICT BY BRITISH AUTHORITIES
* WHO DID NOT BENEFIT FROM REGULAR CONSULAR SERVICES.

* ALL AVAILABLE AND RELEVANT INFORMATION ON THE ABOVE MENTIONED
* PROTECTED PERSONS IS BEING TRANSMITTED TO THE POWER ON WHICH THEY
* DEPEND, ACCORDING TO THE THIRD AND FOURTH GENEVA CONVENTIONS OF
* 12 AUGUST 1949.

* TRACING AND MAILING SERVICES

* SINCE 17 JANUARY, THE CENTRAL TRACING AGENCY (CTA) HAS REGISTERED
* ABOUT 100 'ANXIOUS FOR NEWS' MESSAGES FROM FAMILIES WITHOUT CON
* TACT WITH THEIR RELATIVES IN IRAQ OR KUWAIT.

0138

MEDICAL ACTIVITIES

* BAHRAIN: 3.5 TONNES OF MEDICINES AND MEDICAL SUPPLIES ARRIVED.
* PERSONNEL INCLUDE A MEDICAL CO-ORDINATOR AND AN SANITATION ENGI
* NEER.

* IRAN: A COMPLETE NORHOSP AND 15 TONNES OF MEDICINES AND MEDICAL
* SUPPLIES DESTINED FOR IRAQ ARRIVED IN TEHRAN. AN ICRC MEDICAL CO-
* ORDINATOR IS POSTED IN TEHRAN.

* JORDAN: A SURGICAL NORHOSP UNIT AND 15 TONNES OF MEDICINES AND
* MEDICAL SUPPLIES DESTINED FOR IRAQ ARRIVED IN AMMAN. PERSONNEL
* INCLUDE ONE ICRC MEDICAL CO-ORDINATOR AND A SANITATION ENGINEER.
* A SURGICAL TEAM COMPOSED OF SIX FINNISH RC AND TWO DANISH RC MEM
* BERS IS READY IN AMMAN FOR INTERVENTION IN THE REGION.

* SYRIA: A COMPLETE WHO BASIC MEDICAL KIT FOR THE PLANNED ICRC
* TRANSIT CAMP ARRIVED. PERSONNEL INCLUDE TWO ICRC NURSES, A SANI
* TATION ENGINEER AND A MEDICAL TEAM (TEN JAPANESE RC MEMBERS).

RELIEF ACTIVITIES

* BAHRAIN: ICRC AND LEAGUE DELEGATION ARE CURRENTLY DEVELOPING
* PLANS FOR ACTION WITH THE KUWAITI RED CRESCENT. MATERIAL HAS BEEN
* PREPARED FOR THIS PROGRAMME.

* IRAN: FOLLOWING A SURVEY IN THE BAHKTARAN PROVINCE, IT WAS
* DECIDED THAT MATERIAL FOR ONE THIRD OF A CAMP MODULE WOULD BE
* SENT TO TEHRAN. MATERIAL FOR CAMP FACILITIES FOR 10,000 PERSONS
* ARRIVED ON FOUR FLIGHTS. ADDITIONAL MATERIAL IS BEING SENT VIA
* THE GERMAN RED CROSS ON WEEKLY FLIGHTS TO TEHRAN.

* JORDAN: ICRC TRANSIT CAMP 1/28 (CAPACITY 5,000 PERSONS) IS
* FUNCTIONAL. AZRAQ 1 CAMP IS FULLY OPERATIONAL, OCCUPANCY WAS AT
* ABOUT 2,000 PEOPLE AS OF 22 JANUARY. THE LEAGUE OF RED CROSS AND
* RED CRESCENT SOCIETIES AND THE JORDAN NATIONAL RED CRESCENT
* SOCIETY IS IN THE PROCESS OF BRINGING CAMP AZRAQ 2 UP TO FULL
* OPERATIONAL CAPACITY (30,000 PERSONS), 1,300 TENTS WERE RECEIVED
* FROM THE UNHCR FOR USE IN AZRAQ 2.

* ON 27 JANUARY, AN ICRC CONVOY BROUGHT ASSISTANCE IN THE FORM OF
* FOOD AND WATER TO ABOUT 5,000 PEOPLE, MOSTLY JORDANIANS AND EGYP
* TIANS, BLOCKED AT THE BORDER IN IRAQ. ICRC DELEGATES TOGETHER
* WITH THE JORDAN NATIONAL RED CRESCENT SOCIETY WILL CONTINUE THIS
* ASSISTANCE AS LONG AS NECESSARY.

* SYRIA: ON 22 AND 23 JANUARY, MATERIAL FOR A TRANSIT CAMP
* WAS SENT BY AIR FROM EUROPE AND CYPRUS TO DAMASCUS. THE MATERIAL
* IS READY FOR DISPATCH TO THE BORDER. A TECHNICAL ASSESSMENT TEAM
* IS EVALUATING POTENTIAL SITES FOR THIS TRANSIT CAMP.

* THE CAMP MODULE (CAPACITY 30,000 PERSONS), TO BE MANAGED BY THE
* BENELUX RED CROSS SOCIETIES (LEAD AGENT IS THE DUTCH RC), WAS
* MOBILIZED. FLIGHTS WITH MATERIAL BEGAN ON 22 JANUARY. SITE
* ASSESSMENT FOR THIS CAMP IS IN PROGRESS.

* THE LEAGUE AND THE ICRC MOBILIZED ADDITIONAL MATERIALS FOR THE
* SYRIAN ARAB RED CRESCENT CAMP PROJECTS IN ABU CHAMAT (NEW CON
* STRUCTION) AND DARAA/SUWEIDA (EXISTING FACILITIES), CAPACITY
* 15,000 PERSONS.

* TURKEY: ONE THIRD OF A CAMP MODULE, TO BE MANAGED BY THE GERMAN
* RED CROSS, IS BEING TRANSPORTED BY LAND. THE ROAD CONVOY COMPOSED
* OF 17 TRUCKS WITH CAMP MATERIAL, 10 OTHER VEHICLES AND TWO AMBU
* LANCES LEFT BONN ON 26 JANUARY AND IS EXPECTED TO ARRIVE IN
* ANKARA ON 31 JANUARY. FROM ANKARA THE CONVOY CAN BE DIRECTED TO 0139
* ANY COUNTRY IN THE REGION ACCORDING TO NEED.

* LOGISTICS

* TRUCKS:
* 2 TRUCKS WERE SENT TO TEHRAN ON 26 JANUARY,
* 4 TRUCKS ARE READY TO BE DISPATCHED FROM EUROPE.

* CARS:
* 7 UNITS WERE DISPATCHED TO TEHRAN, DAMASCUS AND AMMAN,
* 35 UNITS BOUGHT OR READY TO BE DISPATCHED FROM GENEVA, GIBRALTAR,
* AND CYPRUS,
* 10 UNITS WILL BE BOUGHT BY THE LEAGUE AND THE ICRC LOCALLY
* FOR USE IN SYRIA AND JORDAN.

* AIRCRAFT:
* 2 AIRPLANES HAVE BEEN LEASED OR ARE READY FOR USE IN THE REGION.

* BOTH AIRCRAFT HAVE BEEN REINSURED BY THE SWISS GOVERNMENT WHICH
* HAS TAKEN OVER FINANCIAL COVERAGE IN CASE OF LOSS THROUGH AN ACT
* OF WAR.

* 9 ICRC CARGO FLIGHTS WERE CARRIED OUT BETWEEN 21 AND 26 JANUARY
* TO DAMASCUS, AMMAN AND TEHRAN,
* 5 CARGO FLIGHTS WERE CARRIED OUT BY THE DUTCH RED CROSS TO
* DAMASCUS.

* THE 14 FLIGHTS CARRIED A TOTAL OF OVER 430 TONNES OF RELIEF
* CARGO.

* FINANCE

* THE ICRC SPECIAL APPEAL FOR INTERNATIONAL RED CROSS AND RED CRES
* CENT ACTION IN THE MIDDLE EAST FOR SFR. 141 MILLION IS BROKEN
* DOWN INTO 50-600/0 DONATIONS IN KIND AND 40-500/0 IN CASH CONTRIBU
* TIONS.

* THE ICRC ESTIMATES THAT SFR. 40 MILLION IN DONATIONS IN KIND HAS
* BEEN MOBILIZED TO DATE. ABOUT SFR. 8 MILLION HAS BEEN RECEIVED IN
* CASH PLEDGES.

* THE ICRC STILL NEEDS CASH CONTRIBUTIONS FOR THE INTERNATIONAL RED
* CROSS AND RED CRESCENT ACTION IN THE MIDDLE EAST.

* FOR FURTHER INFORMATION PLEASE CONTACT SO/REX.

* BEST REGARDS,

* CHRISTIAN KORNEVALL
* SO/REX, ICRC, GENEVA

0140

7-7

원 본

# 외 무 부

종 별 :

번 호 : GVW-0235 일 시 : 91 0204 1800

수 신 : 장 관(국기,중근동)

발 신 : 주 제네바 대사대리

제 목 : 걸프전 관련 ICRC 활동

연: GVW-0186

연호, 표제관련 ICRC 추가 자료( NO.13) 을별첨 송부함.

첨부:상기 자료( GVW(F)-0052). 끝

(대사대리 박영우-국장)

국기국 중아국

PAGE 1

91.02.05 09:07 WG

외신 1과 통제관

0141

GVW(F)-0052 02.4 1800

* ,(3Q:
* UPDATE NO. 13 ON INTERNATIONAL RED CROSS AND RED CRESCENT ACTIO
* N IN
* THE MIDDLE EAST "GVW-235 첨부"

* 1 FEBRUARY 1991

* SUMMARY

* AIR BOMBARDMENTS CONTINUE AND SIGNIFICANT GROUND FIGHTING HAS B
* EGUN
* IN THE REGION.

* ON 1 FEBRUARY THE ICRC'S PRESIDENT MADE A SOLEMN APPEAL TO THE
* BEL
* LIGERENTS. ON 31 JANUARY AN ICRC MEDICAL CONVOY CROSSED INTO IR
* AQ
* FROM IRAN. ICRC VISITS TO POWS HELD BY THE ALLIED FORCES ARE CO
* NTI
* NUING. SEVERAL THOUSAND PEOPLE STRANDED AT THE IRAQI/JORDANIAN
* BORDER
* HAVE BEEN ASSISTED. ADDITIONAL RELIEF SUPPLIES HAVE ARRIVED IN
* THE
* REGION.

* ICRC'S PRESIDENT MAKES APPEAL

* ON 1 FEBRUARY, ICRC PRESIDENT CORNELIO SUMMARUGA SOLEMNLY APPEA
* LED TO
* THE BELLIGERENT PARTIES, IN THE NAME OF ALL CIVILIAN AND MILITA
* RY
* VICTIMS OF THE CONFLICT:

* TO HAVE DUE REGARD FOR HUMANITARIAN CONSIDERATIONS.
* HE REMINDED THEM THAT THE LAW OF WAR MUST BE UPHELD,
* THAT METHODS AND MEANS OF WARFARE ARE NOT UNLIMITED,
* THAT WEAPONS WITH INDISCRIMINATE EFFECTS OR LIKELY
* TO CAUSE DISPROPORTIONATE SUFFERING AND SEVERE DAMAGE
* TO THE ENVIRONMENT ARE PROHIBITED. HE ALSO REITERATED
* THAT THE WOUNDED, SHIPWRECKED, PRISONERS OF WAR AND
* CIVILIANS HAVE TO BE PROTECTED AND CARED FOR ACCORDING
* TO THE GENEVA CONVENTIONS OF 12 AUGUST 1949.

* PROTECTION AND TRACING ACTIVITIES

* PRISONERS OF WAR, MISSING IN ACTION, AND CIVILIAN INTERNEES

* SINCE 28 JANUARY, IN ACCORDANCE WITH THE THIRD GENEVA CONVENTIO
* N OF
* 12 AUGUST 1949:
* THE ICRC WAS NOTIFIED BY THE US NATIONAL INFORMATION BUREAU OF
* THE
* CAPTURE OF 68 MEMBERS OF THE IRAQI ARMED FORCES.

* ON 28 AND 30 JANUARY, ICRC DELEGATES VISITED RESPECTIVELY 91
* AND 14 IRAQI POWS HELD BY THE UNITED STATES ARMED FORCES IN SAU
* DI
* ARABIA.

* ALL AVAILABLE AND RELEVANT INFORMATION ON THE ABOVE-MENTIONED P
* RO
* TECTED PERSONS ARE BEING TRANSMITTED TO THE POWER ON WHICH THEY
* DEPEND, ACCORDING TO THE THIRD GENEVA CONVENTION OF 12 AUGUST 1
* 949.

5-1 0142

1991-02-04 19:34 KOREAN MISSION GENEVA 2 022 791 0525 P.01

* MAILING AND CING

* ALL MESSAGES 'ANXIOUS FOR NEWS' FROM FAMILIES HAVING NO CONTACT
* S WITH
* THEIR RELATIVES IN IRAQ, REGISTERED BY THE CENTRAL TRACING AGEN
* CY
* SINCE 17 JANUARY, WERE FORWARDED TO THE ICRC DELEGATION IN BAGH
* DAD.

* THE FIRST SEVEN MESSAGES 'ANXIOUS FOR NEWS' FROM IRAQI POWS VIS
* ITED
* BY THE ICRC IN SAUDI ARABIA, ADDRESSED TO THEIR RELATIVES IN IR
* AQ,
* HAVE ALSO BEEN FORWARDED TO THE ICRC DELEGATION IN BAGHDAD.

* MEDICAL ACTIVITIES

* ON 31 JANUARY, AFTER HAVING NOTIFIED ALL PARTIES CONCERNED, FOU
* R ICRC
* DELEGATES - INCLUDING A MEDICAL DOCTOR -LEFT TEHRAN FOR BAKHTAR
* AN
* PROVINCE WITH 19 TONNES OF MEDICINE AND MEDICAL/SURGICAL MATERI
* AL IN
* A CONVOY OF TWO TRUCKS PROVIDED BY THE IRANIAN RED CRESCENT SOC
* IETY.
* AFTER CROSSING THE IRANIAN/IRAQI BORDER,THE MATERIAL WAS TRANFE
* RRED
* ONTO VEHICLES OF THE IRAQI RED CRESCENT. THE CONVOY LED BY ICRC
* DELE
* GATES IS NOW ON THE WAY TO BAGHDAD. THESE FOUR ICRC DELEGATES W
* ILL
* REINFORCE THE DELEGATION IN BAGHDAD, BRINGING THE NUMBER OF ICR
* C
* EXPATRIATES IN THE COUNTRY TO EIGHT.

* IN JORDAN, MEDICAL MATERIAL AND SURGICAL TEAMS ARE BEING PREPAR
* ED FOR
* ENTRY INTO IRAQ. A MEDICAL EVALUATION HAS BEEN MADE AND FIRST A
* ID
* IS BEING PROVIDED FOR SEVERAL THOUSANDS REFUGEES AT THE
* IRAQI/JORDANIAN BORDER.

* IN BAHRAIN, AN ICRC MEDICAL COORDINATOR AND A SANITARY ENGINEER
* HELD
* DISCUSSIONS WITH THE AUTHORITIES OF BAHRAIN AND WITH OFFICIALS
* OF THE
* KUWAITI RED CRESCENT.

* IN JERUSALEM, A MEMORANDUM OF UNDERSTANDING WAS SIGNED BETWEEN
* THE
* EPISCOPAL CHURCH OF JERUSALEM + THE MIDDLE EAST AND THE ICRC CO
* NCERN-
* ING THE PLACING OF AN ICRC SURGICAL TEAM IN THE ARAB AHLI HOSPI
* TAL IN
* GAZA. ISRAELI AUTHORITIES HAVE GIVEN THEIR CONSENT. THE ICRC W
* ILL
* DISPATCH A FOUR-MEMBER FINNISH RED CROSS SURGICAL TEAM TO THIS
* HOS
* PITAL ON 5 FEBRUARY.

* IN LEBANON, THE ICRC PROVIDED ASSISTANCE TO MEDICAL STRUCTURES
* IN THE
* PALESTINIAN REFUGEE CAMP OF RACHADIYE, NEAR SIDON, FOLLOWING RE
* CENT
* BOMBARDMENTS.

5-2 0143

* IN THE MIDDLE EAST
* · BAHRAIN: FINANCIAL AND IN-KIND RESOURCES IN SUPPORT OF THE KUWA
* ITI
* RED CRESCENT, IN RESPONSE TO THE APPEAL MADE BY THE LEAGUE OF T
* HE RED
* CROSS AND RED CRESCENT SOCIETIES, WHICH IS NOW INTEGRATED INTO
* THE
* INTERNATIONAL RED CROSS AND RED CRESCENT ACTION, HAVE BEEN MOBI
* LIZED.

* THE FOLLOWING ITEMS ARE STILL NEEDED:
* 2,820 FAMILY SIZE TENTS
* 2,500 COOKING SETS
* 10 GENERATORS WITH EMERGENCY LIGHTING SYSTEMS
* 35 FIRE EXTINGUISHERS

* TRANSPORT OF RELIEF ITEMS FOR THE KUWAITI RED CRESCENT PROGRAMM
* E WILL
* BE ARRANGED BY THE LEAGUE.

* EGYPT: A RECENTLY ARRIVED DELEGATE OF THE LEAGUE OF THE RED CRO
* SS AND
* RED CRESCENT SOCIETIES IS WORKING TOGETHER WITH THE EGYPTIAN RE
* D
* CRESCENT TO SET UP RECEPTION CENTRES FOR RETURNEES.

* IRAN: MATERIAL, MOSTLY PROVIDED BY THE GERMAN RED CROSS, FOR TW
* O
* CAMPS - EACH WITH A CAPACITY OF 5,000 PERSONS - PLUS TWO TRUCKS
* HAVE
* BEEN FLOWN INTO TEHRAN FROM FRANKFURT AND CYPRUS AND ARE NOW GO
* ING
* THROUGH CUSTOMS. WITH THE AGREEMENT OF THE AUTHORITIES OF THE I
* SLAMIC
* REPUBLIC OF IRAN, A SITE FOR THE FIRST CAMP WAS CHOSEN NEAR THE
* TOWN
* OF GILAN-E-GHARB IN BAKHTARAN PROVINCE AND CONSTRUCTION WORK HA
* S
* STARTED.

* JORDAN: SINCE 27 JANUARY, THE ICRC HAS BEEN ASSISTING APPROXIMA
* TELY
* 5,000 PEOPLE EITHER STRANDED AT THE IRAQI BORDER POST IN TREBIL
* OR IN
* THE NO MAN'S LAND. EVERY DAY TRUCKS CROSS INTO IRAQ FROM JORDAN
* TO
* DISTRIBUTE FOOD AND WATER TO THESE PERSONS. IN ADDITION, 5,000
* BLAN
* KETS WERE PROVIDED FOR PROTECTION AGAINST THE COLD.

* AMONG THOSE ASSISTED WAS A GROUP OF 151 VIETNAMESE NURSES WHO H
* AD
* ALSO BEEN GIVEN FOOD BY THE ICRC DELEGATION IN BAGHDAD BEFORE T
* HEY
* COULD LEAVE FOR THE JORDAN BORDER.

* AS THEY CROSS THE BORDER, THE REFUGEES RECEIVE ADDITIONAL ASSIS
* TANCE
* AT THE ICRC TRANSIT CAMP T 1/28 IN THE NO MAN'S LAND BEFORE THE
* Y CON
* TINUE THEIR JOURNEY TO AMMAN. YESTERDAY EVENING 280 PERSONS REM
* AINED
* OVERNIGHT IN T 1/28.

5-3 0144

1991-02-04 19:36 KOREAN MISSION GENEVA 2 022 791 0525 P.03

* SYRIA: SIX CH▬ ERED FLIGHTS CARRYING MA▬▬IAL FOR THE BENELUX
* CAMP
* MODULE HAVE BEEN MADE FROM AMSTERDAM TO DAMASCUS. THESE FLIGHTS
* WERE
* ORGANIZED BY THE DUTCH RED CROSS, LEADING AGENT FOR THIS MODULE
* .

* THE FRENCH RED CROSS HAS PREPARED MATERIAL TO UPGRADE THE FACIL
* ITIES
* OF THE SYRIAN ARAB RED CRESCENT SOCIETY'S YOUTH CENTRES AT THE
* JORDA
* NIAN/SYRIAN BORDER WHICH WILL BE USED AS REFUGEE CENTRES.

* TURKEY: THE ROAD CONVOY COMPOSED OF 29 VEHICLES OF THE GERMAN R
* ED
* CROSS WILL ARRIVE THIS EVENING IN ANKARA. FOR THE TIME BEING, T
* HE
* MATERIAL, READY TO BE DEPLOYED IN ANY COUNTRY IN THE REGION ACC
* ORDING
* TO NEED, HAVE BEEN STORED IN A WAREHOUSE KINDLY PROVIDED BY THE
* TURK
* ISH RED CRESCENT.

* MEDICAL MATERIAL AND VEHICLES WHICH WILL INCREASE THE PREPAREDN
* ESS OF
* THE TURKISH RED CRESCENT SOCIETY HAVE BEEN MOBILIZED BY THE CAN
* ADIAN
* AND SWISS RED CROSS SOCIETIES.

* OTHER RELIEF ACTIVITIES
* . THE NORDIC CAMP MODULE, WITH THE DANISH RED CROSS AS ITS LEADIN
* G
* AGENT, IS READY FOR IMMEDIATE DISPATCH TO THE REGION.

* . OTHER RED CROSS SOCIETIES - INCLUDING THOSE OF AUSTRIA, CANADA,
* CZECHOSLOVAKIA, FINLAND, NORWAY, POLAND, PORTUGAL, SPAIN, SWEDE
* N,
* SWITZERLAND AND THE UNITED STATES - HAVE ALSO PROVIDED ADDITION
* AL
* MATERIAL NEEDED FOR THE ACTION OF THE INTERNATIONAL RED CROSS A
* ND RED
* CRESCENT IN THE MIDDLE EAST.

* PERSONNEL

* IN RESPONSE TO THE ICRC'S APPEAL AND UPDATES, RED CROSS AND RED
* CRES
* CENT SOCIETIES MADE PERSONNEL AVAILABLE FOR THE INTERNATIONAL R
* ED
* CROSS AND RED CRESCENT ACTION IN THE MIDDLE EAST. THESE PERSONS
* WILL
* BE MOBILIZES AS NEEDS ARISE. THE FOLLOWING SOCIETIES HAVE RESPO
* NDED:
* ALGERIA, AUSTRIA, AUSTRALIA, BELGIUM, BRAZIL, CANADA, CHILE, DE
* NMARK,
* DOMINICAN REPUBLIC, FINLAND, FRANCE, GERMANY, ICELAND, ITALY, J
* APAN,
* MALAYSIA, NETHERLANDS, NEW ZEALAND, NORWAY, SWEDEN, SWITZERLAND
* ,
* THAILAND, TUNISIA, TURKEY, YEMEN.

0145

5-4

1991-02-04 19:36 KOREAN MISSION GENEVA 2 022 791 0525 P.04

TOTAL P.05

*                                   COORDINATION

*      THE OVERALL RESPONSIBILITY AND COORDINATION OF THE INTERNATIONA
* L RED
*      CROSS AND RED CRESCENT ACTION IN THE MIDDLE EAST, WHICH INCLUDE
* S
*      ACTIVITIES OF THE LEAGUE OF RED CROSS AND RED CRESCENT SOCIETIE
* S AND
*      OF NATIONAL RED CROSS AND RED CRESCENT SOCIETIES, LIES WITH THE
*  ICRC.

*                                   FINANCE

*      FINANCIAL SUPPORT IS STILL NEEDED TO COVER CASH EXPENDITURES AS
* SOCIATED
*      WITH THESE ACTIVITIES. TO DATE, THE ICRC HAS RECEIVED CONTRIBU-
*      TIONS/PLEDGES/INDICATIONS FOR APPROXIMATELY SFR. 20 MILLION FOR
*  ITS
*      SPECIAL APPEAL LAUNCH LAUNCHED ON 17 JANUARY. THE ICRC URGES GO
* VERN
*      MENTS AND NATIONAL SOCIETIES TO FORWARD PLEDGES AND TO FORMALLY
*      PLEDGE INDICATIONS.

*      FOR FURTHER INFORMATION, PLEASE CONTACT SO/REX.

*      BEST REGARDS,

*      CHRISTIAN KORNEVALL
*      SO/REX, ICRC

5-5

0146

1991-02-04 19:37 KOREAN MISSION GENEVA 2 022 791 0525 P.05

| 분류기호 문서번호 | 국기20335- | 협조문용지 ( 2181-2 ) | 결재 | 담당 | 과장 | 국장 |
|---|---|---|---|---|---|---|
| | | | | 오연주 | | |
| 시행일자 | 1991. 2. 8. | | | | | |
| 수 신 | 중동아프리카국장 | 발 신 | 국제기구조약국장 (서 명) | | | |
| 제 목 | ICRC 총재 감사서한 | | | | | |

국제적십자위원회(ICRC)의 Sommaruga 총재는 아국이 1990.12 걸프만 사태 지원 명목으로 ICRC에 3만미불을 특별 지원키로 결정했음을 통보한 차관 명의의 서한에 대한 감사 답신을 별첨과 같이 송부해온바, 귀국 업무에 참고하시기 바랍니다.

첨부 : 상기 Sommaruga 총재 서한 1부. 끝

0147

6158

# 기 안 용 지

| 분류기호<br>문서번호 | 국기20347- | (전화 : 720-4050 ) | 시 행 상<br>특별취급 | |
|---|---|---|---|---|
| 보존기간 | 영구 . 준영구.<br>10. 5 . 3 . 1. | 장 관 | | |
| 수 신 처<br>보존기간 | | | | |
| 시행일자 | 91. 2. 8. | | | |

| 보조기관 | | 협조기관 | | 문 서 통 제 |
|---|---|---|---|---|
| 국장 | 전 결 | | | 검열 1991. 2. 8 |
| 과장 | | | | |
| | | | | |
| 기안책임자 | 오영주 | | | 발 송 인 |

| 경 유<br>수 신<br>참 조 | 대한적십자사총재 | 발신명의 | | 1991. 의무부 |
|---|---|---|---|---|
| 제 목 | ICRC 총재 감서서한 | | | |

1. 당부 공문 국기 20347-63893 관련입니다.

2. 국제적십자위원회(ICRC)의 Sommaruga 총재는 아국이 1990.12 걸프만사태 지원 명목으로 ICRC에 3만미불을 특별 지원키로 결정했음을 통보한 유종하 의무차관(장관 대리)의 서한에 대한 감사 답신을 별첨과 같이 송부해 온바, 귀사 업무에 참고하시기 바랍니다.

첨부 : 상기 Sommaruga 총재 서한 1부. 끝

0148

2/6 오
1. 서한 차관 공람
2. 서한 사본 아중동국, 한적 송부

# 주 제 네 바 대 표 부

제네(정) 20358-129 1991. 2. 1

수신 : 장관

참조 : 국제기구조약국장

제목 : ICRC총재 감사서한

대 : 국기 20347-650(91.1.17)

연 : GVW-2867(90.12.28)

당지 국제적십자위원회(ICRC)의 Sommaruga총재는 아국이 걸프만사태 지원 명목으로 ICRC에 대해 3만미불을 특별지원키로 결정했다는 연호 유종하차관의 서한에 대한 답신을 통해 아국의 특별지원에 대해 감사를 표시해 왔는바, 동 답신을 별첨 송부합니다.

첨부 : Sommaruga총재 서한 1부. 끝.

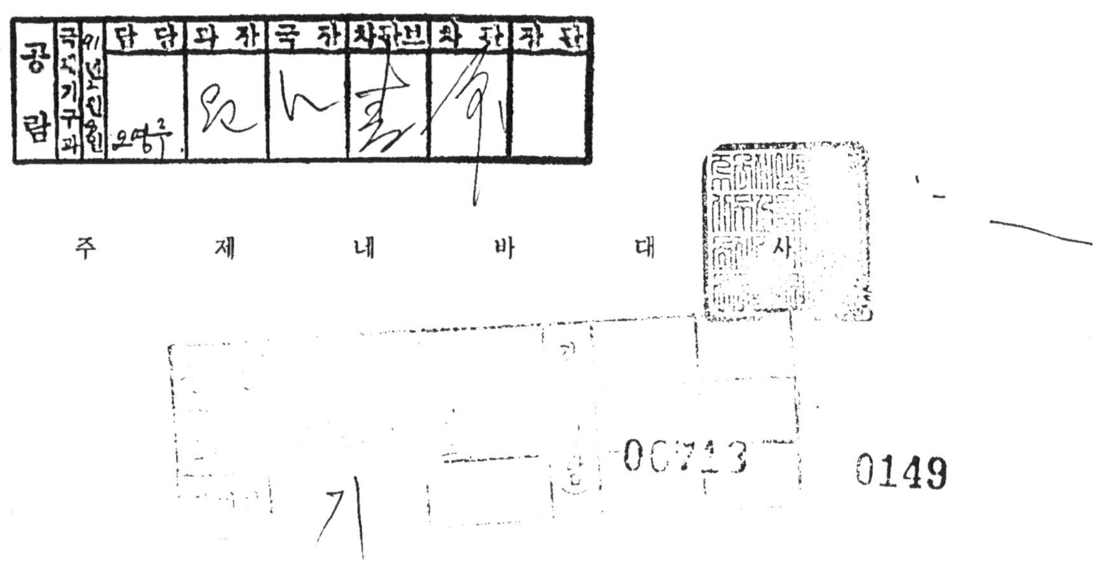

주 제 네 바 대 사

0149

Geneva, 29 January 1991

LE PRÉSIDENT

Sir,

It is with deep gratitude that I acknowledge receipt of the contribution of US$ 30,000 for budget year 1990 which the Government of Korea has made to the International Committee of the Red Cross for its activities in aid of civilians gathered on the border between Iraq and Jordan.

During the last four months of 1990, the ICRC assisted more than 200,000 persons fleeing the Gulf conflict. Since its opening on 12 September through 31 December, Azrak I camp provided water, shelter, and some material relief to close to 70'000 persons; it served more than 275'000 meals. The transit camp 1/28 gave short term emergency help to 43'300 persons in transit through Jordan during this period; its medical dispensary gave about 4'500 medical consultations.

His Excellency
Mr. Chong Ha Yoo
Acting Minister of Foreign Affairs

Seoul

Republic of Korea

0150

19, AVENUE DE LA PAIX, CH-1202 GENÈVE - TÉL. 022 / 734 60 01

In view of the urgency and magnitude of the humanitarian tasks facing the ICRC in that part of the world, I highly appreciate the generous support the Government of Korea has given to our activities.

I am confident that the ICRC will be able to count on your Government's support for its Emergency Appeals also in the future.

On behalf of those affected by the events, I should like to renew my thanks to the Government of Korea for its confidence and financial support, and ask you to accept, Sir, the assurance of my highest consideration.

Cornelio Sommaruga

0151

# 외 무 부

종 별 :

번 호 : GVW-0289 일 시 : 91 0212 1800

수 신 : 장관(국기,중근동)

발 신 : 주 제네바 대사대리

제 목 : 걸프전 관련 ICRC 활동

연: GVW-0235

연호, 표제 관련 ICRC 자료 ( NO.14) 를 별첨 송부함.

첨부: 상기자료 끝

(GVW(F)-62)

(대사대리 박영우-국장)

국기국 중아국

PAGE 1

91.02.13 06:28 DA

외신 1과 통제관

0152

* UPDATE NO. 14 ON INTERNATIONAL RED CROSS AND RED CRESCENT ACTION
* IN THE MIDDLE EAST

* 10 FEBRUARY 1991

GVW(지)-0062 102 12 1800
GVW-209 2011

*
* INTRODUCTION

* INTENSIVE AIR STRIKES CONTINUED IN THE REGION. IT IS STILL NOT
* POSSIBLE TO MAKE AN ACCURATE ASSESSMENT OF HUMANITARIAN NEEDS
* ARISING FROM THE SITUATION. AT THIS POINT, THERE HAS BEEN NO
* MAJOR CIVILIAN DISPLACEMENT TO THE COUNTRIES NEIGHBOURING IRAQ.

* THE ICRC PURSUES EFFORTS TO CARRY OUT ITS PROTECTION AND
* ASSISTANCE ACTIVITIES IN THE MIDDLE EAST ON BEHALF OF CIVILIANS
* AND PRISONERS OF WAR ACCORDING TO THE THIRD AND FOURTH GENEVA
* CONVENTIONS OF 12 AUGUST 1949. VISITS HAVE BEEN MADE TO IRAQI
* PRISONERS OF WAR HELD BY THE ALLIED FORCES. IT IS A MAJOR CONCERN
* FOR THE ICRC THAT IT HAS NOT YET RECEIVED A RESPONSE FROM THE
* IRAQI AUTHORITIES REGARDING VISITS TO ALLIED PRISONERS OF WAR
* HELD BY THE IRAQI ARMED FORCES.

* CONTACTS WITH ICRC DELEGATES IN IRAQ ARE DIFFICULT BUT REGULAR.
* FIVE ADDITIONAL ICRC DELEGATES CROSSED INTO IRAQ WITH THE ICRC
* CONVOY ON SATURDAY.

* PROTECTION AND TRACING ACTIVITIES

* PRISONERS OF WAR (POWS), MISSING IN ACTION AND CIVILIAN INTERNEES

* IN ACCORDANCE WITH THE THIRD GENEVA CONVENTION, THE ICRC WAS
* NOTIFIED BY THE UNITED KINGDOM AND UNITED STATES' NATIONAL
* INFORMATION BUREAUX OF THE CAPTURE OF 40 MEMBERS OF THE IRAQI
* ARMED FORCES. ON 30 JANUARY THE ICRC VISITED 214 IRAQI POWS AND
* BETWEEN 3 AND 6 FEBRUARY VISITED 635 IRAQI POWS HELD BY THE
* KINGDOM OF SAUDI ARABIA OR THE UNITED STATES ARMED FORCES IN THE
* KINGDOM OF SAUDI ARABIA. SOME OF THESE POWS AFTER HAVING BEEN
* TRANSFERRED FROM A TRANSIT CENTRE TO A CAMP, WERE VISITED A
* SECOND TIME BY THE ICRC.

* ALL THE RELEVANT INFORMATION AVAILABLE ON THE ABOVE MENTIONED
* PROTECTED PERSONS IS BEING TRANSMITTED TO THE POWER ON WHICH THEY
* DEPEND ACCORDING TO THE THIRD GENEVA CONVENTIONS OF 12 AUGUST
* 1949.

* TRACING AND MAILING SERVICES

* SINCE 17 JANUARY, THE ICRC CENTRAL TRACING AGENCY HAS REGISTERED
* 204 'ANXIOUS FOR NEWS' MESSAGES CONCERNING 420 PERSONS FROM
* FAMILIES WHO HAVE NO CONTACT WITH THEIR RELATIVES IN IRAQ OR
* KUWAIT. ALL MESSAGES ARE BEING FORWARDED TO THE ICRC DELEGATION
* IN BAGHDAD. THE ICRC RESOLVED TWO TRACING CASES CONCERNING
* FAMILIES WHO HAD LEFT IRAQ.

* MEDICAL ACTIVITIES

* A MEDICAL CO-ORDINATOR ARRIVED IN BAGHDAD WITH THE FIRST ICRC
* CONVOY FROM IRAN ON 31 JANUARY.

* A SECOND ICRC CONVOY WITH 15 TONNES OF MEDICINES AND MEDICAL
* SUPPLIES, PROVIDED IN PART BY THE IRANIAN RED CRESCENT, WENT INTO
* IRAQ ON 9 FEBRUARY.

62-2-1

0153

TOTAL P.01

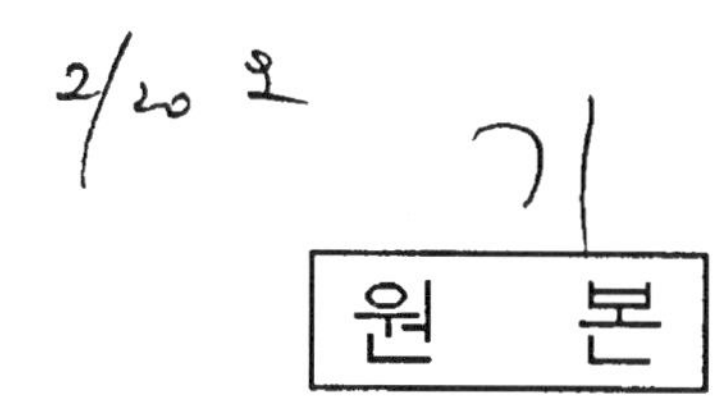

# 외 무 부

종 별 :

번 호 : GVW-0323 일 시 : 91 0219 1850

수 신 : 장관(국기,중근동)

발 신 : 주제네바대사대리

제 목 : 걸프전 관련 ICRC 활동

연: GVW-0289

연호, 표제관련 ICRC 자료( NO.15) 를 별첨송부함.

첨부: 상기자료.끝.

(대사대리 박영우-국장)

국기국 중아국

PAGE 1

91.02.20 06:43 CG

외신 1과 통제관

0154

* UPDATE NO. 15 ON INTERNATIONAL RED CROSS AND RED CRESCENT ACTION
* IN THE MIDDLE EAST

GUW(CH)-0067 1021/P185
// GUW-0323 첨부 //

* 19 FEBRUARY 1991

* INTRODUCTION

* THE NUMBER OF CIVILIAN CASUALTIES RESULTING FROM THE CONFLICT IN
* THE MIDDLE EAST IS RISING. A GROUND ATTACK APPEARS IMMINENT.

* ICRC DELEGATES IN BAGHDAD HAVE NOTED A STEADY DETERIORATION IN
* THE LIVING CONDITIONS OF THE CIVILIAN POPULATION. THE ICRC IS
* ALSO CONCERNED ABOUT THE PLIGHT OF CIVILIANS IN OTHER PARTS OF
* IRAQ AND IN KUWAIT, TO WHICH IT HAS NOT YET HAD ACCESS.

* MISSIONS TO THE REGION

* DURING A VISIT TO AMMAN ON 16 AND 17 FEBRUARY, THE ICRC PRESIDENT
* MET WITH QUEEN NOUR AND THE CROWN PRINCE HASSAN OF JORDAN. MR.
* SOMMARUGA ALSO MET WITH THE JORDANIAN VICE-MINISTER OF THE
* INTERIOR, THE IRAQI AMBASSADOR IN JORDAN, YASSER ARAFAT, CHAIRMAN
* OF THE PLO AND DR. ABU GOURA, PRESIDENT OF THE JORDAN NATIONAL
* RED CRESCENT SOCIETY. THESE MEETINGS PERMITTED THE ICRC TO
* REITERATE THE ORGANIZATION'S MANDATE FOR THE PROTECTION AND
* ASSISTANCE OF THE VICTIMS OF THE CONFLICT ACCORDING TO THE GENEVA
* CONVENTIONS AND THE GLOBAL APPROACH OF THE RED CROSS AND RED
* CRESCENT ACTION IN THE MIDDLE EAST.

* THE ICRC DELEGATE GENERAL, MR. GNAEDINGER VISITED BAGHDAD BETWEEN
* 14 AND 16 FEBRUARY WHERE HE HELD TALKS WITH THE IRAQI MINISTER
* OF HEALTH AND THE IRAQI RED CRESCENT.

* MR. BELAOUANE, PRESIDENT OF THE ALGERIAN RED CRESCENT SOCIETY,
* ALSO WAS ON MISSION IN BAGHDAD.

* DIPLOMATIC ACTIVITIES

* A NOTE VERBALE WAS SENT BY THE ICRC TO THE 27 PARTIES TO THE
* CONFLICT IN THE MIDDLE EAST REGARDING THE PROTECTION OF THE
* CIVILIAN POPULATIONS IN KUWAIT AND IRAQ, THE POSSIBILITY OF
* ESTABLISHING NEUTRALIZED ZONES, MODALITIES FOR THE EVACUATION OF
* THE WOUNDED AND FOR THE FREE PASSAGE OF RELIEF CONVOYS. THE ICRC
* ONCE AGAIN OFFERED ITS SERVICES TO FACILITATE THE REALIZATION OF
* THESE OBJECTIVES.

* THE SANCTIONS COMMITTEE OF THE UNITED NATIONS WAS INFORMED BY THE
* ICRC OF THE TRANSPORT OF FOOD AND WATER PURIFICATION EQUIPMENT
* INTO IRAQ.

* PROTECTION AND TRACING ACTIVITIES

* PRISONERS OF WAR, MISSING IN ACTION AND CIVILIAN INTERNEES

* IN ACCORDANCE WITH THE THIRD GENEVA CONVENTION OF 12 AUGUST 1949,
* THE ICRC IS REGULARLY NOTIFIED BY THE STATES PARTY TO THE
* COALITION OF THE CAPTURE OF MEMBERS OF THE IRAQI ARMED FORCES.
* THE INSTITUTION RECEIVES CAPTURE CARDS FROM IRAQI PRISONERS OF
* WAR WHO WISH TO INFORM THEIR FAMILIES OF THEIR WHEREABOUTS.
* BETWEEN 17 JANUARY AND 14 FEBRUARY THE CENTRAL TRACING AGENCY IN
* GENEVA REGISTERED FILES FOR 301 IRAQI POWS.

3-1

0155

TOTAL P.01

* THE ICRC DELEGATES IN SAUDI ARABIA CONTINUED VISITS TO IRAQI
* POWS. FOR NOTIFICATION PURPOSES, THE DELEGATES CONCENTRATED ON
* REGISTERING ALL POWS HELD BY THE DETAINING POWER.

* ALL AVAILABLE AND RELEVANT INFORMATION ON THE ABOVE-MENTIONED
* PROTECTED PERSONS IS TRANSMITTED TO THE POWER ON WHICH THEY
* DEPEND, ACCORDING TO THE THIRD GENEVA CONVENTION.

* IN SPITE OF THE ICRC'S EFFORTS, THE INSTITUTION HAS NOT YET
* RECEIVED NOTIFICATION FROM THE IRAQI AUTHORITIES OF THE CAPTURE
* OF MEMBERS OF THE COALITION FORCES. THUS, THE ICRC DOES NOT YET
* HAVE ACCESS TO THESE PRISONERS OF WAR.

* TRACING AND MAILING SERVICES

* SINCE 17 JANUARY, THE CENTRAL TRACING AGENCY HAS REGISTERED 342
* 'ANXIOUS FOR NEWS' MESSAGES CONCERNING 699 PERSONS FROM FAMILIES
* WHICH HAVE NO CONTACT WITH THEIR RELATIVES IN KUWAIT AND IRAQ.

* MEDICAL AND SANITATION ACTIVITIES

* THE ICRC DELEGATION CONFIRMS THAT THERE IS A SEVERE LACK OF
* DRINKING WATER IN BAGHDAD BECAUSE OF DAMAGE TO THE SUPPLY SYSTEM
* AND LACK OF FUEL AND ELECTRICITY. WATER PURIFICATION SYSTEMS ARE
* NON-FUNCTIONAL WHICH MEANS THERE IS A RISK FOR SPREAD OF VARIOUS
* INFECTIOUS DISEASES. THE DELEGATION WILL CARRY OUT SURVEYS IN
* MAJOR URBAN AREAS SHORTLY IN ORDER TO HAVE A MORE COMPREHENSIVE
* PICTURE OF THE SITUATION. THE ICRC IS REGULARLY IN CONTACT WITH
* THE IRAQI MINISTRY OF HEALTH.

* IN VIEW OF THE URGENT NEED FOR WATER, THE ICRC IS SENDING A
* MOBILE WATER PURIFICATION UNIT, FROM THE ITALIAN RED CROSS, TO
* BAGHDAD AS A FIRST RESPONSE TO THIS PROBLEM. THIS UNIT HAS THE
* CAPACITY FOR PURIFYING AND PACKAGING 80,000 LITRES OF WATER A
* DAY. STORAGE AND DISTRIBUTION UNITS WITH THE CAPACITY TO SUPPLY
* 500,000 LITRES PER DAY HAVE ALSO BEEN MOBILIZED TO SERVE
* HOSPITALS AND VULNERABLE GROUPS.

* THE ICRC HAS FACILITATED THE TRANSPORT OF MEDICAL MATERIALS PUT
* AT ITS DISPOSAL BY THE RED CROSS AND RED CRESCENT SOCIETIES AND
* DONOR GOVERNMENTS. A CONVOY WHICH LEAVES 19 FEBRUARY FROM TEHRAN
* CARRIES AN ADDITIONAL 10 TONNES OF MEDICINES AND MEDICAL
* SUPPLIES.

* FOLLOWING THE VISIT OF THE VICE-PRESIDENT OF THE MOROCCAN RED
* CRESCENT SOCIETY TO ICRC HEADQUARTERS IN GENEVA LAST WEEK, THE
* MOROCCAN GOVERNMENT IS SENDING 60 TONNES AND THE MOROCCAN RED
* CRESCENT SOCIETY 40 TONNES OF MEDICINES AND MEDICAL SUPPLIES TO
* TEHRAN FOR USE IN IRAQ AND KUWAIT. THE YEMENITE RED CRESCENT
* SOCIETY SENT 30 TONNES OF MEDICINES AND MEDICAL SUPPLIES TO
* TEHRAN. THE ALGERIAN, SUDANESE, TUNISIAN AND YEMENITE RED
* CRESCENT SOCIETIES HAVE MEDICAL TEAMS PREPARED TO INTERVENE IN
* IRAQ ON SHORT NOTICE.
*

* RELIEF ACTIVITIES

* THE LEAGUE OF RED CROSS AND RED CRESCENT SOCIETIES' DELEGATE IN
* EGYPT REPORTED THAT MORE THAN 16,000 EVACUEES FROM IRAQ AND
* KUWAIT HAVE RETURNED TO EGYPT SINCE 17 JANUARY. RETURNEES ARE
* PROVIDED WITH FOOD AND BLANKETS, AS NEEDED, BEFORE BEING TRANS-
* PORTED TO THEIR GOVERNORATE OF ORIGIN. IN YEMEN, THE YEMENITE RED
* CRESCENT SOCIETY RECEIVES DAILY 30-40 FAMILIES WHICH HAVE LEFT
* KUWAIT AND IRAQ IN ITS TRANSIT CAMPS.

3-2 0156

* THE ICRC CONTINUES TO MEET HUMANITARIAN NEEDS AT THE JORDANIAN/
* IRAQI BORDER WHERE APPROXIMATELY 2,500 PEOPLE WAIT TO CROSS INTO
* JORDAN.

* THE ABOVE-MENTIONED ICRC CONVOY FROM TEHRAN TO IRAQ ALSO CARRIES
* FOODSTUFFS FOR EMERGENCY STOCK AND ESSENTIAL ITEMS FOR THE
* DELEGATION IN BAGHDAD SUCH AS FUEL. THE CONVOYS ARE ORGANIZED
* WITH THE EFFICIENT HELP OF THE IRANIAN RED CRESCENT SOCIETY. THE
* SUPPORT OF THE ISLAMIC REPUBLIC OF IRAN IS ESSENTIAL TO THE
* OPERATION OF THE INTERNATIONAL RED CROSS AND RED CRESCENT ACTION
* IN THE MIDDLE EAST.

* THE NETHERLANDS RED CROSS SENT A TOTAL OF 66.3 TONNES OF VARIOUS
* RELIEF ITEMS WITH SEVERAL FLIGHTS FROM AMSTERDAM AND MOMBASA TO
* DAMASCUS FOR THE BENELUX CAMP MODULE IN SYRIA.

* THE GERMAN RED CROSS CONVOY LEAVES ANKARA 19 FEBRUARY FOR TEHRAN
* WITH 25 VEHICLES, 16 OF WHICH ARE LORRIES, CARRYING 1/3 OF A CAMP
* MODULE. THE LORRIES WILL REMAIN IN IRAN AT THE DISPOSITION OF THE
* ICRC FOR FUTURE CONVOYS TO IRAQ.

* ONE THIRD OF A CAMP MODULE PREPARED BY THE NORDIC RED CROSS
* SOCIETIES (DANISH RC, LEAD AGENT) IS EN ROUTE TO TEHRAN BY LORRY
* AND BY AIR. THE SWEDISH RED CROSS ORDERED 8 VOLVO TRUCKS WHICH
* WILL BE SENT TO TEHRAN IN MARCH.

* THE AMERICAN RED CROSS PREPARED ONE COMPLETE CAMP MODULE, THE
* CANADIAN RED CROSS HAS MOBILIZED PART OF A CAMP MODULE. THE
* MATERIAL FROM BOTH RED CROSS SOCIETIES WILL BE TRANSFERRED
* SHORTLY TO CYPRUS.

* FINANCE

* THE ICRC THANKS DONORS FOR THE GENEROUS CONTRIBUTIONS IN KIND AND
* IN CASH AND REQUESTS FURTHER CASH CONTRIBUTIONS TO CARRY ON WITH
* THIS IMPORTANT OPERATION FOR THE VICTIMS OF THE WAR IN THE MIDDLE
* EAST.

* FOR FURTHER INFORMATION PLEASE CONTACT SO/REX.

* BEST REGARDS,

* CHRISTIAN KORNEVALL
* SO/REX, ICRC, GENEVA

0157

TOTAL P.02

원 본

# 외 무 부

종 별 :

번 호 : GVW-0357 일 시 : 91 0225 1900

수 신 : 장 관(국기,중근동)

발 신 : 주 제네바 대사대리

제 목 : 걸프전 관련 ICRC 활동

연: GVW-0323

연호, 표제관련 ICRC 자료 (NO.16 및 17)를 별첨 송부함.

첨부: 상기 자료

( GVW(F)-0078). 끝

(대사 박수길-국장)

국기국 1차보 2차보 중아국 정문국 청와대 안기부

PAGE 1

91.02.26 08:54 WG

외신 1과 통제관

0158

GVW(F) 0018 10225 1800

* UPDATE NO. 14 ON INTERNATIONAL RED CROSS AND RED CRESCENT ACTION
* IN THE MIDDLE EAST

"GVW-0357 첨부"

* 22 FEBRUARY 1991

* INTRODUCTION

* NEW DIPLOMATIC EFFORTS WERE MADE TOWARD A POLITICAL SOLUTION TO
* THE CONFLICT IN THE MIDDLE EAST. LIVING CONDITIONS FOR CIVILIANS
* IN IRAQ CONTINUE TO DETERIORATE.

* ICRC ACTIVITIES IN IRAQ

* UPON HIS RETURN FROM A MISSION IN IRAQ, THE ICRC DELEGATE GENERAL
* FOR THE MIDDLE EAST, MR. GNAEDINGER, REITERATED THE FOLLOWING
* THREEE OBJECTIVES FOR ICRC ACTIVITIES IN THE MIDDLE EAST:

* 1) PURSUE CONTACTS WITH ALL PARTIES CONCERNED FOR THE PROTECTION
* OF ALL POWS RESULTING FROM THE CONFLICT IN THE MIDDLE EAST,

* 2) RESPOND TO THE NEEDS OF THE CIVILIAN POPULATION IN KUWAIT AND
* IRAQ WITH MEDICAL AND RELIEF ASSISTANCE,

* 3) ASSESS AND RESPOND TO THE NEEDS OF PERSONS PROTECTED BY THE
* FOURTH GENEVA CONVENTION IN IRAQ, IN PARTICULAR, THIRD-PARTY
* NATIONALS IN KUWAIT AND IRAQ,

* THERE ARE PRESENTLY 11 ICRC DELEGATES IN BAGHDAD.

* THE ICRC IS CURRENTLY MAKING AN INDEPTH SURVEY OF PRESENT
* CONDITIONS IN BAGHDAD AND INTENDS TO EXTEND THE SURVEY TO OTHER
* AREAS IN IRAQ TO ASSESS THE NEEDS OF THE CIVILIAN POPULATION. THE
* ENERGY SYSTEMS FOR ELECTRICITY AND FUEL AS WELL AS THE SANITATION
* SYSTEM IN BAGHDAD HAVE BEEN SEVERELY DAMAGED. THEREFORE,
* TRANSPORT IS DIFFICULT, ELECTRICITY AND GAS SERVICES ARE LIMITED,
* DISTRIBUTION OF POTABLE WATER HAS BEEN INTERRUPTED, SEWAGE
* SYSTEMS HAVE BEEN SEVERELY AFFECTED.

* FOOD IS AVAILABLE BUT PRICES ARE INCREASING SIGNIFICANTLY. A
* RATIONING SYSTEM IS IN EFFECT FOR BASIC FOODSTUFFS BUT DISTRIBU-
* TION IS HAMPERED BECAUSE OF THE SITUATION.

* STOCKS OF MEDICINES ARE DEPLETED IN PHARMACIES IN BAGHDAD.

* THE ICRC INTENDS TO INTERVENE WITH SANITATION, MEDICAL AND RELIEF
* ASSISTANCE:

* THE ICRC INTENDS TO RE-ESTABLISH WATER PURIFICATION AND DISTRIBU-
* TION SYSTEMS BY PROVIDING SPARE PARTS FOR DAMAGED WATER PURIFICA-
* TION EQUIPMENT. AS AN EMERGENCY MEASURE, A MOBILE WATER PURIFICA-
* TION UNIT WILL BE SET UP TO SUPPLY WATER TO HOSPITALS AND
* VULNERABLE GROUPS.

* MEDICINES AND MEDICAL SUPPLIES WILL BE DISTRIBUTED TO HOSPITALS
* AND DISPENSARIES. THE ICRC, AS A NEUTRAL AND INDEPENDENT
* INTERMEDIARY BETWEEN IRAQ'S MINISTRY OF HEALTH AND ITS USUAL
* SUPPLIERS, WILL FACILITATE THE IMPORT OF MEDICINES AND MEDICAL
* SUPPLIES. IN CO-ORDINATION WITH THE IRAQI RED CRESCENT, THE ICRC
* WILL INTERVENE WITH MEDICAL PERSONNEL AS NEEDED.

0159

* THE ICRC INTENDS TO PROVIDE FOODSTUFFS TO THIRD-PARTY NATIONALS
* IN KUWAIT AND IRAQ AS WELL AS TO VULNERABLE GROUPS AMONG THE
* IRAQI POPULATION.

* THE UN SECURITY COUNCIL APPROVED THE DELIVERY OF A MOBILE WATER
* PURIFICATION UNIT, MEDICAL SUPPLIES AND EMERGENCY STOCKS OF FOOD
* BY THE ICRC TO IRAQ. NEGOTIATIONS FOR ADDITIONAL SHIPMENTS OF
* FOODSTUFFS ARE UNDER WAY.

* PROTECTION AND TRACING ACTIVITIES

* PRISONERS OF WAR, MISSING IN ACTION AND CIVILIAN INTERNEES

* IN ACCORDANCE WITH THE THIRD GENEVA CONVENTION OF 12 AUGUST 1949:

* THE ICRC IS REGULARLY NOTIFIED BY THE STATES PARTY TO THE
* COALITION OF THE CAPTURE OF MEMBERS OF THE IRAQI ARMED FORCES.
* THE ORGANIZATION ALSO RECEIVES THE CAPTURE CARDS OF THOSE WHO
* WANT TO INFORM THEIR FAMILIES OF THEIR WHEREABOUTS.

* ICRC DELEGATES IN SAUDI ARABIA HAVE CONTINUED THEIR VISITS TO
* IRAQI POWS, WITH PARTICULAR ATTENTION TO THE REGISTRATION OF ALL
* POWS BY THE DETAINING POWERS FOR NOTIFICATION PURPOSES.

* ALL AVAILABLE AND RELEVANT INFORMATION ON THE ABOVE-MENTIONED
* PROTECTED PERSONS IS TRANSMITTED TO THE POWER ON WHICH THEY
* DEPEND, ACCORDING TO THE PROVISIONS OF THE THIRD GENEVA CONVEN-
* TION.

* IN SPITE OF NUMEROUS EFFORTS, THE ICRC HAS NOT YET BEEN NOTIFIED
* BY THE IRAQI AUTHORITIES OF THE CAPTURE OF MEMBERS OF THE
* COALITION FORCES. ICRC DELEGATES STILL DO NOT HAVE ACCESS TO
* THESE PRISONERS OF WAR. SINCE 17 JANUARY, THE ICRC SUBMITTED
* REPORTS INDICATING 60 MEMBERS OF THE COALITION FORCES MISSING IN
* ACTION.

* IN ACCORDANCE WITH THE FOURTH GENEVA CONVENTION, BETWEEN 11 AND
* 15 FEBRUARY, ICRC DELEGATES VISITED THREE IRAQIS PLACED IN
* ASSIGNED RESIDENCE IN FRANCE.

* TRACING AND MAILING SERVICES

* SINCE 17 JANUARY, THE CENTRAL TRACING AGENCY HAS REGISTERED 557
* 'ANXIOUS FOR NEWS' MESSAGES FROM FAMILIES WHICH HAVE NO CONTACT
* WITH THEIR RELATIVES IN IRAQ OR KUWAIT.

0160

6-2

* MEDICAL ACTIVITIES

* AN ICRC SANITATION ENGINEER IS DOING A SURVEY OF NEEDS IN
* BAGHDAD. THE MOBILE WATER PURIFICATION SYSTEM AND A TEAM OF
* TECHNICIANS IS BEING FLOWN INTO TEHRAN. THE WATER PURIFICATION
* EQUIPMENT WILL BE TRANSFERRED TO BAGHDAD SHORTLY.

* A DONATION OF MEDICINES AND MEDICAL SUPPLIES FROM THE MOROCCAN
* GOVERNMENT FOR USE IN IRAQ ARRIVED BY AIR IN TEHRAN TODAY. A
* SHIPMENT FROM THE MOROCCAN RED CRESCENT SOCIETY WILL BE SENT NEXT
* WEEK.

* THE INDIAN RED CROSS SOCIETY ANNOUNCED THAT A SHIPMENT OF 15
* TONNES OF MEDICINES AND MEDICAL SUPPLIES WILL BE SENT TO TEHRAN
* ON 23 FEBRUARY.

* THE NORDIC RED CROSS SOCIETIES HAVE ASSEMBLED 80 TONNES OF
* MEDICINES AND MEDICAL SUPPLIES WHICH WILL BE FLOWN TO TEHRAN THIS
* WEEKEND FOR TRANSFER TO IRAQ.

* RELIEF ACTIVITIES

* THE SURVEY OF THE KURDISTAN PROVINCE IN NORTHERN IRAN HAS BEEN
* COMPLETED. A SURVEY OF THE CONDITIONS IN THE KHUZESTAN PROVINCE
* IN SOUTHERN IRAN WAS BEGUN. THE IRANIAN RED CRESCENT IS CON-
* STRUCTING A REFUGEE CAMP JOINTLY WITH THE ICRC IN THE BAKHTARAN
* PROVINCE.

* THE ICRC CONTINUES HUMANITARIAN INTERVENTION FOR 300 DIVERSE
* THIRD-PARTY NATIONALS AT TREBIL ON THE IRAQI/JORDANIAN BORDER.
* THE EGYPTIAN NATIONALS WHO HAD BEEN BLOCKED AT THIS POINT HAVE
* RETURNED TO EGYPT.

* THE ICRC INTERVENED WITH ISRAELI AUTHORITIES ON BEHALF OF
* PALESTINIANS BLOCKED AT THE BRIDGES ON THE JORDAN RIVER.

* A FRENCH RED CROSS REPRESENTATIVE ARRIVED IN DAMASCUS TO DISCUSS
* THE FRENCH RED CROSS RELIEF ACTIVITIES WITH THE SYRIAN ARAB RED
* CRESCENT SOCIETY.

FINANCE

IN RESPONSE TO THE APPEAL SENT OUT ON 17 JANUARY FOR SFR. 141
MILLION FOR THE INTERNATIONAL RED CROSS AND RED CRESCENT ACTION
* IN THE MIDDLE EAST DONORS HAVE GENEROUSLY PLEDGED MORE THAN SFR.
21 MILLION IN CASH AND MORE THAN SFR. 30 MILLION AS CONTRIBUTIONS
IN KIND. THESE DONATIONS ARE FOR USE IN IRAQ, KUWAIT AND
NEIGHBOURING COUNTRIES AFFECTED BY THE CONFLICT.

0161

6-3

5.c' - 0-16' LENINPROTOCOL 105 P04

* THE FOLLOWING CASH CONTRIBUTIONS AND PLEDGES RECEIVED TO DATE ARE
* LISTED BELOW:

| * GOVERNMENT | AMOUNT IN SFR. | NATIONAL SOCIETY | AMOUNT IN SFR. |
|---|---|---|---|
| * AUSTRALIA | 980,000 | AUSTRIA | 3,075 |
| * CANADA | 1,618,700 | BRAZIL | 25,200 |
| * FINLAND | 701,000 | CANADA | 1,750 |
| * ITALY | 2,260,000 | HUNGARY | 1,000 |
| * JAPAN | 3,780,000 | INDONESIA | 31,500 |
| * SPAIN | 630,000 | JAPAN | 368,500 |
| * SWEDEN | 2,250,000 | MONACO | 25,000 |
| * UNITED KINGDOM | 6,182,500 | UNITED KINGDOM | 123,650 |
| * UNITED STATES | 1,260,000 | UNITED STATES | 252,000 |

*
*
* CASH PLEDGES ARE STILL NEEDED FOR THIS OPERATION. SOME MAJOR
* DONORS HAVE NOT YET RESPONDED DIRECTLY TO THIS APPEAL BUT HAVE
* MADE SIGNIFICANT CONTRIBUTIONS TO THEIR NATIONAL SOCIETIES'
* ACTIVITIES IN THE FRAMEWORK OF THE INTERNATIONAL RED CROSS AND
* RED CRESCENT ACTION IN THE MIDDLE EAST. FUTURE PLEDGES AND
* CONTRIBUTIONS TO THE INTERNATIONAL RED CROSS AND RED CRESCENT
* ACTION WILL BE MENTIONED IN COMING UPDATES.

* FOR FURTHER INFORMATION PLEASE CONTACT SO/REX.

* BEST REGARDS,

* CHRISTIAN KORNEVALL
* SO/REX, ICRC, GENEVA

*

* +++
* ++++
415519 KOGE CH

0162

6-4

UPDATE NO. 17 ON INTERNATIONAL RED CROSS AND RED CRESCENT ACTION IN THE MIDDLE EAST

25 FEBRUARY 1991

## INTRODUCTION

THE GROUND BATTLE STARTED EARLY THIS MORNING. THE ICRC HAS STEPPED UP ITS ACTIVITY LEVEL IN ORDER TO MEET EXISTING AND UPCOMING NEEDS BY SENDING MEDICAL EQUIPMENT, FIELD HOSPITALS AND MEDICAL PERSONNEL TO THE AREA.

THE ON-GOING PROTECTION AND TRACING ACTIVITIES IN THE REGION, AS DESCRIBED IN UPDATE NO. 16, ARE BEING REINFORCED IN ORDER TO COPE WITH THE NEW SITUATION. THE HIGHEST PRIORITY OF THE ICRC STILL REMAINS ACCESS TO KUWAIT IN ORDER TO CARRY OUT A PROTECTION AND ASSISTANCE PROGRAMME FOR VICTIMS OF THE CONFLICT.

## MEDICAL ACTIVITIES

THE ICRC NOW HAS FOUR FIELD HOSPITALS MOBILIZED TO BE INSTALLED OR ALREADY IN PLACE AS FOLLOWS:

IN AMMAN - A FIELD HOSPITAL WITH MEDICAL EQUIPMENT AND SUPPLIES, PROVIDED BY THE NORWEGIAN RED CROSS, HAS BEEN STORED.

A SECOND NORWEGIAN FIELD HOSPITAL IS ON ITS WAY FROM BAKTARAN TO AHWAS, IRAN.

ALSO IN AHWAS - A COMPLETE FIELD HOSPITAL, PROVIDED BY THE SWEDISH RED CROSS IS BEING MOBILIZED FOR IMMEDIATE DISPATCH IN ORDER TO BE OPERATIONAL AS NEEDS ARISE.

THE IRANIAN GOVERNMENT AND RED CRESCENT SOCIETY HAVE GIVEN THEIR FULL SUPPORT IN ORDER TO FACILITATE THE ICRC ACTIVITIES IN IRAN FOR IRAQ.

IN BAHRAIN - A COMPLETE FIELD HOSPITAL, PROVIDED BY THE FINNISH RED CROSS, IS BEING MOBILIZED FOR IMMEDIATE DISPATCH IN ORDER TO BE OPERATIONAL AS NEEDS ARISE.

FOUR MORE FIELD HOSPITALS TO BE PROVIDED BY THE NORWEGIAN RED CROSS (2 UNITS), THE GERMAN RED CROSS, AND THE AUSTRIAN RED CROSS ARE ON STAND-BY AND READY TO LEAVE.

MEDICAL TEAMS (ABOUT 150 PERSONS IN TOTAL) FROM THE TUNISIAN AND ALGERIAN RED CRESCENT SOCIETIES ARE BEING PREPARED TO LEAVE FOR IRAQ.

0163

6-5

*
* IN THE SANITATION FIELD, THE ICRC HAS RECEIVED MORE PRECISE
* INFORMATION FROM ITS DELEGATION IN IRAQ CONCERNING THE WATE
* R
* SITUATION IN BAGHDAD. THE ICRC HAS MOBILIZED A SECOND WATE
* R
* LINE FOR THE CITY. THE OPTION TO HAVE A THIRD WATER LINE FO
* R
* OTHER URBAN AREAS HAS BEEN SECURED. THE NEXT CONVOY COMING
* TO
* BAGHDAD WILL MAINLY INCLUDE SANITATION EQUIPMENT.

* RELIEF

* THE GERMAN RED CROSS CONVOY - WHICH INCLUDES 17 TRUCKS, 5
* LAND-CRUISERS AND 2 AMBULANCES - ARRIVING IN TEHRAN TODAY A
* ND
* CARRYING RELIEF MATERIALS COMPRISING ONE-THIRD OF A CAMP
* MODULE, HAS BEEN RE-DIRECTED TOWARDS IRAQ. AFTER DELIVERY O
* F
* THESE RELIEF SUPPLIES IN BAGHDAD, THE ICRC WILL USE THESE
* VEHICLES FOR TRANSPORT BETWEEN BAGHDAD AND TEHRAN.

* BEST REGARDS,

* CHRISTIAN KORNEVALL
* SO/REX, ICRC, GENEVA

* +++
* +++++
415519 KOGE CH
* 414226A CCR CH
* 24-02-91 22:21

16.11.90.22:23

0164

6-6

# 기 안 용 지

| 분류기호 문서번호 | 국기20300- | (전화 : 720-4050 ) | 시 행 상 특별취급 | |
|---|---|---|---|---|
| 보존기간 | 영구 . 준영구. 10. 5 . 3 . 1. | 차 관 | 장 관 | |
| 수 신 처 보존기간 | | | | |
| 시행일자 | 91.3.11. | | | |

| 보조기관 | 국장 | | 협조기관 | 기획관리실장 | 문 서 통 제 |
|---|---|---|---|---|---|
| | 과장 | | | 미주국장 | |
| | | | | 중동아프리카국장 | |
| 기안책임자 | 오영주 | | | 총무과장 | 발 송 인 |

| 경 유 수 신 참 조 | 건 의 | 발신명의 | | |
|---|---|---|---|---|
| 제 목 | 걸프사태 관련 국제기구 구호사업 지원 | | | |

1. 걸프전쟁 종결후 전쟁지역이 극심한 인적.물적 피해를 겪고 난민이 증대함에 따라, UN 관련기구 및 국제적십자사(ICRC)등에서는 적극적인 구호활동을 전개하는 한편 동 구호사업에 필요한 사업비 지원을 각국에 요청하고 있습니다.

2. 상기관련, 아국의 걸프사태 지원의 일환으로 아국과 긴밀한 협조 관계를 유지하고 있는 유엔고등판무관실(UNHCR) 및 국제적십자사(ICRC)측에 아래와 같이 사업비를 지원할 것을 건의하오니 재가하여 주시기 바랍니다.

/계속/

0165

- 아 래 -

1. UNHCR 사업 지원

o 지 원 액 : $15,000

o 지원사유 : 아국이 현재 UNHCR에 납부하는 부담금 2만불은 UNHCR 전체예산의 0.12%에 해당하는것으로 유엔에서 책정한 아국 분담율 0.22%의 절반수준에 불과하므로,UNHCR의 걸프전 구호 사업에 특별 지원함으로써 동기구에 대한 유엔의 아국분담율에 상응하는 기여가능(UNHCR은 91년 아국부담금으로 5만불 납부요청)

2. ICRC 사업 지원

o 지 원 액 : $30,000

o 지원사유 : 걸프전 발발후 동지역에서 적극적으로 인도적 구호 사업을 전개하고 있는 ICRC에 특별지원함으로써, 걸프 복구사업에 대한 아국의 적극적 참여가시화 (아국은 현재 ICRC에 연 15만불을 부담금으로 지불 하고 있으나 ICRC는 연 25만불 지원을 요청중임)

- 2 -

0166

3. 사업비 지원총액 : $45,000

4. 사업비 송금처 : 주제네바 대표부

5. 예산항목 : 정무활동, 해외 경상이전비. 끝

| 분류기호<br>문서번호 | 국기20300-<br>66 | 협조문용지<br>( 2181-2 ) | 결재 | 담당 | 과장 | 국장 |
|---|---|---|---|---|---|---|
| 시행일자 | 1991. 3. 23. | | | (서명) | (서명) | (서명) |
| 수 신 | 총무과장 | 발 신 | 국제기구조약국장 (서 명) | | | |
| 제 목 | 특별지원금 지급 의뢰 | | | | | |

별첨과 같이 재가를 득한 걸프사태 관련 국제기구 특별사업에 대한 지원금 송금을 아래와 같이 의뢰하오니 필요한 조치를 취하여 주시기 바랍니다.

- 아 래 -

1. 사업비 지원내역

   ㅇ UNHCR : $ 15,000

   ㅇ ICRC : $ 30,000

2. 사업비 지원총액 : $ 45,000

3. 사업비 송금처 : 주제네바 대표부

4. 예산항목 : 정무활동, 해외경상 이전비

첨부 : 상기 재가문서 사본 1부. 끝

0168

| | 분류번호 | 보존기간 |
|---|---|---|
| | | |

# 발 신 전 보

번 호 : WGV-0355 910325 1453 DQ 종별 :

수 신 : 주 제네바 대사. 총영사

발 신 : 장 관 (국기)

제 목 : 걸프사태 관련 특별지원비 송금

본부는 걸프사태 관련한 UNHCR과 ICRC의 구호 사업에 각각 $15,000과 $30,000을 지원키로 결정하여 총 $45,000을 송금조치중이니 수령후 UNHCR, ICRC 사무국에 납부~~하고 결과 보고~~바람. 끝

(국제기구조약국장 문동석)

| 보안통제 | |
|---|---|

| 앙고재 | 91년 3월 24일 | 국기과 | 기안자 성명 | | 과 장 | | 국 장 | | 차 관 | 장 관 |
|---|---|---|---|---|---|---|---|---|---|---|
| | | | | | | | 전결 | | | |

| 외신과통제 |
|---|
| |

0169

4/20 오
시분 즐[illegible]

# 대 한 적 십 자 사

(755 - 9301)

한적섭 91 - 1056 1991. 4. 19

수신 외무부장관

참조 국제기구조약국장

제목 걸프전쟁에 따른 한적 모금 현황 통보

1. 지난 1. 17 시작된 걸프전쟁 희생자를 구호하기 위하여 국제 적십자운동은 전쟁희생자를 보호, 원조하며 난민구호,의료활동, 심인업무등을 수행하기 위한 의연금을 각국 정부 및 적십자사를 통하여 지원받을 수 있도록 호소하여 온바 있습니다.

2. 이에따라 정부당국과 대책을 협의한 결과 당사의 역량만으로는 이러한 호소에 대응하기 어려운 형편임을 감안하여 중동진출 국내 주요 기업체에 동참하도록 총재명의 공한으로 요청한 결과 4. 18 현재 별첨내역과 같이 총 미화 27만불의 현금이 본사에 기탁되었음을 알려 드리니 참고 하시기 바랍니다.

발송 1991. 4. 19 대한적십자사

첨부 : 걸프전쟁 희생자 지원 기업체 성금현황 1부 끝

총 재 김 상 협

| 접 수 | 1991. 4. 19 | 전 재 (공 람) |
|---|---|---|
| 처 리 | 71 10897 | |

0170

## 걸프전쟁 희생자 한국기업체 성금 현황

| | 업체명 | 대표자 | 기탁자 | 액수 | 날자 |
|---|---|---|---|---|---|
| 1 | 선경건설 | 회장 최종현 | 전무 김기용 | 미화 15,000불 | 2.9 |
| 2. | 삼양사 | 회장 김상하 | 상무 박종헌 | " | 2.26 |
| 3. | 금호그룹 | 회장 박성용 | 전무 이득산 | " | 2.28 |
| 4. | 유 공 | 사장 김항덕 | 대리 박우종 | " | 3.4 |
| 5. | 럭키금성 | 회장 구자경 | 부사장 이문호 | 미화 50,000불 | 3.5 |
| 6. | 동아건설 | 사장 유영철 | 사장 유영철 | 미화 15,000불 | 3.6 |
| 7. | 쌍용정유 | 회장 이승원 | 부사장 이상온 | 미화 30,000불 | 3.7 |
| 8. | 한진해운 | 사장 이근수 | 상무 김윤기 | 미화 10,000불 | 3.8 |
| 9. | 경인에너지 | 부회장 성낙정 | 차장 김용래 | 미화 20,000불 | 3.8 |
| 10. | 극동정유 | 사장 장홍선 | 차장 유광현 | 미화 10,000불 | 3.12 |
| 11. | 극동건설 | 사장 김세중 | 차장 이용흡 | 미화 10,000불 | 3.15 |
| 12. | (주)대우 | 회장 김우중 | 부장 김우일 | 미화 15,000불 | 3.16 |
| 13. | 삼성종합건설 | 회장 박기석 | 과장 백영석 | 미화 20,000불 | 4.1 |
| 14. | 꽃동네 | 회장 오웅진 | 신부 오웅진 | 미화 10,000불 | 4.1 |
| 15. | (한석)서울지사 | | | 미화 20,000불 | 4.18 |

총 미화 270,000불

0171

# 지 출 처

| 기관 | 금액 | 송금일 | 지 원 목 적 |
| --- | --- | --- | --- |
| 1. ICRC | 10만불 | 3.14 송금 | 걸프전 희생자 지원 |
| 2. ICRC | 8만불 | 3.19 총재결재 | 걸프전 희생자 지원 |
| 3. 연맹 | 9만불 | 3.19 총재결재 | 걸프전 희생자 지원(5만불)<br>이란적신월사의 쿠르드난민 지원(2만불)<br>터키적신월사의 쿠르드난민 지원(2만불) |

0172

4/25 일

# 주 제 네 바 대 표 부

제네(정) 20358-386　　　　　　　　　　　　1991. 4. 19.

수신 : 외무부장관

참조 : 국제기구조약국장

제목 : ICRC의 특별 예산 사업 지원 요청

연 : GVW-0105

1. 당지 국제 적십자 위원회 (ICRC)는 걸프전 종전이후 중동지역에서의 ICRC활동 관련 각국에 대하여 별첨과 같이 특별예산 지원 (Emergency Appeal)을 요청하고 있는바 참고하시기 바랍니다.

2. ICRC는 1.17 걸프전 발발당시 특별 예산 소요를 141 백만 서서프랑으로 추정하였으나 최근 동 특별 예산 소요를 188.2 백만 서서프랑으로 상향조정하였다 하며, 현재 각국으로 부터 84.2 백만 서서프랑 (현금, 현물 및 용역)이 모금되었다 하니 참고 바랍니다. 끝.

주 제 네 바 대 사

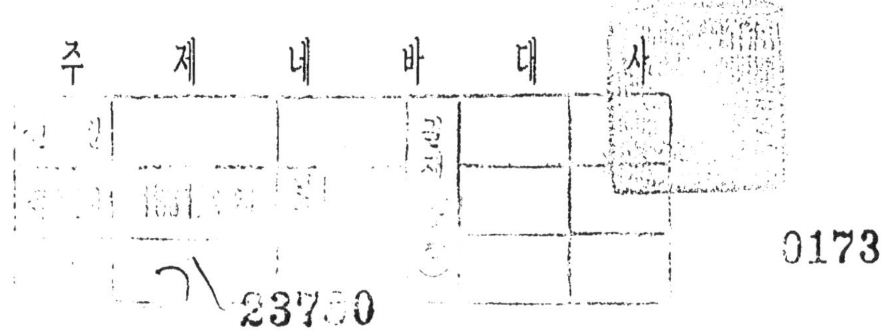

0173

MEMO-TELEX CH
414226Z CCR CH
CI
STORED MSG REF 22144
RYANG LEE

ICRC, GENEVA

REVISED ICRC SPECIAL EM
FOR ICRC OPERATIONS IN T

9 APRIL 1991

8 INTRODUCTION

IN VIEW OF THE FURTHER DETERIORATION OF CONDITIONS IN IRAQ AND THE URGENT NEED FOR HUMANITARIAN AID IN IRAQ AND THE NEIGHBOURING COUNTRIES, THE ICRC LAUNCHES A REVISED SPECIAL EMERGENCY APPEAL FOR ITS OPERATIONS IN THE MIDDLE EAST. THIS APPEAL COVERS ICRC OPERATIONS IN THE FOLLOWING COUNTRIES: IRAN, IRAQ, JORDAN, KUWAIT, SAUDI ARABIA, SYRIA AND TURKEY.

ON 17 JANUARY 1991, THE ICRC LAUNCHED A SPECIAL EMERGENCY APPEAL FOR THE INTERNATIONAL RED CROSS AND RED CRESCENT ACTION IN THE MIDDLE EAST FOR SFR. 141 MILLION. BASED ON THE OBJECTIVES OUTLINED BELOW, A DETAILED BUDGET OF PAST AND PROJECTED OPERATIONAL EXPENDITURE FROM 1 JANUARY - 30 SEPTEMBER 1991 WAS ESTABLISHED. THE ICRC OPERATIONAL BUDGET, AMOUNTING TO SFR. 188.2 MILLION, INCLUDES THE EXPENDITURE OF THE INTERNATIONAL RED CROSS AND RED CRESCENT ACTION IN THE MIDDLE EAST WHICH ENDED ON 25 MARCH 1991. TO DATE, DONORS HAVE GENEROUSLY RESPONDED WITH CONTRIBUTIONS FOR AN ESTIMATED SFR. 84.2 MILLION IN CASH, KIND AND SERVICES.

THEREFORE, THE ICRC APPEALS FOR
++ SFR. 104 MILLION ++
TO CARRY OUT ITS HUMANITARIAN ACTION IN THE MIDDLE EAST.

THE PRESENTATION OF THIS SPECIAL EMERGENCY APPEAL IS OUTLINED BY PROGRAMME ACCORDING TO THE STANDARD ICRC BUDGETING PROCEDURES. THE ICRC WILL REPORT ON OPERATIONS IN THE MIDDLE EAST THROUGH FUTURE UPDATES AND THE STANDARD REPORTING SYSTEM.

PROTECTION AND TRACING

OPERATIONAL OBJECTIVES:

- REGISTER, VISIT AND REPATRIATE ALL PRISONERS OF WAR ACCORDING TO CUSTOMARY ICRC PROCEDURES AND THE 7 MARCH MEMORANDUM OF UNDERSTANDING, ALL PRISONERS OF WAR CAPTURED AND CIVILIANS INTERNED SINCE THE BEGINNING OF THE CONFLICT ON 2 AUGUST 1990,

- RESOLVE MISSING IN ACTION CASES AND CASES OF CIVILIANS UNACCOUNTED FOR,

-

0174

- TRANSMIT RED CROSS MESSAGES AND RESOLVE TRACING CASES OPENED SINCE THE BEGINNING OF THE CONFLICT,

- PROTECT DETAINED PERSONS AND PERSONS IN OCCUPIED TERRITORIES,

THE RESOURCES INVOLVED IN CARRYING OUT THE PROTECTION AND TRACING PROGRAMME INCLUDE OVER 100 ICRC DELEGATES, PICAL, WATER AND SANITATION

OBJECTIVES FOR WATER AND SANITATION OPERATIONS:

IN THE AREAS AFFECTED BY THE CONFLICT (ACCORDING TO NEED)

- PROVIDE PERSONS LIVING IN THE MOST AFFECTED URBAN AREAS WITH A MINIMUM OF POTABLE WATER,

- PROVIDE THE IDENTIFIED VULNERABLE GROUPS WITH PURIFIED WATER IN PLASTIC BAGS (MINIMUM OF 2 LITRES OF POTABLE WATER PER DAY PER PERSON),

- SUPPLY THE EXISTING WATER PURIFICATION STATIONS STILL ABLE TO FUNCTION WITH THE NECESSARY AMOUNT OF CHEMICALS SO THAT POTABLE WATER CAN BE DISTRIBUTED THROUGH THESE SYSTEMS,

- TOGETHER WITH THE WATER AND SANITATION AUTHORITIES, IDENTIFY THE EQUIPMENT AND SPARE PARTS NEEDED TO RESTORE A MINIMUM WATER SUPPLY.

THE HUMAN AND MATERIAL RESOURCES INVOLVED IN THIS PROGRAMME INCLUDE MORE THAN 40 EXPATRIATES AS WELL AS FIVE MOBILE WATER PURIFICATION UNITS AND SPARE PARTS, MORE THAN 1,000 TONNES OF CHEMICALS FOR WATER PURIFICATION, WATER PURIFICATION EQUIPMENT AND SPARE PARTS FOR EXISTING WATER PURIFICATION STATIONS, AT LEAST 100 WATER STORAGE TANKS, 125 WATER TANKER TRUCKS, TEN 110 KVA GENERATORS AND 25 WATER PUMPS.

OBJECTIVES FOR MEDICAL OPERATIONS:

IN THE AREAS AFFECTED BY THE CONFLICT (ACCORDING TO NEED)

- PROVIDE MEDICINE, MEDICAL SUPPLIES AND EQUIPMENT TO HOSPITALS AND MEDICAL FACILITIES DEALING WITH DISEASES SUCH AS DIARRHOEA AND ILLNESSES RELATED TO LACK OF POTABLE WATER,

- PROVIDE MEDICINE, MEDICAL SUPPLIES AND EQUIPMENT, AND MEDICAL PERSONNEL TO HOSPITALS AND MEDICAL FACILITIES WHICH LACK BASIC MEDICAL MATERIAL AND STAFF,

- SET UP ICRC FIELD HOSPITALS.

THE RESOURCES INVOLVED IN MEETING THESE OBJECTIVES INCLUDE ABOUT 80 EXPATRIATES, ABOUT 1,000 TONNES OF MEDICINE, MEDICAL SUPPLIES AND EQUIPMENT, AT LEAST 3 FIELD HOSPITALS, AMBULANCES AND TRANSPORT FOR STAFF AND MATERIALS.

0175

RELIEF

OBJECTIVES FOR THE RELIEF PROGRAMME:

- PROVIDE BASIC RELIEF ITEMS, INCLUDING FOODSTUFFS AND NON-FOOD, TO IDENTIFIED VULNERABLE GROUPS AMONG THE CIVILIAN POPULATION, AS WELL AS TO HOSPITALS, ORPHANAGES AND OTHER SOCIAL INSTITUTIONS IN THE AREAS AFFECTED BY THE CONFLICT.

- ASSIST WITH FOOD AND OTHER RELIEF ITEMS DISPLACED PERSONS IN IRAQ AND REFUGEES IN NEIGHBOURING COUNTRIES WHERE OTHER ORGANIZATIONS ARE UNABLE TO WORK BECAUSE OF SECURITY REASONS.

THE RESOURCES INVOLVED IN MEETING THE RELIEF OBJECTIVES INCLUDE:

APPROXIMATELY 45 EXPATRIATES, 8 COMPLETE CAMP MODULES (CAPACITY 30,000 PERSONS), 3 TRANSIT CAMP MODULES (CAPACITY 5,000 PERSONS), 60,000 FULL FOOD RATIONS PER MONTH FOR IRAQ, BLANKETS, TENTS, FOOD AND OTHER RELIEF ITEMS FOR UP TO 400,000 KURDISH REFUGEES IN IRAN, RUNNING COSTS FOR CAMPS IN IRAN AND JORDAN, FLEET OF MORE THAN 30 ICRC TRUCKS AND OVER 60 RENTED TRUCKS, VEHICLES FOR RELIEF PERSONNEL, AND NECESSARY FUEL, PERMANENT AND TEMPORARY WAREHOUSES FOR RELIEF STOCKS, COSTS FOR RELIEF FLIGHTS.

FINANCE

SUMMARY OF ICRC SPECIAL EMERGENCY BUDGET FOR THE MIDDLE EAST

| PROGRAMMES | TOTAL (IN MILLIONS OF SFR.) |
| --- | --- |
| PROTECTION AND TRACING | 12.4 |
| DISSEMINATION | 0.2 |
| MEDICAL AND SANITATION | 37.7 |
| RELIEF | 119.8 |
| OPERATIONAL SUPPORT | 6.3 |
| CO-OPERATION WITH NATIONAL SOCIETIES | 4.9 |
| OVERHEAD | 6.9 |
| | ------ |
| TOTAL BUDGET 1.1.91 - 30.9.91 | IIMW |

INCLUDING KIND AND SERVICES VALUED AT SFR. 75.2 MILLION

THE ICRC HAS RECEIVED SFR. 44.2 MILLION IN CASH CONTRIBUTIONS AND PLEDGES AND APPROXIMATELY SFR. 40 MILLION IN KIND AND SERVICES. CASH EXPENDITURES FOR HUMANITARIAN OPERATIONS UNTIL THE END OF MARCH TOTAL SFR. 31 MILLION.

THE ICRC APPEALS TO DONORS FOR AN ADDITIONAL SFR. 104 MILLION TO CARRY OUT ITS HUMANITARIAN ACTION IN THE MIDDLE EAST.

FOR A DETAILED SUPPLEMENTARY DOCUMENT ON THE ABOVE SPECIAL EMERGENCY APPEAL OR FURTHER INFORMATION PLEASE CONTACT SO/REX.

BEST REGARDS,

JEAN DE COURTEN
DIRECTOR OF OPERATIONS, ICRC, GENEVA

0176

+++

| 정 리 보 존 문 서 목 록 | | | | | |
|---|---|---|---|---|---|
| 기록물종류 | 일반공문서철 | 등록번호 | 2021010202 | 등록일자 | 2021-01-27 |
| 분류번호 | 721.1 | 국가코드 | XF | 보존기간 | 영구 |
| 명 칭 | 걸프사태 : 외국인 수송 및 난민 지원, 1990-91. 전3권 | | | | |
| 생 산 과 | 중근동과/해외이주과/국제기구과 | 생산년도 | 1990~1991 | 담당그룹 | |
| 권 차 명 | V.3 기타 | | | | |
| 내용목차 | 1. 이란 난민 지원, 1991<br>2. UNESCO 지원, 1990<br>* 요르단 및 이집트 난민자녀 특별교육을 위한 자금 지원 요청<br>3. 걸스카우트 평화의 주머니 보내기 운동 | | | | |

0001

1. 이란 난민 지원, 1991

0002

| 관리번호 | 91-455 |
|---|---|

원 본

# 외 무 부

종 별 : 지 급

번 호 : IRW-0038 일 시 : 91 0117 1900

수 신 : 장관(중근동,건설부,기정)

발 신 : 주 이란 대사

제 목 : 주재국의 구호물자 지원요청

1. 본직은 금 1.17(화) 주재국 외무부 아주대양주국 ROUIS SEPHAT 심의관과 면담한 바, 요지 아래보고함.

가. 구호물자 지원 요청

-페만사태에따라 이란은 이라크로부터 10 만명이상 수십만명(주로 방글라데시, 태국, 필리핀등 아주지역 국민 및 이라크인)의 피난민이 올것으로 예상함.

-이란정부는 인도적인 견지에서 동인들의 이란입국을 허용키로 하였으며, 국경근처에 피난민 캠프를 설치코자함.

-동 난민수용에 대비, 이란은 국제적십자의 지원을 이미 요청하였는바, 아국에서도 천막, 의약품, 의료단, 식량, 발전기등을 긴급 지원하여줄것을 요청함.

-본직은 본국과 협의후 회보할것이라 답변하였으니, 적의 검토회시바람.

나. 이라크내 아국근로자의 이란대피

-당지 체류중인 현대건설 임원은 본사로부터 이라크내에 잔류중인 아국인 22명 및 태국인 방글라데시 근로자(숫자미상)의 이란 대피 가능성에 대비토록 지시를 받았다고 당관에 통보하고, 당관의 지원을 요청함.

-본직은 상기 아국인 및 제 3 국 근로자에대한 입국사증 발급, 동인들을 접수하기 위한 당관직원 및 현대건설 임원의 국경지역 방문허가 및 국경지역에서 테헤란까지의 교통편 제공등을 요청한바, SEPHAT 심의관은 원칙적으로 협조를 약속하고 관계기관과 협의, 결과를 통보해 주겠다고 말함.

-당관은 일단 상기 아국인및 제 3 국 근로자의 명단(160 명)을 SEPHAT 심의관에 수교하고, 국경도착시 일단 접수하여줄것을 요청한대대해 이를 수락하고, 곧 국경초소에 전달하겠다고 답변함.(면담 3 시간이후, 당관은 외무부 당직을통하여 동명단이 FAX 로 국경지역 주정부에 전달되었음을 확인함)

| 중아국 | 장관 | 차관 | 1차보 | 2차보 | 청와대 | 안기부 | 건설부 |
|---|---|---|---|---|---|---|---|

PAGE 1

91.01.18 06:21

외신 2과 통제관 CF

0003

-주재국측의 국경지역 방문허가를 받는대로 당관직원등을 파견할예정임.끝
(대사 정경일-국장)
예고:91.6.30 까지

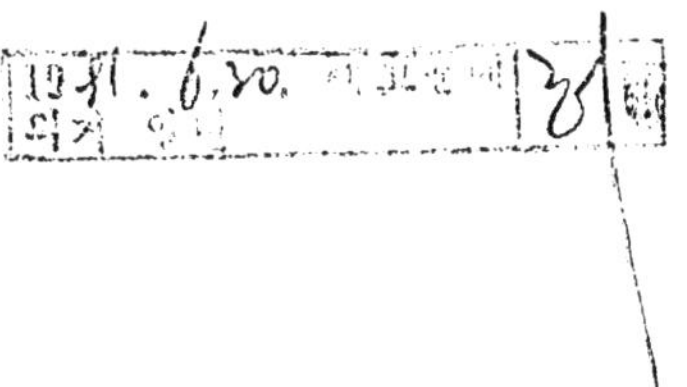

PAGE 2

0004

## AID TO THE DISPLACED PERSONS

1/24/91

- THE UNITED STATES DOES NOT OBJECT TO THE ROKG OR GOJ PROVIDING IRAN WITH HUMANITARIAN ASSISTANCE FOR THE CARE AND REPATRIATION OF GULF DISPLACED PERSONS.

- AT THE SAME TIME HOWEVER, THE U.S. BELIEVES THAT THE U.N.-COORDINATED MULTILATERAL RELIEF EFFORT NOW UNDERWAY IN ALL FOUR ASYLUM STATES (JORDAN, SYRIA, TURKEY, IRAN) IS THE BEST WAY TO ASSURE 1) ADEQUATE CARE FOR ALL DISPLACED PERSONS AND 2) THE PROPER AND EFFECTIVE USE OF ALL CASH AND IN-KIND CONTRIBUTIONS.

- BILATERAL CONTRIBUTIONS TO THE ASYLUM STATES, WHILE NOT INAPPROPRIATE, CONSTRAIN FLEXIBILITY IN RESPONDING TO DISPLACED PERSONS MIGRATIONS. U.N. AND OTHER RELIEF PLANNERS DO NOT AT THIS POINT HAVE A SOLID INDICATION AS TO HOW THE NEXT LARGE OUTFLOW WILL DEVELOP, THAT IS, WHICH AMONG THE FOUR COUNTRIES WILL BE MOST SEVERELY IMPACTED. COMMITMENTS OF RESOURCES TO THE U.N. REGION-WIDE, MULTILATERAL EFFORT PROVIDE MAXIMUM FLEXIBILITY FOR THE INTERNATIONAL COMMUNITY TO RESPOND TO DISPLACED PERSONS EMERGENCIES WHEN AND WHERE THEY OCCUR.

- WE ENCOURAGE THE ROKG AND THE GOJ TO ASSIST THE GULF DISPLACED PERSONS WITH CASH AND IN-KIND CONTRIBUTIONS TO THE U.N. PLAN OF ACTION AND THE APPEAL OF THE INTERNATIONAL COMMITTEE OF THE RED CROSS (ICRC). TO DATE, THE U.N. HAS RECEIVED PLEDGES OF DOLS 61 MILLION TO THE ESTIMATED PLAN BUDGET OF OVER DOLS 175 MILLION. INFORMATION ON DONOR RESPONSE TO THE ICRC APPEAL IS NOT YET AVAILABLE.

- USG ASSISTANCE TO DATE FOR GULF DISPLACED PERSONS HAS GENERALLY BEEN CHANNELLED THROUGH THE MULTILATERAL EFFORT. IN RESPONSE TO THE LATEST ICRC APPEAL AND U.N. PLAN OF ACTION, BOTH OF WHICH INCLUDE RELIEF OPERATIONS IN IRAN, USG CONTRIBUTIONS ARE AS FOLLOWS:

O ICRC - DOLS 1 MILLION

O UNHCR - DOLS 1 MILLION

O IOM - DOLS 750,000

0005

O UNDRO - DOLS 250,000 (EARMARKED FOR THE TURKISH RED CRESCENT)

- IN ADDITION TO THE ABOVE, THE USG IS COMMITTING FOOD SUPPLIES TO THE WORLD FOOD PROGRAM TO ASSIST IN THE MULTILATERAL RELIEF EFFORT.

---

GULF DISPLACED PERSONS MIGRATION SINCE JANUARY 1

---

- SINCE JANUARY 15, THE OUTFLOW OF DISPLACED PERSONS FROM IRAQ AND KUWAIT HAS BEEN VERY SMALL.

T

- RELIABLE REPORTS ABOUT MIGRATION TO IRAN RANGE FROM 1,000 TO 8,000.

- AS OF JANUARY 21, 3,000 FOREIGN NATIONALS WERE IN JORDAN AWAITING REPATRIATION. WE BELIEVE THAT AN ESTIMATED 8,000 EGYPTIAN NATIONALS WHO ENTERED JORDAN LAST WEEK HAVE BEEN REPATRIATED OR ENROUTE HOME TO EGYPT.

- SO FAR, DISPLACED PERSON MIGRATION TO SYRIA AND TURKEY HAS BEEN NEGLIGIBLE.

- DESPITE THE ABOVE, IT IS VERY POSSIBLE THAT LARGE NUMBERS OF DISPLACED PERSONS WILL ULTIMATELY FLEE IRAQ AND KUWAIT. BETWEEN AUGUST AND OCTOBER 1990, OVER 1 MILLION DISPLACED PERSONS SOUGHT REFUGE IN THE ABOVE-MENTIONED ASYLUM STATES AND SAUDI ARABIA.

- IN COOPERATION WITH HOST GOVERNMENTS, U.N. PLANNING AND PREPARATIONS ARE UNDERWAY IN JORDAN, SYRIA, TURKEY, AND IRAN FOR THE CARE AND REPATRIATION OF LARGE OUTFLOWS OF DISPLACED PERSONS. ICRC PREPARATIONS ARE ALSO UNDERWAY IN THESE FOUR COUNTRIES; IN ADDITION, ICRC IS MAKING ADVANCE PREPARATIONS FOR EVENTUAL OPERATIONS IN IRAQ AND KUWAIT.

0006

| 관리 번호 | 91-54 |
|---|---|

| | 분류번호 | 보존기간 |
|---|---|---|
| | | |

# 발 신 전 보

WJA-0395 910128 1446 DP

번 호 : 종별 :

수 신 : 주 일 대사. ~~총영사~~

발 신 : 장 관 (마그)

제 목 : 걸프전쟁 난민지원

걸프전쟁후 난민의 주변국 유입이 진행되고있는 가운데 ICRC (국제적십자사) 등 국제기구 및 이란등 주변국으로부터 아국의 긴급 구호지원 요청이 있는바 동 검토에 참고코자하니 일본의 걸프전쟁 난민 관련 지원현황을 지급 파악 (대국제기구 및 이란, 기타주변국) 보고바람. 끝.

(중동아국장 이 해 순)

예고 : 91.12.31. 까지.

검토필(1991.6.30.)

| 보안 통제 | |
|---|---|

| 앙 고 재 | 91년 1월 28일 | 중근동과 | 기안자 성명 | | 과 장 | 심의관 | 국 장 | | 차 관 | 장 관 | 외신과통제 |
|---|---|---|---|---|---|---|---|---|---|---|---|
| | | | | | | | 전결 | | | | |

0007

| 報告畢 |
| --- |
| |

# 長官報告事項

1991. 1 . 28 .
中東.아프리카局
마그레브 課( 3 )

題 目 : 걸프事態 難民 救護金 對 이란 支援

이란 政府는 걸프事態 難民의 이란 流入事態와 관련 我國에 救護 支援을 要望하였는바, 향후 推進方案을 아래와 같이 報告합니다.

## 1. 이란側 要請內容

(1.17. 이란 外務部 亞洲大洋洲局 審議官, 駐 이란 大使에 要請)

- 걸프事態로 이라크로부터 수십만명의 難民流入豫想(주로 아시아人)
- 人道的 견지에서 이란 入國 許容 및 難民 收容 캠프設置 豫定
- 同 難民 收容에 對備, 我國의 천막, 醫藥品등 緊急支援 要望

## 2. 美國側 意見

(美洲局長의 駐韓 美大使館 Hendrickson 參事官 協議結果 1.24.자 意見書 提示)

- 人道的 견지에서 걸프事態 難民 救護를 위한 對 이란 支援 反對않함.
- 단, 難民 救護活動은 유엔, 國際赤十字社등 主導下의 多者的支援이 効果的 이라고 判斷함.

미주국장 [서명]

| 앙 고 재 | 마그 과 | 1991년 1월 29일 | 담 당 | 과 장 | 심의관 | 국 장 |
| --- | --- | --- | --- | --- | --- | --- |
| | | | [서명] | [서명] | [서명] | [서명] |

0008

## 3. 支援方案

ㅇ 이란 政府에 15만불 상당의 國産品을 支援하되 品目은 駐 이란 大使의 建議를 받아 決定함.

ㅇ - 支援金 규모(15만불)는 국산 앰블란스 약 10대 購入費를 기초로 算定

ㅇ - 財源은 걸프事態 分擔金중 豫備費(현재 잔액 194만불)에서 支出

| 參 考 |
|---|

ㅇ 我國의 對國際機構 支援現況 (計 56만불)

- IOM : 50 만불
- ICRC : 3 만불 (豫備費)
- UNESCO : 3 만불 (豫備費)

ㅇ 걸프事態 難民現況 (美側 提供資料)

- 90.8월-10월간 100만명이 요르단, 터키, 이란, 시리아, 사우디에 流入
- 91.1.15.이후 이란에 1,000-8,000명 流入 推定
- 91.1.21.현재 요르단에 3,000명 殘留 (8,000명 本國 旣送還)
- 시리아와 터키에 流入된 難民은 극히 적음.

0009

# 대 IRAN 차량 공급 검토

1991. 1. 29.

1. 검토품목

   가. BESTA AMBULANCE

   나. TRUCK K3500 33S

   다. COMBI BUS

2. 해상운임

   가. '91. 1. 29. 현재 IRAN 국영선사를 통하여 PUSAN 항에서 IRAN 의 BANDAR ABBAS 항까지의 요율은 U$ 140.-/CBM 수준임.

   나. 그러나, GULF 만 사태 진행 상황에 따라 요율도 변동될 수 있으며, 경우에 따라서는 SERVICE 가 중단될 가능성도 있음.

   다. 유첨의 품목별 원가계산서는 현재의 요율을 기준으로 함.

3. 보험료

   가. '91. 1. 29. 현재 대이란 수출 차량의 PUSAN 항에서 BANDAR ABBAS 항까지의 DIRECT 운송 보험료율은 0.376% 이며, 유첨의 원가계산서는 이 요율을 기준으로 함.

   나. 다만, 보험요율은 GULF 만 사태의 추이에 의거 시간별로 변화 되므로 향후 선적 시점에서 변동될 수 있음.

0010

# 품 목 별 원 가 계 산 서

1991. 1. 29.

o ITEM : BESTA AMBULANCE WITH STANDARD EQUIPMENT

o COST BREAKDOWN

- F.O.B. : U$ 15,730.-
  - 차 량 : U$ 14,300.-
  - S/PARTS : U$ 1,430.-

- FREIGHT : U$ 1,968.40
  U$ 140 X 14.06CBM

- INSURANCE : U$ 74.81
  CIF X 1.1 X RATE (0.376%)

- MARGIN : U$ 314.60 ( FOB X 2% )

---

CIF ISTANBUL : U$ 18,087.81

0011

# 품 목 별 원 가 계 산 서

1991. 1. 29.

o ITEM : TRUCK 3 TON K3500 33S WITH STANDARD EQUIPMENT

o COST BREAKDOWN

- F.O.B. : U$ 11,362.-
  - 차 량 : U$ 10,329.-
  - S/PARTS : U$ 1,033.-

- FREIGHT : U$ 3,246.60
  U$ 140 X 23.19CBM

- INSURANCE : U$ 61.62
  CIF X 1.1 X RATE (0.376%)

- MARGIN : U$ 227.24 ( FOB X 2% )

---

CIF ISTANBUL : U$ 14,897.46

0012

# 품 목 별 원 가 계 산 서

1991. 1. 29.

o ITEM : AM 815 COMBI BUS (LHD) 24+1 SEATS WITH STANDARD EQUIPMENT

o COST BREAKDOWN

- F.O.B. : U$ 21,637.-
  - 차 량 : U$ 19,670.-
  - S/PARTS : U$ 1,967.-
- FREIGHT : U$ 3,634.40
  - U$ 140 X 25.96CBM
- INSURANCE : U$ 106.75
  - CIF X 1.1 X RATE (0.376%)
- MARGIN : U$ 432.74 ( FOB X 2% )

---

CIF ISTANBUL : U$ 25,810.89

0013

| 관리번호 | 91-58 |
|---|---|

원 본

# 외 무 부

종 별 : 지 급

번 호 : JAW-0439 일 시 : 91 0129 1849

수 신 : 장관(마그,아일)

발 신 : 주 일 대사(일정)

제 목 : 걸프전쟁 난민 지원

대 : WJA-0395

대호 관련, 당관 강대현 서기관이 주재국 외무성 인권난민과 도도 수석사무관으로부터 청취한 일본의 지원현황을 하기 보고함.

1. 개요(90-91 년)

0 ICRC, UNDRO 등 국제기관에 대한 지원 : 총 6 천만 불

0 요르단 정부에 대한 물자원조 : 약 1 억 5 천만엥

2. 상세내용

가. 91 년도 지원내용

0 국제기관을 통한 헌금

- UNDRO 에 3,800 만불 지원결정(1.14)

- UNDRO 는 금번 걸프전 관련 약 40 만명의 난민이 유출될 것으로 보고, 이의 지원을 위해 약 1 억 7 천 5 백만불 경비가 소요될 것으로 상정, 당장 필요한 제 1 단계의 경비로서 3,800 만불을 긴급지원하여 줄것을 1.11 유엔등 국제기관에 요청하였는바, 동 금액 전액을 일정부가 부담하기로 결정한 것임.

0 물자원조

- UNDRO 를 통해 요르단정부에 1,700 만엥 상당의 모포를 제공키로 결정(1.12)

- 요르단 정부에 직접 1,286 만엥 상당의 모포, 석유곤로, 생선통조림 전달(1.19)

0 난민수송

- IOM 과 난민수송을 위한 민간 수송기 4 대(JAL 3 대, ANA 1 대) 제공키로 챠타 계약 체결(1.28), 소요경비는 일정부가 UNDRO 에 제공키로 한 3,800 만불중에서 충당

- 동 챠타기로 요르단에서 이집트로 피난한 베트남인 963 명 및 태국인 82 명을 우선 베트남 및 태국으로 수송할 예정이며, 제 1 진으로서 카이로에서 베트남인 580

중아국 장관 차관 1차보 2차보 아주국 청와대 안기부

PAGE 1

91.01.29 19:51

외신 2과 통제관 CF

0014

명을 태운 JAL 기 2 대가 금 1.29 밤 나리따에 도착, 바로 호지명시로 출발 예정

나. 90 년도 지원내용

0 ICRC 의 요청에 따라 요르단 피난밀 구제활동 자금으로 적십자 국제위원회에 200 만불, UNDRO 에 800 만불 제공(8.29)

- 동 금액은 ICRC 가 요청한 전체지원 요청액의 56 퍼센트에 해당하는 액수라고 함.

0 요르단등에 대한 아시아계 피난민 지원을 위해 UNDRO 를 통해, 1,200 만불제공(9.4)

0 요르단 정부에 9,800 만엥 상당의 의료품, 텐트, 모포, 베이비 분유등 지원 (9 월상순)

0 요르단 정부에 1,750 만엥 상당의 모포, 건빵, 텐트류 지원(9.19)

0 요르단 정부에 300 만엥 상당의 건빵제공(10.5)

3. 참고로, 이란등 여타 주변국에 대한 직접지원은 현재까지는 없다고 하며, 다만 UNDRO 에 제공키로한 3,800 만불중에서 요르단에 40 만불, 이란에 40 만불, 터키에 10 만불, 시리아에 10 만불, 이집트에 20 만불을 난민지원금으로 해당국에 제공토록 UNDRO 측과 합의되어 있다고 함. 끝

(대사 이원경-국장)

예고:91.12.31. 까지

검토필(1991.6.30.)

PAGE 2

0015

| 관리번호 | 91-468 |
|---|---|

| 분류번호 | 보존기간 |
|---|---|
| | |

# 발 신 전 보

번 호 : WIR-0118 910129 1530 BX 종별 :

수 신 : 주 이란 대사. 총영사

발 신 : 장 관 (마그)

제 목 : 걸프사태 난민구호지원

대 : IRW-0038

1. 걸프사태 난민의 이란유입 사태와 관련한 이란정부의 대호 구호지원 요청에 대해 검토한결과, 이란정부에 15만불 상당의 국산차량을 지원키로 했음.

2. 아국은 걸프사태 난민구호를 위해 국제이주기구(IOM), 국제적십자사 및 유네스코등 국제기구에 56만불을 이미 기탁했는바 참고바람.

3. 지원코자하는 국산차량의 가격(CIF)을 다음 통보하니 15만불 범위내에서 이란측과 종류 및 수량을 협의한후 보고바람.

- Ambulance : $18,000 - 19,000
- Combi Bus(25인승) : $26,000 - 27,000
- Truck (3t) : $15,000 - 16,000

(중동아국장 이 해 순)

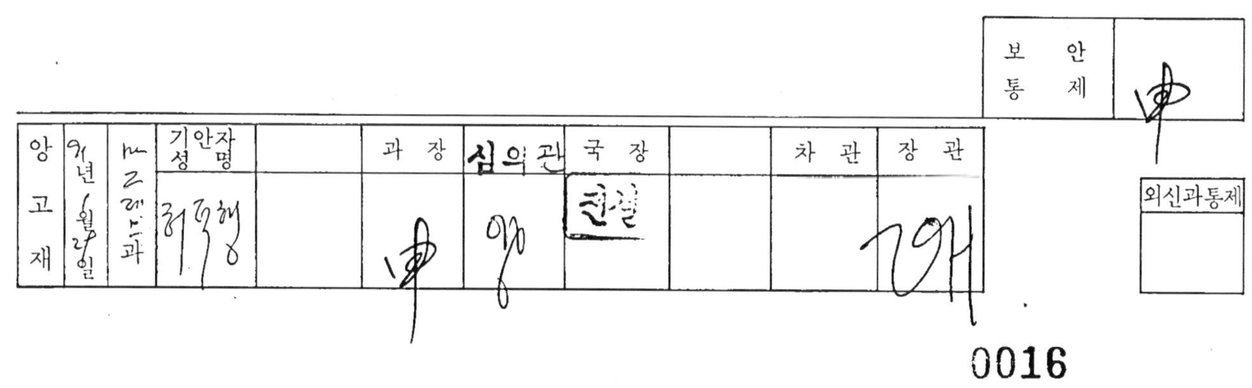


0016

| 관리 번호 | 91-457 |
|---|---|

| | 분류번호 | 보존기간 |
|---|---|---|
| | | |

# 발 신 전 보

WIR-0149 910206 1751 ER

번 호 : 종별 :

수 신 : 주 이란 대사. ~~총영사~~

발 신 : 장 관 (마그)

제 목 : 걸프사태 난민구호지원

대 : IRW-0038

연 : WIR-0118

대호 걸프사태 난민구호를 위한 아국의 15만불 지원계획에 대한 이란측의 반응 및 지원품목 조속 확인 보고바람. 끝.

(중동아국장 이 해 순)

검토필(1991.6.30.)

| | | | | | | | | | 보안 통제 | 3/6 |
|---|---|---|---|---|---|---|---|---|---|---|
| 앙 고 재 | 91년 2월 6일 | 마그 과 | 기안자 성명 | | 과장 | | 국장 | | 차관 | 장관 |

외신과통제

0017

| 관리 번호 | 91-72 |
|---|---|

원 본

# 외 무 부

종 별 :

번 호 : IRW-0124 일 시 : 91 0207 1030

수 신 : 장관(마그)

발 신 : 주 이란 대사

제 목 : 걸프사태 난민구호 지원

대:WIR-0149

본직은 예년(1990 년)의 예와같이 공관장회의 일시귀국전 주재국 외무장관과의 면담을 요청하고 있으며, 이때 대호 원조를 포함한 다음사항을 거론할예정임.걸프사태등으로 주재국 장관의 일정이 여의치 않을경우 내주초(일요일 2.10 또는 월요일 2.11) 차관과 면담하고 결과보고하겠음.

1. 외무장관 취임 축전에대한 사의전달 (기송부된 답전은 주재국 외무부에이미전교)

2.15 만불원조

3.AFKO 및 효성 정지점장문제. 끝

(대사정경일-국장)

예고:91.12.31 까지

검토필(1991.6.30.)

중아국

PAGE 1

91.02.07 16:30

외신 2과 통제관 BN

0018

| 관리 번호 | 91-78 |
|---|---|

원 본

# 외 무 부

종 별 :

번 호 : IRW-0136 일 시 : 91 0210 1630

수 신 : 장관(중근동)

발 신 : 주 이란 대사

제 목 : 걸프사태관련 난민지원

대:WIR-0149

본직은 주재국 외무장관이 NAM 회의참석차 벨그라드에 출장중 이므로 BOURJERDI 차관에게 대호 난민구호 원조내용을 알렸던바, 동차관은 이란 으로서는 현금을 주면 좋겠으나 어려울경우, 차량종류를 선정, 혁명기념일이 끝나는 2.16 에알려 주겠다고 답변 하였기보고함. 끝

(대사정경일-국장)

예고:91.6.30 까지

1991.6.30. 예고문에 의거 일반

중아국

PAGE 1

91.02.11 06:58

외신 2과 통제관 FE

0019

| 관리번호 | 91-456 |
|---|---|

| | 분류번호 | 보존기간 |
|---|---|---|
| | | |

# 발 신 전 보

WIR-0181 910221 1810 CG

번 호 :

종별 :

수 신 : 주 이란 대사. ~~총영사~~

발 신 : 장 관 (중동이)

제 목 : 걸프사태 관련 난민지원

연 : WIR-0118, 0149

대 : IRW-0136

걸프사태 난민구호를 위한 국산차량 지원건은 물품발주 및 선적, 운송에 상당한 시일이 소요되므로 조속한 물품선정이 필요한바, 주재국측의 희망~~사항~~ 차종 조속 파악 보고바람. 끝.

(중동아국장 이 해 순)

검토필(1991.6.30.)

| 보안통제 | |
|---|---|

| 앙고재 | 91년 2월 21일 | 중동2과 | 기안자 성명 | | 과장 | 심의관 | 국장 | | 차관 | 장관 |
|---|---|---|---|---|---|---|---|---|---|---|
| | | | | | | | 전결 | | | |

외신과통제

0020

| 관리번호 | 91-132 |
|---|---|

원 본

# 외 무 부

종 별 :

번 호 : IRW-0186 일 시 : 91 0225 1000

수 신 : 장관(중동일)

발 신 : 주 이란 대사

제 목 : 걸프사태관련 난민지원

대:WIR-0181

대호관련, 당관은 외무부 아주대양국 ROHIS SEFAT 심의관및 한국담당과장등에게 조속한 품목선정을 요청하고있으나, 동인들은 주재국적십자사(적신월사)와의 협의지연등으로 품목선정이 지연되고있다고 설명하고있음을 양지바람. 주재국측에 계속 독촉, 조속 결과 보고토록 하겠음. 끝

(대사정경일-국장)

예고:91.12.31 까지

중아국

PAGE 1

91.02.25 16:06

외신 2과 통제관 BA

0021

| 관리<br>번호 | 91-<br>212 |
|---|---|

원 본

# 외 무 부

종 별 :

번 호 : IRW-0235 일 시 : 91 0312 1400

수 신 : 장관(중동일)

발 신 : 주 이란 대사

제 목 : 걸프사태관련 난민지원

대:WIR-0181

표제관련, 주재국 외무부 BOURJERDI 차관은 금 3.12(화) 아국의 지원품목으로 앰브란스를 희망한다고 통보하여왔음. 끝

(대사 정경일-국장)

예고:91.12.31 까지

검토필(1991.6.30.)

중아국

PAGE 1

91.03.12 22:03

외신 2과 통제관 CW

0022

| 관리 번호 | 91-208 |
|---|---|

| | 분류번호 | 보존기간 |
|---|---|---|
| | | |

# 발 신 전 보

번　　호 : WIR-0242　　910314 1933　FK 종별 :

수　　신 : 주　　이란　　대사. ~~총영사~~

발　　신 : 장　관　　(중동이)

제　　목 : 걸프사태관련 난민지원

대 : IRW-0235

1. 대호 귀주재국 외무차관의 요청대로, 걸프난민 구호물자로 앰브란스 8대를 지원코자하니 ~~발송요망~~ 하역 항구명 및 수신처를 파악 지급 보고바람.

2. 앰브란스의 카타로그는 차파편 송부예정임. 끝.

(중동아국장 이 해 순)

예고 : 91.12.31. 까지

검토필(1991.6.20.

| 보안 통제 | 高 |
|---|---|

| 앙 고 재 | 91년 3월 14일 | 중동1과 | 기안자 성명 | | 과 장 | 심의관 | 국 장 | | 차 관 | 장 관 |
|---|---|---|---|---|---|---|---|---|---|---|
| | | | 허덕행 | | 高 | | 전결 | | | |

| 외신과통제 |
|---|
| |

0023

9462 기 안 용 지

| 분류기호<br>문서번호 | 중동이20005- | (전화 : ) | 시 행 상<br>특별취급 | |
|---|---|---|---|---|
| 보존기간 | 영구·준영구.<br>10. 5. 3. 1. | 장 관 | | |
| 수 신 처<br>보존기간 | | | | |
| 시행일자 | 1991. 3.14. | | | |

| 보조기관 | 국 장 | 전 결 | 협조기관 | | 문 서 통 제 |
|---|---|---|---|---|---|
| | 심의관 | | | | 검인 1991. 3.15 문서통제관 |
| | 과 장 | | | | 발 인 |
| 기안책임자 | 허 덕 행 | | | | 발송 1991. 3.15 외무부 |

| 경 유<br>수 신<br>참 조 | 주 이란 대사 | 발신명의 | |
|---|---|---|---|
| 제 목 | 걸프사태 관련 난민지원 | | |

대 : IRW-0235

걸프난민 구호물자로 귀주재국에 지원예정인 앰브란스외 카타로그를 별첨과 같이 송부합니다.

첨 부 : 동 카타로그 2부. 끝.

0024

1505-25(2-1) 일(1)갑 190㎜×268㎜ 인쇄용지 2급 60g/㎡
85. 9. 9. 승인 "내가아낀 종이 한장 늘어나는 나라살림" 가 40-41 1990. 5. 28

| 관리 번호 | 91-244 |
|---|---|

원 본

# 외 무 부

종 별 :

번 호 : IRW-0261 일 시 : 91 0319 1500

수 신 : 장관(중동이)

발 신 : 주 이란 대사

제 목 : 걸프사태관련 난민지원

대:WIR-0242

대호 아래보고함.

1. 하역항구:BANDAR ABBAS

2. 수신처:RED CRESCENT OF THE ISLAMIC REPUBLIC OF IRAN

VILLA AVENUE, CORNER OF TALEGHANI CROSS TEHRAN, IRAN. 끝

(대사정경일-국장)

예고:91.12.31 까지

검토필(1991.6.30.)

중아국

PAGE 1

91.03.19 22:55

외신 2과 통제관 FI

0025

# 一般豫算検討意見書

199 1 . 3 . 21. 중동2 課

| 事業名 | 걸프사태 난민 구호지원 | | |
|---|---|---|---|
| 支辨科目 | 細項 | 目 | 金額 |
| | 121 | 341 | $146,064.00 |

| 検討意見 | |
|---|---|
| 主務者 | 정무활동, 해외경상이전 이월액에서 집행 |
| 擔當官 | 〃 |
| 調整官 | 〃 |

0026

# 기 안 용 지

| 분류번호<br>문서번호 | 중동이20005- | (전화 : ) | 시 행 상<br>특별취급 | |
|---|---|---|---|---|
| 보존기간 | 영구 · 준영구<br>10. 5. 3. 1. | 차 관 | 장 관 | |
| 수 신 처<br>보존기간 | | 전 결 | | |
| 시행일자 | 1991. 3.20. | | | |

| 보조기관 | | 협조기관 | | 문서통제 |
|---|---|---|---|---|
| 국 장 | | | 기획관리실장 | |
| 심의관 | | | 총 무 과 장 | |
| 과 장 | | | 기획운영담당관 | |
| 기안책임자 | 허 덕 행 | | | 발 송 인 |

| 경유<br>수신<br>참조 | 건 의 | 발신명의 | | |
|---|---|---|---|---|
| 제 목 | 걸프사태 난민구호지원 (이란) | | | |

걸프전쟁으로 인한 이라크 난민의 이란유입 사태와 관련한 이란정부의 요청에 따라 다음과 같이 엠블란스 8대를 구호물자로 지원 코자하니 재가하여 주시기 바랍니다.

/계속.../

0027

- 다 음 -

1. 지원내역 (단위 : $)

| 품 목 | 단 가(CIF) | 수 량 | 금 액 |
| --- | --- | --- | --- |
| 엠블란스(기아 Besta) | 18,258 | 8 | 146,064 |

2. 선적일정

o 91.4.30 까지 선적, 이란 Bandar Abbas 항 하역

3. 지출근거

o 정무활동, 해외경상이전, 걸프만사태 관련 주변피해국 지원 예비비 (이란 난민)

첨 부 : 1. (주) 고려무역의 견적서 및 수출계약서

2. 관련 보고서 및 전문. 끝.

0028

# 誓　約　書

受　信 ： 外務部長官

題　目 ： 걸프만 事態에 따른 供與用 物品供給

弊社는 貴部가 主管하는 表題 事業이 緊急支援 및 秘密維持를 要하는 國家的 事業임을 認識하고, 今般 IRAN 國에 供與하는 BESTA AMBULANCE 物品을 供與契約 締結함에 있어 아래 事項을 遵守할 것을 誓約하는 바입니다.

1. 物品供給 契約時 品質 價格面에서 一般 輸出契約과 最小限 同等한 또는 보다 有利한 條件을 適用한다.

2. 締結된 契約은 보다 誠實하고 協助的인 姿勢로 履行한다.

3. 同 契約 內容은 業務上 目的 以外에는 公開하지 않는다.

1991 年 3 月 15 日

會 社 名 ： 株式會社 高 麗 貿 易

代 表 者 ： 代表理事 高 一 男

(署名 및 捺印)

0029

# 輸 出 契 約 書

"甲" 外 務 部

중동 2 課長 鄭 鎭 鎬

"乙" 株式會社 高 麗 貿 易

代表理事 副社長 高 一 男

上記 "甲" "乙" 兩者間에 다음과 같이 輸出契約을 締結한다.

第 1 條 : 輸出物品의 表示

別 添

第 2 條 : "甲" 은 上記 第1條의 物品貨金을 船積書類 受取後 "乙" 에게 支給한다.

第 3 條 : "乙" 은 上記 第1條의 物品을 1991 . 4 . 30. 까지 PUSAN PORT 港 (또는 空港) 에서 BANDAR ABBAS 行 船舶(또는 航空機) 에 船積하여야 한다. 但, 불가피한 事由로 船積이 遲延될 境遇에는 1990. 12. 21. 外務部長官과 "乙" 間에 締結된 輸出代行業體 指定 契約書 第4條 規定에 依하여 "乙" 은 "甲" 에게 船積 遲延事由書를 提出하고 "甲" 은 同 遲滯償金 免除 與否를 決定한다.

第 4 條 : "乙" 은 船積完了後 7日 以內에 "甲" 이 船積物品 通關에 必要한 諸般 船積書類를 "甲" 또는 "甲" 의 代理人에게 提出 또는 現地公館에 送付하여야 한다.

- 1 -

0030

第 5 條 : 上記 船積物品의 品質保證 期間은 船積後 1 年間으로 하며, 이 期間中 正常的인 使用에도 不拘하고 製造不良이나 材質 또는 조립상의 하자가 發生할 境遇 "乙" 의 責任下에 解決한다.

本 契約에 明示되지 않은 事由에 對하여는 걸프만 事態 供與品 輸出 代行 契約書에 따른다.

1991 年 3 月 15 日

"甲" 外 務 部

중동 2 課長 鄭 鎭 鎬

"乙" 株式會社 高麗貿易

서울特別市 江南區 三成洞

代表理事 副社長 高 一



0031

(別　添)

| DESCRIPTION | Q'TY | U/P | AMOUNT |
| --- | --- | --- | --- |
| | | C.I.F. BANDAR ABBAS | |
| BESTA AMBULANCE WITH<br>4X4, POWER STEERING<br>AND STANDARD EQUIPMENT<br>(WITH 10% RECOMMENDED SPARE PARTS) | 8UNITS | @$ 18,258.- | U$ 146,064.- |
| TOTAL : | | | U$ 146,064.- |

0032

# 원 가 계 산 (1. BESTA AMBULANCE)

단위 : U$

| 비 고 | F. O. B. | F | | | I | | | M (FOB X 2%) | 합 계 |
|---|---|---|---|---|---|---|---|---|---|
| | | C B M | 단 가 | 송 료 | 기 준 가 (CIFx1.1) | 요 율 | 보 험 료 | | |
| | 1. 차량 (기아자동차)<br>14,300 X 8 대<br>= 114,400.-<br><br>2. 부품 (동서교역)<br>1,430 X 8 셋트<br>= 11,440.-<br>- - - - - - - - - -<br>합 계 : 125,840.- | 127.95104 | 135.- | 17,273.39 | 160,670.40 | 0.27% | 433.81 | 2,516.80 | 146,064.- |

0033

심의관 :

| 분류기호<br>문서번호 | 중동이<br>20005- 16 | 협 조 문 용 지<br>( ) | 결<br>재 | 담 당 | 과 장 | 국 장 |
|---|---|---|---|---|---|---|
| 시행일자 | 1991. 5. 9. | | | [서명] | [서명] | [서명] |
| 수 신 | 총무과장 (외환계) | 발 신 | 중동아프리카국장 (서명) | | | |
| 제 목 | 경비지불의뢰 | | | | | |

걸프사태 관련 이란 지원용 난민구호 물자가 '91.4.30 선적된바 동 경비를 다음과 같이 지불하여 주시기 바랍니다.

- 다 음 -

1. 지불금액 : $146,064

2. 지 불 처

o (주) 고려무역

o 구좌번호 : 100-53470-1341 (한미은행 본점)

3. 지출근거 : 정무활동 해외경상이전, 걸프사태관련 지원금 예비비 (이란 난민구호)

첨 부 : 1. 재가공문사본 1부.

2. 관련계약서, 선적서류 및 원가계산서 사본 각 1부. 끝.

0034

16305

# 기 안 용 지

| 분류기호 문서번호 | 중동이 20005- | (전화 : ) | 시 행 상 특별취급 | |
|---|---|---|---|---|
| 보존기간 | 영구·준영구. 10. 5. 3. 1. | 장 관 | | |
| 수 신 처 보존기간 | | | | |
| 시행일자 | 1991. 5.9. | | | |

| 보조기관 | 국 장 | 전 결 | 협조기관 | | 문 서 통 제 |
|---|---|---|---|---|---|
| | 심의관 | | | | 1991. 5. 09 |
| | 과 장 | | | | |
| 기안책임자 | 허 덕 행 | | | | 발 송 인 |

| 경 유 수 신 참 조 | 주 이란대사 | 발신명의 | | 1991. 5. 09 |
|---|---|---|---|---|
| 제 목 | 걸프사태 난민구호 물자선적 | | | |

1. 걸프사태관련 난민구호물자로 엠뷸란스8대 및 동 부품이 '91.4.30 선적된바, 동 선적서류를 별첨과 같이 송부합니다.

2. 동 지원물자는 '91.6.15경 귀지 Bandar Abbas 항 입항 예정입니다.

첨 부 : 동 선적서류 2 부. 끝.

0035

1505-25(2-1) 일(1)갑 190㎜×268㎜ 인쇄용지 2급 60g/㎡
85. 9. 9. 승인 "내가아낀 종이 한장 늘어나는 나라살림" 가 40-41 1990. 5. 28

# 株式會社 高麗貿易

電 話 : (02) 737-0860
F A X : (02) 739-7011
TELEX : KOTII K34311

서울 特別市 江南區 三成洞 159番地
貿易會館 빌딩 11層
TRADE CENTER P.O. BOX 23,24.

수 신 : 외무부 중동 2과장

제 목 : 걸프만 사태 관련 지원물대 송금 신청

폐사는 귀부와의 계약에 의거하여 아래와 같이 걸프만 사태 관련 지원물품을 기 선적하였아오니 송금조치 하여 주시기 바랍니다.

- 아 래 -

1. 선적물품 내역

| 품 목 | 수 량 | 금 액 | 선적일 | 도 착 예정일 | 선 명 | 선적항 | 도착항 |
|---|---|---|---|---|---|---|---|
| BESTA 4x4 AMBULANCE WITH POWER STERING | 8 UNITS | U$ 132,784.- | 4/30 | 6/15 | HOJIN V-09 | ULSAN | BANDAR ABBAS |
| SPARE PARTS | 8 SETS | U$ 13,280.- | | | | | |
| 합 계 | | U$ 146,064.- | | | | | |

2. 비 고

걸프만 사태 관련 IRAN 지원 계약분 ('91. 3. 15.) U$ 146,064.- 전량 선적 기일 ('91. 4. 30.) 내 선적 완료.

3. 송 금 처 : 한 미 은 행 본 점

구좌번호 : 100-53470-1341

예 금 주 : (주) 고 려 무 역. 끝.

1 9 9 1 年 5 月 3 日

鍾 路 輸 出 本 部 海 外 事 業 팀 

0036

원 본

# 외 무 부

종 별 :

번 호 : IRW-0583 일 시 : 91 0729 1200

수 신 : 장관(중동일,중동이)

발 신 : 주 이란 대사대리

제 목 : 걸프사태 난민구호물자

대:중동이 20005-16305

1.표제 구호물자 아국산 앰블랜스 8대는 7.28(일)도착항구인 BANDAR ABBAS 에서 간단한 전달식을 갖고, 주재국 적신월사 측에 무위전달되었음.

2.BANDAR ABBAS 적신월사 지부에서 개최된 전달식에는 주재국 적신월사 국제부장, 지역지부장및 주정부인사들이 참석하였으며 다수신문, TV 기자들이 동전달식을 취재하였음. 당관에서는 전참사관 및 홍충웅영사가 출장, 참석하였음.끝

(대사대리-국장)

중아국 1차보 중아국 외정실 안기부

PAGE 1

91.07.29 17:31 WG

외신 1과 통제관

0037

2. UNESCO 지원, 1990

0038

| 분류기호<br>문서번호 | 국기20350-<br>232 | 협조문용지<br>( 2181-2 ) | 결 | 담당 | 과장 | 국장 |
|---|---|---|---|---|---|---|
| 시행일자 | 1990. 12.10. | | 재 | 허강일 | | |
| 수 신 | 중동아프리카국장, 미주국장 | 발 신 | 국제기구조약국장 (서명) | | | |
| 제 목 | 유네스코의 걸프사태 관련 난민자녀 특별 교육 자금 지원 요청 | | | | | |

1. 유네스코 사무국은 주 유네스코 아국 대사앞 별첨 공한을 통하여 유네스코가 걸프만 사태로 안하여 어려움을 겪고 있는 요르단 및 이집트 난민 청소년들의 특별 교육을 위하여 총 189만 미불이 소요되는 특별 사업 계획을 수립하였음을 알려오면서 아국이 동 소요자금의 일부를 긴급 지원해줄것을 요청하여 왔습니다.

2. 별첨 주 유네스코 대사의 관련공문 및 유네스코 사무국의 주유네스코 대사앞 공한을 검토하시어 상기 자금지원에 관한 귀국 입장 및 지원시 귀국예산 사용 가능성에 대하여 회신하여 주시기 바랍니다.

첨부 : 상기 공문 및 공한 사본 1부. 끝

0039

1505－8일(1) 190㎜×268㎜(인쇄용지 2급 60g /㎡)
85. 9. 9 승인 "내가아낀 종이 한장 늘어나는 나라살림" 가 40－41 1988. 1. 29.

주 유 네 스 코 대 표 부

유네 (정) 760 - 166 1990.11.30.

수 신 : 장 관

참 조 : 국제기구 조약국장

제 목 : 걸프 사태 관련 난민 자녀 특별 교육 지원요청

1. 유네스코 사무국 A. CHIBA 대외사업 조정 국장은 11.27. 자 본직앞 서한을 통하여 걸프 사태로 인해 귀국한 요르단 및 이집트 난민 (48만명)의 초.중등학교 취학 자녀 9 만여명의 교육 문제와 관련하여 유네스코 사무국이 특별 사업 계획을 수립하였음을 알리면서, 총 189 만미불이 소요되는 동사업에 아국에서 일부를 긴급 지원해 줄 것을 요청해 왔는 바, 본건 검토후 동처리 방안에 관한 본부 입장을 지시하여 주시기 바랍니다.

2. 상기 서한에 의하면, 동 취학 자녀들은 6-17 세의 초.중.고등학생들로서 현재 교육이 중단되어 있는 상태라고 하며, 소요 경비 내역은 아래와 같음을 참고로 보고합니다.

경비내역 : - 교과서 구입 (90 만불)
- 장비 (칠판, 지도 및 기초 장비) (30만불)
- 교실 40 개 건축 (이집트 및 요르단에 각 20 개 교실) (48만불)
- 기타경비 (21만불)

계 189만불

첨부 : 서한 사본 1 부. 끝.

주 유 네 스 코 대

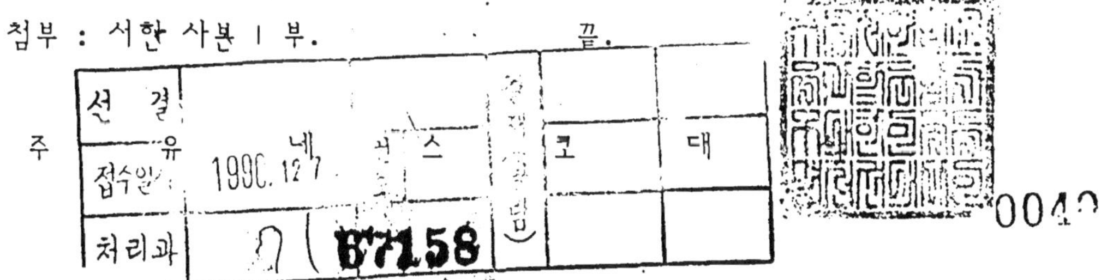


0042

united nations educational, scientific and cultural organization
organisation des nations unies pour l'éducation, la science et la culture

7, place de Fontenoy, 75700 Paris
1, rue Miollis, 75015 Paris

téléphone : national (1) 45.68.10.00
international + (33.1) 45.68.10.00
télégrammes : Unesco Paris
télex : 204461 Paris
270602 Paris
téléfax : 45.67.16.90

référence : BAO/ESP/90/091 — 21 November 1990

Dear Ambassador,

I have the honour to refer to the emergency educational needs of school-age children repatriated to the Hashemite Kingdom of Jordan and the Arab Republic of Egypt as a result of the present crisis between the Republic of Iraq and the State of Kuwait. By mid-September 1990, some 180,000 Jordanian nationals and some 300,000 Egyptians have returned to their home countries from Iraq and Kuwait. According to the Governments of Jordan and Egypt, the repatriates include - respectively - 40,228 and 50,000 school-age children who require immediate accommodation in educational institutions at the primary and secondary levels. Both governments have asked Unesco for emergency assistance to help them meet the educational needs of these schoolchildren.

The purpose of this letter is to provide information on these needs and to seek financial support from the donor community to enable Unesco to extend basic assistance to minimize the disruption to these children's education. The programme budget of US$ 1,892,000 set out is based on the assessments made by Unesco's regional offices in Amman and Cairo in collaboration with the educational authorities of the two countries concerned. Given the continuing influx of returning nationals as well as foreigners whose repatriation to their home country may not be feasible in the near future, the budget estimates of this emergency programme may have to be adjusted as the situation evolves.

In Egypt, the repatriates are concentrated in the urban centres of Cairo, Alexandria, Tanta and Assiut, where they are receiving help from family members and the local community. While the Government is making every possible effort to facilitate their reintegration, insufficient public funds are restricting the provision of social services. Repatriates, as at 20 September 1990, include some 50,000 school-age children between the age of 6-17 years who need to be accommodated in primary and secondary schools.

.../...

H.E. Mr. HAHM Tae-Hyuk
Ambassador extraordinary and
Plenipotentiary
Permanent Delegate of the
Republic of Korea to Unesco
Unesco House

0041

The Ministry of Education of Jordan reports that, as at 10 October 1990, the repatriates who have returned to the country include 31,110 primary school-age children and 9,118 secondary school students. Most of the returning population live in the urban area of Amman, which comprises almost half of the total population of Jordan. Significant numbers of repatriates are also found in the regions of Zarka, Irbid, Balqa and Jerash.

In both Jordan and Egypt, despite an appreciable improvement in the gross enrolment ratio in recent years, capacities to meet the demand at the primary school level are still inadequate. At the primary level in Egypt, the gross enrolment ratio stands at some 90%, while at the secondary level it is just under 70%. In Jordan, the annual population growth rate of 3.8% over the past decade has been placing added pressure on the Government in its attempts to cope with the high demand for school entry.

In these circumstances, repatriate pupils and students are forced to compete with local children to obtain entry to schools or are causing the pupil-teacher ratio to rise to an unacceptably high level. The difficulties confronting repatriated families in finding employment and lodging and in meeting other priority needs, thus risk being compounded by serious interruption or disturbance to the education of their children, unless measures are taken immediately to expand school facilities, increase the number of teachers, and provide for the distribution of textbooks and school supplies.

In identifying measures required to reinforce the educational infrastructure and absorption potential of the main areas where the repatriates have settled or are likely to settle, the educational authorities of Jordan and Egypt have estimated the financial needs at some US$ 5.65 million for Jordan and US$ 50 million for Egypt.

As it is not within the scope of Unesco's mandate to subsidize the salaries of teachers or to finance the entire cost of the Member States' emergency activities, the Organization has agreed to draw up a programme proposal for limited educational assistance and to appeal to the international donor community to mobilize financial resources for the implementation of the proposed activities.

The estimated budget, presented as an Annex to this letter, covers the partial costs of purchasing the most essential textbooks and school equipment for some 90,000 target beneficiaries. The programme budget also includes the cost of the procurement of building materials and technical assistance for the construction of 40 additional classrooms (20 each in Jordan and Egypt) which, of course, is far from meeting the actual needs but is intended to lessen the pressure in areas with the highest concentration of repatriates.

.../...

0042

Unesco's operational support costs, included in this budget, are to cover technical assistance for the construction work and monitoring of the purchase and distribution of textbooks, educational supplies and equipment. Unesco's programme support and administration costs are to meet expenses such as staff travel in connection with the programme, as well as communication and general office administration costs exceeding amounts foreseen under the regular budget appropriation. In view of the humanitarian nature of the proposed activities, the standard 13% overhead costs generally charged by Unesco for programme execution has exceptionally been waived by the Director-General.

To avoid further disruption to the lives of tens of thousands of children affected by the present political crisis in the region and to help them in the difficult process of reintegration, we appeal to the generosity of your Government for a special contribution to enable Unesco to fulfil one of its mandated responsibilities. Unesco has so far committed US$ 100,000 to initiate the procurement of school textbooks and educational supplies. Given our existing budgetary constraints, the implementation of the limited emergency programme set out in the annex - costed at US$ 1,892,000 - is conditional on prompt financial support being made available. We would therefore be grateful if you would inform Unesco as soon as possible of your Government's readiness to contribute to this emergency programme.

I should like to thank in advance all those whose early response to this appeal will enable us to meet the very urgent educational needs arising from the crisis in the Gulf region.

Yours sincerely,

for A. Chiba
Director
Bureau for the Co-ordination
of Operational Activities

0043

# UNESCO PROGRAMME OF EMERGENCY EDUCATIONAL ASSISTANCE TO DISPLACED CHILDREN IN EGYPT AND JORDAN AFFECTED BY THE CRISIS BETWEEN IRAQ AND KUWAIT

Estimated Budget
(in US dollars)

| ITEMS | EGYPT | JORDAN | TOTAL |
|---|---|---|---|
| A. Textbooks (including cost of transport and distribution) | 500,000 | 402,000 | 902,000 |
| B. School equipment and teaching materials (blackboards, maps and other basic equipment) | 150,000 | 150,000 | 300,000 |
| C. Classroom construction materials (20 each) | 240,000 | 240,000 | 480,000 |
| D. Local contract fees for supervision of construction work | 25,000 | 25,000 | 50,000 |
| E. Unesco operational support costs (technical assistance, cost of project personnel) | 40,000 | 40,000 | 80,000 |
| F. Unesco programme and administration costs at Headquarters and Field Offices | 40,000 | 40,000 | 80,000 |
| | 995,000 | 897,000 | |
| GRAND TOTAL FOR EGYPT AND JORDAN: | | | 1,892,000 |

0044

12/14 에
지원가능문의 없음
기

| 분류기호<br>문서번호 | 마그20005-156 | 협 조 문 용 지<br>(　　　　) | 결재 | 심의관<br>담 당 | 과 장 | 국 장 |
|---|---|---|---|---|---|---|
| 시행일자 | 1990.12.12. | | | | | |
| 수 신 | 국제기구조약국장 | 발 신 | 중동아프리카국장 (서명) | | | |
| 제 목 | 유네스코의 걸프사태 관련 난민자녀 특별교육 | | | | | |

대 : 국기 20350-232 (90.12.10)

1. 아국은 걸프사태 관련 주변피해국 지원에 적극 참여하고 있어 대호 유네스코를 통한 이집트, 요르단 난민학생특별교육에도 성의를 표하는 것이 바람직하다고 생각합니다.

2. 재원은 걸프만사태 관련국 지원경비에서 지출이 가능할 것으로 사료됩니다.

끝.

0045

1505 - 8 일 (1)　　190㎜×268㎜(인쇄용지 2급 60g / ㎡)
85. 9. 9 승인 "내가아낀 종이 한장 늘어나는 나라살림"　가 40-41 1990. 7. 9.

12/14 허
기

# 협조문용지

| 분류기호 문서번호 | 미북 0160- 997 | (전화 : 720-4648) | 결재 | 담당 | 과장 | 심의관 |
|---|---|---|---|---|---|---|
| 시행일자 | 1990.12.13 | | | | | |
| 수 신 | 국제기구조약국장 | 발 신 | 미주국장 (서명) | | | |
| 제 목 | UNESCO의 걸프사태 관련 난민자녀 특별 교육자금 지원 요청 | | | | | |

대 : 국기 20350-232

1. 대호 관련, 당국으로서는 UNESCO 사업에 대한 지원 원칙에 동의함을 통보드립니다.

2. 상세 지원 규모는 타국의 지원 규모를 감안, 결정함이 좋을 것으로 사료됩니다. 끝.

0046

| | 분류번호 | 보존기간 |
|---|---|---|
| | | |

# 발 신 전 보

번 호 : WUC-0253 901220 1428 DY 종별 :

수 신 : 주 유네스코 대사. 총영사

발 신 : 장 관 (국기)

제 목 : 걸프사태 관련 난민자녀 특별교육 지원

대 : 유네(정) 760-166(90.11.30)

1. 걸프만 사태 주변 피해국 지원에 참여하는 일환으로 본부는 대호 유네스코의 표제사업 경비의 일부 지원을 실무적으로 검토하고 있음.

2. 아국의 지원 결정시 지원 규모 검토에 참고코자 하니 타회원국들의 지원금액 (파악 가능시) 수준을 파악, 보고바람.

3. 지원시 정파일정 마감에 따라 지원금을 본부에서 유네스코 사무국으로 직송할 경우에 대비하여 유네스코 관련부서의 송금구좌 번호를 파악, 보고바람. 끝

(국제기구조약국장 문동석)

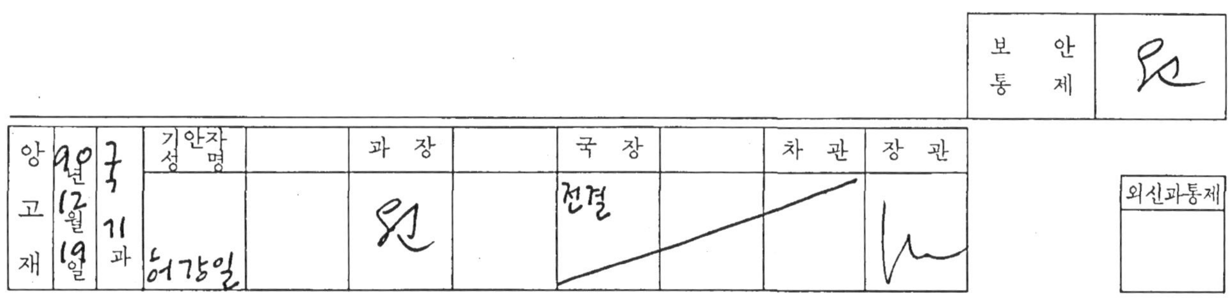

| 보안통제 | |
|---|---|

| 앙고재 | 90년 12월 19일 | 국기과 | 기안자 성명: 허강일 | | 과장 | | 국장: 전결 | | 차관 | 장관 |
|---|---|---|---|---|---|---|---|---|---|---|

외신과통제

0047

12/21 오(허)
UNESCO 사무
5만불 지원 계기

| 분류기호 문서번호 | 미그20005- 162 | 협조문용지 ( ) | 결재 | 담 당 | 과 장 | 국 장 |
|---|---|---|---|---|---|---|
| 시행일자 | 1990.12.20. | | | | | |
| 수 신 | 수신처참조 | 발 신 | 중동아프리카국장 (서명) | | | |
| 제 목 | 걸프사태관련 지원예산 집행 | | | | | |

1. 걸프사태 관련 지원업무 협의를 위해 부내 대책회의가 90.12.19(수) 15:00 별첨과 같이 개최되었는바 동 회의결과에 따라 귀국실 소관사항에 대해 필요한 조치를 취하고 결과를 당국으로 알려 주시기 바랍니다.

2. 특히 미집행 예산에 대한 사고이월 신청에 필요하니 집행 되었거나 집행이 예상되는 사업비 내역 및 금년중 집행이 불가능한 사업비에 대한 미집행 및 이월사유를 조속 당국으로 송부하여 주시기 바랍니다.

3. 동 예산은 정무활동 해외경상이전비이니 예산집행시 참고 바랍니다. 끝.

첨부 : 걸프사태관련 부내 대책회의결과 1부.

수신처 : 기획관리실장, 미주국장, 국제기구조약국장, 국제경제국장, 영사교민국장. 끝.

0048

1505 - 8 일 (1) 190㎜×268㎜ (인쇄용지 2급 60 g/㎡)

# 걸프사태 관련 피해국 지원
# 부내 대책회의 결과

## 1. 회의개요

ㅇ 일 시 : 90.12.19.(수) 15:00 중동아국장실

ㅇ 이혜순 중동아프리카국장(주재)

- 양태규 중동아국 심의관
- 조일환 북미과장
- 김의기 중근동과장
- 신국호 마그레브과장
- 정달호 법무담당관
- 김의식 경리계장
- 허덕행 마그레브과 서기관
- 정용칠 경협 2과 사무관
- 김광규 기획예산사무관
- 정혜웅 법무담당관실 사무관

(보고사항)

ㅇ 걸프사태 피해국 지원업무 추진현황(마그레브과장)

(토의사항)

ㅇ 예산집행절차

- 대행업체 지정 및 계약

ㅇ 예산 사고이월 조치

ㅇ 지원업무 실국별 분담

0049

(결정사항)

ㅇ 예산집행절차

- 대개도국 무상원조 사업시와 같은 방식으로 대행업체 지정계약후 건별로 다시 개별 계약체결

- 예산회계법상 비밀유지, 긴급지원실시 필요시 수의계약 체결가능 (법무담당관)

ㅇ 예산이월사용

- 90년도 지원금 1억 7천만불중 EDCF차관 4천만불, 쌀 지원금 1천만불을 제외한 1억 2천만불(860억원) 예산 배정

- 재무부로부터의 자금영달은 90년도 집행가능분만 신청(미집행분도 91년도 이월가능하나 일단 국고환수되므로 가능한 금년도 집행예정분만 신청키로함)

- 각 관계부서별 90년도 집행예정분 파악, 마그레브과에서 종합, 경리계에서 재무부에 신청

* 주요집행 예상금액
대미지원 6,500만불, IOM 및 UNESCO 지원 55만불, 행정비 20만불
계 6,575만불

5만불

ㅇ 지원업무분장

- 대미지원(미주국)
- 주변국 물자지원(중동아국)
- 주변국 EDCF 지원(국제경제국)
- IOM 지원(영사교민국)
- UNESCO(국제기구국)
- 레바논 지원(중동아국)
- 의료지원(미주국, 중동아국)
- 쌀지원(국제경제국)
- 행정비 및 예비비(중동아국 주관)

0050

# 기 안 용 지

| 분류기호<br>문서번호 | 국기20300- | (전화 : 720-4050 ) | 시 행 상<br>특별취급 | |
|---|---|---|---|---|
| 보존기간 | 영구 . 준영구.<br>10. 5 . 3 . 1. | 차 관 | 장 관 | |
| 수신처<br>보존기간 | | 전결 | | |
| 시행일자 | 90.12.21. | | | |

| 보조기관 | 국장 | | 협조기관 | 기획관리실장<br>미주국장<br>중동아프리카국장<br>총무과장 | 문서통제 |
|---|---|---|---|---|---|
| | 과장 | | | | |
| 기안책임자 | 오영주 | | | | 발송인 |

| 경유<br>수신<br>참조 | 건의 | 발신명의 | |
|---|---|---|---|
| 제목 | 걸프만사태 관련 유네스코 특별사업지원 | | |

1. 유네스코 사무국은 주유네스코 아국 대사앞 별첨 공한을 통하여 유네스코가 걸프만 사태로 인하여 여려움을 겪고 있는 요르단 및 이집트 난민 청소년들의 특별교육을 위하여 총 189만 미불이 소요되는 특별 사업계획을 수립하였음을 알려오면서, 아국이 동 소요자의 일부를 긴급 지원해 줄것을 요청하여 왔읍니다.

/계 속/

0051

2. 1항 관련, 아국의 걸프만사태 지원의 일환으로 유네스코에 아래와

같이 사업비를 지원할 것을 건의하오니 재가하여 주시기 바랍니다.

- 아 래 -

1. 사업비 지원액 : $30,000

2. 사업비 송금처 : 주유네스코 대표부

3. 예산항목 : 정무활동 해외경상 이전비

첨부 : 상기 주유네스코 공한 사본 1부. 끝

0052

# UNESCO PROGRAMME OF EMERGENCY EDUCATIONAL ASSISTANCE TO DISPLACED CHILDREN IN EGYPT AND JORDAN AFFECTED BY THE CRISIS BETWEEN IRAQ AND KUWAIT

Estimated Budget
(in US dollars)

| ITEMS | EGYPT | JORDAN | TOTAL |
|---|---|---|---|
| A. Textbooks (including cost of transport and distribution) | 500,000 | 402,000 | 902,000 |
| B. School equipment and teaching materials (blackboards, maps and other basic equipment) | 150,000 | 150,000 | 300,000 |
| C. Classroom construction materials (20 each) | 240,000 | 240,000 | 480,000 |
| D. Local contract fees for supervision of construction work | 25,000 | 25,000 | 50,000 |
| E. Unesco operational support costs (technical assistance, cost of project personnel) | 40,000 | 40,000 | 80,000 |
| F. Unesco programme and administration costs at Headquarters and Field Offices | 40,000 | 40,000 | 80,000 |
| | 995,000 | 897,000 | |
| GRAND TOTAL FOR EGYPT AND JORDAN: | | | 1,892,000 |

0053

| 분류기호 문서번호 | 국기20350-285 | 협조문용지 ( 2181-2 ) | 결재 | 담당 | 과장 | 국장 |
|---|---|---|---|---|---|---|
| 시행일자 | 1990. 12. 21. | | | | | |
| 수 신 | 중동아프리카국장 | 발 신 | 국제기구조약국장 (서명) | | | |
| 제 목 | 걸프만사태 관련 지원예산 요청 | | | | | |

연 : 국기 20350-232

대 : 마그 20005-162

1. 연호로 통보한바와 같이 유네스코는 걸프만사태 관련 요르단 및 이집트 난민 청소년들의 특별교육을 위해 총 189만 미불이 소요되는 특별 사업 계획을 수립하고 있으며, 아국에게 동소요자금의 일부를 긴급 지원해 줄것을 요청한바 있읍니다.

2. 1항관련, 아국의 걸프만사태 지원의 일환으로 유네스코측에 5만불을 지원코저 함을 알려드립니다. 끝

0054

원 본

# 외 무 부

종 별 :

번 호 : UCW-0296 일 시 : 90 1222 1200

수 신 : 장관(국기)

발 신 : 주 유네스코 대사

제 목 : 걸프사태 관련 난민자녀 특별교육 지원

대: WUC-0253

연:유네(정)760-166

1.유네스코 사무국 표제사업 담당관 MRS YANG에의하면,금일 현재까지 사무국에 공식적으로 지원규모를 통보해온 국가는 없으나, 일본,서독,화란및 북구제국이 동사업지원 문제를 호의적으로검토하고 있는 것으로 알고 있다고 하며,동 지원금접수 송금구좌는 아래와 같음을 보고함.

구좌명칭: EMERGENCY RELIEF FUND 431,SUB-ACCOUNT FORGULF CRISIS

구좌번호: UNESCO US DOLLAR ACCOUNT 77666,CHASEMANHATAN BANK

거래은행 주소:18, BLD MALESHERBES B.P.450,75361PARIS CEDEX 08 FRANCE

2. 상기 담당관에의하면,유네스코 사무국이 표제사업 지원을 요청한 대상 국가들은 아국을포함한 서구 선진제국 등 36개 국가라고밝히면서,인도주의와 국제협력의정신에입각하여 상징적 의미에서라도 아국의 참여가긴요함을 부연한바 있음을 참고로 보고함.끝.

(대사 함태혁-국장)

국기국

PAGE 1

90.12.22 21:35 CT

외신 1과 통제관

0055

| 분류기호 문서번호 | 국기20350-285 | 협조문용지 (2181-2) | 결재 | 담당 | 과장 | 국장 |
|---|---|---|---|---|---|---|
| 시행일자 | 1990. 12. 24. | | | 오영주 | (서명) | (서명) |
| 수 신 | 중동아프리카국장 | 발 신 | 국제기구조약국장 | | | (서 명) |
| 제 목 | 걸프만사태 관련 지원예산 요청 | | | | | |

연 : 국기 20350-232

대 : 마그 20005-162

1. 연호로 통보한바와 같이 유네스코는 걸프만사태 관련 요르단 및 이집트 난민 청소년들의 특별교육을 위해 총 189만 미불이 소요되는 특별사업 계획을 수립하고 있으며, 아국에게 동 소요자금의 일부를 긴급 지원해 줄것을 요청한바 있습니다.

2. 1항 관련, 아국의 걸프만사태 지원의 일환으로 유네스코측에 3만불 지원을 추진하고자 하니 걸프만사태 아국 지원금 소요내역으로 반영하여 주시기 바랍니다.

첨부 : 상기 주제네바 대표부 공한 사본. 끝

0056

| 분류기호 문서번호 | 국기20350-285 | 협조문용지 ( 2181-2 ) | 결재 | 담당 | 과장 | 국장 |
|---|---|---|---|---|---|---|
| 시행일자 | 1990. 12. 24. | | | | | |
| 수 신 | 중동아프리카국장 | 발 신 | 국제기구조약국장 (서 명) | | | |
| 제 목 | 걸프만사태 관련 지원예산 요청 | | | | | |

연 : 국기 20350-232

대 : 마그 20005-162

1\. 연호로 통보한바와 같이 유네스코는 걸프만사태 관련 요르단 및 이집트 난민 청소년들의 특별교육을 위해 총 189만 미불이 소요되는 특별사업 계획을 수립하고 있으며, 아국에게 동 소요자금의 일부를 긴급 지원해 줄것을 요청한바 있습니다.

2\. 1항 관련, 아국의 걸프만사태 지원의 일환으로 유네스코측에 3만불 지원을 추진하고자 하니 걸프만사태 아국 지원금 소요내역으로 반영하여 주시기 바랍니다.

첨부 : 상기 주제네바 대표부 공한 사본. 끝

0057

6388ㄷ

# 기 안 용 지

| 분류기호 문서번호 | 국기 20333- | (전화: 720-4050 ) | 시 행 상 특별취급 | |
|---|---|---|---|---|
| 보존기간 | 영구 . 준영구. 10. 5 . 3 . 1. | 장 관 | | |
| 수 신 처 보존기간 | | | | |
| 시행일자 | 90.12. 28. | | | |

| 보조기관 | | | 협조기관 | | 문서통제 |
|---|---|---|---|---|---|
| | 국장 | 전 결 | | | |
| | 과장 | (서명) | | | 1990.12.28 통제관 |
| | | | | | |
| 기안책임자 | | 허강일 | | | 발 송 인 |

| 경 유 수 신 참 조 | 유네스코한위 사무총장 | 발신명의 | | 발송 1990.12.28 외무부 |
|---|---|---|---|---|
| 제 목 | 걸프만사태 관련 유네스코 특별 교육사업 지원 | | | |

1. 유네스코 사무국은 별첨 공한을 통하여 유네스코가 걸프만 사태로 인하여 교육이 중단된 요르단 및 이집트 난민 청소년들의 특별 교육을 위하여 총189만 미불이 소요되는 특별 사업계획을 수립하였다고 하면서, 동 소요자금의 일부를 아국이 긴급 지원해줄 것을 요청하여 온바 있습니다.

/계 속/

0058

2. 당부는 걸프만사태 발생이후 주변 피해국 원조활동에

적극 참여하여 오고 있는 바, 이의 일환으로 ~~아국의 기본입장에 따라~~ 상기 유네스코 특별교육

사업에 3만미불을 지원키로 결정하고 유네스코측에 기송금 조치하였으니

업무에 참고하시기 바랍니다.

첨부 : 유네스코 사무국 공한 사본 1부. 끝

0059

| 분류기호 문서번호 | 국기20300- 290 | 협조문용지 ( 2181-2 ) | 결재 | 담당 | 과장 | 국장 |
|---|---|---|---|---|---|---|
| 시행일자 | 1990. 12. 28. | | | | | |
| 수 신 | 총무과장 | 발 신 | 국제기구조약국장 (서 명) | | | |
| 제 목 | 특별지원금 지급 의뢰 | | | | | |

별첨과 같이 재가를 득한 걸프만사태 관련 유네스코 특별사업에 대한 지원금 송금을 아래와 같이 의뢰하오니 필요한 조치를 취하여 주시기 바랍니다.

- 아 래 -

1. 사업비 지원액 : $30,000(유네스코 사무국)

2. 송금처

o 구좌명칭 : EMERGENCY RELIEF FUND 431,
SUB-ACCOUNT FOR GULF CRISIS

o 구좌번호 : UNESCO US DOLLAR ACCOUNT 77666, CHASEMANHATAN BANK

o 거래은행 주소 : 18, BLD MALESHERBES B.P. 450,
75361 PARIS CEDEX 08 FRANCE

3. 예산항목 : 정무활동, 해외 경상이전

첨부 : 재가문서 사본 1부. 끝

0060

| | 분류번호 | 보존기간 |
|---|---|---|
| | | |

# 발 신 전 보

번 호 : WUC-0256 901228 1049 FC 종별 :

수 신 : 주 유네스코 대사. 총영사

발 신 : 장 관 (국기)

제 목 : 걸프만사태 관련 난민자녀 특별교육 지원

대 : 유네(정) 760-166(1)

UCW-0296(2)

본부는 걸프만사태 아국 지원금으로 유네스코의 표제 사업에 3만 미불을 지원키로 결정하고, 동 지원금을 대호(2)로 통보한 송금 구좌로 연내 직송 조치할 예정임. 끝

(국제기구조약국장 문동석)

| 보안 통제 | |
|---|---|

| 앙 고 재 | 90년 12월 28일 | 국기과 | 기안자 성명 | | 과 장 | | 국 장 | | 차 관 | 장 관 |
|---|---|---|---|---|---|---|---|---|---|---|
| | | | | | | | 전결 | | | |

| 외신과통제 |
|---|
| |

0061

3. 걸스카우트 평화의 주머니 보내기 운동, 1991

0062

서울특별시종로구안국동163
광화문사서함277 ☎ 733－4347, 5893
FAX : 738－3013

Girl Scouts of Korea

National Headquarters
P.O.Box (K) 277, Seoul, Korea

한걸 제 91-35　　　　　　1991. 3. 12.

수 신 외무부장관

참 조 중동국장

제 목 걸스카우트'평화의 주머니 보내기'운동안내및 협조요청

1. 118개국 800만명의 회원들이 활동하고 있는 걸스카우트는 소녀와 여성을 위한 국제단체로 전세계에서 가장 크고 유일한 사회교육단체로서 다양한 프로그램활동과 스카우트의 훈련을 통해 소녀들에게 올바른 국가관과 사회관을 심어주고 책임있는 세계의 민주시민으로 육성케 함을 그 목적으로 하고 있습니다.

2. 본연맹에서는 1991년도 특별사업으로 "평화 - 단 하루만이라도"라는 주제아래 걸스카우트 평화운동을 전개하여 걸스카우트 소녀들로 하여금 우리 주위의 어렵고 소외된 이웃을 돌아보고, 자신의 것을 나누도록 지도하며, 그 일환으로 국.내외 불우이웃들에게 '걸스카우트 평화의 주머니'를 보내고자 합니다.

3. 이에따라 걸프전쟁으로 인해 많은 고난을 받고 있는 중동 지역에도 위로의 편지와 함께 평화의 주머니를 보내 깊은 인류애를 전하고자 합니다.

4. '평화의 주머니'에는 전국의 걸스카우트 소녀들이 평화모금 활동을 통해 모은 기금으로 각종 문구류와 생필품류등이 담겨져 전달될 예정임을 양지하시고 다음 사항을 참고하시어 금번 사업이 성공적으로 개최될 수 있도록 협조하여 주시기 바랍니다.

0063

한걸 제 91-35 1991. 3. 12.

- 다 음 -

1. 사업명 : 걸스카우트 평화운동
"평화의 주머니 보내기"
2. 기 간 : 1991년 연중 (집중기간 : 4-5월)
3. 대상국 : 1) 쿠웨이트, 이라크, 기타 걸프전쟁으로 피해를 입은 지역
2) 기타 난민들이 많은 지역
4. 평화의 주머니 품목 : 문구류및 생필품류
예) 필기류, 세면도구, 바느질세트, 손수건, 가위, 자, 고무 손톱깍기, 색연필, 티슈, 면도기, 로션, 양말, 스타킹 속내의등
5. 총수량 : 10,000개 (각대별 2개, 5000대 x 2대)
20,000개로 총량 아프리카지역도 도착
6. 수거및 전달방법
1) 각 지방연맹은 '걸스카우트 평화의 주머니 보내기' 운동에 참여를 희망하는 대에서 자발적으로 마련한 평화의 주머니를 수거하여 중앙연맹으로 송부한다.
2) 중앙연맹은 각지방연맹에서 보내온 평화의 주머니를 외무부와 대한항공의 도움을 받아 현지로 전달한다.
7. 연락처 : 한국걸스카우트연맹 기획부
(전화 : 733 - 4347, 732 - 8718)

0064

8. 협조요청사항

1) 금번 사업에 관련된 정보제공

2) 현지 전달처 결정

3) 평화의 주머니 전달 대행

*별 첨 : 1) 평화운동 사업계획서 1부. 끝.

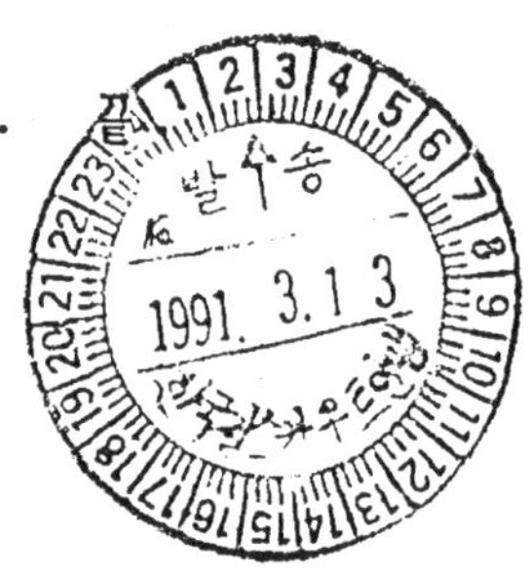


한 국 걸 스 카 우 트 연 맹

0065

1991년도 특별사업

# 걸스카우트 평화운동
# "평화—단 하루만이라도"

1991. 3.

한국걸스카우트연맹

0066

- 목 차 -



0067

# 취 지 문

스카우트운동의 창시자 로버트 베이든 포엘경은 세계평화를 향한 모든 조치중 그 첫단계는 모든 국가의 자라나는 세대를 절대적인 정의에 따라 지도되도록 훈련시키는 것이라고 정의하고, 수많은 소녀, 소년들이 전 세계에 퍼져서 전 인류의 평화와 행복을 이룩하는데 크게 기여한다는 것을 생각하는 것은 얼마나 가슴벅찬 일인가 하고 강조하였다.

이처럼 걸스카우트운동의 궁극적인 목표는 세계평화라고 할수 있고 스카우트 운동을 통해 이 세계는 조금이라도 더 나은 세상이 되어갈 것이다.
걸스카우트 세계연맹은 1988년 UN으로부터 세계평화의 해 (1986년)에 전 세계 걸스카우트들이 펼쳤던 사업들과 그간의 공헌을 인정받아 평화의 전달자 ( The Peace Messenger )란 칭호를 부여받았다.

이밖에도 걸스카우트 세계연맹은 1990년 6월 싱가폴에서 개최된 제 27차 걸스카우트 세계대회에서 오늘날 전세계적으로 가장 강조되어야하는 것은 "평화"라고 의견을 모으고 UN이 정한 세계 평화의 날(9월 세번째 화요일)을 전회원들이 기념하고, 그 주간 역시 걸스카우트 평화주간으로 설정하여 전세계적으로 기념키로 결정하기도 하였다.

한국걸스카우트연맹은 1985년 세계 청소년의 해를 맞아 "참여, 발전, 평화"란 주제아래 1985년부터 1987년까지 사랑의 뜨개질, 특별행사 "평화의 메아리", 평화패치를 달자등 다양한 사업을 전개하였다. 오늘 우리사회를 보다 평화로운 사회로 만드는데 앞장서고자 이 "평화 운동"의 불을 다시 지펴 "평화 -단 하루만이라도"라는 활동주제를 가지고 대대적인 국민운동을 전개코자 한다.

- 1 -

0068

평화운동은 누구보다 나 자신이 주체가 되어 일상생활에서 부터 이루워져야 하고, 모든 사회의 기초 공동체인 가정에서부터 믿음과 사랑이 되살아나야 한다. 가정의 평화가 이루워짐으로써, 이웃과 지역사회에 가지 그 씨앗을 뿌리게 되고 결실을 거두게 될것이다.

전국의 걸스카우트는 실천적 이념의 추구자로서 진정한 평화의 전달자가 될 수 있도록 우리의 이념인 "선서와 규율"을 생활화하고, 가정과 학교등 자신이 속한 곳의 평화를 위해 노력하고, 우리 이웃의 평화를 위해 내가 갖고 있는 것을 나누어야 할 것이다.

평화실천을 위한 우리들의 다짐

1. 우리 걸스카우트는 걸스카우트의 이념인 선서와 규율을 생활화 하고, 말과 행동으로 우리의 주위를 밝히는 평화의 진단자가 됩니다.

2. 우리 걸스카우트는 행복한 가정을 만들기위해 노력함으로써 걸스카우트 평화운동을 지역사회로 확산시켜 나갑니다.

3. 우리 걸스카우트는 우리보다 어려운 이웃을 위해 내가 가지고 있는 것을 나누어 가짐으로써 우리 사회를 보다 평화롭게 만듭니다.

4. 걸스카우트 평화운동은 "지금, 여기서, 나에게서 부터" 시작합니다.

- 3 -

0070

## 평화실천을 위한 실천과제 (예시)

| 실 천 과 제 | 실 천 방 향 (예) |
|---|---|
| 화목한 가정 이루기 | 1. 나의 일은 내 손으로 합니다.<br>2. 하루 한번이라도 부모님과 가족을 위한 착한 일을 합니다.<br>3. 온 가족이 정기적으로 대화의 시간을 갖습니다.<br>4. 우리가 앞장서서 가족놀이를 이끕니다. |
| 질서있는 생활하기 | 1. 약속을 지킵니다.<br>2. 거짓말을 안합니다.<br>3. 바르게 인사합니다.<br>4. 고운 말을 씁니다.<br>5. 조용하고 예의있게 말합니다.<br>6. 공중도덕과 교통질서를 지킵니다. |
| 밝고 깨끗한 생활환경 만들기 | 1. 아껴쓰고, 나눠쓰고, 바꿔쓰고, 다시 씁시다.<br>2. 일회용 생활용품을 아껴씁니다.<br>3. 쓰레기는 가능한 적게 버리고 분리 수거 합니다.<br>4. 야외에서 생긴 쓰레기는 반드시 다시 가져 오고, 버려진 쓰레기는 줍습니다.<br>5. 길거리에 침이나 껌을 뱉지 않습니다.<br>6. 샴푸, 린스, 세제, 스프레이를 덜 사용합니다.<br>7. 환경오염을 일으키는 수은 건전지는 다 쓴후 철저히 처리토록 계몽합시다.<br>8. 우리 지역의 도로를 깨끗이 합시다. |

평화실현을 위한 실천과제 (예시)

| 실 천 과 제 | 실 천 방 향 (예) |
| --- | --- |
| 서로 돕는 사회 만들기 | 1. 우리 주위에 있는 불우이웃을 찾아 우리가 갖고 있는 것을 나누어 줍니다.<br>2. 이웃들에게 평화의 신문로 평화의 꽃씨를 보냅니다.<br>3. 헌혈운동에 참여합니다.<br>4. 불우이웃을 위해 한달에 한끼 절식합니다.<br>5. 불우이웃을 위해 평화모금을 조성합니다.<br>6. 모든 모임에서 걸스카우트 평화의 노래를 보급하고, 건전한 프로그램을 제공하여 평화로운 분위기를 만들어 냅니다. |

## 걸스카우트 평화운동 전개방안

| 사 업 명 | 기 간 | 내 용 |
|---|---|---|
| 평화의 엽서 보내기 | 연 중<br>(집중기간<br>4월, 9월) | . 전대원과 지도자들이 평화의 소망을 담은 엽서 (중앙연맹 제작 배부)를 송부<br>. 수량 : 200,000매<br>. 참가인원 : 600,000명 (1매당 3명 연결) |
| 평화 캠페인 | 9월 평화주간<br>(9월 17일<br>집중실시) | 평화의 물결이 전국에 퍼져 나갈 수 있도록 대국민 홍보활동을 펼친다.<br>. 배부자료 : 스틱카, 책갈피꽂이,<br>포스터등 (중앙연맹 제작, 배부)<br>. 캠페인 내용 : 가두캠페인, 평화행진등 |
| 평화의 주머니 보내기 운동 | 연 중<br>(집중기간 4월) | . 걸프전쟁 피해자나 난민, 국내불우이웃, 오지지역 특수대 대원들에게 생필품을 전달한다.<br>. 품목 : 문구류및생필품<br>. 방법 : 해당금액을 모아 현금을 보내 구입하거나 배부된 주머니에 직접 해당 항목을 넣어 준비한다. |
| 걸스카우트 일일일선 생활화 | 연 중 | . 걸스카우트의 표어인 일일일선을 생활화 한다. |
| 평 화 모 금 | 연 중 | . 평화사업에 동참하는 뜻으로 연중 모금사업을 전개한다.<br>. 모금방법 : 대집회등 행사 상설 모금함 비치<br>걸스카우트 쿠키판매등<br>(* 목적사업 추후 안내) |



0073

| 사 업 명 | 기 간 | 내 용 |
|---|---|---|
| 대별, 지역별 평화사업 전개 | 연 중 | 각대나 연합대, 지역별로 그 지역사회에 평화를 가져올 수 있는 사업을 정해 정기적인 활동을 전개한다. |
| 평화운동 사례발표회 | 9월 평화주간 및 연말 | 지구, 지방연맹별로 그간 대나 지역별로 실시한 평화사업중 우수사업을 선정 발표회를 가짐으로써 서로의 정보를 교환하고, 전국적으로도 사례발표회를 개최하여 지역사회에 걸스카우트의 활동을 알린다. |

- 7 -

0074

| | 분류번호 | 보존기간 |
|---|---|---|
| | | |

# 발 신 전 보

번 호 : WKU-0013 910315 1723 FD 종별 :

수 신 : 주 수신처 참조 대사 ~~/총영사~~ WYM -0108 WSS -0083 WMT -0038 WJO -0257

발 신 : 장 관 (중동일)

제 목 : 걸스카우트 평화의 주머니 보내기 운동

1. 한국 걸스카우트 연맹에서는 91년도 걸스카우트 평화운동의 일환으로 걸프전으로 인해 고난을 받고 있는 중동지역에 각종 문구류, 생필품류 등이 담겨져 있는 평화의 주머니를 쿠웨이트, 이라크, 기타 난민들이 많은 지역에 송부할 계획에 있음.

2. 상기 연맹측은 4-5월경 까지 약 2만여봉지를 수집 목표로 필기류, 세면도구, 바느질세트, 손수건, 가위, 자, 고무, 손톱깍기, 색연필, 티슈, 면도기, 양말, 스타킹, 속내의 등을 수집한다 하는바, ~~현지 필요물품, 수량, 전달시기등 귀견 보고바람. 끝.~~ 수집되는대로 일국당 4-5천개씩 보낼 예정이니 수령인의 명세를 보고바람.

(중동아국장 이 해 순)

수신처 : 주 쿠웨이트 (~~바레인 경~~유), 예멘, 수단, 모리타니, 요르단 대사

| 보안통제 | 7h |
|---|---|

| 앙고재 | 91년 3월 15일 | 중동1과 | 기안자 성명 | | 과 장 | 심의관 | 국 장 | | 차 관 | 장 관 |
|---|---|---|---|---|---|---|---|---|---|---|
| | | | 서명 | | 7h | 서명 | 전결 | | | 서명 |

| 외신과통제 |
|---|
| |

0075

원 본

# 외 무 부

종 별 :

번 호 : KUW-0026 일 시 : 91 0317 1100

수 신 : 장관(중동일)

발 신 : 주 쿠웨이트대사

제 목 : 걸스카웃 평화의 주머니운동

대: WKU-13

1. 주재국에는 GIRL'S CLUB (회장: CROWNPRINCE) 이라는 단체가 걸스카웃과 유사한 기능을 가지고 있었으나 걸프전으로 인해 현재는 소재가 불명인 상태임.

2. 따라서 동 단체의 복귀상태를 보아 가면서 적절한 시기에 수령단체 또는 기관을 선정, 보고하겠음.

끝.

(대사-국장)

중아국

PAGE 1

91.03.18 05:54 DA

외신 1과 통제관

0076

| 관리번호 | 91/148 |
|---|---|

# 외 무 부

종 별 : 지 급

번 호 : SSW-0134 일 시 : 91 0320 1400

수 신 : 장관(경이,중동일,중동이)

발 신 : 주 수단 대사

제 목 : 무상원조

대:WSS-84,83 및 경이 20615-4675

1. 본직이 금 3.20. 외무성으로 ABDEL AHMADI 정무차관보를 방문(ABU HAJ 차관은 부재중), 대호 설탕등 지원계획을 통보한 바, 차관보는 내륙 운송비용을 주재국이 부담하는 조건으로 이를 수령하겠다고 하였음.

2. 정무차관보는 또한, 걸스카웃 지원품을 수령할 기관과 91 무상원조 계획의 지원 희망 품목에 대하여도 조속 통보하여 주겠다고 하고, 아국 정부와 국민의 이와 같은 지원에 진심으로 감사한다고 함. 끝.

(대사 이우상-국장)

예고:91.12.31 일반

경제국 2차보 중아국 중아국

PAGE 1

91.03.21 04:52

외신 2과 통제관 DO

0077

원 본

# 외 무 부

종 별 :

번 호 : YMW-0202 일 시 : 91 0324 1400

수 신 : 장 관(중동일,정문)

발 신 : 주 예멘 대사

제 목 : 평화의 주머니 보내기 운동

한국걸스카웃 연맹에 공급
박애자
(김애자 씨와)

대:1. WYM-0108

2. 정문 20521-33067

3. 정문 20521-5613

1. 본직은 3.23 주재국 청년 체육성 DR. MUHAMEDAHMED AL-KABAB 장관을 면담, 한국 걸 스카우트가 주재국 난민(걸프 사태로 귀환 근로자)에 대한 작은 성의의 표시로 평 화의 주머니 5,000개를 전달할 뜻이 있음을 전하였는바, 동 장관은 이에감사를 표시하고 이는 향후 양국 걸 스카우트 관계는 물론 양국 관계 증진에 하나의 계기가 될것으로 믿는다고 언급하였음. (평화의 주머니 수령처: MINISTRY OF YOUTH SPORTS)

2. 또한 동 장관은 대호 2의 운동 용구를 기증해준대 대해 사의를 표명하고 계속적인 지원을 요청 하였으며, 대호 3의 91 보이 스카우트 잼보리에 주재국에서 20명이 참가할 예정이라고 말하고 이들에 대한 바레인-서울 왕복 항공료를 지원해줄것을 요청하였음. ? 이부분 회신을 (김애자)

3. 동 장관은 이자리에서 박철언 청년 체육성 장관께 취임 축하의 뜻을 전달해줄 것을 아울러 요망 하였음.

4. 당관 의견:

동 장관은 면담 과정에서 아국의 다국적군 지원사실을 상기 시켰는바, 이는 아국의 대 예멘 난민지원이 미미 했음을 아쉬워한 것으로 사료됨. 주재국은 걸프 사태로 외환 사정이 극도로 악화된점을 감안, 잼보리 참가자들에 대한 항공료의 지원이없을 경우 대부분 참가가 어려울것으로 판단됨.

끝.

(대사 류 지호-국장)

중아국 정문국

PAGE 1

91.03.25 21:56 DA

외신 1과 통제관

0078

| 분류기호 문서번호 | 중동일 720-13510 | 기안용지 (720-2327) | | 시 행 상 특별취급 | |
|---|---|---|---|---|---|
| 보존기간 | 영구.준영구 10. 5. 3. 1 | 장 | | 관 | |
| 수 신 처 보존기간 | | | | | |
| 시행일자 | 1991. 3. 28. | | | | |
| 보조기관 국 장 | 전결 | 협조기관 | | 문서통제 | |
| 심의관 | | | | 1991. 3. 29 통제관 | |
| 과 장 | | | | | |
| 기안책임자 | 박종순 | | | 발송인 | |
| 경 유 / 수 신 / 참 조 | 한국걸스카우트연맹총재 | 발신명의 | | 발송 1991. 3 29 외무부 | |
| 제 목 | 평화의 주머니 보내기 운동 | | | | |

1. 한걸제 91-35 (91.3. 12) 귀공문과 관련된 사항입니다.

2. 걸프전으로 인해 고난을 받고있는 중동지역 일부 국가에 대해 91년도 걸스카우트 평화운동의 일환으로 귀 연맹이 추진하고 있는 각종 문구류, 생필품류 등이 담겨져있는 평화의 주머니 보내기 사업계획은 예멘, 모리타니아, 수단, 요르단등 수혜 예정국가들로 부터 좋은 반응을 얻고 있음을 우선 알려드립니다.

3. 특히, 주 예멘 아국대사는 3.23. Dr. Muhamedahmed Al-Kabab 예멘 청년 체육성장관 면담시, 아국 걸스카우트가 예멘 난민(걸프사태로 귀환한 근로자)에 대한 성의의 표시로 /계속 . . .

0079

평화의 주머니 5,000개를 전달할 뜻이 있음을 전하였는데 동 장관은

이에 감사를 표시하고, 이는 향후 한.예멘 양국 걸스카우트 관계는

물론 양국관계 증진에 하나의 계기가 될것으로 믿는다고 언급

하였다고 보고 해 왔음을 참고로 통보해 드립니다.

3. 상기 관련, 평화의 주머니 수령 기관(또는 단체)은 예멘의 경우

청년 체육부(Ministry of Youth Sports)이며 기타국가(요르단,

모리타니아, 수단, 쿠웨이트, 이라크)의 경우는 파악되는 대로

관련사항과 함께 귀 연맹에 추후 별도 통보할 예정임을 양지

하시기 바랍니다.

4. 귀연맹의 이같은 평화운동 사업전개를 통하여 상호간 깊은 인류애를

나누고 이를 바탕으로 우의를 더욱 다질수 있을 것으로 사료되는바

향후에도 이런한 사업들이 계속 확대될수 있기를 바라며

적절한 홍보도 필요할 것으로 생각됩니다. 끝

0080

원 본

# 외 무 부

종 별 :

번 호 : JOW-0412 일 시 : 91 0429 1530

수 신 : 장 관(중동일)

발 신 : 주 요르단 대사

제 목 : 걸스카운트 평화의 주머니 보내기 운동

대:WJO-0257

1.대호 평화의 주머니 주재국 수령인은 다음과같음

PRESIDENT DR. AHMED ABU GHURA

JORDAN NATIONAL RED CRESCENT SOCIETY(JNRCS)

P.O. BOX 10001, AMMAN-JORDAN

2.이라크 난민들에 대한 평화의 주머니도 요르단JNRCS를 통해 이라크 INRCS 에 전달 할수있다함

3.주재국에도 걸스카운트 연맹이 있으나 동기구 및기능이 미미하여 대호 운동등난민 구호관계는 주로JNRCS 에서 주로 취급하고 있음.

(대사 박태진-국장)

걸스카우트 (김현주) 연맹 총무부장에게 기통보 (5/02 11:30)

중아국

PAGE 1

91.04.29 23:56 FD

외신 1과 통제관

0081

원 본

# 외 무 부

종 별 :

번 호 : KUW-0286 일 시 : 91 0616 1400

수 신 : 장관(중동일)

발 신 : 주 쿠웨이트 대사

제 목 : 걸 스카웃 평화의 주머니운동

대:WKU-13(91.3.15)

연:KUW-26(91.3.17)

1.대호, 주재국 수령처를 다음과같이 보고함.

DEPARTMENT OF PHYSICAL EDUCATION AND SCOUT

MINISTRY OF EDUCATION(ATTENTION OF MR.AL-JIMAZJASSIM),KUWAIT.

2.참고로 현재의 회원수는 450여명이라 하며 전쟁전에는 650명 정도였다함.

끝

(대사-국장)

중아국

PAGE 1 91.06.16 23:04 DA

외신 1과 통제관

0082

91. 12. 18 10:43 *GIRL SCOUT NHQs P02

한국걸스카우트연맹

Girl Scouts of Korea

National Headquarters
P.O. Box (K) 277, Seoul, Korea

팩시밀리 송부 안내

| 발신 | 발신자 : 한국걸스카우트연맹 | 부서 : 기 획 부 |
|---|---|---|
| 수신 | 수신처 : 외 무 부 | 일자 : 1991 년 12월 17일 |
| | 부 서 : 중 동 국 | 시간 : (오전) (오후) |
| | 수신자 : 주 독 용 사 무 관 | 총매수 : 1 매 |
| | 팩스번호 : 720 - 26 5 | 회답 : (불필요) (필요) |

만일, 송매이서를 수령치 못하거나 불분명한 점이 있으시면 즉시 연락바랍니다.

송 부 사 항

제 목 : 평화의 주머니 중동지역 전달 현황

내 용 : 걸스카우트 소녀들의 정성으로 모은 우정의 선물
"평화의 주머니"의 중동지역 송부내용을 알려드립니다.
참조하시고 문의시 아래 연락처로 연락바랍니다.
- 기획부 : 730 - 5320

총 5개국 910개.

0083

91. 12. 10 10:47 GIRL SCOUT P01

## 평화의 주머니 중동지역 전달 현황

| 국 명 | 수 신 처 | 수량 | 전달일시 | 주 소 |
|---|---|---|---|---|
| 수 단 | 수단 걸가이드 연맹 | 200 | 10월 10일 | The Sudan Girl Guides Association, P.o.Box 294, Khartoum, Sudan Mrs, Um Salamasaeid (Tel: 249 11 80536 |
| 요르단 | 요르단 걸가이드 연맹 | 200 | 10월 17일 | AL KIYADA AL AAMA LE-KASHAFET WA MORSHIDAT AL ORDON, P.O.Box 1794 Amman, Jordan (Mrs. Abla Abu Nowar, Tel No: 962 6 604 701) 우편 |
| 방글라데시 | 방글라데시 걸가이드 연맹 | 200 | " | Bangladesh Girl Guides Association, Guide House, New Bailey Road, Dhaka 1000, Bangladesh (Mrs. Zeba Rasneed Choudhury, Tel: 880 240 14 74) 우편 |
| 쿠웨이트 | 쿠웨이트 걸가이드 연맹 | 110 | 8월 15일 | Ministry of Education Department of Physical Education & Scouts Kuwait Sheikha Khalid ALL Shaheen POX 5241, Kuwait * 인편으로 전달함. |
| 4개국 | | 710 | | |

* 요청국중 모리타니아, 예멘, 이라크 등은 수송등의 어려움으로 인해 수송하지 못했음.

0084

외무부, 중동아국 구부홍사무관님께

1. 시에라레온 (10월17일, 200개 수송)

주소) The Sierra Leone Girl Guides Association.
1, George Street, P.O.BOX 254,
Freetown, Sierra Leone.
(FAX NO : +232-22-26892)

2. 우간다. (10월17일, 200개 수송)

주소) The Uganda Girl Guides Association
Baden-Powell House, Buganda Road,
P.O.Box 696. Kampala. Uganda.

0085

| | 분류번호 | 보존기간 |
|---|---|---|
| | | |

# 발 신 전 보

번 호 : WUG-0343 911219 1717 WG 종별 :

수 신 : 주 우간다 대사. 총영사

발 신 : 장 관 (중동일)

제 목 : 평화의 주머니 송부

1. 한국 걸 스카웃연맹은 91년 평화운동의 일환으로 귀 주재국측에 평화의 주머니 200개를 10.17.자로 선박우편으로 송부했다하니 참고 바람. (기도착 했다 함)
   수신처 : THE UGANDA GIRL GUIDES ASSOCIATION
   BADEN-POWELL HOUSE, BUGANDA ROAD,
   P.O.BOX 696. KAMPALA, UGANDA

2. 평화의 주머니는 일종의 구호품으로서 필기류, 세면도구, 바느질셋, 손수건, 가위, 자, 고무, 손톱깎기, 색연필, 티슈, 면도기, 양말, 스타킹, 속내의등이 내용물임. 끝.

(중동아프리카국장 이 해 순)

| 보안 통제 | |
|---|---|

| 앙 고 재 | 91년 12월 19일 | 중동1과 | 기안자 성명 | | 과 장 | 심의관 | 국 장 | | 차 관 | 장 관 |
|---|---|---|---|---|---|---|---|---|---|---|
| | | | 주 | | | | 전결 | | | |

| 외신과통제 |
|---|
| |

0086

| | 분류번호 | 보존기간 |
|---|---|---|
| | | |

# 발 신 전 보

번 호 : WSR-0221 911219 1717 WG 종별 :

수 신 : 주 시에라레온 대사대리대사. ~~총영사~~

발 신 : 장 관 (중동일)

제 목 : 평화의 주머니 송부

1. 한국 걸 스카웃연맹은 91년도 평화운동의 일환으로 귀 주재국측에 ~~표제~~ 평화의 주머니 200개를 10.17.자로 선박우편으로 송부했다하니 참고 바람.

수신처 : THE SIERRA LEONE GIRL GUIDES ASSOCIATION
1, GEORGES STREET, P.O.BOX 854, FREETOWN

2. 평화의 주머니는 일종의 구호품으로서 필기류, 세면도구, 바느질셋, 손수건, 가위, 자, 고무, 손톱깎기, 색연필, 티슈, 면도기, 양말, 스타킹, 속내의등이 내용물임. 끝.

(중동아프리카국장 이 해 순)

| 보 안 통 제 | |
|---|---|

| 앙 고 재 | 91년 12월 19일 | 중동1과 | 기안자 성 명 | | 과 장 | 심의관 | 국 장 | | 차 관 | 장 관 |
|---|---|---|---|---|---|---|---|---|---|---|
| | | | 주 | | | | 전결 | | | |

외신과통제

0087

| | 분류번호 | 보존기간 |
|---|---|---|
| | | |

# 발 신 전 보

번 호 : WSS-0366 911219 1716 WG 종별 :

수 신 : 주 수 단 대사. ~~총영사~~

발 신 : 장 관 (중동일)

제 목 : 평화의 주머니 송부

대 : SSW - 0134 (91.3.20)

대호 관련, 한국 걸 스카웃연맹은 귀 주재국측에 ~~표제~~ 평화의 주머니 200개를 10.10.자로 항공편 송부했다하니 참고 바람. (대우협조)

수신처 : MRS. UM SALAMASAEID
THE SUDAN GIRL GUIDES ASSOCIATION
P.O.BOX 294, KHARTOUM, SUDAN 끝.

(중동아프리카국장 이 해 순)

| 보 안 통 제 | |
|---|---|

| 앙 고 재 | 91년 12월 19일 | 중동1과 | 기안자 성 명 | | 과 장 | 심의관 | 국 장 | | 차 관 | 장 관 |
|---|---|---|---|---|---|---|---|---|---|---|
| | | | 주 | | | | 전결 | | | |

| 외신과통제 |
|---|
| |

0088

| | 분류번호 | 보존기간 |
|---|---|---|
| | | |

# 발 신 전 보

번 호 : WJO-0741 911219 1716 WG 종별 :

수 신 : 주 요르단 대사. 총영사

발 신 : 장 관 (중동일)

제 목 : 평화의 주머니 송부

대 : JOW - 0412 (91.4.29)

대호 관련, 한국 걸 스카웃연맹은 귀 주재국측에 ~~표제~~ 평화의 주머니 200개를 10.17.자로 선박우편으로 송부했다하니 참고 바람.

수신처 : MRS. ABLA ABU NOWAR,
AL KIYADA AL AAMA LE KASHAFET
WA MORSHIDAT AL ORDON.
P.O.BOX 1794 AMMAN, JORDAN 끝.

(중동아프리카국장 이 해 순)

| 보 안 통 제 | |
|---|---|

| 앙 고 재 | 91년 12월 19일 | 중동1과 | 기안자 성 명 | | 과 장 | 심의관 | 국 장 | | 차 관 | 장 관 |
|---|---|---|---|---|---|---|---|---|---|---|
| | | | 주 | | | | 전결 | | | |

| 외신과통제 |
|---|
| |

0089

| | 분류번호 | 보존기간 |
|---|---|---|
| | | |

# 발 신 전 보

번 호 : WKU-0519 911219 1715 WG 종별 :

수 신 : 주 쿠웨이트 대사. 총영사

발 신 : 장 관 (중동일)

제 목 : 평화의 주머니 송부

대 : KUW - 0286 (91.6.16)

대호 관련, 한국 걸 스카웃은 귀 주재국측에 ~~표재~~ 평화의 주머니 110개를 8.15. 인편으로 전달했다하니 참고 바람.

수신처 : SHEIKHA KHALID AL SHAHEEN

DEPT. OF PHYSICAL EDUCATION AND SCOUTS, MINISTRY OF EDUCATION.

P.O.BOX 5241, KUWAIT 끝.

(중동아프리카국장 이 혜 순)

| 보안통제 | |
|---|---|

| 앙고재 | 91년 12월 19일 | 중동1과 | 기안자 성명 | | 과장 | 심의관 | 국장 | | 차관 | 장관 |
|---|---|---|---|---|---|---|---|---|---|---|
| | | | 주 | | | | 전결 | | | |

외신과통제

0090

원 본

# 외 무 부

종 별 :

번 호 : KUW-0822 일 시 : 91 1221 1700

수 신 : 장관(중동일)

발 신 : 주쿠웨이트대사

제 목 : 평화의주머니

대:WKU-0519

1.평화의 주머니를 쿠웨이트 관계자에게 전달한경과를 자세히 알려주시기바람.

2.이와같은 일은 당연히 현지대사관과 협조하여시행하여야 대주재국 성과를 높일수있을터이므로,앞으로는 그렇게 되도록 조처해주시기바람.끝

(대사-국장)

중아국

PAGE 1

91.12.22 11:44 CJ

외신 1과 통제관

0091

| | 분류번호 | 보존기간 |
|---|---|---|
| | | |

# 발 신 전 보

번 호 : WYM-0391 911227 1132 WG 종별 :

수 신 : 주 예 멘 대사. /총영사

발 신 : 장 관 (중동일)

제 목 : 평화의 주머니 송부

대 : YMW 0202 (91.3.24)

대호 관련, 한국 걸스카웃연맹은 귀 주재국 청년체육부 앞으로 평화의 주머니 300개를 우편 송부예정이라 하는바, 수령자성명 및 주소를 지급 알려주기 바람. 끝.

(중동아프리카국장 이 해 순)

| 보안 통제 | |
|---|---|

| 앙 고 재 | 91년 12월 26일 | 중동1과 | 기안자 성명 | | 과 장 | 심의관 | 국 장 | | 차 관 | 장 관 |
|---|---|---|---|---|---|---|---|---|---|---|
| | | | 주 | | | | 전결 | | | |

| 외신과통제 |
|---|
| |

0092

원 본

# 외 무 부

종 별 :

번 호 : YMW-0699 일 시 : 91 1230 1600

수 신 : 장 관(중동일)

발 신 : 주 예멘 대사

제 목 : 평화의 주머니

대:WYM-0391

대호 관련,수령자 성명 및 주소는 아래와 같음.

--- 아 래 ---

1. 수령자 성명:

MRS.FATEN HAMOOD ESA'A

DIRECTOR GANERAL OF GIRL SCOUT

2. 주소:

P.O.BOX.2414,MINISTRY OF YOUTHSPORTS

REPUBLIC OF YEMEN

(대사 류 지호-국장)

중아국

PAGE 1 91.12.31 08:41 DQ

외신 1과 통제관

0093

******* Goldfax GF-2 ******* -JOURNAL- *********** DATE 1992-01-03 *** TIME 09:47 ********

| NO. | DATE | TIME | DURATION | IDENTIFICATION | X/R | DOC | COM | DIAGNOSTIC |
|---|---|---|---|---|---|---|---|---|
| 31 | 01-03 | 09:43 | 00:03'54 | 7383013 | XMT | 02 | OK | 8004402C2800 |

************************************************************************ - - *********

0094

외교문서 비밀해제: 걸프 사태 17

# 걸프 사태 외국인 수송 및 난민 지원

초판인쇄 2024년 03월 15일
초판발행 2024년 03월 15일

지은이 한국학술정보(주)
펴낸이 채종준
펴낸곳 한국학술정보(주)
주 소 경기도 파주시 회동길 230(문발동)
전 화 031-908-3181(대표)
팩 스 031-908-3189
홈페이지 http://ebook.kstudy.com
E-mail 출판사업부 publish@kstudy.com
등 록 제일산-115호(2000. 6. 19)

ISBN 979-11-6983-977-8 94340
979-11-6983-960-0 94340 (set)


책에 대한 더 나은 생각, 끊임없는 고민, 독자를 생각하는 마음으로 보다 좋은 책을 만들어갑니다.